CONSTITUTIONAL AND ADMINISTRATIVE LAW

AUSTRALIA
The Law Book Company Ltd.
Sydney : Melbourne : Brisbane

CANADA & U.S.A.
The Carswell Company Ltd.
Agincourt, Ontario

INDIA
N. M. Tripathi Private Ltd.
Bombay

ISRAEL
Steimatzky's Agency Ltd.
Jerusalem : Tel Aviv : Haifa

MALAYSIA : SINGAPORE : BRUNEI
Malayan Law Journal (Pte.) Ltd.
Singapore

NEW ZEALAND
Sweet & Maxwell (N.Z.) Ltd.
Wellington

PAKISTAN
Pakistan Law House
Karachi

CONSTITUTIONAL
AND ADMINISTRATIVE LAW

BY

O. HOOD PHILLIPS

Q.C., D.C.L., M.A.(OXON.), J.P.
*Pro-Vice-Chancellor, Vice-Principal and Barber Professor
of Jurisprudence in the University of Birmingham*

FIFTH EDITION

OLD EDITION

LONDON
SWEET & MAXWELL
1973

First Edition . . 1952
Second Edition . . 1957
Third Edition . . 1962
Fourth Edition . . 1967
Fifth Edition . . 1973

Published in 1973 by
Sweet & Maxwell Limited of
11 New Fetter Lane, London,
and printed in Great Britain
by The Eastern Press Limited
of London and Reading

SBN Hardback 421 15470 5
Paperback 421 15480 2

PREFACE TO THE FIFTH EDITION

As in the previous editions, innumerable alterations and additions have been made to meet the many rapid changes in the law and practice covering so wide a field. Cutting out or abridging existing matter to prevent the book growing too long is perhaps the most time-consuming part of preparing a new edition. Thanks to the forbearance of my publishers—the manuscript reached them twelve months behind schedule—the text has actually been reduced by 190 pages.

The treatment of the Legislative Supremacy of Parliament has been divided into two chapters (Chaps. 3 and 4), the latter dealing more fully with the question whether Parliament can bind itself or its successors, including the new aspect of membership of the European Communities. Some of the views expressed in my *Reform of the Constitution* (1970) find a place in this book, such as the invalidity of the " Parliament Act 1949 "; but I have not developed here my suggestion that we should return to the Triennial Act 1694 with regard to the life of Parliament, although I think that the reduction to three years would both revive public interest in Parliament and also restrict the freedom of the Prime Minister (or, preferably, the Cabinet) to use the timing of a dissolution as a political weapon. The chapter on the " High Court of Parliament " has been rearranged to include the Parliament Acts, so that Parliament as a whole is dealt with before each of the two Houses. The revised chapter on the Cabinet and Prime Minister deals with recent trends in Cabinet committees and also the question whether we now have " Prime Ministerial government." Account has been taken of many reforms in parliamentary procedure, especially in financial legislation; developments in the scrutiny of administration, including the new Expenditure Committee; the Bill to reform the House of Lords introduced and dropped in 1968; the report of the Select Committee on Parliamentary Privilege of 1967, not yet implemented in the main; and the reports of a number of parliamentary and other committees, and the Law Commission, White Papers, Blue Papers and Green Papers.

Emergency powers have been brought forward to Part III on the Central Government, the police are given a separate chapter in Part IV on Justice and Police, the system of courts has been omitted, while the Immigration Act 1971 and the Fugitive Offenders Act 1967 have necessitated the rewriting of the chapter in Part V now entitled " Nationality, Immigration and Extradition."

The chapter on Local Government has been rewritten to take account of the Local Government Act 1972. The process of shortening Part VI on Administrative Law has helped revision of such topics as the Parliamentary Commissioner, parliamentary scrutiny of delegated legislation, administrative and domestic tribunals, and Crown privilege. At the same time Judicial Control of Public Authorities has reverted to its former two chapters, dealing respectively with liability and remedies.

Part VII on the Commonwealth has been further abridged, the chapter on protectorates and trust territories disappearing. The treatment of associated states has been revised. More countries have abolished appeals to the Privy Council. No attempt has been made to record detailed changes with regard to particular Commonwealth countries, which now include the republics of Sri Lanka and Bangladesh.

Recent statutes include European Communities Act 1972, Northern Ireland (Temporary Provisions) Act 1972, Representation of the People Act 1969, Industrial Relations Act 1971, Courts Act 1971, Criminal Justice Act 1972, Race Relations Act 1968, Post Office Act 1969, and Tribunals and Inquiries Act 1971. Among the more interesting cases included are *Nissan* v. *Att.-Gen.*, *Schmidt* v. *Secretary of State for Home Affairs*, *Madzimbamuto* v. *Lardner-Burke*, *Ghani* v. *Jones*, *Durayappah* v. *Fernando*, *Padfield* v. *Minister of Agriculture, Fisheries & Food*, *Anisminic* v. *Foreign Compensation Commission*, *Dorset Yacht Co. Ltd.* v. *Home Office*, *Conway* v. *Rimmer*, *Rediffusion (H.K.) Ltd.* v. *Att.-Gen. of Hong Kong*, *R.* v. *Caird*, *Cheney* v. *Conn*, *R.* v. *Jordan* and the enterprising litigation of Messrs. *Blackburn* and *McWhirter*.

We still await the report of the Constitutional Commission set up by the Government in 1969 under the chairmanship of the late Lord Crowther, which was expected in 1972. The present would seem to be an unfortunate time to consider setting up a regional system based on anything like the Northern Ireland model, or reverting to the English Heptarchy. Perhaps the reasons that inspired the setting up of this Commission are no longer valid.

The referendum held in Northern Ireland on March 8, 1973, evidently boycotted by a large section of the public, resulted in an overwhelming vote in favour of the province remaining part of the United Kingdom.

Mr. Whitelaw's White Paper on *Northern Ireland Constitutional Proposals* was published on March 20, 1973. The following are among the more important proposals. There will be a Northern Ireland Assembly of about eighty members, elected by a kind of proportional representation for a fixed term of four years. There will be committees of the assembly, whose members will reflect the balance of parties, associated with each department; the chairmen of these committees will be the political heads of the departments and will collectively form the executive. There will continue to be a Secretary of State for Northern Ireland who will be a member of the United Kingdom Cabinet, and the office of Governor will be abolished. The intention is that the executive would no longer be solely based upon any single party. The assembly will have power to legislate on most matters affecting Northern Ireland; but certain matters of national importance will be excluded from its competence, and there will be some matters on which it will be able to legislate only with the agreement of the United Kingdom Parliament. Measures of the assembly will have the force of law when approved by the Queen in Council. The assembly will be debarred from passing legislation of a discriminatory nature. It is proposed to enact a charter of human rights. Certain executive functions will be reserved to the United Kingdom Government, namely, the appointment to certain judicial offices, the conduct of public prosecutions, elections and the franchise, and emergency measures. The Government favours, and is prepared to facilitate, arrangements for consultation and co-operation between Northern Ireland and the Republic of Ireland.

The Australian Government began discussions in January 1973 with a view to the removal of the remaining limitations on the Commonwealth of Australia in relation to the United Kingdom Parliament and the Privy Council, but the states may wish to retain direct appeals in state matters from their courts.

The Joint Committee on Delegated Legislation ((1971–72) H.L. 184; H.C. 475) recommended that for the technical scrutiny of delegated legislation a Joint Scrutiny Committee should be set up in place of the existing Special Orders Committee of the Lords and the Statutory Instruments Committee of the Commons; that there should be a specific mention of *vires* in the list of grounds on which the Committee could draw an instrument to the special attention of both Houses; and that no motion for an affirmative order should be moved until it has been considered and reported on by the Joint Committee. A Joint Scrutiny Committee was accordingly set up in February 1973.

For the consideration of the merits of delegated legislation the Joint Committee on Delegated Legislation recommended that a Standing Committee of the Commons should be established to which statutory instruments and draft statutory instruments would be referred for debate. A Standing Committee on Statutory Instruments was accordingly set up in March 1973.

With regard to delegated legislation resulting from membership of the European Communities, the Joint Committee on Delegated Legislation (*supra*) was concerned only with instruments or draft instruments laid before Parliament by a Minister to implement or supplement Regulations or Directives. Delegated legislation made under the European Communities Act will be subject to ordinary technical scrutiny like other delegated legislation, but it may repeal or amend existing Acts of Parliament. The amount of delegated legislation resulting from accession to the European Communities is thought unlikely to make more than a relatively small addition to the number of instruments already scrutinised by the Statutory Instruments Committee; and it should be possible (with the recommended improvements in procedure) for Parliament to maintain a watch over delegated legislation arising out of the EEC without over-straining the parliamentary machinery.

The Select Committee on European Secondary Legislation in its interim report in February 1973 recommended arrangements for informing Members of Parliament about legislative proposals going before the Council of Ministers of the EEC, and these recommendations have been accepted by the Government. The Chancellor of the Duchy of Lancaster (Mr. John Davies) is the Minister responsible for co-ordinating departmental action on EEC matters. Council legislation (self-operating Regulations and Directives requiring U.K. legislation) is expected to be contained in about 300 instruments annually. For each EEC legislative proposal the Government will give to members details of its general effect, the Ministry responsible, how it would affect United Kingdom law, whether legislation would be required to implement it, its policy implications, and the date on which it is likely to be considered by the Council of Ministers. The Chancellor of the Duchy of Lancaster is expected to make a regular monthly statement in the Commons to accompany a list of subjects likely to be on the agenda of the next meeting of the Council, and if the subject warrants it he can arrange for a regular ministerial report to the House after each month's meeting of the Council. Members will then be able to table questions and ask for adjournment debates on proposed EEC Regulations raising important policy issues. The Select Committee's final report was expected in March 1973, and this may recommend a Joint Standing Committee for the discussion and criticism of draft Community regulations.

The Home Secretary (Mr. Carr) announced in the House of Commons on February 23, 1973, that he intended to introduce arrangements by the end of 1973 for an independent element for *ex post facto* review of the handling of complaints against police officers. The actual investigation into such complaints must continue to be carried out by the police, and the arrangements will ensure that a police officer will not be put in jeopardy twice in relation to the same offence.

The Parliamentary Commissioner for Administration is to combine his role with that of Health Service Commissioner for England and Wales after the passing of the National Health Service Reorganisation Act. Separate legislation authorising the appointment of a Health Service Commissioner for Scotland has been passed, and the same person is expected to be appointed Commissioner in all three countries. Complainants will have direct access to the Commissioner, but the health authorities concerned will have the necessary opportunity to investigate the complaint and to reply. The Commissioner will not investigate complaints concerning the exercise of clinical judgment by doctors and other staff; and this procedure will not apply where other statutory procedures exist, *e.g.* service committees for medical and allied practitioners, or where the matter can be pursued through the courts or before a tribunal.

Once more I have to thank Mr. G. D. Kinley of King's College, London, for kindly advising me of recent constitutional developments in the Isle of Man.

O. H. P.

March 1973.

CONTENTS

PART I

INTRODUCTION

xi

PART II

PARLIAMENT

PART III

THE CROWN AND THE CENTRAL GOVERNMENT

PART IV

JUSTICE AND POLICE

PART V

RIGHTS AND DUTIES OF THE INDIVIDUAL

PART VI
ADMINISTRATIVE LAW

PART VII

THE COMMONWEALTH

TABLE OF STATUTES

xxi

TABLE OF COMMONWEALTH STATUTES

Isle of Man

TABLE OF CASES

Part 1

INTRODUCTION

CHAPTER 1

THE NATURE OF CONSTITUTIONAL AND ADMINISTRATIVE LAW

THE constitutional law of a state is the law relating to the constitution of that state. It is therefore desirable at the outset to discuss briefly the terms " Law," " State " and " Constitution."

Law

Many attempts have been made to define this apparently simple term, and for these the reader is referred to books on legal theory which English writers commonly call jurisprudence. We are concerned with state law (municipal law), and it will be sufficient for our present purpose to define the law of a state as consisting of those rules of conduct which are enforced by the duly constituted courts of that state. This would not be an adequate definition for the student of jurisprudence, or the science of law in general; for it does not explain whence the courts derive their authority to lay down the law, nor why the courts in administering justice look to certain sources and not to others, and look to those sources in a certain order and in a certain way. To say that the law is the law because the courts declare it to be so would be like defining an acid as that which turns litmus paper red. Litmus paper provides a convenient working test whereby the chemist determines whether a given liquid is acid or alkali, but it does not explain what acids and alkalis are in themselves. Similarly, enforcement by the courts is a sort of litmus test which may be used to distinguish between legal and non-legal rules of conduct. Enforcement by the courts does not necessarily mean specific enforcement, but usually takes the form of punishment or some other treatment (in criminal law), or an order to pay damages or to deliver up property (in civil law).

This criterion is admittedly imperfect when applied to constitutional and administrative law. In the first place, many decisions in English administrative law are made by tribunals other than the ordinary courts. These tribunals, however, are created by Acts of Parliament; their jurisdiction, composition and powers are defined by statute, and their decisions—whether subject to appeal to the courts or not—are recognised and enforced by the courts. Again, law cannot be enforced against the government, though it can be enforced against members of the government individually. Nor can law be enforced against Parliament or either House of Parliament, although the courts may make a declaration as to the law in relation to either of the Houses, and law may be enforced against members of either House personally. Actions in tort or contract may be brought against a government department representing the Crown, but the judgment cannot be enforced by execution.[1] The law is not enforceable against the Queen in her personal capacity, but this is not of practical importance. Statutory " duties " may be declared by Parliament to be unenforceable in the courts, such as the duty of the Railways Board to provide railway services under the Transport Act 1962; and the performance of certain functions by the Speaker under the Parliament Acts may not be questioned in the courts. Moreover " the law and custom of Parliament," although it is recognised by the ordinary courts, is enforced by the Houses of Parliament through their officers, and is both historically and analytically a distinct branch of British constitutional law.[2]

Some recent writers find the essential element of legal rules to be their recognition as obligatory, by legislative and executive as well as by judicial officers.[3] But the question remains, what would happen (or what ought to happen) if a given rule were broken? We still need the formal distinction between rules which the courts enforce and rules which they do not enforce. If constitutional conventions were called laws, then we should have to distinguish between judicially-enforced laws and non-judicially-enforced laws.[4]

Legal rules, with these modifications, are thus distinguished from rules of public morality which are not enforced by the courts, although they may in some cases, *e.g.* constitutional conventions (such as the responsibility of members to Parliament), be recognised as existing by the courts. Although constitutional conventions are not laws as here defined, a study of them is essential to the understanding of a constitution—especially the British Constitution—and a description of the more important conventions is always included in books on British constitutional law.[5]

Legal rules are also distinguished from rules of private morality or ethics which are not enforced by the courts, *e.g.* the moral obligation to carry out a freely made bargain which is not unlawful but which for some reason (such as absence of consideration) lacks legal sanction.

---

1 Crown Proceedings Act 1947.
2 See Chap. 11; and for Standing Orders, Chap. 9.
3 See *e.g.* A. L. Goodhart, *English Law and the Moral Law* (1955) pp. 46–65.
4 See further, O. Hood Phillips, " Constitutional Conventions: A Conventional Reply " (1964) 8 J.S.P.T.L. 60; and *post*, Chap. 5.
5 See Chap. 5; also Chaps. 6, 15 and 35.

The contents of ethics and law overlap to a great extent, *e.g.* murder, theft and slander; but there are many rules of ethics which the law does not seek to enforce, such as the commandment to honour our parents; and many legal rules which are not intrinsically moral, such as the husband's general liability to pay tax on his wife's income.

Law includes not only the sum total of particular laws, whether statutory or otherwise, but also the complex interrelations between those laws, as well as the technique—judicial precedent, statutory interpretation and so on—by which the law is administered.

The state

This is another very difficult term to define, and a full discussion of this question also falls within the province of jurisprudence or political theory. For present purposes, however, we may define a state as an independent political society occupying a defined territory, the members of which are united together for the purpose of resisting external force and the preservation of internal order. No independent political society can be termed a state unless it professes to exercise both these functions; but no modern state of any importance contents itself with this narrow range of activity. As civilisation becomes more complex, population increases and a social conscience arises, the needs of the governed call for increased attention; taxes have to be levied to meet these needs; justice must be administered, commerce regulated, educational facilities and many other social services provided.

A fully developed modern state is expected to deal with a vast mass of social problems, either by direct activity or by supervision or regulation. In order to carry out these functions, the state must have agents or organs through which to operate. The appointment or establishment of these agents or organs, the general nature of their functions and powers, their relations *inter se* and between them and the private citizen, form a large part of the constitution of a state.

The constitution of a state

The word "constitution" is used in two different senses, the abstract and the concrete. The constitution of a state in the abstract sense is the system of laws, customs and conventions which define the composition and powers of organs of the state, and regulate the relations of the various state organs to one another and to the private citizen. A "constitution" in the concrete sense is the document in which the most important laws of the constitution are authoritatively ordained. A country, such as our own, which has no "written" constitution as explained below, has no constitution in the concrete sense of the word. It should be clear from the context which meaning is being employed.

Written and unwritten constitutions

A constitution is said to be " written " when the most important constitutional laws are specially *enacted*. Probably all civilised states, except the United Kingdom, New Zealand and Israel,[6] now have written or enacted constitutions. Those who attain power in a nation, whether as a result of a war of liberation or civil war or otherwise, usually put into the form of legislative enactment the manner in which the state is to be organised, government carried on and justice administered. The most important laws constituting the basis of the state are specified in one formal document or a series of formal documents which are binding on the courts and all persons concerned. Thus the United States of America, the U.S.S.R., Switzerland and France have written constitutions.[7] So have most members of the Commonwealth, whose constitutions were originally delegated by Parliament.[8]

It is not practicable for a written constitution to contain more than a selection of constitutional laws. It is invariably supplemented, within the limits prescribed by the constitution, by amendments passed in the prescribed manner; by organic laws, and other legislation passed in the ordinary way from time to time to fill in gaps; usually also by judicial decisions interpreting the written documents; and by customs and conventions regulating the working of the machinery of government.[9] Organic laws are a special class of laws for the passing of which a constitution prescribes some special procedure, but which do not amount to constitutional amendments.

---

6 H. E. Baker, *The Legal System of Israel* (2nd ed. 1968); E. Likhovski, *Israel's Parliament* (1972): there are " basic laws," but no constitution has been drawn up yet.

7 Compilations of texts include A. J. Peaslee, *Constitutions of the Nations* (2nd ed. 1955). For particular constitutions, see E. S. Corwin, *The Constitution and What it Means Today* (12th ed.); B. Schwartz, *American Constitutional Law* (1955); Max Beloff, *The American Federal Government* (1959); C. Hughes, *The Federal Constitution of Switzerland*; P. Campbell and B. Chapman, *The Constitution of the Fifth Republic* (1958); Dorothy Pickles, " The Constitution of the Fifth French Republic " (1959) 22 M.L.R. 1; Wm. Pickles, " The French Constitution of October 4th, 1958 " [1960] P.L. 228; Maurice Duverger, *Les Institutions françaises* (1962) pp. 144–147.

8 The Constitution of New Zealand is still largely unwritten: J. L. Robson, *New Zealand: The Development of its Laws and Constitution* (2nd ed. 1967) Chap. 1; K. J. Scott, *The New Zealand Constitution* (1962) Chap. 1.

9 Wheare, *Modern Constitutions*, Chaps. 3, 7 and 8. See, *e.g.* Munro, *The Constitution and Government of the United States* (4th ed.) pp. 76–88; Dawson, *The Government of Canada*, pp. 69–72; H. W. Hoswill, *Usages of the American Constitution* (1925).

Flexible and rigid constitutions

A more significant classification of the types of constitution is that into " flexible " and " rigid," metaphors given currency by the late Lord Bryce.[10] A *flexible* constitution was defined by Dicey as " one under which every law of every description can legally be changed with the same ease and in the same manner by one and the same body." Dicey defined a *rigid* constitution as " one under which certain laws generally known as constitutional or fundamental laws cannot be changed in the same manner as ordinary laws." [11] The distinction is of great importance in relation to constitutional amendment.

Where the constitution is rigid, certain provisions are distinguished from others in that some *special procedure* is necessary for their alteration, if they are legally alterable at all. Most European and American constitutions are rigid. The method of amending " fundamental " or " constitutional " laws varies in different constitutions: it may be the legislature sitting in a special way (as in France) or with a prescribed majority or a prescribed quorum (as in Belgium), the convention of a special constituent body (as in the United States), the consultation of the component members of a composite state (as in the United States and Swiss Federations), or a referendum of the electorate (as in Switzerland and Australia). Amendment of the United States Constitution, for example, requires either initiation by two-thirds of both Houses of Congress and ratification by the legislatures of three-fourths of the states, or initiation by two-thirds of the states and ratification by conventions in three-fourths of the states.

A subdivision of rigid constitutions can be drawn according to whether the special amending procedure is within the sole power of the legislature, or whether some outside agency has to be brought in. In the latter case the constitution may be said to be supreme over the legislature.

Sometimes a constitution or part of it may not be legally alterable at all, as certain articles of the Constitution of the German Federal Republic (1949), the " basic articles " of the Constitution of the Republic of Cyprus (1960), the " fundamental rights " in the Indian Constitution (1950),[12] and the representation of a state in the United States Senate (unless that state consents); or it may be unalterable

---

[10] Bryce, *Studies in History and Jurisprudence*, Vol. I, Essay 3. Other descriptive names considered by Bryce were moving and stationary, or fluid and solid (crystallised); *op. cit.* pp. 131–132. Lord Birkenhead L.C. preferred " controlled " and " uncontrolled ": *McCawley* v. *The King* [1920] A.C. 691 (P.C.). *Cf.* Wheare, *op. cit.* Chap. 6.

[11] Dicey, *Law of the Constitution* (10th ed.) pp. 126 *et seq.*, 146–150.

[12] *Golak Nath* v. *State of Punjab*, A.I.R. 1967 S.C. 1643 (Supreme Court of India). This reversal of previous decisions has been much criticised.

before a certain time, *e.g.* certain provisions of the United States Constitution before 1808. In such cases any alteration would legally amount to revolution.

It is unnecessary and it may be confusing to draw a distinction, as Dicey does in the first definition quoted, between the relative ease and difficulty of amending a law; this is not a distinction of which lawyers can take account, for it depends on political and psychological factors. It may be more difficult to pass a British statute facilitating divorce or the sale of intoxicating liquors or street betting than to pass a French statute reducing the period of office of the President of the Republic from seven to five years.

Unwritten constitutions are in practice flexible but written constitutions are not necessarily rigid. The Constitution of Singapore is written but entirely flexible while the constitutions of the Australian states are written and largely flexible.[13]

Fundamental laws and judicial review of legislation

Those who frame a rigid constitution seem to be placed in a dilemma. They may give the power to interpret the constitution, and to declare legislation invalid *ex post facto* as being repugnant thereto, to the ordinary courts, or to a special constitutional court. Here the final and supreme power would appear to be vested in the courts, which would usually be contrary to the intention of the framers of the constitution. Why should the judges, whose function is primarily judicial, set up their own views in opposition to the will of a popularly elected legislative assembly? Two answers may be suggested: first, the judges may be appointed by the executive which initiates legislation and presumably keeps in touch with public opinion; or, alternatively, the " will of the people " is supposed to be embodied in the constitution in a more permanent way than it is represented in the legislative assembly of the day.

On the other hand, if the legislature itself is given authority to interpret the constitution, what guarantee is there that it will ever hold itself to be wrong? In other words, how can the constitution in this case be rigid at all? Dicey saw this difficulty and stated the paradox that the " fundamental laws " in the continental type of " rigid " constitution placing restrictions on the authority of the ordinary legislature without giving power of judicial review, so far from being laws of a particularly sacrosanct character are found on analysis not to be laws at all. When the courts are not given and have not

---

[13] R. D. Lumb, *The Constitutions of the Australian States* (Brisbane, 2nd ed. 1965): these state constitutions are subject to the Colonial Laws Validity Act 1865, and to certain fundamental principles such as the monarchy.

assumed authority to declare legislation unconstitutional, the constitutional restrictions on legislative activity—though in fact they may
be carefully observed—appear on Dicey's view to be merely constitutional conventions resting on the force of public opinion.[14]

It is comparatively rare for the courts to have jurisdiction to
review legislation except in federal states, such as Switzerland [15]
and the federal members of the Commonwealth, where some check is
necessary to preserve the respective rights of the federation and its
component members.[16] The United States is the classic example of
a federation in which each state as well as the federation has a completely rigid constitution. Here the state courts have jurisdiction to
declare state legislation repugnant to the state constitution; and the
federal courts have jurisdiction to declare provisions of state constitutions, state legislation and federal legislation repugnant to the
Federal Constitution. It is not strictly accurate to say that the courts
declare legislation void: when cases are brought before them
judicially, they may declare that an alleged right or power does not
exist or that an alleged wrong has been committed because a certain
statute relied on is unconstitutional. Under the influence of Chief
Justice Marshall the American Supreme Court first assumed the power
of declaring Federal legislation unconstitutional in *Marbury* v. *Madison* (1803),[17] and the power of declaring state legislation repugnant
to the Federal Constitution in *Fletcher* v. *Peck* (1810).[18] It may be
added by way of further justification that, not only is the United
States a federation, but the executive is not responsible to the legislature and so there is not the same reason for the will of the legislature
to prevail. The Republic of Ireland, on the other hand, is a unitary
state, with an executive legally as well as conventionally responsible
to the legislature, whose Constitution gives the Supreme Court some
power of review.

The modern alternative to review of legislation by the ordinary
courts is not necessarily the complete absence of any review of constitutionality. A special constitutional court may be set up for such
cases, as in the Constitutions of the Republic of Cyprus (1960), West
Germany,[19] and Italy.[20]

[14] *Cf.* Bryce, *op. cit.* pp. 193–198.
[15] C. Hughes, *The Federal Constitution of Switzerland*; Geoffrey Sawer, *Modern Federalism* (1969) Chap. 10.
[16] Judicial review obtains in dependent territories of the Commonwealth, however, because their legislatures are regarded as subordinate to the British Parliament; *post*, Chap. 34.
[17] 1 Cranch 137.
[18] 6 Cranch 87.
[19] E. McWhinney, *Constitutionalism in Germany and the Federal Constitutional Court* (1962).
[20] Malcolm Evans, " The Italian Constitutional Court " (1968) 17 I.C.L.Q. 602.

Another device is to establish a constitutional council to which Bills may be referred *before* being submitted to the Head of State for his assent. Thus the Constitution of the Fifth French Republic (1958) provides for a *Conseil constitionnel* composed of former Presidents of the Republic and nine other members, three being appointed by each of the President of the Republic, the President of the National Assembly and the President of the Senate. Before organic laws are promulgated, the Council must examine them to ensure that they do not conflict with the constitution. The President of the Republic, the Prime Minister or the President of either House may also submit ordinary laws to the Council before they are promulgated. If a provision is declared unconstitutional it cannot be promulgated or come into force. There is no appeal against decisions of the Constitutional Council, which are binding on all public, administrative and judicial authorities. This device differs from judicial review in that the *Conseil* is not a court, and judicial review operates *ex post facto*.

The Constitutions of the Irish Republic and India expressly recognise the distinction between fundamental rights safeguarded by the courts against amendment otherwise than by the appropriate procedure, and "directive principles of social (or state) policy" for the general guidance of the legislature but which are not cognisable by any court. Such directive principles of state policy are morally binding on the legislature, but can scarcely be called laws.

The scope of constitutional law

The constitutional law of a state is the law relating to its constitution. Where the constitution is written, even though it may have to be supplemented by other materials, it is fairly easy to distinguish the constitutional law of a state from the rest of its legal system; but where, as in Britain, the constitution is unwritten, it is largely a matter of convenience what topics one includes in constitutional law, and there is no strict scientific distinction between that and the rest of the law. It follows from what has been said that constitutional law deals, in general, with the distribution and exercise of the functions of government, and the relations of the government authorities to each other and to the individual citizen. It includes the rules—though the nature of these is difficult to define—which identify the lawmaking authorities themselves, *e.g.* the legislature and the courts.[21]

More specifically, constitutional law embraces that part of a country's laws which relates to the following topics, among others: the method of choosing the Head of State, whether king or president;

21 See H. L. A. Hart, *The Concept of Law* (1961) pp. 107–108.

his powers and prerogatives; the constitution of the legislature; its powers and the privileges of its members; if there are two Chambers, the relations between them; the status of Ministers and the position of the civil servants who act under them; the armed forces and the power to control them; the relations between the central government and local authorities; treaty-making power; citizenship; the raising and spending of public money; the general system of courts, and the tenure and immunities of judges; civil liberties and their limitations; the parliamentary franchise and electoral boundaries; and the procedure (if any) for amending the constitution.

Administrative law

A distinction is commonly drawn in continental countries between constitutional law and administrative law, but because English law is not codified or officially systematised English jurists have found difficulty in determining the distinction. Sir Ivor Jennings contended that administrative law, like other branches of law, ought to be defined according to its subject-matter, namely, public administration. Administrative law then determines the organisation, powers and duties of administrative authorities.[22] This description is in accordance with continental and American usage,[23] and is now generally accepted in this country.

What specially distinguishes administrative authorities from private individuals is the extent of their powers. An important aspect of administrative law is the control exercised by courts or tribunals over those powers, especially in relation to the rights of citizens. The remedy of the citizen may be left to the jurisdiction of the ordinary courts, or the matter may be regulated by special rules and adjudicated by special courts or by administrative tribunals. A system of administrative courts or tribunals is not essential for the existence of administrative law, as is shown by the experience of Belgium, which did not set up a *Conseil d'Etat* until 1946; but the fact that France has long possessed special administrative tribunals—notably the *Conseil d'État*—which in appropriate cases oust the jurisdiction of the ordinary civil courts, has no doubt helped towards the systematisation of administrative law in that country.[24]

---

22 Jennings, *The Law and the Constitution* (5th ed.) p. 217.
23 L. Neville Brown and J. F. Garner, *French Administrative Law* (2nd ed. 1973); B. Schwartz, *American Administrative Law; French Administrative Law and the Common-Law World*.
24 L. Neville Brown, " The Reform of the French Administrative Courts " (1959) 22 M.L.R. 357; M. Letourneur and J. Méric, *Conseil d'Etat et Juridictions Administratives* (1955); Maurice Duverger, *Les Institutions françaises* (1962) Part IV. For an earlier period, see C. J. Hamson, *Executive Discretion and Administrative Control*.

Where there is a written constitution, as in France and the United States, it is easier to demarcate administrative law from constitutional law, although neither the French *droit administratif* nor American administrative law is codified. Where the constitution is unwritten, as in this country, it is largely a matter of convenience what aspects of public law we choose to treat as administrative law.[25]

The functions of government

Montesquieu in *L'Esprit des Lois* (1748) [26] following attempts by Aristotle [27] and Locke,[28] divided the powers of government into: (i) the legislative power; (ii) the executive power in matters pertaining to the law of nations, and (iii) the power of judging; and so we get the first statement of the modern classification to which we are now accustomed, *viz.*: (i) legislative, (ii) executive, and (iii) judicial.

We may attempt a general description of the various governmental functions in the modern state on the following lines:

(i) *The legislative function* is the making of new law, and the alteration or repeal of existing law. Legislation is the formulation of law by the appropriate organ of the state, in such a manner that the actual words used are themselves part of the law: the words not only contain the law, but in a sense they constitute the law. Legislation may take the form of the decree of a personal ruler, whether king or dictator; or it may be issued by an autocratic body or by a democratic assembly wholly or partly elected by the people. Without a legislative body of some sort a state could not provide law readily enough to meet modern conditions.

Two methods of direct lawmaking are found in some states: the *referendum* by which certain measures have to be submitted for approval to the electorate before being enacted by the legislature; and the *initiative* by which certain kinds of measures may be proposed by a specified number of the electors for enactment.[29] The referendum is usually a method for amending federal constitutions.

(ii) *The executive or administrative function* is the general and detailed carrying on of government according to law, including the framing of policy and the choice of the manner in which the law may be made to render that policy possible. In recent times, especially

---

25 *Post*, Chap. 2; and Part VI.
26 Bk. XI, Chap. 6.
27 Aristotle, *Politics*, Vol. IV (transl. Jowett).
28 John Locke, *Second Treatise of Civil Government* (1690) Chap. 12.
29 Wheare, *op. cit.* Chap. 6; A. B. Keith, *British Cabinet System* (2nd ed. Gibbs) pp. 256–260; H. J. Laski, *Introduction to Politics*, pp. 66–68; Philip Goodhart, *Referendum* (1971).

since the industrialisation of most civilised countries, the scope of this function has become extremely wide. It now involves the provision and administration or regulation of a vast system of social services—public health, housing, assistance for the sick and unemployed, welfare of industrial workers, education, transport and so on—as well as the supervision of defence, order and justice, and the finance required therefor, which were the original tasks of organised government.

(iii) *The judicial function* consists in the interpretation of the law and its application by rule or discretion to the facts of particular cases. This involves the ascertainment of facts in dispute according to the law of evidence. The organs which the state sets up to exercise the judicial function are called courts of law or courts of justice.

Although the above classification of the functions and corresponding powers of government, based on a material or functional analysis, may be useful in helping one to arrange the facts and to think about the problems of government, the categories are inclined to become blurred when one attempts to apply them to the details of a particular constitution. Some hold that the true distinction lies not in the nature of the powers themselves, but rather in the procedure by which they are exercised. Thus legislation involves a formal and instantaneous act designed to establish general rules by which all disputes shall be settled; administration is a continuing and mainly informal process aimed at preventing disputes in classes of cases and does not create rights by establishing precedents; adjudication presupposes an existing dispute in a particular case, is governed by strict rules of procedure and evidence and tends to create rights by establishing precedents.

Others hold that the distinction is organic or formal. Thus administration consists of the operations, whatever their intrinsic nature may be, which are performed by administrators; and administrators are all state officials who are neither legislators nor judges.[30] This last doctrine seems to be as difficult to apply as the functional or material conception of governmental functions. Thus in the Constitution of the Fifth French Republic not only has the Parliament other powers than the strictly legislative, but the lawmaking power is divided between the Parliament (*loi*) and the government (*règlement*), so that the Parliament may only make laws dealing with matters enumerated in article 34, while all other matters fall within the province of ministerial regulation.[31]

---

[30] Jennings, *op. cit.* pp. 24–25. For a contrast between the conceptual and the functional approach, see Griffith and Street, *Principles of Administrative Law* (4th ed.).

[31] B. Nicholas, " Loi, Règlement and Judicial Review in the Fifth Republic " [1970] P.L. 251.

Doctrine of the separation of powers

The doctrine of " the separation of powers " as usually understood is derived from Montesquieu,[32] whose elaboration of it was based on a study of Locke's writings [33] and an imperfect understanding of the eighteenth-century English Constitution. Montesquieu was concerned with the preservation of political liberty. " Political liberty is to be found," he says, " only when there is no abuse of power. But constant experience shows us that every man invested with power is liable to abuse it, and to carry his authority as far as it will go . . . . To prevent this abuse, it is necessary from the nature of things that one power should be a check on another. . . . When the legislative and executive powers are united in the same person or body . . . there can be no liberty. . . . Again, there is no liberty if the judicial power is not separated from the legislative and the executive. . . . There would be an end of everything if the same person or body, whether of the nobles or of the people, were to exercise all three powers."

A complete separation of powers, in the sense of a distribution of the three functions of government among three independent sets of organs with no overlapping or co-ordination, would (even if theoretically possible) bring government to a standstill. What the doctrine must be taken to advocate is the prevention of tyranny by the conferment of too much power on any one person or body, and the check of one power by another. There is an echo of this in Blackstone's *Commentaries* (1765): " In all tyrannical Governments . . . the right of making and of enforcing the laws is vested in one and the same man, or the same body of men; and wheresoever these two powers are united together there can be no liberty "; and this doctrine was taken over by the fathers of the American Constitution.

The question whether the separation of powers (*i.e.* the distribution of the various powers of government among different organs), in so far as is practicable, is desirable, and (if so) to what extent, is a problem of political theory and must be distinguished from the question which alone concerns the constitutional lawyer, namely, whether and to what extent such a separation actually exists in any given constitution. As a matter of fact the doctrine has not received much acceptance either in its country of origin or in other European countries. Governmental powers are co-ordinated by the effective part of the executive—the Council of Ministers or Cabinet—which is created by, but in fact controls, the legislature in which its members sit. The executive in some democratic countries is made responsible

[32] *L'Esprit des Lois*, Chap. XI, pp 3–6.
[33] Locke, *Second Treatise of Civil Government*, Chaps. 12–13.

to the legislature; but in totalitarian states the executive has acquired complete domination over both the legislature and the judiciary. The doctrine has received its main application in democratic countries by the securing of the independence of the courts from the control of the executive.[34]

The United States Constitution goes farther than any other in applying the doctrine. Thus the federal executive power is vested in the President, the federal legislative power is vested in Congress, and the federal judicial power is vested in the Supreme Court. The President and his Cabinet are not members of Congress (except that the Vice-President presides over the Senate), and they are not responsible to Congress. The President holds office for a fixed term and he is not necessarily of the same political party as the majority in either House of Congress. The President and Cabinet cannot initiate Bills or secure their passage through Congress, but he may recommend legislation in a message to Congress. But the separation of powers is by no means complete, the three branches of government being connected by a system of "checks and balances." Madison's theory was that one branch must not have the whole of another branch vested in it, nor obtain control over another branch. The chief danger in a republic with a representative legislature was, he thought, that the legislature (rather than the executive) would encroach on the other departments.[35] Thus the President may veto measures passed by Congress, though his veto may be overridden by a two-thirds vote of both Houses. The President has the power to negotiate treaties, but they must be ratified by a two-thirds vote of the Senate. The Senate may refuse to confirm certain appointments made by the President, notably that of judges of the Supreme Court; and the judges of that court, although appointed for life, may be removed by impeachment. The power of judicial review of legislation was assumed by the Supreme Court, and was not expressly conferred—although it may perhaps be implied—by the constitution. The three branches of government are therefore interrelated; they act as checks on each other. The problem that may have to be faced before long is whether the draftsmen of the constitution, in their zeal to prevent too great a concentration of power, did not provide restraints that unduly hamper the working of government.[36]

---

[34] The separation of powers, in the sense of the vesting of the judicial power exclusively in the courts, was read into the Ceylon Constitution of 1947: *Liyanage* v. *R.* [1967] A.C. 259 (P.C.).

[35] *The Federalist*, Nos. 47 and 48 (1788).

[36] See, *e.g. Youngstown Sheet & Tube Co.* v. *Sawyer*, 343 U.S. 579 (1952) (the "Steel Seizure Case"); B. Schwartz, *American Constitutional Law*, Chap. 7.

The rule of law and fundamental rights

Many modern constitutions incorporate certain " fundamental rights " such as personal freedom, equality before the law, freedom of property, free elections, freedom of speech, freedom of conscience and worship, freedom of contract, the right of assembly, the right of association and family rights. They are always restricted, expressly or impliedly, by some such concepts as " public order " or " due process of law "; and the courts may or may not have jurisdiction to review legislation that infringes such rights. Formulations of natural rights date from the second half of the eighteenth century, the revolutionary period in America and France. Both countries borrowed largely from English experience and thought, especially as embodied in the writings of Locke [37] and, in the case of America, Coke's commentary on Magna Carta and Blackstone's *Commentaries* (1765). For Blackstone the absolute rights of Englishmen were the rights of personal security, personal liberty and private property.

The American Declaration of Independence (1776) states that all men are created equal, and among their inalienable rights are life, liberty and the pursuit of happiness. The American " Bill of Rights " consists of ten amendments added in 1791 to the Federal Constitution of 1787.[38] These rights include free exercise of religion, freedom of speech and the press, peaceable assembly, petition for redress of grievances (1st Amendment); security of persons, houses, papers and effects from unreasonable searches and seizures (2nd Amendment); no deprivation of life, liberty or property without due process of law [39] (5th Amendment); and freedom from excessive bail or fines and from cruel or unusual punishments (8th Amendment). The American Constitution had already provided that the writ of habeas corpus should not be suspended, that no *ex post facto* law should be passed, and that the trial of all crimes, except in cases of impeachment, should be by jury.[40] Later amendments abolished slavery, and preserved the franchise from discrimination on grounds of race, colour or sex. The constitutions of individual American states also contain Bills of Rights.

A Declaration of the Rights of Man was prefaced to the French Constitution of 1791, and was confirmed by the preambles to the Constitutions of 1946 and 1958.

A Universal Declaration of Human Rights was adopted by the

---

[37] *Two Treatises of Civil Government* (1690); see Bk. II, " Of Civil Government."
[38] A Bill of Rights was intentionally excluded from the original United States Constitution for the reasons given by Hamilton in *The Federalist*, No. 88.
[39] " Due process of law " may be traced back to (1354) 28 Edw. III, c. 3.
[40] The Statute of Provisors 1351–52, c. 4, required for a criminal charge indictment or presentment of good and lawful people of the neighbourhood.

General Assembly of the United Nations in 1948,[41] and this was followed by the European Convention for the Protection of Human Rights and Fundamental Freedoms drawn up at Rome in 1950.[42] The Convention came into force in 1953. The European countries which have signed the Convention, including the United Kingdom,[43] guarantee to all persons within their jurisdiction a number of rights and freedoms. In so far as they do not already exist in their laws, the countries which have signed the European Convention are under an obligation to introduce the necessary legislation. The rights concerned are a more detailed version of those contained in the Universal Declaration of 1948. They are still expressed in very general terms, and the necessary limitations are not stated. There is an enforcement machinery, partly adoptive, through the European Commission of Human Rights, the Committee of Ministers of the Council of Europe and the European Court of Human Rights.

Meanwhile the International Commission of Jurists, which is affiliated to UNESCO, has attempted with considerable success to give material content to " the rule of law," an expression used in the Universal Declaration of Human Rights. Its most notable achievement so far has been the *Declaration of Delhi, 1959*.[44] This resulted from a congress held in New Delhi attended by jurists from more than fifty countries (including Lord Denning and Mr. Justice Devlin), and was based on a questionnaire circulated to 75,000 lawyers. " Respect for the supreme value of human personality " was stated to be the basis of all law.

The " rule of law," according to the Declaration of Delhi, relates to:

  (i) the legislature: there is a right to representative and responsible government; and there are certain minimum standards or principles for the law, including those contained in the Universal Declaration and the European Convention, in particular, freedom of religious belief, assembly and association, and the absence of retroactive penal laws;

  (ii) the executive: especially that delegated legislation should be subject to independent judicial control, and that a citizen who

---

[41] H. Lauterpacht, *International Law and Human Rights*. The Declaration is set out at pp. 428–434.

[42] A. H. Robertson, *Human Rights in Europe* (1963); *European Institutions* (3rd ed. 1973). [43] (1953) Cmd. 8969; confirmed periodically since.

[44] " Declaration of Delhi " (1959) 2 Jo.Int.Com. of Jurists, pp. 7–43; " The Rule of Law in a Free Society " *Report of International Congress of Jurists* (New Delhi, 1959). See further, N. S. Marsh, " The Rule of Law as a Supra-National Concept " *Oxford Essays in Jurisprudence* (ed. A. G. Guest, 1961) Chap. 9; N. S. Marsh, " Civil Liberties in Europe " (1959) 75 L.Q.R. 530; A. H. Robertson, *Human Rights in the World* (1972).

is wronged should have a remedy against the state or government;

(iii) the criminal process: a " fair trial " involves such elements as certainty of the criminal law, the presumption of innocence, reasonable rules relating to arrest, accusation and detention pending trial, the giving of notice and provision for legal advice, public trial, right of appeal, and absence of cruel or unusual punishments;

(iv) the judiciary and the legal profession: this requires the independence of the judiciary, and proper grounds and procedure for removal of judges; and imposes a responsibility on an organised and autonomous legal profession.

Declarations of Rights in various forms have been incorporated into a number of constitutions of Commonwealth countries in recent years, including India, the Federation of Malaysia, Malta, Nigeria, and other African countries.[45] Canada enacted in 1960 a " Bill of Rights " which is of a peculiar nature in that it does not bind the Canadian Parliament against express repeal or amendments, but it operates in the courts as a presumption of interpretation in the absence of express words to the contrary.[46]

The attitude of the British Constitution to such matters is discussed in the next chapter.

[45] Sir Kenneth Roberts-Wray, " Human Rights in the Commonwealth " (1968) 17 I.C.L.Q. 908.
[46] R. v. Drybones (1969) 9 D.L.R. (3d) 473 (S.C.); and note by F. M. Auburn in (1970) 86 L.Q.R. 306.

CHAPTER 2

GENERAL CHARACTERISTICS OF THE
BRITISH CONSTITUTION

Unitary Constitution

The United Kingdom [1]

The British Constitution is unitary as opposed to federal or con-
federal. The United Kingdom is a union of England and Wales (Laws
in Wales Act 1536) with Scotland, forming Great Britain (Union with
Scotland Act 1706),[2] and Northern Ireland (Union with Ireland Act
1800; Government of Ireland Act 1920). The state for the purpose of
international relations is the United Kingdom, although it is often
popularly but inaccurately referred to as " Great Britain," " Britain "
or " England." The appropriate adjective for our constitution,
Parliament and so on would be " United Kingdom," [3] although again
that commonly used is " British " or " English." Scotland has a
distinct system of private law, and the House of Lords is the final court
of appeal from Scotland in civil cases only. Northern Ireland has
its own subordinate and limited Parliament,[4] but its electors are also
represented in the United Kingdom Parliament.

The British Islands

The United Kingdom together with the Isle of Man and the
Channel Islands comprise the British Islands (Interpretation Act

---

[1] Post, Chap. 33. For a recent discussion, see D. G. T. Williams, " The Constitution
of the United Kingdom " [1972 B] C.L.J. 266.

[2] A Personal Union of the Crowns of England and Scotland was constituted in 1603
when James VI of Scotland succeeded Elizabeth I as James I of England. The
name " Great Britain " was suggested by Francis Bacon: " Brief Discourse Touching the Happy Union of the Kingdoms of England and Scotland," Spedding, *Letters
and Life of Francis Bacon*, Vol. III, pp. 90 *et seq.*
There was also a Personal Union of Great Britain and Hanover from the
accession of George I to the British throne in 1714 until the death of William IV
in 1837, Victoria being disqualified from succeeding to the throne of Hanover.
It was held in *Isaacson* v. *Durant* (*Stepney Election Petition*) (1886) 17 Q.B.D. 54,
that Hanoverians after the death of William IV ceased to owe allegiance to the
British Sovereign. The Act of Settlement 1700 provided that England should not
be obliged to engage in any war for the defence of Hanover without the consent
of Parliament.

[3] Formerly in overseas dominions of the Crown, the United Kingdom Parliament
was called the " Imperial Parliament."

[4] The Northern Ireland Parliament was suspended for twelve months from March 30,
1972, by the Northern Ireland (Temporary Provisions) Act 1972 in view of the
political situation in Northern Ireland. By the Act, the suspension may be extended
by Order in Council beyond the twelve-month period.

1889, s. 18). The Isle of Man has been under the allegiance of the Crown since the reign of Henry IV. The Channel Islands were formerly part of the Duchy of Normandy which remained to the King of England when the rest of Normandy reverted to France in the thirteenth century. These are not part of the United Kingdom, nor have they ever been colonies.[5] They have their own legislatures. Parliament legislates for the Isle of Man in certain topics, but the Channel Islands assert that legislation for them by Act of Parliament or Order in Council requires their consent and local registration. These islands are part of Her Majesty's dominions, and persons born in them are British subjects by birth. The British Nationality Act 1948 includes their citizens among citizens of the United Kingdom and colonies, although as a mark of their unique association with the Crown they may, if they desire, be known as " citizens of the United Kingdom, Islands and Colonies."

Possible devolution

Following a recent resurgence of Scottish and Welsh nationalism, suggestions were put forward for the further devolution of governmental powers in Scotland and Wales, and perhaps to the various regions of England.[6] A Constitutional Commission was set up by the government in 1969 under the chairmanship of the late Lord Crowther, with the following terms of reference: " to examine the present functions of the central legislature and government in relation to the several countries, nations and regions of the United Kingdom; to consider, having regard to developments in local government organisation and in the administrative and other relationships between the various parts of the United Kingdom, and to the interests of the prospertity and good government of Our people under the Crown, whether any changes are desirable in those functions or otherwise in present constitutional and economic relationships; to consider also, whether any changes are desirable in the constitutional and economic relationships between the United Kingdom and the Channel Islands and the Isle of Man." The Commission was expected to report in 1972. It will be seen that the terms of reference are not confined to devolution of powers. The resurgence of Scottish and Welsh nationalism as an electoral force may prove to be only temporary. National or regional devolution can hardly sustain a form of government midway between the central and local levels unless the nations or regions have taxing power and a certain degree of financial autonomy, which would raise considerable legal and constitutional problems.

5 *Post*, Chap. 33.
6 See J. P. Mackintosh, *The Devolution of Power* (1968); D. M. Walker, " The Constitution and the Proposed Scottish Convention," 1970 S.L.T. 117.

Unwritten Constitution

The British Constitution is said to be " unwritten " [7] because it is not embodied in any enactment or formally related series of enactments. The laws of the constitution comprise three kinds of rules: statute law, common law, and custom (especially parliamentary custom). To these we must add constitutional conventions if we are to understand modern developments and the manner in which the constitution works.

The sources of the legal rules are the same as for English private laws, namely, statutes, judicial precedents, customs and books of authority,[8] except that under the third head we must include parliamentary custom. Treaties are not in themselves sources of municipal (*i.e.* national) law, as they are in some countries.

Statutes

These consist of Acts of Parliament and subordinate legislation.

Some of the principles and detailed rules of the British Constitution are contained in formally unrelated Acts of Parliament, such as the Act of Settlement 1700; the Parliament Acts 1911 and 1949; the Government of Ireland Act 1920; the Crown Proceedings Act 1947; and the British Nationality Act 1948. Laws intended to bind both Houses of Parliament are put into the form of Acts, *e.g.* Provisional Collection of Taxes Acts, the Laying of Documents before Parliament (Interpretation) Act 1948 and the Royal Assent Act 1967. There are also a few important documents of a quasi-legislative nature, such as Magna Carta 1215 (and subsequent reissues and confirmations by King and Parliament [9]), and the Bill of Rights 1688 (passed by a " convention " Parliament, but deemed to have the force of statute); and at least two Acts of Parliament which have a peculiar status—the Union with Scotland Act 1706, based on a treaty negotiated by the English and Scottish Parliaments, and the Statute of Westminster 1931, based on conventions agreed between the United Kingdom and the British Dominions at that time.

Subordinate legislation consists mainly of legislation made by persons or bodies to whom the power has been delegated by Parlia-

---

[7] Sir Kenneth Wheare prefers to say that Britain " has no written Constitution ": *Modern Constitutions*, p. 19.

[8] See O. Hood Phillips, *A First Book of English Law* (6th ed.) Part II.

[9] The version of Magna Carta that became law for subsequent times was that of Henry III (1225); and the authoritative text was that of (1297) 25 Edward I, later understood as expounded by Coke in his Second Institute. Obsolete provisions—not including Cap. 14 (forbidding excessive fines) and Cap. 29 (Caps. 39 and 40 of 1215)—were repealed in the nineteenth century by Statute Law Revision Acts. See *The Great Charter* (New York, 1965) ed. Griswold; Alec Samuels, " Magna Carta as living law " (1969) 20 N.I.L.Q. 49. Confirmations by Edward I (1297) and Edward III (1324) were largely repealed by the Statute Law (Repeals) Act 1969.

ment. Parliament confers on the Queen in Council the power to legislate by Orders in Council, a method which is useful for filling in the more important details giving effect to the principles of the enabling Act, and also valuable in times of emergency when Parliament may not be in session. Legislative powers are also frequently delegated by Parliament to individual Ministers, local government authorities and public corporations. Delegated legislation issued by Ministers usually takes the form of orders, rules or regulations, and these in appropriate cases are mostly published as Statutory Instruments. Delegated legislation made by local authorities is known as by-laws, and is published by the local authority concerned.

Judicial precedents

Many of the principles of British constitutional law are to be inferred from decisions of the courts in particular cases, such as the extent of the liberties of the citizen, determined in disputes between individuals and the executive. Such cases arise incidentally, as it were, in the ordinary course of litigation. They will most commonly be found in the decisions of the Queen's Bench Division (previously the Court of King's Bench), which not only grants damages for breach of legal rights but also has a special jurisdiction in proceedings for habeas corpus, certiorari, prohibition and mandamus; in the decisions of the Court of Appeal and the House of Lords on appeal therefrom, and the Judicial Committee of the Privy Council in appeals from British overseas territories.[10]

Examples of judicial precedents laying down important principles of constitutional law, chosen from hundreds of cases that might be cited, are: *Anderson* v. *Gorrie* [11] (immunity of judges); *Ashby* v. *White* (1704) [12] (*ubi jus ibi remedium*); *Att.-Gen.* v. *Wilts United Dairies* (1922) [13] (no power to levy money without authority of Parliament); *Campbell* v. *Hall* [14] (no prerogative power to legislate for colony with representative assembly); *Entick* v. *Carrington* [15] (general warrant illegal); *Johnstone* v. *Pedlar* [16] (" act of state " no defence in tort as regards act committed in relation to a friendly alien in this country); *Case of Proclamations* [17] (the King cannot create offences

---

[10] The influence of equity on constitutional law has been comparatively slight, although the remedies of injunction and declaration were equitable in origin: see Hanbury, " Equity in Public Law " (*Essays in Equity*, p. 80).

[11] [1895] 1 Q.B. 668.

[12] 2 Ld.Raym. 938.

[13] 91 L.J.K.B. 897.

[14] (1774) 1 Cowp. 204; Lofft 655.

[15] (1765) 19 St.Tr. 1029, 1066.

[16] [1921] 2 A.C. 262.

[17] (1610) 12 Co.Rep. 74.

by proclamation); *Stockdale* v. *Hansard* [18] (Commons cannot change law by claiming new privileges); *Wason* v. *Walter* [19] (defence of qualified privilege extends to unauthorised reports of parliamentary debates).

Custom

A custom in private law is a rule of conduct which has not been adjudicated upon by the courts, but which would be recognised and enforced by the courts if the matter came before them. It is based on usage, but in order that it may be recognised by the courts as law, a custom must be: (i) regarded by those subject to it as obligatory; (ii) certain; (iii) reasonable; (iv) of immemorial antiquity; and (v) it must have been in existence continuously. These are the main tests which English courts apply to an alleged local custom, and they would presumably apply the same tests to an alleged general custom not hitherto adjudicated upon. The traditional doctrine was that the common law of England consisted of the general "customs of the realm." It is true to a certain extent that the early common law consisted of general immemorial customs; but it is almost certain that general customs are no longer a creative source of English private law, as they have all become embodied by judicial recognition and enforcement in the system of case law or else have been displaced by legislation.

Custom (largely feudal in origin) has been a source of important parts of our constitutional law, for example, the royal prerogative and parliamentary privilege.[20] As Plucknett said: "Feudal custom includes the relationship of Crown and nobles until the moment when this body of custom separates and becomes, first, the law of the prerogative, and then later still combines with the custom of the King's High Court of Parliament to form modern constitutional law." [21] The royal prerogative is now regarded as part of the common law. The law and custom of Parliament, including parliamentary privilege, is a special kind of customary law—recognised, but not developed, by the ordinary courts—which is not of immemorial antiquity. There may still be some customary constitutional laws which have not had occasion to be recognised by the courts but which would be so recognised if the question came before them, for example, such rules (not being statutory or merely conventional) as prescribe the forms according to which acts of the Crown are to be performed. If so, customs of this kind would hardly require immemorial antiquity,

---

[18] (1839) 9 Ad. & E. 1.
[19] (1869) L.R. 4 Q.B. 73.
[20] But much of parliamentary privilege is not of "immemorial antiquity": Parliament itself may be said to have originated with Edward I.
[21] T. F. T. Plucknett, *A Concise History of the Common Law* (5th ed.) p. 309.

but would rest rather on the necessity of there being some form (such as sealing and counter-signature) by which the Crown's acts can be authenticated.

Books of authority

The general rule applied by English courts is that textbooks, however eminent their authors, and whether or not they were judges, are not authoritative. Between later authors and some of the earlier writers, however, there is a difference of authority so great as virtually to amount to a difference in kind. Some of the earlier textbooks are treated by the courts as authoritative statements of the law of their time, and therefore of present law if it is not shown to have been changed, which may be quoted and relied on in court on the authority of their authors. The statements of such writers are presumed to be evidence of judicial decisions that have been lost, and they are therefore accepted if not contrary to reason. This is chiefly to be explained by the difficulty of ascertaining the law of early times, and of course it only applies in the absence of statutes and reported decisions on the point. Whether a textbook will be treated as authoritative in this special sense is determined by the tradition of the legal profession and the practice of the courts, and depends on such factors as the reputation of the author and the date when the book was written.

Among the books of authority that are most important as sources of English constitutional law are Fitzherbert's *Abridgment* (1516), Brooke's *Abridgment* (1568), Glanvill's *Tractatus de Legibus et Consuetudinibus Angliae* (c. 1189), Bracton's treatise of the same name (c. 1250),[22] Littleton's *Tenures* (c. 1470), Fitzherbert's *Natura Brevium* (1543), Coke's *Institutes of the Laws of England* (1628–1644), Hale's *History of the Pleas of the Crown* (published in 1736, sixty years after the author's death),[23] Hawkins' *Pleas of the Crown* (1716), Foster's *Crown Cases* (1762),[24] and Blackstone's *Commentaries on the Laws of England* (1765).[25] Of these Blackstone's *Commentaries*, being the most general and elementary as well as the most recent, have not such a high authority on points of detail as Hale, Hawkins and Foster.

Flexible constitution

The British Constitution is said to be " flexible " because any principle or rule of the constitution can be altered by the same body

22 See *Case of Prohibitions* (*Prohibitions del Roy*) (1607) 12 Co.Rep. 63.
23 See *R. v. Casement* [1917] 1 K.B. 98, at pp. 141–142.
24 See *Joyce v. Director of Public Prosecutions* [1946] A.C. 347.
25 See *e.g. Thomas v. Sawkins* [1935] 2 K.B. 249; *R. v. St. Edmundsbury and Ipswich Diocese* (*Chancellor*) [1948] 1 K.B. 195.

and in the same manner as any other law. In other words, there is no formal distinction between laws that are specifically "constitutional" or "fundamental" and those that are not. The body which has the power to alter the constitution, or any other rules of law, is the Queen in Parliament, and the procedure is the same as for any other legislation. There are no laws that cannot be repealed or altered in this way, that is to say, none that are "entrenched." [26] The flexibility of the British Constitution is a corollary of the fact that there is no written constitution or "higher law" binding on Parliament, and the consequent legislative supremacy of Parliament (*infra*). The courts therefore have no power to "review" parliamentary legislation and to declare it unconstitutional.[27]

It follows also that the distinction drawn between British constitutional law and administrative law or other branches of English law, and the selection of the contents of each, are matters of convenience, guidance being sought from tradition and comparison with other constitutions.

Legislative supremacy of Parliament [28]

The most important characteristic of British constitutional law is the legislative supremacy (formerly called "sovereignty") of the United Kingdom Parliament. Positively this means that Parliament can legally pass any kind of law whatsoever: negatively it means that there is no person or body whose legislative power competes with it or overrides it. We may call it the one fundamental law of the British Constitution.[29]

Constitutional or limited Monarchy

The British political system is in form monarchical. But it is a limited or "constitutional" monarchy, as opposed to an absolute or strong monarchy. That is to say, the governmental powers which as a matter of legal form are vested in the Queen are in practice exercised according to the laws, customs and conventions of the constitution; and they are exercised either by the Queen on the advice of her

---

[26] *Cf. McWhirter* v. *Att.-Gen.*, *The Times*, July 1, 1972 (C.A.); summons for declaration that accession to EEC would be contrary to the Bill of Rights, struck out as an abuse of the process of the court.

[27] For a discussion of the question whether this country ought to have a written and entrenched constitution, and (if so) how this might be brought about, see O. Hood Phillips, *Reform of the Constitution* (1970).

[28] See further, Chaps. 3 and 4.

[29] Taken with the Parliament Acts 1911 and 1949 and the convention that the Queen will not refuse the Royal Assent to Bills, this virtually means the supremacy of a majority of the House of Commons: "That is really all the British Constitution that there is": Kenneth Pickthorn, M.P. (1956) 550 H.C.Deb., col. 1821.

Ministers or by the Ministers in her name. This principle applies both to the Queen's common law (" prerogative ") powers and to her statutory powers. It is a product of English political history from the seventeenth century, and is secured by means of constitutional conventions.

Responsible Parliamentary government

Parliamentary government

Parliament itself does not govern, nor is it capable of doing so. The expression " parliamentary government " is somewhat misleading, and means government by the executive in and through Parliament. Parliament exercises supreme control over all branches of government. Besides its supreme lawmaking power, Parliament supervises the general conduct of the executive. It makes and unmakes state offices and government departments, controls their finances, asks questions concerning the carrying out of their duties, and debates motions of confidence. Parliament also reorganises the system of courts, though it does not in practice interfere with the conduct of litigation. All this is a matter partly of law, partly of custom and partly of convention.

Responsible government

Ministers are responsible to Parliament—more particularly to the House of Commons. They defend their conduct there, and continuance in office depends on retaining the confidence of the Commons. This is mainly a matter of constitutional convention.[30] The key to responsible parliamentary government lies in the Cabinet system, which ensures that Ministers are members of the legislature, that they must retain the confidence of the Commons, and that they can appeal to the electorate to return an assembly that will support their policy.

Responsible parliamentary government of this kind may be found in a republican régime, as in India. It is in marked contrast to the presidential system that exists, for example, in the United States, where the executive power is vested in the President, who is not a member of Congress and whose continuance in office does not depend on the support of the House of Representatives.[31]

Representative government

It is implied in what has been said of the British Constitution that the legislature " represents " the people in a general way.

30 See *post*, Chaps. 5 and 15.
31 In addition to the " executive " type of President (*e.g.* U.S.A.) and the " parliamentary " type of President (*e.g.* India), there are other varieties of the presidential system, *e.g.* in South America and Africa.

Responsible government involves representative government, though the converse is not necessarily true. A general election nowadays is in effect the election of a prime minister, the leader of a political party with a certain programme. Political parties are a development since 1688. They rest almost entirely on convention or merely political fact, though their existence was assumed by the Ministers of the Crown Act 1937, which defined the Leader of the Opposition and granted him a salary.[32]

Representative government presupposes that the electors are free to organise themselves in political parties, and (within reasonable limits) to express their views and to criticise the government. The party system is inevitable in a democratic country, since men disagree about political ends and means. It is " a convenient device to enable the majority to have their way and the minority to have their say." [33]

Although, as George Tierney said, it is the duty of the Opposition to oppose, the responsible aspect of the party system is brought out in the expression " His Majesty's Opposition," which was coined— originally as a joke—by J. C. Hobhouse early in the last century.

Representative government is now assisted also by secret ballot, universal adult suffrage,[34] independent Boundary Commissions, and a strict limitation of the powers of the House of Lords as against the House of Commons.[35]

Importance of constitutional conventions [36]

The word " conventions," as used by constitutional lawyers, refers to rules of political practice which are regarded as binding by those whom they concern—especially the Sovereign and statesmen—but which would not be *enforced* by the courts if the matter came before them. The lack of judicial enforcement distinguishes conventions from laws in the strict sense. This is an important formal distinction for the lawyer, though the politician may not be so interested in the

---

32 See now, Ministerial Salaries Consolidation Act 1965.

33 S. D. Bailey, *The British Party System* (Hansard Society, 1952) p. xii For the political parties, see also Sir Ivor Jennings, *Party Politics*, Vol. II; *The Growth of Parties* (1961); I. Bulmer-Thomas, *The Growth of the British Party System* (1965); Robert McKenzie, *British Political Parties*; C. S. Emden, *The People and the Constitution* (2nd ed.); Greaves, *The British Constitution* (3rd ed.) Chap. 6; A. Lawrence Lowell, *The Government of England* (1931) Vol. I, Chaps. 24–30; Vol. II, Chaps. 31–37.

34 *Post*, Chap. 8. Direct " participation " of the people at the national level is not practicable, even if it were thought desirable; see Bernard Crick, " ' Them and Us ': Public Impotence and Government Power " [1968] P.L. 8; and see Crick, *In Defence of Politics* (1962; Pelican, 1964) Chap. 3 (" A Defence of Politics Against Democracy ").

35 *Post*, Chap. 6.

36 See further, *post*, Chap. 5.

distinction. Privileges enforced by each House are also excluded from
the definition of conventions.

Conventions are found to a greater or less extent in most countries
that have written constitutions. This is so not only in the Commonwealth countries but also, for example, in the United States. There
the method of electing the President and the manner of choosing
the President's Cabinet are governed largely by convention. What
is characteristic of the British Constitution is the extremely important
part played by conventions. Not only do the British have no written
constitution, but they have been reluctant to stereotype their rules
of government in the form of statutes. Many important political
developments have been effected since 1688 without recourse to legal
forms at all. It is constitutional conventions that describe and explain
how the constitution works, how it lives and grows. Their general
purpose is to adapt structure to function. In this way the strong
monarchy of 1688 has become a limited monarchy with responsible
parliamentary government.

Independence of the judiciary [37]

The justices of the Royal courts, which grew up in Norman and
Plantagenet times, were the King's servants: down to the time of the
Stuarts they usually held office during the King's pleasure and, like
other Crown servants, could be dismissed by the King at will. This
fact doubtless affected some of the judicial decisions given in the reigns
of James I and Charles I. After the revolution of 1688, judges of
superior courts were appointed " during good behaviour," but there
was doubt whether at common law this referred merely to good
behaviour in relation to the King. Eventually the Act of Settlement
1700 provided that " Judges commissions be made *quamdiu se bene
gesserint*, and their salaries ascertained and established, but upon
the address of both Houses of Parliament it may be lawful to remove
them." The first and third of those provisions have been substantially
re-enacted by the Judicature Acts and Appellate Jurisdiction Acts
now in force. Their effect is that judges of the *superior* British
courts may not be removed except for misbehaviour in their office
or (probably) conviction of some serious offence. Removal is by
the Crown. Removal may be on an Address by both Houses of
Parliament, but it is not certain whether such an Address is necessary.
This question is discussed more fully in Chapter 19.

There are now statutory retiring ages for Lords of Appeal in
Ordinary, Supreme Court judges, Circuit judges, county court judges
and magistrates. County court judges and justices of the peace are

[37] See further, *post*, Chap. 19.

removable at the instance of the Lord Chancellor for misconduct, and in some cases incompetence, under various statutes.[38]

The provision as regards the ascertainment and establishment of salaries is secured by the practice of passing permanent Acts [39] defining judicial salaries and charging them on the Consolidated Fund. The executive, therefore, cannot bring pressure to bear on the judges by threatening to reduce their salaries, nor do their salaries come up for annual review (with opportunity for discussion of their conduct) by the House of Commons as do most estimates of public expenditure.

As the body of Ministers or " the government " has in practice come to play the part in public affairs formerly played by the Sovereign, the modern significance of the independence of the judges is that they are free from control or influence by the government in the administration of justice. Even the Houses of Parliament do not seek to interfere in the conduct of litigation; not only are the judges' salaries charged on the Consolidated Fund, but it is a parliamentary custom that questions should not be asked in the House about the conduct of the courts in particular cases.

A different, though relevant, principle is the immunity of judges from ordinary civil or criminal proceedings taken against them in respect of the discharge of their judicial functions, in order that the law may be administered freely and without fear or favour. No civil proceedings lie against a judge of a superior court for anything said or done by him in his judicial capacity, even if malicious or in bad faith (*Anderson* v. *Gorrie*).[40] A judge of an inferior court, *e.g.* county court or court-martial, is similarly immune if he was acting within his jurisdiction (*Heddon* v. *Evans*).[41]

No strict separation of powers

On the other hand there is not, and never has been, a strict separation of powers in the English Constitution. Historically the Crown has been an element in the exercise of all three kinds of powers— legislative, executive and judicial. A court cannot effectively adjudicate unless it has such executive power as enables it to conduct its proceedings without interference and to secure the enforcement of its decisions. Justices of the peace have administrative or ministerial, as well as judicial, functions. Central government departments and

---

[38] Colonial judges hold office at the pleasure of the Crown (unless local legislation provides otherwise), and the Act of Settlement did not apply to them: *Terrell* v. *Secretary of State for the Colonies* [1953] 2 Q.B. 482.

[39] Strictly, there are no *permanent* Acts, *i.e.* Acts which Parliament cannot repeal or amend. The expression here refers to Acts passed for an indefinite period, as contrasted with Acts passed for some definite period, *e.g.* Annual Acts.

[40] [1895] 1 Q.B. 668.

[41] (1919) 35 T.L.R. 642. See further, *post*, Chap. 19.

local authorities have lawmaking and adjudicatory powers delegated to them by statute. The government, including the Cabinet, is composed of members of the legislature. The House of Lords has both legislative and judicial functions, and the Lord Chancellor has executive functions as well. And Parliament, whose original functions were of a judicial nature, has power to do anything under the form of an Act of Parliament.

No distinct system of administrative law

Administrative law, as we have seen,[42] determines the organisation, powers and duties of administrative authorities. It is the law relating to public administration. English law, of course, contains both general principles and detailed rules relating to the structure of administrative authorities, their functions and powers, and the supervision of the relations between them and the private citizen. Administrative authorities include Ministers and central government departments, local government authorities, public corporations, and their officers and servants. There are numerous statutes concerning their organisation, and conferring the powers necessary for the exercise of their functions relating to such matters as public health, education, transport, planning, housing, national insurance, electricity supply and so on. Administrative authorities are kept within their powers partly by the courts, and partly by a miscellaneous number of special or administrative tribunals such as transport tribunals, national health insurance tribunals and planning tribunals. But there is no *system* of administrative law in this country—still less a *system* of administrative courts. The state of affairs was described by a former Lord Chief Justice as " administrative lawlessness." [43] The topics covered by administrative law in England have to be picked out, as a matter of choice, from the general body of our constitutional law. They comprise, roughly, the topics covered by Part VI of this book. The rest of our constitutional law would then deal with the monarchy and the royal prerogative, especially in relation to foreign affairs, the armed forces and aliens; Parliament; nationality and citizenship; the general principles relating to the rights of the individual; the courts; and the Commonwealth.

This view has slowly gained ground among academic lawyers. At first, English writing on administrative law tended to deal mainly with the delegation to the executive of legislative and judicial powers,[44]

---

[42] *Ante*, p. 11.
[43] Lord Hewart, *The New Despotism* (1929).
[44] *e.g.* Carr, *Delegated Legislation; Concerning English Administrative Law*; Robson, *Justice and Administrative Law* (3rd ed.); Allen, *Law and Orders* (3rd ed.); *Administrative Jurisdiction*.

not because administrative law is confined to these topics but largely because the great influence of Dicey [45] made them controversial ground and they revealed tendencies that were resented by the more conservative and individualist members of the legal profession.[46] Dicey's attitude was due not only to his political predilections in favour of individual liberty as against government " interference," but also to a misunderstanding of the French *droit administratif* which led to the false assumption that there could be no administrative law without a separate system of administrative courts.[47] More recently, however, English authors have produced monographs or textbooks covering a much wider field or specific aspects.[48]

The first judicial mention of " administrative law " in the courts was by Lord Reid in *Ridge* v. *Baldwin* (1964) [49] where he said: " We do not have a developed system of administrative law—perhaps because until fairly recently we did not need it." The Law Commission has been asked to review the existing remedies for the judicial control of administrative acts with a view to evolving a simpler and more effective procedure.[50]

The rule of law

History of the doctrine

The " rule of law " is an ambiguous expression, and may mean different things for different writers. The idea that the rulers as well as the governed should be subject to law is found in one form in Aristotle, who said that " the rule of the law is preferable to that of any individual." [51] Bracton, writing in the thirteenth century, adopted the theory generally held in the Middle Ages that the world was governed by law, human or divine; and held that " the King himself ought not to be subject to man but subject to God and to the law, because the law makes him king." [52] The same view is also

---

[45] Dicey, *Law of the Constitution* (10th ed.) Chap. 12.
[46] See Lord Hewart, *The New Despotism*; Cmd. 4060 (1932), *Report of the Committee on Ministers' Powers.*
[47] See, however, Dicey's article, " *Droit Administratif* in Modern French Law " (1901) 17 L.Q.R. 302, on changes in French administrative law after 1872.
[48] *e.g.* Griffith and Street, *Principles of Administrative Law* (4th ed. 1972); H. W. R. Wade, *Administrative Law* (3rd ed. 1971); S. A. de Smith, *Judicial Review of Administrative Action* (2nd ed. 1968); J. F. Garner, *Administrative Law* (3rd ed. 1970); D. C. M. Yardley, *A Source Book of English Administrative Law* (2nd ed. 1970). And see H. W. R. Wade, " Anglo-American Administrative Law: Some reflections " (1965) 81 L.Q.R. 357; J. D. B. Mitchell, " The Causes and Effects of the Absence of a System of Public Law in the United Kingdom " [1965] P.L. 95.
[49] [1964] A.C. 40.
[50] *Law Commission Report: Administrative Law* (Law Com. No. 20) (1969), Cmnd. 4059; *Law Commission Published Working Paper No. 40, Remedies in Administrative Law* (1971). [51] *Politics*, Vol. III, p. 16 (transl. Jowett, ed. Davis).
[52] " Ipse autem rex non debet esse sub homine sed sub Deo et sub lege, quia lex facit regem ": *De Legibus et Consuetudinibus Angliae*, f. 5 b.

expressed in the Year Books of the fourteenth and fifteenth centuries.[53] Such superior law governed kings as well as subjects and set limits to the prerogative. On that ground Fortescue, in the middle of the fifteenth century, based his argument that there could be no taxation without the consent of Parliament.[54] During the conflict between King and Parliament in the reigns of the early Stuarts, the doctrine propounded by Coke was the superiority of the traditional common law over King and executive; but the common lawyers (including Coke in his later life) were in alliance with Parliament, and this theory had to be combined with the new doctrine of the supremacy of Parliament. What was supreme, therefore, was the law for the time being; that is to say, the common law subject to such changes as King in Parliament might make from time to time.[55]

This view eventually prevailed with the revolution of 1688, although the law now regarded as supreme was not the common law (subject to parliamentary change) in the narrow sense, but the whole of English law, both statute law and case law, in whatever courts it was administered. The rule of law, therefore, precludes arbitrary action on the part of the Crown or members of the government—although as a matter of fact the government can generally secure the passing by Parliament of such laws as it wants.

Dicey's doctrine of the rule of law

It is as long ago as 1885 that Dicey first published his *Law of the Constitution*, based on lectures he gave as Vinerian Professor of English Law at Oxford, in which his purpose was to deal " only with two or three guiding principles which pervade the modern constitution of England." [56] The three distinguishing characteristics of the English Constitution that he chose to explain and illustrate were " the Sovereignty of Parliament, the Rule of Law, and the Conventions of the Constitution." [57] A large part of the book was devoted to an exposition of his doctrine of the " rule of law," [58] and this has had a profound influence among those who think and write about the constitution, as well as those who work it.

---

[53] See *Report of Committee on Ministers' Powers* (1932) Cmd. 4060, pp. 71–72.
[54] *De Laudibus Legum Angliae*, Chap. 18; *The Governance of England*, Chap. 3.
[55] Holdsworth, *History of English Law*, Vol. II, pp. 441–442; Vol. X, pp. 647–649. See also F. W. Gough, *Fundamental Law in English Constitutional History* (1955); cf. Roscoe Pound, *The Development of Constitutional Guarantees of Liberty* (1957); McIlwain, *The High Court of Parliament*, Chap. 2.
[56] Preface to 1st ed. (1885).
[57] Dicey, *Law of the Constitution* (8th ed. 1914) p. xvii.
[58] Dicey, *Law of the Constitution* (10th ed.) Part II. H. W. Arndt, " The Origins of Dicey's Concept of ' The Rule of Law ' " (1957) 31 A.L.J. 117, points out that Dicey elaborated and expanded the ideas of W. E. Hearn in *The Government of England* (1867), to which Dicey made a general reference in the Preface to his first edition.

For Dicey the expression " the rule of law " included three distinct though kindred conceptions:

(i) The absence of arbitrary power. No man is above the law. No man is punishable except for a distinct breach of law, established in the ordinary legal manner before the ordinary courts.

(ii) Equality before the law. Every man, whatever his rank or condition, is subject to the ordinary law and the jurisdiction of the ordinary tribunals. This Dicey contrasted with the French *droit administratif*, under which the responsibility of public officers for their official acts is decided by a distinct system of administrative courts.

(iii) The general principles of the British Constitution—especially the liberties of the individual, such as personal liberty, freedom of speech and public meeting—are the result of judicial decisions in particular cases. The constitution is judge-made.

Dicey's doctrine has been chiefly criticised with regard to the notion of equality before the law and the topic of administrative law.[59]

The first principle (" No man is punishable," etc.) applies generally in criminal law. Criminal courts usually have a wide discretion with regard to punishment, but this favours the citizen as it is a discretion downwards from a statutory maximum. The principle excludes, as a general rule, preventive detention, compulsory acquisition of goods and direct enforcement of administrative decisions, although preventive detention by order of the Home Secretary was authorised by Parliament during the two World Wars. Parliament *could* confer wide discretionary or even arbitrary powers on the executive, but for extra-legal reasons it seldom does so except in an emergency, for example, the emergency powers granted in wartime.[60]

However, so many exceptions have to be made at the present day to the doctrine that all persons have equal rights and duties before the law that the statement is of doubtful value. Public authorities have many powers that the ordinary person has not got. Thus local authorities have statutory power under certain conditions to buy land compulsorily, and the police have special powers of arrest and search by common law and statute. Ministers have wide powers of delegated legislation, and the rights and obligations of the individual are now

---

[59] See, *e.g.* E. C. S. Wade in Dicey, *Law of the Constitution* (10th ed.) pp. xcvi–cli; Jennings, *op. cit.* Chap. 2, s. 1 and Appendix II; " In Praise of Dicey " (1935) 13 *Public Administration* 123; B. Schwartz, *French Administrative Law and the Common-Law World*, Chap. 10. For a re-appraisal of Dicey's doctrine, see F. H. Lawson, " Dicey Revisited " (1959) *Political Studies*, Vol. VII, pp. 109, 207. For other versions of the rule of law, see Wade and Godfrey Phillips, *Constitutional Law* (8th ed.) Chap. 5; A. L. Goodhart, " The Rule of Law and Absolute Sovereignty " (1958) 106 Univ. Pennsylvania Law Rev. 943.
[60] Or the current emergency in Northern Ireland.

decided in many cases not by the ordinary courts but by special or administrative tribunals or by juvenile courts. Judges and ambassadors have immunity from being sued in the courts, although the immunity of judges actually favours " the rule of law." The immunity of trade unions from being sued in tort conferred by the Trades Disputes Act 1906, which Dicey noted in his later editions, has now been modified by the Industrial Relations Act 1971. In one important respect we are paradoxically nearer to Dicey's " rule of law " than when he wrote, for the common law immunity in tort of the Crown (in effect, the government) was largely removed by the Crown Proceedings Act 1947.[61]

The appointment of the Parliamentary Commissioner for Administration ("Ombudsman") in 1967 is another important development. His function is to investigate complaints of injustice to citizens resulting from faulty administration on the part of a government department, not amounting to illegality.[62] Proposals are also about to be implemented to establish commissioners to investigate similar complaints against local authorities and the National Health Service.

Dicey admitted that in his discussion of the French *droit administratif* [63] he was concentrating chiefly on the period before 1872; but it has been considerably developed in the last 100 years and his account is very largely out of date. The existence of administrative law does not necessarily involve special administrative courts, as is shown by the fact that Belgium before 1946 had a *droit administratif* without such separate courts. The essence of administrative law is that different principles should apply in relation to the official acts of public authorities and officers. These are not confined to liability to pay compensation for injury caused to private individuals. In any event, *droit administratif* is looked upon by the French as a protection for the individual, not as a privilege for public officials.[64] Dicey misunderstood, or exaggerated, certain aspects of the French *droit*

---

61 An anomalous exception was the exemption of the Post Office and its employees under section 9 of that Act, which has been substantially re-enacted in the Post Office Act 1969.

The " ticket system " authorised by the Road Traffic and Roads Improvement Act 1960 is not an exception to the rule of law, as the penalty mentioned on the ticket would only be paid if the person wishes to admit liability; otherwise the ordinary process of prosecution remains. Traffic wardens authorised by the Act remain under the control of the police.

62 Parliamentary Commissioners Act 1967; *post*, Chap. 29.

63 Dicey, *op. cit.* Chap. 12; *cf.* A. V. Dicey, " *Droit Administratif* in Modern French Law " (1901) 17 L.Q.R. 302; " The Development of Administrative Law in England " (1915) 31 L.Q.R. 148 (based on the case of *Local Government Board* v. *Arlidge* [1915] A.C. 120).

64 Hauriou, *Précis Elémentaire de Droit Administratif* (4th ed.) pp. 252–253; P. Weil, " The Strength and Weakness of French Administrative Law " [1965] C.L.J. 242; L. Neville Brown and J. F. Garner, *French Administrative Law* (1967) Chap. 10.

administratif in his own day, although he modified some of his statements in his later writings. Administrative law in England includes such matters as the organisation and powers of public authorities, the judicial control of public authorities, administrative tribunals and the judicial control of delegated legislation. If French administrative law provides compensation for excess or abuse of power *ex post facto*, English administrative law seeks to deter public officials from exceeding their powers in the first instance.

Dicey's treatment of the " rights of the subject " in British constitutional law also calls for comment here. It is not easy to see how it is related to the other parts of his doctrine. It is true that the rights of the individual are mostly to be inferred from judicial decisions [65] and are therefore part of the common law, especially if such enactments as the Bill of Rights 1688 be regarded mainly as declaratory. That such rights are *part* of the ordinary law is a necessary consequence of the fact that the British Constitution is unwritten; but the fundamental principle both in the ordinary English law and in British constitutional law is the legislative supremacy of Parliament, so that it cannot be said with exactness that either the principles or the decisions are *derived* from the others.

General conclusion

In so far as Dicey's general statement of the rule of law may be taken to involve the existence in the English Constitution of certain principles almost amounting to fundamental laws, his doctrine is logically inconsistent with the legislative supremacy of Parliament. Dicey attempted to reconcile the two notions by saying that parliamentary sovereignty favours the rule of law because the will of Parliament can be expressed only in the form of an Act, which must be interpreted by the courts; and that the rule of law favours parliamentary sovereignty, as any additional discretionary powers that the government needs can only be obtained from Parliament.[66] His doctrine is a political theory, in some of its aspects connected with the doctrine of the separation of powers. From another point of view it implies moral restrictions on the legislative activity of Parliament, its juridical nature resembling the " directive principles of state policy " found in the Constitutions of the Republic of Ireland and India.

The significance of this kind of doctrine for the English lawyer is that it finds expression in three ways. First, it influences legislators. The substantive law at any given time may approximate to the " rule

---

[65] But statutes have curtailed some (*e.g.* Public Order Act 1936) and modified others (*e.g.* Habeas Corpus Acts). See further, *post*, Chaps. 23–25.
[66] Dicey, *op. cit.* Chap. 13.

of law," but this only at the will of Parliament. Secondly, its principles provide canons of interpretation which express the individualistic attitude of English courts and of those courts which have followed the English tradition. They give an indication of how the law will be applied and legislation interpreted. English courts lean in favour of the liberty of the citizen, especially of his person: they interpret strictly statutes which purport to diminish that liberty, and presume that Parliament does not intend to restrict private rights in the absence of clear words to the contrary. But Parliament could pass an Act requiring the judges to interpret social legislation freely in favour of the administration. Thirdly, the rule of law is a rule of evidence: everyone is prima facie equal before the law. A person, whether an executive officer or not, may have peculiar rights, powers, privileges or immunities; but, if so, he must prove them. In this sense, the government is subject to law.

The most valuable version of "the rule of law" so far is that formulated by the International Commission of Jurists at Delhi in 1959.[67]

The British Constitution and Human Rights [68]

The British Constitution contains no fundamental rights in the strict sense. Being unwritten and flexible, the constitution in any of its parts can be changed in the same way as any other part, namely, by ordinary Act of Parliament. And the legislative supremacy of Parliament means that there is no legal limit to the extent to which Parliament can abridge or abolish rights that in other countries may be regarded as "fundamental." The practical checks are the influence of public opinion, the vigilance of the Opposition, and the restrictive interpretation of the courts. The rights of the individual in English law are the *residue* of freedom that is left after legislative and executive powers have been defined, and their extent can only be determined by examining the restrictions placed on the activity of the individual and the enjoyment of his property.[69]

The traditional view in this country has been that statements of the "rights" of the individual are very misleading unless they are properly qualified, and when qualified they almost amount to truisms.

---

[67] *Ante*, p. 17.
[68] See J. E. S. Fawcett, *The Application of the European Convention on Human Rights* (1969); A. H. Robertson (ed.), *Human Rights in National and International Law* (1970); Ian Brownlie, *Basic Documents on Human Rights* (1971); *cf.* D. R. Gilmour, " The Sovereignty of Parliament and the European Commission of Human Rights " [1968] P.L. 62. And see C. C. Morrisson, " Restrictive Interpretation of Sovereignty-limiting Treaties: the practice of the European Human Rights Convention System " (1970) 19 I.C.L.Q. 361.
[69] See *post*, Chaps. 22–25.

A citizen's person or property may not be interfered with—unless it may. A person is not liable for what he speaks or writes—unless he is. No liability attaches to one who takes part in a public meeting— unless it does. The British attitude is much more concerned with judicial enforcement, with the provision of effective remedies administered by an independent and incorruptible judiciary, than with the formulation of general principles on paper.

Nevertheless, there has been a strong movement since the War— both within the Commonwealth and outside—to define fundamental or human rights, and such definitions or declarations have come to form an important part of a new international concept of " the rule of law." [70] The United Kingdom ratified the European Convention on Human Rights in 1951,[71] and extended its obligations under the Convention to her dependencies in 1953.[72] Later she accepted the compulsory jurisdiction of the European Court, and recognised the right of individuals to bring petitions against her before the European Commission.[73] The European Convention, however, is not incorporated into British constitutional law. It is binding on her morally and in international law, but as a matter of constitutional law there is, and can be, no obligation on Parliament to bring English law into line with the Convention.[74] In fact, the view is taken that what the British Constitution lacks in formally guaranteed rights is more than compensated by judicial remedies that are in practice effective against both the executive and private individuals.[75] In one or two matters English law did actually fall below the standards worked out by recent international congresses of jurists; for example, there was no right of appeal against the refusal of habeas corpus in criminal cases, nor where a person was committed to prison for contempt of court; but in both these instances the law was reformed by the Administration of Justice Act 1960.

---

[70] *Ante*, p. 17n.
[71] (1953) Cmd. 8969; (1954) Cmd. 9221.
[72] (1954) Cmd. 9045.
[73] (1966) Cmnd. 2894; prolonged (1972) Cmnd. 5026. The Commission in February 1971 rejected the claim by Miss Bernadette Devlin, M.P., that Britain had not given her a fair trial when she was convicted of riotous behaviour during street fighting in the Londonderry disturbances of 1969. In September 1971 the Commission heard a complaint about the admission of Kenya Asians to Britain, and helped to secure a friendly settlement of the case.
[74] For the somewhat analogous question of Britain's adherence to the EEC, see *post*, Chap. 4.
[75] See *Human Rights in the United Kingdom* (1967) C.O.I. No. R. 5625/67.

CHAPTER 3

THE LEGISLATIVE SUPREMACY OF PARLIAMENT

I. HISTORICAL INTRODUCTION

The chief of the three distinguishing characteristics of the British Constitution that Dicey chose to describe in his *Law of the Constitution* was called by him the " sovereignty " of Parliament.[1] In Dicey's day the prevailing juristic theory in this country was Austin's doctrine of sovereignty, which supposed that in every mature legal system there was some person or body—the " Sovereign " [2]—vested with unlimited power to make law.[3] Austin himself did not apply his own doctrine consistently to the British Constitution. Dicey's treatment, in which he ascribed sovereignty to the United Kingdom Parliament, was more consistent.[4]

The doctrine of sovereignty in the theory of municipal law as opposed to international law, however, is now out of fashion, and the continued use of the term " sovereignty " in the present context tends to prejudice discussion of the lawmaking power of the United Kingdom Parliament, with which legislature we are here concerned. A body may have supreme (highest) power without necessarily being sovereign (unlimited) in Austin's sense, nor do we need to assert or imply here that there must be a sovereign authority in every legal system. We have therefore headed this chapter " The Legislative Supremacy of Parliament."

The establishment of parliamentary supremacy was a product of the revolution of 1688.[5] Before then the chief rivals were, first,

---

[1] Chaps. 1–3 (10th ed. 1959); *cf.* Professor E. C. S. Wade's Introduction, at pp. xxxiv–xcvi.

[2] The doctrine of sovereignty was derived by Austin from Bodin, Hobbes and Blackstone. In the Middle Ages the King ruled (subject to custom and advice) and was called the Sovereign, but " the Sovereign " as applied to the modern constitutional monarch is a courtesy title.

[3] John Austin, *The Province of Jurisprudence Determined* (1832). There are many editions and commentaries, notably H. L. A. Hart's edition (1954) and Jethro Brown's *The Austinian Theory of Law* (1906). Most English textbooks on jurisprudence contain criticisms of Austin's theory. The most recent critique is in H. L. A. Hart, *The Concept of Law* (1961).

[4] Dicey, *op. cit.* pp. 71–76. Dicey suggests indeed that Austin's general theory of sovereignty was a deduction from the position of the British Parliament.

[5] Sir Thomas Smith in *De Republica Anglorum* (1589) discussed the " absolute " power of Parliament: Bk. 2 (ed. Alston) Chap. 1, pp. 48–49; but he was probably referring to Parliament as the highest court, " absolute " in this context meaning " not subject to appeal."

the King or King in Council, and then the common law courts. Later the House of Commons acting by resolution occasionally threatened a breach in the authority of the Parliament as a whole.[6]

The King as lawmaker

Parliament emerged as an effective body in the fourteenth century.[7] In the reign of Henry VI the Lords and Commons framed the statutes and the King assented in much the same fashion as at the present day. Nevertheless it would seem that the King continued to legislate on matters of lesser or temporary importance. Whether there was a significant distinction between the terms " statute " and " ordinance," the former applying to Parliament and the latter to royal legislation, has long been a matter of controversy, but Plucknett thought those terms were synonymous.[8]

Proclamations

The Statute of Proclamations 1539, which gave to proclamations the force of law, was of very limited scope and short-lived. Intended for emergencies, it provided that (except for cases of heresy) proclamations might not impose the death penalty, take away a subject's property or conflict with existing statutes, customs or common law. This Act was repealed in the first year of Edward VI. Notwithstanding its repeal, Mary and Elizabeth I continued to make and enforce proclamations concerning imports and also certain religious matters. In the reign of James I the Commons complained of the abuse of proclamations. The opinion of Chief Justice Coke and four of his colleagues was sought and given in the *Case of Proclamations* (1610),[9] when James I wanted to prohibit by proclamation the building of new houses in London in order to check the overgrowth of the capital, and the manufacture of starch from wheat so as to preserve wheat for human consumption. The opinion was to the effect that no new offence can be created by proclamation; the only prerogative possessed by the Crown is that which is conferred by the law of the

---

[6] *Stockdale* v. *Hansard* (1839) 9 Ad. & E. 1; *Case of the Sheriff of Middlesex* (1840) 11 Ad. & E. 273; *post*, Chap. 11. The attitudes of trade unions towards the Industrial Relations Act 1971 is widely regarded as a modern threat to the authority of Parliament.

[7] A. F. Pollard, *Evolution of Parliament* (2nd ed.) Chap. 2.

[8] T. F. T. Plucknett, *Statutes and their Interpretation in the Fourteenth Century*, p. 34. See also S. E. Thorne, *Introduction to a Discourse upon the Exposition and Understanding of Statutes* (Huntington Library, 1942); H. G. Richardson and G. O. Sayles, *Law and Legislation from Aethelberht to Magna Carta* (1966); " The Early Statutes " (1934) 50 L.Q.R. 201, 540.

[9] 12 Co.Rep. 74; 2 St.Tr. 723.

land; but that to prevent offences the King can by proclamation warn his subjects against breaches of the existing law, in which case a breach would be the more serious.

The suspending and dispensing powers

By virtue of the *suspending* power the King claimed to postpone indefinitely the general operation of a given statute; by virtue of the *dispensing* power he relieved particular offenders or classes of offenders from the statutory penalties they had incurred. In the reign of Henry VII it was held that the King could at common law dispense with *mala prohibita* but not *mala in se*.[10] Subject to this restriction, both the suspending and dispensing powers were accepted as part of the prerogative in the sixteenth and seventeenth centuries. The Stuarts used these prerogatives to subvert established laws. James II issued a proclamation that a Declaration of Indulgence, suspending the operation of all laws against Roman Catholics, should be read in all the churches; but in the *Seven Bishops' Case* (1688)[11] the Primate and six bishops were acquitted by a jury on a charge of seditious libel for signing a petition claiming that to read the declaration would be illegal and against their conscience. The right of the subject to petition the King was also confirmed.

In *Thomas* v. *Sorrell* (1674)[12] the plaintiff claimed a penalty for selling wine without a licence contrary to a statute of 12 Charles II. The jury returned a special verdict that they had found a patent of 9 James I incorporating the Vintners Company and granting them permission to sell wine without a licence, *non obstante* an Act of 7 Edward VI forbidding such sale. The judges decided that the King might dispense with an individual breach of a penal statute by which no man was injured, or with the continuous breach of a penal statute enacted for the King's benefit. In *Godden* v. *Hales* (1686)[13] a collusive action was brought to test the King's *dispensing* power. Sir Edward Hales accepted appointment as colonel of a regiment, and was sued for a penalty for neglecting to take the oaths of supremacy and allegiance and to receive the Sacrament according to the Test Act of 25 Charles II. Hales pleaded a dispensation of James II. The court held that the dispensation barred the right of action, as the King had a prerogative to dispense with penal statutes in particular cases for reasons of which the King was the sole judge.

The Bill of Rights 1688 declared: " That the pretended power of

---

10 Y.B.Mich. 11 Hen. VII, no. 35 (1495) *per* Fineux C.J.; see Holdsworth, *History of English Law*, Vol. VI, pp. 218–219.

11 12 St.Tr. 371.

12 Vaughan 330.

13 11 St.Tr. 1166; 2 Shower 275.

suspending of laws or the execution of laws by regal authority without consent of Parliament is illegal; that the pretended power of *dispensing* with laws or the execution of laws by regal authority *as it hath been assumed and exercised of late* is illegal." Projected legislation, stating in what cases dispensation should be legal, was never passed.[14] It is by virtue of the words " as it hath been assumed and exercised of late " in relation to the dispensing power that the prerogative right to pardon was retained. These words were also relied on as legalising a dispensation granted by Elizabeth I in 1566 in the *Eton College* case (1815)[15] where, owing to their insertion, a fellow of Eton College was allowed to hold a living in conjunction with his fellowship.

Monopolies

Formerly the granting of monopolies by the monarch was presumed to inflict a hardship on the public. In the *Case of Monopolies* (1602)[16] Darcy, a servant of Elizabeth I and grantee of the sole rights of importing and making playing-cards, sued Allein for interfering with his grant. The court held that the grant was a monopoly and void, and that the Queen could not exercise her dispensing power to confer private gain on an individual contrary to statutes of Edward III, and Edward IV, which imposed a penalty on the importation of certain goods and were enacted for the public good. The grant of monopolies is now governed by Patent Acts.[17]

Taxation

It was supposed to have been settled by Magna Carta and by legislation in the reigns of Edward I and Edward III that taxation beyond the levying of customary feudal aids required the consent of Parliament. One of the central themes of English constitutional history was the gaining of control of taxation and national finance in general by Parliament, and in particular the Commons; for this control meant that the King was not able to govern for more than short periods without summoning Parliament, and Parliament could insist on grievances being remedied before it granted the King supply. This applied at least to *direct* taxation. With regard to *indirect* taxation different considerations might apply. Down to the early seven-

---

[14] Holdsworth, *op. cit.* Vol. VI, pp. 215–225, 240–241.

[15] *King's College, Cambridge* v. *Eton College*, P.Wms. 53; Broom, *Constitutional Law*, p. 503.

[16] *Darcy* v. *Allein*, 11 Co.Rep. 84b. For the background of this case, see D. R. Seaborne Davies, " Further Light on the Case of Monopolies " (1932) 48 L.Q.R. 394.

[17] The Crown's right to make use of patents is preserved by the Crown Proceedings Act 1947, s. 3; *cf. Feather* v. *The Queen* (1865) 6 B. & S. 257.

teenth century import duties, for example, were regarded rather as licences or concessions than as taxes and, further, the royal prerogative relating to foreign affairs—and hence the regulation of foreign trade in the national interest—was relevant. Issue was joined in two famous cases in the reigns of James I (the "Case of Impositions") and Charles I (the "Case of Ship-Money").

In *Bate's Case* (*Case of Impositions*) (1606) [18] Bate, a Levant merchant, refused to pay a duty imposed by letters patent of James I on the import of currants, contending that the imposition was contrary to a statute of Edward III which declared that such taxation required the consent of Parliament. The Court of Exchequer gave judgment unanimously for the King. Their reasons were that foreign affairs, and therefore foreign commerce, were within the absolute power of the King; as the King could prohibit the importation of goods, still more could he tax imported goods; and the court must accept the King's statement that the purpose of the tax was to regulate foreign trade. Coke and Popham C.JJ. thought this decision was right.[19] The judgment has been condemned by some modern historians, but it may well have been warranted by the law of that time in so far as it rested on the prerogative power to regulate foreign trade. This power, however, was liable to be abused, and danger also lay in dicta treating the matter as a question of revenue within the "absolute" (*i.e.* inalienable) powers of the Crown. It was in the debate on impositions in 1610, says Holdsworth,[20] that the supremacy of the King in Parliament over the King out of Parliament was first asserted by James Whitelocke.

The Petition of Right 1628 was occasioned largely by *Darnel's Case* (*The Five Knights' Case*) (1627),[21] where the defendants were imprisoned for refusing to pay a forced loan. The Petition of Right was assented to by Charles I, and has always been regarded as having statutory force although largely superseded by the Bill of Rights. It forbad tallages, aids, forced loans, benevolences, taxes and suchlike charges "without common consent by Act of Parliament." [22]

While this document was still fresh in men's minds, Charles I (after consulting the judges) imposed under the Great Seal a direct tax known as ship-money, to be used to furnish ships for the navy. The tax was

[18] 2 St.Tr. 371. See further Holdsworth, *History of English Law*, Vol. VI, pp. 42–48; G. D. G. Hall, " Impositions and the Courts 1554–1606 " (1953) 69 L.Q.R. 200.

[19] 12 Co.Rep. 33.

[20] *Some Lessons from our Legal History*, pp. 124–125.

[21] 3 St.Tr. 1.

[22] Tallages were imposts set by the King as landlord on his own demesne lands, aids were free-will offerings by tenants to their lord in time of need, and benevolences were extorted free-will offerings. These methods of raising money were not invented by the Stuarts, but were known in the fourteenth and fifteenth centuries.

charged first on the seaport towns, which had the primary responsibility for finding ships and men for the national defence, and then on the inland counties. In *R. v. Hampden (Case of Ship-Money)* (1637) [23] proceedings were taken against John Hampden, a Buckinghamshire gentleman, for refusing to pay the amount of £1 assessed on him. The majority of the judges in the Court of Exchequer Chamber gave judgment for the King. The gist of their decision was that the King's prerogative to defend the realm in time of danger overrode the general principle that taxation required the consent of Parliament, and that the King was sole judge both of the existence of an emergency and also of the steps to be taken to meet the danger. It is difficult to criticise this decision in the light of the law at that time. The precedents were conflicting, and Hampden's counsel did not place much reliance on the Petition of Right. The verdict of most historians has been against the correctness of the decision, which they put down to the subservience of the judges to the King. Even if the decision was right in law, it had implications that were politically dangerous. The judgment itself was declared void by the Long Parliament in 1641.

The eventual solution was political rather than legal, for the revolution of 1688 meant that Parliament henceforth controlled the King. The Bill of Rights 1688 accordingly settled the matter for the future, as regards both direct and indirect taxation, by declaring that " levying money for or to the use of the Crown by pretence of prerogative without consent of Parliament for longer time or in other manner than the same is or shall be granted is illegal." It may be noted that the Statute of Tenures 1660 had confirmed the abolition of military tenures, and no revenue was derived from that source after 1645.[24]

An attempt by the government (which in modern times represents the Crown) to levy money without express statutory authority was *Att.-Gen. v Wilts. United Dairies* (1921).[25] The Attorney-General sought to recover £15,000 from Wilts. United Dairies, representing a fee of 2d. a gallon on milk purchased by them under licence from the Food Controller, which was granted under statutory orders made in virtue of Regulations issued under the Defence of the Realm (Consolidation) Act 1914. The House of Lords unanimously upheld the decision of the Court of Appeal that the charge was *ultra vires* as a levy of money for the use of the Crown without the authority of Parliament. Lord Buckmaster stated that neither the Act creating the

---

23 3 St.Tr. 825. See further Holdsworth, *History of English Law*, Vol. VI, pp. 48–54; D. L. Keir, " The Case of Ship-Money " (1936) 52 L.Q.R. 546.
24 For the " sovereignty " of Parliament in the eighteenth century, see Holdsworth, *op. cit.* Vol. X, pp. 526–531.
25 37 T.L.R. 884; 91 L.J.K.B. 897.

Ministry of Food, nor the Regulations issued under the Defence of the Realm Act, directly or by inference enabled the Food Controller to levy payment. The charges to the extent of £18,000,000 were validated retrospectively by the War Charges (Validity) Act 1925. Parliament can, of course, expressly delegate the power to levy such charges, and did so in the Second World War.[26]

In 1954 it was discovered that the Post Office had for many years been inadvertently charging licences for wireless sets without the power to do so, since no regulations with the consent of the Treasury had been issued as required by the Wireless Telegraphy Act 1904. The Post Office repaid the plaintiff's licence and costs,[27] and the charge for wireless licences was validated retrospectively by the Wireless Telegraphy (Validation of Charges) Act 1954.

The Judges and a Higher Law [28]

There are dicta in the common law courts down to the seventeenth century to the effect that there is a law of nature or reason superior even to Acts of Parliament. The most celebrated example is *Dr. Bonham's Case* (1610),[29] in which Coke C.J. presided over the King's Bench. The question was whether Dr. Bonham was liable to pay a fine, half to the Crown and half to the Royal College of Physicians, under the charter of the College which had been confirmed by Act of Parliament. The Court gave judgment for Bonham on the ground that the College had no jurisdiction over those practising outside London; but Coke's report of the judgment goes on to say that " when an Act of Parliament is against common right and reason, or repugnant, or impossible to be performed, the common law will controul it, and adjudge such act to be void." This statement was obiter, and is also inconsistent with what Coke says in his *Institutes*.[30]

In *Day* v. *Savadge* (1615)[31] the question was whether Day, as a freeman of the City of London, was exempt from wharfage duty on a bag of nutmegs. On behalf of the Corporation it was contended that by a statute of 7 Ric. II disputes as to the customs of the City

---

[26] Emergency Powers (Defence) Act 1939, s. 2.

[27] *Davey Paxman & Co. Ltd.* v. *Post Office* (action settled) *The Times*, November 16, 1954.

[28] J. W. Gough, *Fundamental Law in English Constitutional History*; Roscoe Pound, *The Development of Guarantees of Liberty* (1957); E. S. Corwin, *The " Higher Law " Background of American Constitutional Law* (reprint 1955).

[29] 8 Co.Rep. 114, 118; *cf.* T. F. T. Plucknett, " Bonham's Case and Judicial Review " (1926) 40 *Harvard Law Review* 30; S. E. Thorne, " Dr. Bonham's Case " (1938) 54 L.Q.R. 543.

[30] 4 Inst. 36. Coke as a Law Officer supported the prerogative, as a judge the supremacy of the common law (which he equated with reason), and as a parliamentarian the sovereignty of Parliament.

[31] Hobart 85, 97.

were to be decided on the basis of a certificate of the mayor and aldermen. Hobart C.J., giving the judgment of the Court of Common Pleas, held that the custom in this case was to be tried by jury and not by certificate, and added obiter: " even an act of parliament, made against natural equity, as to make a man judge in his own case, is void in itself; for *jura naturae sunt immutabilia,* and they are *leges legum.*" This dictum may be taken as illustrating a logical impossibility or moral limitation, or merely as traditional rhetoric. Again in *City of London* v. *Wood* (1701),[32] where the Court of Common Pleas gave judgment for Wood on a writ of error from the Mayor's Court in an action for the recovery of a forfeiture to the City of London under a by-law made by virtue of an Act of Parliament, Holt C.J. is reported to have approved Coke's dictum in *Dr. Bonham's Case,* saying: " an Act of Parliament can do no wrong, though it may do several things that look pretty odd," and adding that an Act of Parliament may not make adultery lawful, though it may dissolve the marriage of A and his wife and make her the wife of B. A last relic of this traditional rhetoric is Blackstone's statement in the second half of the eighteenth century that no human laws are of any validity if contrary to the " law of nature." [33]

The modern view, however, is that expressed by Willes J. in *Lee* v. *Bude & Torrington Ry.* (1871) [34]: " It was once said that if an Act of Parliament were to create a man judge in his own cause, the court might disregard it. That dictum, however, stands as a warning rather than an authority to be followed. . . . Are we to act as regents over what is done by Parliament with the consent of the Queen, lords and commons? I deny that any such authority exists."

II. THE NATURE OF PARLIAMENTARY SUPREMACY [35]

The " Legislative Supremacy of Parliament " means that Parliament (*i.e.* the Queen, Lords and Commons in Parliament assembled) can pass laws on any topic affecting any persons, and that there are no " fundamental " laws which Parliament cannot amend or repeal in the same way as ordinary legislation. Dicey [36] was following the tradition of Coke [37] and Blackstone [38] when he said that Parliament has " the

---

[32] 12 Mod. 669, at pp. 687–688. This report is, however, considered to be unreliable,
[33] Bl.Comm., Vol. I, p. 41.
[34] L.R. 6 C.P. 576, 582.
[35] Dicey, *op. cit.*; H. W. R. Wade, " The Basis of Legal Sovereignty " [1955] C.L.J. 172, and review in [1954] C.L.J. 265; O. Hood Phillips, *Reform of the Constitution* (1970) Chaps. 1 and 7.
[36] Dicey, *op. cit.* pp. 39–40.
[37] 4 Inst. 36.
[38] Bl.Comm., Vol. I, pp. 160–162.

right to make or unmake any law whatever," and further that " no person or body is recognised by the law of England as having the right to override or set aside the legislation of Parliament."

Legislative supremacy as thus defined is a legal concept. The supremacy of Parliament, being recognised and acted on by the courts, is a principle of the common law. It may indeed be called the one fundamental law of the British Constitution, for it is peculiar in that it could not be altered by ordinary statute, but only by some fundamental change of attitude on the part of the courts resulting from what would technically be a revolution. Parliament could not, of course, confer this authority on itself. Thus the first Acts of the Convention Parliaments of 1660 and 1689, legalising their own authority, confirmed the result of revolutions; and the American Colonies Act 1766,[39] asserting the authority of Parliament to legislate for the American colonies, was merely declaratory.

On the other hand a state may be a sovereign state and yet have a legislature which is not unlimited and courts with jurisdiction to review its legislation. Thus the 1947 Constitution of Ceylon (an independent sovereign state within the Commonwealth) required for its amendment the Speaker's certificate that not less than two-thirds of the members of the House of Representatives voted in favour. It was held by the Privy Council in *Bribery Commissioner* v. *Ranasinghe* [40] that the Bribery Tribunal by which the respondent had been convicted was not lawfully appointed, because the Act under which it was appointed was passed by the ordinary legislative procedure, whereas it required a constitutional amendment relating to the appointment of judicial officers. This is also the principle that emerges from the South African case *Harris* v. *Minister of the Interior* (" the Cape coloured voters case "),[41] in so far as that case is relevant to the present context. The question in issue was the validity of the Separate Representation of Voters Act 1951, which was passed by the two Houses sitting separately and thus infringed section 152 of the South Africa Act 1909, which Act formed the basis of the Constitution. This section provided that no repeal or alteration of section 35 (qualification of Cape coloured voters) should be valid unless the Bill was passed by both Houses sitting together and the third reading was agreed to by not less than two-thirds of the members of both Houses. It was held by the Appellate Division of the Supreme Court of South Africa that the Separate Representation of Voters Act was invalid as

---

[39] Repealed by the Statute Law Revision Act 1964.
[40] [1965] A.C. 172.
[41] [1952] (2) A.D. 428; *sub nom. Harris* v. *Dönges* [1952] 1 T.L.R. 1245. See D. V. Cowen, *Parliamentary Sovereignty and the Entrenched Sections of the South Africa Act* (1951).

the South Africa Act was a superior law to the Union Parliament, which it created. Whether the Union Parliament was called a " sovereign " legislature was a matter of definition: the Parliament functioning bicamerally was restricted in certain respects, but anything it could not do in that way could be done by a two-thirds majority in the Parliament functioning unicamerally.[42]

The legislative supremacy of the British Parliament, as well as being a legal concept, is also the result of political history and is ultimately based on fact, that is, general recognition by the people and the courts. It is therefore at the same time a legal and a political principle.[43]

The doctrine of the legislative supremacy of Parliament has been so firmly established that it has scarcely been challenged in the courts. In R. v. Jordan [44] J, who had been sentenced to imprisonment for offences under the Race Relations Act 1965, applied for legal aid to enable him to apply for habeas corpus on the ground that the Race Relations Act was invalid as being in curtailment of free speech. The Divisional Court, dismissing the application, held that Parliament was supreme and there was no power in the courts to question the validity of an Act of Parliament, adding that the ground of the application was completely unarguable. In Cheney v. Conn [45] a taxpayer contended that the Finance Act 1964 conflicted with the Geneva Conventions incorporated in the Geneva Conventions Act 1957, and that it was contrary to international law that part of his tax should go to the construction of nuclear weapons. Ungoed-Thomas J. held that there was no conflict between the two Acts; the Finance Act prevailed over international conventions, which are an executive act of the Crown; and that what Parliament enacts cannot be unlawful. When Canon Selwyn made an application questioning the validity of the Royal Assent to the Irish Church Disestablishment Act 1869 as being inconsistent with the Coronation Oath and the Act of Settlement, Cockburn C.J .and Blackburn J. in refusing the application said: " There is no judicial body in the country by which the validity of an act of parliament can be questioned. An act of the legislature is superior in authority to any court of law . . . , and no court could pronounce a judgment as to the validity of an act of parliament " (ex p. Selwyn).[46] In Hall v. Hall [47] the plaintiff claimed that the

---

42 The desired legislation was eventually passed by changing the composition of the Senate; see Collins v. Minister of the Interior [1957] (1) A.D. 552.

43 Professor H. L. A. Hart calls it " the ultimate rule of recognition," which may be regarded both as an external statement of fact and as an internal criterion of validity: The Concept of Law, p. 108.

44 [1967] Crim.L.R. 483; 9 J.P.Supp. 48.

45 [1968] 1 W.L.R. 242.   46 (1872) 36 J.P. 54.

47 (1944) 88 S.J. 383 (Hereford C.C.). The judgment as reported appears to beg the question.

Probate Act 1857, on which the defendant based the title to a house, had not really received the Royal Assent as he challenged the Royal Succession from the days of James II. The county court judge said he could not ignore a statute that had been acted on for more than eighty years, and that in any event Parliament could validate all titles by passing an Indemnity Act. In *Vauxhall Estates Ltd.* v. *Liverpool Corporation* [48] and *Ellen Street Estates Ltd.* v. *Minister of Health* [49] counsel unsuccessfully argued that a later Act could not repeal the provisions of an earlier Act, with which it was inconsistent, except by express words. That contention, said Scrutton L.J. in the latter case, " is absolutely contrary to the constitutional position."

In an appeal to the House of Lords in *Edinburgh and Dalkeith Ry.* v. *Wauchope* (1842), [50] where it had been suggested in the Scottish court below that a private Act might not be applicable against a person whose rights were affected but who had not been given prior notice, [51] Lord Campbell pronounced the following dictum: " All that a Court of Justice can do is to look to the Parliament roll: if from that it should appear that a Bill has passed both Houses and received the Royal Assent, no Court of Justice can enquire into the mode in which it was introduced into Parliament, nor into what was done previous to its introduction, or what passed in Parliament during its progress in its various stages through both Houses." In another case concerning a private Act, *Lee* v. *Bude and Torrington Ry.* (1871), [52] Willes J. said: " Acts of Parliament are the law of the land and we do not sit as a Court of Appeal from Parliament." [53]

---

48 [1932] 1 K.B. 733 (D.C.) *post*, p. 55.
49 [1934] 1 K.B. 590 (C.A.) *post*, p. 55.
50 8 Cl. & F. 710.
51 And see *Pickin* v. *British Railways Board* [1972] 3 W.L.R. 824 (C.A.).
52 L.R. & C.P. 576.
53 Other judicial dicta that may be cited are: " The supremacy of Parliament. . . . That sovereign power can make and unmake the law ": *per* Lord Denman C.J. in *Stockdale* v. *Hansard* (1839) 9 Ad. & E. 1; " Whereas . . . you may canvass a rule and determine whether or not it was within the power of those who made it, you cannot canvass in that way the provisions of an Act of Parliament ": *per* Lord Herschell L.C. in *Institute of Patent Agents* v. *Lockwood* [1894] A.C. 347, 359; " Parliament is supreme. It can enact extraordinary powers of interfering with personal liberty. If an Act of Parliament . . . is alleged to limit or curtail the liberty of the subject or vest in the executive extraordinary powers of detaining a subject, the only question is what is the precise extent of the powers given ": *per* Lord Wright in *Liversidge* v. *Anderson* [1942] A.C. 206; " Parliament has absolute sovereignty and can make new legal creatures if it likes ": *per* Scott L.J. in *National Union of General and Municipal Workers* v. *Gillian* [1946] 1 K.B. 81; " Parliament is omnipotent ": *per* Vaughan Williams L.J. in *R.* v. *Local Government Board, ex p. Arlidge* [1914] 1 K.B. 160, 175–176; " Nothing we do or say could in any degree affect the complete power of the legislature by Act of Parliament to carry out the present scheme, or any other scheme ": *per* Atkin L.J. in *R.* v. *Electricity Commissioners* [1924] 1 K.B. 171; " Parliament could do anything . . . being omnipotent ": *per* Harman J. in *Hammersmith Borough Council* v. *Boundary Commission, The Times*, December 15, 1954.

Examples of subject-matter

Examples of the positive aspect of the legislative supremacy of Parliament as regards subject-matter are the Septennial Act 1715, extending the maximum duration of the existing and future Parliaments from three to seven years; the Parliament Acts 1911 and 1949, restricting the power of the House of Lords to withhold its assent to public Bills (especially money Bills), and reducing the maximum duration of a Parliament to five years; the prolongation of its own life by annual Acts to eight years by the Parliament that passed the Act of 1911, and annual prolongations during the last war of the life of the Parliament that was elected in 1935; the Act of Settlement 1700, which regulated the succession to the throne on the failure of Queen Anne's issue, and His Majesty's Declaration of Abdication Act 1936, which varied that succession; the Union with Scotland Act 1706, by which the English Parliament extinguished itself and transferred its authority to the new Parliament of Great Britain; the Government of Ireland Act 1920 and the Irish Free State Agreement Act 1922, dissolving the union between Great Britain and Ireland (which had been created by the Union with Ireland Act 1800), setting up a subordinate legislature in Northern Ireland [54] and giving Dominion status to the Irish Free State [55]; the Defence of the Realm Acts and Emergency Powers (Defence) Acts of the two World Wars, conferring extremely wide—though temporary—powers on the government [56]; Acts of Indemnity legalising acts which when they were done were illegal; and other kinds of retrospective legislation, of which notable examples are the War Damage Act 1965, [57] and the Northern Ireland Act 1972 legalising retrospectively to 1920 the use of troops in Northern Ireland for certain civilian purposes.

The absence of " fundamental " laws means, as we have seen in Chapter 2, that the courts have no jurisdiction to declare an Act of Parliament void as being *ultra vires* or " unconstitutional."

Composition

Parliament is also free to alter its own composition. The composition of the House of Commons may be affected by redistribution

---

[54] *Cf.* Northern Ireland (Temporary Provisions) Act 1972.
[55] Recognised as the independent Republic of Ireland by the Ireland Act 1949.
[56] See especially, Emergency Powers (Defence) (No. 2) Act 1940, authorising Defence Regulations to make provision " for requiring persons to place themselves, their services and their property at the disposal of His Majesty."
[57] Reversing the decision of the House of Lords as regards war damage in *Burmah Oil Co.* v. *Lord Advocate* [1965] A.C. 75. Other examples of retrospective legislation include Marriage Validation Acts, the War Charges (Validity) Act 1925, the Truck Act 1940, the Charitable Trusts (Validation) Act 1954, the Wireless Telegraphy (Validation of Charges) Act 1954, and Finance Act 1960, s. 39. And see A. L. Goodhart, " Ex Post Facto Penal Offences," in *United Nations Year Book on Human Rights* (1955).

of seats, alteration of the franchise or changes in the disqualifications for membership. The composition of the House of Lords has been affected by extending the qualification of Scottish peers, and the creation of life peerages and Lords of Appeal. Parliament could confine membership of the House of Lords to life peers. Indeed, Parliament could abolish the House of Lords, perhaps without its own consent under the provisions of the Parliament Acts; and it could abolish the monarchy, though that would require the Royal Assent. It would be idle to speculate on the abolition of the House of Commons, as such an event postulates a completely different kind of constitution.

Persons and areas

With regard to persons and areas, since Parliament is the Parliament of the United Kingdom its Acts are presumed to apply to the United Kingdom and not to extend further: if an Act is not intended to apply to Wales,[58] Scotland or Northern Ireland, or if it is intended to apply outside the United Kingdom, e.g. to a colony, this must be expressly stated.[59] Parliament can define the country's territory,[60] fishery limits,[61] and continental shelf.[62] It can penalise offences of an international character,[63] the broadcasting of election propaganda from abroad,[64] the operation of private radio stations outside territorial waters,[65] and the destruction of animals and plants in Antarctica.[66]

Parliament could, according to the traditional theory of English law, legislate for the whole British Commonwealth[67]; but it is presumed not to intend to legislate for aliens abroad.[68] In fact, Parliament very seldom legislates with regard to acts done in foreign territory, except in so far as it entitles the Crown to make laws under Foreign

---

[58] References to " England " in Acts of Parliament after 1967 no longer include Wales: Welsh Language Act 1967.

[59] R. v. Martin [1956] 2 Q.B. 272, per Devlin J.

[60] Island of Rockall Act 1972.

[61] Fishery Limits Act 1964; cf. Territorial Waters Order in Council 1964.

[62] Continental Shelf Act 1964.

[63] Hijacking Act 1971.

[64] Representation of the People Act 1949, s. 80.

[65] Marine etc. Broadcasting (Offences) Act 1967; passed as a consequence of R. v. Kent Justices, ex p. Lye [1967] 2 K.B. 153 (D.C.); Post Office v. Estuary Radio [1967] 1 W.L.R. 1396 (C.A.).

[66] Antarctic Treaty Act 1967. Acts of this kind are usually based on international treaties.

[67] But with regard to the independent members of the Commonwealth, cf. post, p. 60.

[68] Cail v. Papayanni (1863) 1 Moo.P.C.(N.S.) 471, 474, per Dr. Lushington; Lopez v. Burslem (1843) 4 Moo. 300, 305, per Lord Campbell; Jefferys v. Boosey (1854) 4 H.L.C. 815, 926, per Parke B. For other presumptions of constitutional importance in the interpretation of Acts of Parliament, see O. Hood Phillips, A First Book of English Law (6th ed.) pp. 140 et seq.

Jurisdiction Acts for overseas territories in which it has acquired jurisdiction, gives effect to international conventions relating to such matters as copyright, or makes certain crimes, e.g. murder or bigamy, committed abroad by citizens of the United Kingdom and colonies [69] punishable when they come within the territorial jurisdiction.

Practical limitations

There are in practice, of course, factors which limit Parliament's ability to pass any laws it likes, or, rather, which limit the choice of measures that the government puts before Parliament for approval. These factors are the concern of the political scientist rather than the student of constitutional law, but it is convenient to mention some of the more important ones briefly here. [70]

Doctrine of the mandate

The government is expected to carry out the policy (if any) indicated at the last general election, by virtue of which it holds its position, and is not expected to act contrary to that policy. This is the general and rather vague doctrine of the " mandate," which seems to have been invented in the latter part of the nineteenth century. The government must, however, deal with emergencies, so that it may be its duty to ignore or even to act against the mandate. In any case, a government that has been in power for some time must meet changing circumstances in all fields of the national life, and is not expected to mark time because it has exhausted its " mandate " (which may have been expressed in very general terms). In Sir Ivor Jennings's words: " The doctrine of the mandate is part of the political cant. It is a stick used by the Opposition to beat the Government. . . . The doctrine is, however, of importance. Though it must necessarily be vague and its operation a matter of dispute, it is recognised to exist." [71]

Public opinion

Parliament must also take account of the even vaguer concept of " public opinion." Public opinion expresses itself through the press, radio, television, trade unions, industrialists, local councillors, party organisations and countless other ways. The manner in which it is interpreted by the government and other Members of Parliament

---

[69] Cf. British Nationality Act 1948, s. 3, as to citizens of other Commonwealth countries.

[70] For legislation in relation to independent members of the Commonwealth, see post, pp. 60 et seq.

[71] Jennings, Cabinet Government (3rd ed.) p. 505. See also C. S. Emden, The People and the Constitution (2nd ed.); G. H. L. Le May, " Parliament, the Constitution and the ' Doctrine of the Mandate ' " (1957) 74 South African Law Journal 33.

must obviously affect Parliament's activities, including the passing of legislation. The moral ideas and ideals of the community, especially as expressed through the leaders of the Churches, make their influence felt. The strength of the Opposition—although *ex hypothesi* a minority in the Commons—is a variable factor, but in our system of parliamentary government the official Opposition must always be taken into respectful account. The government's legislative proposals must stand up to debate, the debates will be reported in the press or be available in *Hansard*, and the government must remember that within a few years at most it will have to face another general election.

Consultation of organised interests

In modern times the government does not in practice introduce legislation affecting well-defined sections of the community without first consulting organisations of the groups specially concerned or interested. In matters affecting industry or trade, for example, the Minister proposing to initiate legislation will consult the employers' associations, chambers of commerce and the trade unions. The National Farmers Union would be consulted in matters affecting agriculture. Any reorganisation of local government would involve discussions with the associations representing the different kinds of local authorities. Professional associations would expect to be consulted in any matter that concerned their professions. Thus the introduction of the National Health Service would have been impossible without the co-operation of the General Medical Council, and reforms in legal procedure are preceded by discussions with the General Council of the Bar and the Law Society.

There is no general legal duty to consult. Still less is the Minister bound to accept the advice given, which will often be conflicting anyway. The practice is to discuss the general principles of the proposed legislation, rather than the draft Bill.[72]

International Law

Treaties do not automatically become part of English law.[73] The principles of international law do not in themselves bind Parliament, although the activities of Parliament are in fact restrained by considerations of international law and the comity of nations.[74] There is a presumption that Parliament does not intend to legislate contrary

---

[72] Sir Ivor Jennings, *Parliament* (2nd ed.) Chap. 7.
[73] *Rustomjee* v. *The Queen* (1876) 2 Q.B.D. 69, 74, *per* Lord Coleridge C.J.; *McWhirter* v. *Att.-Gen.*, The Times, June 30, 1972 (C.A.) *per* Lord Denning M.R.
[74] See *Cheney* v. *Conn* [1968] 1 W.L.R. 242, *ante*, p. 47; *Chung Chi Cheung* v. *The King* [1939] A.C. 160, 167–168 (P.C.) *per* Lord Atkin; Holdsworth, " The Relation of English Law to International Law " *Essays in Law and History*, p. 260; *History of English Law*, Vol. XIV, pp. 22–33.

to the principles of international law, and a statute would be interpreted as far as possible so as not to conflict with them [75]; but the
legal power of Parliament to make laws contrary thereto remains,[76]
and redress would have to be sought by diplomatic action and not
through the courts. Where a statute is clear and unambiguous the
" comity of nations " is irrelevant (per Lord Porter in *Theophile* v.
Solicitor-General [77]), for the sovereign power of Parliament extends
to breaking treaties (per Diplock L.J. in *Salomon* v. *Customs and
Excise Commissioners* [78]).

This principle is well illustrated by the case of *Mortensen* v.
Peters.[79] Mortensen, a Danish citizen and captain of a Norwegian
ship, was convicted by the High Court of Justiciary of infringing the
Herring Fishery (Scotland) Act 1889, which forbad trawling in the
Moray Firth, although the acts done took place outside the three-mile
limit. Diplomatic representations were made to the Foreign Office,
and the Crown remitted the fine, although it recognised that the Court
was right to apply the Act of Parliament. Shortly afterwards an Act
was passed [80] providing that prosecutions should not be brought under
the Act of 1889 for trawling outside the three-mile limit, but that fish
caught by prohibited methods might not be landed or sold in the
United Kingdom.

---

[75] *The Zamora* [1916] A.C. 77 (P.C.); *Co-operative Committee on Japanese Canadians*
v. *Att.-Gen. for Canada* [1947] A.C. 87, 104 (P.C.); cf. *Polites* v. *The Commonwealth* (1945) 70 C.L.R. 60 (High Ct. Austr.).
[76] Cf. *Sovereignty within the Law*, by Arthur Larson, C. Wilfred Jenks and Others
(1966).
[77] [1950] A.C. 186, 195.
[78] [1967] 2 Q.B. 116 (C.A.).
[79] 1906, 14 S.L.T. 227; 8 F (Ct. of Sess.) 93.
[80] Trawling in Prohibited Areas Prevention Act 1909.

CHAPTER 4

CAN PARLIAMENT BIND ITS SUCCESSORS? [1]

I. SUBJECT-MATTER OF LEGISLATION

Express or implied repeal

Coke introduces a section of his *Institutes* with the heading:
" Acts against the power of the Parliament subsequent bind not . . .
for it is a matter in the law of the Parliament, *quod leges posteriores
priores contrarias abrogant*." [2] Blackstone supports this, stating that
a clause in an Act prohibiting repeal could be repealed along with
the Act itself. [3] Dicey follows this tradition, but many readers have
gained the impression that it is an apparent exception to the sovereignty of Parliament as he understood it. The paradox is verbal only,
however, as will be seen if the proposition is expressed in another
way, " Parliament is not bound by its predecessors." Thus the
marginal note to Coke's statement reads: " Subsequent Parliaments
cannot be restrained by the former "; and Blackstone explains that
" the legislature, being in truth the sovereign power, is always of
equal, always of absolute authority: it acknowledges no superior
upon earth, which the prior legislature must have been, if its ordinances
could bind a subsequent Parliament."

The Treason Act 1495 provided that any Act made contrary
thereto should be void and of no effect. Bacon commenting on this
says: " a supreme and absolute power cannot exclude itself; neither
can that which is in its nature revocable be made fixed." [4] And
Herbert C.J. said in *Godden* v. *Hales* (1686) [5]: " if an Act of Parlia-

---

1 Dicey, *Law of the Constitution* (10th ed.) pp. 64–70; Anson, *Law and Custom of
the Constitution*, Vol. 1 (5th ed. Gwyer) pp. 7–8; H. W. R. Wade, " The Basis
of Legal Sovereignty " [1955] C.L.J. 172, and review in [1954] C.L.J. 265; E. C. S.
Wade and G. Godfrey Phillips, *Constitutional Law* (8th ed. 1970) Chap. 4; Hood
Phillips, *Reform of the Constitution* (5th ed.) Chap. 4, pp. 151–156. *Cf.* Sir Ivor
Jennings, *The Law and the Constitution* (5th ed.) Chap. 4; D. V. Cowen, " Legis-
lature and Judiciary: Reflections on the Constitutional Issues in South Africa "
(1952) 15 M.L.R. 282; (1953) 16 M.L.R. 273; B. Beinart, " Parliament and the
Courts " [1954] *South African Law Review* 135; G. Marshall, *Parliamentary
Sovereignty and the Commonwealth* (1957) Chap. 4, and *Constitutional Theory*
(1971) Chap. 3; R. F. V. Heuston, *Essays in Constitutional Law* (2nd ed. 1964)
Chap. 1; J. D. B. Mitchell, *Constitutional Law* (2nd ed. 1968) Chap. 4; S. A. de
Smith, *Constitutional and Administrative Law* (1971) Chap. 3.
2 4 Inst. 42–43.   3 1 Comm. 90–91.
4 *History of Henry VII*, p. 133.
5 11 St.Tr. 1165, 1197.

54

ment had a clause in it that it should never be repealed, yet without question, the same power that made it may repeal it." It is true that Parliament apparently thought it necessary in 1705 to pass two Acts [6] in order to naturalise Princess Sophia, Electress of Hanover (who was abroad), without her having to take the oath of allegiance at Westminster as required by the Naturalisation Act 1609; but it is submitted that one Act would have been sufficient, the Act of 1609 being regarded not as binding Parliament until repealed or amended but as being directed towards petitioners and officials.

The power of *express* repeal is so well established that it has not been contested in the courts. Lord Reid has said extrajudicially: " It is good constitutional doctrine that Parliament cannot bind its successors." [7] There are two cases, however, in which it has been argued by counsel that a provision in an earlier Act precluded *implied* repeal in a later Act. The Acquisition of Land (Assessment of Compensation) Act 1919, s. 7 (1), stated: " The provisions of the Act or order by which the land is authorised to be acquired . . . shall . . . have effect subject to this Act, and so far as inconsistent with this Act those provisions shall cease to have or shall not have effect. . . ." The marginal note (which is not binding) to section 7 reads: " Effect of Act on existing enactments." In *Vauxhall Estates Ltd.* v. *Liverpool Corporation* [8] the plaintiffs claimed that compensation for land compulsorily acquired from them should be assessed on the basis of the Act of 1919 and not on the less favourable terms provided by the Housing Act 1925. The Divisional Court held that even if the Act of 1919 could be construed as intended to govern future as well as existing Acts assessing compensation, which construction was doubtful, yet the relevant provisions must be regarded as impliedly overridden by the inconsistent provisions of the Act of 1925. In *Ellen Street Estates Ltd.* v. *Minister of Health* [9] a similar argument on the relation between the provisions for compensation contained in the Act of 1919 and the Housing Acts 1925 and 1930 was raised in the Court of Appeal. Here the decision that the Housing Acts impliedly repealed the Act of 1919 in so far as they were inconsistent with it was part of the ratio. " The Legislature cannot, according to our constitution," said Maugham L.J., " bind itself as to the form of subsequent legislation, and it is impossible for Parliament to enact that in a subsequent statute dealing with the same subject-matter there can be no

[6] 4 & 5 Anne, c. 14 and c. 16. See *Att.-Gen.* v. *Prince Ernest Augustus of Hanover* [1957] A.C. 436, *per* Viscount Simonds.
[7] " The Judge as Law Maker " (1972) 12 J.S.P.T.L. 22, 25.
[8] [1932] 1 K.B. 733.
[9] [1934] 1 K.B. 590; approving *Vauxhall Estates Ltd.* v. *Liverpool Corporation*, *supra.* Cf. F. M. Auburn, " Trends in Comparative Constitutional Law " (1972) 35 M.L.R. 129.

implied repeal. If in a subsequent Act Parliament chooses to make it plain that the earlier statute is being to some extent repealed, effect must be given to that intention just because it is the will of the Legislature."

Three problems however call for special treatment in this context, namely, Acts of Union, Independence Acts conferring independence on countries that formerly came under the authority of Parliament, and the European Communities Act 1972.

(a) Acts of Union

Union with Ireland. The Union with Ireland was negotiated by commissioners,[10] and based on Acts of the British and Irish Parliaments in response to messages from the Crown. The Union with Ireland Act 1800, passed by the British Parliament, provided that the Kingdoms of Great Britain and Ireland should be united " for ever " into one Kingdom, by the name of the United Kingdom of Great Britain and Ireland; and that the United Kingdom should be represented in one and the same Parliament. It further provided that the government and doctrine of the United Church of England and Ireland should be and should remain " for ever " assimilated to those of the existing Church of England, and that the continuance of the United Church should be deemed " an essential and fundamental part " of the Union of the two Kingdoms. Nevertheless, the Church of Ireland was disestablished by the Irish Church Act 1869,[11] some fifty years before the political Union itself was partly dissolved by the creation of the Irish Free State. Although there was much opposition in this country to the disestablishment of the Church of Ireland, it does not seem to have been based on the theory that the union of the Churches was legally indissoluble. Similarly, the difficulties preceding the separation of the Irish Free State from the United Kingdom by the Irish Free State (Constitution) Act 1922 were political and not legal.

When the secession of Eire (the Republic of Ireland) from the Commonwealth was recognised by the United Kingdom Parliament in the Ireland Act 1949 the following declaration was inserted in section 1 (2): " It is hereby declared that Northern Ireland remains part of His Majesty's dominions and of the United Kingdom, and it is hereby affirmed that in no event will Northern Ireland or any part thereof cease to be part of His Majesty's dominions and of the United Kingdom without the consent of the Parliament of Northern Ireland." This must be taken to be an expression of present intention, which is not legally binding on Parliament. It is submitted that

---

10 There was no formal treaty between Great Britain and Ireland.
11 *Ex p. Selwyn* (1872) 36 J.P. 54; *ante,* p. 47.

Parliament could expressly repeal or amend this section, or pass an ordinary Act inconsistent with it. The declaration may also be taken as expressing a convention, based both on agreement and on analogy to self-governing colonies, that the status of Northern Ireland, since it has responsible, though subordinate self-government, should not be altered without its consent. The declaration was repeated in the Northern Ireland (Temporary Provisions) Act 1972,[12] which would not be necessary if Parliament were bound by the 1949 Act.

Union with Scotland.[13] The Union was preceded by a treaty negotiated by the Parliaments of England and Scotland through commissioners. The Articles of Union were ratified first by the Scottish Parliament (" Estates "), which also passed Acts for securing the Presbyterian Church government and concerning the election of Scottish representatives to the Parliament of Great Britain, which Acts were to be part of the terms of the Union. Then the English Parliament ratified the terms approved by the Scottish Estates, together with an Act for the security of the Church of England. While Englishmen refer to the English Act of Union, Scotsmen tend to refer to the " Treaty."

The Union with Scotland Act 1706, passed by the English Parliament, provided that the two Kingdoms of England and Scotland should for ever after be united into one Kingdom by the name of Great Britain (Art. I); the United Kingdom of Great Britain should " be represented by one and the same Parliament " to be styled the Parliament of Great Britain (Art. III); that (subject to a common public law) Scots law was to remain as before but alterable by the Parliament of Great Britain, except that no alterations should be made " in laws which concern private right except for evident utility of the subjects within Scotland " (Art. XVIII). Article XIX preserved the Court of Session and Court of Justiciary as superior Scottish courts in all time coming, subject to regulations made by the Parliament of Great Britain for the better administration of justice. The Act incorporated an Act for securing the Protestant religion and

---

12 This Act suspended the Northern Ireland institutions for one year because of the emergency there. *Cf.* H. Calvert, *Constitutional Law of Northern Ireland* (1968) Chap. 1; Professor Calvert admits at p. 32 that his contrary arguments " are very tentative and find little support in the authorities."

The Taxation of Colonies Act 1778 provided that Parliament would not impose any taxes on colonies in North America or the West Indies, except such duties as might be expedient for the regulation of commerce.

13 Dicey and Rait, *Thoughts on the Union between England and Scotland* (1920); G. M. Trevelyan, *Ramillies and the Union with Scotland*, Chaps. 12–14. *Cf.* T. B. Smith in *The British Commonwealth*, Vol. I, Part II, *Scotland*, pp. 641–650; " The Union of 1707 as Fundamental Law " [1957] P.L. 99; *British Justice: The Scottish Contribution* (1961) pp. 201–213; K. W. B. Middleton, " New Thoughts on the Union between England and Scotland " (1954) 66 *Juridical Review* 37; J. D. B. Mitchell, " Sovereignty of Parliament—Yet Again " (1963) 79 L.Q.R. 196.

Presbyterian government in Scotland, paragraph 2 of which required professors of Scottish universities to subscribe to the Confession of Faith (a religious test), and paragraph 4 of which states that this Act with the establishment therein contained " shall be held and observed in all time coming as a fundamental and essential condition of any treaty or union to be concluded betwixt the two Kingdoms without any alteration thereof or derogation thereto in any sort for ever."

It was clearly intended that the Union itself should be permanent, and that certain provisions—concerning, or mainly concerning, the Scottish Church—should be unalterable. One of these, relating to Scottish professors subscribing to the Confession of Faith, was repealed by the Universities (Scotland) Act 1853. With regard to changes in Scots private law, it is not certain whether Parliament or the Scottish courts are supposed to have the power to determine whether they are for the " evident utility " of Scottish citizens. The main question is whether Parliament has power to repeal the provisions relating to the Presbyterian Church in Scotland.

The orthodox view, at any rate among English writers, is that at the Union the English and Scottish Parliaments extinguished themselves and at the same time transferred their powers to the new Parliament of Great Britain, and it is assumed that the Parliament of Great Britain inherited and developed the characteristics of the English Parliament, including sovereignty.[14] If so, this means that the United Kingdom Parliament, although morally bound by the terms of the Union with regard to the Scottish Church, might legally repudiate them.[15] In the Scottish courts, however, doubt has been expressed whether this view is sound. *McCormick* v. *Lord Advocate* [16] (the " Royal Numeral Case ") arose out of the official use in Scotland of the title " Elizabeth II," which was adopted by royal proclamation under a power conferred by the Royal Titles Act 1953. The Court of Session held that the Treaty did not prohibit the use of the numeral, and that the petitioners had no legal title or interest to sue. Either of these reasons would have been sufficient for the decision, but the Court added obiter that it was not satisfied that the Royal Titles Act would be conclusive if it had been repugnant to the Treaty, although in any

---

[14] It is commonly said that the Scottish Parliament was not recognised as having sovereignty; but *cf.* Erskine, *Inst.* i, 1, 19; Stair, Bk. I, Tit. IV, 61.

[15] So Blackstone, *Commentaries*, Introduction, para. 4 note; Austin, *The Province of Jurisprudence Determined* (ed. Hart) Lecture 6, pp. 256–257; Maitland, *Constitutional History*, p. 332. Dicey and Rait, *op. cit.* pp. 252–254 thought that the declaration concerning the Scottish Church, though not a legal limitation, represented a moral restriction and a warning.

[16] 1953 S.C. 396; 1953 S.L.T. 255. See T. B. Smith, " Two Scots Cases " (1953) 69 L.Q.R. 512–516; Middleton, *op. cit.*

event the court would have no jurisdiction to review a governmental act of this kind. " The principle of the unlimited sovereignty of Parliament," said Lord Cooper, " is a distinctively English principle which has no counterpart in Scottish constitutional law . . . . I have difficulty in seeing why it should have been supposed that the new Parliament of Great Britain must inherit all the peculiar characteristics of the English Parliament but none of the Scottish Parliament, as if all that happened in 1707 was that Scottish representatives were admitted to the Parliament of England." Here we have Scottish obiter dicta to the effect that Parliament is bound by the fundamental terms of the Treaty (or Act of Union), although the effect of the dicta is considerably reduced by the disclaimer of jurisdiction to review governmental acts done under unconstitutional legislation, and *a fortiori* (presumably) to review the unconstitutional legislation itself.

But to hold that Parliament is bound by certain articles of the Union—whatever that may mean in the absence of a judicial power of review—raises difficulties that appear to be insoluble in legal terms. It implies that there is a fundamental law to which Parliament is subordinate. Then what happens if this subordinate Parliament infringes the fundamental law? To say that the Union would be terminated involves the assumption that England and Scotland are still separately identifiable nations. If Parliament cannot alter these fundamental terms, who can? There might come a time when the Presbyterian Church was no longer a majority church in Scotland. How can the wishes of the Scottish people be known? The Members of Parliament for Scottish constituencies are a minority in the Commons and they are not necessarily Scotsmen. There is no provision in the Treaty for appointing commissioners to negotiate a revision, or for holding a plebiscite in Scotland. As a matter of legal theory the conclusion must be that the doctrine of sovereignty or legislative supremacy has developed since the Union as a characteristic of the United Kingdom Parliament. It is highly probable that the House of Lords in its judicial capacity would hold this view if the matter came before it although there is no appeal from Scottish courts to the House of Lords in criminal cases.[17]

---

[17] Professor T. B. Smith ([1957] P.L. 99) argues that the twofold ratification constituted both a treaty *jure gentium* and a fundamental law for the Union, whereas the Acts of Parliament of each country bound the subjects within that country alone as ordinary legislation. The Treaty *qua* Treaty ceased to exist by merger of the parties at the Union. What is left, Professor Smith contends, is the " fundamental law " which cannot be altered except by (technical) revolution. On the question of judicial review, he admits that a private individual would seldom have a title to sue, and the Lord Advocate would presumably agree with the government of which he was a member.

(b) *Grants of Independence*

Another special problem is whether Parliament can continue to legislate for members of the Commonwealth that have been granted independence. After the growth of conventions relating to self-governing colonies, the next legislative stage was section 4 of the Statute of Westminster 1931. This provides that an Act of the United Kingdom Parliament passed thereafter shall not extend, or be deemed to extend, to a Dominion (as therein defined) as part of the law of that Dominion unless it is expressly declared in the Act concerned that that Dominion [18] has requested, and consented to, its enactment. The definition of " Dominion " for this purpose now covers Canada, Australia and New Zealand.[19] This provision enacted what was already an established convention, which was also recited in the preamble to the Statute. It is a statement of Parliament's intention, and also a direction to the courts, which are only concerned with the presence or absence of a declaration in the Act of a Dominion's request and consent. The Statute did not purport to terminate Parliament's power to legislate for the Dominions altogether. It was contemplated that such request and consent might still be forthcoming in particular cases, as happened, for example, in connection with Australian and New Zealand emergency powers during the war and with the Cocos Islands Act 1955, which transferred the Cocos Islands to Australia. Further, reservations were made with regard to the power of constitutional amendment in some of the Dominions, which they would otherwise have had under section 2, so that as recently as 1964 we find Parliament amending the Canadian Constitution at Canada's request.[20]

Lord Sankey L.C. in *British Coal Corporation* v. *The King* [21] said obiter that as a matter of " abstract law " Parliament could repeal this Statute either expressly or by passing legislation inconsistent with it; but, he added, " that is theory and has no relation to realities." More recently, in *Blackburn* v. *Attorney-General* [22] Lord Denning M.R. went so far as to say obiter; " We have all been brought up to believe that, in legal theory, one Parliament cannot bind another and

---

[18] The request and consent required are those of the government of the Dominion concerned, and in the case of Australia those of its Parliament also.

[19] The Statute originally applied also to Newfoundland (now a province of Canada), and to South Africa and the Irish Free State (later Eire or the Republic of Ireland), which are no longer within the Commonwealth.

[20] British North America Act 1964, empowering the Canadian Parliament to legislate with regard to old age pensions.

[21] [1935] A.C. 500, 520.

[22] [1971] 1 W.L.R. 1037, 1040 (C.A.) *post*, p. 64. And see *McWhirter* v. *Att.-Gen.*, *The Times*, July 1, 1972 (C.A.): plaintiff might not argue that joining the EEC would be contrary to the Bill of Rights, which declared that the powers of government were vested in the Crown.

that no Act is irreversible. But legal theory does not always march alongside political reality. Take the Statute of Westminster 1931, which takes away the power of Parliament to legislate for the Dominions. Can anyone imagine that Parliament could or would reverse that Statute? Take the Acts which have granted independence to the Dominions and territories overseas. Can anyone imagine that Parliament could or would reverse these laws and take away their independence? Most clearly not. Freedom once given cannot be taken away. Legal theory must give way to practical politics." But Salmon L.J. was content to remark; " As to Parliament, in the present state of the law, it can enact, amend and repeal any legislation it pleases."

If section 4 of the Statute of Westminster is regarded primarily as a rule of construction addressed to the courts,[23] it seems probable that British courts would continue to regard Parliament as unrestricted by it, at least so far as the monarchies are concerned [24]; but that the courts of the country (former " Dominion ") concerned—in so far as they could not construe such Act as not being intended to infringe the section—would decline to apply an offending British statute, and an appeal to the Privy Council could be prevented by local legislation where such appeals have not already been abolished. It is the attitude of the local courts that matters, since section 4 refers to alteration of *the law of a Dominion*, not to alteration of *the law in this country*. Such a divergence of judicial decisions in this country from those in other parts of the Commonwealth would be a reflection in the courts of a (technical) revolution that had already taken place in the political sphere.[25]

It has been suggested above that the local court would, if possible, construe an Act of Parliament as not being intended to apply to the Dominion, unless passed at its request and with its consent. This is borne out by *Copyright Owners Reproduction Society* v. *E.M.I. (Australia) Pty Ltd.* (1958) [26]; where the High Court of Australia held that Copyright Acts of 1928 and 1956 did not apply to Australia.

[23] See K. C. Wheare, *The Statute of Westminster and Dominion Status* (5th ed.) Chap. 6, s. 3. And see further *post*, Chap. 35.

[24] A republic is not one of Her Majesty's Dominions, and it may be that on this ground an Act of Parliament would not be construed as extending to it.

[25] s. 2 (2) of the Statute of Westminster allows the Dominions to pass laws repugnant to United Kingdom legislation, but to say that this would enable the Dominions to nullify a repeal of the Statute begs the question.

[26] 100 C.L.R. 597. The Acts concerned were the Copyright Order Confirmation (Mechanical Instruments: Royalties) Act 1928, and the Copyright Act 1956. The draftsmen of the 1956 Act indicated that the repeal of the Copyright Act 1911 was not intended to affect the law of any country other than the United Kingdom. And see H. R. Gray, " The Sovereignty of the Imperial Parliament " (1960) 23 M.L.R. 647.

Dixon C.J. said that even before 1931 there was a strong convention that the United Kingdom Parliament would not legislate for a Dominion without its consent: there was therefore in Australian courts a rule of construction that, in the absence of evidence of such consent, a United Kingdom Act was not intended to apply to that Dominion.

The " Dominion status " of 1931, by the further development of constitutional conventions in relation to the countries concerned, has become independence within the Commonwealth. The grant of independence to a number of former dependent territories from 1947 onwards has been done by separate Acts of Parliament. As regards legislative powers, the Independence Acts for Ceylon (1947) and Ghana (1957) followed the Statute of Westminster,[27] but the Act for Nigeria (1960) and those that followed did not contemplate that the country concerned would in future request the United Kingdom to legislate for it. The post-war Independence Acts have gone further than the Statute of Westminster by expressly divesting the United Kingdom Government of any responsibility for the government of those countries.

A distinction might be drawn between the mere transfer of the *legislative* powers of Parliament, *e.g.* under the Statute of Westminster, and the transfer also of the *governmental* powers of the United Kingdom as under the post-war Independence Acts. Where in relation to a particular territory the sovereignty of the Crown as head of the United Kingdom Government has been transferred to a sovereign state, or in such a way as to make the transferee a sovereign state—recognised as such by other countries, and becoming a member of the United Nations—it seems absurd to say that Parliament can still legislate for such territory. Could Parliament cancel the cession of Heligoland to Germany,[28] or even repudiate the independence of the United States? [29] The distinction between the method used in 1931 and the method used after 1947, however, is probably no longer significant. When the courts recognise the political fact that territory formerly under the authority of Parliament has become independent of that authority, then Parliament can no longer alter the law of that

---

[27] The Indian Independence Act 1947 followed the Status of the Union Act 1934 (South Africa) in providing that Acts of the United Kingdom Parliament would not extend thereto unless adopted by its own legislature.

[28] Anglo-German Agreement Act 1890.

[29] By the Treaty of Paris 1783, signed between Great Britain and the United States of America, Britain acknowledged the United States to be free, sovereign and independent states; and relinquished all claims to the government, property and territorial rights of the same. This was an act of the prerogative. But statutes of 1782 relating to trade with America and American loyalists (23 Geo. III, c. 26, 39, 80) implied that the United States were no longer British colonies: *Doe* d. *Thomas* v. *Acklam* (1824) 2 B. & C. 778.

territory; although it may pass laws in relation to persons or acts in such territory as in any other " foreign " country, which are enforceable in the courts of this country.[30]

The legislative supremacy of Parliament, then, is a concept of British public law. It is recognised by the courts of the United Kingdom [31] and its dependencies,[32] and is enforced by those courts in relation to persons and property which are or which come within their jurisdiction. Thus if Parliament purported to revoke the independence of Uganda, this would affect the legal status of citizens of Uganda in this country.

(c) *European Communities Act 1972* [33]

The Treaties by which the United Kingdom agreed to join the European Communities (the " Common Market ") [34] were executive acts, which required an Act of Parliament to give effect to them in this country. The European Communities Act 1972, s. 2 (1), gives effect to rights and obligations created by or arising under the Treaties, *i.e.* created by the Treaties themselves and by existing and future Community Regulations which take effect directly as law in the member states. With regard to future Community Regulations this is a constitutional innovation, and they constitute a new kind of delegated or subordinate legislation in this country. Section 2 (2) confers power to give effect by Statutory Instrument to Community Directives, which set out objects to be achieved but leave it to each member state to decide the method of achieving them. Schedule 2 provides that such Statutory Instrument, if made without a draft having been approved by resolution of each House, shall be subject to annulment by resolution of either House; and the lawmaking

---

[30] *Ante*, p. 50.

[31] But as to Scotland, *cf. ante*, p. 58.

[32] *i.e.* colonies and other dependencies from whose courts appeal lies to the Privy Council.

[33] *Legal and Constitutional Implications of United Kingdom Membership of the European Communities* (1967) Cmnd. 3301; H.L.Deb., May 8, 1967, cols. 1202–1204; *The United Kingdom and the European Communities* (1971) Cmnd. 4715.

See also Geoffrey Howe, " The European Communities Act 1972 " (1973) 49 *International Affairs* 1; S. A. de Smith, " The Constitution and the Common Market " (1971) 34 M.L.R. 597; Andrew Martin, " The Accession of the United Kingdom to the European Communities: Jurisdictional Problems " (1968–9) 6 C.M.L.R. 7; N. M. Hunnings, " Constitutional Implications of Joining the Common Market," *ibid.* p. 50; Mitchell, Kuipers and Gall, " Constitutional Aspects of the Treaty and Legislation relating to British Membership " (1972) 9 C.M.L.R. 134.

[34] The Communities are the European Economic Community (EEC), the European Coal and Steel Community (ECSC) and the European Atomic Energy Community (EURATOM). Accession was effective from January 1, 1973.

power so delegated does not extend to taxation, retrospective law-making, sub-delegation or the creation of criminal offences punishable beyond certain limits. Section 3 provides that for the purpose of legal proceedings, the meaning of the Treaties and the validity or meaning of any Community Instrument are questions of law which, if not referred to the European Court, are to be determined in accordance with the principles laid down by that court.[35]

" Community law " is concerned with customs duties; agriculture; free movement of labour, services and capital; transport; restrictive trade practices; and the regulation of the coal, steel and nuclear energy industries. Most domestic law, such as criminal law, contract, tort, land law and family law, remains unaffected. Even where Community law has direct internal effect, it does not affect citizens in their private capacity, but imposes monetary penalties under civil proceedings relating to industrial and commercial activities. The effect of the European Communities Act is to override existing English law so far as inconsistent, and Parliament is expected to refrain from passing legislation inconsistent with Community law for the time being in force.

It has been widely objected that Parliament, by passing the European Communities Act, would be surrendering a large part of its " sovereignty "[36] to the Community institutions, and that as there is no time limit in the Treaties Parliament would be binding itself for ever. In *Blackburn* v. *Attorney-General*[37] the plaintiff sought declarations to the effect that the government, by signing the Treaty of Rome, would surrender in part the sovereignty of Parliament and would surrender it for ever, which would be in breach of the law. The Court of Appeal decided that the statements of claim disclosed no course of action and should be struck out. The Treaty of Accession to EEC was a prerogative act, and the question with regard to Parliament was hypothetical.

Successive Lord Chancellors in the House of Lords and extra-judicially have denied either that Parliament would surrender its sovereignty or that the Act could be irreversible—Lord Kilmuir and Lord Dilhorne in the House of Lords in 1962, Lord Gardiner in the House of Lords in 1967, and Lord Hailsham of St. Marylebone in 1971.[38] Lord Gardiner[39] pointed out that the United Kingdom has

35 See L. Blom-Cooper Q.C. and G. Drewry, *Final Appeal: A Study of the House of Lords in its Judicial Capacity* (1972) Chap. 20 (" European Postscript "). On the delegated legislation aspects, see further, Chap. 28.
36 We have already suggested that the term " sovereignty " is better applied to states than to legislatures.
37 [1971] 1 W.L.R. 1037; *The Times*, March 15, 1971 (C.A.).
38 322 H.L.Deb., cols. 195–208.
39 H.L.Deb., May 8, 1967, cols. 1202–1204.

accepted restraints on its legislative power to take account of obligations arising out of such treaties as the United Nations Charter, the European Convention on Human Rights, NATO and GATT. The Treaty obligations are reciprocal; all the members remain sovereign states; the United Kingdom would take part in the making of new Regulations (which is virtually always unanimous), and also in the judicial work of the EEC tribunals. Lord Hailsham [40] has said there are stacks of treaties designed to last for indefinite periods, some designed to last for ever, and that most peace treaties fall under one of these heads. He saw membership of the Community not as a derogation from sovereignty, but as sovereignty plus the advantages of membership. Other members of the EEC do not regard the Treaty as overriding their written constitutions. Lord Gardiner has said: "Under the British constitutional doctrine of Parliamentary sovereignty no Parliament can preclude its successors from changing the law . . . . There is in theory no constitutional means available to us to make it certain that no future Parliament would enact legislation in conflict with Community law"; but he added that repeal of the Act would be a breach of *international* obligations, unless it was justified by exceptional circumstances and had the approval of the other members. Again, Lord Diplock has said: "If the Queen in Parliament were to make laws which were in conflict with this country's obligations under the Treaty of Rome, those laws and not the conflicting provisions of the Treaty, would be given effect to as the domestic law of the United Kingdom." [41] Mr. Harold Wilson is reported to have said in February 1972 [42] that a future Labour Government would withdraw from the EEC if it could not satisfactorily renegotiate the terms for British membership: it would recognise "the British constitutional doctrine that one Parliament cannot bind its successors."

Any conflicts between later Acts of Parliament and Community law are likely to be inadvertent. Implied conflict might be prevented by an Interpretation Act, providing that (unless the context expressly stated otherwise) a self-styled "Community Act" should be read subject to Community law; or Parliament might pass every year a European Communities (Annual) Act removing current conflicts. [43]

---

[40] At the Mansion House: *The Times*, July 14, 1971. Lord Hailsham has also said: " either Dilhorne or Kilmuir got every leading lawyer . . . to discuss this very question and they came to the same conclusion ": *The Listener*, July 13, 1972, p. 40.

[41] " The Common Market and the Common Law " (1972) 6 *Law Teacher* 3, 5.

[42] In Bonn: *The Times*, February 5, 1972.

[43] H. W. R. Wade, " Sovereignty and the European Communities " (1972) 88 L.Q.R. 1. See also F. A. Trindade, " Parliamentary Sovereignty and the Primacy of European Community Law " (1972) 35 M.L.R. 375.

But Parliament could not be required to pass, nor could it be prevented from repealing, such legislation.[44]

II "MANNER AND FORM" OF LEGISLATION

The next question is whether Parliament can bind its successors as to the "manner and form" [45] of legislation, that is, as regards its own procedure.

Authentication of Acts of Parliament

There must be some rules logically prior to Parliament by which an act can be recognised as the act of Parliament.[46] This is not a matter of limitation, but identification. The principle applies to all legislatures, and is not a problem relating specifically to "sovereignty." For many centuries, except during the revolutionary Commonwealth period in the seventeenth century, "Parliament" has meant the Monarch, the Lords and Commons in Parliament assembled. "There is no Act of Parliament," says Coke,[47] "but must have the consent of the Lords, the Commons and the Royal Assent of the King, and as it appeareth by Records and our Books, whatsoever passeth in Parliament by this threefold consent, hath the force of an Act of Parliament." It has been a custom since the reign of Edward III for the Lords and Commons to deliberate separately,[48] but Parliament's formal acts until 1967 were always done by one body in the Parliament chamber.[49] The legislative formula for ordinary Acts of Parliament has long been established as follows: "Be it enacted by the Queen's most Excellent Majesty, by and with the advice and consent of the Lords Spiritual and Temporal, and Commons, in this present Parliament assembled, and by the authority of the same, as follows . . . ." [50] It will be noticed that this formula does not refer to the Houses of Lords and Commons.

The chief original sources for Acts of Parliament before 1849 are the Statute Rolls and Parliament Rolls, consisting of inrollments in

---

[44] See further, *post*, pp. 75–76.
[45] The expression is taken from the Colonial Laws Validity Act 1865, s. 5, and ultimately from the Foreign Jurisdiction Act 1843.
[46] These rules are both common law and fact, *ante*, p. 47.
[47] 4 Inst. 25.
[48] A. F. Pollard, *Evolution of Parliament* (2nd ed.) pp. 120–123.
[49] Pollard, *op. cit.* p. 123. And see Chitty, *Prerogatives of the Crown*, p. 75; " That which constitutes law is the concurring assent of all the branches of the legislature, wherever it may originate, whatever may happen to be the form of it." For the giving of the Royal Assent, and the Royal Assent Act 1967, see *post*, p. 100.
[50] Different formulae are used for Finance and Appropriation Acts, private Acts, and Acts passed under the special procedure of the Parliament Acts.

Chancery and proceedings in Parliament. We also have most of the original Acts since Henry VII, *i.e.* the drafts from which the Clerk of the Parliaments made up the inrollments. Since 1849 the Queen's printer has made two vellum prints authenticated by the proper officers of each House, one of which is kept in the House of Lords and the other deposited in the Public Record Office. Except in rare cases of doubt, printed copies of the statutes are sufficient—the King's (Queen's) printer's copies for Acts passed since 1713, and Statutes of the Realm for statutes passed down to that year.[51]

It appears from *The Prince's Case* (1606) [52] that it was sometimes difficult to determine the authenticity of earlier Acts, and that a statute (even though recited as coming from the King) would be accepted as an Act of Parliament if it was entered on the Parliament Roll and had always been allowed as an Act. In *Heath* v. *Pryn* (1670) [53] counsel challenged the Parliament Act 1660 on the ground that the Lords and Commons were not summoned by the King's writ, but the Court of King's Bench said: "the Act being made by the King, Lords and Commons they ought not now to pry into any defects of the circumstances of calling them together." The recital of the assent of the Monarch, Lords and Commons is generally taken to be conclusive, and it is doubtful whether *a litigant* would be allowed to attempt to prove that one of these assents had not in fact been given. On the other hand, *either House* might have the privilege of asserting by reference to its journals that it had not agreed to the Bill, or that amendments proposed by one House had not been agreed by the other. Although the question of the authentication of Acts is sometimes brought into discussions about the legislative supremacy of Parliament, it is more appropriately described by Erskine May as "Subsidiary Points in connection with Legislative Procedure." [54] Under the Parliament Acts, however, the Speaker's certificate is stated to be conclusive.

Courts not concerned with procedure in Parliament

Centlivres C.J. in *Harris* v. *Minister of the Interior* [55] suggested that a Bill passed by both Houses of the British Parliament sitting together would not be an Act of Parliament, as otherwise a Conservative Prime Minister who had lost his majority in the Commons

---

[51] See O. Hood Phillips, *A First Book of English Law* (6th ed.) pp. 109–110, 112.
[52] 8 Co.Rep. 1a.
[53] 1 Vent. 14.
[54] *Parliamentary Practice* (18th ed.) pp. 556–559. And see Craies, *Statute Law* (7th ed.) pp. 37–38.
[55] 1952 (2) S.A. (A.D.) 428, 470. And see R. T. E. Latham, "The Law of the Commonwealth" (in *Survey of British Commonwealth Affairs*, Vol. I, ed. Hancock) pp. 523–524.

could get a Bill passed by the Lords and Commons sitting together.
But Centlivres C.J. took as his example a particular case which would
be constitutionally objectionable. It may be replied, conversely, that
it would be absurd for a court to deny validity to an Act passed
unanimously by both Houses sitting together. There seems to be
no strictly legal objection to the Lords and Commons debating and
voting in a joint sitting. The matter seems now to be one of the
Commons' privileges and of constitutional convention. If it is one
of the Lords' privileges also, both Houses would have to agree before
a joint sitting could be held. It is submitted that the courts would
not wish to involve themselves in these procedural matters.

The decision of the Court of Appeal in *Ellen Street Estates Ltd.* v.
Minister of Health [56] is a precedent for saying that Parliament cannot
bind its successors as to the form of subsequent legislation by providing that there shall be no *implied* repeal of an Act.

The judgment of the House of Lords in *Edinburgh and Dalkeith
Ry.* v. *Wauchope* [57] may be relied on in relation to public as well as
private Acts (although as to public Acts the statement was obiter),
to the effect that the courts will not concern themselves with the
procedure by which a Bill passed through either House, such as the
customary three readings. Suppose that when a Labour Government
was in office Parliament had passed an Act providing that no Bill
to implement Britain's joining the EEC should have effect unless
approved by the electorate in a referendum. If Parliament under a
subsequent Conservative Government passed a European Communities
Act without a referendum being held, it is submitted that no court
would hold the latter Act void. Again, suppose that the Industrial
Relations Act 1971 contained a provision that it might not be repealed
or amended unless the Bill for that purpose was approved by the
votes of not fewer than two-thirds of the members of the House of
Commons. [58] It is submitted that if Parliament under a future Labour
Government passed an Act purporting to repeal or amend the
Industrial Relations Act, the courts would hold the subsequent Act
valid even though it could be shown that it had received fewer than
two-thirds of the votes of the members of the Commons. Similarly
with an Act to alter the status of Northern Ireland as part of the
United Kingdom. [59]

It is submitted that the courts would regard these as procedural
matters. This does not mean that if Parliament made such statutory

---

[56] [1934] 1 K.B. 590; *ante*, p. 55.
[57] 8 Cl. & Fin. 710; *ante*, p. 48; *cf. post*, p. 183.
[58] Such a provision would require a government to have the unusual majority of more
than 200 in the Commons.
[59] *Ante*, p. 56.

provisions they would be "void." Steps taken under them to hold a referendum or to obtain the approval of the Northern Ireland Parliament would be lawful. What we are saying is that the same Parliament, or a subsequent Parliament (probably of a different political complexion), could repeal these provisions or simply ignore them. There is no reason why a later Act should be accorded less authority than an earlier one.

Contrary arguments

It has been argued by Sir Ivor Jennings and others that the requirement of a referendum or the approval of some outside body such as the Parliament of Northern Ireland would constitute, not a procedural requirement, but a change in the *composition* of Parliament (which for this purpose would include the electorate or the Northern Ireland Parliament, as the case might be) and so be binding on the legislature. This view, if followed through to its logical conclusion, would lead to absurd results, for by the law and custom of Parliament all the elements constituting Parliament must be summoned to Westminster by Royal Writs to deliberate, vote and hear the Royal Assent.

Alternatively it has been argued by followers of D. V. Cowen that a requirement such as a special majority in either or both Houses would constitute a *redefinition* of " Parliament " for this purpose, so that in the case proposed above " Parliament " would mean the Queen, Lords and the Commons approving by a majority of not less than two-thirds. This " *redefinition*," it should be noticed, would be done not by some higher law as in the South African case of *Harris* v. *Minister of the Interior* [60] but by Parliament itself. To say that Parliament (while retaining its existing composition) can redefine *itself* in this way begs the question. It is a fiction or formula designed to avoid classifying the matter as " procedural." In so far as this argument differs from the " composition " argument, also, it would lead to the consequence that the word " Parliament " as applied to the United Kingdom Parliament could have an indefinite number of meanings.

The unicameral New Zealand Parliament is similarly not limited by a higher law,[61] and an " uncontrolled " [62] constitution can be

---

[60] D. V. Cowen's original argument referred to the meanings of " Parliament " in different sections of the constituent South Africa Act.

[61] *Cf.* the dictum of Moller J. at first instance in *R.* v. *Fineberg* [1968] N.Z.L.R. 119. And see J. W. Bridge, " Legislative Competence of the New Zealand Parliament " [1969] P.L. 112.

[62] See *McCawley* v. *R.* [1920] A.C. 691 (P.C.) *per* Lord Birkenhead L.C.

amended by implication by an ordinary statute.[63] The Electoral Act passed by the New Zealand Parliament in 1956 included section 189 which states that certain provisions relating to such matters as the life of Parliament, the franchise and secret ballot, may not be repealed or amended except by a majority of 75 per cent. of all the members of the House of Representatives or by a simple majority of votes in a referendum. Section 189 did not itself require this special procedure for its own repeal or amendment. It has been argued, that in any event in order to alter these electoral provisions it would be necessary to repeal section 189; but, secondly, that section 189 is probably binding on the New Zealand Parliament as a " redefinition " of the legislature for this purpose.[64] Most New Zealand lawyers and politicians at the time, however, admitted that the sanction provided by section 189 was merely moral and conventional,[65] and it is submitted that this is the correct view. The reason why the legislature did not try to " entrench " section 189 itself was that it recognised that such an attempt would be ineffectual.

The arguments concerning " manner and form " or " redefinition " in relation to the United Kingdom Parliament have also prayed in aid cases concerning legislatures that are subordinate to a higher law, or controlled constitutions. The first and best known of these is *Attorney-General for New South Wales* v. *Trethowan*.[66] The New South Wales legislature had passed an Act in 1929 providing that no Bill to abolish the Legislative Council (the Upper House) should be presented to the Governor for his assent unless it had been approved at a referendum, and that this provision should also apply to any Bill to repeal or amend the Act. After a change of government in 1930 two Bills were introduced, one to repeal the Act of 1929 and the other to abolish the Legislative Council. The Privy Council held that if they received the Governor's assent without being approved at a referendum the Acts would be void, because they would not have been passed in the " manner and form " required by the law in force in New South Wales. It is clear from the judgment of the Privy

---

[63] *Kariapper* v. *Wijesinha* [1968] A.C. 717 (P.C.); *cf. Ibralebbe* v. *R.* [1964] A.C. 900 (P.C.): no implied repeal of entrenched provisions. And *cf. R.* v. *Drybones* (1969) 9 D.L.R. (3d) 473 (S.C. Canada) on Canadian Bill of Rights.

[64] See *e.g.* Aikman, *New Zealand, its Laws and Constitution* (2nd ed. Robson) pp. 66–69.

[65] See *e.g.* K. J. Scott, *The New Zealand Constitution* (1962) pp. 6–9.

[66] [1932] A.C. 526 (P.C.) on appeal from the High Court of Australia in *Trethowan* v. *Peden* (1931) 44 C.L.R. 394. The case could have been argued on the question whether an injunction would lie to prevent the Bills from being presented to the Governor for the Royal Assent, but the Australian High Court allowed special leave to appeal to the Privy Council only on the question of " manner and form." See also *The State (Ryan)* v. *Lennon* [1935] I.R. 170, on the amending power of the Irish Free State legislature; O. Hood Phillips, " Ryan's Case " (1936) 52 L.Q.R. 241.

Council, and has been confirmed since by the Australian High Court,[67] that the decision in *Trethowan's* case was based on the ground that New South Wales (although no longer a " colony ") was still subject to the Colonial Laws Validity Act 1865, which recognises the law-making power of a representative colonial legislature provided that its laws are passed " in such manner and form as may from time to time be required by any Act of Parliament . . . or colonial law for the time being in force in the said colony." " The answer depends," said Lord Sankey L.C. in that case, " entirely upon a consideration of the meaning and effect of section 5 of the Act of 1865." The limitation placed on itself by the New South Wales legislature in 1929 was therefore binding on it in 1930 *by virtue of the Colonial Laws Validity Act,* a " higher law " passed by a legislature to which it was legally subordinate. The case is no authority whatsoever for saying that the United Kingdom Parliament can bind itself in this way.

The application of the " manner and form " argument to the United Kingdom Parliament appears to have been initiated by an obiter dictum of Dixon J., as he then was, in the Australian High Court in *Trethowan's* case.[68] His lordship suggested that if the United Kingdom Parliament passed legislation concerning the abolition of the House of Lords similar to that passed by the New South Wales legislature in 1929, it would be unlawful to present a repealing or abolition Bill for the Royal Assent; and if it was found possible (*sic*) to raise the question for judicial decision the court would be bound to pronounce it unlawful to do so; further that, if such Bill did receive the Royal Assent without being submitted to a referendum, the courts might (*sic*) be called upon to consider whether the supreme legislative power in respect of the matter had in truth been exercised in the manner required for its authentic expression and by the elements in which it had come to reside. He concluded that the answer was " not clear." In a later Australian case,[69] however, Dixon C.J. said that in Australian law an injunction ought not to be granted in connection with the legislative process,[70] that therefore *Trethowan's* case was probably wrongly decided, and the remedy was judicial review after the Royal Assent had been given. He implied that it was unlikely that such a case could be brought before the courts in the United Kingdom. The disinclination of English courts to intervene

---

[67] *Clayton* v. *Heffron* (1960) 105 C.L.R. 214; G. Sawer in [1961] P.L. 131. And see *per* Dixon C.J. in *Hughes and Vale Pty. Ltd.* v. *Gair* (1954) 90 C.L.R. 203. *Cf.* W. Friedmann, " Trethowan's Case, Parliamentary Sovereignty and the Limits of Legal Change " (1950) 24 A.L.J. 103.

[68] 44 C.L.R. 426. The dictum seems to have been inspired by counsel's argument.

[69] *Hughes & Vale Pty. Ltd.* v. *Gair* (1954) 90 C.L.R. 203.

[70] It might be regarded as a breach of privilege: *Clayton* v. *Heffron* (1960) 105 C.L.R. 214.

by injunction in the process of private Bill or delegated legislation is shown in several decisions.[71] *A fortiori* they are unlikely to intervene in the process of public Bill legislation, which is a matter within the cognisance of Parliament, apart from the fact that an injunction cannot be brought against an officer representing the Crown.[72] In *Harper* v. *Home Secretary,*[73] where an injunction was refused to restrain the Home Secretary from presenting a draft electoral boundaries order (approved by both Houses) to the Privy Council, Lord Evershed M.R. pointed out that *Trethowan's* case was concerned with a strictly limited legislature, and said: " That seems to me quite a different case from the present. We are here in no sense concerned with a Parliament or legislature having limited legislative functions according to the constitution."

In *Rediffusion (Hong Kong) Ltd.* v. *Attorney-General of Hong Kong* [74] the Privy Council held that no declaration or injunction lay to restrain the colonial legislature of Hong Kong from debating, passing and presenting to the Governor a copyright Bill, although it might, if enacted by the Governor's assent, be void under the Colonial Laws Validity Act 1865, s. 5, as being repugnant to United Kingdom statute. The principle of this decision would clearly rule out declaration or injunction as ways of preventing the presentation of a Bill to the Queen for the Royal Assent.

What we have said about cases concerning subordinate legislatures applies also to two appeals to the Privy Council from Ceylon, which are sometimes cited in this context. The reason for the invalidity of the Bribery Tribunal in *Bribery Commissioner* v. *Ranasinghe,*[75] and of the special court in *Liyanage* v. *R.*[76] was that the setting up of these judicial institutions had not been done by the special legislative procedure of constitutional amendment required by the written [77] Con-

---

71 *Bilston Corporation* v. *Wolverhampton Corporation* [1942] 1 Ch. 391 (statutory obligation not to oppose application for private Bill); *Hammersmith Borough Council* v. *Boundary Commission for England, The Times,* December 15, 1954 (forwarding of Boundary Commission's report to Home Secretary); *Merricks* v. *Heathcoat-Amory* [1955] Ch. 567 (ministerial marketing scheme); *Harper* v. *Home Secretary* [1955] Ch. 238 (C.A.). And see W. S. Holdsworth (1943) 59 L.Q.R. 2 (denying jurisdiction of courts in such cases); Z. Cowen, " The Injunction and Parliamentary Process " (1955) 71 L.Q.R. 336.
72 Crown Proceedings Act 1947, s. 21.   73 [1955] Ch. 238, *supra.*
74 [1970] A.C. 1136; O. Hood Phillips, " Judicial Intervention in the Legislative Process " (1971) 87 L.Q.R. 321. *Cf.* G. Sawer, " Injunction, Parliamentary Process, and the Restriction of Parliamentary Competence " (1944) 60 L.Q.R. 83: suppose an Act expressly authorises the citizen and the courts to intervene by injunction?
75 [1965] A.C. 172. *Cf.* G. Marshall, " Parliamentary Sovereignty: A Recent Development " (1966–67) 12 McGill L.J. 523.
76 [1967] 1 A.C. 259.
77 The Ceylon Constitution of 1947 was not merely " written," but contained entrenched clauses subject to judicial review.

stitution of Ceylon, although that country was a sovereign state.
In the *Ranasinghe* case Lord Pearce said that there was no analogy
to the British Constitution, which has no instrument governing the
forms of the lawmaking power.

Attempts have been made to suggest drafting formulae by which
Parliament might bind itself, but none of them would be effective to
prevent repeal or amendment by a later Act.[78]

Parliament Acts [79]

Public Acts (with one specific exception) may, in certain circumstances, be passed by the Queen and the Commons without the consent
of the Lords under the Parliament Acts 1911 and 1949. It has been
argued that by the Parliament Acts Parliament has bound itself for the
future as to the manner and form of legislation, or that for this
purpose " Parliament " now consists of the Queen and the Commons.
It is submitted that both arguments are unsound. In the first place,
the Parliament Acts do not limit the powers of Parliament. All Bills
(including Money Bills) must be sent to the Lords, and the Lords have
the opportunity of agreeing to them all if they wish. What the
Parliament Acts do is to alter the usual procedure for public Bills by
limiting the time during which the Lords may deliberate: after that
time a Bill may be sent for the Royal Assent although the Lords have
not agreed to it. This is an alternative permissive procedure, which
only comes into play after the prescribed period if the Lords do not
consent to a Bill in the form approved by the Commons. Again, the
five-year maximum life of Parliament is effective in that, if Parliament
is not dissolved by prerogative by the end of five years, it would be
dissolved automatically by the Parliament Act 1911; but Parliament can
during the five-year period pass an Act in the ordinary way extending
or reducing its life.[80]

Secondly, the Parliament Acts do not alter the composition of
Parliament. When an Act is passed by the Queen and the Commons
under the provisions of the Parliament Acts, the enacting formula
must state that this is done in accordance with the provisions of those

---

[78] *e.g.* Keir and Lawson, *Cases in Constitutional Law* (4th ed. 1954) p. 7: an Act
providing that no Bill to repeal it should have effect unless approved by a
referendum (passage omitted from later editions); J. L. Montrose, *Precedent in
English Law and other Essays* (1968) and J. D. B. Mitchell, *Constitutional Law*
(2nd ed. 1968) p. 89, cite the National Insurance Act 1965, s. 116, which reproduced
certain departmental regulations but provided that their validity might be determined
as though they remained delegated legislation. Montrose, *op. cit.* pp. 283–284, also
suggested the application of Interpretation Acts and the maxim *generalia specialibus
non derogant* as possible limitations on the doctrine that Parliament cannot bind
itself.

[79] See further, *post*, Chap. 6.

[80] Parliament in fact extended its life during both World Wars.

Acts (which include the sending of the Bill to the Lords),[81] and so it may best be regarded as a kind of subordinate or delegated legislation.[82]

Indeed, we may doubt whether the measure calling itself " the Parliament Act 1949 " is valid.[83] The Parliament Act 1911, of course, received the consent of the House of Lords; but the " Parliament Act 1949 "—designed to reduce still further the period during which the Lords might delay a public Bill other than a Money Bill—did not receive the consent of the Lords but purported to be passed in accordance with the provisions of the Parliament Act 1911. It therefore offended against the general principle of logic and law that delegates (the Queen and Commons) cannot enlarge the authority delegated to them. We are not, of course, arguing—as it is impossible in English law to argue—that an Act of Parliament is invalid; what we are questioning is whether the measure called " the Parliament Act 1949 " bears the character of an Act of Parliament. In other words we are contending that the Parliament Act 1911, as an enabling Act, cannot itself be amended by subordinate legislation of the Queen and Commons. At the time of writing no Act has purported to be passed without the consent of the Lords " in accordance with the provisions of the Parliament Acts 1911 and 1949," and so no legislation yet stands in jeopardy as depending on the doubtful effectiveness of the " Act " of 1949.

Regency Acts [84]

The Regency Acts 1937–53 provide that if the Sovereign is under eighteen years of age, the royal functions shall be exercised by a Regent appointed under the provisions of the Acts. The Regent may assent to Bills, except Bills altering the succession to the throne or repealing the Acts securing the Scottish Church. It is clear that the Regent and the two Houses could not repeal these exceptions, not because Parliament has bound its successors, but because legislation passed with the Regent's assent is a kind of subordinate or delegated legislation which must keep within the limits prescribed by the Regency Acts. On the other hand it seems that a Sovereign under the age of eighteen could assent to Bills, including Bills excepted from

---

81 A number of procedural provisions must be complied with, as to which the Speaker's certificate is stated to be conclusive: Parliament Act 1911, s. 3. *Cf. Akar* v. *Att.-Gen. of Sierra Leone* [1970] A.C. 853 (P.C.).

82 H. W. R. Wade [1954] C.L.J. 265; [1955] C.L.J. 193.

83 Hood Phillips, *Reform of the Constitution*, pp. 18–19, 91–93; letter from the author to *The Times*, July 15, 1968; Graham Zellick, " Is the Parliament Act *Ultra Vires*? " (1969) 119 New L.J. 716. See further, *post*, Chap. 6.

84 See further, *post*, Chap. 12.

the Regent's authority and Bills to repeal or amend the Regency Acts themselves,[85] for a Sovereign is never an infant at common law and Parliament is not bound by the procedure provided by the Regency Acts. This does not mean that these provisions of the Regency Acts are " void." They are valid and effective so long as they remain unrepealed in that, if a Regent is appointed, Bills assented to by him (subject to the two exceptions) will be recognised as valid statutes.

Conclusion

The problem raised in this chapter is known to logicians as the problem of " self-referring propositions." The view put forward here is that, as a matter of logic and law, a legislature cannot bind itself—whether as to subject-matter or the manner and form of legislation—unless it is directed or empowered to do so by some " higher law," that is, some (logically and historically) prior law *not laid down by itself*.[86] That superior law might be either a written constitution creating the legislature and containing entrenched provisions, or some general principle like natural law or the supremacy of international law. With regard to the former, as Lord Pearce said in *Bribery Commissioner* v. *Ranasinghe* [87]: " in the Constitution of the United Kingdom there is no governing instrument which prescribes the law-making powers and the forms which are essential to those powers." As to the latter, to recognise such an overriding legal principle in this country would be contrary to established judicial authority.[88]

The question has been discussed here in the light of the probable attitude of the British courts at the present time. It is possible, as has been suggested,[89] that our courts might change their attitude towards the lawmaking power of Parliament in the future—for example, with regard to express [90] conflicts between late Acts of Parliament and Community law or with regard to legislation implementing with-

---

[85] H. W. R. Wade [1955] C.L.J. 193n.

[86] Hood Phillips, *Reform of the Constitution*, pp. 155-157. See Alf Ross, " On Self-Reference and a Puzzle in Constitutional Law " (1969) LXXVIII *Mind*, p. 1; H. Kelsen, *General Theory of Law and State* (1945) pp. 124-128.

[87] [1965] A.C. 172.

[88] *Ante*, Chap. 3. For the supremacy of international law generally, see H. Kelsen, *The Pure Theory of Law* (2nd ed. transl. Max Knight, 1967), Chap. 7; and in relation to Human Rights, see B. A. Wortley, *Jurisprudence* (1967) Parts 4 and 5.

[89] Sir Leslie Scarman, " Law and Administration: A Change in Relationship " (1972) 50 *Public Administration* 253; S. A. de Smith, " The Constitution and the Common Market: A Tentative Appraisal " (1971) 34 M.L.R. 597, at pp. 612 *et seq.*; D. G. T. Williams, " The Constitution of the United Kingdom " [1972B] C.L.J. 266, at pp. 289 *et seq.*; F. M. Auburn, " Trends in Comparative Constitutional Law " (1972) 35 M.L.R. 129.

[90] Implied conflict is a matter of interpretation; see *post*, Chap. 28.

drawal from the EEC. This speculation posits judicial recognition of the supremacy of international law (and therefore of the obligations arising out of the Treaty of Rome) over the national legal system, which would be a reversal of judicial thinking.[91] But judges should follow revolutions, not make them. Meanwhile, our judges can be dismissed from office on an address from both Houses of Parliament, and the House of Lords as the final court of appeal is itself strictly part of Parliament.

It appears that the only way by which the legislature of this country could become legally limited would be for the United Kingdom Parliament to extinguish itself, after surrendering its powers [92] to a new written constitution with entrenched provisions (*e.g.* as to abolition of the Second Chamber, the life of Parliament, membership of EEC, and a Bill of Rights) and judicial review—a constitution limiting the powers of the new legislature *and to which the new legislature would owe its existence.* The new constitution could either be drafted by the existing Parliament, or its drafting could be entrusted to a constituent assembly, the new constitution perhaps receiving the extra moral sanction of an inaugural referendum. In either case there would be a *breach of continuity* between the old and the new constitutions.

---

[91] J. D. B. Mitchell, " Constitutional Aspects of the Treaty and Legislation relating to British Membership " (1972) 9 C.M.L.Rev. 134, argues that the Treaty has given rise to *a new legal order*, which binds the United Kingdom unless it renounces the Treaty; but British courts would be unlikely to accept this continental doctrine as a self-limitation by Parliament, and it could not have been imposed on this country by the Crown (*Case of Proclamations* (1610) 12 Co.Rep. 74; *The Zamora* [1916] 2 A.C. 77).

[92] *Cf.* A. V. Dicey, *England's Case against Home Rule* (3rd ed. 1887) pp. 241–245.

CHAPTER 5

CONSTITUTIONAL CONVENTIONS [1]

I. THE NATURE AND PURPOSE OF CONSTITUTIONAL CONVENTIONS

Nature of constitutional conventions

Some study of constitutional conventions is necessary in order to understand the working of the British Constitution. In drawing the distinction between the laws and conventions of the Constitution, Dicey was anticipated by a number of nineteenth-century writers, notably by E. A. Freeman in his *Growth of the English Constitution* (1872); but the significance of conventions in the working of the British Constitution, and therefore the importance of their study for an understanding of our constitution, were brought out by the emphasis Dicey placed upon them. Conventions are sometimes called "unwritten laws," but this is very confusing because according to the generally accepted doctrine they are not laws at all. "Unwritten law" in our system is a term properly applied to the common law. Again, conventions are sometimes called "customs." This is liable to cause confusion with customary law, which not only is law in the strict sense but requires for its validity (as conventions do not) immemorial antiquity.[2]

The working definition of constitutional conventions suggested here is: *rules of political practice which are regarded as binding by those to whom they apply, but which are not laws as they are not enforced by the courts or by the Houses of Parliament.*

This definition *distinguishes* constitutional conventions from:

　(i) *mere practice, usage, habit or fact,* which is not regarded as obligatory, such as the existence of political parties (fact), or the habit of Chancellors of the Exchequer in carrying from

---

1 See Dicey, *Law of the Constitution* (10th ed.) Chaps. 14 and 15; *cf.* Professor E. C. S. Wade's *Introduction*, pp. cli–cxci; Sir Ivor Jennings, *The Law and the Constitution* (5th ed.) Chap. 3; *Cabinet Government* (3rd ed.) Chap. 1; *Parliament* (2nd ed.) Chap. 3; G. Marshall and G. C. Moodie, *Some Problems of the Constitution* (3rd ed. 1964) Chap. 2; K. C. Wheare, *Modern Constitutions* (1951) Chap. 8; *The Constitutional Structure of the Commonwealth* (1960); S. A. de Smith, *The New Commonwealth and its Constitutions* (1964) Chaps. 1–3; O. Hood Phillips, "Constitutional Conventions: A Conventional Reply" (1964) 8 J.S.P.T.L. 60; "Constitutional Conventions: Dicey's Predecessors" (1966) 29 M.L.R. 137.

2 For common law, see O. Hood Phillips, *A First Book of English Law* (6th ed. 1970) Chap. 1; and for custom or customary law, *op. cit.* Chap. 13. Some customary laws are "conventional" or contractual, *ibid.*

Downing Street to the House of Commons a dispatch case supposed to contain his " Budget " speech. If the persons concerned are not aware that they are under an obligation to act in a certain way, there is no convention. On the other hand, the opinion that they are bound is not conclusive as they may be mistaken.[3] The precise content of some conventions is uncertain, since they must be flexible enough to meet changing circumstances; and as that which is not certain cannot be obligatory, it is sometimes difficult to distinguish between obligatory rules and non-obligatory practice, e.g. the consultation of outside interests when social welfare legislation is being drafted[4];

(ii) *non-political rules, i.e.* rules of conduct which are not referable to the needs of constitutional government, e.g. ethical or moral rules, or the almost invariable custom of crowning the Queen Consort, which has no constitutional significance[5];

(iii) *rules enforced by the courts, i.e. laws.* Judicial enforcement does not necessarily, or indeed usually, imply specific enforcement. In public law it usually involves an action for damages, declaration or injunction, habeas corpus, certiorari or one of the other prerogative orders; or it may involve a criminal prosecution or a defence to a criminal charge.[6] Sir Ivor Jennings,[7] while admitting that there was this formal distinction between laws and conventions, contended that there was no distinction of substance. The distinction may perhaps be comparatively unimportant for the political scientist or the politician, but it is surely of vital importance for lawyers. Some criticise the distinction on the ground that there may be laws with no judicial sanction.[8] It is true that laws cannot be enforced against the government as a body or against either House of Parliament; but they can be enforced against individual Ministers personally,[9] or (subject to parliamentary privilege, which is itself part of the law) against individual members of either House; and judgment may be delivered (though not executed) against a government

---

[3] Marshall and Moodie, *op. cit.* p. 36.
[4] See E. C. S. Wade in Dicey, *op. cit.* at pp. cliv–clv.
[5] In *Queen Caroline's Claim* (1821) 1 St.Tr.(N.S.) 949, the Privy Council held that the Queen Consort has no legal right to be crowned.
[6] In *Madzimbamuto* v. *Lardner-Burke* [1969] 1 A.C. 645 the Privy Council held that the convention under which the United Kingdom Parliament did not legislate for Southern Rhodesia without the consent of the government of that colony, although important as a convention, had no effect in limiting the powers of the United Kingdom Parliament.
[7] Jennings, *Law and the Constitution* (5th ed.) p. 117.
[8] *e.g.* J. D. B. Mitchell, *Constitutional Law* (2nd ed. 1968) pp. 34–39.
[9] *Raleigh* v. *Goschen* [1893] 1 Ch. 73.

department.[10] Parliament sometimes imposes " duties " on public authorities but goes on to say that such duties are not to be enforced by judicial proceedings. For example, the Transport Act 1962 provided that it should be the duty of the Railways Board to provide railway services (s. 3 (1)), but that this should not be construed as imposing any duty or liability enforceable by proceedings before any court (s. 4 (1)). On analysis it appears that from a legal point of view such " duties " are properly classed as powers. The statutory requirement that a Governor-General shall direct the issue of writs has been construed to be directory, not mandatory [11]; and the requirement that a Minister shall lay certain instruments before Parliament would probably be interpreted in the same way.[12] The judicial enforcement test does not—as has been suggested—deny the name of " law " to the principles applied and the decisions made by administrative tribunals, for these tribunals are created by statute, and their decisions are if necessary controlled or given effect to by the courts even where there is no appeal from the former to the latter;

(iv) *rules enforced by the Houses of Parliament* through their officers, *e.g.* the Speaker and the Serjeant-at-Arms, notably parliamentary procedure and privilege (part of " the law and custom of Parliament," which is itself part of the common law in the wide sense). These may, however, overlap constitutional conventions. Thus some parts of parliamentary practice constitute conventions, such as the protection of minorities in debate and the party composition of committees. Standing Orders are often said to be examples of constitutional conventions; but on analysis they will be found to consist partly of law, partly of mere practice, and only to a small extent of convention.[13]

The fact that the courts to not *enforce* constitutional conventions does not necessarily mean that the courts do not recognise their existence. Thus the responsibility of the Home Secretary to Parliament was one of the reasons for the decision of the House of Lords in *Liversidge* v. *Anderson* [14]; and the Judicial Committee of the Privy Council in *British Coal Corporation* v. *The King* [15] mentioned

[10] Crown Proceedings Act 1947.
[11] *Simpson* v. *Att.-Gen.* [1955] N.Z.L.R. 271 (C.A. of New Zealand).
[12] *Post*, Chap. 28.
[13] *Post*, Chap. 9.
[14] [1942] A.C. 206; but the Home Secretary was also required by statutory regulation to report monthly to Parliament.
[15] [1935] A.C. 500; W. Ivor Jennings, " The Statute of Westminster and Appeals " (1936) 52 L.Q.R. 173.

the conventions regulating what was then called Dominion status, and also the convention that the Crown invariably accepts the Judicial Committee's advice. In *Carltona Ltd.* v. *Commissioners of Works* [16] Lord Greene M.R. referred to the convention of a Minister's responsibility to Parliament for the acts of his officials.

Legislation may recognise or presuppose conventions. Thus the Ministers of the Crown Act 1937 implied a knowledge of the existence of the Prime Minister, the Leader of the Opposition and the Cabinet; and the preamble to the Statute of Westminster 1931 recites several conventions of inter-Commonwealth relations. Conventions are capable of being formulated in statute, *e.g.* the Statute of Westminster 1931, s. 4, and they have been incorporated (with or without justiciable effect) in various Commonwealth constitutions.[17]

The laws of the constitution could stand alone, although the constitution would then be antiquated and static; but the conventions would be meaningless without their legal context. Every constitutional convention is closely related to some law or laws, which it implies. The conventions forming the Cabinet system, for example, presuppose the laws relating to such matters as the Queen's royal prerogative, the office and powers of Ministers (except the Prime Minister), the constitution of government departments, and the composition of Parliament. There are thus layers, as it were, of laws, conventions and facts (political practice); and any one situation may be governed by a number of layers of this kind, perhaps including a statute which implies the existence of a convention.

The purpose of constitutional conventions

Conventions are a means of bringing about constitutional development without formal changes in the law.[18] This they often do by regulating the exercise of a discretionary power conferred on the Crown by the law. It must not be supposed that conventions are peculiar to unwritten constitutions. They are found to a greater or less extent in written constitutions as well. Canada and Australia, for example, observe the main British constitutional conventions, and many conventions have been developed in the United States relating to such matters as the method of electing the President, his choice and use of a Cabinet, and " senatorial courtesy " in making appoint-

---

16 [1943] 2 All E.R. 560.

17 *Adegbenro* v. *Akintola* [1963] A.C. 614 (P.C.) *per* Viscount Radcliffe; *cf. Ningkan* v. *Government of Malaysia* [1970] A.C. 379; see K. J. Keith, " The Courts and the Conventions of the Constitution " (1967) 16 I.C.L.Q. 542 .

18 Conventions therefore change in accordance with the underlying ideas of government: see Holdsworth, " The Conventions of the Eighteenth-Century Constitution " (1932) 17 *Iowa Law Review* 161.

ments to office. [19] This informal method of change is more adaptable than a series of statutes or constitutional amendments. The general tendency is towards democracy, due regard being had to the protection of minorities and their right to be heard.

The ultimate object of most conventions is that public affairs should be conducted in accordance with the wishes of the majority of the electors. The reason why the Ministry must be chosen from the party or parties enjoying a majority in the Commons is that, on the assumption that the majority of the Commons reflect the views of the majority of the electors,[20] a Ministry so selected will be most likely to give effect to the will of the nation as a whole. And this is also the reason why the Queen should act on the advice of Ministers, why Ministers should resign if defeated in the Commons, and why the House of Commons should have a political ascendancy over the House of Lords, especially in matters of finance.

To ensure that the power of government shall be exercised in accordance with the popular will, that will must be ascertained from those best qualified to know it, namely, the elected representatives of the people; hence the convention requiring Parliament to be summoned annually. If there is reason to suppose that the government no longer represents the will of the country, the Ministry may properly advise a dissolution in order to enable the electorate, through a new Parliament, to obtain a new Ministry more in accordance with its views.

In this way the legal framework of 1688—a strong monarchy limited in certain specific ways—has become a " constitutional " monarchy, that is to say, a democratic political system with a hereditary Head of State practically bereft of governmental powers. To meet current political ideas and social needs, conventions have facilitated the growth of the Cabinet system; changed the emphasis on the functions of Parliament, which is now largely occupied in representing the views of the electors by criticising the government's activities and debating their measures; and developed the autonomy of other Commonwealth countries.

Conventions also make the legal constitution work by providing means for co-operation in the practice of government. In particular, the Cabinet system co-ordinates the work of the various government departments among themselves, and promotes co-operation between the departments and Parliament and between the Ministry and the Queen. Similarly, the conventions governing inter-Commonwealth

---

[19] H. W. Horwill, *The Usages of the American Constitution* (1925).
[20] Owing to our system of voting in territorial constituencies, a majority in the Commons may, however, represent a minority of the voters.

relations enable the members of the Commonwealth, although independent, to co-operate to a great extent in their defence and foreign policy.

How and when do conventions become established?

It is wrong to suppose that constitutional conventions are analogous to customary law in that they must necessarily have existed a long time, or even from time immemorial. A moment's thought will show that this cannot be so, for the conventions of our constitution mostly date from a time later than the Revolution of 1688, and in most cases a good deal later. Many conventions are indeed based on usage, although this is not necessarily of long standing. Some conventions, however—especially among those concerned with Commonwealth relations—are based on agreement,[21] and we know exactly when and how they were formulated.

It is not easy to say precisely how or when conventions based on usage come into existence. Every act by the Queen or a responsible statesman is a " precedent " [22] in the sense of an example which may or may not be followed in subsequent similar cases, but it does not necessarily create a binding rule. For that it must be generally accepted as creating a rule by those in authority. A long series of precedents all pointing in the same direction is very good evidence of a convention, but this is not possible in the case of recent precedents. Thus the fact that no monarch has refused the Royal Assent to a Bill since Queen Anne clearly points to the existence of a convention that the Royal Assent should not be refused; but can we say that the Queen may in no circumstances refuse the Prime Minister's request to dissolve Parliament?

Sir Ivor Jennings suggested two requirements for the creation of a convention: (i) general acceptance as obligatory, and (ii) a reason or purpose referable to the existing requirements of constitutional government. Thus one precedent might create a convention while a long series of precedents might not. Owing to Cabinet secrecy, posthumous biographies and prejudiced autobiographies, it is often difficult to find out whether the actors thought they were obeying a binding rule.[23]

Why are conventions observed?

What is it that induces obedience to these extra-legal or conventional rules? The answer seems to be that obedience is yielded

---

21 This is the sense in which international lawyers speak of " conventions."
22 The word " precedent " is not, of course, used here in the technical sense of a legal (judicial) precedent.   23 *Cabinet Government* (3rd ed.) pp. 5–13.

to the conventions because of the consequences that would plainly ensue if they were disregarded. Thus if Parliament were not summoned annually the army and air force could not lawfully be maintained, an important part of the public revenue, namely, income tax, could not be lawfully raised, and even less could be lawfully spent.[24] If the Queen appointed as Prime Minister someone who did not enjoy the confidence of the majority of the Commons, he and his colleagues could be defeated in the lower House. If a government after defeat in the House declined to resign or ask for a dissolution, the Commons could paralyse the business of government by withholding supplies or refusing to agree to the continuance in force of the Army and Air Force Acts. Even if a government succeeded in carrying on for a time in disregard of Parliament, it would cease to be in touch with the will of the electors and would forfeit their favour, assuming this had not been already lost by the recourse to extra-parliamentary government.

Some conventions are not always observed if special circumstances warrant a departure from established practice, but if they were not regularly observed they would not be, or would cease to be, conventions.[25] It is the reason or purpose for which they stand that both leads to their development and secures their observance. The " agreement to differ " in 1932, whereby certain Liberal members of the Cabinet were permitted by their colleagues to disagree openly on the majority's fiscal policy, was alleged to be justified by the necessity of preserving the National (Coalition) Government in view of the " economic crisis "; but it did not work, and the recalcitrant members soon resigned office.[26]

Dicey rejected the answer that observance of constitutional conventions is secured by " public opinion," on the ground that it begs the question, which is, why does public opinion appear to be sufficiently strong to ensure the observance of the conventions?[27] In the past, respect for conventions was established by the threat of impeachment, greatly influenced by public opinion; but a stronger sanction was needed, and impeachment has in practice become obsolete as being unnecessary in view of the development of ministerial responsibility to Parliament. Dicey concluded that the sanction of constitutional

---

[24] That is, so long as the practice continues of authorising these matters by annual Acts or statutory provisions having force for one year only.

[25] F. D. Roosevelt broke the American convention against standing for the office of President for a third term. He was elected and later re-elected for a fourth term; but an amendment to the Constitution has since been passed limiting the tenure of office to two terms.

[26] Keith Middlemas and John Barnes, *Baldwin* (1969) Chap. 24.

[27] Dicey, *op. cit.* Chap. 15.

conventions is to be found in the fact that a person who persisted in the breach of convention would inevitably be led into a breach of the law " sooner or later "—in one place he says " immediately." Thus if Parliament were not summoned in any one year, so that the annual Finance and Appropriation and Army Acts [28] expired, the collection of much of the national revenue (especially income tax), the expenditure of most of the public funds and the maintenance of a standing army and enforcement of military discipline would be illegal under the Bill of Rights.

Dicey only dealt, however, with one group of conventions, though admittedly the most important, namely, those that regulate the relations between the executive and Parliament, especially those between the government and the House of Commons. No breach of law would follow if Standing Orders relating to the rights of minorities were not followed in conducting the business of either House, nor (by English law) if the United Kingdom Parliament legislated for an independent member of the Commonwealth without its consent, nor (assuming it to be a constitutional convention, as distinct from the practice of the court, that they should not) if lay peers took part in a trial in the House of Lords.

Further, certain qualifications must be made even in the case of those conventions to which Dicey's argument applies. If a government that was committing breaches of convention retained the confidence of the Commons it could procure the alteration of the law, as it did with the Provisional Collection of Taxes Act 1913, following the decision of *Bowles* v. *The Bank of England*,[29] or the passage of an Act of Indemnity, thus indicating that the convention in question was considered undesirable or to have lost its purpose. Even if the government lost the confidence of the Commons, it might remain in office for some months without breaking the law owing to the time-lag between the lapsing of the Finance Act (fixing the standard rate of income tax and authorising most of the expenditure) and the Army Act and the beginning of the next financial year when the Commons must be asked for fresh supplies.

For the reasons stated above, however, it is submitted that it is not necessary to go as far as Dicey. The question why conventions are observed is a political or psychological question. One might equally ask what motives induce people to obey the law, since fear of the legal sanction only operates on some of the people some of

---

[28] His argument is not affected by the modern procedure whereby the Army and Air Force Acts are continued in force for twelve months at a time by Orders in Council subject to affirmative resolution of both Houses.

[29] [1913] 1 Ch. 57.

the time.[30]   As a matter of fact, statesmen probably observe the conventions because they wish the machinery of government to go on and because they hope to retain the favour of the electorate.[31]

II. CLASSIFICATION AND ILLUSTRATION OF CONSTITUTIONAL CONVENTIONS

Constitutional conventions may be classified into three main groups:
   (1) relating to the exercise of the royal prerogative and the working of the Cabinet system;
   (2) regulating the relations between the Lords and Commons, and proceedings in Parliament; and
   (3) regulating the relations between the United Kingdom and the independent members of the Commonwealth.

The first group is the most important, and forms the main theme of Dicey's discussion (*supra*).   The second group has lost much of its importance as convention since the passing of the Parliament Acts.   The third group has developed almost entirely since Dicey's day.

It is difficult to say to what extent conventions, in the sense in which we have defined them, exist in English local government, *e.g.* as to the election of mayor and chairmen of committees, having regard to the state of the parties on the council.   The practice varies greatly from one local authority to another, and is often not consistent over a period within the same authority.   Further, political scientists who have examined this question tend to ignore the distinction between rules regarded as obligatory and mere practice.[32]

1. Conventions relating to the exercise of the royal prerogative and the working of the Cabinet system

The Sovereign could legally declare war or make peace; dissolve Parliament at any time, and need not summon another for three years; she could refuse her assent to measures passed by both Houses of Parliament; she could at any time dismiss her Ministers and appoint others, and so on.   The exercise of these powers, however, is either

---

[30] See Bryce, *Studies in History and Jurisprudence*, Vol. II, Essay IX.
[31] Marshall and Moodie, *op. cit.* pp. 40–41, suggest that the sanction for the observance of conventions is that a breach of convention is likely to lead to a *change* of law; see *ante*, p. 83n.
[32] See R. S. B. Knowles, " Local Government Practices—or Conventions? " (1958) 122 J.P. 856; E. S. Walker, " Conventions in Local Government " (1959) 123 J.P. 234; H. Maddick and E. P. Pritchard, " The Conventions of Local Authorities in the West Midlands " (1958) *Public Administration* 145; (1959), 135.

restricted altogether or regulated by conventions, of which the following are some of the most important.

(i) The Queen must invite the most influential leader of the party or group commanding a majority of the House of Commons to form a Ministry. The person so called on is the " Prime Minister." In law the Prime Minister until recently did not exist, and even now he is only referred to incidentally in a few statutes, notably the Ministerial Salaries Consolidation Act 1965 (salary and pensions).[33]

(ii) The Queen must appoint as her other Ministers such persons as the Prime Minister advises her to appoint. Ministers should have seats in either the House of Commons or the House of Lords. The latter convention is illustrated by the appointment by Mr. Harold Wilson of Mr. Cousins and Mr. Gordon Walker to ministerial posts after the Labour victory in the general election in October 1964. Neither was a Member of Parliament: Mr. Cousins was a trade union official, and Mr. Walker (who was appointed Foreign Secretary) had actually been defeated at Smethwick in the recent election. In January 1965 they stood as candidates in by-elections facilitated by the grant of life peerages to two Labour M.P.s. Mr. Cousins was elected, but Mr. Walker was again defeated and resigned office next day. (By law the Queen can appoint and dismiss Ministers at her pleasure).

(iii) The body of Ministers so appointed become the " government," and an inner ring of them is called the " Cabinet." Cabinet Ministers are always made Privy Councillors, if not such already. The Cabinet is entirely the product of convention, and is unknown to the law except for a few incidental references in statutes such as the Ministerial Salaries Consolidation Act 1965 [34] and the Parliamentary Commissioner Act 1967.

(iv) The Queen is bound to exercise her legal powers in accordance with the advice tendered to her by the Cabinet through the Prime Minister. She has the right to be kept informed and to express her views on the questions at issue, but not to override ministerial advice. This advice is expected to be unanimous.

(v) The Queen must assent to every Bill passed by the Houses of Parliament, or passed by the House of Commons only in accordance with the Parliament Acts. A Sovereign has not refused assent to a Bill since Queen Anne refused her assent to the Scottish Militia Bill in 1707, and the exercise of this prerogative today would be un-

[33] Replacing the Ministers of the Crown Act 1937.
[34] Replacing the Ministers of the Crown Act 1937. It has also been suggested that it has become a convention that the Opposition leaders should form a Shadow Cabinet; D. R. Turner, *The Shadow Cabinet in British Politics* (1969).

constitutional. (No Bill has the force of law until the Queen gives her assent, but there is no law requiring her to give it.)

(vi) Parliament must be summoned to meet at least once each year. The observance of this convention is secured by the practice (probably itself also a convention) of limiting to one year at a time the statutory authority covering the raising and spending of part of the revenue and the maintenance of the Army and Air Force. (By the Meeting of Parliament Act 1694 Parliament must be summoned at least once in three years.)

(vii) The government is entitled to continue in office only so long as it enjoys the confidence of a majority of the House of Commons. The Prime Minister is bound to tender the resignation of himself and his colleagues, or to advise the Sovereign to dissolve Parliament, if his government is defeated on the floor of the House on a major issue. Owing to party discipline the defeat of a government with a party majority in the House of Commons is very rare in modern times. Gladstone's second government was defeated on the Budget in 1885 and made way for a minority Conservative administration under Salisbury. In the following year Gladstone's third government was defeated on the Home Rule Bill and he advised a dissolution. The last occasion on which a government was forced to resign after defeat in the House of Commons was in 1895 on a snap vote of censure for the inadequate supply of cordite for the army. The Labour Government was defeated by one vote on the floor of the House in May 1970 on a clause in the Administration of Justice Bill giving power to the Commercial Court to sit in private, but there was no question of resignation. Minority Conservative and Labour Governments were defeated in the Commons in 1924. Ramsay MacDonald's minority Labour Government was defeated twelve times in eight months, but the Prime Minister announced that he would not resign unless defeated on a major issue. Even though the government has not been defeated in the Commons, a Prime Minister is further entitled to advise a dissolution if there are good grounds for thinking that it no longer enjoys the confidence of the electors. (By law, subject to the Meeting of Parliament Act 1694 and the Parliament Act 1911—fixing the maximum duration of a Parliament at five years —the Queen has power to summon and dissolve Parliament at her pleasure.)

(viii) The Ministers are collectively responsible to Parliament for the general conduct of the affairs of the country. This collective responsibility requires that on a major question Ministers should be of one mind and voice. If any Minister does not agree with the policy of the majority in the Cabinet, he must resign or (if the matter is a minor one) at least keep quiet about it.[35]

(ix) Ministers are also individually responsible to Parliament for the administration of their departments. A Minister must be prepared to answer questions in the House concerning matters for which he is administratively responsible, and if a vote of censure is passed against him he must resign his office. Standing Orders of the House of Commons assume the existence of the former convention by prescribing days and times for questions. (By law, Ministers are individually responsible to the Sovereign.)

(x) Ministers are expected to disembarrass themselves of any company directorships or shareholdings that would be likely, or might appear, to conflict with their official duties.

(xi) A government should not advise the Crown to declare war, make peace or conclude a treaty unless there is ample ground for supposing that the majority of the Commons approve of the policy. (By law the power to make war and peace and to enter into international treaties is vested in the Queen, who is not bound to consult advisers [36] or Parliament, though the Bill of Rights prevents her from imposing taxation to meet financial commitments.)

2. Conventions regulating the relations between the Lords and Commons, and proceedings in Parliament

The House of Commons being the representative assembly, its will ought ultimately to prevail in cases of conflict with the House of Lords, which is mainly hereditary and partly nominated. Since medieval times the Commons have claimed the right to control national finance, that is, the levying of taxation and the supervision of the expenditure of public money.

Each House must have power to control the conduct of its own proceedings free from outside interference, and in course of time the Houses have evolved rules and customs, privileges and practice regulating legislative procedure and the conduct of debate.

The following are some of the most important conventions in this group:

(i) In cases of conflict the Lords should ultimately yield to the Commons. (Perhaps the Parliament Acts 1911 and 1949—by defining the period during which the Lords may delay public Bills, other than a Bill to extend the maximum duration of Parliament—have rendered this convention unnecessary.) Until the Parliament Act 1911 was

---

[35] Post, Chap. 15.
[36] Foreign countries, however, might well be unwilling to enter into a treaty that was not authenticated by the signature or seal of some senior Minister.

passed it was legitimate for a Ministry, when an important measure was rejected by the Lords, to advise the Sovereign as a last resort to create a sufficient number of peers to ensure its passage in the Upper House. The Treaty of Utrecht was ratified by this method in 1712; and the Reform Act 1832 and the Parliament Act 1911 were passed by the threat of recourse to it. (The Parliament Act 1911 made recourse to this expedient for the future unnecessary and perhaps improper.)

(ii) Proposals involving the expenditure of public money may only be introduced on behalf of the Crown by a Minister in the House of Commons. Standing Orders provide that a financial resolution shall only be proposed by a Minister on behalf of the Crown. There may be elements here of parliamentary custom and privilege, as well as constitutional convention. (The Parliament Act 1911 assumes, without expressly stating, that Money Bills will be introduced in the Commons.)

(iii) The business of the House of Commons is arranged informally " behind the Speaker's Chair " between the Prime Minister or Leader of the House and the Leader of the Opposition. The latter is a product of convention more recent than the Prime Minister, and fulfils the function of a sparring partner. Charles James Fox is generally regarded as the first Leader of the Opposition, when the younger Pitt became Prime Minister in 1783. (The Ministers of the Crown Act 1937 first gave the Leader of the Opposition a salary payable out of the Consolidated Fund; and the Ministerial Salaries and Members' Pensions Act 1965 gave salaries to the Leader of the Opposition in the House of Lords and the Chief Opposition Whips in both Houses. These salaries are charged on the Consolidated Fund.) A member may, so far as his Chief Whip is concerned, safely absent himself from a debate if he obtains a " pair " from among members of the other party.

(iv) The majority in Parliament must not stifle minorities. It is a duty of the Speaker to protect minorities in debate, and so far as possible he calls on speakers from alternate parties.

(v) The political parties are represented in parliamentary committees in proportion to the number of their adherents in the House. (The Ministers of the Crown Act 1937 indirectly recognised the existence of political parties in its definition of the Leader of the Opposition.)

(vi) Peers who do not hold or have not held high judicial office do not take part when the House of Lords is sitting in its judicial capacity. (The Appellate Jurisdiction Acts provide for the appointment of a certain number of Lords of Appeal in Ordinary, but there is no law that lay peers may not sit as well.) This rule is perhaps rather one of parliamentary practice or the practice of the court than a " convention," as it is not of a political nature referable to the needs of constitutional government.[37]

(vii) We may say that there is a convention that the Houses of Parliament will not entertain, or pass, a private Bill without providing for adequate notice to be given to persons affected and allowing them an opportunity to state objections. The Standing Orders relating to private business, which are alterable in detail, presuppose this convention.[38]

3. Conventions regulating the relations between the United Kingdom and other members of the Commonwealth

A number of conventions have grown up, or have been formulated, regulating the relations between the United Kingdom and the independent members of the Commonwealth, providing methods of co-operation and communication among the members of the Commonwealth and concerning negotiations between them and foreign countries. Many of these conventions were formulated as resolutions of Imperial Conferences between the wars, though that did not give them legal effect. The following are some of the most important of this group of conventions:

(i) The Parliament of the United Kingdom may not legislate for a former dependent territory that is now an independent member of the Commonwealth except at its request and with its consent. (This convention is recited in the preamble to the Statute of Westminster 1931, and enacted as section 4 of that Act. It has also been enacted in various Independence Acts.)

(ii) Any alteration in the law touching the succession to the throne or the Royal Style and Titles requires the assent of the Parliaments of Canada, Australia and New Zealand as well as of the Parliament of the United Kingdom. (This convention is recited in the preamble to the Statute of Westminster 1931.) The same convention may apply to the other members in the Commonwealth.

(iii) The Queen in appointing the Governor-General of an independent Commonwealth country acts on the advice of the Prime Minister of that country.

(iv) The Governor-General is the representative of the Queen, not of the British Government, and acts on the advice of the government of the Commonwealth country concerned.

(v) The governments of the United Kingdom and the independent members of the Commonwealth keep each other informed with regard

---

[37] See further, *post*, p. 136.
[38] *Cf. Edinburgh and Dalkeith Ry.* v. *Wauchope* (1842) 8 Cl. & F. 710.

to the negotiation of treaties and the conduct of foreign affairs, and none of them can commit the others to active participation without their consent.

The Crown or the Governor-General would not be bound by English law to observe these last three conventions, but such conventions may be enacted in the constitutions of Commonwealth countries. Conventions (iii) and (iv) are not applicable to Commonwealth countries that have become republics, and is doubtful whether convention (ii) is applicable to them.[39]

[39] See further, *post*, Chap. 35.

Part II

PARLIAMENT

CHAPTER 6

" THE HIGH COURT OF PARLIAMENT "

I. Historical introduction

In origin Parliament was not primarily a lawmaking body, nor are its functions exclusively legislative at the present day. A "parliament" was a council summoned to discuss some important matter, and the name is still appropriate to its present activity of debating policy and questioning and criticising the government. The title given it in the Book of Common Prayer, "the High Court of Parliament," reminds us that Parliament was, and still is, a court—the highest court in the land. The word "court" (*curia*) has a number of meanings. It may mean the place where the Sovereign is, a body of judges appointed to administer the law, or a place where justice is administered. Coke, in his treatment of the jurisdiction of the courts, deals first with "The High and most Honourable Court of Parliament,"[1] and says that "the Lords in their House have power of Judicature, and the Commons in their House have power of Judicature, and both Houses together have power of Judicature."[2]

The distant precursor of Parliament was the *Curia Regis*, in which the judicial, executive and legislative powers were fused. Its remotest ancestor, the Witenagemot, also exercised all three functions of government. In the early Middle Ages the common law courts split off from the council, and the latter may be said to have separated from Parliament in the reign of Richard II. Appeal by writ of error passed to what came to be called the House of Lords. Adjudication was one of the essential elements in the early Parliaments, notably those of Edward I.[3] The statutes of the Lords Ordainers (*temp.* Edward II in 1311) ordained that the King should hold a parliament at least once a year in which pleas that had been delayed or about which the judges differed should be recorded and determined.

Professor Sayles has suggested that three factors combined to produce the early Parliaments: (i) the King's desire to expedite the processes of administration and law by the provision of means for

---

[1] 4 Inst. 3, 4.
[2] 4 Inst. 15.
[3] Maitland, *Memoranda de Parliamento* (1893); McIlwain, *The High Court of Parliament* (1910) Chap. 3; Baldwin, *The King's Council during the Middle Ages*, Chaps. 1 and 12; Pollard, *Evolution of Parliament* (2nd ed 1926) Chap. 2; Pike, *Constitutional History of the House of Lords*, Chap. 4.

resolving difficulties; (ii) the desire of the barons to control the government by establishing a method of proper consultation; and (iii) the popular desire to get abuses removed and grievances remedied through ready access to an institution which could grant the highest justice.[4]

Judicial functions

Before treating of the legislative functions of Parliament, which today are at least of equal importance to its general supervision of the government of the country, we may preserve a historical sense by glancing at its remaining judicial functions. These include:

(1) The appellate jurisdiction of the House of Lords, both civil and criminal.

(2) The judicial functions of the Lords and Commons within the sphere of their privileges.[5]

(3) The jurisdiction of the Lords and the Commons in committees dealing with private Bills.[6]

(4) The judicial functions of the Lords with regard to claims to ancient peerages.[7]

These are discussed later in their appropriate chapters. Here we will mention impeachment and attainder (now in practice obsolete) and trial of peers (abolished),[8] to which we may add a note on Committees and Tribunals of Inquiry.

Impeachment

Impeachment was a judicial proceeding against any person, whether lord or commoner, accused of state offences beyond the reach of the law, or which no other authority in the state would prosecute. The Commons were the accusers, and the Lords were judges both of fact and law.

The first recorded case of impeachment occurred in 1376, when two lords and four commoners were charged with removing the staple from Calais, lending the King money at usurious interest, and buying Crown debts for small sums and then paying themselves in full out of the Treasury. Bacon was impeached in 1621 for misconduct in

---

4 G. O. Sayles, *The Medieval Foundations of England* (2nd ed. 1950) Chap. 27. And see H. G. Richardson and G. O. Sayles, " Parliament and Great Councils in Medieval England " (1961) 77 L.Q.R. 213, 401.

5 *Post*, Chap. 11.

6 *Post*, Chap. 9.

7 *Post*, Chap. 7.

8 For the history of impeachment, attainder and trial of peers, see Stephen, *History of the Criminal Law* (1883) Vol. I, Chap. 5.

the office of Lord Chancellor: the large fine was remitted and the King set him at liberty, but he was banned from public office for the rest of his life.

The Act of Settlement 1700 provides that a pardon under the Great Seal *before* the Lords have passed sentence cannot be pleaded by way of defence to an impeachment. This provision arose out of *Danby's Case* (1679).[9] Danby was impeached in connection with a letter written by him to the English ambassador at Versailles with the approval of Charles II, who wrote on the letter: " This letter is writ by my Order.—C.R." The last two cases of impeachment were those of Warren Hastings, Governor-General of India (1787),[10] and Lord Melville, formerly treasurer to the Admiralty (1805).[11] Both were acquitted.

Impeachment may be said to be now obsolete. So far as Ministers are concerned this is mainly due to the development of the conventions relating to collective ministerial responsibility to Parliament.[12] A recent report of the Select Committee of the House of Commons on Parliamentary Privilege suggested that this procedure should now be abolished by legislation.[13]

Acts of Attainder [14]

An Act of Attainder, though it served the same purpose as impeachment, was strictly a legislative and not a judicial act. It was an Act of Parliament finding a person guilty of an offence, usually a political one of a rather insubstantial kind, and inflicting a punishment on him. The subject of the proceedings was allowed to defend himself by counsel and witnesses before both Houses. One of the first Acts of Attainder of which we know was that of the Duke of Clarence in 1477, and from about that time until James I's reign this procedure was commonly used instead of impeachment. Attainder was later used occasionally down to 1715. It has not been used since the early eighteenth century when Cabinet government was beginning to develop. We may therefore describe it as possible but in practice obsolete.

9 11 St.Tr. 599.
10 *Impeachment of Warren Hastings* (1787) *Lords' Journals*, Vol. XXXVII, p. 678; (1795) *Lords' Journals*, Vol. XL, p. 388; P. J. Marshall, *The Impeachment of Warren Hastings* (1965); Keith Feiling, *Warren Hastings.*
11 *Impeachment of Lord Melville* (1805) 29 St.Tr. 549.
12 May, *Parliamentary Practice* (17th ed.) p. 40; but *cf.* G. W. Keeton, " Legal Responsibility for Political Acts " [1948] C.L.P. 15. Keeton, *The Passing of Parliament*, Chap. 4, suggests that the critical moment was in 1742, when Walpole's opponents failed to impeach him.
13 *Report from Select Committee on Parliamentary Privilege* (1967) H.C. 34.
14 Lord Justice Somervell, " Acts of Attainder " (1951) 67 L.Q.R. 306.

Trial of peers

The privilege of peers to be tried by the House of Lords for treason or felony, or misprision of either, could be traced back to the *judicium parium* of Magna Carta, c. 39, though the law did not become settled until well after 1215. If Parliament was sitting the House was presided over by the Lord Chancellor as the Lord High Steward. If Parliament was not sitting, the Lord High Steward acted as judge, sitting with a jury of peers. The last trial of a peer before the House of Lords was that of Baron de Clifford for manslaughter in 1935. He was acquitted.[15] The so-called privilege, which could not be waived and entailed great expense, was abolished by the Criminal Justice Act 1948.

Committees and Tribunals of Inquiry

A *Select Committee of Inquiry* may be set up by either House to investigate any matter of public interest, and such a committee may include persons who are not Members of Parliament. This method was first used in 1689 to investigate the conduct of the war in Ireland, but Parliament is a political body and voting tends to be on party lines.

The Tribunals of Inquiry (Evidence) Act 1921 therefore provides that on a resolution of both Houses on a matter of urgent public importance, a *Tribunal of Inquiry* may be appointed by the Queen or a Secretary of State with all the powers of the High Court as regards examination of witnesses and production of documents. It was under this Act that the Porter Tribunal was appointed in 1936 to inquire into a Budget leakage through J. H. Thomas (Secretary of State for the Colonies); the Lynskey Tribunal was set up in 1948 to inquire into allegations of bribery and corruption arising out of the use of " contact men " to approach Ministers [16]; and in 1957 Parker L.J. presided over an inquiry into allegations of improper disclosure of information relating to the raising of the bank rate. The Vassall spy case was the subject of a Tribunal of Inquiry under Lord Radcliffe in 1963. If a person refuses to answer relevant and essential questions or to produce documents, the matter may be referred to the High Court to be dealt with as contempt of court. The latter power was invoked at the Vassall inquiry, when two journalists refused to reveal the source of their information, one being sentenced to six months' imprisonment and the other to three months.[17]

---

[15] R. v. *Baron de Clifford*, *The Times*, December 13, 1935, pp. 15–16; *Proceedings on the Trial of Lord de Clifford* (H.M.S.O. 1936).   [16] (1949) Cmd. 7616.
[17] *Att.-Gen.* v. *Clough* [1963] 1 Q.B. 773 (Lord Parker C.J.): Clough never in fact served his sentence as the source revealed itself and he confirmed it; *Att.-Gen.* v. *Mulholland* and *Att.-Gen.* v. *Foster* [1963] 2 Q.B. 477 (C.A.).

An objection to Tribunals of Inquiry is that all sorts of allegations may be made against individuals which are not—and sometimes cannot be—made the substance of criminal or other judicial proceedings.[18] It is an inquisitorial investigation, usually in public without a jury. There are no strict rules of evidence, no right of appeal, no right to legal representation, and no opportunity to meet allegations made by witnesses. A Royal Commission recommended in 1966 that the inquisitorial powers of tribunals should be retained, with certain safeguards (some of which would require amendment of the 1921 Act) for persons appearing before or taking part in such inquiries.[19]

II. The meeting of Parliament

Royal prerogative in relation to Parliament

A " parliament " lasts from the summons of the legislature until its sittings are terminated by dissolution or lapse of time. During a single parliament there may be a number of sessions—before 1914 generally not more than one a year, since 1918 usually two a year. A session is terminated by prorogation. Within a session there are a number of sittings separated from each other by adjournments, which can be brought about by motion of each House.

The exercise of the royal prerogative is necessary to summon, to prorogue or (before the expiration of the statutory period) to dissolve Parliament. The royal proclamation which dissolves one Parliament also summons the next. Before 1965 the control, use and occupation of the whole of the Palace of Westminster rested with the Lord Great Chamberlain on behalf of the Queen. When the House of Commons was sitting, control of that side of Parliament was delegated by him to the Serjeant-at-Arms acting for the Speaker; but during parliamentary recesses and at weekends control reverted to the Lord Great Chamberlain. In 1965 the Queen handed over control of the Palace of Westminster to the two Houses themselves, and since then the Speaker has been in control of the House of Commons whether it was sitting or not.

Sovereign's presence in Parliament

The Sovereign, although in constitutional theory present in the High Court of Parliament as in other courts, does not now in practice

[18] See G. W. Keeton, *Trial by Tribunal* (1960).
[19] *Royal Commission on Tribunals of Inquiry* (1966) Cmnd. 3121. And see Sir Cyril Salmon, *Tribunals of Inquiry* (Lionel Cohen Lectures, 1967); *Report of Inter-departmental Committee on Tribunals of Inquiry and Contempt* (Salmon L.J.) (1969) Cmnd. 4078.

visit Parliament in person, except to read the speech from the Throne in the Lords' Chamber at the opening of a new Parliament or session. Other royal functions performed in whole Parliament, such as prorogation, dissolution or giving the Royal Assent to Bills, are now done by royal proclamation or commission under the Great Seal.

A convention to ensure freedom of debate forbids the Sovereign to be present in either House sitting separately. As regards the Commons, the Sovereign was not present in the Middle Ages, but occasional intrusions were made in the seventeenth century. The Lords, on the other hand, were the Great Council and the Sovereign's presence was necessary in early times; but the practice of attending was dying out in the Stuart period and ceased on the death of Queen Anne.

Royal Assent to legislation

The Queen may still give the Royal Assent in person in Parliament, but this has not been done since 1854. The Royal Assent Act 1967 provides that the Royal Assent, signified by letters patent under the Great Seal signed with Her Majesty's own hand, may also be: (a) pronounced by commissioners in the presence of both Houses in the House of Lords in the manner customary since George III's reign [20]; or (b) notified to each House separately by the Speaker of that House. The latter method is new and avoids interrupting the proceedings of the Commons by a summons from Black Rod. The customary method (a) is still used at the time of prorogation.

When the Royal Assent is given to a public or local Bill the words " La Reine le veult " are pronounced by the Clerk of the Parliaments. For a private Bill the words " Soit fait comme il est désiré " are used, and for a Money Bill the following: " La Reine remercie ses bons sujets, accepte leur bénévolence, et ainsi le veult." If the Queen were to refuse her assent, which would now be unconstitutional, the tactful formula " La Reine s'avisera " (The Queen will think about it), would be used.

Frequency of Parliaments

In early times Sovereigns generally pleased themselves when they would convene Parliament. In the reign of Charles I the Long Parliament passed the first Triennial Act (1640), which enacted that a Parliament should be held in every third year; and made provision for the issue of writs for the election of the Commons if the King omitted to do so for these years. In the reign of Charles II this

---

[20] Under the Royal Assent by Commission Act 1541, which was repealed by the 1967 Act.

was repealed by the Triennial Act 1664, which provided that the sitting of Parliament should not be discontinued for over three years; but it laid down no machinery for the summoning of Parliament if the clause were disregarded. The provision that a Parliament should be held once at least in three years was re-enacted in the Meeting of Parliament Act 1694, which is still in force.[21]

The Bill of Rights 1688 meanwhile declared (s. 13) that for the redress of all grievances and for the amending, strengthening and preserving of all laws, Parliament ought to be held " frequently." The real security, however, for the frequent—indeed annual—meeting of Parliament consists (as we saw in Chapter 5) in the practice of passing annual Finance Acts and annual orders continuing the Army and Air Force Acts. In modern times it is necessary to keep Parliament in almost constant session, not only to legislate but to supervise the government of the country, to say nothing of dealing with emergencies.

Summons of a new Parliament

When the Queen is advised by the Prime Minister to dissolve, a proclamation is published dissolving the existing Parliament and fixing the date for the meeting of the new Parliament. The proclamation also announces the making of an Order in Council directing the Lord Chancellor of Great Britain and the Governor of Northern Ireland to issue the necessary writs. The Clerk of the Crown in Chancery then prepares writs, which are sent to the temporal peers and the twenty-six Lords Spiritual. The judges are also summoned to attend and advise, but (unless they are peers) they do not attend, though they may be asked to advise the House of Lords sitting as the final court of appeal. The returning officers are instructed by writs to cause election to be made of a member to serve in Parliament for the constituency mentioned, and to return the name to the Crown Office in Chancery.[22]

Meeting of a new Parliament

On the appointed day each House assembles in its own chamber until the Gentleman Usher of the Black Rod requires attendance of the Commons at the bar of the Lords. As many members as space permits, and as have the inclination, then proceed with the Assistant Clerk of the Parliaments (Clerk to the House of Commons) to the

---

[21] The Act of 1694 also fixed the maximum life of Parliament at three years; *post*, p. 103.

[22] The issue of writs to returning officers is governed by the Representation of the People Act 1949, as modified by the Local Government Act 1972.

" bar," a line which is deemed to mark the boundary of the Lords' Chamber. Unless the Sovereign is present, the commission for opening Parliament is then read by the Lord Chancellor. The Commons are then bidden by him to retire and proceed to the election of a Speaker. The election of Speaker ends the day.

Next day the new Speaker proceeds with the Commons to the bar of the House of Lords. He announces his election, which is confirmed by the Lord Chancellor in the name of the Sovereign. It is not certain whether the Sovereign's approval is required by law; but it is always sought and has only once been refused, by Charles II in the case of Sir Edward Seymour in 1678. After this the Speaker claims certain ancient privileges of the House. The Sovereign, if present, reads the Queen's speech. If she is absent her speech is read by the Lord Chancellor. It is drafted by the Cabinet, and outlines the government's policy with regard to foreign affairs and legislation. After this the Commons retire, and each member of either House proves his right to membership. Then members of both Houses take the statutory oath or affirmation of allegiance.

Adjournment

Either House may adjourn its *sittings* for any given number of hours, days, weeks or months; but the Crown has a statutory power to issue a proclamation ordering resumption of business when both Houses stand adjourned for more than fourteen days. A proclamation may be issued giving one day's notice in an emergency.[23]

Prorogation

Prorogation terminates a *session* of Parliament. It is effected by command of the Queen—acting by convention on the advice of the Cabinet—such command being signified to both Houses either by the Lord Chancellor (in the Queen's presence or by commission) or by proclamation. In either case the date for the new session is stated, but statutes enable the Crown by proclamation to accelerate or defer the next meeting of a Parliament that stands prorogued.[24] The interval between two sessions is called a recess.

The progress of public Bills (including private Members' Bills) is liable to be stopped by prorogation. This rule has been subject to criticism, and has recently been modified.[25] The Houses commonly

---

[23] Meeting of Parliament Acts 1797 and 1870; Parliament (Elections and Meeting) Act 1943.

[24] Meeting of Parliament Act 1797; Prorogation Act 1867; Meeting of Parliament Act 1870; Parliament (Elections and Meeting) Act 1943.

[25] *Post*, Chap. 9.

pass resolutions allowing private Bills to be proceeded with in the next session. It is probably better that Parliament should have to clear its books, as it were, at the end of the session rather than that the order paper should become cluttered by a number of stale Bills and motions. Prorogation also keeps the government up to the mark in the attempt to complete its legislative programme. A Minister is sometimes content to drop a Bill and bring in an improved version later.

Prorogation may be preceded by the signification of the Royal Assent to Bills that have passed both Houses, and the Queen's Speech surveying the work of the past session.

Beginning of a new session

At the beginning of each session (except the first session of a Parliament) when the Speaker returns from the Lords to the House of Commons, a Bill for the Suppression of Clandestine Outlawries is formally read the first time. This practice preserves the right of the House to initiate Bills not foreshadowed in the Queen's Speech, and in particular the ancient right of the Commons to air grievances before granting the Sovereign supplies. The Speaker then reads a copy of the Queen's Speech to the House, and a loyal address of thanks to Her Majesty for the speech is moved and seconded. On that question amendments may be moved, and a general debate on the address takes place, in which the government programme is discussed and criticised.

A similar debate on the Queen's Speech, in the form of a loyal address, takes place in the House of Lords after the formal first reading of the Select Vestries Bill.

Duration of Parliament

The Meeting of Parliament Act 1694 provided that no Parliament should last for more than three years. This provision was repealed at the time of the Scottish rising by the Septennial Act 1715, which provided that a Parliament could continue for a period not exceeding seven years. The latter provision in its turn was repealed by the Parliament Act 1911, which provides (s. 7) that the maximum life of a Parliament shall be five years. This period can, of course, be extended by Act of Parliament,[26] but it has only been done in wartime and the practice has been to extend the period for one year at a time. Thus the Parliament that passed the Parliament Act 1911

---

[26] Such a Bill may not be passed without the consent of the Lords under the provisions of the Parliament Act 1911; see *post*, p. 109.

survived until after the Armistice in 1918, and the Parliament elected
in 1935 lasted until 1945.

The life of Parliament is terminated by lapse of time, *viz.* five
years under the provisions of the Parliament Act 1911, or by a dissolution. In practice, the government makes an opportunity favourable
to its own interest to advise a dissolution during the fifth year if no
crisis has occurred before then.

Parliament and the demise of the Crown

Formerly Parliament expired when the Sovereign died, but this
inconvenient rule was abolished by various statutes. On the demise
of the Crown, Parliament (if sitting) is to proceed to act, and if
prorogued or adjourned is to meet immediately without the usual
form of summons.[27] When Parliament has expired or been dissolved,
the old Parliament is to meet and continue for six months (subject
to prorogation or dissolution) if there is a demise of the Crown before
the date fixed for the assembly of the new Parliament.[28] The duration of an existing Parliament is not affected by a demise of the
Crown.[29] All members of both Houses must take the oath of
allegiance to the new Sovereign.

Dissolution

A dissolution by the Sovereign in person is possible, but Parliament has only been dissolved in that way once, in 1818, since the
reign of Charles II. Parliament is now invariably dissolved by Royal
Proclamation, expressed to be issued with the advice of the Privy
Council.

III. THE LORDS AND COMMONS IN CONFLICT [30]

Earlier conflicts

In the reign of Charles II the Commons passed resolutions denying
the right of the Lords to introduce or amend Money Bills. They
did not specifically deny the right of the Lords to reject a Money Bill,
a right which the Lords continued formally to claim, although before
1860 they exercised it extremely rarely. In 1832 there was a serious
controversy over the Reform Bill. William IV, much against his

---

27 Succession to the Crown Act 1707.
28 Meeting of Parliament Act 1797.
29 Representation of the People Act 1867.
30 This section is confined to conflicts over legislation and finance. The two Houses
    have also on occasion been in conflict on judicial issues (*post*, Chap. 7) and over
    their privileges (*post*, Chap. 11).

inclination, supported Lord Grey by threatening to use the prerogative power of creating sufficient peers to carry the measure in the House of Lords. This power was actually exercised by Queen Anne in 1712 in order to ensure approval of the Treaty of Utrecht.

In 1860 the Lords exercised their legal right of rejecting Money Bills by throwing out a measure for the repeal of the paper duty. Three resolutions to the following effect were carried in the Commons: (1) that the right of granting aid and supplies to the Crown is in the Commons alone; (2) that, although the Lords could legally reject Money Bills, yet the exercise of that power was regarded by the lower House with peculiar jealousy; (3) that the Commons had the power so to impose and remit taxation and to frame Bills of Supply that the right of the Commons as to the matter, manner, measure and time might be maintained inviolate.[31] In the following year, Gladstone being then Chancellor of the Exchequer, the opposition of the peers was overridden by tacking the provision regarding paper duties on to a general financial measure for the services of the year. The House of Lords, therefore, had to face the alternative of passing the provision they disliked, or of rejecting the whole financial provision for the year. They shrank from the latter alternative.

In 1869 the Irish Church Disestablishment Bill was violently opposed by the Lords, in spite of the clearly expressed wishes of the electorate, but the difficulty was surmounted by Lord Cairns's influence. Another memorable dispute concerned the rejection in 1872 of a Bill to abolish the purchase of Army commissions. The warrant authorising the purchase of commissions was cancelled by exercise of the prerogative, and so the Government attained their object without a direct conflict between the two Houses. There was considerable friction between the two Houses when the Lords at first rejected the Representation of the People Bill in 1884, but mutual concessions were made by Salisbury and Gladstone. The next dispute was over Gladstone's second Home Rule Bill in 1893, but as the Lords were in this instance supported by the electorate their position was for the time being maintained.

Events leading to the Parliament Act 1911 [32]

In 1905–06 the Liberals were returned to power with a gigantic majority, only to find that their principal measures continued to be

---

[31] C. S. Emden, *Selected Speeches on the Constitution*, Vol. I, pp. 141–142.

[32] See Anson, *Law and Custom of the Constitution*, Vol. I (5th ed. Gwyer) pp. 304–308; Jennings, *Parliament* (2nd ed.) pp. 408 *et seq.*; Harold Nicolson, *King George V*, pp. 102–104, 125–139, 148–158; Roy Jenkins, *Mr. Balfour's Poodle* (1954); *Asquith*, Chaps. 14 and 15; R. C. K. Ensor, *England 1870–1914*, pp. 422 *et seq.*

rejected or drastically amended by the upper House. In 1907 the Commons passed a resolution to the effect that the power of the Lords to alter or reject Bills passed by the Commons should be so restricted that the will of the Commons should prevail within the lifetime of a single Parliament. This resolution as explained by Campbell-Bannerman, the Prime Minister, afterwards with some expansion formed the basis of the Parliament Act 1911. In 1908-09 Liberal measures—notably the Licensing Bill—were again thrown out by the Lords.

The climax was reached in 1909 when the Finance Bill, containing Lloyd George's Budget, was thrown out in its entirety. The Commons resolved that this action was " a breach of the Constitution, and a usurpation of the rights of the Commons." Edward VII refused to promise Asquith, the Prime Minister, to create enough peers to swamp the Lords until the government's financial policy had been endorsed by the electorate. Parliament was dissolved. In the general election of January 1910 the government lost many seats, but retained its majority with the help of Irish Nationalist and Labour members. The Lords then passed the Finance Bill, which had been reintroduced by the Commons. The Parliament Bill was introduced in the Commons in April; but Edward VII died, and a conference of party leaders was formed to try to reach a settlement and to preserve King George V from a constitutional crisis at the beginning of his reign. Lord Lansdowne, leader of the Conservative peers, proposed that when a Bill had been rejected three times by the House of Lords, the matter should be decided by referendum.[33] Another suggestion was that deadlocks over non-financial Bills should be resolved at a joint sitting of both Houses, with the Speaker of the Commons as chairman. Other Lords' amendments would exclude from the operation of the Parliament Bill certain fundamental or constitutional matters, including Irish Home Rule. The conference broke down, mainly on the application of the Bill to Home Rule, and in November the Cabinet advised another dissolution. It is now clear that the second general election was embarked on in deference to the wishes of Edward VII expressed shortly before his death. The Cabinet also asked the new King to promise to create a sufficient number of peers to pass the Parliament Bill, and advised that his intention should not be published unless and until the actual occasion should arise. About 400 additional peers [34] would have been needed. The King

---

[33] And see Philip Goodhart M.P., *Referendum* (1971) Chap. 2.

[34] The provisional list of nominees later published shows that most of them had no male issue, so that the number of new hereditary peerages would in fact not have been large.

felt that he had no alternative but to assent to the advice of the Cabinet.

The following general election made little difference to the position of the parties. The Lords proposed a number of amendments to the Parliament Bill which the Commons rejected, and in the summer of 1911 the Prime Minister divulged the King's promise to create a sufficient number of peers to force the Bill through the Lords. The Parliament Bill was eventually passed by the Lords in August 1911 with the help of a large number of abstentions, a majority of seventeen (131–114) voting against the Lords insisting on their amendments.

The Parliament Act 1911 [35] in effect abolished the Lords' power to reject Money Bills (as therein defined); and substituted for their power to reject other public Bills a power to delay them (with one important exception) for two years spread over three sessions. The important exception was a Bill to extend the life of Parliament.

Events leading to the Parliament Act 1949 [36]

In the general election of 1945 the Labour Party said that they would not allow the House of Lords to thwart the will of the people, but they did not ask for a mandate for its abolition or reform. There was a mandate for the nationalisation of certain industries, not including iron and steel. The House of Lords did not reject the Labour Government's nationalisation measures in 1945–47: they suggested a number of useful technical amendments, but did not insist on any amendments to which the Commons did not agree. It seemed likely, however, that the Lords would reject the Iron and Steel Bill.

In 1947 the Commons passed a Parliament Bill (in the form which eventually became the Parliament Bill 1949) designed to reduce the period of the Lords' delaying power in the case of public Bills other than Money Bills from two years to one year, spread over two sessions instead of three. The object of introducing this Bill at that stage was to ensure the passing of the Iron and Steel Bill, and perhaps further nationalisation measures, in spite of the opposition of the Lords in the fourth year of the existing Parliament. The Conservative majority in the Lords opposed the Parliament Bill on the grounds that (*inter alia*) it did not reform the membership of the upper House, the nation had expressed no desire for it, and it would go far to expose the country to the dangers of single chamber government.

A Conference of Party Leaders, representative of the three main parties in each House, was convened in 1948. [37] It was agreed that

---

[35] *Post*, p. 108.
[36] See Jennings, *op. cit.* pp. 428–434.
[37] (1948) Cmd. 7380.

the discussion should treat the composition and powers of the House of Lords as interdependent, but so far as concerned powers the terms of reference were limited to the delaying power. The Conservative leaders regarded twelve months from the third reading in the Commons as the shortest period acceptable. The Labour leaders regarded the maximum period acceptable as nine months from the third reading in the Commons or one year from the second reading, whichever might be the longer in a particular case. The difference between the parties was more than a matter of three months, for it revealed a cleavage of opinion as to the purpose of the delaying power. The Labour view was that each House should have a proper time for the consideration of amendments to Bills proposed by the other. In effect this meant that *the Commons* should have time to think again. The Conservative view was that in the event of serious controversy between the two Houses on a measure on which the view of the electorate is doubtful, a sufficient time should elapse to enable *the electorate* to be properly informed of the issues involved and for public opinion to crystallise and express itself. This does not necessarily involve a general election. The Conference therefore broke down, and the Lords then rejected the Parliament Bill at its second reading. The Bill was eventually passed in 1949 *without the consent of the Lords* under the provisions of the Parliament Act 1911, it being necessary to introduce an extra short session for the purpose.[38]

The Parliament Act 1949 was remarkable as being an important constitutional measure that included a retroactive provision (the proviso to section 1) extending to Bills introduced before the Parliament Bill itself. The Iron and Steel Bill was not in fact forced through under these provisions. The Commons compromised [39] on the Lords' amendment to postpone the date of its coming into operation until after the next general election, which the government lost. The 1949 Act made no change with regard to Money Bills as the Lords could scarcely be allowed a shorter period to consider them than the month allowed by the 1911 Act.

The Parliament Acts 1911 and 1949

The provisions of the 1911 Act, as amended in 1949, are to the following effect: After reciting (*inter alia*) that it was eventually

---

[38] The Parliament Act 1949 has been described as anti-democratic in so far as, by reducing the delaying power of the Lords, it reduces the opportunities of the electorate to express their views and correspondingly enlarges the powers of the Ministry: C. S. Emden, *The People and the Constitution* (2nd ed.) p. 307.

[39] The compromise was to reject the Lords' amendment, but to undertake to postpone the appointment of the proposed corporation until a date that would arrive after the general election.

intended to substitute for the existing House of Lords a second chamber constituted on a popular instead of a hereditary basis, it is provided that:

Section 1.—(1) If a *Money Bill*, having been passed by the Commons and sent to the House of Lords at least one month before the end of the session, is not passed by the Lords without amendment within one month after it has been sent up, the Bill, unless the Commons direct to the contrary, shall be presented to the Sovereign and become an Act of Parliament on the Royal Assent being signified, notwithstanding that the House of Lords have not consented to the Bill.

(2) A Money Bill means a public Bill which, in the opinion of the Speaker of the House of Commons, contains *only* provisions dealing with the following topics:

imposition, repeal, remission, alteration or regulation of taxation (not including local rates);

imposition for any financial purposes of charges on the Consolidated Fund or the National Loans Fund,[40] or on money provided by Parliament, or the variation of such charges;

supply;

appropriation, receipt, custody, issue or audit of accounts of public money;

raising or guarantee of any loan (not including loans by local authorities) or the repayment thereof; or

subordinate matters incidental to the above topics or any of them.[41]

(3) There shall be endorsed on a Money Bill when sent up to the Lords, and when presented to the Sovereign for assent, a certificate signed by the Speaker that the Bill is a Money Bill. Before so certifying the Speaker is to consult, if practicable, two members to be appointed from the Chairmen's Panel [42] at the beginning of the session by the Committee of Selection.

Section 2.—(1) If any *public Bill* [43] (*other than a Money Bill or a Bill containing any provision to extend the maximum duration of Parliament beyond five years*) [44] is passed by the Commons in *two* [45]

---

[40] National Loans Act 1968.

[41] For a discussion of this definition, see Jennings, *op. cit.* pp. 416 *et seq.*; Lord Campion, *Introduction to the Procedure of the House of Commons* (3rd ed.) p. 293.

[42] Composed of the Chairmen of Standing Committees of the Commons.

[43] Not including a Bill for confirming a Provisional Order; s. 5.

[44] See *post*, p. 113. This exclusion from the Parliament Act 1911 was the only Lords' amendment agreed at a late stage of the proceedings on the Bill. Professor Denys Holland, in a letter to *The Times* of June 29, 1968, expressed the view that this exception could be repealed or amended without the consent of the Lords under

successive sessions (whether of the same Parliament or not),[46] and, having been sent to the Lords at least one month before the end of the session, is rejected by the Lords in each of these sessions, that Bill shall, on the *second*[45] rejection by the Lords, unless the Commons direct to the contrary, be presented to the Sovereign for the Royal Assent and thereupon become an Act of Parliament without the consent of the Lords. But the foregoing provision is not to take effect unless *one year*[45] has elapsed between the date of second reading in the first of the sessions in the Commons and the date of its passing the Commons in the *second*[45] session.[47]

(2) When a Bill is presented to the Sovereign for assent under this section, the signed certificate of the Speaker[48] that the requirements of this section have been complied with shall be endorsed thereon.

(3) A Bill shall be deemed to be rejected by the Lords if it is not passed by them without amendment or with amendments agreed to by both Houses.

(4) A Bill shall be deemed to be the same Bill as a former Bill sent up to the Lords in the preceding session if, when sent to the Lords, it is identical with the former Bill or contains only such alterations as are certified by the Speaker to be necessary owing to lapse of time since the date of the former Bill, or to represent amendments made by the Lords in the former Bill in the preceding session and agreed to by the Commons.

The Commons may, if they choose, in the *second*[45] session suggest further amendments without inserting them in the Bill, and such suggested amendments, if agreed to by the Lords, shall be treated as amendments agreed to by both Houses; but the exercise of this power by the Commons shall not affect the operation of this section in the event of rejection of the Bill by the Lords.

Section 3. The Speaker's certificate " *shall be conclusive for all purposes,*[49] *and shall not be questioned in any court of law.*" It

---

the provisions of the Parliament Acts. The author in a letter to *The Times* of July 15, 1968, disputed this view on the ground that delegates (the Queen and the Commons) cannot enlarge their powers.

[45] Amendment made by the Parliament Act 1949.

[46] Prescribing more than one *session* enables both Houses to think again: a compromise is possible, or the Bill may be dropped.

[47] A minimum *time* limit is also prescribed because the government could arrange one-day sessions.

[48] It has been suggested that it would be more satisfactory if a certificate of such importance were issued by a Joint Committee of the two Houses or a High Court judge.

[49] This expression could cover the Lords and the Sovereign.

may be noticed that the Parliament Acts do not describe the Speaker's functions thereunder as "duties." [50]

Section 4. When a Bill is sent up for the Royal Assent without the consent of the Lords the enacting formula is as follows:

"Be it enacted by the Queen's most excellent Majesty, *by and with the advice and consent of the Commons* in this present Parliament assembled, *in accordance with the provisions of the Parliament Acts 1911 and 1949,* and by authority of the same, as follows."

Section 6. "Nothing in this Act shall diminish or qualify the existing rights and privileges of the House of Commons." [51]

Section 7. "Five years shall be substituted for seven years as the time fixed for the maximum duration of Parliament under the Septennial Act 1715." [52]

Measures not covered by the Parliament Acts

These include: (i) a Bill to extend the maximum duration of Parliament (s. 2 (1)); (ii) Bills to confirm Provisional Orders (s. 5); (iii) Finance and other Supply Bills not certified as " Money Bills "; (iv) private Bills; (v) Statutory Instruments [53] or other subordinate legislation; and (vi) Bills introduced into the Lords.

Conclusion

Apart from the 1949 Act itself, only two other Acts have received the Royal Assent in accordance with the provisions of the Parliament Act 1911, namely, the Government of Ireland Act 1914 and the Welsh Church Act 1914. The former in fact never came into force as it was postponed by the outbreak of war and eventually superseded by the Government of Ireland Act 1920; the latter became law with some modifications.

Differences between the two Houses can normally be composed without recourse to the Parliament Acts. When the House of Lords sends back a Bill with amendments, a Committee of the House of Commons (if it disagrees with the amendments) sends the amended Bill back again with a statement of its reasons for so doing, and a

---

50 *Cf. ante,* p. 79, concerning the argument that there may be legal duties that are not enforceable in the courts.
51 This preserves the various privileges of the Commons, especially in relation to financial measures, *e.g.* that they should only be introduced in the lower House, and that the Lords should not amend a Money Bill. See *post,* Chap. 10.
52 A shorter maximum life of Parliament is advocated: O. Hood Phillips, *Reform of the Constitution,* pp. 52–54.
53 If the Lords reject a Statutory Instrument the Minister can introduce a new version, which the Lords are not likely to reject, *e.g.* Statutory Order imposing further economic sanctions on Rhodesia in 1968.

settlement is often reached by conferences between the party leaders. If the Lords are opposed to a Bill sent up by the Commons, they generally propose amendments on the Committee stage rather than vote against the second reading. Most amendments in the upper House are in fact introduced by the government to improve the drafting of their own Bills. Nowadays the Lords would very rarely reject or insist on their amendments to a government Bill. The question in practice only arises when a Labour Government is in office.

In the debate on the War Damage Bill 1965 the Marquess of Salisbury, a Conservative elder statesman, suggested that the House of Lords should only insist on its amendments: (i) if the question raises issues important enough to justify such drastic action; and (ii) if the issue is one which can be readily understood by the people and on which the Lords can expect their support, an issue on which the House of Lords would really be acting as the watchdog of the people.[54] The policy of Lord Carrington, when Leader of the Conservative Opposition, was that the Lords should not insist on their opposition to a government Bill for which there is a mandate; but that they may impose delay if the constitution is at risk, or public opinion is so clearly against the government that the electorate ought to be consulted before the proposed law is enacted. Thus the Lords did not insist on their amendment to the War Damage Bill 1965, which (by omitting the *ex post facto* provision) would have frustrated the main purpose of the Bill[55]; but in 1969 the Opposition moved a number of " wrecking " amendments in Committee to a Redistribution of Seats Bill, which they regarded as gerrymandering and therefore unconstitutional, and the amendments were passed by a majority greater than the number of hereditary peers present. The Lords then rejected a revised Bill, which the government dropped.[56]

The 1968 reform proposals

The Parliament (No. 2) Bill 1968, introduced by the Labour Government, would have reduced the period of delay to *six months* from the day on which the House of Lords disagreed in the case of a public Bill sent up by the Commons, other than a Money Bill, a Bill to extend the maximum duration of Parliament or a Bill to confirm a Provisional Order. A resolution of the Commons to present such a Bill for the Royal Assent without the Lords' consent would not be

---

54. (1965) 266 H.L.Deb. cols. 784–785.
55. Which was to nullify the decision of the House of Lords in *Burmah Oil Co.* v. *Lord Advocate* [1965] A.C. 75, *post*, p. 238.
56. The House of Lords rejected in Committee a clause in the Education (Miscellaneous Provisions) Bill 1970, which was construed by the Opposition as enabling the Secretary of State to pay grants for students' mistresses.

affected by prorogation or dissolution. If the Lords postponed an overt disagreement by delaying tactics, the Commons would have power to resolve that the Bill be treated as having been disagreed by the Lords. There was also provision to the effect that resolutions of the Lords concerning the making, coming into operation or continuance in force of subordinate legislation could be overridden by the Commons. Sections 2 and 5 of the Parliament Act 1911 and the whole of the Parliament Act 1949 would have been repealed.

Is the " Parliament Act 1949 " a valid Act of Parliament? [57]

We have already raised doubts on the validity of the measure calling itself the " Parliament Act 1949." [58] It is a mistake to suppose that Parliament in 1911 " conferred " on the House of Lords power to " delay " legislation for certain periods, and that " Parliament " in 1949 reduced this period. At common law the consent of the Lords was essential to the passing of any legislation. In 1911 the power of the Lords to reject Bills was restricted, but the upper House retained thereafter any power that was not expressly abrogated. The Parliament Act 1911 may be said to have delegated a lawmaking power to the Monarch and the Commons under certain specific conditions, and it is submitted that it is not open to them as delegates to enlarge that power as they purported to do in 1949. If this principle is sound in relation to a reduction of the delaying period, it probably also applies to a Bill to abolish the Second Chamber (the existence of which is implied by the provisions of the Parliament Act 1911), and perhaps also to a Bill to alter the composition of the House of Lords. It may well be that the consent of the Lords would be necessary for the validity of any of these measures.

The provision of section 3 of the Parliament Act 1911 that the Speaker's certificate shall be conclusive for all purposes, and shall not be questioned in any court of law, certainly appears to raise a difficulty; but the House of Lords in its judicial capacity has decided that where a statute states that an instrument such as an order or certificate shall be " conclusive evidence " or words to that effect, this implies that the instrument has been properly made, and does not extend to some purported order or certificate which was beyond the power of the maker to make.[59] This principle could be applied to a certificate signed by the Speaker in misconstruction of the power conferred on him by the Parliament Act 1911.

---

[57] Hood Phillips, *op. cit.* pp. 91–93; letter from the author to *The Times*, July 15, 1968. And see G. Zellick, " Is the Parliament Act *Ultra Vires*? " (1969) 119 New L.J. 716.

[58] *Ante*, p. 74.

[59] *Anisminic* v. *Foreign Compensation Commission* [1969] 2 A.C. 147.

IV. THE PREROGATIVE OF DISSOLUTION [60]

Although in law the Queen may dissolve Parliament when she likes, her conduct would be unconstitutional (*i.e.* contrary to convention) if she did so without or against the advice of her Ministers. In what circumstances it is constitutionally proper for the Prime Minister (or the Cabinet) to refuse a dissolution, and whether the Queen is necessarily bound by convention to dissolve when advised to do so, are questions discussed in the following paragraphs.

The conventions governing the exercise of the prerogative power to dissolve Parliament are in *normal* circumstances the following:

(a) The Sovereign should dissolve Parliament when advised by the Prime Minister to do so.

(b) The Sovereign should not dissolve Parliament unless advised by the Prime Minister to do so.

(c) The Prime Minister has the power to choose the time of dissolution, within the five-year period prescribed by the Parliament Act 1911. (This power of timing is a weapon of great political importance in the hands of the government, and especially of the Prime Minister.)

(d) If the government is defeated in the House of Commons on a major question of policy, or on a vote of confidence, the government must either ask for a dissolution or resign. Rosebery resigned in 1895 after being defeated on the cordite vote, and was succeeded by Salisbury, but nowadays it is much more likely—and probably more correct—that a dissolution would be advised.

If the government party is defeated at a general election, the Prime Minister should tender the resignation of the government at once, and the Opposition will take over. At one time, before party unity was as definite as it is now, it was the practice to await defeat in the Commons.

It was formerly the practice for the timing of a dissolution to be a Cabinet matter. In 1918 Lloyd George and Bonar Law, the party leaders in a Coalition Government, alone made the decision, the lapse of time since the last general election in 1910 having apparently caused Ministers to forget what the practice was.[61] Lloyd George

---

[60] Sir Ivor Jennings, *Cabinet Government* (3rd ed. 1959) pp. 412–428, and Appendix III; J. P. Mackintosh, *The British Cabinet* (2nd ed. 1968); A. B. Keith, *The British Cabinet System* (2nd ed. Gibbs) pp. 279–305; Anson, *Law and Custom of the Constitution*, Vol. I (5th ed. Gwyer) pp. 325–330; Dicey, *Law of the Constitution* (10th ed.) pp. 432–437. See also B. E. Carter, *The Office of Prime Minister* (1956) pp. 273–294; E. A. Forsey, *The Royal Power of Dissolution of Parliament in the British Commonwealth* (1943); H. V. Evatt, *The King and His Dominion Governors*; Enid Campbell, " The Prerogative Power of Dissolution: Some Recent Tasmanian Precedents " [1961] P.L. 165; B. S. Markesinis, *The Theory and Practice of Dissolution of Parliament* (1972).

[61] Ivor Jennings, *Parliament must be Reformed* (1941); L. S. Amery, *Thoughts on the Constitution* (2nd ed.) p. 23.

consulted a number of Coalition colleagues about dissolution in 1922, because he had difficulty in making up his mind,[62] but it has not been a formal Cabinet matter since 1910. The Prime Minister, of course, consults a few intimate colleagues (not necessarily the modern "Inner Cabinet"), the Chief Whip and the Chairman of the party; but it is desirable to restore the balance of ministerial power by reverting to the convention that dissolution should be advised by, and granted to, the Cabinet.[63]

Defeats in successive by-elections do not compel a government to resign unless they wipe out its majority in the Commons, though Balfour resigned in 1905 when Parliament was not in session.[64]

The main problems that arise are, whether there are any exceptional circumstances in which the Sovereign may: (i) dissolve Parliament without, or against, the advice of the Prime Minister; (ii) dismiss a Ministry that refuses to advise a dissolution; or (iii) refuse a dissolution when advised by the Prime Minister to dissolve.

1. Dissolution without or against advice

There is no instance in this country in modern times of a Sovereign attempting to dissolve Parliament without or against the advice of the Ministry. It seems that, apart from convention, the Queen cannot now in practice dissolve Parliament without or against the advice of her Ministers, because a dissolution involves an Order in Council (which requires the approval of the Lord President of the Council) and proclamations and writs of summons under the Great Seal (which is affixed by the Lord Chancellor). She might dissolve Parliament orally in the House of Lords, but proclamations and writs would still be required for the holding of elections and the summoning of the new Parliament. The Queen may take the initiative in proposing a dissolution, and then if the Ministers agree with her they adopt her policy as their own; but if Ministers refuse to advise a dissolution, they could only be dismissed.

2. Dismissal of a Government that refuses to advise a dissolution

The last occasion in this country when a Ministry was dismissed was that of the North-Fox Coalition in 1783. During the Irish Home Rule controversy of 1913, Dicey expressed the opinion that the King might dismiss a Ministry that refused to advise a dissolution if he had reason to think that their policy, although supported by

---

[62] Lord Beaverbrook, *The Decline and Fall of Lloyd George* (1963) Chaps. 7, 8, 11.
[63] O. Hood Phillips, *Reform of the Constitution* (1970) pp. 44–45, 51–52.
[64] C. S. Emden, *The People and the Constitution* (2nd ed. 1956) pp. 277–280; Mackintosh, *op. cit.* pp. 208–209.

the House of Commons, was not approved by the electorate. On the other hand, although there might be an argument for dissolution if the Sovereign thought the government had lost its majority in the country,[65] it is very doubtful whether she is sufficiently in touch with public opinion to judge the attitude of the electorate or to anticipate its decision on all items of the government's policy. Only most exceptional circumstances would justify the dismissal of a Ministry, such as unconstitutional conduct like introducing Bills for unnecessary or indefinite prolongations of the life of Parliament, gerrymandering of constituencies or fundamental modifications of the electoral system in the interests of one party.[66]

Dismissal of a Ministry would be a last resort, for the evil to be expected from inaction by the Sovereign would have to be weighed against the evil of bringing the Crown into the political arena. And the Sovereign would have to be satisfied, presumably from the advice of the Leader of the Opposition (which normally cannot be sought unless the government resigns), that an alternative government was willing to take office.[67]

3. Refusal of dissolution

Down to the early nineteenth century the defeat of the government at a general election was regarded as a rebuff to the Sovereign. Since the Reform Act 1832 the prestige of the Sovereign has been dissociated from the fate of governments and there has been no instance of refusal to dissolve the British Parliament. George V is said to have refused (at least temporarily) to dissolve Parliament in 1910 and the Cabinet decided to resign; but he later agreed to a dissolution.[68] In 1918 the King only agreed to Lloyd George's request for a dissolution with justifiable reluctance: it is not certain whether Lloyd George would have resigned if the request had been refused.[69]

The question whether the Sovereign could still constitutionally refuse to dissolve Parliament when advised by Ministers to do so was raised in 1923–24, and again in 1950. In 1923 Ramsay MacDonald was appointed Prime Minister of a minority Labour Government which could only count on a majority in the House of Commons so long as it retained the support of a sufficient number of Liberals. Lord Cave, the Lord Chancellor in the previous administration, advised George V's private secretary, Lord Stamfordham, that if no

---

65 Cf. Adegbenro v. Akintola [1963] A.C. 614 (P.C.).
66 Jennings, op. cit. p. 412.
67 The Sovereign can, and will, dismiss individual Ministers on the Prime Minister's advice, but the Prime Minister usually persuades an unwanted Minister to resign.
68 Jennings, op. cit. pp. 414–415.
69 Ibid. p. 425.

constitutional reason exists for the request of a dissolution the Sovereign may properly refuse the request, provided he is assured that other Ministers are prepared to carry on the government. He went on to say that if a statesman is asked to form a government and makes it a condition of accepting office that the Sovereign will grant a dissolution in the event of a new government being defeated in the House of Commons, the Sovereign is under no obligation to give such a promise, and he should not give such an assurance unless it is the only way of securing that the government of the country will be carried on.[70]

Asquith (a former Liberal Prime Minister) said that " the Crown is not bound to take the advice of a particular Minister to put its subjects to the tumult and turmoil of a series of general elections so long as it can find other Ministers who are prepared to give contrary advice. The notion that a Minister who cannot command a majority in the House of Commons . . . is invested with *the right* to demand a dissolution is as subversive of constitutional usage as it would, in my opinion, be pernicious to the paramount interests of the nation at large." When the minority Labour Government was defeated in the Commons in 1924, George V did not want to grant a dissolution but did so after consulting Conservative and Liberal leaders, who were unwilling to combine in the existing House. Lord Attlee thought that the King might legitimately have refused a dissolution to Ramsay MacDonald, but he added: " I fancy it was thought impolitic to refuse the request of the first Labour Prime Minister." [71] The view that a Sovereign is not bound to grant a dissolution when asked for, provided that he can obtain other Ministers to take responsibility for the royal refusal, was supported by Keith, who added: " The right to a dissolution is not a right to a series of dissolutions. The King could not, because a Ministry had appealed and lost an election, give them forthwith another without seeming to be endeavouring to wear out the resistance of the electors to the royal will." [72]

Refusal of a dissolution would be proper if, but only if, there was general agreement inside and outside the House of Commons that a general election should be delayed pending further developments of the situation, for where the view of the people can be gathered without a dissolution it would be absurd to insist upon it. Another possible case would be where a government which is normally supported by a majority in the House of Commons is defeated by a snap vote, the result of which can be rectified or overlooked. As Anson said, the uniform practice for more than a century that

---

[70] R. F. V. Heuston, *Lives of the Lord Chancellors 1885–1940* (1964) pp. 432–435.
[71] " The Role of the Monarchy," *Observer*, August 23, 1959.
[72] Keith, *op. cit.* p. 301.

the Sovereign should not refuse a dissolution when advised by her Ministers to dissolve has been largely due to the observance of another convention, namely, that dissolutions should not be improperly advised.

The other view is that the Sovereign's right to withhold a dissolution has become obsolete, and that the convention that she must in all circumstances accept the advice of the Prime Minister provides her with a clear and simple rule about which there can be no mistake.[73] Sir Ivor Jennings denied that it is a *convention* that a dissolution may not be refused, since Victoria, Edward VII, George V and their Prime Ministers all thought there was a right to refuse a dissolution [74]; but he said that while the Queen's personal prerogative is maintained in theory, there are hardly any circumstances in which it can be exercised in practice. He pointed out, however, that this assumed a continuance of the two-party system. " If the major parties break up," he wrote,[75] " the whole balance of the Constitution alters; and then, possibly, the Queen's prerogative becomes important." Some writers who adopt the " new " doctrine which deprives the Queen of any discretion, would make an exception where a Prime Minister requests a second dissolution immediately after being defeated at a general election, provided that an alternative government could be formed.[76]

The former opinion, which allows a limited personal prerogative to the Sovereign, is the better one. It is more in consonance with the traditions of British parliamentary government, and it has tended to be adopted in other Commonwealth countries. It was supported by Viscount Simon (a former Lord Chancellor) in April 1950 [77] when the Labour Government had been returned with a majority of only six in the Commons.[78] Attlee, who was Prime Minister in 1950, later expressed the opinion that if the government had been defeated in the House at that time, George VI would have been within his rights in sending for the Leader of the Opposition if he thought a working majority in the House could have been obtained by him.[79]

The reason for the general convention that the Sovereign is bound by the advice of her Ministers is not applicable if they do not represent the wishes of the electorate (or the Commons). Among

---

73 Lord Chorley, letter to *The Times*, April 26, 1950.
74 *Law and the Constitution* (5th ed.) p. 135.
75 *Cabinet Government* (3rd ed.) pp. 427–428.
76 G. Marshall and G. C. Moodie, *Some Problems of the Constitution* (3rd ed. 1964) pp. 50–57.
77 Letters to *The Times*, April 24 and 27, 1950.
78 And see Wheeler-Bennett, *King George VI*, pp. 771–775.
79 " The Role of the Monarchy," *loc. cit.*

the factors that would have to be taken into account before the Sovereign could properly refuse a dissolution would be the time that has elapsed since the last dissolution, whether the last dissolution took place at the instance of the present Opposition, whether the question in issue is of great political importance, the supply position,[80] whether Parliament is nearing the end of its maximum term, whether the Prime Minister is in a minority in the Cabinet, whether there are more than two main parties, and, perhaps, whether there is a war on.

---

[80] The grant of a dissolution must be dependent on supply having been voted to the Crown for the period that would elapse before the meeting of the new Parliament.

CHAPTER 7

THE HOUSE OF LORDS

Historical introduction

The origin of the House of Lords is to be found in the Great Council (*magnum concilium*) of Norman times, and even in the earlier Witenagemot.[1] The *magnum concilium* of the Norman and early Plantagenet Kings was a council of the chief men of the nation, summoned by the King because of their wealth or skill. Wealth and power went with the holding of land, which was in the main hereditary. The connection between summons to early Parliaments and what later became peerage lies in the confused theory of " baronage." " *Baron* " was the Norman-French for " man," " the King's barons " were the King's men. Baronage was connected in early times both with jurisdiction and with tenure. In the thirteenth century those who were summoned individually to the King's Council in Parliament were the holders of a barony (*baronia*), probably not less than 13⅓ knights' fees. The lesser barons during the course of that century ceased to be summoned collectively through the sheriffs, but were represented in Parliament by the knights of the shire and thus became commoners.

The next development is the notion of " peerage." A person who had received a summons to Parliament and had taken his seat, acquired not only a right to be summoned in future but a hereditary right to be summoned which descended to his heirs. The ordinary meaning of the word " peer " is simply " equal," and it was a later refinement of " peer " that gave it the meaning of one who was entitled to be tried for treason or felony by the King's Council in Parliament.

A peerage has been held to be an incorporeal hereditament,[2] and is classed as real property.[3] The principles laid down in peerage cases apply retrospectively and are regarded by the House of Lords as always having been the law, that is, back to 1290 or 1295.[4]

The older method of creating peerages was by writ of summons

---

[1] Pike, *Constitutional History of the House of Lords*, Chap. 4.
[2] *Nevil's Case* (1605) 7 Co.Rep. 33; *Grey de Ruthyn Peerage Case* (1640) Collins' Claims 244; *Lord Cowley* v. *Countess Cowley* [1901] A.C. 450.
[3] *Buckhurst Peerage Case* (1876) 2 App.Cas. 1.
[4] *e.g. Fitzwalter Barony Case* (1668) Collins' Claims 268; *Clifton Peerage Case* (1763) Collins' Claims 291; *Norfolk Peerage Case* [1907] A.C. 10; *Berkeley Peerage Case* (1861) 8 H.L.C. 79.

to Parliament, followed by the person summoned taking his seat. Baronies were created in this way in the reign of Edward I. A peerage by writ, as it was called, descended to the heirs general, *i.e.* male and female, lineal and collateral. The usual method of creating peerages in more recent times has been by letters patent, which give the grantee a right to a summons. A peerage by patent descends in accordance with the limitation in the patent, which is generally (though not invariably) to the lineal heirs male. A peerage may not be granted for an estate of inheritance not known to the common law.[5]

In order to establish his right to attend Parliament, a new peer presents his letters patent and writ of summons to the Lord Chancellor at the Woolsack. Other peers present their writs of summons at the table of the House. If a peer is entitled to a writ of summons but does not receive one, he may petition the Crown.[6] A person entitled, however, is under no obligation to apply for the writ if he does not wish to do so, and it is the custom that a writ of summons is only issued to a consenting party (*Re Parliamentary Election for Bristol South-East* [7]).

Peerage claims

The House of Lords, acting on the advice of its Committee for Privileges, can itself and of its own motion determine the validity of the creation of a new peerage and the question whether the grantee is entitled to a writ of summons. An example is the *Wensleydale Peerage Case* (1856).[8] The House also has the privilege of deciding whether anyone other than the original grantee is entitled to sit.[9]

A claim to an *existing* peerage, which is in abeyance [10] or the title to which is disputed, is made by petition to the Crown through the Home Secretary, and is referred by him to the Attorney-General. The Crown may accept or reject the claim on the Attorney-General's report, but if—as is often the case—there is some doubt, it is the practice for the Crown to refer the matter to the House of Lords. The House in turn refers the question to its Committee for Privileges, which hears the arguments of the claimant or his counsel and of the Attorney-General on behalf of the Crown, and reports to the House. The Committee for Privileges consists of sixteen peers and four Lords

5 *Wiltes Peerage Case* (1869) L.R. 4 H.L. 126.
6 *Bristol Peerage Case* (1626) 3 Lords' Journals 544.
7 [1964] 2 Q.B. 257; [1961] 3 W.L.R. 577. Gorman J. described this as a convention, and said there was no constitutional convention to the contrary; but it would be better to describe it as parliamentary custom.
8 5 H.L.C. 958.
9 *Viscountess Rhondda's Claim* [1922] 2 A.C. 339.
10 *e.g.* because it descended to two or more females in the same degree.

of Appeal. In a peerage claim three Lords of Appeal must be present.[11] The House of Lords may summon the judges to advise the House on a matter of peerage law.[12] Although lapse of time is no legal bar to a peerage claim,[13] the modern practice is that a petition will not be entertained if a peerage has been in abeyance for more than one hundred years.[14]

There is no precedent for proceedings in a peerage claim being taken in an ordinary court of law, and a court has no jurisdiction to determine even incidentally any question relating to a dignity.[15]

I. COMPOSITION OF THE HOUSE OF LORDS

The Lords Spiritual

The twenty-six Lords Spiritual now consist by statute of the Archbishops of Canterbury and York, the Bishops of London, Durham and Winchester, and twenty-one other diocesan bishops of the Church of England in order of seniority of appointment. They are summoned on their "faith and love." [16] In the Middle Ages archbishops and bishops could attend Parliament both as holders of important offices of state and as tenants-in-chief or holders of baronies. Their presence was not due to any theory of the "three estates" of clergy, barons and commons.[17] Until the Reformation the Lords Spiritual formed a large part, sometimes a majority, of the House of Lords. It was not certain at the time of Elizabeth I, when Acts of Supremacy and Uniformity were passed, whether a Bill that was opposed unanimously by the Lords Spiritual was valid.[18] The bishops were excluded during the Commonwealth period.

Hereditary peers

The bulk of the Lords Temporal consists of the holders of hereditary peerages of England and Scotland (created before the Union of England and Scotland), of Great Britain (created after

---

11 H.L., Standing Order 65.
12 Palmer, *Peerage Law in England*, pp. 231–235.
13 *Hastings Peerage Case* (1840) 8 Cl. & Fin. 144 (peerage unclaimed for 450 years); *Camoys Peerage Case* (1839) 6 Cl. & Fin. 789 (peerage called out of abeyance after 420 years).
14 Sir Geoffrey Ellis, *Earldoms in Fee* (1963) Chaps. 8, 13.
15 *Earl Cowley* v. *Countess Cowley* [1901] A.C. 450. *Cf.* an election court; see *Re Parliamentary Election for Bristol South-East* [1964] 2 Q.B. 257, *post*, Chap. 8.
16 The summons now omits the *praemunientes* clause: Crown Office (Writs of Summons) Rules 1969.
17 "Those who pray, those who fight, those who work": Maitland, *Constitutional History*, p. 75.
18 Maitland, "The Reformation," in *Cambridge Modern History*, II, p. 571.

the Union with Scotland and before the Union with Ireland) and of the United Kingdom (created since the Union with Ireland). Their ranks in order of precedence are dukes, marquesses, earls, viscounts, and barons, but these distinctions do not affect their rights as Lords of Parliament. There are more than 800 hereditary peers, although a relatively small number now attend regularly. Changing ideas and the institution of life peerages have led to the creation of few hereditary peerages in recent years.[19]

Peers of Scotland

The Union with Scotland Act 1706 provided that sixteen representative peers of Scotland should be elected by the Scottish peers to each Parliament. The Peerage Act 1963, s. 4, repealed that provision and provides that all peers of Scotland may sit and vote in the House of Lords.

Representative peers of Ireland

The Union with Ireland Act 1800 provided that twenty-eight representative peers of Ireland should be elected to the House of Lords for life by the Irish peers. After the Irish Free State was established in 1922 there was no machinery for the election of Irish peers to replace those who died, and the last one in fact died in 1961. The Committee for Privileges held in 1966 that the right to elect Irish representative peers no longer existed [20]; and the relevant enactments, including the provisions of the Union with Ireland Act, were repealed by the Statute Law (Repeals) Act 1971.[21]

Hereditary peeresses

In *Viscountess Rhondda's Claim* (1922) [22] the Committee for Privileges held that a hereditary peeress in her own right was not entitled to a writ of summons to the House of Lords, in spite of the general provisions of the Sex Disqualification (Removal) Act 1919.[23] The Peerage Act 1963, s. 6, now provides that the small class of hereditary peeresses may sit and vote in the House of Lords.

[19] The former custom in the political field was for ex-Prime Ministers to be created earls, ex-Cabinet Ministers viscounts, and other ex-Ministers barons. For Lord Chancellors, see *post*, p. 125n.

[20] *Earl Antrim's Petition* [1967] A.C. 691; *cf*. Lord Dunboyne, " Irish Representative Peers: Counsel's Opinion 1924 " [1967] P.L. 314 (Opinion of F. H. Maugham and W. A. Greene); C. E. Lysaght, " Irish Peers and the House of Lords " (1967) 18 N.I.L.Q. 277.

[21] See (1970) Cmnd. 4546, Law Commission, No. 37; statute law revision, 3rd Report.

[22] [1922] 2 A.C. 339.

[23] As a matter of fact, during the debate on the 1919 Bill the Lords rejected a Commons amendment declaring that " public function " included sitting and voting in the House of Lords: May, *Parliamentary Practice* (17th ed.) p. 192.

Disclaimer of hereditary peerages

The main object of the Peerage Act 1963 was to permit the disclaimer of hereditary peerages.[24] Section 1 allows the holder of a hereditary peerage (other than an Irish peerage) to disclaim the peerage for his life. A peer who succeeded before the passing of the Act had one year in which to disclaim, or, if under age, he may disclaim within one year after attaining his majority. A peer who succeeds after the passing of the Act may generally disclaim within one year of his succession or attaining his majority; but section 2 provides that a member of the House of Commons who succeeds to a peerage has only one month from succession in which to disclaim; and similarly a candidate for election to the House of Commons who succeeds to a peerage has, if he is elected to that House, one month in which to disclaim.

Disclaimer of a peerage is irrevocable. A peer who disclaims is divested of the peerage and any offices or privileges attaching thereto. No other hereditary peerage may at any time be conferred on him. On the other hand, he is relieved of the disqualification from voting for and being elected to the House of Commons. Disclaimer does not affect any rights of property (s. 3). It is anomalous that the Act makes disclaimer of a peerage operate for life only: succession on death to the peerage is not affected, though no writ of acceleration may be issued to the heir. The Peerage Act does not deal with courtesy titles, which are matters of the Queen's pleasure and not of law.[25]

Life peers and life peeresses [26]

In order to increase the number of those who could be expected in the circumstances of today to attend and take part in debates regularly—especially those who are not Conservatives—the Life Peerages Act 1958 gave Her Majesty power by letters patent to confer on any person (man or woman) a peerage for life, entitling him or her to rank as a baron and (unless disqualified by law) to receive writs of summons to attend the House of Lords and to sit and vote therein. No limit is set to the number of life peers.

The Conservative Government's case for the Bill was that if a Second Chamber is necessary, it must contain an Opposition. Some

---

[24] *Report of Joint Committee on House of Lords Reform* (1962) H.L. 23 and H.C. 38. For earlier report, see (1961–62) H.L. 125 and H.C. 262. *Cf. Re Parliamentary Election for Bristol South-East* [1964] 2 Q.B. 257; [1961] 3 W.L.R. 577; *post*, Chap. 8.

[25] *e.g.* Lord Lambton, M.P., who disclaimed the Earldom of Durham. The Commons, however, regarded his mode of address in the House as a matter of privilege.

[26] O. Hood Phillips, " Lords and Ladies for Life " (1958) 1 *Oxford Lawyer* 21.

life peers might be independent, but in recruiting for the Opposition the intention was that the Prime Minister should consult the Leader of the Opposition and accept his suggestions. There were in 1972 about 230 life peers (including 30 baronesses), Mr. Wilson when Labour Prime Minister having created over one hundred.

The Lord Chancellor [27]

The Speaker of the House of Lords is the Lord High Chancellor of Great Britain, who is Keeper of the Great Seal. He presides over the House from " the Woolsack," a seat traditionally stuffed with wool, the emblem of England's medieval prosperity. The Speaker of the Lords need not be a peer, the Woolsack being notionally outside the limits of the Chamber.[28] As the officer who issues the writs of summons he is present ex officio. He has not the powers of the Speaker of the Commons for maintaining order in the House. Questions of order are settled by the House itself, and in debate peers address the House and not the occupant of the Woolsack. The Lord Chancellor in debate speaks as a politically minded peer, standing a few feet away from the Woolsack. On a division he votes first, and has no casting vote. He gives preliminary rulings on peerage claims, subject to reference to the Committee for Privileges.

The Lord Chancellor is the principal legal and constitutional adviser of the government, a Minister of the Crown and almost invariably a member of the Cabinet. As he has been called the Keeper of the Queen's Conscience since the time of Elizabeth I, it is often said that it would be unconstitutional—if not illegal—to appoint a Roman Catholic to the office.[29] The Lord Chancellor is also the

---

[27] See Viscount Hailsham, *The Duties of a Lord Chancellor* (Holdsworth Club, University of Birmingham, 1936); Lord Schuster, " The Office of the Lord Chancellor " (1949) 10 C.L.J. 175; Lord Gardiner, *The Trials of a Lord Chancellor* (Holdsworth Club, University of Birmingham, 1968); Lord Hailsham of St. Marylebone, " The Problems of a Lord Chancellor " (Holdsworth Club, University of Birmingham, 1972); R. F. V. Heuston, *Lives of the Lord Chancellors 1885–1940* (1964) Introduction.

[28] Before the reign of George III the Speaker of the Lords was sometimes a commoner called Lord Keeper (of the Great Seal), *e.g.* Sir Nicolas Bacon (1558) and his son Sir Francis Bacon (1617); but the latter was a nephew of Lord Burghley, and a year later was appointed Lord Chancellor with a peerage. Modern practice was to make the Lord Chancellor a viscount or baron on appointment, and to promote him to earl or viscount if his period of office continued for some years; but Gerald Gardiner Q.C. was appointed a life peer as Lord Gardiner in 1963 in anticipation of his taking office after the general election of 1964, and Quintin Hogg Q.C. was appointed a life peer as Lord Hailsham of St. Marylebone on taking office in 1970, being disqualified from holding a hereditary peerage after having renounced his viscountcy.

[29] Viscount Simon, Lord Chancellor, said in a debate in the House of Lords in 1943 that enabling legislation would be advisable: (1942–43) 127 H.L.Deb., cols. 464–467. *Cf.* counsel's opinion for Lord Russell of Killowen C.J. in 1910 on the construction of the ancient and ambiguous statutes: R. B. Haldane, *An Autobiography* (1929)

head of the judiciary, presiding over the House of Lords sitting as the final court of appeal, and over the Judicial Committee of the Privy Council when he is present.[30] He therefore performs legislative, executive and judicial functions of great importance. He is also President of the Court of Appeal, the High Court and the Chancery Division.[31] He does not in practice sit in these latter courts, the senior judge of the Chancery Division now being called Vice-Chancellor; but he is responsible for regulating their business through the Rule Committee. His salary, partly judicial and partly as Speaker of the House of Lords, is charged on the Consolidated Fund. The Lord Chancellor certifies, in cases of doubt, who is the Leader of the Opposition in the House of Lords for the purpose of the latter's salary and that of the Chief Opposition Whip.[32]

The Lord Chancellor recommends the appointment of High Court and Circuit judges; and he appoints and removes recorders, stipendiary magistrates and justices of the peace in England [33] and Wales. He is the patron of some hundreds of benefices in the Church of England. The Land Registry and the Public Trustee Office are under his control, and he has general responsibility for court records.[34]

The Lord Chancellor has the prime responsibility for keeping law reform and the revision of statute law under constant review, especially by appointing and considering the reports of the Law Commission (Law Commissions Act 1965).[35] The Courts Act 1971 [36] transfers from local authorities to the Lord Chancellor responsibility for the staffing and accommodation of the new crown courts and circuit courts. A similar responsibility for magistrates' courts may also be transferred to him in the future. Proposals for a Ministry of Justice have been considered more than once, but so far Lord Birkenhead's view has prevailed, that it is valuable to have the holder

pp. 67–68. Plowden, who was a Roman Catholic, is said to have declined an invitation from Elizabeth I to be Lord Chancellor, as he would incur that Queen's displeasure if he had charge of Her Majesty's conscience: Richard O'Sullivan Q.C., *Edmund Plowden* (Middle Temple, 1952) p. 20.

30 *Cf. post*, p. 139.

31 Supreme Court of Judicature (Consolidation) Act 1925.

32 Ministerial Salaries Consolidation Act 1965.

33 The Chancellor of the Duchy of Lancaster is responsible for the appointment of county court judges and justices of the peace within the Duchy of Lancaster.

34 Land Registration Act 1925, Public Trustee Act 1906 and Public Records Act 1958. There is an advisory committee on public records under the Master of the Rolls.

35 See *Proposals for English and Scottish Law Commissions* (1965) Cmnd. 2573. The Home Secretary, however, is concerned with reform of the criminal law.

36 Based on the Report of the Royal Commission on Assizes and Quarter Sessions (Beeching) 1966–69 (H.M.S.O.) 1969.

of the highest judicial office as a link between the judiciary and the executive.[37]

The Lord Chancellor's small department has a Permanent Secretary, who is also Clerk of the Crown in Chancery, and a Clerk of Commissions. The Crown Office in Chancery seals and issues writs and other documents.

Lords of Appeal in Ordinary

In the middle of the nineteenth century attention was drawn to the dearth of qualified lawyers in the House of Lords, which in one of its capacities is the highest court of appeal. The only solution, if the appellate jurisdiction of the House of Lords was to be retained, was to make a limited number of judges Lords of Parliament for life, or at least during their tenure of office; and, as at common law a peer could not be created for a term of years, and as the House had ruled that a peer for life would not be allowed by parliamentary custom to take his seat (*Wensleydale Peerage Case*, 1856),[38] two Lords of Appeal in Ordinary were introduced by the Appellate Jurisdiction Act 1876. Their maximum number has been gradually increased to eleven.

As members of the upper House, the "Law Lords" (including retired Lords of Appeal,[39] and the Presidents of the Supreme Court who are peers) take part in debates on legislation affecting the law and the courts; but there is a convention that when they speak on controversial non-legal matters they generally do so in a purely personal capacity.

Disqualifications from membership of the House

The following persons are disqualified from sitting and voting in the House of Lords:

(i) aliens (Act of Settlement 1700, s. 3; *cf.* British Nationality Act 1948, 4th Sched.);

(ii) persons under twenty-one years of age (Standing Order No. 2, 1685);

---

[37] Viscount Birkenhead, *Points of View* (1922). And see *Report of Machinery of Government Committee* (1918) Cd. 9230; R. M. Jackson, *The Machinery of Justice in England* (6th ed. 1972) Chap. 7; G. Gardiner and A. Martin, *Law Reform Now* (1963) pp. 7–10.

Lord Hailsham thinks that having the Lord Chancellor near the apex of government helps to *preserve* the separation of powers.

[38] 5 H.L.C. 958. An account of this case is given in Pike, *op. cit.* pp. 372–384.

[39] Lords of Appeal in Ordinary were at first Lords of Parliament during tenure of office only, but since the Appellate Jurisdiction Act 1887 they are entitled to sit in the House for life with the dignity of baron.

(iii) persons convicted of treason or an arrestable offence and sentenced to death or imprisonment for more than one year (Forfeiture Act 1870; Criminal Justice Act 1948);
(iv) bankrupts, unless the bankrupt is discharged with a certificate that the bankruptcy was caused by misfortune and not misconduct (Bankruptcy Acts);
(v) a member who has been expelled by sentence of the House acting in its *judicial* capacity (*i.e.* on impeachment), unless pardoned by the Crown.[40]

Members of the boards of public corporations who are peers are not disqualified from sitting but they are subject to the convention (the Addison Rules 1951) that, although they may exercise their right to speak in the House, the parent Minister and the government are alone responsible to Parliament. Members of such boards, therefore, should not give information to the House concerning the detailed work of the boards, nor should they answer questions about it.

Standing Orders relating to attendance

The House has power to enforce attendance, although this has not been exercised since 1841; but it is not within the power of the House to exclude members who habitually do not attend.[41] At the time of the passing of the Life Peerages Act 1958, Standing Order No. 21 was amended so as to provide that " Lords are to attend the sittings of the House or, if they cannot do so, obtain leave of absence." They need not apply for leave of absence, however, if they intend to attend as often as they reasonably can. A lord may apply for leave of absence for a session, or the remainder of a session or the remainder of the Parliament. On the summoning of a new Parliament, the Lord Chancellor is to ask every lord whether he wishes to apply for leave of absence. At the beginning of every subsequent session the Lord Chancellor is similarly to ask every lord whose leave of absence has come to an end, or who (though not granted leave of absence) did not attend during the preceding session. A lord who has been granted leave of absence is expected not to attend until the period has expired. If a lord having been granted leave of absence wishes to attend during the period, he is expected to give at least one month's notice, after which the leave comes to an end. About 200 peers apply for leave of absence.

The revised Standing Order relating to attendance ought to be

---

40 The House of Lords as a legislative chamber cannot disqualify one of its members: May, *Parliamentary Practice* (17th ed.) pp. 108, 192.
41 *Report by the Select Committee on the Powers of the House in Relation to the Attendance of its Members* (1956) H.L. (7) (66–1) (67).

considered together with the Life Peerages Act. Together they should ensure the regular attendance of an adequate number of competent peers, while at the same time discouraging sporadic forays by the " backwoodsmen." The average attendance since the Life Peerages Act has been rather more than 200.

Expenses of attendance up to a certain amount per day, plus travelling expenses, have been reimbursed since 1957. When attendance has become stabilised, a salary for all peers attending regularly may be introduced.

Officers of the House

The *Chairman of Committees*, who holds office for the session, takes the Chair when the House is in Committee, and is Deputy Speaker of the House. He also superintends all matters relating to private Bills.

The offices of *Gentlemen Usher of the Black Rod* and *Serjeant-at-Arms of the House of Lords* were amalgamated in 1971. The holder executes warrants of commitment or attachment under the rules of the House, carries the black wand surmounted by a golden lion which is used as the Mace of the Lords, and desires the attendance of the Commons when necessary.[42]

The *Clerk of the Parliaments* is appointed by the Crown, and is removable only on an address from the House. He is head of the staff of the House, keeps the minutes and journals, and pronounces the Royal Assent to Bills.

II. MODERN FUNCTIONS OF THE HOUSE OF LORDS [43]

Most legislatures contain—in addition to a representative assembly directly elected by popular vote—a Second Chamber, upper House or Senate, elected indirectly or by some different method, or nominated. This in spite of the apparent dilemma propounded by the Abbé Sieyès, that if a Second Chamber dissents from the First, it is mischievous, while if it agrees it is superfluous. In a federation a Second Chamber is regarded as essential in order to preserve the rights of the individual states. In a unitary state a Second Chamber is generally thought desirable in order to admit into the legislature persons with special kinds of experience or representing special minority interests, and

[42] *Cf. ante*, p. 100.
[43] K. C. Wheare, *Legislatures* (1963) Chap. 8; Sir Ivor Jennings, *Parliament* (2nd ed. 1957) pp. 395–402; Sir John A. Marriott, *Second Chambers*; *The Federalist*, LXII–LXVI; S. D. Bailey (ed.) *The Future of the House of Lords* (Hansard Society, 1954); P. A. Bromhead, *The House of Lords and Contemporary Politics, 1911–1957* (1958); Lord Chorley, " The House of Lords Controversy " [1958] P.L. 216.

also to provide opportunity for second thoughts about policy and legislation. As this country has no written constitution, if we had a unicameral legislature our governmental system and laws would be at the mercy of a majority of one in the House of Commons, and moreover the House of Commons could prolong its own life indefinitely. There are, therefore, strong reasons for retaining a Second Chamber of some kind, although of course the one we possess came into being for very different reasons. The House of Lords, as we have seen, emerged from the ancient *magnum concilium*, whereas the representation of the Commons was a medieval and novel addition.

The most important function of the House of Lords in modern times is debating on motions and taking part in the legislative process. Government Bills (except Money Bills) which are not politically controversial [44] and private members' Bills may be initiated there, although most Bills are sent up from the House of Commons. The upper House is specially useful for revising Bills sent up from the lower House. It relieves the Commons of much Committee work in the consideration of private Bills and subordinate legislation, and it also plays some part in the scrutiny of the administration. The House of Lords acts as a brake on important constitutional innovations, the effect of the Parliament Acts being to change the power of rejecting Bills to a power of delaying them. Most important of all, the House of Lords remains a safeguard against extensions of the life of Parliament at the will of the Commons alone.

On the other hand, the Lords have no effective power over finance. Their debates do not affect the fate of governments,[45] the practice being to " move for papers " and then to withdraw the motion rather than press it to a vote.

The Lords have several other functions which are not of political importance. They are hereditary advisers of the Crown and have in theory the right of individual audience with the Sovereign; but this right is not now exercised except by Ministers who are Privy Councillors. Being part of the High Court of Parliament, the House of Lords retains certain judicial functions: it is the court of final appeal, it has the privilege of determining who is entitled to sit and vote in the House, it has the power to enforce its privileges and to punish for contempt, and it would try impeachments if they were still brought.

The Bryce Conference 1917–18 formulated the following description of the *functions* of the Second Chamber:

---

44 *e.g.* Crown proceedings, courts, Commonwealth and capital punishment.
45 The House of Lords defeated the Government on a motion of confidence in January 1968 concerning the withdrawal of forces east of Suez and defence cuts. This had no practical effect.

(1) The examination and revision of Bills brought from the House of Commons, which is often obliged to limit its debating time. The problem here is, when does revision amount to interference with the will of the Commons? Actually, " revision " means the proposal of amendments, which (if not proposed by the government itself) the Lords would seldom insist on if the government (and therefore the Commons) opposed them. The usefulness of the upper House in this connection may be illustrated from the fact that the Lords proposed about 1,200 amendments to the nationalisation Bills of 1946–47, of which 95 per cent. were accepted by the Commons. They proposed 300 amendments to the Criminal Justice Bill 1967, all but six of which were accepted; and they passed 341 amendments to the Industrial Relations Bill 1971, about half of them moved by the government to meet proposals made by Opposition peers.

(2) The initiation of Bills dealing with subjects of a comparatively non-controversial character, which may have an easier passage through the House of Commons if they have been fully discussed. But it is not easy to define " non-controversial."

(3) The interposition of so much delay (and no more) in the passing of a Bill into law as may be needed to enable the opinion of the nation to be adequately expressed upon it. This would be specially needed, said the Bryce committee, with regard to Bills affecting the fundamentals of the Constitution or introducing new principles of legislation, or raising issues on which the opinion of the country may appear to be almost equally divided. But how long, or how short, is " reasonable " delay? The delaying power is controversial. Many thought that the power left by the Parliament Act 1911 was still too great; some think that there should be no delaying power at all; and others think that the control gained by the Cabinet over the Commons by reason of the party system makes it all the more necessary that the Lords should have power to prevent a dictatorship by the Cabinet.

(4) Full and free discussion of large and important questions, unconnected with specific legislative proposals, such as those of foreign policy, when the House of Commons cannot find sufficient time for them. Such discussions may often be all the more useful if conducted in an assembly where debates and discussions do not involve the fate of the government. In the fifty-odd years that have elapsed since the Bryce report, moreover, other media for the discussion of broad questions of policy have developed, such as newspapers, radio and television.

As regards *powers*, the Bryce conference [46] considered that the

46 Cd. 9038, p. 5.

Second Chamber ought not to have equal powers with the House of Commons, nor aim at becoming its rival. In particular, it should not have the power of making or unmaking Ministries or enjoy equal rights in dealing with finance. Precautions should be taken as far as possible to secure that no one set of political opinions should predominate. The Second Chamber should aim at ascertaining the views of the nation as a whole.

III. PROPOSALS FOR REFORM IN COMPOSITION [47]

It is owing to the hereditary element that most demands for the abolition or reform of the House of Lords have been made. The ancient relation between hereditary peerage and Lordship of Parliament is now commonly seen to be unnecessary and undesirable. A number of proposals for reform have been made in the present century, in particular by a Select Committee set up by Lord Rosebery in 1908, Lord Lansdowne in 1911, the Bryce Conference in 1917, the Government in 1922, and the Conferences of Party Leaders on the Parliament Bills of 1947 and 1968. It should be noticed that the preamble to the Parliament Act 1911 recited that Parliament intended eventually " to substitute for the House of Lords as it at present exists a Second Chamber constituted on a popular instead of hereditary basis." On the other hand, it would be misleading to suppose that the present House is mainly composed of " the aristocracy," for most hereditary peerages have been created after 1906 and since 1958 most new creations have been life peerages.

The Bryce Conference of 1917–18 [48] considered five alternative methods of composition in order to secure the predominance of the popular element in the House, viz. (a) nomination, (b) direct election by large constituencies, (c) election on a regional basis by groups of local authorities, (d) selection by a joint Standing Committee of both Houses, and (e) election by the House of Commons. They recommended that the Second Chamber should consist of about 325 members, of whom three-quarters would be indirectly elected by panels of members of the House of Commons in regional groups for twelve

---

[47] McKechnie, *Reform of the House of Lords*, Chaps. 6 and 9; Lees-Smith, *Second Chambers in Theory and Practice*, Chaps. 11 and 12; Jennings, *Parliament* (2nd ed.) pp. 434–453; *Conference on the Reform of the Second Chamber* (1918) Cd. 9038; *Agreed Statement on Conclusion of Conference of Party Leaders* (1948) Cmd. 7380; R. C. Fitzgerald, " The House of Lords and its Reform " [1948] C.L.P. 69; S. D. Bailey, *The Future of the House of Lords* (Hansard Society, 1954); Bernard Crick, *The Reform of Parliament* (2nd ed. 1968) Chap. 6; A. Wedgwood Benn, *The Privy Council as a Second Chamber* (1957); *House of Lords Reform* (1968) Cmnd. 3799; O. Hood Phillips, *Reform of the Constitution*, Chap. 4.

[48] (1918) Cd. 9038, pp. 6 *et seq.*

years, retiring in rotation; and one-quarter would be elected by a joint Standing Committee of both Houses, similarly for twelve years. To these would be added the Lord Chancellor and the Law Lords if the Second Chamber was to continue to discharge judicial functions.

The Conference of Party Leaders that met in 1948 following the opposition of the House of Lords to the new Parliament Bill, agreed that the following proposals for the reform of the composition of the upper House should be further considered if (as proved not to be the case) agreement could be reached on the extent of the delaying power:

" (1) The Second Chamber should be complementary to and not a rival to the Lower House, and, with this end in view, the reform of the House of Lords should be based on a modification of its existing constitution as opposed to the establishment of a Second Chamber of a completely new type based on some system of election.

(2) The revised constitution of the House of Lords should be such as to secure as far as practicable that a permanent majority is not assured for any one political Party.

(3) The present right to attend and vote based solely on heredity should not by itself constitute a qualification for admission to a reformed Second Chamber.[49]

(4) Members of the Second Chamber should be styled ' Lords of Parliament ' and would be appointed on grounds of personal distinction or public service. They might be drawn either from Hereditary Peers, or from commoners who would be created Life Peers.

(5) Women should be capable of being appointed Lords of Parliament in like manner as men.[50]

(6) Provision should be made for inclusion in the Second Chamber of certain descendants of the Sovereign, certain Lords Spiritual and the Law Lords.

(7) In order that persons without private means should not be excluded, some remuneration would be payable to members of the Second Chamber.[51]

(8) Peers who were not Lords of Parliament should be entitled to stand for election to the House of Commons, and also to vote at elections in the same manner as other citizens.[52]

(9) Some provision should be made for the disqualification of a

---

49 *Cf.* Life Peerages Act 1958.
50 See now Life Peerages Act 1958 and Peerage Act 1963.
51 Expenses for attendance have been payable since 1957; *ante*, p. 129.
52 Peerage Act 1963 allows renunciation of hereditary peerages.

member of the Second Chamber who neglects, or becomes no longer able or fitted, to perform his duties as such." [53]

As the Opposition (Conservative) leaders did not reach agreement with the Government (Labour) leaders on the powers of the House of Lords—in particular, the period of delay, which they regarded as involving a question of principle—these proposals were dropped; and the Parliament Act 1949, confined to reducing the Lords' delaying power, was passed without the agreement of the Lords under the provisions of the Parliament Act 1911.[54]

The Parliament Bill 1968 [55]

An attempt was made by the Labour Government in 1968 to devise a reformed Second Chamber that would be suitable in composition and function, but would preserve as far as possible the historical continuity of the House of Lords without interfering with hereditary titles. Direct election was turned down as it would lead to rivalry with the House of Commons; nomination for the life of Parliament was also rejected because it would reflect the political complexion of the lower House. Little was said about indirect election, for example by regions, partly because regional institutions have not been developed; or about nomination for a fixed term, although that device (together with life peers) might be an appropriate solution.

The solution adopted was a two-tier scheme of voting members and other (non-voting) members of the House of Lords. Voting peers would be peers of the first creation, that is, life peers and first holders of hereditary peerages who had made a declaration that they wished to take advantage of this qualification. There would be about 230 voting peers, who would lose their voting right at the age of 72, or by failing to attend two-thirds of the meetings in a session without excuse. Non-voting members would be those peers by succession who had already received or applied for a writ of summons before the commencement of the Act. Non-voting members would retain the right to move any motion, and to take part (otherwise than by vote) in any proceedings of the House or a Committee. Attendance regulations would be modified for Ministers, Lords of Appeal and Lords Spiritual, the numbers of which last would be gradually reduced from twenty-six to sixteen. All peers, including the Lords Spiritual, would be entitled to vote at parliamentary elections, and any peer

[53] (1948) Cmd. 7380, p. 3.
[54] *Ante*, Chap. 6.
[55] *House of Lords Reform* (1968) Cmnd. 3799.

not entitled to sit in the House of Lords would be qualified to stand for election to the House of Commons.

The problem of the party complexion of a reformed House of Lords brings out two apparently conflicting principles. The first is that an effective Second Chamber must possess a degree of genuine independence of the government; the second is that a government must expect normally to pass its measures without undue delay, though subject to scrutiny. The solution adopted in the 1968 Bill was to ensure that the government would have a majority of (say) 10 per cent. of the *party* membership, but not an overall majority including cross-benchers. These last would in theory hold the balance of power, but they are not organised as a group.

The creation of new peers (presumably life peers) would continue to be done by prerogative, that is, on the advice of the Prime Minister, but the preamble to the Bill referred to the policy expressed in the White Paper, namely, (a) to preserve the balance of parties and non-party members among voting peers, and (b) to include voting peers with knowledge of the various countries, nations and regions of the United Kingdom. The Prime Minister would be expected to consult the leaders of other parties over the choice. An incoming government would achieve its majority of about 10 per cent. over other parties by new creations during its first months of office. A reviewing committee to report periodically on the state of the parties in the House was suggested in the White Paper, though it was not mentioned in the Bill. Who would appoint such a committee? It was implied that the committee would take account of the state of parties in the Commons, which changes over a period as a result of by-elections; but if the total number of voting peers were not fixed there would be nothing to prevent a Prime Minister from threatening to swamp a reformed upper House.

The Bill was substantially agreed by the leaders of each side in both Houses; but the more extreme back-benchers on both sides of the Commons revolted on the ground that the government would have too much patronage and the Prime Minister too much discretion, especially as it was contemplated that voting peers would be paid full salaries. The Bill was then dropped.

IV. THE HOUSE OF LORDS AS THE FINAL COURT OF APPEAL

Before the Appellate Jurisdiction Act 1876 [56]

The early doctrine was that ultimate jurisdiction in the administration of justice lay with " the King in his Council in Parliament,"

[56] Holdsworth, *History of English Law*, I, Bk. i, Chap. 4.

and in the fifteenth century it was held [57] that this jurisdiction in error belonged not to Parliament as a whole, but to the House of Lords which had been part of the Council. Error from the equitable jurisdiction of the Court of Chancery was not established until the case of *Shirley* v. *Fagg* (1675).[58]

Since the dispute with the Commons over the case of *Skinner* v. *East India Company* (1666) [59] the Lords have not attempted to exercise an original jurisdiction in civil cases. The only criminal jurisdiction exercised at first instance by the House of Lords was the trial of peers for treason and felony, and trial on impeachment.[60]

The House of Lords assumed appellate jurisdiction in civil cases from Scottish courts (the Court of Session) soon after the Union, although this jurisdiction was not expressly conferred by the Union with Scotland Act 1706. The earliest case to attract public attention was *Greenshields* v. *Magistrates of Edinburgh* in 1711.[61]

The Union with Ireland Act 1800 conferred on the House of Lords appellate jurisdiction in civil cases from Irish courts.

Lay peers in the House

Few of the Lords had adequate legal qualifications, and the House discouraged reports of its proceedings,[62] so that the House of Lords was scarcely regarded as a regular and ordinary court of justice before the end of the eighteenth century.[63] The last reported occasion on which lay peers attempted to take part in the strictly judicial proceedings of the House was *O'Connell* v. *The Queen* (1844) [64] on a writ of error from the Court of Queen's Bench in Ireland, in which the conviction of Daniel O'Connell for criminal conspiracy was quashed. This case may be said to have established the convention or practice that lay members do not take part when the House of Lords is sitting as a court of appeal. The Lord Chancellor, Lord Lyndhurst, ignored the votes of the lay peers. A discussion followed,

---

[57] (1485) Y.B. 1 Hen. VII, P. pl. 5.
[58] 6 St.Tr. 1122.
[59] 6 St.Tr. 710.
[60] *Ante*, Chap. 6.
[61] Robertson 12; Dicey and Rait, *Thoughts on the Union between England and Scotland*, pp. 194–195; A. D. Gibb, *Law from Over the Border*, pp. 9–11; A. S. Turberville, *The House of Lords in the Eighteenth Century*, pp. 94–95, 139–141.
[62] Regular reports of House of Lords cases began with the authorised reports of Dow (1812–1818).
[63] Pollock's Preface to Volume I of the Revised Reports; Turberville, *op. cit.*; " The House of Lords as a Court of Law, 1784–1837 " (1946) 52 L.Q.R. 189.
[64] 11 Cl. & Fin. 155, 421–426. The legally qualified peers present were Lord Lyndhurst L.C., and Lords Brougham, Campbell, Cottenham and Denman. The lay peers present included Lord Wharncliffe, the Earl of Stradbroke, the Marquess of Clanricarde and the Earl of Verulam. Clarke and Finelly cite previous examples of lay peers taking parts in judicial decisions in 1695, 1697, 1703 (*Ashby* v. *White*), 1769, 1773, 1775 and 1783.

during which the legally qualified peers emphasised the argument that a peer who had not heard the whole proceedings should not vote. The lay peers eventually withdrew on the ground that only those qualified should vote. It appears, however, that Earl Spencer, a layman, sat in about 1860 [65]; and that the second Lord Denman (son of the Chief Justice and a barrister of fifty years' standing) sat throughout, spoke and voted in *Bradlaugh* v. *Clarke* (1883),[66] his vote (which was ignored) not affecting the result.[67]

Three is the quorum under Standing Orders of the House of Lords in both its legislative and judicial capacities, and it appears that the leading case of *Rylands* v. *Fletcher* (1868) [68] was heard by Lord Cairns L.C. with one other legally qualified peer (Lord Colonsay, former President of the Court of Session) and a lay peer—probably a Lord Spiritual—within call to form a quorum.[69]

There was wide criticism in the last century both of the House of Lords as a court of appeal and of the system of two-tier appeals. The attempt by virtue of the prerogative to create Baron Parke [70] a life peer with the right to sit and vote in the House of Lords had failed.[71] Lord Selborne, Liberal Chancellor, introduced the Supreme Court of Judicature Bill 1873, which in its original form would have given the final appeal in English cases to a new Court of Appeal while retaining the Lords' jurisdiction in Scottish and Irish cases. The opposition to the abolition of the House of Lords' jurisdiction was largely due to the fear that this would undermine the remaining powers of the hereditary House. Also, the Scots and Irish would not want their appeals to go to an English Court of Appeal. This Act as amended came into force at the beginning of 1876.[72]

From the Appellate Jurisdiction Act 1876 [73]

Meanwhile a Bill introduced by the Conservative Chancellor, Lord Cairns, met most of the criticisms that had been made of the House

---

[65] See *Re Lord Kinross* [1905] A.C. 468, 476.
[66] 8 App.Cas. 354.
[67] Lord du Parcq, " The Final Court of Appeal " in (1949) C.L.P. 4 6; *cf.* R. E. Megarry in (1949) 65 L.Q.R. 22–24. Lord Denman is not mentioned in the law report: Megarry, *Miscellany at Law*, pp. 11–13. Lord Denman also attempted to vote in *Bain* v. *Fothergill* (1874) L.R. 7 H.L. 158, but his vote was not counted. It has been questioned whether lay peers sat in *Hutton* v. *Upfill* (1850) 2 H.L.C. 674, 647n., and *Hutton* v. *Bright* (1852) 3 H.L.C. 341; see Lord Denning, " From Precedent to Precedent " (Romanes Lecture, 1959) pp. 26–28.
[68] L.R. 3 H.L. 330.
[69] R. F. Heuston, " Who was the Third Lord in *Rylands* v. *Fletcher?* " (1970) 86 L.Q.R. 160.
[70] He was not a peer, but a baron (*i.e.* judge) of the Court of Exchequer.
[71] *Wensleydale Peerage Case* (1856) H.L.C. 958; *ante*, p. 127.
[72] Supreme Court of Judicature Acts 1873–1875.
[73] See L. Blom-Cooper Q.C. and G. Drewry, *Final Appeal: A Study of the House of Lords in its Judicial Capacity* (1972).

of Lords as an appellate court. This became the Appellate Jurisdiction Act 1876. It provided for appeals in civil cases to be heard
by the House of Lords from the new English Court of Appeal, in
addition to appeals from the courts of Scotland and Ireland (s. 3).

The Act of 1876 created salaried Lords of Appeal in Ordinary,
who must either have held high judicial office for at least two years
or be practising barristers of not less than fifteen years' standing
(s. 6). Their number, at first two, has been gradually increased by
subsequent statutes. It provided that there should be present at the
hearing of an appeal at least three of the following Lords of Appeal:
(1) the Lord Chancellor, (2) the Lords of Appeal in Ordinary, and
(3) such peers of Parliament as hold or have held " high judicial
office " as therein defined. The last group includes ex-Lord Chancellors (s. 5). In important cases the court usually consists of five
members.

The Act further provided that the House of Lords may hear
appeals during any prorogation of Parliament (s. 8), and that arrangements may be made for the hearing of appeals by the Lords of Appeal
in the name of the House of Lords during a dissolution of Parliament
(s. 9). The origin of the court is preserved, however, in the form
to be used on an appeal, viz. a petition to the House of Lords praying
that the matter may be reviewed before Her Majesty the Queen in
her Court of Parliament (s. 4). The Lords give their opinions in
the form of speeches, and an appeal is won or lost on a vote in the
House.

One effect of the Appellate Jurisdiction Act 1876 was to increase
the importance of the House of Lords as an English court of common law. Previously it had been more important for Scottish appeals,
while English appeals had usually been cases in equity.[74]

Appeals to the House of Lords in criminal cases, as distinct from
jurisdiction on writ of error, were not introduced until the Criminal
Appeal Act 1907, which created the Court of Criminal Appeal.
Criminal appeals since 1966 lie from the criminal division of the Court
of Appeal.[75]

Appeals from Irish courts since 1922 are confined to Northern
Ireland, but include criminal cases.

Lord Cairns had suggested a Judicial Committee of the House of
Lords, sitting throughout the year in a separate courtroom. This
did not occur until a change of practice at the end of the last war.
The court used to sit in the House of Lords debating chamber when

[74] Robert Stevens, " The Final Appeal: Reform of the House of Lords and Privy
Council, 1867–1876 " (1964) 80 L.Q.R. 343.
[75] Criminal Appeal Act 1968, consolidating the Criminal Appeal Act 1966 and other
statutes.

the House was not sitting for legislative business. During the last
war it was often impossible for peers to get home before the nightly
air-raids started, so the House decided to meet at 2.30 p.m. instead
of 4.30 p.m. As the House cannot sit in two places at once, it was
resolved to refer appeals temporarily to an " Appellate Committee "
consisting of Law Lords sitting in a committee room. This arrangement
has become permanent.

After hearing argument the Appellate Committee then reported to
the House, where the appeal was considered and the vote taken.
Since 1963 the opinions of the Lords of Appeal whether in civil or
criminal appeals are no longer, as a general rule, delivered orally in
the House. When the House meets for the delivery of opinions their
Lordships confine themselves to stating that, for the reasons given
in their opinions, they would allow or dismiss the appeal. The question
is then put from the Woolsack and the answer made. Copies of the
opinions are available for counsel an hour beforehand.[76] This practice
is similar to that employed by the Judicial Committee of the Privy
Council and saves time for both judges and counsel.

The earlier sitting of the House clashes with the sittings of the
Appellate Committee. This has meant that since the war it has been
very difficult for the Lord Chancellor to sit judicially, except for about
a fortnight in January and a fortnight in October when the courts
are sitting but Parliament is not.[77]

In cases of difficulty their Lordships may summon the judges of
the Queen's Bench Division (formerly the Court of Queen's Bench)
for advice, but this has only been done four times since the creation
of Lords of Appeal in Ordinary in 1876. The advice of the judges
was usually accepted, as in *Mersey Docks and Harbour Board* v.
Gibbs (1866),[78] but not always, as in *Allen* v *Flood* (1898),[79] this
being the last English case in which the judges were summoned. The
last occasion in a Scottish appeal was *Free Church of Scotland*
(*General Assembly*) v. *Lord Overtoun* (1904).[80]

The House had no authority to summon Chancery judges unless
they were peers.

76 *Practice Direction* (*H.L.*) (*Delivery of Opinions*) [1963] 1 W.L.R. 1382.
77 Lord Gardiner, *The Trials of a Lord Chancellor* (Holdsworth Club, University of
   Birmingham, 1968) pp. 2–3.
78 L.R. 1 H.L. 93.
79 [1898] A.C. 1.
80 [1904] A.C. 515.

CHAPTER 8

THE HOUSE OF COMMONS

I. MEMBERSHIP OF THE HOUSE OF COMMONS

Historical introduction [1]

Simon de Montfort, leader of the rebel forces against Henry III, may be called the founder of the House of Commons, though not the founder of Parliament. His innovation in 1265 was to summon not only the knights from each shire—there were precedents for this—but also two burgesses from each borough. This action was not based on any theory of representative government (which originated in ecclesiastical organisations before the thirteenth century), but in order to counteract the power of the King.

Edward I revived the idea of summoning the knights and burgesses in 1275 primarily, it is supposed, for financial purposes. Parliament was in a formative stage in his reign, and some of his most important statutes were passed in the absence of the Commons. There was still no clear distinction between Council and Parliament. The Commons became more regularly established during the reign of Edward III, although as a body they were not of much influence before the end of the fourteenth century. The division of Parliament into two Houses may be said to have taken place in the reign of Edward III. Petitions involving judicial decisions were dealt with by the Council and the courts. The elected knights and the burgesses were concerned with common petitions and requests by the King for aids. In time they came to form a House of Commons, meeting in the Chapter House of Westminster Abbey, appointing a Speaker to reply in the parliament chamber to the King's requests and demanding that their common petitions be made statutes. [2]

The knights were elected in the county court by the freeholders. The borough franchise varied according to the customs and privileges of the various boroughs. For centuries members of the House of Commons consisted of knights and burgesses so elected.

Since 1774 a candidate for a parliamentary election need not have any connection with his constituency. In 1858 the property qualification was abolished. From the time of Elizabeth I penal

---

[1] For a survey and guide to the literature, see Taswell-Langmead, *English Constitutional History* (11th ed. Plucknett) Chap. 6.
[2] A. F. Pollard, *The Evolution of Parliament* (2nd ed.) pp. 117–128.

statutes against papists, Protestant dissenters and others, and the requirement of a parliamentary oath that could conscientiously be taken only by Anglicans, virtually excluded non-Anglicans from Parliament for a long time. Civil disabilities against dissenters were removed in 1828, and Roman Catholics were admitted to Parliament by the Roman Catholic Relief Act 1829. The oath was later made acceptable to Jews.[3] Quakers and others who objected to taking an oath were allowed to make an affirmation.[4] Women were admitted to the House of Commons in 1918.[5]

Offices or places of profit from or under the Crown, and pensions at the pleasure of the Crown

The Act of Settlement 1700, s. 6, would have provided that " no person who has an office or place of profit under the King, or receives a pension from the Crown, shall be capable of serving as a member of the House of Commons," but this provision was repealed before it came into force. The Succession to the Crown Act 1707, passed at the time of the union with Scotland, provided by section 24 that no person who held any office or place of profit under the Crown *created after 1705*,[6] and no person having any pension from the Crown *during pleasure*, should be capable of being elected or of sitting or voting as a member of the House of Commons. Section 25 provided that if a member of the House of Commons accepted any office of profit from the Crown, his election should become void but he should be capable of being re-elected. One who sat and voted as a member when disqualified was liable to pay a heavy fine at the suit of a common informer, although it seems that no common informer actions were ever brought for this purpose. Section 25, requiring re-election of a member on appointment to office, should probably be taken to apply only to offices existing in 1705.[7]

Pensions from the Crown were a disqualification only if they were held " during pleasure," or (according to the Pensioners Civil Disabilities Relief Act 1869) for any term or number of years. This disqualification by 1957 extended to very few persons, such as those who held small pensions in the Civil List, for it did not apply, *e.g.* to holders of civil or military service pensions.

3 Jews Relief Act 1858.
4 Promissory Oaths Act 1868; Oaths Act 1888 (atheists). *Cf. Bradlaugh* v. *Gossett* (1884) 12 Q.B.D. 271.
5 Parliament (Qualification of Women) Act 1918.
6 The date of an intervening Act, the Succession to the Crown Act 1705, which was repealed in order to take account of the Union.
7 While section 24 refers to offices or places held *under* the Crown, section 25 specifies offices accepted *from* the Crown, which are probably limited to appointments made directly by the Crown and not through the medium of a Minister, *i.e.* senior ministerial offices and Household offices.

By the end of the eighteenth century three principles were established: (i) certain non-ministerial offices were incompatible with membership of the House of Commons; (ii) the control of the government over the House through members who were office-holders must be limited; but (iii) a certain number of Ministers must be members of the House in order that Parliament could control the executive. A series of statutes after 1707 therefore converted the distinction between the holders of "old" offices (qualified) and "new" offices (disqualified) into a distinction between the holders of *political* offices (qualified within limits) and *non-political* offices (disqualified), by disqualifying or suppressing many old offices of a non-ministerial nature and providing for the eligibility of the ministerial heads of newly created departments, subject to the necessity for re-election if already members.[8]

Number of Ministers in the House of Commons

A limit was set to the number of Ministers and Secretaries of State, respectively, who might sit in the House of Commons. The Ministers of the Crown Act 1937 abolished the distinction in this respect between Secretaries of State and other Ministers, but limited the total number who might sit in the Commons. There remained a residual number of Ministers who were excluded, and who therefore by convention had to sit in the House of Lords.[9]

Government contractors, i.e. persons who held contracts for or on account of the public service, were disqualified by the House of Commons (Disqualification) Acts 1782 and 1801, the purpose being to exclude those who contracted to supply goods to government departments and who might therefore be under the influence of the government. Actions by common informers were brought under these Acts for the penalty of £500 a day for sitting and voting while so disqualified.[10] The House of Commons Disqualification (Declaration of Law) Act 1931 declared that the scope of the Acts was confined to contracts for furnishing or providing money to be remitted abroad, and wares and merchandise to be used in the service of the public.[11]

---

8 Certain offices to which a member was appointed continued to vacate the seat but allowed re-election, until the requirement of re-election was finally abolished in 1926: Re-election of Ministers Acts 1919 and 1926. Gladstone inadvertently vacated his seat in 1859 by accepting the post of Lord High Commissioner of the Ionian Islands: Sir Philip Magnus, *Gladstone*, p. 135.

9 *Cf.* House of Commons Disqualification Act 1957 and Ministers of the Crown Act 1964 (*infra*).

10 *Forbes* v. *Samuel* [1913] 3 K.B. 706; *Burnett* v. *Samuel* [1913] 3 K.B. 742. Forbes's original claim for £46,500 was reduced in the statement of claim to £17,500. Judgment was given for the defendant in both cases on technical grounds, the judge clearly disliking common informer actions.

11 *Cf. Re Sir Stuart Samuel* [1913] A.C. 514 (advisory opinion of the Privy Council).

The House of Commons Disqualification Act 1957 repealed the enactments disqualifying the holders of offices or places of profit under the Crown and of persons holding pensions from the Crown, and instead disqualifies the holders of *specified* offices.

The disqualification of government contractors was also removed by the Act of 1957 (*infra*), since there was no evidence of corruption in the last hundred years and it was impossible to remove anomalies.[12]

Miscellaneous existing disqualifications

There are several disqualifications from membership which are not affected by the House of Commons Disqualification Act 1957.

1. *Aliens*,[13] *i.e.* persons who are not British subjects or Commonwealth citizens, and are not citizens of the Republic of Ireland (British Nationality Act 1948).

2. *Persons under twenty-one years of age.*[14]

3. *Persons suffering from mental illness.* " Lunatics " and " idiots " were disqualified at common law. The Mental Health Act 1959, s. 137, now provides that the Speaker must be notified when a member is detained as a person suffering from mental illness. The Speaker must then obtain a medical report. If the detention is confirmed by this report, and the member is still detained as a mental patient according to a second medical report six months later, his seat is vacated.

4. *Peers and peeresses* are disqualified by the law and custom of Parliament,[15] except that by statute Irish peers are no longer disqualified.[16] The wives and eldest sons of peers, who have courtesy titles, may sit.

5. *Clergy* who have been episcopally ordained, including clergy of the Church of England and the Church of Ireland (House of Commons (Clergy Disqualification) Act 1801; *Re MacManaway*[17]),

12 Until 1969 the Post Office was a government department, supplying telephone services, etc.
13 *R.* v. *Cassel* [1916] 1 K.B. 595; *R.* v. *Speyer* [1916] 2 K.B. 858.
14 Parliamentary Elections Act 1695. It appears that before 1832 several infants sat in the Commons " by connivance," including Charles James Fox and Lord John Russell.
15 *Report from the Committee of Privileges: Petition concerning Mr. Anthony Neil Wedgwood Benn* (1961) H.C. No. 142; *Re Parliamentary Election for Bristol South-East* [1964] 2 Q.B. 257; [1961] 3 W.L.R. 577; G. Borrie, " The Wedgwood Benn Case " [1961] P.L. 349. See also *Beresford-Hope* v. *Lady Sandhurst* (1889) L.R. 23 Q.B.D. 79 (C.A.). And *cf.* now, renunciation of peerage: Peerage Act 1963; *ante*, p. 124.
16 Peerage Act 1963 (non-representative Irish peers); Statute Law (Repeals) Act 1971.
17 [1951] A.C. 161 (P.C.).

and Roman Catholic priests (Roman Catholic Relief Act 1829); but not clergy of the Church in Wales (Welsh Church Act 1914).

Ministers of the (Presbyterian) Church of Scotland are also disqualified by the Act of 1801.[18]

6. *Prisoners.* Persons convicted of treason or felony were disqualified at common law, although by the Forfeiture Act 1870 this did not apply to a sentence of less than twelve months' imprisonment. The present rule is that if a member is sentenced to imprisonment for any period the Speaker is to be informed of the nature of the offence and the sentence, but the prisoner remains a member unless a motion is passed to expel him.[19]

7. *Bankrupts*, until five years after discharge, unless the bankrupt is discharged by the court with a certificate to the effect that his bankruptcy was caused by misfortune and not by his misconduct (Bankrupcty Acts 1883–1914).[20] But a member may continue to sit until the House takes notice of his bankruptcy and orders him to withdraw.

8. *Corrupt and illegal practices.* Various statutes constituted certain kinds of conduct at parliamentary elections " corrupt " or " illegal " practices. These have now been consolidated by the Representation of the People Act 1949.[21] The consequences so far as disqualification from sitting in the House of Commons is concerned are:

(a) If a candidate who has been elected is reported by an election court personally guilty, or guilty by his agents, of any corrupt or illegal practice, his election is void (s. 139 (1)).

(b) A candidate is also incapable of being elected for the constituency concerned: (i) for ten years if reported personally guilty of a corrupt practice; (ii) for seven years if reported guilty by his agents of a corrupt practice or personally guilty of an illegal practice; and (iii) during the Parliament for which the election was held if reported guilty by his agents of an illegal practice (s. 139 (2)).

[18] See, further, *Report from the Select Committee on Clergy Disqualification* (1953) H.C. No. 200. The Committee recommended that no change in the law on this topic should be at present made, as did the Select Committee on the House of Commons Disqualification Bill (1956) H.C. No. 349.

[19] Miss Bernadette Devlin M.P. was sentenced to six months' imprisonment in Northern Ireland in 1969 for encouraging petrol bomb attacks against the police. She served her sentence, but was not expelled.

[20] The bankruptcy laws of Scotland and Northern Ireland make somewhat different provisions.

[21] For corrupt and illegal practices, see *post*, p. 160. L. M. Helmore, *Corrupt and Illegal Practices* (1967) gives an account of the trial of the Exeter election petition in 1911.

(c) A candidate reported by an election court personally guilty of a corrupt practice is incapable for five years of being elected to the House of Commons, and if already elected shall vacate his seat (s. 140 (3)).

(d) A person convicted of a corrupt practice on indictment or by an election court is subject to the incapacities mentioned in (c) above (s. 151).[22]

The House of Commons Disqualification Act 1957

From time to time Indemnity Acts were passed to indemnify members who had become disqualified unwittingly through holding certain offices or places of profit from or under the Crown,[23] and usually the election was validated also.[24] A Select Committee was set up in 1941, and recommended the passing of an Act to reform and consolidate the law on this subject.[25] The matter was taken up again after the war,[26] and the House of Commons Disqualification Act 1957 was passed. It deals with a particular range of problems, and is not an exhaustive code of disqualification from membership.[27] The main provisions of the Act are as follows:

Section 1. Disqualification of holders of certain offices and places. A person is disqualified for membership of the House of Commons if he falls into any of the following categories:

(1) (a) *Judicial offices.* The holders of the judicial offices specified in Part I of the First Schedule. These include judges of the High Court and the Court of Appeal, circuit judges [28] and stipendiary magistrates, but not justices of the peace.

(b) *Civil service.* Civil servants, whether established or not, and whether whole or part time. Service regulations require that if a civil servant becomes a candidate for parliamentary election, he must resign his office.[29]

(c) *Armed forces.* Members of the regular armed forces of the Crown. Service regulations forbid members of the regular forces from standing for Parliament.[29] It was discovered that this regulation

---

22 *Cf.* s. 152 (mitigation and remission of incapacities).
23 See *ante,* pp. 141–142.
24 *Cf.* Charles Beattie Indemnity Act 1956, which did not validate the election because with more care Mr. Beattie would have discovered his position.
25 *Report of the Select Committee on Offices or Places of Profit under the Crown* (1941) H.C. Pap. 120.
26 *Special Report from the Select Committee on the House of Commons Disqualification Bill* (1956) H.C. No. 349; Charles Doughty Q.C., M.P., " House of Commons Disqualification " [1957] P.L. 340.
27 See *ante,* pp. 143–145 as to aliens, minors, peers, clergy, etc.
28 Courts Act 1971, s. 17 (5).
29 Servants of the Crown (Parliamentary Candidature) Order 1960.

provided a means of getting service engagements terminated,[30] and the Home Secretary therefore appointed an advisory committee in 1963 to report to the appropriate Service Minister whether they were satisfied that such applications were bona fide.

(d) *Police forces.* Members (*i.e.* full-time constables) of any police force maintained by a police authority.

(e) *Foreign legislatures.* Members of the legislature of any country outside the Commonwealth. Members of such legislatures would generally be disqualified as aliens, but this provision disqualifies those with dual nationality and members of the legislature of the Republic of Ireland.

(f) *Commissions and Tribunals, etc.* Members of the commissions, tribunals and other bodies specified in Part II of the First Schedule. These include the boards of the nationalised industries, and many other statutory bodies whose members are appointed by the Crown, *e.g.* the various electricity and gas boards and councils, the British Transport Commission, the National Coal Board, the Transport Tribunal, the Lands Tribunal and the University Grants Committee. The list is constantly being extended by statute, *e.g.* members of local government commissions [31] and members of the Council on Tribunals.[32] The reason for the disqualification of members of public corporations is that some Minister is in the last resort responsible for them to Parliament and it would impair his responsibility if members of these boards could sit in the House of Commons.

Certain other offices. The holders of various offices specified in Part III of the First Schedule, including ambassadors and high commissioners, boundary commissioners, the Comptroller and Auditor-General, judge-advocates, Parliamentary Commissioner, and certain officials who act as returning officers at elections. These are disqualified either because they are appointed by the Crown or because their office is incompatible with membership of the House of Commons.

Section 1 (2). *Offices disqualifying for particular constituencies.* The holder of any office described in Part IV of the First Schedule is disqualified from membership for any constituency specified in the Schedule in relation to that office. A lord-lieutenant or sheriff, for example, is disqualified in relation to any constituency in the area for which he is appointed.

---

[30] Some years ago a large number of service-men applied for release from the forces for the purpose of contesting by-elections, 175 at Colne Valley and 496 at Rotherham: *The Times*, February 19, 1963.
[31] Local Government Act 1958.
[32] Tribunals and Inquiries Act 1971.

Section 1 (4). *Effect of section* 1 (*holders of certain offices*). A person is not disqualified for membership of the House of Commons by reason of holding any office or place of profit except as provided in the Act. Conversely, a person is not disqualified for appointment to any office or place by reason of his being a member of that House.[33]

The First Schedule containing the list of offices mentioned above may be amended by Order in Council, following a resolution of the House of Commons—a remarkable example of delegated legislation; and Her Majesty's printer is required to print copies of the Act with the First Schedule as amended from time to time by Order in Council or other Acts (s. 5).

Section 2. *Ministerial offices.*[34] The Act of 1957 provided that not more than seventy holders of the "ministerial offices" specified in the Second Schedule might sit and vote at any one time in the House of Commons: of these not more than twenty-seven might be holders of the offices specified in Part I of that Schedule, which contained the senior political offices (other than the Lord Chancellor), including those which are normally of Cabinet rank. The Ministers of the Crown Act 1964, s. 3, raised from seventy to ninety-one the maximum number of Ministers who may sit and vote in the House of Commons, and removed the limit (twenty-seven) on the number of holders of senior ministerial offices who may sit and vote in the House. It is thus possible for all senior Ministers, except the Lord Chancellor, to sit in the Commons.[35]

Section 4. *Stewardship of the Chiltern Hundreds, etc.* It was established by the early seventeenth century that a member could not resign his seat. If a member wished to relinquish his seat, therefore, it has been the practice since about 1750 to apply to the Chancellor of the Exchequer for the Stewardship of the Chiltern Hundreds. The office has for long been a sinecure, but it is technically an "office of profit under the Crown" and therefore under the previous law disqualified the holder from further membership of the

---

[33] The latter provision negatives what is called "reverse disqualification."

[34] These statutory provisions should be distinguished from the *convention* that Ministers shall disembarrass themselves of any company directorships or shareholdings which would be likely, or which might appear, to conflict with their official duties.

[35] Mr. Wilson, the new Prime Minister in 1964, wanted to increase the number of Ministries, and also to give a large number of members of his party experience of office without creating more peerages. The House of Commons Disqualification Act 1957 appeared to take him by surprise. Pending the passing of the Ministers of the Crown Act 1964, Mr. Wilson circumvented the Act of 1957 by appointing to fourteen offices not specified in the Schedule and to twelve offices without remuneration. His conduct, which was not officially challenged by the Opposition, was contrary to the spirit if not the letter of the statute. See note by A. E. W. Park (1965) 28 M.L.R. 338.

Commons. In order to preserve this interesting historical relic, section 4 of the Act of 1957 provides that the Stewardship of the Chiltern Hundreds and three similar offices shall be treated as included among the disqualifying offices listed in Part IV of the First Schedule (*supra*).[36]

Section 6. Effect of disqualification, and provision for relief. If a person disqualified for membership is elected, his election is void; and if a member of the House becomes disqualified his seat is vacated. If, however, the disqualification has been removed the House may, if it appears proper to do so, direct that the disqualification shall be disregarded; but such order is not to affect proceedings on an election petition or the determination of an election court.[37]

Section 7. Jurisdiction of Privy Council as to disqualification. Any person who claims that a person purporting to be a member of the House of Commons is disqualified by the Act of 1957 may apply to Her Majesty in Council for a declaration to that effect. The application is referred to the Judicial Committee in the same way as an appeal from a court under the Judicial Committee Act 1833, s. 3. As regards disqualification under the Act of 1957, this is an alternative method to an election petition, though without the time limit. The Judicial Committee may direct an issue of fact to be tried in the High Court,[38] whose decision shall be final. A declaration may not be made, however, if an election petition is pending or has been tried, or if the House of Commons has directed that the disqualification shall be disregarded.

It should be noticed that the House itself may resolve that a case be referred by the Crown to the Judicial Committee under section 4 of the Judicial Committee Act 1833 for an advisory opinion on a point of law, and this could include any legal disqualification, whether arising under the House of Commons Disqualification Act or not. This was in fact done in the case of MacManaway.[39]

Section 8. Relaxation of obligation to accept office. No member of the House of Commons or candidate for a parliamentary election may be *required* to accept any office which would disqualify him from membership. This relaxation does not apply to any obligation, statutory or otherwise, to serve in the armed forces of the Crown. It appears that the office of sheriff is the only other office which is by

---

[36] There are four offices, enabling four members to resign in quick succession, *viz.* Steward or Bailiff of the Chiltern Hundreds, and Steward or Bailiff of the Manor of Northstead. The Chancellor of the Exchequer usually grants them alternately.

[37] The obligation of the House to make an order implementing the finding of an election court under the Representation of the People Act 1949, s. 124 (5), remains; *post*, p. 164.

[38] Or the Court of Session or the High Court in Northern Ireland.

[39] *Re MacManaway* [1951] A.C. 161; *ante*, p. 143.

custom regarded as obligatory. Sheriffs were formerly required to remain in the county during their year of office, and therefore could not sit in the House.[40] In 1626 Charles I excluded Coke and four other members by " pricking " them sheriffs against their will,[41] but the Commons resolved in 1675 that it was a breach of privilege to appoint a member of the House as sheriff.[42] Section 8 of the 1957 Act was inserted *ex abundante cautela*, in case the government should be able to exclude members of the Opposition by appointing them to disqualifying offices.

A candidate's consent to nomination at a parliamentary election must contain a statement that he is aware of the provisions of the Act, and that, to the best of his knowledge and belief, he is not disqualified from membership of the House of Commons (s. 11).

Crown pensioners[43] and government contractors[44] are no longer disqualified from membership (s. 9).

The Act repealed in whole or in part a large number of Acts from 1693 onwards,[45] including all provisions whereby common informers could sue for penalties in respect of disqualifications covered by the Act.[46]

Payment of Members

In medieval times knights, citizens and burgesses received a few shillings a day from their constituencies. This right was balanced by statutory penalties for non-attendance, which are now obsolete. Although called wages, these payments were intended as expenses, and they too became obsolete with the fall in the value of money.

As a result of the decision in *Amalgamated Society of Railway Servants* v. *Osborne* (1910)[47] declaring that a " political levy " by trade unions on their members was illegal, the House of Commons resolved that members who were not Ministers should receive a salary under the annual Appropriation Act payable out of the Consolidated Fund. The salary has been increased by statute from time to time. Allowances for secretarial, postal, travel and other expenses

---

[40] 4 Co.Inst. 48.

[41] Holdsworth, *History of English Law*, V, pp. 448–449.

[42] Wittke, *Parliamentary Privilege*, p. 38.

[43] *Ante*, p. 141.

[44] *Ante*, p. 142.

[45] *e.g.* the House of Commons (Disqualification) Act 1693; the Succession to the Crown Act 1707, ss. 24, 25, 27 and 28; the House of Commons (Declaration of Law) Act 1931; and the Ministers of the Crown Act 1937, s. 9.

[46] The Common Informers Act 1951, which abolished the common informer procedure generally, did not extend to this procedure in relation to parliamentary disqualifications.

[47] [1910] A.C. 87 (H.L.). *Cf. post*, Chap. 25 (trade unions).

may also be claimed.[48] Thus the idea of the amateur in politics has largely given way to the professional politician, an inevitable change that may not be all gain to our political life.

The Speaker [49]

The practice of the Commons having a spokesman arose gradually in the Middle Ages. The first two members who may be regarded as holding a definite office as Speaker were Sir Peter de la Mere and Sir Thomas Hungerford in the years 1376 and 1377. The Commons appear always to have elected their Speaker. For some time he also attended the King's Council, and his position as liaison between the Commons and the King was for long a dangerous one.

The Speaker is elected by the Commons from their own number at the beginning of each new Parliament. After informal consultations between the leaders of the parliamentary parties, a new Speaker (selected from the government party) is proposed by a government supporter, and seconded by an Opposition supporter. The election is then normally unanimous. It was, however, opposed in 1895 and 1951, and again in 1971 when there was a division on the motion for the election of Mr. Selwyn Lloyd.[50] As we have seen, it is a convention that the Sovereign should be asked for, and should give, consent to the choice of Speaker.[51]

The Speaker of the previous Parliament is usually re-elected unanimously, if he is still a member and willing to stand. Re-election by the House has not been opposed since 1835.[52]

A Speaker takes no active part in a parliamentary election campaign, and it was thought by some to be a convention that he should not be opposed in his constituency at a general election. However, Sir Harry Hylton-Foster was opposed by Labour and Liberal candidates at the general election in 1964; he stood as an Independent, and conducted the election successfully on a non-party basis. In order

---

[48] See *Sixth Report from Select Committee on House of Commons (Services), Session 1968–69; Services and facilities for Members* (1969) H.C. 374.

[49] See Dasent, *The Speaker of the House of Commons*; May, *Parliamentary Practice* (18th ed.) pp. 223 *et seq.*; Sir Ivor Jennings, *Parliament* (2nd ed.) pp. 63 *et seq.*; Taswell-Langmead, *op. cit.* pp. 207–211.

[50] There was no other nomination, and the motion was carried by a large majority. The minority were not against Mr. Selwyn Lloyd himself, but the method of selection: they objected that there had not been enough consultation of members by the party leaders.

[51] *Ante*, p. 102.

[52] A Select Committee on Procedure recommended in 1972 that the " Father of the House," instead of the Clerk to the House, should preside over the election of the Speaker, and also that he should propose the re-election of a Speaker, and that all candidates for election after the first should be put to the House in the form of an amendment to the original motion.

that a constituency may not be virtually disfranchised, it has been suggested that the Speaker should have a fictitious constituency or none at all, so that on a member's election as Speaker there would be a by-election in the constituency which returned him to Parliament. On the other hand, it would be incorrect to say that the Speaker's constituency is disfranchised, because the member who fills that office continues to look after the interests of his constituents.

The Speaker is the channel of communication between the Commons and the Queen, and between the Commons and the Lords. Hence his title of " Speaker " or spokesman. On his appointment he claims from the Sovereign certain " ancient and undoubted " privileges of the House at the beginning of each Parliament.[53]

The Speaker presides over the House, except when it is in Committee.[54] When in the chair he maintains order, and guides the House on all questions of privilege and practice. He is expected to be impartial between political parties, and especially to protect the rights of minorities in the House and to ensure that they have their say. The Speaker does not take part in debate. He does not vote unless there is a tie, in which case he usually votes in such a way as not to make the decision of the House final: for example, he will generally vote in favour of the introduction of a Bill, and against an amendment to a Bill on the report stage. He gives advice and rulings on procedure; signs warrants of committal for contempt, and reprimands members and strangers for misconduct; and signs warrants for the issue of writs for by-elections.

The Speaker has the duty under the Parliament Acts 1911 and 1949 of certifying " Money Bills," and giving his certificate that the procedure for overriding the House of Lords has been complied with. If it were doubtful which was the largest party in opposition to the government in the House of Commons, or who was the leader in the House of such party, the Speaker would issue a certificate for this purpose, which would be binding and conclusive (Ministerial Salaries Consolidation Act 1965, s. 4).

The Speaker has an official residence, and his salary is payable out of the Consolidated Fund.[55] This means that it is payable by permanent legislation, and does not come up for annual review and perhaps debate. In precedence he ranks next after the Lord President of the Council (Order in Council 1919). When he retires, it is customary to bestow on him a peerage [56] and a statutory pension.

---

[53] Post, Chap. 11.
[54] Until 1870 he sometimes spoke in Committee.
[55] House of Commons (Speaker) Act 1832; House of Commons Officers Act 1834; Ministerial Salaries Consolidation Act 1965.
[56] Formerly a viscountcy; now probably a life peerage.

The Clerk of the House has custody of all the records of the House, makes entries of what takes place in the House, and from these materials prepares the Journals. He indorses Bills sent up to the Lords. Hitherto when the Commons retire to elect a Speaker the Clerk of the House has occupied the chair.

The Serjeant-at-Arms is appointed by the Crown by letters patent under the Great Seal. The present practice is for the Queen to discuss the appointment informally with the Speaker, who sounds the feelings of the party leaders. The Lancastrian Kings first appointed one of the Serjeants-at-Arms (originally royal bodyguards) to attend the Commons, and the Commons came to use him to protect their privileges because through him they could arrest or imprison offenders without having to take proceedings in the courts. During session he attends, with the mace,[57] the Speaker when the latter enters and leaves the House.

It is the duty of the Serjeant-at-Arms to carry out directions for maintaining order, and to arrest strangers who have no business in the House. With the mace in his hands he can arrest without warrant anyone who obstructs the Speaker's procession. He executes the Speaker's warrants for contempt, and when ordered to do so brings persons in custody before the bar of the House. He or his assistants serve processes of the House. When a person is arrested by order of the House, the Serjeant-at-Arms keeps the prisoner in his custody until arrangements are made for his bestowal elsewhere. The Metropolitan Police on duty in the precincts come under his orders when the House is in session.

The Chairman of Ways and Means is a member elected at the beginning of each Parliament to preside over committees of the whole House.[58] He maintains order in Committee and can "name" members, but where a suspension is necessary the Speaker reoccupies the chair. The closure can be applied by the Chairman in Committee.

The Chairman of Ways and Means also acts as Deputy Speaker, and by the Deputy Speaker Act 1855 he can exercise the Speaker's statutory functions. In both capacities he is expected to show the same political impartiality as the Speaker. He also has important duties in conjunction with the Chairman of Committees of the House of Lords relating to private Bills. There is a Deputy Chairman of

---

[57] The mace, at first both a weapon and the Serjeant's emblem of office, has come to be regarded as the symbol of the authority of the House; but during prorogation the Serjeant-at-Arms reverts to being a member of the royal household, and the mace is returned to the Lord Chamberlain. See article in *The Times*, December 31, 1956, and letter from Edward F. Iwi to *The Times*, December 11, 1961.

[58] And formerly over the Committee of Ways and Means.

Ways and Means, who may also act as Deputy Speaker. Neither the Chairman nor the Deputy Chairman of Ways and Means speaks or votes except in his official capacity. Hence their offices, and that of the Speaker, are called the three " non-voting " offices.

Government and Opposition Whips [59]

The Government Whips consist of the Chief Whip (the Parliamentary Secretary to the Treasury),[60] the Deputy Chief Whip (the first Junior Lord of the Treasury) and the Junior Whips (the other four Junior Lords of the Treasury, and the Treasurer, Comptroller and Vice-Chamberlain of the Household). The Government Chief Whip is responsible to the Prime Minister and Leader of the House for fitting the government's programme of business into the time available during the session. He and the Chief Whips of the other parties constitute the " usual channels " through which business communications pass between the parties.

It is the duty of the Whips, whether acting for the government or not, to see that their parties are fully represented at important divisions and to arrange " pairs." They also keep their leaders informed of the state of feeling in the party. Again, they act as intermediaries between the leaders of the party and the constituency organisations, and can often influence the local association in its choice of candidate. The Ministers of the Crown Act 1964 for the first time provided a salary for the Assistant Government Whips.

II. PARLIAMENTARY FRANCHISE AND ELECTIONS

Modern history of the parliamentary franchise [61]

The modern history of the parliamentary franchise begins with the Representation of the People Act 1832 (" the Reform Act "). Roughly we may say that the franchise was extended by means of property qualifications from the landed gentry and borough caucuses to the middle classes. The indirect consequences of this Act and its successors were immense. The Commons became the predominant element in the government of the country, the Crown became

---

[59] " Whip," originally " whipper-in," is a term derived from the hunting field.

[60] Formerly known as the patronage secretary, as it was through him that the patronage of the Treasury was administered and appointments to departments under its control were made.

[61] Sir Ivor Jennings, *Party Politics I: Appeal to the People* (1960); D. E. Butler, *The Electoral System in Britain since 1918* (2nd ed. 1963).

detached from politics, and governments recognised that they depended on the will of the electorate.[62]

The Representation of the People Act 1867, by introducing certain occupation and lodger qualifications in the boroughs, gave the vote to many urban workers, who were shortly to reap the benefits of the Education Act 1870. The Representation of the People Act 1884 extended the lodger and householder qualifications to counties, thus giving the vote to many agricultural workers.

The Representation of the People Act 1918 introduced adult male suffrage, and for the first time gave the vote to women,[63] but only at the age of thirty. The Act provided for both a residence and a business premises qualification. The Representation of the People (Equal Franchise) Act 1928 assimilated the franchise for men and women of twenty-one years (the "flapper vote"). The Representation of the People Act 1945 assimilated the local government franchise to the parliamentary franchise in so far as every parliamentary elector was to have the local government franchise, and also abolished the spouse's qualification in respect of business premises. The Representation of the People Act 1948 laid down that no elector should have more than one vote at a general election, and abolished the business premises qualification and the university franchise.[64]

The Representation of the People Act 1969, s. 1, lowered the minimum age of voting from twenty-one to eighteen years, in spite of an almost unanimous recommendation of a Speaker's Conference on Electoral Law in 1968 that the minimum age of voting should be twenty years.[65] This provision added about three million electors.

Qualifications for the franchise

These are now laid down mainly in the Representation of the People Acts 1949 and 1969.

[62] The proportion of the electorate to the population was raised from 3 to 4 per cent. by the Act of 1832, from 18 to 47 per cent. by the Act of 1918, and to 65 per cent. by the Act of 1928.

[63] Before 1832 women in boroughs could transfer voting rights to their husband, and in burgage boroughs also to their son, son-in-law or nephew; but there is no evidence that women ever voted at parliamentary elections in that period: Porritt, *The Unreformed House of Commons*, pp. 39–40, 78.

[64] The university franchise was granted to Oxford and Cambridge Universities in the reign of James I: the other British universities were added from time to time: see Lord Salter, *Memoirs of a Public Servant* (1961) Chap. 19; Butler, *op. cit.* Chap. 5. The Conservative Opposition regarded it as virtually a breach of convention for the Government to reject a recommendation of a Speaker's Conference that the business premises qualification and university representation should be retained; see *Report of All-Party Speaker's Conference on Electoral Reform and Redistribution of Seats* (1944) Cmd. 6534.

[65] Cmnd. 3717, *Departmental Report on the Law relating to Parliamentary Elections.*

In order to qualify as a parliamentary elector in any constituency, a person must:

    (i) be eighteen years of age on the date of the poll [66];

    (ii) be a British subject (*i.e.* a citizen of the United Kingdom and Colonies [67] or of any Commonwealth country) or a citizen of the Republic of Ireland [68];

    (iii) not be subject to any legal incapacity (*infra*); and

    (iv) be *resident* in the constituency on the qualifying date (October 10).

The Electoral Register [69]

The Electoral Register is published on February 15, and remains in force for twelve months from February 16. Thus a householder in 1973 should include on the form British subjects or Irish citizens resident at that address on October 10 who are eighteen or over, or will have their eighteenth birthday during the life of the Register, *i.e.* by February 15, 1975. These latter may vote as soon as they become eighteen.

"Resident" means *ordinarily* resident at the qualifying date.[70] There is no longer any period of residence required. Students residing in college or a hall of residence (or, presumably, in lodgings) are entitled to be registered in that constituency (*Fox* v. *Stirk*).[71]

Electors' lists are displayed in town halls, public libraries and the main post offices from November 28 to December 16, and during this period claims to be included in the list may be made to the electoral registration officer.

A person is not entitled to vote in any constituency unless he is registered in the register of parliamentary electors for that constituency, nor at a general election is he entitled to vote in more than one constituency.

[66] For the purposes of the Representation of the People Acts a person attains a given age at the commencement of the relevant anniversary of his birthday, and not (as at common law) at the commencement of the previous day.

[67] See British Nationality Act 1948.

[68] This is a result of the anomalous provision of section 2 of the Ireland Act 1949, whereby citizens of the Republic of Ireland are not to be regarded as aliens.

[69] Electoral Registers Act 1953. The names of occupiers of property over 21 and under 65 who are liable for jury service are marked as jurors on the Register.

[70] Such persons include: (a) those who normally live at that address but are temporarily away, *e.g.* on holiday, as students, in hospital, or as reservists; (b) resident guests (but not short-stay visitors); (c) lodgers and resident domestics; (d) anyone who will be away working for not more than six months; and (e) merchant seamen.

[71] *Fox* v. *Stirk and Bristol Electoral Registration Officer*; *Ricketts* v. *Cambridge City Electoral Registration Officer* [1970] 2 Q.B. 463 (C.A.). *Cf. Tanner* v. *Carter* (1885) 16 Q.B.D. 231 (period of residence then required); *R.* v. *Hurst (Judge)*, *ex p. Smith* [1960] 2 Q.B. 133 (Ruskin College student's name removed from register although he was not a party to the proceedings). And see Susan Maidment, "The Case of the Student Voters" [1971] P.L. 25.

Apart from residence qualification any of the following persons has the right, on making a " service declaration," to be entered on the register as a *service voter*: (i) a member of the forces; (ii) a person employed in the whole-time service of the Crown in a post outside the United Kingdom; and (iii) the wife of a person having a service qualification, who is residing outside the United Kingdom to be with her husband.

Disqualifications for the franchise

The following are subject to legal incapacity from voting, either under the Acts of 1949 and 1969 or under the pre-existing law [72]:

  (i) Aliens (*cf. supra*).
  (ii) Minors (under eighteen years of age).
  (iii) Peers, except Irish peers.[73]
  (iv) Offenders in prison, *i.e.* convicted persons while detained in penal institutions.[74]
  (v) A person who has been reported by an election court personally guilty, or who has been convicted, of a *corrupt* practice is disqualified for *five years* from voting at any parliamentary election. In the case of an illegal practice the five-year disqualification is limited to that constituency.[75]

Conduct of elections [76]

The conduct of elections is now governed mainly by the consolidating Representation of the People Act 1949, the Representation of the People Act 1969, the House of Commons (Redistribution of Seats) Acts 1949 and 1958, and the Election Commissioners Act 1949.

Writs for a general election are issued by the Crown under the Great Seal, which is kept by the Lord Chancellor.

---

[72] The Representation of the People Act 1949 and the Mental Health Act 1959 are silent about the franchise of mentally disordered persons. A mentally disordered person detained (voluntarily or under restraint) is presumably entitled to vote by post, provided he is on the register and is capable of signing the application form for a postal vote; but a mental hospital would not be accepted as an address for registration.

[73] *Ante*, p. 123. The former convention that peers should not take part in parliamentary election campaigns was broken in the general election of 1909–1910, and the sessional order was restricted in 1910 to peers who were lords-lieutenant: Roy Jenkins, *Mr. Balfour's Poodle*, pp. 73–74.

[74] Representation of the People Act 1969, s. 4, taking account of the abolition of the distinction between felonies and misdemeanours. A prison would not be accepted as an address for registration.

[75] Representation of the People Act 1949, ss. 140 (3), (4) and 151; *cf.* s. 152 (mitigation and remission of incapacities). For corrupt and illegal practices, see *post*, pp. 160–161.

[76] For an historical account, see Jennings, *op. cit.* Chaps. 1 and 3.

By-elections

When a casual vacancy occurs in the House of Commons the Speaker, on the motion of a member, issues a warrant for the issue out of the Chancery of a writ for the holding of a by-election in that constituency. Polling is to take place not less than eleven or more than twenty days after issue of the writ. There is no legal obligation on the part of any member to move during the lifetime of the Parliament. The convention, practice or custom is that, when Parliament is in session, a by-election writ is moved by the Chief Whip of the party that previously held the seat at such time as suits that party's convenience; and that when Parliament is in recess members do not instruct the Speaker to issue his warrant for a new writ. The average time for the issue of by-election writs is three-and-a-half months after the seat becomes vacant, either because the party concerned is waiting for a new electoral register or because it is waiting until its electoral chances improve.[77] It is widely held that there ought to be a statutory period within which a by-election writ should be issued, and several private members' Bills to this effect have recently been introduced without success.

Constituencies

Four permanent and independent Boundary Commissions for England, Scotland, Wales and Northern Ireland were set up in 1944. By the House of Commons (Redistribution of Seats) Acts 1949 and 1958, the Commissions are to keep under review the representation in the House of Commons of the part of the United Kingdom with which they are concerned, and to submit reports to the Home Secretary as to the redistribution of seats at intervals of not less than ten or more than fifteen years. The criteria to be applied as far as practicable include numerical equality of voters between constituencies, respect for the boundaries of natural local communities, the distance to be travelled between parts of a single constituency, and the balance between the several parts of the United Kingdom. The reports are to be laid before Parliament by the Secretary of State as soon as may be, together with a draft Order in Council giving effect (with or without modifications[78]) to their recommendations.[79] If the draft Order is approved by resolution of each House, the Secretary of State

---

[77] When writs for by-elections for five Labour-held seats were issued on October 13, 1969, one seat had been vacant since February 19 and another since March 7.

[78] A statement of the reasons for any modifications must accompany the draft Order.

[79] The court will not grant an injunction to restrain the Home Secretary from submitting to Her Majesty draft Orders in Council alleged to be *ultra vires*, nor will it grant a declaration against either the Home Secretary or the Boundary Commission: *Harper* v. *Home Secretary* [1955] Ch. 238 (C.A.); *Hammersmith Borough Council* v. *Boundary Commission, The Times*, December 15, 1954.

must submit it to Her Majesty in Council, and the Order will take effect on the dissolution of Parliament.

The number of constituencies allotted is not substantially greater or less than 613 for Great Britain (including at least seventy-one for Scotland and thirty-five for Wales) and twelve for Northern Ireland. The number is 630 at present. Parliamentary constituencies are still divided into county and borough constituencies. Every constituency is to return a single member.[80] The electorate of each constituency is to be as near as practicable to its " electoral quota," which is about 60,000 at present.

The Act of 1949 provides that the validity of an Order in Council when made may not be called in question in any legal proceedings.

The court has refused to grant a mandatory injunction against a Boundary Commission to withdraw its recommendations after they had been reported to the Home Secretary: *Hammersmith Borough Council* v. *Boundary Commission for England* [81]; and the Court of Appeal has upheld the refusal to grant an injunction to restrain the Home Secretary from submitting to Her Majesty draft Orders in Council alleged to be *ultra vires*: *Harper* v. *Home Secretary*.[82] On the other hand, when in 1969 an elector applied for mandamus ordering the Home Secretary to lay before Parliament draft Orders in Council implementing the report of a Boundary Commission, the court did not disclaim jurisdiction on the ground of parliamentary privilege or otherwise; but the application was dismissed by consent when the Attorney-General assured the court that the Home Secretary undertook to perform this statutory duty.[83]

This last case arose out of the fact that Mr. Callaghan, the Home Secretary, had refrained from introducing draft Orders in Council to give effect to the latest recommendations of the Boundary Commission, on the ground that a major reorganisation of local government was envisaged and it was desirable that parliamentary and local government boundaries should as far as practicable be the same. Instead he introduced a House of Commons (Redistribution of Seats) Bill implementing the Commission's recommendations for Greater London,

---

[80] It was admitted by the Royal Commission on Electoral Systems ((1910) Cd. 5163) that our electoral system does not profess to provide representation of all parties in proportion to their voting strength: " A general election is in fact considered by a large portion of the electorate of this country as practically a referendum on the question of which of two governments shall be returned to power " (para. 126). The French system fosters groups of parties resulting in coalitions and compromise Ministries. Proposals for proportional representation or the alternative vote were decisively rejected by the Speaker's Conference on Electoral Reform in 1944 (Cmd. 6534).

[81] *The Times*, December 15, 1954.

[82] [1965] Ch. 238.

[83] *R.* v. *Home Secretary, ex p. McWhirter, The Times*, October 21, 1969.

the government of which had been reorganised in 1963, but not the recommendations relating to the provinces. This Bill failed to pass the House of Lords, and lapsed.[84] Mr. Callaghan then laid the draft Orders before Parliament, thus avoiding a possible order of mandamus, but moved that they should be *not* approved. The Orders were accordingly rejected by means of the Government's majority, which device made a mockery of the whole procedure.[85] The draft Orders were eventually re-introduced by the new Government and approved by both Houses after the general election of 1970.

Returning and registration officers

The returning officers are the sheriffs of counties, the chairmen of district councils and the mayors of London boroughs.[86] Most of their duties, however, are delegated to the *registration* officers, *i.e.* town clerks and clerks to county and district councils who are disqualified from membership.

The principal duty of the registration officer is to prepare and publish each year a register of parliamentary electors for each constituency in his area, and a register of local government electors.[87] He also adjudicates on claims and objections to the inclusion of names on the Register. An appeal from his decision lies to the county court. The registration officer must also prepare each year a list of persons found guilty of corrupt and illegal practices, for publication at the same time as the Register. He must further keep a list of *absent voters*, and the addresses to which their ballot papers are to be sent. Absent voters are: (1) service voters and (2) persons unable, or likely to be unable, for certain reasons (including physical incapacity and change of address) to go in person to the poll, who have made application to vote by post.[88] He must also keep a record of electors for whom *proxies* have been appointed, and a postal proxies list. Two classes of persons may vote by proxy: (1) service voters and (2) persons unable, or likely to be unable, to go to the poll by reason of the nature of their occupation or service in Her Majesty's reserve or auxiliary forces. The proxy is appointed on the application of the elector by the registration officer.

84 See *ante*, p. 112.
85 Lord Shawcross Q.C., in a letter to *The Times*, October 16, 1969, said that it seemed to involve "an almost unbelievable cynicism in regard to our legal and constitutional processes."
86 Local Government Act 1972.
87 These registers are to be combined, as far as practicable, with "L" marked against the names of persons registered as local government electors only.
88 The question whether people away from home on holiday should be entitled to vote by post was referred to the Speaker's Standing Electoral Advisory Conference in 1970.

Returning officers, registration officers, presiding officers and others who commit breaches of their official duties are liable for penalties under section 50 of the Representation of the People Act 1949, but no action for damages now lies against them: cf. Ashby v. White (1703).[89]

Election campaign

Part II of the Representation of the People Act 1949, as amended by the Representation of the People Act 1969, makes detailed provisions in relation to election campaigns. A candidate must submit a nomination paper to the returning officer within the prescribed time between a dissolution of Parliament and polling day. The nomination must be signed by the proposer and seconder, and eight other electors.[90]

A candidate is required to have an election agent, though he may be his own agent.[91] Stringent limits are set on the permissible amount of election expenses, and the purposes for which they may be incurred. Election expenses must be paid through the election agent, and they must be declared and published.

Corrupt practices include personation, bribery, treating and undue influence.[92] These were ill-defined offences at common law. Corrupt practices continued after the Reform Act 1832, and a significant improvement only came with the Parliamentary Elections Act 1868.[93] Their virtual elimination followed the Act of 1883,[94] which set a limit to election expenses.[95]

Illegal practices include false statements as to candidates; corruptly inducing a person's withdrawal from candidature; use of unauthorised premises; broadcasting on radio or television in the United Kingdom items about a constituency pending a parliamentary or local government election without the consent of any candidate who takes part in the

---

[89] 2 Ld.Raym. 938.
[90] Before the Ballot Act 1872 candidates were nominated by oral declaration to the presiding officer on the public " hustings."
[91] Most candidates are adopted by the committee of the constituency branch of their party, and sitting Members of Parliament are usually re-adopted in the same way; cf. Nigel Nicolson, *People and Parliament* (1958). Party " primaries " have been held in a few constituencies in recent years, in which the candidate is adopted on the vote of the party members present.
[92] Representation of the People Act 1949, ss. 47, 99–101.
[93] *Post*, p. 163.
[94] Corrupt and Illegal Practices Prevention Act 1883.
[95] Cornelius O'Leary, *The Elimination of Corrupt Practices in British Elections, 1868–1911* (1962). The maximum expenditure permitted to a candidate is £100 personal expenses, plus £750, plus an amount related to the number of entries in the electoral register. Parliamentary election in 1970 cost a successful candidate an average of £2,212, two-thirds of which was for printing and stationery: *Election Expenses*, H.C. Paper 305.

item [96]; broadcasting on radio or television from outside the United Kingdom in connection with a parliamentary or local government election otherwise than as arranged by the British Broadcasting Corporation [97]; payment for exhibition of election notices, except to a commercial advertising agent; not printing the name and address of the printer on election publications; employment of paid canvassers; and any other payments contrary to, or in excess of, those allowed by the Acts.[98]

There is scope for difference of opinion as to what exactly constitutes an election expense, e.g. advertisements by the sugar industry against nationalisation (" Mr. Cube," 1950). In *R*. v. *Tronoh Mines Ltd*.[99] McNair J. held that section 63 (1) (*b*) of the Act of 1949 (which prohibits expenses not authorised by election agent on issuing advertisements) is intended to prohibit expenditure on advertisements *supporting a particular candidate in a particular constituency*, which, it authorised by the election agent, would form part of the election expenses for that constituency: it is not intended to prohibit expenditure on advertisements supporting the interest of a particular party generally in all constituencies, at any rate at the time of a general election, and not supporting a particular candidate in a particular constituency. In *Grieve* v. *Douglas-Home*[1] an action was brought to have Sir Alec Douglas-Home's election at the general election in 1964 declared void, on the ground that he had not included in his return the expenses of party political broadcasts on behalf of the Conservative Party. It was held that no corrupt or illegal practice had been committed by anyone, as the motive of the BBC and ITA in presenting party political broadcasts was to give information to the public, and not to promote Sir Alec's election to Parliament.

The ballot

The Parliamentary and Municipal Elections Act 1872, commonly known as the " Ballot Act," made the vitally important innovation of substituting a secret ballot (by placing a cross on a ballot paper in a polling booth) for open election at the hustings. These provisions are now contained in the Representation of the People Act 1949. Each

---

[96] Representation of the People Act 1969, s. 9 (1)–(4).

[97] Representation of the People Act 1949, s. 80 (1), as amended by Representation of the People Act 1969, s. 9 (5).

[98] Representation of the People Act 1949, ss. 91–98. The restriction on the use of private motor-vehicles was removed by the Representation of the People (Amendment) Act 1958; and expenditure on music, torches, flags and banners was permitted by the Representation of the People Act 1969, s. 10.

[99] [1952] 1 All E.R. 697; [1952] 1 T.L.R. 461.

[1] *The Times*, December 24, 1964 (Scottish Election Court: Lords Migdale and Kilbrandon).

voter's ballot paper has a number printed on the back, which number is also printed on the counterfoil as it may be necessary in later *judicial* proceedings to discover whether there has been personation or plural voting; but such strict precautions as are humanly possible are made to ensure that no unauthorised person can ascertain, by a comparison of the ballot paper with the counterfoil, for which candidate a given elector voted.

A description of the candidate, not exceeding six words, is now allowed if desired in the nomination paper and on the ballot paper. The object is to enable a candidate's party to be shown, which was previously forbidden. This provision (s. 12) of the Representation of the People Act 1969 was contrary to the recommendation of the Speaker's Conference, and there are arguments on both sides of the question.

The Election Commissioners Act 1949 gives power to establish a commission to inquire into allegations of bribery and corrupt and illegal practices at elections. The commission is not to try election petitions (*infra*), but a commission may be constituted if, after the report of an election court or a Committee of the Commons or a public petition, it appears that such practices are widespread in a particular constituency.

Disputed elections

The King and Council originally settled election disputes, but as early as the reign of Richard II the Commons began to remonstrate against this practice. James I in the proclamation summoning his first Parliament specifically forbad the choice of bankrupts and outlaws. Sir Francis Goodwin was elected (against his will) for Buckinghamshire, but the Clerk of the Crown refused to receive the return on the ground that Goodwin was an outlaw, and Sir John Fortescue, a Privy Councillor, was elected in his place. The case of *Goodwin* v. *Fortescue* (1604) [2] followed, the real struggle being in the background between the Commons and the King. The Commons disputed Goodwin's outlawry, and contended that in any event outlawry did not disqualify him. The King and the Commons consented to submit the dispute to the judges, but no such reference took place. Finally, James admitted the right of the Commons to judge disputed election returns.[3] The Commons' privilege was confirmed by the

[2] 2 St.Tr. 91.
[3] The Commons later claimed the privilege of settling the rights of electors, and this gave rise to the celebrated cases of *Ashby* v. *White* and *Paty's Case*, *post*, Chap. 11.

Court of Exchequer Chamber and the House of Lords during the protracted litigation in *Barnardiston* v. *Soame* (1674–1689).[4]

After *Goodwin* v. *Fortescue* disputed elections were tried first for a time by Select Committees of the House, then by a committee of the whole House, the decisions tending to be made on party lines, and from 1770 by Select Committees under the provisions of various statutes. Eventually the Parliamentary Elections Act 1868, passed after the very corrupt general election of 1865, handed jurisdiction in disputed elections over to the Court of Common Pleas, proper safeguards being added to secure to the Commons their privileges. By the Parliamentary Elections and Corrupt Practices Act 1879 this jurisdiction was, with similar safeguards, committed to two judges of the High Court.

Election court

These provisions are now re-enacted in Part III of the Representation of the People Act 1949. An election petition may be presented by: (a) a person who voted or had the right to vote, (b) a person claiming to have had the right to be elected or returned, or (c) a person alleging that he was a candidate.[5] The election court consists of two judges of the Queen's Bench Division, acting without a jury. They have the powers of the High Court, and may sit in the constituency for which the election was held. Discovery and interrogatories are allowed. If the person elected is found to be disqualified, and if the electors knew the facts on which his disqualification was based, the election court may declare the candidate with the next highest number of votes to have been elected.[6] If the circumstances warrant, an election may simply be held to be void.

Appeal lies on a question of law with the leave of the High Court to the Court of Appeal, whose decision is final, the Commons not being willing that such questions should be decided by the House of Lords.

---

[4] (1674) 6 St.Tr. 1063, 1092; (1689) 6 St.Tr. 1119; Broom, *Constitutional Law* (2nd ed.) pp. 800, 839. This was an action against the sheriff for falsely and maliciously making a double return at the Suffolk by-election in 1672. The Parliamentary Elections (Returns) Act 1689, which subsequently allowed such an action, was repealed by the Representation of the People Act 1949; see Robin L. Sharwood, " *Barnardiston* v. *Soame*: a Restoration Drama " (1964) 4 *Melbourne Univ. Law Rev.* 502.

[5] *Cf.* application to the Judicial Committee of the Privy Council for a declaration under the House of Commons Disqualification Act 1957, s. 7; *ante*, p. 148.

[6] See *Re Parliamentary Election for Bristol South-East* [1964] 2 Q.B. 247; [1961] 3 W.L.R. 577; *ante*, p. 143. This case was heard in London. See also *Beresford-Hope* v. *Lady Sandhurst* (1889) L.R. 23 Q.B.D. 79; *Re Mid-Ulster Election Petition, Beattie* v. *Mitchell* [1958] N.I. 143; *Re Fermanagh and South Tyrone Election Petition, Grosvenor* v. *Clarke* [1958] N.I. 151.

The election court certify their finding to the Speaker. Section 124 of the 1949 Act provides that the House shall order the certificate and report to be entered in their Journals, and shall give the necessary direction for confirming or altering the return, or for issuing a writ for a new election, as the case may be [7]

---

[7] The Commons have the privilege, however, of deciding whether a person who has been duly elected shall be allowed to sit in the House; *post*, Chap. 11.

CHAPTER 9

PARLIAMENTARY PROCEDURE [1]

I. THE NATURE OF PARLIAMENTARY PROCEDURE

THE functions of Members of Parliament are not only, or indeed primarily, legislation (including taxation) but cover the discussion of policy and current affairs, and—especially in the Commons—the supervision of national finance and scrutiny of the administration. This chapter deals with parliamentary procedure generally, and the ordinary legislative process; while the next chapter covers national finance and scrutiny of the administration. The emphasis, for obvious reasons, is on the House of Commons.

Content

The content of parliamentary procedure may be divided into the following parts:

1. *Forms of proceeding, e.g.* the various stages in the passing of a Bill; the process of debate by motion, question and division; the methods by which the Commons control the administration in supply, questions to Ministers and motions for the adjournment.

2. *Machinery,* including the officers of each House (especially the Speaker of the Commons), committees and " Whips."

3. *Rules of procedure* in the strict sense, *i.e.* directions which govern the working of the forms of proceeding and the machinery of each House; *e.g.* the rule that a public Bill may be presented without an order of the House; the rule that the principle of a Bill is decided

---

[1] The standard work of reference is Erskine May's *Treatise on the Law, Privileges, Proceedings and Usages of Parliament,* commonly known as May's *Parliamentary Practice* or " Erskine May." The 18th edition (1971) is by the Clerk of the House of Commons. Book II covers proceedings on public business, and Book III proceedings on private business. The appendix contains the Standing Orders of the House of Commons relating to public business (H.C. 162, 1970–71).

See also Anson, *Law and Custom of the Constitution* (Vol. I, 5th ed. Gwyer, 1922) Chap. 6; Lord Campion, *Introduction to the Procedure of the House of Commons* (3rd ed. 1958); Sir Ivor Jennings, *Parliament* (2nd ed. 1957); C. R. Niven, *Notes on Parliamentary Procedure* (Hansard Society); *Parliamentary Reform, 1933–1960* (Hansard Society, 2nd ed. 1967); *The Commons in Transition* (ed. Hanson and Crick, 1970); K. Bradshaw and D. Pring, *Parliament and Congress* (1972); C. J. Boulton, " Recent Developments in House of Commons Procedure " (1969–70) *Parliamentary Affairs,* p. 61; Bernard Crick, *The Reform of Parliament* (2nd ed. 1968).

on the second reading; and the rules regulating the powers and duties of the Speaker in the conduct of debate and the maintenance of order.

4. *Parliamentary conventions, i.e.* rules not enforced by the Chair but by the public opinion of the House; for example, the rule that the selection of particular votes to be discussed in debates on Supply rests with the Opposition.

Rules of procedure vary considerably in importance, that is to say, in the extent to which they are essential or useful to the exercise of their functions by each House. At one end of the scale is the Standing Order of the House of Commons that expenditure must be proposed by the Crown, which is of great constitutional importance; at the other end come rules, such as that the " Ayes " divide to the right and the " Noes " to the left, where it does not matter what the rule is so long as there is one.

Historical development

The forms and rules show traces of their origin in various stages of historical development. So far as the development of the Commons procedure is concerned, Lord Campion (a former Clerk of the House of Commons) has suggested the following periods:

(i) From the establishment of Parliament to the beginning of the Commons Journals, during which period constitutional forms came to be settled (c. 1300–1547).

(ii) The period of " ancient usage," from the beginning of the Journals to the Restoration (1547–1660).

(iii) The period of later " parliamentary practice," from the Restoration to the great Reform Act (1660–1832).

(iv) The period of modern Standing Orders (from 1833 to the present day).[2]

Sources of parliamentary procedure

The sources of parliamentary procedure may be classified as follows:

(i) *Practice, i.e.* the unwritten part of procedure;

(ii) *Standing Orders*; also Sessional Orders and *ad hoc* resolutions;

(iii) *Rulings from the Chair, i.e.* by the Speaker or Chairman of Committees;

(iv) *Acts of Parliament* regulating certain aspects of the procedure of both Houses.

[2] Campion, *op. cit.* p. 5.

The greater part of the procedure of the House of Commons is unwritten, and has to be collected from the Journal [3] (made from the Votes and Proceedings [4]), reports of debates [5] and personal experience. Standing Orders are merely appendant to the unwritten part, which they presuppose.[6] The well-known rules that a Bill is " read " three times, and that certain kinds of amendments may be moved on the second or third reading, are not contained in Standing Orders but are part of unwritten practice. In ascertaining what is the practice of the House reliance is placed on precedents as recorded in the Journals. The practice before 1832 was evolved mainly in order to facilitate and encourage debate.

Standing Orders are passed in the ordinary way by resolution of the House; but it is expressly provided that they shall last beyond the end of the session, otherwise they would be terminated by pro rogation. The main purpose of Standing Orders relating to public business is to enable more business to be done by speeding up debate.[7] Sessional Orders are passed for the session only, and ad hoc Orders or resolutions for the particular occasion; the former are often experimental, and both are used to regulate the order of business. A Standing Order or a Sessional Order can be set aside by an Order of the same kind, and either can be suspended by an ad hoc Order. An express Order of any kind overrides a rule of practice.

The function of the Speaker or Chairman in giving rulings is mainly interpretative and declaratory, and involves the application of practice and Standing Orders in particular circumstances as they arise.

Acts of Parliament modifying parliamentary procedure are few. They are passed in order to bind both Houses, so that one House cannot change the rule without the other. Some of the more important examples are the Exchequer and Audit Departments Act 1866, the Parliamentary Elections Act 1868,[8] the Parliament Acts 1911 and 1949, the Provisional Collection of Taxes Act 1968 and the Statutory Orders (Special Procedure) Acts 1945 and 1965. Acts of Parliament, of course, have overriding authority over the Orders of both Houses or either of them.

[3] The permanent official record of the proceedings of the House, compiled from the minute books of the Clerks at the table, and published annually.
[4] The daily record of the proceedings of the House.
[5] For " Hansard," see post, p. 203.
[6] The bulk of House of Commons Standing Orders in fact relate to private business, i.e. the procedure on private Bills. For the division of the content of Standing Orders into laws, customs and conventions, see ante, pp. 79, 89.
[7] See Ilbert, Parliament (3rd ed. Carr) pp. 117–118. Cf. Lord Chorley, " Bringing the Legislative Process into Contempt " [1968] P.L. 52, 54: " the caterpillar speed of the legislative process is really one of its outstanding values."
[8] Now the Representation of the People Act 1949, Part III.

The House of Lords procedure contains a larger proportion of Standing Orders. Their purpose is rather to declare practice than to accelerate business. About a quarter of the Lords Standing Orders relate to privileges.

The rules relating to private business (*i.e.* private Bills) are mainly contained in a separate set of Standing Orders of each House.

II. PROCEDURE IN THE COMMONS

Order of business

The House meets at 2.30 p.m.[9] on Mondays to Thursdays, and at 11 a.m. on Fridays. The usual order of business on Mondays to Thursdays is:

(1) prayers; (2) business taken immediately after prayers, *e.g.* motions for new writs, and presentation of public petitions[10]; (3) questions for oral answer, and private notice questions; (4) business taken after questions, *e.g.* ministerial statements,[11] proposals to move the adjournment under S.O. No. 9 (urgency motions), consideration of Lords amendments, raising matters of privilege; (5) business taken "at the commencement of public business," *e.g.* introduction (first reading) of public Bills, and government motions regulating the business of the House; (6) consideration of report of Committee of Privileges; (7) public business, *i.e.* mainly "Orders of the Day" (including the stages of public Bills and Committees of the whole House) and notices of motion; (8) certain business motions by Ministers; (9) business exempted from the ten-o'clock rule (including Finance, Consolidated Fund, and Appropriation Bills); (10) adjournment motions. Many of these items are omitted on Thursdays.

If the House has not previously adjourned, it sits until half an hour after the motion for adjournment has been proposed, either at 10 p.m. (Friday 4 p.m.) for ordinary business or at the conclusion of exempted business. Sittings on Saturday are rare, and on Sunday are confined to emergencies.

[9] The mornings are largely occupied by committee work " upstairs," by Ministers in their departments and by lawyers in the courts. Morning sittings were introduced as an experiment in 1966 for less important and non-contentious business, but were abandoned as a failure after a time in exchange for a Standing Order allowing a Minister to move that a debate continuing after 10 p.m. be suspended until the following morning. The Select Committee on Procedure 1969–70 recommended that the House should meet at 2.20 p.m.

[10] It is an ancient liberty of the citizen to petition Parliament to remedy some grievance: *Chaffers* v. *Goldsmid* [1894] 1 Q.B. 186, although a member cannot be compelled to present a petition. However, few petitions are presented nowadays and they are no longer debated in the House, so that they have lost their importance. Their place may be said to have been taken by members' questions.

[11] A new class of " ministerial written statements " has been made available at the end of question time since 1972.

Questions [12]

The first recorded parliamentary question was in the House of Lords in 1721. The device of the parliamentary question was slow to develop in the eighteenth century owing to the conservatism of procedure; the existence of alternative methods of airing grievances, such as petitions and moving for papers; members' lack of control over many aspects of the administration; the inability of the government to provide much information; and the limited publicity given at that time to parliamentary proceedings. It was after 1832 that the practice really developed, especially in the House of Commons. Until 1881 questions were read out, often at great length.

The modern method is for questions to be put down and numbered on the notice paper. Unless the Speaker gives special leave, written notice of intention to ask a question must be delivered to the Clerk of the House at the table beforehand. Where an oral answer is required, an asterisk is affixed to the notice. A member is now limited to two oral questions a day, and he may not " pre-empt " time by giving more than three weeks' notice of a question.[13] If there is no asterisk, or the member is not in the House or the question is not reached by the time-limit, the Minister concerned has the answer printed and circulated with the votes. The member may, however, postpone his question. Opinions must not be asked, and purely legal questions are not allowed, nor may a question refer to any debate that has occurred in either House in the current session.

Questions may not be asked that bring the name of the Sovereign or the influence of the Crown directly before Parliament, or that cast reflections on the Sovereign or the Royal Family. Imputations on private character are not permitted, but imputations on official character may be made with certain reservations. Questions may not be put on matters pending in a committee till the report of that committee is issued. A question must be a question: argument or statements of fact are not permitted. The Clerks at the table give preliminary advice to members, but the Speaker is sole judge of the propriety of a question.

Questions addressed to a Minister [14] must relate either to: (i) public affairs with which he is officially connected, (ii) proceedings

---

[12] *Select Committee on Procedure: Question Time* (1969–70) H.C. 198.   See P. Howarth, *Questions in the House* (1956); D. N. Chester and N. Bowring, *Questions in Parliament* (1962).

[13] The Select Committee on Procedure 1964–65 recommended that a member should be limited to eight questions a month, and the Select Committee on Procedure 1969–70 recommended greater brevity in question and answer.

[14] Questions may be asked of non-official members relating to Bills, motions or other matters concerned with the business of the House for which they are responsible, *e.g.* the Chairman of the Kitchen Committee.

pending in Parliament, or (iii) matters of administration for which he is *responsible*, that is, which come within the work of his department, or his official duties or powers.[15]　A Minister may decline to answer a question on the ground of public policy, and the Foreign Secretary is on this account allowed great latitude. A Minister may also decline to answer a question or to supply information on security grounds, as did Sir Anthony Eden in 1956 in connection with Commander Crabb, the "frogman." The Prime Minister cannot be questioned on the date proposed for the dissolution of Parliament. The Home Secretary is not directly responsible for the police outside the Metropolitan Police area, although his general responsibility for the English police was increased by the Police Act 1964.[16]

The public corporations set up under various nationalisation Acts have given rise to a problem of considerable constitutional importance. How far are questions relating to them admissible and to what extent is a Minister, who has a general control over the policy of such a corporation, expected to answer questions arising out of its operations? This question, which is bound up with the entire constitutional framework of such corporations, has been much debated in Parliament, and it cannot be said that a satisfactory solution has yet been found.[17]

The asking of questions is now one of the most important functions of Parliament. Questions are asked in order to focus attention on matters of topical interest either to individual constituents or to the public generally. Owing to the publicity given by the Press— and questions are in time to catch the evening papers—the practice is indulged in more for the benefit of the electorate than of the House. "If I want to get something done I write to the Minister," said Sir Austen Chamberlain; "if I want to cause trouble I put down a parliamentary question." When a Minister's reply is not considered satisfactory, supplementary questions may be asked. "Originally, questions were asked in order to secure an answer," says Sir Ivor Jennings [18]; "Today they often serve as pegs on which to hang a more insidious ' supplementary.' "

Owing to the strictness of party discipline in modern times, debates tend to run on party lines. Question time therefore constitutes an important check on the activities of the executive. It is then that

---

15 (1958–59) 599 H.C.Deb. cols. 1181–1182.

16 The Secretary of State for Scotland has a similar responsibility for the Scottish police. Before the abolition of the death penalty for murder in 1965 it was ruled that the Home Secretary might not be questioned about the exercise of the prerogative of mercy in cases where persons had been sentenced to death but before execution or commutation of sentence, although limited discussion was not precluded afterwards. *Cf.* Geoffrey Marshall, " Parliament and the Prerogative of Mercy " [1961] P.L. 8.

17 See further, *post*, Chap. 27.

18 Jennings, *op. cit.* p. 106.

the private member comes into his own, for he can put forward the grievances of individual citizens who have suffered at the hands of government departments. A good deal of time is taken up in some government departments in looking up the facts and " briefing " the Minister. When used skilfully by members of the Opposition, the asking of questions may be made a source of considerable embarrassment to the government. On the other hand, a disadvantage of the institution of question time is that it tends to foster a spirit of timidity among civil servants.

If a member remains unsatisfied with an answer, he may give notice that he intends to raise the question on the adjournment. The *motion for adjournment* of the House provides a half-hour at the end of the day in which almost any matter not involving legislation may be discussed. There is no division as adjournment is automatic when the time-limit is reached.

Rules of debate

The rules of debate that have been developed over the years are designed to ensure orderly conduct, the dignity of the House and the right of a minority to be heard. A debate is always on a motion, *e.g.* " that this Bill be read a second time "; and every matter is determined on a question put by the Speaker and resolved by the House in the affirmative or negative. A member who wishes to speak must rise in his place and " catch the Speaker's eye." Privy Councillors have generally a right to priority in being called upon to speak: this gives an advantage to present and former Cabinet Ministers at the expense of back-benchers. A member may only speak once in the House to the same question, except to raise points of order or to correct misrepresentations of fact. All remarks must be addressed to the Chair.[19]

There are rules to ensure relevancy and to avoid repetition. No reference may be made to the House of Lords under that name (it is commonly referred to as " another place "); nor to any matter *sub judice* in a court of law. The name of the Queen must not be mentioned either disrespectfully or in order to influence the House.[20] No treasonable or seditious words are allowed, nor may a person speak to obstruct business. Members must not be referred to by name,

---

[19] In most assemblies this is an excellent rule as an aid in maintaining order. It is in contrast to the practice in the House of Lords, where it is evidently not needed and peers address the House.

[20] Disraeli when Prime Minister, with Queen Victoria's approval, obtained the permission of the House in 1876 to use the Queen's name in debate, in order to rebut a statement made in a public speech that the Queen had asked two previous Prime Ministers for the title of Empress of India: Robert Blake, *Disraeli* (1966) p. 563.

but as " the Hon. Member for Camford," etc. nor may any offensive expressions against members be used or personal charges made. If a member refuses to withdraw an objectionable remark, he may be suspended. No allusion may be made to a debate of the same session on any question not at the time under discussion. A member may refer to notes but must not read his speech. A member who has a direct pecuniary interest in a question should declare his interest if he speaks, and must not vote on it.[21]

Urgency motions

Under Standing Order No. 9 a member who has given proper notice to the Speaker may, immediately after Questions, move the adjournment on " *a specific and important matter that should have urgent consideration.*" If the Speaker rules that the matter is proper to be discussed under the Standing Order, and the House gives leave, the motion is usually debated at the commencement of public business next day, but exceptionally at 7 p.m. on the same day. Before 1967 the Standing Order specified " a definite matter of urgent public importance," but Speakers came to interpret this so strictly that only fifteen such debates were allowed in twenty years. The Select Committee in 1967 thought that the right number would be about five emergency debates per session.[22]

Suspension of member

When a member contumaciously declines to accept a ruling of the Speaker, *e.g.* by refusing to " withdraw " an offensive remark, or is guilty of misbehaviour or flagrantly breaks the rules of the House, the Speaker may be asked to " name " him. The question is then put that the member be suspended from the service of the House, and if the motion is carried he is suspended on the first occasion until the fifth day, on the second occasion in the same session until the twentieth day, and on a subsequent occasion until further order or until the end of the session. A suspended member must withdraw from the precincts of the House.

[21] A Select Committee in 1969 recommended that in any debate, or communication with other members or with Ministers or civil servants, a member should disclose any relevant pecuniary interest or benefit, whether direct or indirect. A Code of Conduct, including restrictions on advocating any matter for which a member directly or indirectly received payment, should be kept under review by the Committee of Privileges. A Register of members' interests was rejected: *Report from Select Committee on Members' Interests* (1969).

[22] *Second Report from Select Committee on Procedure 1966–67* (*urgent and topical debates*) H.C. 282. Emergency debates were held in January 1971 on the Dutsche case and in February 1971 on the liquidation of Rolls-Royce.

Divisions

When the Speaker closes a debate by " putting the question," he first senses the feeling of the House by asking members to say " Aye " or " No," but in any important matter the members challenge the Speaker's opinion and he orders a division. Electric bells are rung, the lobbies are cleared, and after two minutes [23] the Speaker puts the question again. Unless the division is then " called off " the members now present divide by filing through the two lobbies, their names being checked and the numbers counted by two members nominated to act as tellers for each lobby. The figures are then read out to the Speaker by the senior teller for the majority.

The quorum of forty, including the Speaker, was established in 1641. If a division reveals that fewer than that number of members are present the business under discussion stands adjourned and the House proceeds to the next business. [24]

Closure

This is a device known as " the Gag " for bringing to an end a debate or a speech at any time. A member moves " that the question be now put," and if the Speaker or Chairman accepts the motion and it is carried in a division, not fewer than one hundred members voting in its support, further debate on the subject must cease. This is used frequently, but the Speaker has a discretion to refuse the closure where he considers that the rights of the minority would be infringed, or that the motion is an abuse of the rules of the House.

" Guillotine " [25]

An allocation of Time (or " Guillotine ") order is a closure by compartments. In order to ensure that the remaining proceedings on a public Bill in the House or in Committee are speeded up, a Minister may move either (a) that specified dates and days be allotted to the various stages of the Bill, or (b) that the Committee shall report the Bill to the House by a certain date, leaving the details to the Business Committee of the House or a business sub-committee of the Committee. This device arouses opposition, and is used sparingly. Voluntary timetabling is usually attempted first; if that fails, which it often does, the government can force its timetable through by means of its majority.

[23] The Lords have four minutes in which to cover the distance to their Chamber.
[24] The " count " has been abolished.
[25] See John Palmer, " Allocation of Time: The Guillotine and Voluntary Time-tabling " (1970) XXIII *Parliamentary Affairs*, p. 232. *Cf.* " Selection of amend-ments (' Kangaroo ') " *post*, p. 179.

Committees of the Commons

The Commons have long made use of committees for various purposes. Sometimes a matter was committed to a single Privy Councillor, more often the committee was a Committee of the whole House. The main function of Standing Committees has been to consider and amend public Bills, thus doing what the House could do if it had time. Select Committees do the kind of things that the House as a whole could not easily do.

Committees of the Commons may be classified as follows:

1. *Committees of the whole House*, *i.e.* the House itself sitting with a Chairman instead of the Speaker.[26] This procedure is less frequent now that it has been abolished for financial legislation.

2. *Standing Committees.* Standing Orders provide for the appointment of as many Standing Committees as may be necessary for the consideration of public Bills, and other business committed or referred to a Standing Committee. They consist of sixteen to fifty members nominated by the Committee of Selection. The Selection Committee is required to have regard to the qualifications of members, and also to the composition of the House. Standing Committees are not only larger and more representative than Select Committees, but their functions and procedure are more similar to those of the House. They take the committee stage of public Bills. New ones are Second Reading Committees, Report Committees, and Finance Bill Committees. The Scottish and Welsh Grand Committees and Scottish Standing Committees are exceptional.

3. *Select Committees.* These are Committees composed of not more than fifteen members specially named, and appointed from time to time or regularly re-appointed to consider or deal with particular matters. They include:

(i) Select Committees for considering public Bills (rarely employed);

(ii) Committees of Enquiry (now largely superseded by Royal Commissions and departmental committees);

(iii) Select Committees on private Bills;

(iv) Sessional Committees re-appointed at the beginning of every session, either under Standing Order or an Order renewed each session, to consider all subjects of a particular nature, or such of them as are referred to it, or to perform other functions of a permanent nature, *e.g.* the Selection Committee, the Standing Orders Committee, the Public Accounts Com-

---

[26] The Serjeant-at-Arms places the Mace on brackets beneath the table. The Chairman does not sit in the Speaker's Chair, but on a chair " at the table " which is ordinarily occupied by the Clerk of the House.

mittee, the Committee of Privileges, the Expenditure Committee, the Select Committee for the Parliamentary Commissioner, the Select Committee on Publications and Debates Reports, the Statutory Instruments Committee, the Select Committee on Nationalised Industries, the House of Commons Services Committee and Select Committees on Procedure.

(v) " Specialist " Committees.[27] A new kind of Select Committee appointed to " scrutinise " the administration either of some subject such as science and technology, or of a particular government department, or of some branch of law such as race relations. The experiment began in 1966. " Specialist " Committees are not necessarily re-appointed after the end of a session. This classification is not precise, as a discussion of them would include the Select Committee on Nationalised Industries set up in 1955 and the new Expenditure Committee (*supra*).

More will be said about some of these Select Committees in the next chapter.

4. *Joint Committees, i.e.* a Select Committee of the Commons sitting with a Select Committee of the Lords, an equal number being chosen from each House. The Chairman may be a member of either House. Joint Committees are set up from time to time to deal with non-political questions that equally concern both Houses, *e.g.* Church of England measures and some private Bills. There is a joint Standing Committee to consider consolidation Bills. A Joint Committee has been set up to review the form, drafting and amendment of legislation, and the practice in preparation of legislation for presentation to Parliament,[28] and a Joint Committee on Delegated Legislation.[29]

III. PROCEDURE ON LEGISLATION

Drafting of Bills [30]

Nearly all government Bills are drafted by Parliamentary Counsel to the Treasury, a staff of barristers or solicitors in the Treasury

---

27 See *Select Committees of the House of Commons* (1970) Cmnd. 4507.

28 *Select Committee on Procedure: Process of Legislation* (1970–71) H.C. 538. For consolidation and revision of statute law, see Consolidation of Enactments (Procedure) Act 1949; Viscount Jowitt, *Statute Law Revision and Consolidation* (Holdsworth Club, University of Birmingham, 1951); Law Commission Act 1965, s. 3; *Law Commission's Second Programme on Consolidation and Statute Law Revision* (1971) H.C. 338.

29 It reported in September 1972: (1971–72) H.L. 184 and H.C. 475.

30 Ilbert, *Mechanics of Law Making* (1913); *Legislative Methods and Forms* (1901); Sir Granville Ram, " The Improvement of the Statute Book " [1951] J.S.P.T.L. 442. See also " The Making and Form of Bills " by one of the Parliamentary

whose office was constituted in 1869. Parliamentary Counsel also advise on amendments proposed during the passage of a Bill.

The government sometimes lends drafting assistance to a private Member's Bill that has passed its second reading. Otherwise private members are responsible for drafting their own Bills.

Classification of Bills

A project of law during its passage through Parliament is called a Bill, and its subdivisions are called clauses. Bills are classified into three kinds:

1. *Public Bills*, *i.e.* measures affecting the community at large or altering the general law. A public Bill applies by description to all persons subject to the authority of Parliament or to certain classes of such persons. Strictly, all public Bills are introduced by members in their capacity as members; but in ordinary language those introduced by Ministers are called " government Bills," and those introduced by private (or unofficial) members are called " private members' Bills." Government Bills are far the most numerous, and are assured of the general support of the government's majority. Little time is allotted to private members' Bills,[31] which must be carefully distinguished from private Bills (*infra*).

2. *Private Bills*, *i.e.* measures dealing with local or personal matters, such as a Bill giving special powers to a local authority or altering a settlement. They apply to particular persons or groups who are named or otherwise identified (*e.g.* by locality). They are promoted by petition by interested persons or bodies outside Parliament, and are governed by special procedure under separate Standing Orders.[32]

3. *Hybrid Bills*, *i.e.* Bills which, although they are introduced as public Bills (mostly by the government, but occasionally by private members), affect private interests in such a way that if they were private Bills preliminary notices to persons affected would have to be given under the Standing Orders. They are governed by a special procedure, which in the middle stages is similar to that on private Bills. The classification is done by a Select Committee, and is difficult in some cases: thus the Bill to nationalise the Bank of England, the London Passenger Transport Bill and the Cable and Wireless Bill were

Counsel, in (1948–49) 2 *Parliamentary Affairs* (Hansard Society) p. 175; Sir Ivor Jennings, *Parliament* (2nd ed.) Chap. 7.

31 *Post*, p. 180.
32 *Post*, p. 182.

held to be hybrid Bills; but the Bills to nationalise gas, electricity and the coal industry were regarded as public Bills.[33]

We must also notice *provisional order confirmation Bills*. These are Bills confirming orders and schemes made by government departments under statutory powers that would otherwise formerly have to be dealt with by private Bills. The delay and expense of private Bill legislation was thus saved, and local authorities in particular during the latter half of the nineteenth century and the first half of the present century acquired powers in this way by ministerial order under various statutes. A provisional order has no effect until confirmed by Parliament. It is scheduled, along with others, to a Provisional Orders confirmation Bill introduced by the Minister.

Ordinary procedure on Public Bills [34]

Most kinds of public Bills may originate either in the Commons or the Lords, but there are certain classes of Bills, such as Money Bills and Bills dealing with the representation of the people, which by parliamentary custom or constitutional convention may originate only in the Commons. In practice many more Bills originate in the Commons than in the Lords, although (as we have seen) the latter method is convenient for non-controversial topics that either require no discussion, such as British North America Acts, or that require technical discussion on non-party lines, such as the Crown Proceedings Act 1947.

Introduction of Bills

A member, whether a Minister or unofficial member, introduces a Bill by presenting it at the table or by motion for leave to introduce it, in either case after giving notice. The former method is usual, as the latter may lead to a debate.

The five stages through which a Bill passes in the legislative process in the House are: (i) first reading, (ii) second reading, (iii) committee stage, (iv) report (or consideration of amendments) stage, and (v) third reading.

(i) *First reading.* The Bill is ordinarily presented in "dummy," *i.e.* a sheet of paper on which is the name of the member and the title of the Bill. The "first reading" is purely formal. The Clerk

---

[33] See R. W. Perceval, " The Origin and Essence of Hybrid Bills " (1949) 2 *Parliamentary Affairs* (Hansard Society) p. 139; W. Craig Henderson, " Procedure on Hybrid Bills " *ibid.* p. 148.
The procedure was amended following the *Report of the Select Committee on Procedure in Committee* (1948) H.C. 191.

[34] For Money Bills and financial clauses, see *post*, Chap. 10.

at the table reads the title only. The Bill is then deemed to have been read a first time, and is ordered to be printed.

(ii) *Second reading.* The member in charge of the Bill moves that it " be now read a second time." The Bill is not actually read, but its main principles are discussed. If no one objects to the Bill, it can be "read" a second time when unopposed business is taken. If it is opposed,[35] it can only come on on one of the days fixed for taking opposed Bills.

In 1965 a suggestion of the Select Committee on Procedure [36] was adopted whereby a Minister, having given ten days' notice, may propose that a public Bill be referred to a *Second Reading Committee* to make a recommendation to the House whether it should or should not be read a second time. The Second Reading Committee is a Standing Committee of sixteen to fifty members nominated for the consideration of each Bill referred to it. This experiment, designed to save time, has been successful, and means that a number of non-controversial Bills and unopposed Bills for which the government are not prepared to find time on the floor of the House can be introduced. The procedure may be used unless at least twenty members object.[37] Bills dealt with in this way can now be carried over to the next session, unless the motion to do so is opposed by twenty members.

The second reading of Bills relating exclusively to Scotland is taken by the *Scottish Grand Committee,* unless ten or more members object. This Committee is composed of all members for Scottish constituencies, together with ten to fifteen other members who rarely take part. Motions dealing with exclusively Scottish matters may also be referred to this Committee.[38]

(iii) *Committee stage.* When a Bill has passed the second reading it goes to one of the Standing Committees, unless the House otherwise orders. If the House otherwise orders it may be referred to a Committee of the whole House (*e.g.* an important constitutional measure, such as the Bill to reform the House of Lords in 1968), or (rarely) to a Select Committee, or (for certain purposes) to a Joint Committee of the two Houses. One part of a Bill may be considered by a Stand-

---

[35] In 1772 a Bill was rejected, thrown about, and kicked out of the House; Anson, *Law and Custom of the Constitution,* Vol. I (5th ed. Gwyer) p. 272.

[36] (1964–65) H.C. 149.

[37] Such objection is not seldom forthcoming: *Select Committee on Procedure: The Process of Legislation* (1970–71) H.C. 538.

[38] The more recent *Welsh Grand Committee* considers matters, though not Bills, relating exclusively to Wales and Monmouthshire. It consists of all members for constituencies in Wales and Monmouthshire, together with not more than five other members. See R. L. Borthwick (1968) *Parliamentary Affairs,* Vol. 21, p. 264; and for both Grand Committees, see J. P. Mackintosh, *The Devolution of Power* (1968) pp. 166–168.

ing Committee and another part by a Committee of the whole House, the advantage of the latter being that all members have an opportunity to take part.

A Bill whose second reading was in the Scottish Grand Committee, unless notice of amendment to the second reading was given by not less than six members, is referred to a *Scottish Standing Committee.* There are two of these Committees. One consists of thirty members for Scottish constituencies, to whom twenty other members may be added, though this is seldom done. The other consists of sixteen to fifty members, of whom not fewer than sixteen represent Scottish constituencies.

For the consideration of a Bill relating exclusively to Wales and Monmouthshire, the Standing Committee must include all the members for constituencies in Wales and Monmouthshire (" Welsh Standing Committee ").

The committee stage is the time for discussing details and proposing amendments. The Bill is taken clause by clause, and amendments are moved in the order in which they come in the clause. In the committee stage the procedure is less formal than in the House; a motion need not be seconded, and a member may speak more than once on the same question. When the clauses are finished new clauses and postponed clauses are considered. After that the schedules, if any, are taken.

Selection of amendments (" *Kangaroo* "). In order to save time, Standing Orders give to the Speaker on the report stage, or a Chairman of Committee, the power to select certain new clauses or amendments for discussion. The rest are voted on without debate. A previous announcement is now made concerning the selection of amendments.[39]

(iv) *Report stage.* The Bill as amended in Committee is then " reported " to the House. It may, with certain restrictions, be further amended as in Committee. If voluntary timetabling fails and the Speaker exercises his power of selection of amendments (*supra*), his reason for not " calling " a particular amendment will often be that it has been fully discussed in Committee.

A Bill whose second reading was in Second Reading Committee or the Scottish Grand Committee may now be sent to a Standing Committee at the report stage (" *Report Committee* ") on the motion of a Minister, unless at least twenty members object.[40]

(v) *Third reading.* After the Bill has been considered on report, it is put down for " third reading." The rule since 1967 has been

39 *Report of Select Committee on Procedure* (1959) H.C. 92, para. 14.
40 Such objection is not seldom forthcoming: (1970–71) H.C. 538.

that debate is only permitted at this stage on the motion of at least six members. Thus third readings, which had tended to become repetitive, have become mainly formal. Much time has been saved in this way. Further, it is now possible (with Second Reading Committees) for some Bills to pass the Commons without ever being debated on the floor of the House.

If there is a debate on third reading, it is on general principles and only verbal amendments can be moved.[41] The Bill as a whole can be opposed in principle by the same method as at second reading. If the motion " that the Bill be now read a third time " is carried— which it almost certainly will be if it is a government Bill—the Bill is deemed to have passed the House. It is now sent up to the House of Lords, endorsed with the words " *Soit baillé aux Seigneurs* " (let it be sent to the Lords).

Private members' Bills

Public Bills may be introduced by private members. Private members do not introduce Bills authorising expenditure, because these require a financial resolution with a recommendation from the Crown. Otherwise private members are free as regards subject-matter, but they have to ballot for priority for the very limited time available. Private members' Bills have precedence over government Bills on ten Fridays in the session, and on ten other Fridays they take a similar precedence but after private members' motions. Private members also have an opportunity to introduce Bills on four days other than Fridays until 7 p.m.

The chance is remote of a private members' Bill reaching the final stage—or even an advanced stage—by the end of the session (when uncompleted Bills expire), unless the government give it their active support.[42] The Parliament of 1965–1970 was remarkable for the number of private members' Bills that did become law, on such important social matters as the death penalty, homosexual offences, censorship of stage plays and abortion. The Government helped by allowing time, but they did not accept responsibility or give help in drafting.[43]

---

41 The Bill may, however, be recommitted to a committee.
42 See A. P. Herbert, *The Ayes Have it: Independent Member*; P. A. Bromhead, *Private Members' Bills in the British Parliament*. It has been suggested that there should be a steering committee, or that private members' Bills should be given priority according to the amount of support they obtain.
43 The Government agreed in 1972 to grant up to £200 towards drafting expenses of members gaining the first ten places in the ballot.

Ten minute rule

A private member who has not won a place in the ballot can take advantage of the "*Ten Minute Rule,*" whereby motions for leave to introduce Bills may be set down at the commencement of public business on Tuesdays and Wednesdays (S.O. No. 13). After the mover has briefly explained the objects of the Bill, another member is allowed to make a short speech in opposition, and the question is then put without further debate. This procedure gives early publicity to controversial measures. Bills under this rule are limited to one a day, and a member is now limited to one such notice in a period of fifteen sitting days.[44]

Special Procedure Orders under the Statutory Orders (Special Procedure) Act 1945 have largely replaced Provisional Order confirmation Bills. The Act of 1945 itself applied to Orders made under Water, Planning and certain other Acts, and the "special parliamentary procedure" also applies where any subsequent Act so specifies. This has been done in a number of statutes. Meanwhile, most provisions for the Provisional Order procedure were converted into the new "special procedure" in 1949,[45] and no further power to make Provisional Orders has been conferred since 1945.

Where the "special parliamentary procedure" applies, statutory effect can be given more cheaply and more quickly to departmental Orders laid before the House. The general principle is that matters of national policy are decided on the floor of the House, but that a procedure similar to private Bill procedure is applied in so far as private rights are affected. Provisions are made for giving notice and for objections by petition. Here it is the opponents, not the promoters, who petition. If a Special Procedure Order gives rise to no objections, or if, after a petition has been heard, the Joint Committee reports the Order without amendments or with amendments to which the Minister agrees, the Order becomes law after the prescribed period without the necessity of a Bill to confirm it. On the other hand, if the Joint Committee report that the Order be not approved or report the Order with amendments to which the Minister does not agree, he may introduce a Bill to confirm it: such Bill is treated as a public Bill, and is deemed to have passed through all its stages up to and including the committee stage.

Procedure in the Lords

The procedure on legislation in the House of Lords resembles generally the procedure in the Commons, although it has greater

---

[44] *Select Committee on Procedure: Ten-Minute Rule Motions* (1969–70) H.C. 141.
[45] Statutory Orders (Special Procedure) (Substitution) Order 1949.

flexibility. If the Lords propose amendments to a Bill sent up by the Commons, the Bill is endorsed " *A ceste bille avecque des amendemens les Seigneurs sont assentus* " and returned to the Commons for consideration. The Commons may assent to the amendments (" *A ces amendemens les Communes sont assentus* "), or dissent from them, or further amend them (" *Ceste bille est remise aux Seigneurs avecque des raisons* ").

Procedure on private Bills [46]

Private Bills are initiated not by Members of Parliament within the House, but by petition from persons or bodies (" promoters ") outside Parliament. The procedure on private Bills is complicated and is governed by a special set of Standing Orders. Local Bills [47] deal with the construction of works, such as harbours, or extend the powers of local authorities or public utilities. There has in recent times been a great decline in the number of local Bills, partly because the purposes they served in the eighteenth and nineteenth centuries (enclosure of commons, construction of railways and canals) have been accomplished, and partly because of the increased use of Public General Acts, Provisional Orders and Special Procedure Orders to effect such purposes more conveniently and cheaply. Personal Bills [47] dealing with family estates are sometimes passed, but this class of Bill is now comparatively rare since their purposes—such as settlements, naturalisation and divorce—are now effected under Public General Acts.

Standing Orders require that full notice shall be given, so that persons affected may come in and oppose.[48] A private Bill is usually introduced by being presented at the table by the Clerk of the Private Bill Office. It is then deemed to have been read a first time. Intricate questions frequently arise as to the *locus standi* of various parties to appear and be heard before the Select Committee. The second reading is the first opportunity the House has to discuss the general principles of the Bill. The Bill usually passes the second reading unopposed or with directions to the Committee to delete or insert certain provisions. When the Bill has passed the second reading it goes either to the Committee on Unopposed Bills or, if opposed at this stage, to a Select Committee. The Select Committee proceeds to hear counsel

---

[46] May, *Parliamentary Practice*, Book III; Jennings, *op. cit.* Chap. 13; O. Cyprian Williams, *The Historical Development of Private Bill Procedure* (1948); Sir Cecil Carr (1950) 66 L.Q.R. 216.

This sketch does not apply to Scottish Bills, for which a special procedure was provided by the Private Legislation Procedure (Scotland) Act 1936; May, *op. cit.* Chap. xl.

[47] " Local " and " Personal " is a House of Lords classification.

[48] *Cf. Edinburgh and Dalkeith Ry.* v. *Wauchope* (1842) 8 Cl. & F. 710.

and witnesses for and against the objects of the Bill, and if it finds that a sufficient case for legislation has been made out, declares the preamble proved.[49] The clauses are then gone through before the contending parties, evidence is taken and arguments of counsel heard, and amendments, if necessary, are made. The Bill, as amended in Committee, is then reported to the House. After third reading, the Bill is sent to the other House.

Although private Bills are subject to a number of formalities that do not apply to other Bills, when they come before either House they are read the same number of times and treated in each stage in a similar way to public Bills. If passed by both Houses, a private Bill receives the Royal Assent in the same way as a public Bill, except that a different form of words is used: *Soit fait comme il est désiré.*

---

[49] In *Pickin* v. *British Railways Board* [1972] 3 W.L.R. 824, the Court of Appeal held that the question whether the court was competent to go behind a private Act of Parliament and investigate whether it had been improperly obtained by the promoters' misleading Parliament, was a triable issue; and if it was proved that there had been an abuse of parliamentary procedure, the court might be under a duty to report the matter to Parliament. And see Mitchell, *Constitutional Law* (2nd ed.) p. 84.

CHAPTER 10

NATIONAL FINANCE AND SCRUTINY OF THE ADMINISTRATION

I. NATIONAL FINANCE [1]

The Crown and the Commons

Erskine May says: " The Sovereign, being the executive power, is charged with the management of all the revenue of the State, and with all payments for the public service. The Crown, therefore, acting with the advice of its responsible ministers, makes known to the Commons the pecuniary necessities of the Government; the Commons, in return, grant such aids or supplies as are required to satisfy these demands; and they provide by taxes, and by the appropriation of other sources of the public income, the ways and means to meet the supplies which they have granted. Thus the Crown demands money, the Commons grant it, and the Lords assent to the grant: but the Commons do not vote money unless it be required by the Crown; nor do they impose or augment taxes, unless such taxation be necessary for the public service, as declared by the Crown through its constitutional advisers." [2]

Four general principles should here be noticed:

(1) a proposal affecting supply for the public service or a charge on the public revenue must be recommended by a Minister (royal recommendation) (" the Crown demands money "). This common law principle is now embodied in Standing Order No. 89, which dates back to 1713.

(2) A proposal to raise or spend public money must be introduced in the House of Commons (" the Commons grant it "). This is part of the custom of Parliament and one of the privileges of the Commons, asserted by resolutions of 1671 and 1678, confirmed in 1860 and 1910 and implied by the Parliament Act 1911. So in the Queen's Speech on the opening, prorogation or dissolution of Parliament, the

---

[1] Erskine May, *Parliamentary Practice* (18th ed. 1971) Chaps. 26–31; Lord Campion, *Introduction to the Procedure of the House of Commons* (3rd ed.) Chap. 8; Sir Ivor Jennings, *Parliament* (2nd ed.) Chap. 9 and Appendix IX; Sir Alexander Johnston, *The Inland Revenue* (1965); *Parliamentary Reform—a survey of recent proposals for the Commons* (Hansard Society, 2nd ed. 1967); K. Bradshaw and D. Pring, *Parliament and Congress* (1972); C. J. Boulton, " Recent Developments in House of Commons Procedure " (1969–70) *Parliamentary Affairs*, p. 61.

[2] May, *op. cit.* p. 676.

Commons are separately addressed when estimates or supply are mentioned; and the principle appears in the enacting formulae of the annual Finance and Appropriation Acts.

(3) Levying money for or to the use of the Crown requires the authority of an Act of Parliament (Bill of Rights 1688). The expenditure of public money also requires parliamentary authority.

(4) The Lords may not *alter* Bills of aids and supplies ("the Lords assent to the grant"), although in theory they may reject them, as any other kind of Bill (subject now to the Parliament Acts). Such Bills include (a) supply to the Crown, becoming a Consolidated Fund Bill, or (b) taxation (Finance Bill). This is similarly a privilege of the Commons, included in the resolutions of 1671 and 1678. Section 6 of the Parliament Act 1911, preserving the Commons' privileges, allows the Commons to choose whether to proceed on the Lords' amendments under the procedure of the Act [3] or under their privileges: in the latter case they may waive their privileges and accept the Lords' amendments.[4]

Public revenue

The national revenue is not solely derived from taxation. The Exchequer derives a certain revenue from the Crown lands, in respect of which and other hereditary Crown revenues Parliament pays over to the Queen a fixed annual sum called the Civil List. In modern times, however, the great bulk of revenue is supplied to the Crown by Parliament for the government of the country. It is the practice to impose some taxes by "permanent Acts" which remain in force until repealed or amended, e.g. stamp duties and death duties, and to impose others by annual Acts, which remain in force for one year only. Thus the annual Finance Act sets out the rates of income tax, customs and excise duties, the collection of which is regulated by permanent Acts such as Income Tax Acts.

All the national revenue of whatever kind goes into the Bank of England, where it is credited to the Exchequer account and is called *the Consolidated Fund*. Before 1787 the various taxes were charged arbitrarily on particular sources of revenue. In that year the younger Pitt established a single Consolidated Fund, and charged public expenditure on it.

Public expenditure

The bulk of public expenditure is authorised by annual Acts

[3] The definition of "Money Bill" in the Parliament Act 1911 is narrower than that for the purposes of Commons procedure.
[4] As in the case of the Inshore Fishery Industry Bill 1946.

("supply services" paid out of "moneys provided by Parliament"), including the armed forces, the civil service and other public services. Permanent Acts cover the Queen's Civil List, and the salaries of judges of the superior courts, the Speaker, the Comptroller and Auditor-General, the Leader of the Opposition and the Parliamentary Commissioner for Administration. These services are charged on "the public revenue" or "public funds" and paid out of the Consolidated Fund or the National Loans Fund. Any surplus left over at the end of the financial year goes automatically by statute to the reduction of the National Debt.[5]

The estimates

The financial year is from April 1 to March 31 (except the income tax year, which is from April 6 to April 5), and does not coincide with the parliamentary session. Every autumn the government departments prepare estimates of their expenditure for the next financial year, based on the policy for each department which has been decided by the responsible Minister with the approval of the Cabinet. The estimates are submitted to the Treasury, which scrutinises them in the interests of economy within the limits of government policy. The Cabinet, which is the umpire in any dispute between the departments and the Treasury, finally settles the estimates. These are presented to the Commons in the spring, divided into classes and votes for the various departments.

The estimates provide the basis for Parliament to authorise specific expenditure by Appropriation Act, and for audit by the Comptroller and Auditor-General.

Supply business

Redress of grievances must come before supply; therefore there must be opportunity for criticism. A fixed number of Supply Days (at present 29) are allotted for the purpose of debating the estimates, excess votes and reports from Select Committees concerning expenditure. They must be completed by August 5, *i.e.* four months from the beginning of the income tax year. After the expiration of the allotted time, remaining estimates are voted on without discussion. The report stage is taken on the last day. From 1621 supply was

---

[5] The National Loans Act 1968 created the National Loans Fund, which replaces the Consolidated Fund for certain purposes. The National Debt is charged on the National Loans Fund, with recourse to the Consolidated Fund. There is a daily balancing of the two funds.

debated in the Committee of Supply, a Committee of the whole House,[6] but since 1967 Supply is taken in the House or the Scottish Grand Committee.

When the estimates are under discussion the debate consists of general criticisms of the conduct or policy of the various Ministers rather than detailed criticisms of the expenditure proposed. Apart from lack of time and of the expert knowledge required to attack the estimates in detail, it is assumed that the government (with its party majority in the House) will win any division. The Opposition are allowed to choose which estimates shall be discussed. If a member wishes to oppose the estimates of a given service, the practice is to do this by moving an amendment to reduce the salary of the Minister in charge by the nominal sum of £100 per annum. If it is not withdrawn it will be defeated, because a division on the estimates is a matter of confidence. Members may not move an increase in the estimates.

The allocation of the sums voted is afterwards embodied in the *Appropriation Act*. The annual Appropriation Act appropriates in detail the application of the amounts to the departments and for the purposes for which they were voted. Similar debates take place on the second and third readings of the Appropriation Bill, which is usually passed in July.

It commonly happens, however, that money is wanted by the departments before the Appropriation Act is passed. Interim statutes called *Consolidated Fund Acts* are therefore passed from time to time, providing votes on account to cover the period from April 1 to the time when the Appropriation Act will be passed; and also providing for supplementary estimates. General debates on relevant government policy take place on the second and third readings of Consolidated Fund Bills. The committee stage, for technical reasons, is usually formal. The annual Appropriation Act (*supra*) following on these deals with the balances of money voted but so far undisposed of, and confirms retrospectively the appropriations made by the Consolidated Fund Acts.[7] The Appropriation Act is itself a final Consolidated Fund Act.

The theory of the Constitution with regard to supply is shown in the special enacting formula of the annual Appropriation Act: "Most

---

[6] The practice of appointing Committees of the whole House for financial business was first employed in the reigns of James I and Charles I, when the Speaker was (or might be) under the influence of the Sovereign. It was continued down to recent times because it enabled all members to take part, but in a less formal atmosphere than a sitting of the House.

[7] The position is further complicated by the fact that the financial year overlaps parliamentary sessions: see the summaries of the annual financial legislation in Campion, *op. cit.* pp. 264–265, and Jennings, *op. cit.* Appendix IV.

Gracious Sovereign, We, Your Majesty's most dutiful and loyal subjects the Commons of the United Kingdom in Parliament assembled, towards making good the supply which we have cheerfully granted to Your Majesty in this Session of Parliament, have resolved to grant unto Your Majesty the sum hereinafter mentioned; and do therefore most humbly beseech Your Majesty that it may be enacted, and be it enacted . . ." etc.

Ways and Means business

The authorisation of ways and means of meeting the supply granted to the Crown was formerly done in the Committee of Supply, another Committee of the whole House, which was abolished in 1967. Near the beginning of the financial year the Chancellor of the Exchequer introduces his " Budget." This consists of: (a) a financial review of the previous year; (b) an estimate of the total amount required for the coming year and proposals (by way of alteration in direct and indirect taxes) for meeting these requirements, and (c) a statement of the government's general financial and economic policy. The biggest item is the standard rate of income tax for the year.

Since 1968–69 the Budget has been introduced into the House, accompanied by a White Paper containing financial explanations and comment in the light of the recent economic situation and probable future developments; and it has then been debated in Standing Committee, the guillotine being imposed.[8] Detailed resolutions are provisionally passed as soon as the Chancellor of the Exchequer has spoken.[9] The Budget debate, mainly on taxation,[10] proceeds on a general resolution, followed by the second reading of the Finance Bill. Constructive amendments on the Finance Bill may be accepted by the Chancellor, because there is no prior consultation of outside interests before the Budget is introduced and there may be technical difficulties in collecting particular taxes. A private member may not propose an increase in any tax, but he may propose a decrease.

When the Budget resolutions have been passed they are embodied in the annual *Finance Act*. This Act contains clauses imposing, renewing or increasing taxes; administrative regulations; and clauses reducing or repealing taxes. Like the Appropriation Act, it must be passed before the summer recess, *i.e.* early August. Supplementary

---

8 In 1969–70 a variation in the new procedure was adopted on account of the general election in June 1970. A Select Committee had suggested in 1965 that if part, at least, of the Finance Bill were taken in Committee, this would produce the greatest single economy in the time spent on the floor of the House: *Third Report from the Select Committee on Procedure* (1964–65) H.C. 276.

9 See Provisional Collection of Taxes Act, *post*, p. 190.

10 Expenditure may be referred to generally, but not in detail.

Budgets and other legislation may be needed during the session to levy money, *e.g.* to increase National Health charges.

The theory of the Constitution with regard to taxation is shown in the special enacting formula of the annual Finance Act: "Most Gracious Sovereign, We, Your Majesty's most dutiful and loyal subjects the Commons of the United Kingdom in Parliament assembled, towards raising the necessary supplies to defray Your Majesty's public expenses, and making an addition to the public revenue, have freely and voluntarily resolved to give and grant unto Your Majesty the several duties hereinafter mentioned; and do therefore most humbly beseech Your Majesty, that it may be enacted, and be it enacted . . ." etc. The Royal Assent is given in the form: *La Reine remercie ses bons sujets, accepte leur bénévolence et ainsi le veult.*

Money Bills

A Finance Bill or other taxing Bill is brought into the House in a Ways and Means resolution, which must be moved before second reading. Standing Order No. 91 provides that a Bill (other than a Bill which is required to be brought in on a Ways and Means resolution) the *main* object of which is the creation of a public charge (*e.g.* expenditure), may either be presented, or brought in on an order of the House, by a Minister; and in either case the creation of the charge need not be authorised by a resolution of the House until the Bill has been read a second time.[11] After the charge has been so authorised, the Bill is proceeded with in the same way as a Bill containing a subsidiary money clause (*infra*). In the usage of the Commons a Bill authorised by the House having the royal recommendation or presented under Standing Order No. 91 is called a "money Bill," and so also in some contexts is a Bill founded on a Ways and Means resolution. A "money Bill" for the purposes of Commons procedure, therefore, is not identical with a "Money Bill" for the purposes of the Parliament Act 1911. A Bill of aids and supplies, such as a Finance Bill, often includes provisions dealing with other subjects. In fact, the Speaker more often than not withholds his certificate under the Parliament Act from a Finance Bill.[12]

Bills containing subsidiary financial clauses

Government Bills whose main object is for other purposes, but which incidentally contain financial clauses, may be introduced in

[11] Consolidated Fund Bills are brought in on Supply resolutions.
[12] *Cf. ante*, p. 109. Among the money Bills which the Speaker has declined to certify was the Bill that became the Finance Act 1911, and which incorporated the provisions of Lloyd George's Budget of 1909 that precipitated the crisis which led to the passing of the Parliament Act 1911.

the ordinary way; but their financial provisions are printed in italics and must be authorised by a resolution of the House, on the motion of a Minister after the second Reading, before they can be considered in Committee.

If a private members' Bill contains a monetary provision, it is printed in italics to indicate that it will need to be covered by a money resolution of the House passed on the recommendation of a Minister, although there is no assurance that a Minister will help.

Where a Bill first introduced into the House of Lords would be incomplete without some financial provision, the latter is left out on third reading in the Lords, and the Bill is sent down to the Commons with blanks to indicate where these provisions have been left out. When the Bill is printed for the Commons the words are put back but enclosed in brackets and underlined, to suggest the sort of financial provision that would be required.[13]

Provisional Collection of Taxes Act 1968

For more than a century before the case of *Bowles* v. *Bank of England* [14] it had been the practice to anticipate the passing of legislation by collecting certain taxes on the authority of resolutions of the Committee of Ways and Means. The legality of so deducting income tax from interest accruing in the Bank of England was successfully challenged by Gibson Bowles M.P. in this case, Parker J. declaring the practice to be a violation of the Bill of Rights. The Provisional Collection of Taxes Act 1913 was therefore passed to legalise the provisional collection of certain taxes within well-defined limits. The law is now consolidated by the Provisional Collection of Taxes Act 1968, which provides that a resolution of the House of Commons continuing, varying or abolishing income tax, purchase tax or duties of customs or excise shall have statutory effect until August 5 if passed in the previous March or April, or for four months if passed at any other time. Such a resolution ceases to have effect unless a Bill relating to the tax is read a second time within twenty-five days.

Securing the legality of public expenditure

The national revenue is paid into the Bank of England to the credit of the Exchequer. Withdrawals are authorised by Consolidated

[13] A Select Committee on Procedure has suggested that Bills with subsidiary financial clauses should be enabled to be introduced into the House of Lords, to help to restore the balance of legislative business: *The Process of Legislation* (1970–71) H.C. 538.

[14] [1913] 1 Ch. 57.

Funds Acts, an Appropriation Act or the National Loans Act. For the purposes of the central government an order under the Royal Sign Manual countersigned by two (Junior) Lords of the Treasury [15] directs the Treasury Commissioners to transfer the moneys granted to the credit of the various government departments. The Treasury Commissioners send an authority to the Comptroller and Auditor-General who, after being satisfied that there is statutory authority for the grant and that all statutory requirements have been complied with, issues a formal direction to the Bank to transfer the money to the account of the Paymaster-General. The latter pays it over to the appropriate departments. The Paymaster-General is a Minister, and his duties as the government's cashier are mainly nominal as they are delegated to the Pay Office of the Treasury. The Comptroller and Auditor-General at the request of the Treasury grants credits on the National Loans Fund for sums payable out of that Fund. These provisions are technical, and not politically important compared with the question of the effectiveness of the control by the Commons over public expenditure.[16]

The Comptroller and Auditor-General

The Comptroller-General of the Exchequer and Auditor-General of the Public Accounts, as his title implies, has two main functions. As Comptroller he must see that no money leaves the Consolidated Fund without statutory authority, and that money which has left the Consolidated Fund is properly applied. As Auditor he audits the accounts of income and expenditure of the government departments, and makes an annual report to the Public Accounts Committee of the Commons. He also examines the accounts of the Consolidated Fund and the National Loans Fund, and reports annually to Parliament.

The Comptroller and Auditor-General's salary is charged on the Consolidated Fund so as to emphasise the non-political nature of his office. He is appointed by letters patent and holds office during good behaviour, being removable only on an address from both Houses.[17] He is the Head of the Exchequer and Audit Department, which has a staff of auditors some of whom are attached to the various government departments. The Department is, of course, closely associated with the Treasury.

---

[15] They are also government " Whips."
[16] *Post*, pp. 192 *et seq.*
[17] Exchequer and Audit Departments Act 1866.

II. SCRUTINY OF THE ADMINISTRATION

It has long been felt that although there is effective legal and parliamentary control over taxation and expenditure, there is inadequate control over the volume of public expenditure. Financial and economic policy is that of the Cabinet, and the party organisation ensures that the Cabinet's proposals will be adopted by Parliament. The Treasury, of which the Chancellor of the Exchequer is the effective head, can only co-ordinate and supervise the other departments within the scope of that policy. For more than a century now there has been a gradual development of a system of Select Committees of the Commons to examine departmental accounts and estimates, and more recently to scrutinise various aspects of the administration.

Public Accounts Committee

This Select Committee was set up in 1861 as part of Gladstone's "cycle of control." It consists of not more than fifteen members appointed at the beginning of each session to examine all appropriation accounts, and it may examine such other accounts laid before Parliament (e.g. of certain public corporations) as it thinks fit (S.O. No. 86). Normally the Committee takes evidence only on accounts commented on by the Comptroller and Auditor-General.[18] It is the custom to elect a member of the Opposition as chairman.

The Public Accounts Committee does not exert much practical control over expenditure, partly because it deals with the accounts of a previous year, and partly because the Commons seldom have time or inclination to debate its reports. The mere existence of the Committee, which cross-examines the chief accounting officer and other senior officers of the departments, nevertheless tends to check proposals for extravagant expenditure. Emphasis has recently shifted from mere accounting to the elimination of waste, better estimating and contracting, and getting value for money.

New presentation of public expenditure

During the 1950s the role of the annual Budget changed. The Budget had come to be regarded as primarily concerned with adjusting the short-term situation in the economy as a whole so as to bring supply and demand into balance in the year in question, but the plan-

---

[18] The Committee and the Comptroller and Auditor-General have in recent years extended their purview to the universities: see *Parliament and Control of University Expenditure* (1967) H.C. 290.

ning of public expenditure can only be done over a longer period. The Plowden Report (1961) [19] emphasised the importance of taking a longer look ahead in planning the economy and estimating expenditure and resources. Its fundamental recommendation was that regular surveys should be made of public expenditure as a whole over a period of years ahead, and in relation to prospective resources. The Treasury began to do this in about 1958 for the Public Expenditure Survey Committee of the Cabinet (PESC) and the civil service. The Commons, however, were not given much of the relevant information, nor had the House adapted its procedure to the new situation.

A new method of presenting detailed information about public expenditure to the Commons was introduced by the Government in 1969.[20] From that time the Government has published a White Paper towards the end of each calendar year, telling Parliament the results of the Government's consideration of the prospect of public expenditure. The White Paper sets out the figures for the whole public sector—including expenditure by local authorities (amounting to nearly one-third), and the capital expenditure of the nationalised industries—for a number of years, showing the likely claims on resources. The first consideration is the order of priorities among objectives, showing their effect on each other. The programmes are broken down by broad areas rather than departmental responsibilities. Each White Paper shows last year's figures, the figures for the year of publication (year 1), and each of the following four years (years 2 to 5). The current and two following years (years 1 to 3) have been decided. The focus of attention is on year 3, which can still be modified. But year 1 is largely over when the House discusses the White Paper, and the preparation of estimates for year 3 is only about a year ahead, so that the degree of commitment for the " focus " year is high. Figures for years 4 and 5 are projections, not decisions. The revenue side is presented at the same time, including projections of receipts from taxation and the trading surpluses of nationalised industries. The new information is an important advance in parliamentary and public discussion of expenditure. The first two-day debate on the first of these White Papers [21] in January 1970 was very thinly attended by members, but it attracted considerable attention in the Press and in industry.

[19] *Control of Public Expenditure*, Cmnd. 1432.
[20] *Public Expenditure: A New Presentation*, Cmnd. 4017.
[21] *Public Expenditure, 1968–69 to 1973–74* (1969) Cmnd. 4234. And see *Public Expenditure to 1975–76* (1971) Cmnd. 4829, which was debated on December 8 and 9, 1971.

Development of " Specialist " Select Committees [22]

The name " Specialist " [23] Committees is given to certain Select Committees of the Commons which have been set up since 1966. to provide an effective machinery for scrutinising the efficiency—not mainly financial—of the administration, without impairing the responsibility of Ministers to Parliament or detracting from the importance of proceedings on the floor of the House.   These Committees are usually composed of about fifteen members.   The government through their majority control their setting-up, terms of reference and abolition. The government also choose the chairman and a majority of the members.   The Committees are not necessarily re-appointed at the beginning of a new session.   They have power to send for persons (especially civil servants), papers and records, and to appoint sub-committees.   Ministers may appear before them.   They have a secretarial staff, and professional and technical advisers.   They may sit in public, at Westminster or locally, and may travel abroad. Their reports may be debated in the House.   The work of the various Committees has come to be co-ordinated by an unofficial liaison group composed of the Chairmen of the Committees, presided over by the chairman of the Public Accounts Committee.   Limiting factors in the number of such Committees include the number of members available, accommodation and staffing.

During the 1960s there was much discussion among Members of Parliament and political scientists about the best method of providing a system of committees to scrutinise the administration that would fit into our system of responsible parliamentary government. There already existed the Select Committees on Statutory Instruments (1944) [24] and Nationalised Industries (1955),[25] and a Select Committee on the Parliamentary Commissioner [26] was set up in 1967 when that official was established.   The modern history may be said to begin

---

[22] *Reports from Select Committee on Procedure* (1964–65) H.C. 303; (1966–67) H.C. 576; *Scrutiny of Public Expenditure and Administration* (1968–69) H.C. 410; *Select Committees of the House of Commons* (1970) Cmnd. 4507.

And see R. S. Lankester, " Specialist Committees in the House of Commons " (1969) XXXVIII *The Table*, p. 64; *The Growth of Parliamentary Scrutiny by Committee*, a symposium by Alfred Morris M.P. and Others (1970); John Mackintosh M.P., *Specialist Committees in the House of Commons: Have they failed?* (University of Edinburgh, 1970); *The Commons in Transition* (ed. Hanson and Crick, 1970); K. C. Wheare, *Government by Committee* (1955); Bernard Crick, *The Reform of Parliament* (2nd ed. 1968); Ronald Butt, *The Power of Parliament* (1970); K. Bradshaw and D. Pring, *Parliament & Congress* (1972); M. Partington, " Parliamentary Committees: Recent Developments " (1969–70) 23 *Parliamentary Affairs* 366; D. R. Shell, " Specialist Select Committees " *ibid.* p. 380; Edmond McGovern (1970) 33 M.L.R. 190.

[23] Some writers prefer the word " Specialised " as the members are not specialists.
[24] *Post*, Chap. 28.
[25] *Post*, Chap. 27.
[26] *Post*, Chap. 29.

with the Report of the Select Committee on Procedure 1964–65. Some Specialist Committees have been "Departmental," that is, concerned with the work of a particular department or departments, e.g. those responsible for Agriculture (1966–69), Science and Technology (1966–67) and Overseas Aid (1969–70). Others are, or have been, " Subject " or " Functional " Committees, e.g. Science and Technology (1966), Race Relations and Immigration (1968) and Scottish Affairs (1968). Subject Committees are now preferred to Departmental Committees. The three last mentioned were re-appointed in the session 1971–72.

Further consideration has been given to making more use of Joint Committees of the two Houses to examine matters that are not controversial in the party political sense. The Select Committee on Procedure 1970–71 [27] supported the proposal that regular use should be made of pre-legislation committees to consider subjects that might later form the basis for legislation; and of post-legislation committees to inquire into difficulties in the application and interpretation of statutes and delegated legislation within a short period after enactment. Both where appropriate might be Joint Committees.

Specialist Committees and the Common Market

The Committee on Procedure [28] has also suggested the need for a Select Committee or a Joint Committee to scrutinise Community delegated legislation,[29] and legislative proposals and other documents from Community institutions; general debates in both Houses on European affairs; the need for both Houses to be kept informed and to scrutinise legislation and legislative proposals of the Communities at every stage; the need to be kept informed of, and the opportunity to debate, proposals for the draft budget and expenditure of the Communities before they are adopted by the Council of Ministers; and to consider what part Select Committees might play in scrutinising and reporting on the policies of the Communities, of other Community governments and of the United Kingdom.

Expenditure Committee

The Select Committee on Procedure 1968–69 proposed a Select Committee on Expenditure to replace and extend the work of the existing Estimates Committee,[30] to consider public expenditure and

---

27 *Select Committee on Procedure: The Process of Legislation* (1970–71) H.C. 538.
28 *Ibid.* and see *Report of Select Committee on Procedure* (1971–72) H.C. 448.
29 And see *post*, Chap. 28.
30 The Select Committee on Estimates was set up in 1912 because the estimates became too complex for the House and the Public Accounts Committee. It was required to examine the estimates presented to the House, and to suggest how the policy

to examine the form of the papers presented to the House. It would have a general sub-committee and various sub-committees. The Public Accounts Committee and the Select Committee on Nationalised Industries would be retained, and the fate of the other Select Committees would be reviewed. These proposals fitted in with general thinking, and something like it would probably have been accepted by the Labour Government. After the general election in 1970 Mr. Whitelaw introduced the Conservative Government's proposals, which were on similar lines.[31] It was recognised that the Chamber must remain the centre of Parliament and the main battleground of political controversy. A broad division was drawn between political controversy in the Chamber and " party non-controversy " in Select Committees. It was not possible to retain all the existing Select Committees and also to have an Expenditure Committee of the kind previously suggested. The new proposals were therefore a compromise. There would be a " dual system " retaining some of the existing committees alongside an Expenditure Committee somewhat larger than the Estimates Committee, which it would replace. The Expenditure Committee would focus its attention on public expenditure rather than on the supply estimates, and would have a wider range. The new committee would not be barred from considering policy behind the figures (as was the Estimates Committee), so Ministers could sometimes give evidence before it. The Expenditure Committee's work would be oriented on the annual White Paper giving five-year projections of public expenditure.

Standing Order No. 87 accordingly provides that there shall be a Select Committee called the Expenditure Committee, consisting of forty-nine members nominated at the beginning of each session. The duties of the Committee are to consider any papers on public expenditure presented to the House of Commons, and such of the estimates as it thinks fit. In particular, the Committee is to consider how, if at all, the policies implied in the figures of expenditure and in the estimates may be carried out more economically, and to examine the form of the papers and of the estimates. The Committee has power to appoint sub-committees.

The Expenditure Committee has a steering sub-committee, whose chairman is a member of the Opposition, and which makes recommendations on the departmental subjects to be tackled. It also has six functional sub-committees of eight members each, viz. Public Ex-

---

implied in them might be carried out more economically. It also considered the form of the estimates. Although looking at past estimates it was concerned with the future, and after 1945 became more interested in policy. The Estimates Committee should not be confused with the Committee of Supply, a Committee of the whole House into which the annual estimates used to be presented for approval.
31 *Select Committees of the House of Commons* (1970) Cmnd. 4507.

penditure (General); Trade and Industry; Employment and Social Services; Defence and External Affairs; Education and Arts; Environment and Home Office.

A Select Committee on Procedure [32] has recommended that the Expenditure Committee should be renamed the Expenditure and Finance Committee, that it should have a Sub-Committee on Taxation and Finance, and that its terms of reference should include: " to consider the existing system of taxation; proposals for major changes in the structure of existing taxes and proposals for new forms of taxation; and to consider the economic implications of different forms of taxation."

CHAPTER 11

PARLIAMENTARY PRIVILEGE [1]

The nature of parliamentary privilege

Privilege, notably freedom from arrest, was originally part of the King's peace. It ensured the attendance of members of the Council, judicial and other public officers, and members of the royal household. From the reign of Henry VIII the Commons as well as the Lords have been left to enforce their own privileges.

Each House exercises certain powers and privileges which are regarded as essential to the dignity and proper functioning of Parliament. The members also have certain privileges, although these exist for the benefit of the House and not for the personal benefit of the members. "As every Court of justice hath laws and customs for its direction," says Coke, "so the High Court of Parliament *suis propriis legibus et consuetudinibus subsistit.* It is *lex et consuetudo parliamenti* that all weighty matters in any Parliament moved concerning the peers of the realm or commons in Parliament assembled, ought to be determined, adjudged and discussed by the course of the parliament, and not by the civil law, nor yet by the common laws of this realm used in more inferior Courts." [2] Erskine May defines parliamentary privilege as "the sum of the peculiar rights enjoyed by each House collectively as a constituent part of the High Court of Parliament,[3] and by members of each House individually, without which they could not discharge their functions, and which exceed those possessed by other bodies or individuals." [4]

Parliamentary privilege is to some extent analogous to royal prerogative; both are exceptional, peculiar and discretionary; and both are part of the common law, not in the sense that they are judge-made, but in the sense that the courts recognise their existence and

---

[1] The chief authority and work of reference on this subject is Erskine May, *Parliamentary Practice* (18th ed. 1971) Chaps. 5–11. See also Anson, *Law and Custom of the Constitution*, Vol. I (5th ed. Gwyer) pp. 153–189, 242–247; Wittke, *Parliamentary Privilege*; Holdsworth, *History of English Law*, Vol. VI, pp. 92–100; Sir Ivor Jennings, *The Law and the Constitution* (5th ed.) pp. 112 *et seq.*; Viscount Kilmuir, *The Law of Parliamentary Privilege* (Athlone Press, 1959); R. F. V. Heuston, *Essays in Constitutional Law* (2nd ed. 1964) Chap. 4; O. Hood Phillips, *Reform of the Constitution* (1970) pp. 75–81.

[2] 4 Inst. 15.

[3] The House of Lords is a court of record, the House of Commons probably not.

[4] May, *op. cit.* p. 64. The power to commit for contempt, however, is not essential to the discharge of its functions; see *post*, p. 207.

198

claim jurisdiction to keep the Crown or the Houses (as the case may be) within the limits so recognised. They differ, however, in that while the royal prerogative is part of the law enforced by the ordinary courts, parliamentary privilege is enforced by each House through its officers. Further, prerogative extends throughout Her Majesty's dominions, while privilege is limited to the United Kingdom.

Privilege is part of " the law and custom of Parliament "—to be collected, says Coke, " out of the rolls of Parliament and other records, and by precedents and continued experience." Some of it has the authority of statute, notably the provision of the Bill of Rights 1688 relating to freedom of speech and debates or proceedings in Parliament. A Bill that concerns the privileges of either House should commence in the House to which it relates.

I. THE PRIVILEGES OF THE COMMONS

The privileges of the Commons have been described as " the sum of the fundamental rights of the House and of its individual Members as against the prerogatives of the Crown, the authority of the ordinary courts of law and the special rights of the House of Lords." [5]   Some are available against the Crown, some against the House of Lords, and others against the citizen. They are much more important at the present day than the privileges of the Lords owing to the predominant position attained by the Commons, and there have been few disputes relating to the Lords' privileges (except in relation to the Commons) in modern times.

These privileges are commonly divided into two classes, namely, those specifically claimed by the Speaker at the opening of a new Parliament and those not so claimed, though the fact of a privilege being claimed by the Speaker carries with it no superior force. Indeed, some of those specifically claimed by the Speaker have been confirmed or limited by statute. The " ancient and undoubted " privileges formally claimed by the Speaker since the sixteenth century are: (i) freedom of speech in debate; (ii) freedom from arrest; (iii) access of the Commons to the Crown through the Speaker [6]; and (iv) that the Crown will place the best construction on the deliberations of the Commons. (This last is not now important.) The Lord Chancellor, on behalf of the Sovereign, declares that they are " most readily granted and confirmed." The privileges not specifically claimed by the Speaker are: (i) the right of the House to regulate

---

5 Redlich and Ilbert, *Procedure of the House of Commons*, Vol. I, p. 46.
6 Privy Councillors have a customary right of individual access, but modern convention requires that the Sovereign should take political advice from Ministers only.

its own composition; (ii) the right to take exclusive cognisance of matters arising within the House; (iii) the right to punish members and strangers for breach of privilege and contempt; (iv) the right of impeachment [7]; and (v) the right to control finance and initiate financial legislation.[8]

1. Freedom of speech and debate

Freedom of speech and debate is the essential attribute of every free legislature, and may be regarded as inherent in the constitution of Parliament (*Haxey's Case*, 1397).[9] Strode's Act 1512 provided " that all suits, etc. against all persons of that particular or any other Parliament . . . for any Bill, or speaking . . . of any matter concerning the Parliament be of none effect." The Stuart lawyers regarded the Act as establishing freedom of debate, but *Strode's Case*,[10] out of which it arose, only concerned indictment in an inferior court for introducing a Bill into Parliament. Sir Thomas More, as Speaker, petitioned Henry VIII for freedom of speech in 1523, but did not consider it a matter of right. From the beginning of Elizabeth I's reign freedom of speech has been regularly claimed as a right,[11] although that monarch did not always respect it. In *R. v. Eliot, Hollis and Valentine* (1629) [12] three members were imprisoned and fined by the Court of King's Bench for " seditious words " spoken in the House, the Court holding that Strode's Act was not a public Act. The Houses in 1641 and 1667 passed resolutions against this judgment, and it was reversed by the Lords on a writ of error in 1668. After this case no legal proceedings were ever taken by the Crown for words spoken in the House.

The Bill of Rights (1688) declares that " the freedom of speech and debates or proceedings in Parliament ought not to be impeached or questioned in any Court or place out of Parliament " (Art. 9). What amounts to a " proceeding in Parliament " has never been defined either by the courts or the Commons. The opinion of the Committee of Privileges in the *Strauss* case (1958) [13] that it covers

---

[7] See Chap. 6.
[8] See Chap. 10.
[9] Rot. Parl., iii, 434 (petition to Parliament for curtailment of King's household expenses). See Taswell-Langmead, *Constitutional History* (11th ed. Plucknett) pp. 174–175, 195.
[10] Taswell-Langmead, *op. cit.* pp. 247–249, 377–378.
[11] J. E. Neale, " The Commons' Privilege of Free Speech in Parliament " *Tudor Studies* (ed. Seton-Watson, 1924).
[12] 3 St.Tr. 294; Taswell-Langmead, *op. cit.* pp. 377–378, 390. The members were also charged with an assault on the Speaker; see *post*, p. 206.
[13] *Infra*. And see *Att.-Gen. of Ceylon* v. *De Livera* [1963] A.C. 103 (P.C.): offer of bribe to member acting in that capacity.

everything said or done by a Member of Parliament *in his capacity as a Member* is surely too wide. The expression obviously covers speaking in debate or on a question and voting in the House on parliamentary business; and it includes action taken by the officers of the House in pursuance of its orders.[14] In *Church of Scientology of California* v. *Johnson-Smith* [15] it was held that parliamentary privilege prevented the reading of reports of parliamentary debates in court in order to prove malice in an action against a member for libel uttered in the course of a television interview. Members are privileged from prosecution under the Official Secrets Acts for disclosures made in the House, and they may not be required to divulge in a court of inquiry the sources of secret information used by them to frame questions in the House, although they should use their immunity with discretion.[16] It has been held to be contrary to Article 9 of the Bill of Rights to impugn the validity of the report of a Select Committee, especially when it has been accepted as valid by the House by being printed in its Journal.[17]

Communications with members

In the *Strauss* case (1958) H. G. Strauss M.P. wrote a letter to a Minister reflecting on the method of disposing of scrap cable by the London Electricity Board (a public corporation administering a nationalised industry). The Minister sent a copy to the chairman of the Board. The Board thereupon instructed their solicitors to commence a libel action against Mr. Strauss if he refused to withdraw his statements. Mr. Strauss raised a question of privilege. The House sought the opinion of the Privy Council on the question whether the House, if it treated the issue of the writ as a breach of privilege, would be acting contrary to the Parliamentary Privilege Act 1770 (which provides that any person may at any time bring any action in any court against any member of either House of Parliament, and that no such action shall be impeached on the ground of privilege). Their opinion was that the Act applies only to proceedings against members in their private capacity, *e.g.* actions for debt, and does not affect the privileges of Parliament, as to which their opinion had not been sought (*Re Parliamentary Privilege Act* 1770).[18] The House decided by a small majority that Strauss's letter was not a proceeding

---

[14] *Bradlaugh* v. *Gossett* (1884) 12 Q.B.D. 271; *post*, p. 206.

[15] [1972] 1 Q.B. 522.

[16] *Duncan Sandys* case (1938) H.C.Pap. 173; (1939) H.C.Pap. 101. Interrogation under the Acts now generally requires the permission of a Secretary of State: Official Secrets Act 1939, s. 1.

[17] *Dingle* v. *Associated Newspapers Ltd.* [1960] 2 Q.B. 405.

[18] [1958] A.C. 331; (1958) Cmnd. 431; note by E. C. S. Wade in (1958) C.L.J. 134.

in Parliament, and that the Electricity Board and their solicitors had therefore not committed a breach of privilege.[19] The action for libel was not in fact brought, but the Minister held an independent inquiry which exonerated the Board.[20]

The Speaker later indicated that parliamentary privilege under the Bill of Rights would cover a letter written by a member to a Minister in response to his invitation made during a parliamentary debate, e.g. supplying information arising out of a question on the order paper.[21]

On the other hand, it was held in Rivlin v. Bilainkin[22] that a defamatory statement in a letter from B to a Member of Parliament concerning the conduct of B's former wife was not protected by parliamentary privilege, as it was not connected with any proceedings in Parliament.

Right to exclude strangers

The Commons have always exercised the right to exclude strangers, that is, persons who are not members or officers of the House. This may be regarded both as a corollary to the principle of freedom of speech, and as necessary for the orderly conduct of business where there is a danger of disorderly interruption. If any member " spies strangers," the Speaker must put the question " that strangers do withdraw." The question is decided by vote, without debate. The resolution if carried operates for the rest of the day's sitting, but does not apply to members of the House of Lords. The Speaker also has the power of ordering strangers to withdraw.

The House may further resolve that the remainder of the day's sitting be a *secret session*, in which case it would be a contempt even for a member to disclose anything said or done unless the House resolves otherwise.[23]

---

19 (1958) 430 H.C.Deb. col. 208; *cf. Fifth Report of the Committeee of Privileges, Session 1956–57.* See S. A. de Smith, " Parliamentary Privilege and the Bill of Rights " (1958) 21 M.L.R. 465; D. Thompson, " Letters to Ministers and Parliamentary Privilege " [1959] P.L. 10.

20 (1958) Cmnd. 605. One difficulty in the *Strauss* case was that the matter concerned a public corporation in its day-to-day administration for which the Minister was not responsible; see *post*, Chap. 27. The common law defence of " qualified privilege " in tort would protect members and constituents who communicate under a duty or common interest, in the absence of malice: *R.* v. *Rule* [1937] 2 K.B. 375 (letter from constituent to M.P. about conduct of police officer and magistrate); *Koolman-Darnley* v. *Gunter, The Times*, April 19, 1967 (C.A.) (letter from Minister to M.P.); *Beach* v. *Freeson* [1972] 1 Q.B. 14 (letter from M.P. to Lord Chancellor and the Law Society). •

21 591 H.C.Deb. col. 811.

22 [1953] 1 Q.B. 485.

23 During the war this procedure was reinforced by Defence Regulations.

Right to restrain publication of reports of proceedings

This is another corollary of the privilege of freedom of speech. The publication of parliamentary debates was forbidden by the House in the seventeenth century. Members at that time desired secrecy of debate to protect themselves from the Crown, and they later desired it to protect themselves from their constituents. Since the case of *Miller* (1771) the Commons have ceased to enforce the orders against the publication of reports of debates, although it was not until after the Reform Act 1832 that reporters' galleries were provided. The publishers of newspapers are, however, liable to be punished for *mala fide* reports.

The series of unofficial reports of parliamentary debates known as *Hansard* from the name of the original publisher, began in 1803. The " House of Commons Debates " have been an official publication of the House since 1909, and are still called " Hansard " although that family is no longer associated with them.[24]

Parliamentary papers

It had long been established that immunity from judicial proceedings attached to a petition containing defamatory matter and circulated only among Members of Parliament (*Lake* v. *King* (1668))[25]; but it was held in *Stockdale* v. *Hansard* (1839)[26] that an order of either House authorising the publication of papers outside Parliament did not render the publisher immune from liability for libel. The latter decision was correct but inconvenient, and it was nullified by the Parliamentary Papers Act 1840. Section 1 provides that proceedings, criminal or civil, against persons for the publication of papers, reports, etc. printed *by order* of either House of Parliament are to be stayed. Section 2 provides that proceedings are to be stayed when commenced in respect of a correct *copy* of an authorised paper, report, etc. These provisions confer what in the law of tort is called " absolute privilege," *i.e.* immunity from judicial proceedings for libel. Section 3 provides that in proceedings for printing any *extract from or abstract of* an authorised paper, report, etc., it is a defence to show that such extract or abstract was published *bona fide* and without malice.[27] This in effect confers " qualified privilege," *i.e.* immunity from judicial proceedings if publication was in good faith and in the absence of

[24] *Cf.* The official report of proceedings contained in *Votes and Proceedings*.
[25] 1 Wms.Saund. 131.
[26] 9 A. & E. 1; *post*, p. 215.
[27] In *Dingle* v. *Associated Newspapers Ltd.* ([1960] 2 Q.B. 405) this defence was applied to an extract from the report of a Select Committee of the House of Commons. Qualified privilege attaches at common law to fair and accurate, although unauthorised, reports of parliamentary proceedings; *Wason* v. *Walter* (1868) L.R. 4 Q.B. 73 (*The Times* report of House of Lords debate).

malice, such as spite or improper motive.[28] The Act declares and enacts that nothing therein affects the privileges of Parliament (s. 4). A member would not be liable if he *bona fide* published an extract from a parliamentary debate for the information of his constituents (*Davison* v. *Duncan* (1887)).[29]

2. Freedom from arrest

Freedom from *civil* arrest was in former times an important privilege necessary for the proper functioning of Parliament, because arrest was often part of the process for commencing civil proceedings by compelling the appearance of the defendant before the court, and also of distress, that is, enforcing a money judgment. Owing to reforms in civil procedure in the nineteenth century, and the abolition of imprisonment for debt by the Debtors Act 1869, this privilege has lost most of its importance and only applies to a few cases, *e.g.* attachment for disobeying a court order for the payment of money.[30] The privilege lasted during a session of Parliament and forty days before and after; and it applied also where Parliament was dissolved or prorogued (*Goudy* v. *Dunscombe*).[31] It formerly covered the servants and property of members, but it had come to be abused to such an extent that it was confined by statute in the eighteenth century to the persons of members.[32]

The privilege of freedom from arrest was never claimed by the Commons in cases of treason, felony (arrestable offence) or breach of the peace. In 1763 the Commons resolved that the privilege did not apply to seditious libel (a misdemeanour or non-arrestable offence), although the member concerned—the notorious John Wilkes—had been released by the King's Bench on the ground of privilege. It does not cover acts prejudicial to the public safety or the defence of the realm under statutory Defence Regulations.[33]

When a Member of Parliament commits a crime he is arrested like anyone else,[34] and if he is convicted the court must notify the Speaker. The papers are then laid before the House at their request, and the

---

[28] *Mangena* v. *Wright* [1909] 2 K.B. 958; *cf. Mangena* v. *Lloyd* (1908) 99 L.T. 824 (protection does not extend to headlines that are not part of the report).

[29] 7 E. & B. 229; *cf. R.* v. *Creevey* (1813) 1 M. & S. 273 (publication by a member in a newspaper of a single defamatory Parliamentary speech for the purpose of injuring an individual).

[30] See *Stourton* v. *Stourton* [1963] P. 302; *post*, pp. 213, 217.

[31] (1847) 1 Exch. 430.

[32] Parliamentary Privilege Acts 1700, 1703, 1737 and 1770.

[33] (1939–40) H.C.Pap. 164 (Re Captain Ramsey M.P.); it would have been otherwise if he had been detained for words spoken in the House.

[34] But as to a crime committed in the House, see *post*, p. 206.

member may be expelled. A member who is imprisoned by order of a court has no special privileges.[35]

3. Right of the House to regulate its own composition

This privilege covers: (i) the filling of casual vacancies, (ii) the determination of disputed election returns, (iii) the determination of legal disqualifications of persons returned to Parliament, and (iv) expulsion of members who are unfit to sit. These powers are exercised within the limits left by statute.

(i) *Filling casual vacancies.* The Speaker issues a warrant for the issue of a writ for an election to fill a casual vacancy.[36]

(ii) *Determination of disputed elections.* As has been seen, the right of the Commons to decide questions of disputed election returns was established as a result of the case of *Goodwin* v. *Fortescue* (1604),[37] and was exercised until the Parliamentary Elections Act 1868. The Representation of the People Act 1949, which re-enacts with amendments the provisions of the Act of 1868 relating to election petitions, leaves nominally intact the privileges of the Commons, who in practice give effect to the findings of election courts.

(iii) *Determination of legal disqualifications.* The House retains the right to determine of its own motion whether a person, who has otherwise been properly elected, is legally disqualified from sitting. If the House holds that the person is disqualified it will declare the seat vacant, and may refuse to admit him or may expel him if he has already been admitted.[38]

(iv) *Expulsion of members who are unfit to serve.* The House may also expel a member who, although not subject to any legal disability, is in its opinion unfit to serve as a member. This is commonly done when a court notifies the Speaker that a member has been convicted of a serious criminal offence. The House cannot prevent an expelled member from being re-elected, as happened several times in the case of John Wilkes between 1769 and 1774, but it can refuse to allow him to take his seat. Similar principles apply to expulsion for breach of privilege or contempt (*Allighan's* case).[39]

---

35 (1970–71) H.C. 185. This report of the Committee of Privileges arose out of the case of Miss Bernadette Devlin, M.P., who was sentenced to six months' imprisonment in 1970 by a court in Northern Ireland.

36 *Cf. ante*, p. 157.

37 2 St.Tr. 91; *ante*, p. 162.

38 The House may seek the opinion of the Privy Council: *e.g.* Re *MacManaway* [1951] A.C. 161.

39 *Post*, p. 208.

4. Exclusive right to regulate its own proceedings

The courts must presume that so august an assembly as the House of Commons discharges its functions lawfully and properly. They will therefore not take cognisance of matters arising within the walls of the House, and they will accept the interpretation put by the Commons upon a statute affecting their internal proceedings.

In *Bradlaugh* v. *Gossett* (1884) [40] Charles Bradlaugh, an atheist who had been elected as member for Northampton, brought an action in the High Court against the Serjeant-at-Arms for an injunction to restrain him from excluding him by force from the House of Commons, and a declaration that the order of the House preventing him from taking the oath was void. The Court gave judgment for the Serjeant-at-Arms on the ground that the privilege of the Commons to regulate its own *internal* proceedings—even where the application of the Parliamentary Oaths Act 1866 was involved—precluded the courts from inquiring into the question. The matter would have been different, said Stephen J., if the Commons had allowed Bradlaugh to sit, and had then purported by resolution to protect him against any statutory penalties at the instance of a common informer to which he might at that time have been liable *in the courts*.

There are dicta by Lord Ellenborough in *Burdett* v. *Abbott* (1811) [41] and by Stephen J. in *Bradlaugh* v. *Gossett* (*supra*) [42] to the effect that the privilege does not cover crimes or breach of the peace committed within the House. Stephen J. in the latter case suggested that the accused in *R.* v. *Eliot, Hollis and Valentine* [43] might have been properly charged in a separate indictment with assaulting the Speaker in the House. Apart from *Eliot's* case no charge against a member for committing a criminal act in Parliament has been heard in the ordinary courts. The answer may depend on whether the act would be regarded as part of the proceedings of the House, and generally a member's contribution to those proceedings is limited to speech or writing.[44] In any event the House can always waive its privileges, including the privilege against arrest in the House, and that is probably what it would do if, for example, one member killed or wounded another during a debate.[45] In *R.* v. *Graham-Campbell,*

---

[40] 12 Q.B.D. 271. See also *Clarke* v. *Bradlaugh* (1881) 7 Q.B.D. 38; *Bradlaugh* v. *Clarke* (1883) App.Cas. 354; *Att.-Gen.* v. *Bradlaugh* (1885) 14 Q.B.D. 667. For the background, see W. L. Arnstein, *The Bradlaugh Case* (1965).
[41] 14 East 1, 128; *post*, p. 215.   [42] 12 Q.B.D. 283.
[43] (1629) 3 St.Tr. 294.   [44] May, *op. cit.* pp. 87–88.
[45] Spencer Percival, the Prime Minister, was shot dead by a madman, John Bellingham, in the lobby of the House of Commons in 1812. During question time in January 1972 Miss Bernadette Devlin M.P. called the Home Secretary a " hypocritical liar " and assaulted him, pulling his hair and knocking off his spectacles. The Speaker called the Orders of the Day before members had the opportunity of raising a question of privilege, and no extra-parliamentary proceedings were taken.

ex p. Herbert (1935) [46] the Divisional Court upheld the refusal of the Chief Metropolitan Magistrate for want of jurisdiction to try alleged breaches of a Licensing Act by the Kitchen Committee of the House; but in any event the Court would probably have been prepared to hold that the Licensing Acts do not apply to the House of Commons, which is part of a royal palace.

5. Power to punish for breach of privilege or contempt

Each House has power to enforce its *privileges* and to punish those —whether members or strangers—who infringe them. Each House also has power (this is one of its privileges) to punish members or strangers for *contempt*. Strictly speaking, " privileges "—and therefore breaches of them—are specific, whereas what constitutes " contempt " is not defined but is determinable by the House. *Contempts* generally are offences against the authority or dignity of the House, such as defamatory or disrespectful writings or statements about the House or its members as such, disobedience to orders of the House, or obstructions to the business or officers of the House. Offences against the authority or dignity of the House cannot be enumerated, the power to punish for contempt being discretionary. An act may be treated as a contempt even though there is no precedent of the offence. A breach of privilege is also a contempt, but a contempt is not necessarily a breach of privilege. Absence of wrongful intent, the truth of derogatory words, or ignorance of the facts does not exonerate, although it may affect the degree of punishment. [47]

The power to *punish* for contempt (as distinct from the ejection of persons who interrupt the proceedings), which has been exercised at least since the middle of the sixteenth century, is a judicial rather than a legislative power and not *necessary* to enable a legislature to function. The power is inherent in the Houses of the British Parliament for the historical reason that they are part of the High Court of Parliament and have been regarded as superior courts. [48] There is a strong argument for conferring the power of punishment on the courts, especially as regards the committal or other punishment of strangers for things said or done outside the House.

[46] [1935] 1 K.B. 594.

[47] *Cf.* contempt of court: Administration of Justice Act 1960, ss. 11, 12; reversing *R. v. Odhams Press, ex p. Att.-Gen.* [1967] 1 Q.B. 73.

[48] *R. v. Richards, ex p. Fitzpatrick and Browne* (1955) 92 C.L.R. 157 (Australian House of Representatives has the same privileges by statute). *Cf. Kielley v. Carson* (1842) 4 Moo.P.C. 63 (although colonial legislature can protect itself, *e.g.* by expelling those who disturb its proceedings, it cannot at common law punish for contempt); *Fenton v. Hampton* (1858) 11 Moo.P.C. 347.

Examples of breach of privilege and contempt

Without attempting to distinguish in the various instances between breach of privilege and contempt, we may give some further examples of these offences drawn from the parliamentary precedents. They include misconduct by strangers in the presence of either House; disobedience to the rules or wishes of either House; publication of false or perverted reports of debates (although with regard to the Commons, this is strictly an aggravation of breach of privilege in publishing reports at all); summoning a member as witness or juror (but the House usually allows a subpoena to be served outside the precincts); molesting a member of the House while he is going to or from it; bribery of a member (this would be contempt both by the member accepting and by the person giving the bribe); intimidation of members, or putting pressure on a member to execute his duties in a certain way (*W. J. Brown's* case, 1947) [49]; molesting or taking judicial proceedings against officers of either House in connection with their official conduct; obstructing or molesting witnesses summoned to either House or a committee thereof.

In *Allighan's* case (1947) [50] Allighan, a member, wrote a newspaper article stating that confidential information relating to parliamentary party meetings was conveyed by M.P.s to newspapers, partly for payment and partly under the influence of drink. The Committee for Privileges found the general statement untrue, but there were two exceptions—Allighan himself and another member who turned out to be Walkden. The House resolved that: (i) in writing the article Allighan was guilty of a " gross contempt " (it would still have been contempt even if the facts stated were true); (ii) he was guilty of " grave contempt " in the manner in which he answered the Committee for Privileges; and (iii) he was guilty of " dishonourable conduct " in accepting payment for disclosing the confidential information. Allighan was expelled from the House. The editor was summoned to the bar of the House: he apologised, was found guilty of " gross contempt " and reprimanded. The case is notable, first, because it recognises private *party* meetings—at least in the Palace of Westminster, during the parliamentary session—held to discuss matters which are before, or to come before, Parliament; and, secondly, because the House claimed to punish " dishonourable conduct " that is neither breach of privilege nor contempt. In *Walkden's* case (1947),[51] which arose out of the above, Walkden was found guilty of " dis-

---

[49] *W. J. Brown's* case (paid secretary of trade union) (1947) H.C.Pap. 118; and note by O. Hood Phillips in (1947) 10 M.L.R. 420.

[50] H.C.Pap. 138; 443 H.C.Deb., 5s., 1096–1200. See note by O. Hood Phillips in (1948) 11 M.L.R. 214.

[51] 443 H.C.Deb., 5s., 1200–1231; 445 H.C.Deb., 5s., 1095–1159. See note by O. Hood Phillips in (1948) 11 M.L.R. 216.

honourable conduct " and was reprimanded. Many members thought that the House had no power to punish for dishonourable conduct by itself. The House later passed a resolution that if any member was guilty of corruptly accepting payment for the disclosure of confidential information on matters to be proceeded with in Parliament, the person who *offered* such payment should incur the " grave displeasure " of the House, and the House would take such action as it might think fit.

There have been a number of instances in recent years of the House complaining of contempt by journalists and others, although it is sometimes content with an apology at the bar of the House and often takes no action at all. Many such affronts to its dignity partake more of the nature of inaccurate and injudicious criticism than attempts to obstruct the proper functioning of the House. An example is the case of Junor (1957), where Junor published an article criticising Members of Parliament for not having protested against the over-generous petrol ration allotted by statutory order to political parties in the constituencies at the time of the Suez crisis: members were condemned for failing, through self-interest, to protest at the unfair discrimination in their own favour. The House resolved that this was " a serious contempt," but in view of Junor's apology at the bar of the House no further action was taken.[52]

In 1969 a meeting of a sub-committee of the Select Committee on Education and Science hearing evidence at Essex University on the relations between students and their universities, had to adjourn to a private room because of persistent interruption by members of the audience. The House resolved that this was a contempt, but decided not to exercise its penal jurisdiction.[53].

Procedure on complaint of a matter of privilege

A member, having given notice to the Speaker, is allowed twenty-four hours in which to raise the matter in the House.[54] If the Speaker rules that there is a prima facie case of privilege or contempt, the matter is usually referred to the Committee of Privileges. If he rules that there is no prima facie case, the member may still move that it be referred to the Committee of Privileges, but the motion then has no priority over other business.

The Committee of Privileges is a sessional Select Committee first set up in 1909. The Leader of the House is chairman, and the Law

[52] The scene is described in *The Times*, January 25, 1957.
[53] *Second Report from the Committee of Privileges* (1968–69) H.C. 308; 782 H.C.Deb. April 28, 1969, cols. 951–982.
[54] Before 1959 a question of privilege had to be raised at the earliest opportunity, which may explain the trivial nature of some of the issues raised: *Select Committee on Procedure* (1959) H.C. No. 92, para. 49.

Officers are members. The Committee has power to summon members or strangers before it. Refusal to appear or to answer, or knowingly to give false answers, is itself a contempt. The Committee's recommendations are reported to the House. The House's decision does not necessarily agree with the Committee's, although it will often do so with modifications.

Methods of punishment

(a) *Expulsion* [55] of a member is regarded rather as a declaration of unfitness than a punishment. It causes a vacancy; but as we have said, the Commons cannot prevent his re-election, although they can refuse to let him take his seat if re-elected. The Commons admitted John Wilkes in 1774 after he had been expelled and re-elected several times. Allighan, who was expelled in 1947, did not seek re-election.

(b) *Imprisonment* of a member or stranger. The former is committed to the Clock Tower; the latter is handed over by the Serjeant-at-Arms to one of Her Majesty's prisons. The warrant is drawn up by the Speaker on the order of the House, and is executed by the Serjeant-at-Arms who may use necessary force and may call on the assistance of the Metropolitan Police. Imprisonment (or " committal ") by the Commons is during the pleasure of the House, but cannot last beyond the end of the session, after which the prisoner would be entitled to release on habeas corpus. The House may, however, re-commit in the next session, as they did in the case of one Grissell in 1880.

(c) *Reprimand* and (d) *Admonition*, the mildest form. In both these forms the Speaker addresses the offender, who is at the bar of the House either in the custody of or attended by the Serjeant-at-Arms; except that a member (unless he is in the custody of the Serjeant) is reprimanded or admonished standing in his place.

The House of Commons has not imposed a fine since *White's Case* (1666), and it is doubtful whether it has the power to do so owing to the uncertainty whether it is a court of record. The power was denied by Lord Mansfield in *R. v. Pitt* and *R. v. Mead*.[56] The House of Lords, as a court of record, has frequently imposed fines.

6. Proposals for reform [57]

A Select Committee on Parliamentary Privilege was appointed in 1966 to review the law of parliamentary privilege as it affects the

55 See Enid Campbell, " Expulsion of Members of Parliament " (1971) 21 U.T.L.J. 15.
56 3 Burr. 1355.
57 *Report from the Select Committee on Parliamentary Privilege* (1967) H.C. 34. And see C. Seymour-Ure, " Proposed Reforms of Parliamentary Privilege: Assessment in the Light of Recent Cases " (1970) XXIII *Parliamentary Affairs* 221.

House of Commons and the procedure by which cases of privilege are raised and dealt with in the House, and to report whether any changes in the law or practice were desirable. The Committee reported in 1967, recommending extensive changes which would meet some of the criticisms that have been made. The first recommendation was that the expression " parliamentary privilege " should cease to be used; that the House should speak of its " rights and immunities," and of " contempt" rather than " breach of privilege." In this the Committee seem to have gone too far to avoid giving the impression that members are, or desire to be, a " privileged class " for, as we have seen, " privileges " are capable of being precisely defined whereas the subject-matter of " contempt " is not.

The other main recommendations were that: (1) the House should exercise its penal jurisdiction as sparingly as possible, and only when the House is satisfied that to exercise it is essential for the reasonable protection of the House, its members or officers from obstruction or substantial interference with the performance of its functions; (2) in the ordinary case where a member has a remedy in the courts, for example in defamation, he should not be permitted to invoke the penal jurisdiction of the House; (3) trivial complaints should be dismissed summarily without investigation; (4) the truth, or reasonable belief in the truth, of allegations should be taken into account in considering whether contempt has been committed; (5) legislation should be passed to extend and clarify the scope of the defences of absolute and qualified privilege available in the courts to actions brought against Ministers and others; for example, absolute privilege should cover things said or done in the Chamber or during proceedings (within the precincts) of a committee of the House, documents authorised by the House, questions and notices of motion, and communications between members and certain other persons (the decision of the House in the *Strauss* case to be reversed); while qualified privilege (which is a defence only in the absence of malice) would cover other communications connected with a member's parliamentary functions; (6) legislation should abolish impeachment, which can only be initiated by the Commons and has been regarded as obsolete since the early nineteenth century; (7) the rules regarding the admission of the public to the House and to committees, the reporting of proceedings of the House and of committees, and the publication of evidence given before Select Committees should be modified; (8) (a) complaints of contempt should no longer be made to the Speaker in the Chamber, except in the case of improper or disorderly conduct taking place in the Chamber itself or a gallery or lobby; but a member should raise his complaint as promptly as is reasonably practicable to the Clerk to the Committee of Privileges (to be called

the " Select Committee of House of Commons Rights "); (b) the
Committee, usually acting through a small sub-committee, would decide
the preliminary question whether there is a prima facie case to justify
full investigation by the Committee; (c) if the matter is fully investigated the Committee (instead of the Leader of the House, as now)
should recommend to the House the appropriate penalty; (9) persons
against whom a complaint is made should be entitled to attend, and to
apply for representation by a lawyer or any other person; and the Committee should be able to permit, or refuse permission for, the calling of
witnesses, with the attendant rights of examination, cross-examination
and re-examination, and of making submissions; (10) legislation should
enable the Committee to authorise legal aid; and (11) legislation
should empower the House of Commons to impose fines and fixed
periods of imprisonment.

These recommendations not only go a long way to meet the
criticisms of parliamentary privilege and the manner in which it is
enforced by the House of Commons, but (if adopted) they should also
make conflicts between the House and the courts less likely.

II. The privileges of the Lords

Privileges of the House

The House of Lords has seldom come into conflict either with
the Sovereign or with the courts in respect of its privileges. The
juridical nature of the privileges of the House of Lords is similar to
that of the privileges of the House of Commons, and strictly both are
parts of the privileges of Parliament. The Lords passed a resolution
in 1704 declaring that neither House has power to create for itself
new privileges not warranted by the known laws and customs of
Parliament, and the Commons assented.[58]

(1) The power to declare the law with regard to its own composition, and to determine the validity of the creation of new peerages
(*Wensleydale Peerage Case*).[59]

(2) The exclusive right to regulate its own internal proceedings.

(3) The power to commit for breach of privilege or contempt for

---

[58] 14 Commons Journals 555.
[59] (1856) 5 H.L.C. 958. The Lord Chancellor, Lord Cranworth, had advised the Prime
Minister, Palmerston, that the creation of a life peerage was legal. " By an
unfortunate, or as some will think, a fortunate, accident, Baron Parke was laid up
with an attack of gout, and was unable to take his seat on the first day of the
session, which otherwise he certainly would have done " (*Memoirs of Duke of
Argyll*, ii, 11). Lord Lyndhurst then raised the matter as a question of privilege
to be dealt with in the Committee of Privileges. Otherwise, he argued, it would
be perfectly legal for the Crown to give patents of nobility to every man in a
company of soldiers, and send them to the House of Peers.

a definite period (*Lord Shaftesbury's Case* (1673)).[60] Where no period is fixed, the person committed is released when Parliament is either prorogued or dissolved.

(4) The power to summon the judges for advice on points of law.

(5) The power to issue a warrant for the release of a peer who is improperly arrested.

Until the Criminal Justice Act 1948 the House of Lords had the power to try peers and peeresses for treason and felony. In theory it still has power to try impeachments instituted by the Commons.

Personal privileges of Peers

These include:

(1) Freedom from civil arrest, that is, except in cases of treason, felony (arrestable offence) or refusal to give security to keep the peace (*Earl of Lonsdale* v. *Littledale* (1793)[61]; *Duke of Newcastle* v. *Morris* (1870)[62]). The person of a peer (whether a Lord of Parliament or not) is by custom and statute[63] " for ever sacred and inviolable " during and for a period before and after a session. The privilege is not now of much importance since the abolition of arrest for debt and as a mesne process in civil cases; but it was held in *Stourton* v. *Stourton*[64] that a peer was privileged from attachment by a court for failing to comply with a court order in matrimonial proceedings. Scarman J. thought the privilege probably applied whether or not Parliament was sitting.

(2) Freedom of speech in Parliament. This privilege is similar to that of the Commons.

III. Conflicts between the Commons and the Courts concerning Privilege

The courts cannot interfere with the decision of either House where any of its undoubted privileges are infringed. On the other hand, neither House can create new privileges. The controversial question is, whether the courts or the House has jurisdiction to decide whether an alleged privilege exists. The conflict between the Commons and the courts on this question has come to a head in two famous pairs of cases—*Ashby* v. *White* and *Paty's Case* at the beginning of the

---

0 1 Mod.Rep. 144. *Cf. Stockdale* v. *Hansard* (1839) 9 A. & E. 1, *per* Lord Denham at p. 127.
1 2 Anst. 356.
2 L.R. 4 H.L. 661.
3 Parliamentary Privilege Acts 1700 and 1703. The privilege extends, or extended, to the servants of peers.
4 [1963] P. 302.

eighteenth century, and *Stockdale* v. *Hansard* and the *Case of the Sheriff of Middlesex* in the first half of the nineteenth century.

In *Ashby* v. *White* (1703–1704) [65] Ashby brought an action on the case for damages against White (the mayor) and the other returning officers for maliciously refusing to accept his vote in the election for Aylesbury. The Court of Queen's Bench (Holt C.J. dissenting) held that no action lay as the Commons had exclusive jurisdiction to determine claims to the franchise; but the House of Lords reversed this judgment on the principle stated by Holt C.J.[66] that where there is a right there is a remedy (*ubi jus ibi remedium*). The Commons passed a resolution that this infringed their privilege of exclusively determining both the qualification of an elector and the right of any person elected. The Lords then passed counter-resolutions.

Paty's Case (*R.* v. *Paty*, or the *Case of the Men of Aylesbury*) (1704) [67] arose out of a similar action by Paty and four other electors of Aylesbury against the returning officers for maliciously refusing their votes. The plaintiffs were committed to prison by order of the Commons for breach of privilege. Habeas corpus proceedings were brought. The Speaker's warrant of commitment stated that Paty had been guilty of " commencing and prosecuting an action at common law against W. White and others, late constables of Aylesbury, for not allowing his vote in the election of members to serve in parliament, contrary to the declaration, in high contempt of jurisdiction, and in breach of the known privileges of this House." The Court of Queen's Bench held (Holt C.J. again dissenting) that the court had no jurisdiction. Holt C.J. held, however, that where—as here—the cause *shown* in the return to the writ was insufficient in law to constitute a breach of privilege or contempt, the plaintiffs ought to be released. The Commons, hearing that plaintiffs' counsel intended to bring a writ of error in the House of Lords, committed the counsel also for " conspiring to make a difference between the Lords and the Commons " [68]; but Queen Anne resolved the deadlock by proroguing Parliament. This set the plaintiffs at liberty, and they went on to win their actions in the courts against the returning officers.[69]

---

[65] 2 Ld.Raym. 938; 3 Ld.Raym. 320; 14 St.Tr. 695; Broom, *Constitutional Law* (2nd ed.) p. 846. And see Turberville, *The House of Lords in the Eighteenth Century*, pp. 58–71.

[66] " It is a vain thing to imagine there should be right without a remedy; for want of right and want of remedy are convertibles . . . and we are to exert and vindicate the Queen's jurisdiction, and not to be frightened because it may come in question in Parliament." The franchise at that time was regarded as a property right.

[67] 2 Ld.Raym. 1105, 1113; 14 St.Tr. 849, 857; Broom, *op. cit.* p. 862.

[68] One of them escaped arrest by climbing out of the window of his chambers in the Temple " by the help of his sheets and a rope."

[69] G. M. Trevelyan, *Ramillies*, p. 25; K. Pickthorn, *Some Historical Principles of the Constitution* (1925) pp. 126–127.

In these two cases the question of the relation between parliamentary privilege and the courts was confused by the fact that the final court of appeal was the House of Lords, and each House was judge of its own privileges. In fact, it was the appeal to the House of Lords in the habeas corpus proceedings to which the Commons mainly objected.

In *Burdett* v. *Abbott* (1811) [70] Sir Francis Burdett, a Member of Parliament, brought an action for trespass against the Speaker for ordering the breaking into his house and his imprisonment in the Tower. The court held that the execution of a process for contempt justified the breaking into the plaintiff's house. The plaintiff had committed serious contempts against the Commons, and the House took no objection to the jurisdiction of the court; but the case is of interest here, because Lord Ellenborough expressed an *obiter dictum* agreeing with the opinion of Holt C.J. in *Paty's Case.*

In *Stockdale* v. *Hansard* (1839) [71] Stockdale sued Hansard, the parliamentary printers, for a libel contained in a report of prison inspectors that had been printed *by order* of the Commons and not only laid before the House but also *put on sale to the public.* The Commons instructed Hansard to plead that the report had been ordered by the Commons to be printed and published and was therefore covered by parliamentary privilege. The Queen's Bench gave judgment for Stockdale, holding that the courts had jurisdiction to determine whether an alleged privilege existed, although if a privilege did exist the House was the sole judge as to how it should be exercised. It found that parliamentary privilege extended to papers circulated among members by order of the House, but not to documents published outside the House, and that no resolution of either House could alter the law of the land. The Commons had previously in 1837 passed a resolution [72] that the publication of parliamentary reports and proceedings was essential for the functions of Parliament; that the House had sole and exclusive jurisdiction to determine the existence and extent of its privileges; that to dispute those privileges by legal proceedings was a breach of privilege; and that for any court to decide on matters of privilege inconsistent with the determination of either House was contrary to the law of Parliament.

The Commons allowed the damages of £100 to be paid " under the special circumstances of the case," but declared that in future cases Hansard should not plead and the parties should suffer for their

[70] 14 East 1; Broom, *op. cit.* p. 968.
[71] 9 Ad. & E. 1.
[72] Following the first action by Stockdale against Hansard for an earlier publication of the same libel, which the defendant won on a plea of justification, *i.e.* that the statement was true.

contempt. Stockdale nevertheless brought another action (the third) against Hansard for another publication of the same report. The defendants did not plead and judgment for £600 damages was given against them by default. The two Sheriffs of London, who jointly filled the office of Sheriff of Middlesex, levied the amount of the damages on Hansard's property, but cautiously refrained from paying the money over to Stockdale. The Commons desired them to refund the money to Hansard: they refused, and were committed for contempt. The *Case of the Sheriff of Middlesex* (1840) [73] was an application for habeas corpus on behalf of the two Sheriffs. The Speaker's warrant of committal produced by the Serjeant-at-Arms stated that the House had resolved that the Sheriff of Middlesex, having been guilty of a contempt and breach of privilege, be committed to custody; but it *did not set forth the facts* constituting the alleged breach of privilege or contempt. The court held that it could not go behind the warrant by inquiring into the facts: it must assume that the House of Commons was exercising its powers properly, and it therefore was not entitled to set the prisoners free.[74]

Stockdale, who had meanwhile been committed to prison by the Commons, commenced a fourth similar action through his solicitor, Howard. Hansard was again ordered not to plead, and judgment was once more entered against him by default. The Commons ordered Howard to attend the House, but he evaded service of the order. The Speaker, instead of having him brought before the House to be adjudged guilty of contempt, issued a warrant for his committal to Newgate, which the Serjeant-at-Arms (Gossett) executed. Howard sued Gossett for damages for unlawful arrest and imprisonment (*Howard* v. *Gossett*, 1845–47 [75]), but the Court of Exchequer Chamber held that the Speaker's warrant was sufficient and the matter clearly within the Commons' privileges. As Stockdale, although in custody, could have instructed other attorneys to prosecute further actions, the Commons secured the passing of the Parliamentary Papers Act 1840, which settled the matter of privilege in relation to the courts so far as concerns the publication of parliamentary papers. This Act, as we have seen,[76] provides that actions shall be stayed on production of a certificate or affidavit that the paper complained of was published by order of either House.

The fact that an Act of Parliament was passed vindicates the judgment of the court in *Stockdale* v. *Hansard* that changes in the

---

[73] 11 Ad. & E. 273. The Court of Queen's Bench in this case included three of the four judges who had decided *Stockdale* v. *Hansard* in the previous year.

[74] One of them was in fact released on the ground of ill-health, and the other was released on the day on which the Parliamentary Papers Bill was introduced.

[75] 10 Q.B. 359, 459; May, *op. cit.* p. 119.

[76] *Ante*, p. 203.

law can only be made by Act of Parliament and not by resolution of either House. A strong Judicial Committee in *Re Parliamentary Privilege Act 1770* [77] referred to " the inalienable right of Her Majesty's subjects to have recourse to her Courts of Law for the remedy of their wrongs "; and Scarman J. in *Stourton* v. *Stourton* [78] said that, where a matter of parliamentary privilege arises in court, the court looks to the common law as declared in judicial decisions rather than to parliamentary practice.

The Commons, however, have never formally admitted—indeed they have more than once denied—the jurisdiction of the courts to determine the existence of privilege. It looks at first sight as if the weapon of committal of parties and counsel for contempt (with no facts shown) would always be effective to prevent actions in the courts; but other counsel can be instructed to appear, and during a recess neither House could interfere with parties or counsel, so that judgment might be obtained and executed before the next meeting of Parliament. On the other hand, the House can recommit at the beginning of the next session. It is obviously unsatisfactory that there should be two sets of tribunals—the Houses of Parliament and the ordinary courts— with competing jurisdictions in a matter that may affect the liberty of the subject. The anomaly could be removed if, as has been suggested above, the Commons would allow an Act to be passed—as they did with the Parliamentary Elections Act 1868—transferring to the courts the exclusive jurisdiction to punish persons (or, at least, strangers) charged with contempt of Parliament. In this way the issue would be tried by an impartial tribunal that was not a party to the case; counsel and witnesses would be heard; the facts, perhaps, found by a jury; and there could be a right of appeal. [79]

[77] [1958] A.C. 331; (1958) Cmnd. 431; *ante,* p. 201.
[78] [1963] P. 302; *ante,* p. 213.
[79] There is a right of appeal in cases of contempt of court under the Administration of Justice Act 1960.

Part III

THE CROWN AND THE CENTRAL GOVERNMENT

CHAPTER 12

THE MONARCHY

Title to the Throne

The title to the Throne is both statutory and hereditary, while a trace of the Anglo-Saxon elective element is still found in the coronation ceremony. The Act of Settlement 1700 [1] settled the Throne on Sophia, Electress of Hanover (granddaughter of James I), and the heirs of her body being Protestants. Sophia's son, George I (1714), succeeded Anne under this Act. Any person who is a papist, or who marries a papist, is excluded from the succession. The successor to the Crown must take the Coronation Oath, sign the declaration prescribed by the Bill of Rights, and be in communion with the Church of England.

The convention is recited in the preamble to the Statute of Westminster 1931 that, since the Crown is the symbol of the free association of the members of the Commonwealth, any alteration in the law touching the succession to the Throne requires the assent of the Parliaments of all the "Dominions" (i.e. now Canada, Australia and New Zealand). [2]

Accession

When a Sovereign dies his successor accedes to the Throne immediately. The automatic succession of the new monarch is sometimes expressed in the maxim "the King never dies." [3] At common law a person is never too young to succeed to the Throne.

As soon as conveniently possible after the death or abdication of a Sovereign, an Accession Council meets to acclaim the new Sovereign. An Accession Council is composed of the Lords Spiritual and Temporal, assisted by members of the Privy Council, with the Lord Mayor and Aldermen of the City of London and the high commissioners of the Commonwealth countries. The new Sovereign takes the oath for the security of the Presbyterian Church in Scotland prescribed by the Union with Scotland Act 1706. Before the first

---

[1] The Act of Settlement was amended by the Union with Scotland and Ireland Acts, and by His Majesty's Declaration of Abdication Act 1936. The legitimacy of the succession based on the Act of Settlement cannot be questioned in court: *Hall* v. *Hall* (1944) 88 S.J. 383 (Hereford C.C.).

[2] Perhaps the assent is now required of all the independent countries of the Commonwealth that recognise Her Majesty as Queen.

[3] *Calvin's Case* (1607) 8 Co.Rep. 1a, 10b.

meeting of Parliament or at his coronation he must declare that he is a faithful Protestant, and promise to uphold the enactments securing the Protestant succession to the Throne.[4]

Coronation

Coronation customarily takes place in Westminster Abbey some months after accession, and is conducted by the Archbishop of Canterbury, assisted by the Archbishop of York.[5] Coronation is not legally necessary. Indeed Edward VIII reigned for nearly a year before abdicating, and was never crowned. If a coronation is held, the following ceremonies are essential: (i) presentation by the Archbishop of Canterbury and recognition by the people in the presence of the hereditary officers of state; (ii) the Coronation Oath (*infra*); (iii) anointing by the Primate; (iv) crowning by the Primate and enthroning; (v) homage by the bishops for the temporalities of their sees, and by peers.[6] These proceedings are organised by the Earl Marshal (Duke of Norfolk).

The Coronation Oath is based on the Coronation Oath Act 1688, and is obligatory by the Act of Settlement as amended by the Acts of Union. The Oath taken by Elizabeth II was to govern the peoples of the United Kingdom of Great Britain and Northern Ireland, Canada, Australia, New Zealand, the Union of South Africa, Pakistan and Ceylon,[7] and her possessions and the other territories to any of them belonging or pertaining, according to their respective laws and customs; to maintain in the United Kingdom the Protestant reformed religion established by law; and to maintain and preserve inviolably the settlement of the Church of England, and the doctrine, worship, discipline and government thereof in England.

Abdication

There is no precedent for a voluntary abdication before 1936, when Edward VIII was given the choice of abdicating or giving up his proposed marriage with Mrs. Simpson, whom the Prime Minister (Mr. Baldwin) and the Dominion Prime Ministers regarded as unsuitable for a King's consort.[8] The King signed an Instrument of

---

[4] Accession Declaration Act 1910.

[5] At the coronation of Elizabeth II in 1953 a minor part was played by the Moderator of the General Assembly of the Church of Scotland.

[6] For a description of the coronation ceremony, see A. B. Keith, *The King and the Imperial Crown*, pp. 20–29.

[7] These were the independent kingdoms or realms in the Commonwealth at that time India was already a republic.

[8] For a background account, see H.R.H. The Duke of Windsor, *A King's Story* (1951) pp. 337–415; G. M. Young, *Stanley Baldwin* (1952) pp. 232–244; J. W. Wheeler-Bennett, *King George VI*, pp. 275–289; Lord Birkenhead, *Walter Monckton* (1969) pt. III; Lord Beaverbrook, *The Abdication of King Edward VIII*.

Abdication declaring his irrevocable determination to renounce the Throne for himself and his descendants. He then sent a message to Parliament asking that a Bill should be passed accordingly to alter the succession to the Throne, and issued a commission to signify his assent thereto. His Majesty's Declaration of Abdication Act 1936 accordingly provided that His Majesty should cease to be King and there should be a demise of the Crown, and the member of the Royal Family then next in succession to the Throne should succeed. It amended the Act of Settlement 1700 by excluding King Edward (thereafter Duke of Windsor) and his descendants from the succession to the Throne, and exempted them from the provisions of the Royal Marriages Act 1772.[9]

The Royal Style and Titles

The Royal Style and Titles are altered from time to time by Act of Parliament, or by proclamation issued thereunder. Several changes have been made in the present century to take account of constitutional developments in the Commonwealth. The preamble to the Statute of Westminster 1931 recites the convention that any alteration of the Royal Style and Titles shall require the consent of the Parliaments of all the "Dominions."[10] On the accession of Elizabeth II, the Sovereign was for the first time proclaimed by different titles in the various independent countries of the Commonwealth. The Royal Titles Act 1953 empowers the Queen to use, in relation to the United Kingdom and all other territories for whose foreign relations the Government of the United Kingdom is responsible, such style and titles as she may think fit having regard to the agreement made between representatives of the member governments of the Commonwealth. The style and titles proclaimed under this Act are: "Elizabeth II by the Grace of God of the United Kingdom of Great Britain and Northern Ireland and of her other Realms and Territories Queen, Head of the Commonwealth, Defender of the Faith."[11]

(ed. A. J. P. Taylor, 1966); J. Evelyn Wrench, *Geoffrey Dawson and our Times* (1935) Chap. 29; K. Middlemas and J. Barnes, *Baldwin* (1969) Chap. 34; J. G. Lockhart, *Cosmo Gordon Lang*, Chap. 32.

[9] For an account of the constitutional steps taken, see W. Ivor Jennings, " The Abdication of King Edward VIII " (1937) 2 *Politica* 287; K. H. Bailey, " The Abdication Legislation in the United Kingdom and in the Dominions " (1938) 3 *Politica* 1 and 147. Consultation with the Dominions is described in Lord Beaverbrook, *op. cit.* and Lord Birkenhead, *op. cit.* The Abdication Act was based on a draft prepared by Sir Frederick Pollock; see *The Pollock-Holmes Letters* (1942) I, pp. xiv–xv, 68–69.

The Duke of Windsor retained his service ranks, and was Governor of the Bahamas from 1940 to 1945. He died in 1972 without issue.

[10] *Cf. ante*, p. 221n.

[11] (1953) Cmd. 8748. See also S. A. de Smith, " The Royal Style and Titles " (1953) 2 I.C.L.Q. 263; and *post*, Chap. 35.

The Royal Family

The Sovereign. The Queen Regnant has the same status and powers as a King. She is the Head of the State. The central government of the country is carried on in her name and on her behalf; she is an essential part of the legislature, and justice is administered in the royal courts in her name. But what were formerly the personal prerogatives of the Sovereign have now become largely the powers and privileges of the government.

The official duties of the Queen in her capacity as Sovereign of the United Kingdom and of the other self-governing Commonwealth monarchies and the remaining colonial territories, Head of the Armed Services, and Supreme Governor of the Church of England and with her special responsibility to the Established Church of Scotland, include: (i) work arising out of the government such as approving and signing submissions, and reading ministerial, Cabinet, parliamentary and diplomatic papers for several hours a day; (ii) private audiences, receiving the Prime Minister and other Ministers, holding a Privy Council and investitures; (iii) attending at state occasions such as the opening of Parliament, Trooping the Colour and religious services; and (iv) exchanging state visits and visiting Commonwealth countries.[12]

Husband of Queen Regnant. Prince Philip, Duke of Edinburgh, is granted precedence next to the Queen. He is a Privy Councillor. At common law he has the status of an ordinary subject, and is not protected by the law of treason.

The Prince of Wales. The life of the Sovereign's eldest son is protected by the Statute of Treasons 1351. When the Sovereign's eldest son is born he immediately becomes by custom Duke of Cornwall. When he succeeds to the Throne, the Duchy of Cornwall immediately vests in his eldest son. The Sovereign may create his or her eldest son Prince of Wales and Earl of Chester by letters patent. Prince Charles was created Prince of Wales and Earl of Chester in 1958, and his investiture as Prince of Wales took place at Caernarvon Castle in 1969.

Princes and princesses of the blood royal. Princes of the blood till summoned by the House of Lords, are commoners. It is usual to give them dukedoms when they come of age. The chastity of the Sovereign's eldest daughter unmarried is protected by the law of treason. The style of " Royal Highness " is conferred by letters

---

[12] *Report from the Select Committee on the Civil List* (1971) H.C. 29, para. 17 and Appendix 13.

patent [13] on the children of Sovereigns, and on the wives and children of the sons of Sovereigns.

Royal marriages. By the Royal Marriages Act 1772 no descendant of the body of George II (other than the issue of princesses married into royal families [14]) may marry without the royal consent signified under the Great Seal and declared in Council, and marriages by these persons without such consent are void (*Sussex Peerage Case* (1844) [15]). Further, all persons solemnising such marriages, or who are privy and consenting thereto, commit an offence. If the royal consent is refused, a descendant of George II aged twenty-five or more may give notice to the Privy Council and may contract a valid marriage at the expiration of twelve months unless Parliament has objected in the interim.[16]

The Regency Acts 1937–1953

The common law made no provision for a regency or the delegation of royal functions when the Sovereign was ill or absent from the realm. Great inconvenience was caused in 1811 by the fact that George III was already considered to be insane [17] and therefore could not in fact give his assent to the appointment of a Regent; and special provision for delegation of royal functions had to be made when George V was seriously ill in 1928. When George VI came to the Throne, his children consisting of two young princesses, it was decided to enact permanent legislation, and this was revised on the accession of Elizabeth II. These matters are now regulated by the Regency Acts 1937–1953.

(i) *Delegation of functions to Counsellors of State.* The Regency Act 1937 authorises the Sovereign to appoint Counsellors of State by letters patent, and to delegate to them such of the royal functions as may be specified in the letters patent, whenever he is absent or intends to be absent from the United Kingdom, or is suffering from infirmity of mind or body not amounting to incapacity such as would warrant a regency under the Act. The persons to be appointed to be Counsel-

---

13 *London Gazette*, February 5, 1864.
14 It is possible that this exception exempts from the provisions of the Act all, or nearly all, those who are in close succession to the Throne at the present day (see C. d'O. Farran, " The Royal Marriages Act 1772 " (1951) 14 M.L.R. 53), but Lord Harewood asked for the royal consent in 1967.
15 11 Cl. & F. 85.
16 It is suggested that the Act should be amended so as to be confined to descendants of George V; and also that a marriage without the royal consent should not be void or punishable, but should merely exclude the parties and their descendants from the succession to the Throne.
17 Medical opinion now is that George III was not insane but suffered from an acute intermittent form of porphyria, a rare metabolic disorder: Ida MacAlpine and Richard Hunter, *George III and the Mad-Business* (1969).

lors of State are the wife or husband of the Sovereign and the four persons next in succession to the Throne, excluding any person who would be disqualified from being Regent. The Regency Act 1953 includes Queen Elizabeth the Queen Mother among the persons who may be appointed Counsellors of State. It is the modern practice, because of the significance of the Monarchy to the Commonwealth, that only members of the Royal Family should be appointed to the exclusion of United Kingdom Ministers.[18] The Counsellors may not be given authority to dissolve Parliament otherwise than at the express instructions of the Sovereign—which may be given by telegraph—or to grant any rank, title or dignity of the peerage.

(ii) *Regency*. (a) The Regency Act 1937 provides that if *the Sovereign is under eighteen years of age* the royal functions are to be performed until he is eighteen by a Regent, who shall act in the name and on behalf of the Sovereign. The Sovereign is deemed to accede to the Throne when he attains the age of eighteen years for the purpose of taking statutory oaths and declarations. The Regent is to be the person of full age next in succession to the Throne who is a British subject resident in the United Kingdom and who is not disqualified on religious grounds. The Regency Act 1953, however, provides that the Duke of Edinburgh shall be Regent if a child of Queen Elizabeth and the Duke of Edinburgh succeeds to the Throne under the age of eighteen, or if a regency is necessary in the lifetime of the Queen. The Regent is to take oaths of allegiance, good government and maintenance of the Protestant religion in England and Scotland. He is empowered to exercise all royal functions, except that he may not assent to a Bill altering the succession to the Throne or repealing the Acts for securing the Scottish Protestant religion and Church.[19]

The Act of 1937 also provides for the *guardianship* of the person of a Sovereign under eighteen years. Of an unmarried Sovereign his or her mother is to be the guardian; of a married Sovereign the Sovereign's spouse will be guardian. If in the first case the Sovereign has no mother or in the second case the Consort is under age, then the Regent will be guardian.

(b) The Regency Act 1937 further provides for the appointment of a Regent if a declaration is made by certain persons that they are " satisfied by evidence which shall include the evidence of physicians that *the Sovereign is by infirmity of mind or body incapable* for the time being of performing the royal functions," or that they are " satisfied by evidence that the Sovereign is for some definite cause *not*

18 See J. W. Wheeler-Bennett, *King George VI*, Appendix A.
19 *Cf. ante*, pp. 74–75.

available " for the performance of those functions.[20] The regency will continue until a contrary declaration is made. The persons who may make such declaration are the wife or husband of the Sovereign, the Lord Chancellor, the Speaker, the Lord Chief Justice and the Master of the Rolls, or any three or more of them. It will be noticed that the person who would be Regent is not one of those who make this declaration. The declaration must be made in writing to the Privy Council, and is to be communicated to the governments of the " Dominions."

The Sovereign's Private Secretary [21]

The post of Private Secretary to the Monarch is comparatively modern. Before the reign of George III the theory was that the Home Secretary was the King's Private Secretary, and it was thought desirable that a person admitted to Cabinet secrets should be a Privy Councillor. George III for many years wrote his own letters, but in 1805, when he was almost blind, he appointed Sir Herbert Taylor his Private Secretary. William IV reappointed Taylor, who had by then become a Privy Councillor. Since the Prince Consort's death in 1861 the office has been regular and officially accepted, its prestige being built up by Sir Henry Ponsonby and Sir Arthur Bigge (Lord Stamfordham), who between them occupied that post from 1870 to 1931, except during Edward VII's reign.

The Sovereign's Private Secretary is always now sworn of the Privy Council. It appears that he informally seeks advice from various sources—governmental, opposition and official—and then briefs the Sovereign. His post is very important as he is concerned with the relations not only between the Sovereign and the British Cabinet, but also between the Sovereign and Governors-General and Commonwealth Prime Ministers.

[20] The Sovereign would not be available, for example, if he were made a prisoner of war.
[21] Wheeler-Bennett, *King George VI*, Appendix B; Arthur Ponsonby, *Henry Ponsonby, Queen Victoria's Private Secretary*, Chap. 3; Sir Ivor Jennings, *Cabinet Government* (3rd ed.) pp. 343–351.

CHAPTER 13

THE ROYAL PREROGATIVE

I. GENERAL NATURE OF THE PREROGATIVE

THE term " royal prerogative " is not a technical one. It is some-times used to cover all the powers of the Sovereign, or at least those which the Sovereign does not share with his subjects. Sometimes it refers to the powers of the Sovereign in relation to his subjects, as distinct from " acts of state " done in relation to foreign affairs. More often, and preferably, it is limited to those powers which the Sovereign has by the common law as distinct from statute—in other words, the common law powers of the Crown.[1]

So far as the executive powers of the Crown are concerned (and for practical purposes these are the most important) it should be pointed out at the beginning that in the last hundred years the govern-ment of the country has been carried on largely under statutory powers. Further we must remember that, in so far as the Crown does exercise prerogative powers, their exercise is governed mainly by constitutional conventions, especially the doctrine of ministerial responsibility. Nevertheless, emphasis on the prerogative does illuminate the historical basis of the Constitution, and it helps to explain much of the theory underlying the forms taken by governmental action.

Historical introduction

The distinction between the natural and politic capacities of the King appears in the sixteenth century.[2] Further subtlety of reasoning led to a distinction in the early seventeenth century between the " absolute " and the " ordinary " powers of the King (*Bate's Case* (1606)[3]). By ordinary powers was meant such powers as those involved in the administration of justice, which had long been exercised without discretion in accordance with definite principles and procedure. The absolute powers we should now call discretionary, for example, the direction of foreign policy and the pardoning of criminals. There arose also a tendency to regard the absolute pre-

---

[1] For " the Crown," see *post*, pp. 230–231.
[2] *Case of the Duchy of Lancaster* (1562) Plowd. 212; *Calvin's Case* (1608) 7 Co.Rep. 1a.
[3] Lane 22; 2 St.Tr. 371; Broom, *Constitutional Law* (2nd ed.) pp. 245 *et seq.*

rogatives as " inseparable," so that even Parliament could not detach them from the Crown (Case of the King's Prerogative in Saltpetre (1607) [4]). One certain principle was that the prerogative was limited by law: " the King hath no prerogative but that which the law of the land allows him " (Case of Proclamations (1610) [5]). Had not Bracton said in the thirteenth century that the King ought to be subject to God and the law, because the law makes him King? [6] Charles I might dispute the application of this principle in certain aspects of government, such as preventive detention (Darnel's Case (1627) [7]) and ship-money (R. v. Hampden (1637) [8]), but the Civil War and the Revolution of 1688 meant that henceforth the Sovereign would accept the limitation of the prerogative by law and its determination by the courts. It is now admitted, of course, that the Sovereign has no powers that are " inseparable " none, that is, which cannot be taken away by Act of Parliament.[9]

Blackstone says: " By the word prerogative we usually understand that special pre-eminence which the King hath, over and above all other persons, and out of the ordinary course of the common law, in right of his regal dignity. It signifies, in its etymology (from prae and rogo) something that is required or demanded before, or in preference to, all others." [10] The essential characteristic of the royal prerogative, then, is that it is unique and pre-eminent. It is not " out of the ordinary course of the common law " in the sense of being above the law; it is part of the Common law, but an exception to the principles that apply to citizens generally. Dicey's description of the royal prerogative as " the residue of discretionary or arbitrary authority, which at any given time is legally left in the hands of the Crown " has been more than once judicially approved.[11] Dicey emphasises the discretionary nature of the prerogative—the word " arbitrary " is misleading—and confines it according to the best usage to common law as distinct from statutory powers.

The prerogative is a residue because Parliament can take away any prerogative and has frequently done so. It is seldom abolished expressly, however, but is impliedly abolished, curtailed or merely suspended (Att.-Gen. v. De Keyser's Royal Hotel Ltd.[12]). Since

---

[4] 12 Co.Rep. 12. See Holdsworth, op. cit. Vol. IV, pp. 202–207.
[5] 12 Co.Rep. 74; 2 St.Tr. 723.
[6] De Legibus et Consuetudinibus Angliae, f. 5b.
[7] 3 St.Tr. 1; Broom, op. cit. pp. 158 et seq.
[8] 3 St.Tr. 825: And see Holdsworth, op. cit. Vol. VI, pp. 19–30; Broom, op. cit. pp. 303 et seq.
[9] Att.-Gen. v. De Keyser's Royal Hotel Ltd. [1920] A.C. 508; infra, pp. 232–233.
[10] Bl.Comm. I, 239.
[11] Dicey, Law of the Constitution (10th ed.) p. 424; approved, e.g. by Lord Dunedin in Att.-Gen. v. De Keyser's Royal Hotel Ltd. [1920] A.C. 508, 526.
[12] [1920] A.C. 508; infra, pp. 232–233.

the prerogative is part of the common law, the Queen cannot claim that a new prerogative has come into existence.[13] It can only be the residue at any given time of the rights and powers which the Sovereign had before the days of Parliament.

A prerogative power is *discretionary* because, although its existence is determinable by the courts, the manner of its exercise is outside their jurisdiction, *e.g.* the recognition of foreign Sovereigns, governments and diplomatic envoys (*Engelke* v. *Musmann* [14]).

Lastly, the prerogatives are *legally* vested in the Queen although this is now largely a matter of form. By custom and convention prerogative powers must be exercised through and on the advice of other persons. The necessity of knowing whether or not an executive act is an expression of the Sovereign's will and of making someone other than the Sovereign legally liable for its consequences has given rise to complex rules determining how the Sovereign's acts are to be authenticated. The forms in which the royal will is expressed are generally by: (i) proclamation, writ, letters patent, grant, or other document under the Great Seal; (ii) Order in Council; or (iii) warrant, commission, order or instructions [15] under the Sign Manual. The discretionary character of prerogative powers has also given rise to the doctrine of ministerial responsibility, the most important development in modern British constitutional history. There are very few occasions nowadays when the Queen can act without or against the advice of her Ministers; these exceptional cases may include the choice of Prime Minister [16] and the dissolution of Parliament or the dismissal of a ministry.[17]

Classification of the prerogative

(i) It is still possible to distinguish between *personal* and *political* prerogatives, that is, between those which the Queen has as a person and those which she has as Head of State. The personal, however, have tended to become absorbed by the political and in consequence they have lost most of their constitutional significance.

The political prerogatives are often spoken of as adhering to " *the Crown.*" Thomas Paine called the Crown " a metaphor shown at the Tower for sixpence or a shilling a piece," [18] and Maitland said the expression was often used as a cover for ignorance.[19] In effect

---

[13] *Case of Monopolies* (1602) 11 Co.Rep. 84b.
[14] [1928] A.C. 433.
[15] *e.g.* to colonial Governors, *post*, Chap. 34.
[16] *Post*, Chap. 15.
[17] *Ante*, Chap. 6.
[18] *Rights of Man* (1791).
[19] *Constitutional History*, p. 418.

" the Crown " is equivalent to the executive or the central government. More precisely it means the Queen in her public capacity, either: (a) in rare cases acting at her own discretion, e.g. choice of Prime Minister in exceptional circumstances; (b) acting on the advice of Ministers, e.g. opening Parliament; (c) acting through or by means of Ministers, e.g. negotiating treaties and pardoning criminals; or (d) Ministers acting on behalf of the Queen. With regard to the last, in modern times many powers are conferred by statute directly on Ministers, e.g. to approve town-planning schemes or to acquire land compulsorily; in theory the Ministers act on behalf of the Queen.

(ii) So far we have spoken of the prerogatives as if they were composed entirely of powers. Another classification shows that this is not so. They can be analysed into: (a) *rights,* e.g. the Crown Estate and *bona vacantia* (but these are regulated largely by statute); (b) *powers,* e.g. to summon Parliament and to make treaties; (c) *privileges,* e.g. to ask for and to receive supply from Parliament; and (d) *immunities,* e.g. exemption from statutes imposing taxes or rates unless expressly mentioned, and from being sued or have property taken in execution (*cf.* Crown Proceedings Act 1947). This method of classification is one of analytical jurisprudence [20] rather than constitutional law, but it may sometimes help to a clearer understanding of the prerogative.

(iii) The most convenient classification for the present day is according to the branch of government to which the various prerogatives relate, *i.e. legislative, judicial* and *executive.* Those which relate to legislation and the administration of justice are mostly " ordinary " prerogatives in the sense used above, while those which relate to the executive are mainly " absolute " [21] or discretionary and regulated by convention.

Personal prerogatives

These consist mainly of immunities and property rights.

(i) " *The King never dies.*" The Common law knows no interregnum. But this theory was of limited effect, because the death of the Sovereign entailed the dissolution of Parliament and the determination of the tenure of offices under the Crown (including judicial offices), until these inconveniences were remedied by various statutes.[22]

(ii) " *The King is never an infant.*" The common law made no

[20] See W. N. Hohfeld, *Fundamental Legal Conceptions.*
[21] *Ante,* p. 228.
[22] For Parliament and the demise of the Crown, see *ante,* p. 104; and for judicial tenure, *post,* Chap. 19. And see Crown Proceedings Act 1947, s. 32.

provision for the Sovereign being a minor; but the contingency is now provided for by the Regency Acts.

(iii) " *The King can do no wrong.*" The Sovereign cannot be sued or prosecuted in the courts.[23] There was a feudal principle that proceedings could not be taken against a lord in his own court; and the royal courts had no jurisdiction over the King. Men came to say that wrong could not be imputed to the Sovereign. The significance of this immunity was greatly diminished by the Crown Proceedings Act 1947, which enables the citizen to sue government departments in contract or tort or for the recovery of property, while leaving unimpaired the Sovereign's personal immunity.[24]

(iv) *Crown private estates.*[25] At common law the general rule is that the same prerogatives attach to estates vested in the Sovereign in her natural capacity as apply to estates vested in the Sovereign in her political capacity in right of the Crown. The Crown Private Estates Acts 1800, 1862 and 1873 now regulate to some extent the disposition of such property. These Acts apply to property belonging to the Sovereign at the time of accession, property devised or bequeathed by any persons not being Kings or Queens of the realm, and property bought out of the privy purse. Sandringham and Balmoral are made subject to rates. Crown private estates may be disposed of by the Sovereign *inter vivos* or by will unless, like the Duchies of Lancaster and Cornwall, they are settled by charter having statutory effect. If undisposed of at the death of the Sovereign, they descend with the Crown and become lands held in right of the Crown.[26]

Effect of statute on the prerogative

A royal prerogative may be expressly abolished by Act of Parliament, as when the Crown Proceedings Act 1947 abolished the immunity of the Crown from being sued in contract and tort. An Act may be passed covering the same ground or part of the same ground as the prerogative, in which case the prerogative is to that extent by necessary implication abrogated, at least so long as the statute remains in force. In *Att.-Gen.* v. *De Keyser's Royal Hotel Ltd.*[27] the respondent's hotel was required by the War Office in the

---

23 The legend perpetuated by Bracton, that writs lay against the King down to Edward I's time, is refuted by other authorities; see Holdsworth, *History of English Law*, Vol. IX, p. 12.

24 It would seem that proceedings against the Queen in her private capacity can now be brought (if at all) only by way of the common law (pre-1860) petition of right; *post*, Chap. 32.   25 (1971) H.C. 29.

26 *Cf.* Crown Estate, *post*, p. 235.

27 [1920] A.C. 508. There was argument about the effect (if any) of the Defence Act 1842, now amended by the Statute Law (Repeals) Act 1969.

First World War. Negotiations broke down over the amount of the rent, and possession was taken compulsorily by the Army Council under the Defence of the Realm Regulations on terms that compensation would be paid *ex gratia.* The respondents gave possession but claimed the right to full compensation under the Defence Regulations. The House of Lords unanimously decided that the statutory Regulations specifying the manner in which compensation was to be assessed must be observed by the Crown. The Crown could not choose, said Lord Sumner, whether or not to act under the prerogative power (assuming that to exist) involving perhaps no compensation or only compensation *ex gratia;* it must act under the statutory power and in accordance with its terms for, as Lord Moulton said, that must be presumed to be the intention of Parliament in passing the statute.

Their Lordships expressed various opinions on the question whether, where a statute impliedly covers the same ground as a prerogative power, the statute *pro tanto* abolishes the prerogative or merges it with the statute (Lord Parmoor); or whether, as Lord Atkinson preferred to say, the prerogative is merely in abeyance so long as the statute remains in force.

II. THE PREROGATIVE IN DOMESTIC AFFAIRS

These consist largely of powers, and in theory of some duties.

1. Executive prerogatives [28]

The prerogatives that may be classed as executive, administrative or governmental are a relic of the powers which the King had when he really governed the country. The government at the present day is largely carried on under statutory powers—a subject too vast for discussion in a general book on constitutional law. Prerogative powers nowadays are mainly of importance in relation to the Civil Service, the armed forces, colonial administration, Commonwealth relations and foreign affairs. Moreover, they have to be read subject to the principle of ministerial responsibility. The government does not have to consult, or even to inform, Parliament before exercising prerogative powers. This is convenient, for many matters falling within the prerogative are not suitable for public discussion before the decision is made or the action performed. On the other hand, the government must feel assured of parliamentary support afterwards, especially in a matter like war or where money will be required.

[28] *Cf.* J. B. D. Mitchell, " The Royal Prerogative in Modern Scots Law " [1957] P.L. 304.

The Sovereign in theory also has duties, but these are not legally enforceable. " The principal duty of the King is, to govern his people according to law," says Blackstone, quoting Bracton and Fortescue to like effect. Blackstone cites the Coronation Oath, but adds that "doubtless the duty of protection is impliedly as much incumbent on the Sovereign before coronation as after." [29] The Sovereign is the general conservator of the peace of the Kingdom,[30] but although the preservation of the peace is a function of the Crown, local police officers are not regarded as Crown servants. In *China Navigation Co.* v. *Att.-Gen.*[31] it was held that there is no duty enforceable by the Courts on the Crown to afford such protection as was asked for in that case, *viz.* armed protection against pirates in foreign waters, and the subject is not obliged to pay for such protection; but if the Crown agrees to provide special protection for payment, such payment can be recovered from the subject.

For our immediate purpose the following is probably the most convenient classification of the prerogatives relating to executive government:

(i) *Appointment and dismissal* of Ministers, other government officials, officers and men of the forces; the appointment and (subject to statute) dismissal of judicial officers.

(ii) *Control of the services.* The Queen is head of the Royal Navy, the Army and the Royal Air Force. The supreme command and government of all forces by sea, land and air, and of all forts and places of strength, is vested in the Crown both by common law and statute. The last time a Sovereign exercised the command of the Army in person was in 1743. The raising of forces, their discipline and payment are now governed by statute,[32] but the movement and disposition of forces lawfully raised is entirely under the control of the Crown.[33] The control of the Civil Service is similarly vested in the Crown.[34]

(iii) *The administration of dependencies.* It is still a function of the Crown to provide for the government of British colonies and other dependencies; and also to make laws for colonies acquired by conquest or cession until Parliament takes over or the colony is granted representative institutions.[35]

---

[29] Bl.Comm. I, Chap. 6.
[30] Bl.Comm. I, 266.
[31] [1932] 2 K.B. 197 (C.A.).
[32] *Post*, Chap. 17.
[33] *China Navigation Co.* v. *Att.-Gen.* [1932] 2 K.B. 197 (C.A.); *Chandler* v. *D.P.P.* [1964] A.C. 763 (H.L.).
[34] *Rodwell* v. *Thomas* [1944] K.B. 596. *Post*, Chap. 16.
[35] *Post*, Chap. 34.

(iv) *Revenue.* The Norman and early Plantagenet Kings had "ordinary" and "extraordinary" revenues, and this terminology was still used at the beginning of the nineteenth century.[36] The "ordinary" revenues consisted of customary hereditary revenues such as feudal dues,[37] *bona vacantia,* income from Crown lands and other miscellaneous sources of income that are now exchanged for the Civil List (*infra*). "Extraordinary" revenues or "aids" were raised from time to time to meet the needs of war or other public emergency.

The Crown Estate consists of lands which have become vested in the Sovereign "in his body politic in right of the Crown," and include the ancient demesne lands of the Crown and lands subsequently acquired by prerogative right, *e.g.* by escheat or forfeiture, the foreshore and lands formed by alluvion. The Crown Estate is managed by the Crown Estate Commissioners, who are subject to the general directions of the Chancellor of the Exchequer and the Secretary of State for Scotland. Their annual reports are to be laid before Parliament.[38]

Bona vacantia include wreck,[39] treasure trove, waifs, estrays, royal mines and royal fish.[40] Land that formerly escheated on failure of heirs goes to the Crown as *bona vacantia* under the Administration of Estates Act 1925. Treasure trove consists of gold or silver in coin, plate or bullion, hidden in the earth or other secret place, and subsequently found without trace of the owner. It is hidden, and not abandoned, treasure. The finding of treasure trove is determined by a coroner [41] and a jury. Treasure trove goes by law to the Crown, and it is therefore an offence to conceal the discovery.[42] Nowadays the Crown as a matter of grace usually compensates the owner of the land and the finder.[43]

It is the privilege of the Crown to demand and receive supply from Parliament for the government of the country.[44] Since the Bill of Rights 1688 it can only be raised and spent by authority of Parliament.

---

[36] Chitty, *Prerogatives of the Crown* (1820) p. 200.

[37] Most of these disappeared with the abolition of military tenure in 1660.

[38] Crown Estate Act 1961.

[39] Regulated by the Merchant Shipping Act 1894.

[40] For these, see Bl. Comm. 1, 290–299; Keith, *The King and the Imperial Crown,* p. 390.

[41] The chief duty of the coroner, whose court dates back to 1194, is to inquire into the cause of death of persons who die suddenly, by violence or in suspicious circumstances (Coroners Courts Acts 1887–1954).

[42] *Lord Advocate* v. *Aberdeen University,* 1963 S.C. 533; 1963 S.L.T. 361.

[43] *Att.-Gen.* v. *Moore* [1893] 1 Ch. 676; *Att.-Gen.* v. *Trustees of the British Museum* [1903] 2 Ch. 598. Notable finds that have been declared treasure trove and placed in the British Museum are a fine collection of Roman silver plate (Mildenhall, 1946), a hoard of 883 Anglo-Saxon coins (Norfolk, 1958), and a hoard of 1,326 medieval gold coins (Newstead Abbey, Notts., 1966).

[44] *Ante,* Chap. 10.

Since the accession of George III in 1760 it has been the custom for each Sovereign to surrender to the Exchequer for life the hereditary revenues held in right of the Crown, in exchange for a fixed annual payment known as the *Civil List*. The revenues of the Duchies of Lancaster and Cornwall are excluded from the surrender. The surrendered revenues are paid into the Exchequer and form part of the Consolidated Fund. The main items of expenditure covered by the Civil List are the salaries and expenses of the royal household and royal bounty, and the Privy Purse (pensions for employees and the maintenance of Sandringham and Balmoral). Provision is also made towards the expenses of performing public duties by certain other members of the Royal Family.[45] The amounts fixed by Parliament on the accession of Queen Elizabeth II in 1952 were increased by the Civil List Act 1972 to offset inflation.

(v) *Ecclesiastical prerogatives.* Elizabeth I was described as the supreme ecclesiastical and temporal " Governor " of the realm by the Act of Supremacy 1558,[46] and the Book of Common Prayer refers to the Sovereign as " our Queen and Governor." The title suggests administrative rather than lawmaking powers; ecclesiastical but not spiritual. " Conceive it thus," says Selden, " there is in the Kingdom of England a college of physicians; the King is supreme governor of those, but not the head of them, nor president of the college, nor best physician." The Queen is advised by the Prime Minister on the appointment of bishops. When a see becomes vacant a *congé d'élire* (licence to elect) is sent to the dean and chapter bidding them elect a bishop; but they are bound to elect the person nominated in the letter missive, a letter accompanying the *congé d'élire*.[47] It is understood that in making or advising on ecclesiastical appointments, the Prime Minister consults the archbishops.

Otherwise, the functions and powers of the Queen in relation to the Church of England are mainly regulated by statute, for example, the calling together and dissolving of the General Synod and the Convocations of Canterbury and York.[48] The Submission of the Clergy Act 1533 requires the Queen's assent and licence for the making of Canons, and also provides that no Canons may be made which are contrary or repugnant to the royal prerogative or the customs, laws or statutes of the realm.

---

[45] *Report from the Select Committee on the Civil List* (1971) H.C. 29.
[46] Repealed, except section 13, by the Statute Law (Repeals) Act 1969. The Act of Supremacy 1534 (repealed in 1554) called Henry VIII the supreme " Head " on earth of the Church of England.
[47] The prerogative and procedure for confirming the election of bishops are preserved by the Ecclesiastical (Jurisdiction) Measure 1963, s. 83 (2).
[48] Synodical Government Measure 1969, modifying the Church of England Assembly (Powers) Act 1919 and the Church of England Convocations Act 1966.

(vi) *The "fountain of honour."* The Queen is the "fountain of honour." [49] The creation of peers is done on the advice of the Prime Minister.[50] Most honours in the United Kingdom are also conferred on the advice of the Prime Minister.[51]

(vii) *Miscellaneous prerogatives.* Other prerogatives or former prerogatives relating to coinage, mining of precious metals, administration of charities, guardianship of infants and mental patients, the use of patents and the creation of boroughs,[52] are now largely regulated by statute. The prerogative to issue the writ *ne exeat regno* (to forbid a person to leave the realm) at the instance of a Secretary of State is obsolescent.[53] The right to publish the Bible and the New Testament does not extend to breach of copyright in modern translations.[54] There is a prerogative to issue free information, *e.g.* a government pamphlet about the Common Market [55]

(viii) *Emergency and defence.* The Crown may use such force as is reasonably necessary to put down riot or insurrection.[56]

The Crown is responsible for the defence of the realm by sea and land, and is the only judge of the existence of danger to the realm from external enemies (*R.* v. *Hampden* (1637) [57]), although it is not the sole judge of the means by which such danger is to be averted, *e.g.* the imposition of taxation or conscription (Bill of Rights 1688). In time of war the Crown may requisition ships, at least British ships in territorial waters, on payment of compensation (*The Broadmayne* [58]), and may enter upon and use the lands of the citizen near the coast in order to repel invasion (*Case of the King's Prerogative in Saltpetre* (1606) [59]). After the danger is over the bulwarks ought to be removed: nothing otherwise was said about compensation in

---

[49] *The Prince's Case* (1606) 8 Co.Rep. 1a, 18b; Bl.Comm. I, 271.
[50] George V in 1924 personally offered Asquith, an ex-Prime Minister, a peerage on the day on which he lost his seat at a general election, when Baldwin was about to succeed MacDonald and the premiership was momentarily vacant; Roy Jenkins, *Asquith*, pp. 505–506.
[51] Some Orders are a matter for the Queen's personal choice. Thus the Queen made the Governor of Southern Rhodesia a K.C.V.O. at the time of U.D.I. in November 1965.
[52] Universities are also common law corporations, although some are regulated by private Acts.
[53] *Felton* v. *Callis* [1969] 1 Q.B. 200 (Megarry J.); the writ *ne exeat regno* will now be issued at the instance of a private person only if the requirements of the Debtors Act 1869, s. 6, are complied with. The writ was issued in 1893, but discharged: *Lewis* v. *Lewis* (1893) 68 L.T. 193 (Ch.D.); and an order was issued by Rowlatt J., vacation judge, sitting in his orchard in about 1912 (letter from D. N. Pritt Q.C. to *The Times*, August 15, 1968).
[54] *Universities of Oxford and Cambridge* v. *Eyre and Spottiswoode* [1964] Ch. 736.
[55] *Jenkins* v. *Att.-Gen.*, *The Times*, August 14, 1971.
[56] See further, *post*, Chap. 18.
[57] 3 St.Tr. 825.
[58] [1916] P. 64; and see *The Sarpon* [1916] P. 306.
[59] 12 Co.Rep. 12.

that case. But in modern times the Crown relies in time of war and other grave emergency on statutory powers, such as the Emergency Powers (Defence) Acts of the late war.[60]

Dicey goes so far as to say: " There are times of tumult or invasion when for the sake of legality itself the rules of law must be broken. The course which the Government must then take is clear. The Ministry must break the law and trust for protection to an Act of Indemnity." [61] If this is so, the duty of the Crown to protect the realm is paramount. Darling J. in *Re Shipton* [62] approved *obiter* the old maxim, *salus populi suprema lex* (the safety of the people is the highest law.

The question whether compensation is payable for loss or damage caused by (lawful) exercise of the prerogative was argued for the first time in the House of Lords as a preliminary question of law in *Burmah Oil Co.* v. *Lord Advocate.*[63] The company's oil installations had been destroyed by order of the British commander of the forces in Burma (then a colony) in 1942, to prevent them from falling into the hands of the invading Japanese forces who would have found them of great strategic value. Their Lordships held by a majority of three to two that, although compensation had never been payable at common law for " battle " damage, whether accidental or deliberate, this was " denial " damage—really economic warfare—and there was no general rule that the royal prerogative can be exercised without compensation. Lord Reid in his majority judgment said that there was no precedent of a claim for compensation in such cases not being paid, and it was therefore payable. Lord Radcliffe in his dissenting judgment said the prerogative was so vague and uncertain that he preferred to base his opinion on the idea of necessity: the Crown had as much a duty as a right to do what it did, and it was not a source of profit to the Crown. With logic equal to Lord Reid's he said there was no precedent of such a claim being paid, and therefore it was not payable.[64]

---

[60] *Post*, Chap. 18.   [61] Dicey, *Law of the Constitution* (10th ed.) pp. 412–413.
[62] *Re Shipton, Anderson & Co. and Harrison Brothers & Co.* [1915] 3 K.B. 676, 684; Bracton, *De legibus et consuetudinibus Angliae*, ff. 93B, 247A; Hobbes, *Leviathan*, ii, 166. This residuary common law of civil necessity was the ground of the advisory opinion of the federal court of Pakistan in 1955 as to the President's powers in a grave constitutional emergency: *Special Reference, 1955*, P.L.D. [1955] F.C. 435. See Sir Ivor Jennings, *Constitutional Problems in Pakistan* (1957) pp. 259 *et seq.*
[63] [1965] A.C. 75. See A. L. Goodhart, " The Burmah Oil Case and the War Damage Act 1965 " (1966) 82 L.Q.R. 97; and note by Paul Jackson in (1964) 27 M.L.R. 709.
[64] In *United States* v. *Caltex* (1952) 344 U.S. 149, a similar case relating to property in the Philippines, the majority of the United States Supreme Court held that no compensation was payable at common law, while the minority thought compensation was payable under the Fifth Amendment to the Constitution (private property not to be taken for public use without just compensation).

The War Damage Act 1965 abolished retrospectively [65] any right which the subject may have had at common law to compensation from the Crown in respect of lawful acts of damage to, or destruction of property done by, or under the authority of, the Crown during, or in contemplation of, a war in which the Sovereign was or is engaged. The Act thus nullified the decision of the House of Lords in the *Burmah Oil Company* case so far as war damage is concerned. It does not deal with unlawful acts by officers or servants of the Crown,[66] nor the mere taking possession of property (requisition or angary).[67] Any payment of compensation by the government for war damage, whether caused by the Crown in prosecution of a war or by enemy action, must therefore be authorised by Act of Parliament.

2. Judicial prerogatives

These are discussed later in Chapter 19 under "The Administration of Justice."

3. Legislative prerogatives

The prerogatives in relation to the legislature include the power to summon, prorogue and dissolve Parliament, and the giving of the Royal Assent to Bills. These have already been discussed in Chapter 6. It has also been seen that the Sovereign has no prerogative power to legislate within the realm (*Case of Proclamations* (1910) [68]).

It is a parliamentary custom that legislation affecting the prerogatives or property of the Crown should be preceded by a message from the Crown; and the Speaker must not allow a Bill that affects the prerogative to be read a third time unless the royal consent has been signified by a Privy Councillor.

[65] Lawyers in both Houses objected strongly to the retroactive effect of the Bill, but: (i) the company had been offered reasonable compensation by successive Chancellors of the Exchequer, and had been warned that if their claim were successful in the courts, legislation would be introduced to indemnify the Crown, *i.e.* the taxpayer; (ii) it is unlikely that the company destroyed the property acting in the belief that there was a common law right to compensation; *cf. Phillips* v. *Eyre* (1870) L.R. 6 Q.B. 1; (iii) the provision in the American Constitution against *ex post facto* laws is interpreted to refer to penal laws: *Calder* v. *Bull* (1798) 3 Dall. 386; (iv) by what method, and on what basis, would compensation be assessed? The Japanese captured the site on the day after the installations were destroyed, and the loss was estimated at anything from nil to £100,000,000; (v) by what common law procedure (*e.g.* petition of right) could compensation have been claimed before the Crown Proceedings Act 1947?

[66] *Cf.* Crown Proceedings Act, 1947, s. 2.

[67] Angary is the power of the Crown in time of war to requisition neutral chattels found within the realm on payment of compensation: *Commercial and Estates Co. of Egypt* v. *Board of Trade* [1925] 1 K.B. 271.

[68] 2 St.Tr. 723; *ante*, p. 39. For prerogative legislation by Order in Council for British dependencies, see *post*, Chap. 34.

The Crown is not bound by an Act of Parliament, except by express words or necessary implication. It was said in some earlier cases that the Sovereign is bound, even though not named therein, by statutes for the public good, for the preservation of public rights, suppression of public wrong, relief and maintenance of the poor, advancement of learning, religion and justice, the prevention of fraud, and by statutes tending to perform the will of a grantor, donor or founder.[69]   In *Bombay Province* v. *Bombay Municipal Corporation*,[70] however, the Judicial Committee held that the inference that the Crown agreed to be bound by a statute could only be drawn if it was apparent from its terms at the time of its enactment that its beneficial purpose would be wholly frustrated if the Crown were not bound.

For the court to hold that Parliament intended an Act to bind the Crown there must be either express words to that effect, *e.g.* Crown Private Estates Acts; Crown Proceedings Act 1947; Law Reform (Limitation of Actions, etc.) Act 1954, s. 5, or words giving rise to such a strong implication that the court cannot reasonably help drawing it (*Att.-Gen.* v. *Donaldson* (1842) [71]). Thus it has been held that houses let by the Crown were not protected by Rent Restriction Acts,[72] royal palaces are not bound by the Licensing Acts,[73] vehicles driven by Crown servants were not subject to a statutory speed limit,[74] the Administrator of Austrian Property was not subject to statutes of limitation,[75] and land occupied by government departments does not require planning permission under Planning Acts.[76]

A corollary of this principle is the immunity of the Crown from income tax and rates, for they can only be imposed by authority of Act of Parliament. The matter was reviewed in *Bank voor Handel en Scheepvaart N.V.* v. *Administrator of Hungarian Property*,[77] where the House of Lords by a majority held that the Custodian of Enemy

---

[69] *Case of Ecclesiastical Persons* (1601) 5 Co.Rep. 14b; *Magdalen College Case* (*Warren* v. *Smith*) (1615) 11 Co.Rep. 66b. In *Willion* v. *Berkley* ((1561) Plowd. 223) counsel argued that the presumption is that the Sovereign " does not mean to prejudice himself or to bar himself of his liberty and privilege."
[70] [1947] A.C. 58.
[71] 10 M. & W. 117; *Gorton Local Board* v. *Prison Commissioners* (1887), reported in [1904] 2 K.B. 165 (local by-laws); *Re Wi Matua's Will* [1908] A.C. 448.
[72] *Tamlin* v. *Hannaford* [1950] 1 K.B. 18; *cf.* Crown Lessees (Protection of Sub-Tenants) Act 1952.
[73] *R.* v. *Graham Campbell, ex p. Herbert* [1935] 1 K.B. 594.
[74] *Cooper* v. *Hawkins* [1904] 2 K.B. 164; since the Road Traffic Act 1930 the Crown has been bound by speed limits subject to certain exceptions.
[75] *Administrator of Austrian Property* v. *Russian Bank for Foreign Trade* (1931) 48 T.L.R. 37 (C.A.).
[76] *Ministry of Agriculture, Fisheries and Food* v. *Jenkins* [1963] 2 Q.B. 317 (C.A.); *Campbell (A. G.) (Arcam)* v. *Worcestershire County Council* (1963) 61 L.G.R. 321 (C.A.).
[77] [1954] A.C. 584.

Property was a servant of the Crown, and that the Crown had a sufficient interest in the disposal of property held by him in that capacity to entitle him to claim exemption from tax on the income. The majority of their Lordships approved of the classification made by Blackburn J. in *Mersey Docks and Harbour Board* v. *Cameron* (1864) [78] that the immunity extends to: (i) the Sovereign personally; (ii) Crown servants, *e.g.* government departments [79]; and land occupied or funds held for Crown purposes by persons in *consimili casu, e.g.* assize courts and judges' lodgings,[80] county courts,[81] police stations [82] and prisons.[83] The difficulty was to decide, first, whether the Custodian of Hungarian Property fell into any of the categories enumerated above, and (if so) whether the property held by him was entitled to Crown immunity. Their Lordships (except Lord Keith) were agreed that the Crown, through the Board of Trade and the Treasury, had sufficient control of him to make him a Crown servant, so that he fell into category (ii).

The question whether the Crown is bound by statutes is a matter of interpretation, but there is a presumption in favour of the prerogative of immunity.[84] The general rule is subject to criticism. It has been suggested that the presumption ought to be reversed by legislation, so that the Crown would be bound by statute unless it was expressly declared not to be bound, or public policy required the exemption of the Crown in a particular case.[85]

III. THE PREROGATIVE IN FOREIGN AFFAIRS

Acts of state

There is no technical definition of " act of state," [86] but the expression is generally used in British constitutional law for an act

---

[78] 11 H.L.C. 443, 465. And see Holdsworth, *History of English Law*, Vol. X, pp. 295–299.

[79] *R.* v. *Stewart* (1857) 8 E. & B. 360. And see *Smith* v. *Birmingham Guardians* (1857) 7 E. & B. 483; *R.* v. *Kent Justices* (1890) 24 Q.B.D. 181; *Wirral Estates* v. *Shaw* [1932] 2 K.B. 247.

[80] *Hodgson* v. *Carlisle Local Board of Health* (1857) 8 E. & B. 116; and see *Coomber* v. *Berkshire Justices* (1883) 9 App.Cas. 61 (H.L.).

[81] *R.* v. *Manchester Overseers* (1854) 3 E. & B. 336.

[82] *Justices of Lancashire* v. *Stretford Overseers* (1858) E.B. & E. 225.

[83] *R.* v. *Shepherd* (1841) 1 Q.B. 170. And see *Territorial, etc. Forces Association* v. *Nichols* [1949] 1 K.B. 35.

[84] *Madras Electric Supply Corporation* v. *Boarland* [1955] A.C. 667 (P.C.). The Crown is not bound by an admission made on its behalf that the statute applies to the Crown: *Att.-Gen. for Ceylon* v. *A. D. Silva* [1953] A.C. 461 (P.C.).

[85] Glanville Williams, *Criminal Law*, I, para. 201. And see H. Street, *Governmental Liability* (1953) pp. 143–152.

[86] See Harrison Moore, *Act of State in English Law* (1906); Holdsworth, " The History of Acts of State in English Law " (1941) 41 *Columbia Law Rev.* 1313; E. C. S. Wade, " Act of State in English Law " (1934) 15 B.Y.I.L. 98.

done by the Crown as a matter of policy in relation to another state, or in relation to an individual who is not within the allegiance to the Crown.[87] The two parts of this definition are best considered separately. Cases on acts in relation to foreign states usually arise out of attempts by private individuals to enforce contract or property rights indirectly accruing, while cases on acts in relation to individuals normally arise out of an attempt to obtain a remedy for a supposed wrong directly resulting; and, as will be seen, the class of individuals against whom acts of state may be done is not free from doubt.

1. Acts of state in relation to foreign states

Acts of state in this class include the declaration of war and peace; the making of treaties; the annexation and cession of territory; the sending and receiving of diplomatic representatives; and the recognition of foreign states and governments. A claimant whose property or contracts are indirectly affected will be unsuccessful in his attempt to use an act of state as a foundation of an action. Such acts are outside the jurisdiction of British courts in the sense that they cannot be questioned. They are non-justiciable. Nor can a citizen claim to enforce directly any rights to which he may be entitled under them.[88] One view is that they are not properly described as an exercise of the " prerogative " as they are not done in relation to British subjects,[89] but there seems to be no good reason why the term " prerogative " should be limited in this way; indeed, Lord Coleridge C.J. described the making of peace and war as " perhaps the highest acts of the prerogative of the Crown." [90]

In *Salaman* v. *Secretary of State for India*,[91] where a claim was brought to enforce an agreement between the Secretary of State for India and the Maharajah of the Punjab, Fletcher Moulton L.J. said: " An act of state is essentially an act of sovereign power, and hence cannot be challenged, controlled, or interfered with by municipal courts." He went on to say that the court must accept an act of state as it is without question; but the court may be called upon to decide whether or not there has been an act of state, and (if so) its nature

---

[87] " An act of the executive as a matter of policy performed in the course of its relations with another State, including its relations with the subjects of that State, unless they are temporarily within the allegiance of the Crown ": Wade, *op. cit.* p. 103.

[88] Unless there is a special statutory provision to this effect, *e.g.* Foreign Compensation Act 1950.

[89] *Per* Warrington L.J. in *Re Ferdinand, Ex-Tsar of Bulgaria* [1921] 1 Ch. 107, 139.

[90] *Rustomjee* v. *R.* (1876) 2 Q.B.D. 69, 73.

[91] [1906] 1 K.B. 613 (C.A.). And see *Secretary of State for India* v. *Kamachee Boye Sahaba* (1859) 13 Moo.P.C. 22.

and extent.[92] Further, the court may have to consider the effect of an act of state on the rights of the government or of individuals. Thus, while the court will not enforce private rights arising under a political treaty,[93] it may be concerned if the treaty creates or modifies rights between the Crown and individuals who are, or who thereby become, subjects. For example, the Crown may recover in the courts debts due to it as a result of annexation, and presumably debts can similarly be recovered from it. The Crown decides what rights and obligations it takes over from the government of a state which it has extinguished by conquest and annexation (*West Rand Central Gold Mining Co.* v. *The King* [94]); and so there is no redress where a colonial government declines to recognise concessions made to British subjects by the former ruler of territory that has been annexed (*Cook* v. *Sprigg* [95]). It will be noticed that in these cases the act of state was not done in relation to British subjects, although it affected their interests.

A declaration of war affects the citizen's trading and contract rights with persons of enemy character, prevents a British subject from becoming naturalised in the enemy state (*R.* v. *Lynch* [96]), and alters the status in this country of nationals of the enemy state. The court must accept the certificate of the Foreign Secretary as to whether the Crown is at war, or has ceased to be at war, with a foreign country (*R.* v. *Bottrill, ex p. Kuechenmeister* [97]). The recognition by the Crown of foreign states, Sovereigns and governments may affect the rights of private individuals because of the immunity from the jurisdiction of the courts which such recognition confers (*Duff Development Co.* v. *Government of Kelantan* [98]). The court must accept the certificate of the Crown as to recognition, although it will examine the declaration in order to see that the proper facts have been considered by the appropriate Ministers.[99] Similar considerations apply to the recognition of diplomatic representatives, which confers diplomatic immunity (*Engelke* v. *Musmann* [1]).

---

[92] *Forester* v. *Secretary of State for India* (1872) L.R.Ind.App., supp. Vol., p. 10; *Musgrave* v. *Pulido* (1879) 5 App.Cas. 102 (P.C.).

[93] *Nabob of the Carnatic* v. *East India Co.* (1793) 2 Ves. 56; *Civilian War Claimants' Association* v. *The King* [1932] A.C. 14.

[94] [1905] 2 K.B. 391 (South African Republic).

[95] [1899] A.C. 572 (annexation of Pondoland to Cape Colony).

[96] [1903] 1 K.B. 444.

[97] [1947] K.B. 41 (C.A.); *post*, p. 244.

[98] [1924] A.C. 797 (H.L.). And as to the Commonwealth, see *Mighell* v. *Sultan of Johore* [1894] 1 Q.B. 149; *Kahan* v. *Pakistan Federation* [1951] 2 K.B. 1003; *Mellenger* v. *New Brunswick Development Corporation* [1971] 1 W.L.R. 604 (C.A.). *Cf. Sultan of Johore* v. *Abubakar Tunku Aris Bendahar* [1952] A.C. 218 (P.C.).

[99] *Sayce* v. *Ameer Ruler Sadig Mohammed Abbasi Bahawalpur State* [1952] 2 Q.B. 390 (C.A.).

[1] [1928] A.C. 433.

An act of state cannot alter the law administered by British courts. Thus in *The Zamora* [2] the Privy Council held that a prerogative Order in Council authorising reprisals could not increase the right of the Crown to requisition neutral ships and cargo. Although prize courts are said to administer " international law," it is such law—having its source in international law—as is recognised by English law. It may be modified by statute, but not by the prerogative.

2. *Acts of state in relation to individuals*

Acts done under the authority of the Crown in relation to individuals have been held to be acts of state, so as to prevent an aggrieved person from obtaining redress for damage done,[3] in the following classes of case. Where the plea " act of state " is successful, this means that the court declines jurisdiction. In such cases the Crown uses " act of state " as a shield in an action brought by a private individual.

(a) An alien outside British territory. In *Buron* v. *Denman* (1848 [4]) the captain of a British warship was held not liable for trespass for setting fire to the barracoon of a Spaniard on the west coast of Africa (not British territory) and releasing his slaves: the captain had general instructions to suppress the slave trade, and his conduct in this case was afterwards approved by the Admiralty and the Foreign and Colonial Secretaries. An act of state in relation to individuals, it was held, may be either previously authorised or subsequently ratified by the Crown. There is probably a prerogative power to exclude aliens from entering British territory, and at any rate aliens have no enforceable right to enter (*Musgrove* v. *Chun Teeong Toy* [5]).

(b) An enemy alien within this country. In *R.* v. *Bottrill, ex p. Kuechenmeister* [6] a German national, who had lived in England since 1928 without being naturalised and was interned by the Home Secretary during the war, was unsuccessful in his application for a writ of habeas corpus, detention by the Crown of an enemy alien being an act of state. A similar principle applies to the deportation of an enemy alien (*Netz* v. *Chuter Ede* [7]).

(c) Formerly acts done by the Crown in British protectorates in relation to the local inhabitants were regarded as acts of state, pro-

---

[2] [1916] 2 A.C. 77.

[3] Act of state may also be a defence to a criminal charge: see Stephen, *History of the Criminal Law*, II, pp. 61–65.

[4] 2 Ex. 167. The case was settled on terms.

[5] [1891] A.C. 491 (P.C.). The entry of aliens into this country is now regulated by statutory regulations.

[6] [1947] K.B. 41 (C.A.).

[7] [1946] Ch. 224.

tectorates being technically foreign countries.[8] This principle probably became untenable after the creation of the new status of British protected persons by the British Nationality Act 1948, but the question is no longer of practical importance.

With regard to British subjects outside British territory, there is no direct judicial authority.[9]

The Crown must claim " act of state " specifically.[10] But the mere plea " act of state " is not enough; the court can examine the facts in order to decide whether what has been done is an act of state. Thus in an action of trespass against the Governor of Jamaica for seizing and detaining the plaintiff's schooner, it was not enough for the defendant to plead that the acts were done by him in the exercise of his discretion as Governor and as acts of state; he had to show that the acts were done under and within the limits of his commission, or that they were really acts of state policy done under the authority of the Crown (*Musgrove* v. *Pulido*).[11]

On the other hand, if a wrong is committed by a servant of the Crown against a British subject or a friendly alien in British territory, it is no defence to plead " act of state." In *Walker* v. *Baird*,[12] where the commander of a British warship had taken possession of a lobster factory belonging to a British subject in Newfoundland, it was held no defence that the commander was acting under the orders of the Crown to implement a treaty with France. And in *Johnstone* v. *Pedlar*[13] the House of Lords held that a United States citizen in Dublin (at that time within the United Kingdom) was entitled to claim from the police commissioner money found on him at the time of his arrest for illegal drilling, " act of state " not being available as a defence to an action brought by the citizen of a friendly state for wrongful detention of property in this country.

In *Nissan* v. *Att.-Gen.*[14] Nissan, a citizen of the United Kingdom and Colonies, was lessee of an hotel in Cyprus, an independent republic

8 R. v. *Earl of Crewe, ex p. Sekgome* [1910] 2 K.B. 576 (C.A.); *Sobhuza II* v. *Miller* [1926] A.C. 518 (P.C.); *Eshugbayi (Eleko)* v. *Government of Nigeria (Officer Administering)* [1931] A.C. 662 (P.C.); R. v. *Ketter* [1940] 1 K.B. 787. Cf. *Ex p. Mwenya* ([1960] 1 Q.B. 241 (C.A.)), where the petitioner was assumed to be a British subject by virtue of local citizenship laws (Federation of Rhodesia and Nyasaland). Cf. K. Polack, " The Defence of Act of State in Relation to Protectorates " (1963) 26 M.L.R. 138; L. L. Kato, " Act of State in a Protectorate —in Retrospect " [1969] P.L. 219.
9 See *Nissan* v. *Att.-Gen.* [1970] A.C. 179 (H.L.) *infra*.
10 *Nissan* v. *Att.-Gen.* [1970] A.C. 179, *infra*.
11 (1879) 5 App.Cas. 102 (P.C.).
12 [1892] A.C. 491 (P.C.).   And see the *General Warrant Cases, post*, Chap. 23.
13 [1921] 2 A.C. 262.
14 [1970] A.C. 179.   See J. G. Collier, " Act of State as a Defence against a British Subject " (1968) C.L.J. 102, and note in (1969) C.L.J. 166; S. A. de Smith in (1969) 32 M.L.R. 427; cf. D. R. Gilmour, " British Forces Abroad and the Responsibility for their Actions " [1970] P.L. 120.

in the Commonwealth. The hotel was occupied by British troops for several months as part of a truce force under an agreement between the Governments of the United Kingdom and Cyprus for the purpose of restoring peace in the civil strife between the Greek and Turkish communities. The British forces then continued to occupy the hotel for a period as part of a United Nations peace-keeping force, on the recommendation of the Security Council of the United Nations and with the consent of the Cyprus Government. Nissan brought an action against the Crown in England, claiming declarations that he was entitled to compensation for damage to the contents of the hotel and the destruction of stores, on the ground that this was a lawful exercise of the prerogative [15]; and that the Crown was liable in damages for trespass to chattels by the British troops.[16] This case was fought on preliminary issues, in particular, whether the acts of the British forces were acts of state.[17] The House of Lords upheld the Court of Appeal in deciding that the acts of the British forces were not non-justiciable as acts of state. Although the agreement of the British Government with the Cyprus Government to send peace-keeping forces to Cyprus was no doubt an act of state, not all acts done incidentally in relation to individual persons or their property (such as occupying a particular hotel or damaging its contents) in the course of executing an act of state are themselves acts of state. All the Law Lords said it was unnecessary to discuss whether the acts of the Crown were an exercise of the prerogative, although Lord Denning M.R. in the Court of Appeal based the liability of the Crown to pay compensation on the exercise of the prerogative, referring to the *Burmah Oil Company* case.

There are a number of dicta in the various judgments concerning " act of state." Lords Morris, Wilberforce and Pearson seemed to think that in some circumstances the Crown might successfully plead act of state against a British subject in relation to property abroad, *e.g.* damage or seizure in armed operations of property which included property of a British subject resident in that country.[18] Lord Reid

---

15 See *Burmah Oil Co.* v. *Lord Advocate* [1965] A.C. 75; *ante*, p. 238.
16 Nissan also claimed that there was a contract by the High Commissioner on behalf of the Crown, with the consent of the Secretary of State, that he would receive compensation for occupation of the hotel.
17 Also on the questions whether there was a contract, express or implied, that he would be compensated (a question of fact left to the trial court); and whether the British troops in the first period were agents of the Cyprus Government, and whether in the second period they were agents of the United Nations, the decision as to both periods being " no."
18 H. W. R. Wade suggests that the test whether " act of state " is a defence to an action for a tort against a British subject should be a matter of geography rather than nationality, *e.g.* British troops seizing Suez Canal damage house of British subject living in Egypt: *Administrative Law* (3rd ed. 1971) pp. 294–296, citing *Cook* v. *Sprigg* [1899] A.C. 572.

stated the traditional doctrine that " act of state " is not available as
a defence to the infringement of the rights of British subjects abroad,
but the majority were doubtful about this.

If allegiance or British nationality is crucial in such cases, who
are " British subjects " for this purpose? The cases say that " British
subjects " everywhere owe permanent allegiance to the Crown, and
friendly aliens in British territory owe temporary allegiance; but since
1948 independent countries in the Commonwealth have their own
separate citizenship; further, some of them are republics and acknow-
ledge the Queen merely as Head of the Commonwealth. There is also
since 1948 the class of British protected persons. The principle that
act of state is no defence might apply to: (i) all persons who are
British subjects under the British Nationality Act 1948; or (ii) British
subjects other than citizens of republics, who do not owe allegiance
to the Queen; or (iii) citizens of the United Kingdom and Colonies,
but not citizens of the realms who owe allegiance to the Queen as
Queen of Canada, etc.; and (iv) British protected persons who are
connected with a territory that has ceased to be a protectorate, protected state or trust territory and who are not citizens of any Commonwealth country.[19] In view of the disintegration of the common law
throughout the Commonwealth, also, the earlier cases may similarly
have to be reviewed on the questions: what is meant in this context
by " British territory," " abroad " and " foreign country? "

Passports [20]

The Secretary of State has a discretion to grant, refuse, impound
or revoke passports, which remain Crown property. A passport
contains a request in the name of Her Majesty to allow the bearer to
pass freely, and to afford him such assistance and protection as may
be necessary. The Crown has a duty to protect its citizens abroad,
although this is not legally enforceable.[21] A passport is not legally
necessary at common law in order to go abroad,[22] but it is universally

---

[19] See British Nationality (No. 2) Act 1964, s. 5; British Protectorates, Protected
States and Protected Persons Order 1965; *post*, Chap. 21.

[20] See W. J. K. Diplock, " Passports and Protection in International Law " (1947)
Grotius Society Transactions 42; Glanville Williams, " The Correlation of
Allegiance and Protection " (1948) 10 C.L.J. 54; L. B. Bondin, " The Constitu-
tional Right to Travel " (1956) 56 *Columbia Law Rev.* 47.

[21] But the obtaining of a British passport, even by an alien, involves allegiance to the
Crown: *Joyce* v. *D.P.P.* [1946] A.C. 347 (H.L.).

[22] Blackstone, following the original version of Magna Carta (1215) said: " by the
common law, every man may go out of the realm for whatever cause he pleaseth,
without obtaining the King's leave."

used as a certificate of identity and nationality.[23] Other countries may refuse entry without possession of one, and therefore transport companies may be expected to refuse to carry passengers abroad without passports.

Treaties

The treaty-making power is an executive power which in British constitutional law is vested in the Crown. A treaty is analogous to a contract between states. Its binding force is a matter of international law. The negotiations are conducted by agents of the Crown, *e.g.* the Foreign Secretary or a diplomatic representative, and are usually made subject to ratification by the Crown under the Great Seal. Treaties are acts of state, and do not in general require parliamentary sanction.[24] Where treaties require ratification by the Crown (*i.e.* treaties between Heads of State, but not commercial or technical agreements at official level), it has been the practice since 1924 to lay them when signed before both Houses of Parliament for twenty-one days before they are ratified (" the Ponsonby Rule ").[25] On important treaties the government initiates a discussion; otherwise the Opposition may ask for a discussion.

There are, however, three classes of treaty which do require confirmation by Parliament [26]:

(i) *Treaties expressly made subject to confirmation by Parliament.* A treaty expressly made subject to confirmation by Parliament will not come into force, either by international law or by English law, unless an Act of Parliament is passed confirming it; for that is a condition in the treaty itself. Such parliamentary sanction is sometimes spoken of as " ratification," but that word is properly used of the final authentication by the Crown. Examples of the requirement of statutory confirmation are the European Communities Act 1972, and the peace treaties with former enemy countries after the last war, which involved the private rights of British subjects, the establishment of offices, the imposition of penalties for breach of their provisions, and the payment of expenses to be provided by Parliament.

---

23 H. W. R. Wade, " Passports and the individual's right to travel " *The Times*, August 7, 1968. The refusal of a passport is sometimes reinforced by putting the onus on the applicant to prove that he is a British subject. Wade argues that discretionary powers should be exercised reasonably and in good faith. *Cf. Ghani* v. *Jones* [1970] 1 Q.B. 693 (C.A.), where the police took and retained Pakistani passports in order to prevent persons suspected of murder from leaving the country.

24 *Att.-Gen. for Canada* v. *Att.-Gen. for Ontario* [1937] A.C. 326 (P.C.).

25 (1924) 171 H.C. Deb. 53, col. 2001.

26 Lord McNair, *The Law of Treaties*, Chap. 2; *Legal Effects of War* (3rd ed.) pp. 397–402; " When do British Treaties involve Legislation? " (1928) B.Y.I.L. 59.

(ii) *Treaties involving an alteration of English law or taxation.*
Any alteration of English law involved in implementing a treaty,
including the imposition of taxes or the expenditure of public money,
would have to be authorised by Act of Parliament either beforehand
or *ex post facto*; for example, the imposition of customs duties or
the taking over by the United Kingdom Government of the public
debt of annexed territory (*Att.-Gen. for Canada* v. *Att.-Gen. for
Ontario*).[27] It was found necessary to pass the Geneva Convention
Act 1937 to implement the convention prohibiting the use of the
Red Cross symbol for mercantile purposes. The courts take no
notice of treaties until enacted by Parliament,[28] and statute prevails
over the terms of a treaty inconsistent therewith.[29]

(iii) *Treaties affecting private rights.* In *The Parlement Belge*
(1879)[30] Sir Robert Phillimore said that treaties affecting the private
rights of British subjects were inoperative without the confirmation
of the legislature. The Crown, therefore, could not by a treaty with
Belgium confer on a private ship engaged in trade the immunities
of a public ship so as to deprive a British subject of the right to
bring proceedings against the ship for damage sustained in a collision.
This is really a particular aspect of (ii) above (treaties involving
an alteration of English law). It is also the reason why Extradition
Acts are required to give legal effect to treaties made for surrendering
persons accused of crimes committed abroad.[31]

By the making of a treaty the Crown may morally bind Parliament
to pass any legislation needed to give full effect to it. The negotiation
of treaties, which must often be done in secret, is less under parliamentary control than almost any other branch of the prerogative,
and Parliament may be met with a *fait accompli*. But there is an
increasing tendency to keep Parliament informed and to invite expressions of opinion before the Crown finally commits itself, as was
done during the Common Market negotiations in 1962-71. This
is only expedient, as the government relies on the support of Parliament, and especially of the Commons. Where legislation will be
required to supplement a treaty, there is probably a convention that

---

27 [1937] A.C. 326, 347 (P.C.) *per* Lord Atkin. This is the effect of the *Case of
   Proclamations* ((1610) 12 Co.Rep. 74) and the Bill of Rights.
28 *Rustomjee* v. *The Queen* (1876) 2 Q.B.D. 69 *per* Lord Coleridge C.J.; *Blackburn* v.
   Att.-Gen. [1971] 1 W.L.R. 1037 (C.A) *per* Lord Denning M.R. See D. G. T.
   Williams, " Prerogative and Parliamentary Control " [1971] C.L.J. 178.
29 *Cheney* v. *Conn* [1968] 1 W.L.R. 292.
30 4 P.D. 129, 154. The Court of Appeal ((1880) 5 P.D. 197) reversed Sir Robert
   Phillimore's decision on the ground that the ship in that case was a public ship,
   but they carefully refrained from expressing disapproval of the principle stated by
   him, which is regarded as good law; applied by MacKenna J. in *Swiss-Israel Trade
   Bank* v. *Government of Malta, The Times,* April 14, 1972.
31 Maitland, *Constitutional History,* pp. 424-425.

Parliament should be consulted in principle before the treaty is concluded. Parliament will also be consulted in very important matters, such as the declaration of war or the conclusion of a peace treaty.

Treaties of cession

Doubt has been expressed whether the Crown can by virtue of the prerogative cede territory, so as to deprive British subjects of their nationality and perhaps property and contract rights.[32] The Crown was persuaded to seek parliamentary approval for the cession of Heligoland to Germany in 1890,[33] and since then it has been the practice to ask Parliament to confirm cessions.[34] Whatever the law may be, this seems to be now the convention. Indeed, convention probably demands that Parliament should be consulted beforehand, as in the case of the cession of Jubaland to Italy in 1927.

Diplomatic representation

It is part of the royal prerogative in relation to foreign affairs to recognise, or to withhold recognition from, foreign states, their heads and governments. Foreign states, their heads, governments and diplomatic envoys recognised by the Crown enjoy immunity from the jurisdiction of English courts, as do public ships and other chattels of foreign states.[35] If a diplomatic envoy commits a breach of the law, the Foreign Secretary may request his government to recall him as persona non grata, as was done in the case of the Swedish Ambassador, Count Gyllenburg, in 1717.

The Diplomatic Privileges Act 1708 arose out of Mattueof's Case,[36] in which the Russian Ambassador had been arrested for debt and taken out of his coach in London. The Court of Queen's Bench was uncertain whether the Sheriff of Middlesex and his assistants were guilty of a criminal offence. Peter the Great demanded that they should be punished with instant death. Queen Anne replied that she could not punish any of her subjects except in accordance with

---

[32] See Anson, Law and Custom of the Constitution, II, ii (4th ed. Keith) pp. 137–142; Holdsworth, " The Treaty-making power of the Crown " (1942) 58 L.Q.R. 177, 183. Cf. Damodhar Gordhan v. Deoram Kanji (1876) 1 App.Cas. 352 (P.C.). And cf. Treaty of Paris 1783, recognising the independence of the former American colonies.

[33] Anglo-German Agreement Act 1890.

[34] e.g. Anglo-Italian (East African Territories) Act 1925; Dindings Agreement Approval Act 1934; Anglo-Venezuelan Treaty (Island of Patos) Act 1942.

[35] Rahimtoola v. Nizam of Hyderabad [1958] A.C. 379 (H.L.); The Parlement Belge (1879) 4 P.D. 129; (1880) 5 P.D. 197; The Porto Alexandre [1920] P. 30. See H. G. Hanbury, " The Position of the Foreign Sovereign before the English Courts " [1955] C.L.P. 1.

[36] (1709) 10 Mod.Rep. 4; Bl.Comm. I, 255–356; Martens, Causes Célèbres du Droit des Gens (1827), I, p. 47.

law. The Act of 1708, which was largely declaratory, was therefore passed, providing that judicial proceedings brought against diplomatic envoys or their servants should be null and void, and that it should be a misdemeanour to commence such proceedings.[37]

The Diplomatic Privileges Act 1964, giving effect to most of the provisions of the Vienna Convention on Diplomatic Relations 1961, replaces the previous law on the privileges and immunities of diplomatic representatives in the United Kingdom. The Act adopts the Continental practice of dividing the members of a diplomatic mission into three classes:

(i) members of the diplomatic staff, who have full personal immunity, civil and criminal, with certain exceptions;

(ii) members of the administrative and technical staff, who enjoy full immunity for official acts, but are liable civilly (though not criminally) for acts performed outside the course of their duties[38];

(iii) members of the service staff, who enjoy immunity for official acts, but are liable both civilly and criminally for acts performed outside the course of their duties.

Privileges and immunities may be withdrawn by Order in Council from any state that grants less to British missions.

The certificate of the Foreign Secretary is conclusive as to whether a person falls into any (and, if so, which) of the above three classes. But the courts for the first time were given power to determine whether an act committed by a member of a diplomatic mission was performed in the course of his duties.

Members of the diplomatic mission of a Commonwealth country or of Ireland and their private servants are entitled, if they are both citizens of that Commonwealth country or Ireland and also citizens of the United Kingdom and Colonies, to the privileges and immunities to which they would have been entitled if they had not been citizens of the United Kingdom and Colonies.

Diplomatic privilege may be waived in any particular case. Where an ambassador or other head of mission is concerned, waiver must be with the consent of his Sovereign (*Re Suarez*[39]); where a subordinate is concerned, waiver must be by the head of the mission.[40] Unless the waiver extends to execution, which is unlikely, judgment in

---

[37] The Queen sent an illuminated copy of the Act to Moscow, which appeased the Czar, and the offenders were discharged at his request. It is uncertain how far the 1708 Act covered the bringing of criminal proceedings. There is no record of a prosecution for contravening the Act.

[38] *Empson* v. *Smith* [1966] 1 Q.B. 426 (C.A.).

[39] *Re Suarez, Suarez* v. *Suarez* [1918] 1 Ch. 187.

[40] *Dickinson* v. *Del Solar* [1930] 1 K.B. 376; *Re Republic of Bolivia Exploration Syndicate Ltd.* [1914] 1 Ch. 139.

such a case cannot be enforced until a reasonable time after the envoy has been recalled.[41]

Under the International Organisations Act 1968 [42] immunities and privileges may be accorded to an international organisation of which the United Kingdom is a member, e.g. United Nations, NATO, EEC; and to persons connected with such organisations. Provision is also made for granting immunities and privileges to judges and suitors of the International Court of Justice, and to representatives of other states attending international conferences in the United Kingdom.

Diplomatic privileges and immunities have been extended to the high commissioners or ambassadors of the independent members of the Commonwealth, Associated States and the Republic of Ireland, their staffs, families and servants; and to certain representatives of Commonwealth governments and of the Government of the Republic of Ireland attending conferences with the British Government.[43] Diplomatic immunity and privileges may also be extended by Order in Council to any international headquarters or defence organisation set up under an arrangement for common defence, e.g. NATO, and the Visiting Forces Act 1952 may be applied to them.[44]

The privileges and immunities of consuls are governed by the Consular Relations Act 1968, which gives effect to the Vienna Convention on Consular Relations; and (as to Commonwealth and Irish consuls) by section 4 of the Diplomatic and other Privileges Act 1971.

---

[41] Re Suarez, supra.
[42] Replacing the International Organisations (Immunities and Privileges) Act 1950, and the European Coal and Steel Community Act 1955.
[43] Diplomatic Immunities (Conferences with Commonwealth Countries and Republic of Ireland) Act 1961.
[44] International Headquarters and Defence Organisations Act 1964.

CHAPTER 14

THE PRIVY COUNCIL

I. THE COUNCIL AS AN INSTRUMENT OF GOVERNMENT

Historical introduction [1]

The *Curia Regis* exercised supreme legislative, executive and judicial powers, subject to general feudal customs. From the *Curia Regis* there developed in course of time the most important institutions of English central government, namely, the Exchequer and the Treasury (12th century), the courts of common law (13th–14th centuries) and Chancery (14th–15th centuries), and the House of Lords, *i.e.* the King's Council in Parliament [2] (14th century).

The Privy Council has been generally regarded as a continuation of the *Curia Regis* after these other bodies had separated, but it may be more precise to say that the *Curia Regis* ceased to exist, and that the Council which emerged as a distinct body in the thirteenth and fourteenth centuries was something new. The Council was used as a powerful instrument of government by the Tudors. In Henry VIII's reign the distinction was first drawn between " Ordinary Councillors," a fairly large number of lawyers and administrators, and " Privy Councillors," a select body of nobles who acted as the King's advisers. As the Tudor period progressed the tendency was for Privy Councillors to be drawn from humbler ranks of society.

Coke, in his treatment of the courts, deals after the High Court of Parliament with " the Councell Board or Table," and says: " This is a most noble, honourable, and reverend assembly of the King and his privy councell in the King's court or palace; with this councell the King himself doth sit at pleasure. These councellors, like good centinels and watchmen, consult of and for the publique good, and the honour, defence, safety and profit of the realm." [3]

Committees composed of some only of the members of the Council were sometimes used by the Tudors for particular purposes or occasions, and temporary or permanent committees were used frequently in the seventeenth century. For various reasons Committees of the whole Council came to be employed in the eighteenth century,

---

[1] Holdsworth, *History of English Law*, Vol. I; Baldwin, *The King's Council during the Middle Ages*; Turner, *The Privy Council, 1603–1784*; Dicey, *The Privy Council*; Williamson, *Studies in the Constitutional History of the Thirteenth and Fourteenth Centuries*.   [2] The House of Lords was not so called until Henry VII's reign.
[3] 4 Inst. 53.

and, indeed, most of the Council's work was then carried on in Committee. Some of these committees in their turn became, or transferred their administrative functions to, separate government departments such as the Board of Trade and the former Boards of Agriculture and Education.

The eclipse of the Privy Council as a practical instrument of government came with the development in the eighteenth century of the Cabinet as the policy-making organ and advisory body of the Crown, which is discussed in the next chapter.

The Privy Council at the present day: the composition of the Privy Council

"The Lords and others of Her Majesty's most Honourable Privy Council," now about three hundred in number, consist of persons who hold or have held high political or legal office, peers, Church dignitaries and persons distinguished in the services and professions. They are appointed by letters patent, and include the Lord President of the Council, all Cabinet Ministers by convention, the two Archbishops by prescription, and customarily some of the leading Commonwealth statesmen, British Ambassadors, the Speaker of the House of Commons, the Lords of Appeal in Ordinary, the Lord Chief Justice, the Master of the Rolls, the President of the Family Division, and the Lords Justices of Appeal.

A new member of the Privy Council must take the oath of allegiance and the special Privy Councillor's oath, which binds him to keep secret all matters committed or revealed to him or that are treated of secretly in Council.[4] An affirmation may be made in lieu of oath.[5] The oath or affirmation probably does not add anything to the obligation later imposed by the Official Secrets Acts. The disclosure of such confidential information requires the consent of the Sovereign, which in practice means the Prime Minister of the day. Privy Councillors must be British subjects. They are addressed as " Right Honourable." Since the Demise of the Crown Act 1901 membership of the Privy Council is apparently not affected by a demise of the Crown.

Functions of the Privy Council [6]

The Privy Council became too unwieldy as an instrument of government. Owing to the development of the Cabinet and government

---

4 For the modern form of Privy Councillor's oath, see Anson, *Law and Custom of the Constitution* (4th ed.) Vol. II, Pt. I, p. 153.   5 Oaths Act 1888.
6 For a descriptive account, see Sir Almeric Fitzroy, *The History of the Privy Council* (1928) pp. 294 *et seq.*

departments, the Council lost most of its advisory and administrative functions and is today little more than an organ for giving formal effect to certain acts done under prerogative or statutory powers.

Proclamations and Orders in Council

The most important acts done by Her Majesty " by and with the advice of her Privy Council " take the form of proclamations or Orders in Council, the former normally being authorised by the latter. Proclamations are employed for such matters as proroguing, dissolving and summoning Parliament [7] and declaring war or peace—solemn occasions requiring the widest publicity. Orders in Council are used when changes in the law are made, and are mostly issued under statutory powers.[8] The nature of an Order in Council may be legislative, e.g. making laws for certain overseas territories and Statutory Instruments dealing with various aspects of the welfare state; executive, e.g. setting up a new government department, issuing regulations for the armed forces, or declaring a state of emergency to exist or to be at an end; or judicial, e.g. giving effect to a judgment (technically advice) of the Judicial Committee of the Privy Council.

Miscellaneous functions

A Privy Council is also summoned for certain special occasions, such as the acceptance of office by newly appointed Ministers, and the annual " pricking " of sheriffs on Maundy Thursday.

Meetings of the Privy Council

Privy Councillors are summoned to attend at Buckingham Palace, or wherever else the Sovereign may be.[9] The quorum is three. Usually four are summoned, being Ministers concerned with the business in hand. The whole Council has not met (except at an Accession) since 1839, when Queen Victoria's forthcoming marriage was announced.

Lord Morrison of Lambeth, a former Lord President of the Council, gave this description of an ordinary meeting: " First of all, before the Council begins, the Lord President is received in Audience. The other Counsellors then enter and, having bowed and shaken hands with the King, take up their position. They stand in a line, headed by the Lord President, who has a List of Business, as the agenda is called. The items in this are already known to His Majesty,

---

7 For a specimen, see Anson, op. cit. (5th ed. Gwyer) Vol. I, pp. 55–56.
8 For the form, see Anson, op. cit. (4th ed. Keith) Vol. II, Pt. I, p. 62.
9 A meeting was held at Buckingham Palace at 12.30 a.m. on March 15, 1968, to issue an Order in Council declaring a special bank holiday on the following day, owing to a gold crisis.

who, as they are read out by the Lord President, approves them or gives any other directions that may be needed. When the business is finished, the proceedings become rather less formal. There is some general conversation; then the Counsellors withdraw, leaving as they entered in accordance with their precedence." [10] According to Viscount Caldecote,[11] a former Lord Chancellor, the Lord President reads out the titles of draft Orders in Council, and the Sovereign perfects the drafts by saying " Approved."

The Orders are authenticated by the signature of the Clerk to the Council and the seal of the Council. The Clerk also records the names of the Councillors present, who are legally responsible for what is transacted.

Committees of the Council

Any meeting of Privy Councillors at which the Sovereign or Counsellors of State are not present can only be a committee.[12] Apart from the Judicial Committee, which is discussed below, there are advisory or *ad hoc* committees concerned with such matters as scientific research, the older universities, and the grant of charters.

II. THE JUDICIAL FUNCTIONS OF THE PRIVY COUNCIL [13]

Historical introduction

Even after the separation of the courts of common law and the Court of Chancery, the King's Council retained some jurisdiction (i) in cases which in some way concerned the state, and (ii) in private cases where the ordinary courts could not provide a remedy. This jurisdiction, especially the latter element, represented the residue of justice that always lay with the King. In the early Middle Ages the Council was not a court of record; it had no seal, and indeed it was not called a " court " at all.[14]

---

[10] Herbert Morrison, " The Privy Council today " (1948) 2 *Parliamentary Affairs* (Hansard Society) p. 10, 12–13. See also Dermot Morrah, *The Queen at Work* (1958) pp. 142–144.

[11] Viscount Caldecote, " The King's prerogative " (1941) 7 C.L.J. 310, 320.

[12] This idea dates from the middle of the eighteenth century.

[13] Holdsworth, *History of English Law*, Vol. I; N. Bentwich, *Privy Council Practice* (3rd ed. 1937) Chap. I; Viscount Haldane, " The Judicial Committee of the Privy Council " (1922) 1 C.L.J. 143; Sir George Rankin, " The Judicial Committee of the Privy Council " (1939) 7 C.L.J. 2; Lord Normand, " The Judicial Committee of the Privy Council—retrospect and prospect (1950) C.L.P. 1; Robert Stevens, " The Final Appeal: Reform of the House of Lords and Privy Council 1867–1876 " (1964) 80 L.Q.R. 343.

[14] Leadam and Baldwin, Introduction to *Select Cases before the King's Council* (Selden Society Publications).

In the Tudor period most of the Council's jurisdiction relating to state offences and cases in which great men were involved was exercised by the Court of Star Chamber. In this period the Court of High Commission was set up to deal with important ecclesiastical causes, and the Court of Requests as a " minor Court of Equity " to hear the suits of poor persons. It was part of the struggle between Parliament and the King in the early seventeenth century that these courts of an " arbitrary " jurisdiction should be attacked as being closely associated with the royal prerogative. The Long Parliament, in the same year in which it abolished the Court of High Commission, also passed a statute commonly known as the Act for the abolition of the Star Chamber 1640. Certain other prerogative jurisdictions, such as those of the Councils of Wales and the Marches and of the North, were also expressly abolished. The Act further declared and enacted that neither His Majesty nor his Privy Council have or ought to have any jurisdiction over the land or chattels of English subjects. Although the Court of Requests was not mentioned, it ceased to function almost immediately afterwards.

The ancient judicial powers of the Privy Council survived only in the form of an appellate jurisdiction from the King's overseas dominions, namely, the Channel Islands, the Isle of Man, the colonies (or " foreign plantations," as they were at first called) [15] and, later, India. In the eighteenth century the Judicial Committees formed for this purpose acquired many of the characteristics of courts; they usually sat in public, and reports began to be published in 1829.

Appeals from the ecclesiastical courts, the Court of Admiralty and the vice-admiralty courts of the colonies were given to the Privy Council by statute in 1832. This statutory extension of the Privy Council's jurisdiction necessitated a reorganisation of its constitution.

The Judicial Committee—composition

The Judicial Committee Act 1833, passed " for the better administration of justice in His Majesty's Privy Council," constituted a Judicial Committee. The Judicial Committee Act 1844 authorised the Queen by Order in Council to admit any appeals to the Privy Council from any court within any British colony or possession abroad, even though such court might not be a court of error or of appeal. Hence appeals lay from the Australian states after federation. It has been questioned whether this Act put the prerogative power on a statutory basis, or merely regulated the manner of its exercise.

[15] *Fryer* v. *Bernard* (1724) 2 P.W. 262.

As a result of the Act of 1833 and various later statutes,[16] the Judicial Committee is composed of:

(a) the Lord Chancellor; the Lord President and ex-Lord Presidents of the Council (who do not sit) [17]; the Lords of Appeal in Ordinary; and the Lords Justices of Appeal (who seldom sit);

(b) ex-Lord Chancellors and retired Lords of Appeal;

(c) selected senior judges or ex-judges of Australia, New Zealand and other Commonwealth countries from which appeal lies.

The quorum is three.

It will be seen that the composition of the Judicial Committee is wider than that of the House of Lords sitting as a final court of appeal.

English, Scottish and Northern Irish barristers, and also certain Commonwealth and colonial practitioners, have the right of audience before the Committee. Privy Council agents consist of English solicitors, Scottish writers to the signet and Northern Irish solicitors, provided that their names are on the Privy Council roll.

Jurisdiction

The Judicial Committee was given the jurisdiction of the Privy Council set out above, namely, appeals from the courts of the Channel Islands, the Isle of Man, the colonies and British India, and from the ecclesiastical courts and the Admiralty Court, to which were later added appeals from prize courts.

Appeals in probate, divorce and admiralty causes (other than prize) were later transferred to the House of Lords. From the Arches Court of Canterbury and the Chancery Court of York the Judicial Committee now hears appeals only in causes of faculty not involving matter of doctrine, ritual or ceremonial.[18] A number of former colonies and protectorates, as well as India, have become independent members of the Commonwealth, and in many cases appeals from their courts to the Judicial Committee of the Privy Council have been abolished by local legislation.[19]

Recent statutes have given a right of appeal to the Judicial

---

[16] Appellate Jurisdiction Acts 1876, 1887 and 1908; Judicial Committee Amendment Act 1895.

[17] The Lord President, Secretaries of State and other laymen often sat until the middle of the nineteenth century; for example, the Duke of Buccleuch, of whom the future Lord Kingsdown said: " Depend upon it, the natives of India would much rather have this case decided by a great Scottish Duke than by lawyers alone ": Stevens, *op. cit.* p. 349.

[18] Ecclesiastical Jurisdiction Measure 1963, s. 8. A faculty is a licence from an ecclesiastical superior to do something, such as putting in a stained-glass window.

[19] For appeals to the Privy Council from courts overseas, see *post*, Chap. 36.

Committee from the tribunals of various medical and other professional organisations having power to strike a member off the register.[20]

It has been suggested that the judicial functions of the Privy Council should be merged with those of the House of Lords, and that the Judicial Committee should become a peripatetic Commonwealth Court.[21] The former idea was often discussed in the nineteenth century. The latter idea is not new, but seems to be no longer practicable in the present stage of Commonwealth development or disintegration.

Procedure

Rules of practice are made under the Act of 1833. Appeals, or requests for leave to appeal, are commenced by petition to the Crown. Usually only one " judgment " is given by the Board. This is in theory a report made to Her Majesty of the reasons why judgment should be given in favour of a particular party; but the Committee is regarded for practical purposes as a court, and the Queen is bound by convention to give effect to its advice, which is done by Order in Council.[22] Indeed, the report is made public before it is sent up to the Sovereign in Council.[23]

The advice was formerly required to be unanimous,[24] but an Order in Council in 1966[25] allowed dissenting opinions to be delivered, and this is sometimes done.

Special reference

Section 4 of the Judicial Committee Act 1833 provides that the Crown may refer to the Committee for an advisory opinion any question of law it may think fit. Thus in 1927 the Committee was asked to give an opinion on the Labrador boundary dispute between Canada and Newfoundland,[26] and in 1924 on the interpretation of the provisions of the Anglo-Irish Treaty of 1921 relating to the settlement of the boundary between Northern Ireland and the Irish Free State.[27] It has been called to advise on the elements of the inter-

---

20 *Post*, Chap. 29.
21 Gerald Gardiner and Andrew Martin, *Law Reform Now* (1963) p. 16; *post*, Chap. 36.
22 *British Coal Corp.* v. *The King* [1935] A.C. 500; *Ibralebbe* v. *R.* [1964] A.C. 900.
23 *Hull* v. *M'Kenna* [1926] I.R. 402, *per* Viscount Haldane.
24 *Cf. Cowie* v. *Remfry* (1846) 5 Moo.P.C. 232.
25 Judicial Committee (Dissenting Opinions) Order in Council, 1966. Lord Pearce delivered a dissenting opinion in *Madzimbamuto* v. *Lardner-Burke* [1969] 1 A.C. 645 (appeal from Southern Rhodesia).
26 (1927) 43 T.R. 289.
27 (1924) Cmd. 2214.

national crime of piracy for guidance in future cases, following the erroneous acquittal of certain Chinese by the Supreme Court of Hongkong, there being no appeal from an acquittal.[28] Its advice has also been sought by the Commons, through the Attorney-General, on disqualifications from sitting in the House.[29] The opinion of the Committee may be required on the validity of legislation of the Northern Ireland Parliament under the Government of Ireland Act 1920.[30]

[28] *Re Piracy Jure Gentium* [1934] A.C. 584.
[29] *Re Sir Stuart Samuel* [1913] A.C. 514; *Re MacManaway, Re House of Common (Clergy Disqualification) Act 1801* [1951] A.C. 161. See also *Re Parliamentary Privilege Act 1770* [1958] A.C. 331.
[30] *Re a Reference under the Government of Ireland Act 1920* [1936] A.C. 352.

CHAPTER 15

THE CABINET AND THE PRIME MINISTER

I. DEVELOPMENT OF THE CABINET [1]

Origins in the Privy Council

The seventeenth and eighteenth centuries saw the growth of the practice of withdrawing the discussion and direction of government policy, as distinct from administration, into the hands of a few of the King's *confidential* advisers. The history of this subject is very obscure, owing to the secrecy of the proceedings and the lack of official and connected records, and the fact that during most of this period the practice was unpopular with Parliament and in the country, and was not openly avowed. The historian's difficulty is further increased by the confusing terminology employed by the writers of that time. The better opinion probably is that the body which we now know as the Cabinet should never at any stage in its history be identified with any particular committee of the Privy Council, such as the Committee for Foreign Affairs. No doubt the use of committees helped to crystallise the form that the Cabinet was to take. The process was further assisted by the appointment of regency councils, known as " the Lords Justices," during the frequent absence abroad of William III, George I and George II. In this case the absence of the King made it necessary to commit resolutions to writing, and even to frame rules of procedure.

In the eighteenth century the members of the Cabinet came to call themselves " His Majesty's servants " or " His Majesty's *confidential* servants." The names given to Charles II's group of confidential advisers were intended as terms of reproach. *Cabinet* was a French word then in vogue for a private room set apart for interviews, and the " Cabinet Council " or " Cabinet " was so called because it met literally or metaphorically in the King's cabinet or closet.

George I attended Cabinet meetings at the beginning of his reign, but very seldom after 1717. The main reasons for his abstention were that he was little interested in English affairs, ignorant of the

---

[1] Turner, *The Cabinet Council, 1622–1784*; A. B. Keith, *The British Cabinet System, 1830–1938* (2nd ed. Gibbs); D. L. Keir, *A Constitutional History of Modern Britain*; M. A. Thomson, *A Constitutional History of England, 1642–1801*; C. S. Emden, *The People and the Constitution*; Richard Pares, *King George III and the Politicians* (1953); Sir Lewis Namier, *Crossroads of Power* (1962) Chaps. 7 and 8.

English language and institutions, and unable to influence policy owing to his dependence for support on the Whig leaders. Both George II and George III seem occasionally to have been present at Cabinet meetings for some special reason. The absence of the Sovereign marks a definite epoch in the development of the power of the principal Ministers, although the decline of the royal power was gradual. Kings in the eighteenth century still exercised influence from their closet, and were " sometimes near, if not present." [2]

A further process of division took place in the reign of George II, when a distinction was drawn between the " inner," " efficient," or " effective " Cabinet and the " outer " or " nominal " Cabinet. The former, also known as the " conciliabulum," had special access to important state papers, while the latter disclaimed responsibility for acts of the Ministry on which they had not been consulted. The inner Cabinet, which may be regarded as the direct ancestor of the modern Cabinet, was in existence at least as early as 1740.[3] The size of the Cabinet had increased from five to about twenty in George III's reign. Indeed, the Cabinet had become considerably larger than Elizabeth I's Privy Council, which numbered only twelve.

Opposition of Parliament

The practice of consulting confidentially a small group of Ministers, which had been intermittent in the reign of Charles I, was habitual in the reign of Charles II, and Parliament objected strongly to the secrecy of the deliberations, for it was difficult to know who were the responsible Ministers and how to enforce that responsibility. In order to put a stop to the practice, and to keep the House of Commons from being contaminated by the Sovereign's influence, Parliament inserted two clauses in the Act of Settlement 1700 to the effect that: (1) matters theretofore discussed in the Privy Council must be dealt with there and not elsewhere, and all resolutions must be signed by the members present, and (2) no person holding a place of profit under the Crown was to sit in the House of Commons. The operation of these provisions was postponed until the death of Queen Anne, by which time they had been repealed, although the second emerged in a modified form in the Succession to the Crown Act 1707.[4]

Growth of political ideas relating to the Cabinet

Political ideas grow gradually. The party system and the principle of the dependence of the government on the confidence of Parliament,

---

[2] Turner, *op. cit.* Vol. II, pp. 92–100.
[3] R. R. Sedgwick, " The Inner Cabinet from 1732 to 1741 " 34 *English Historical Review* 290–302.   [4] *Ante*, Chap. 8.

and especially of the House of Commons, were developing in the eighteenth century.[5] The Cabinet often had political unity. Walpole, during his long period of office between 1721 and 1742, was skilful both in holding the favour of the King, partly through his friendship with Queen Caroline, and also in controlling the Commons, largely through bribery. At first the King chose as members of his Cabinet persons whom he liked and could trust. Eventually he had imposed upon him such advisers as Parliament, or the chief Ministers or the Prime Minister, wanted. There was an intermediate stage when the King no longer chose but could obstruct: when he was cajoled into accepting Ministers whom he did not like but to whom he did not profoundly object. This stage is illustrated by the long opposition of George II to the elder Pitt.

It was still possible for George III to hold a personal ascendancy during the earlier part of his reign by trading on the lack of political unity among his Ministers, manipulating the two Houses, and making use of "honorary" members of the Cabinet. Some time during his reign, however, the Cabinet established the right to consider matters without reference from the King. The normal course had been for departmental matters to go from the Minister concerned to the King, and thence to the Cabinet if the King so willed. It now came to be recognised that, if the King had not actually a duty to consult the Cabinet, he was generally expected to do so. The King consulted Ministers individually in the closet, but they could agree beforehand in the ante-room what they would say. When the Cabinet were all of one party (which was not always so) they sometimes met, not as the King's advisers but as party leaders; and this paved the way for the Cabinet to become the general initiator of policy. The decline of the King's influence after the fall of the North Ministry in 1782 was accentuated by "the mental derangement which afflicted George III, the contemptible personal character of George IV, and the negligible qualities of William IV." [6] The younger Pitt asserted the necessity of having the King's confidence. In 1803 he insisted that it was essential that there should be "an avowed and real minister, possessing the chief weight in the Council and the principal place in the confidence of the King." [7]

The turning point came with the Reform Act 1832, which soon showed that henceforth a Ministry would depend on the support of a majority in the House of Commons, and ultimately on the electorate. Peel accepted responsibility for the King's action in forcing Melbourne

---

[5] See Sir Ivor Jennings, *Party Politics*, Vol. II, "The Growth of Parties" (1961), for an account of the development of political parties since 1783.

[6] Keir, *op. cit.* pp. 381–382.

[7] Quoted, Keith, *op. cit.* pp. 16–17.

to resign in 1834. The King granted Peel a dissolution, but he was returned with a minority and remained out of office until 1841. In the latter year the Whig Ministry was defeated in the Commons on the budget, but preferred to retain office. Peel moved a resolution that their continuance in office in such circumstances was at variance with the spirit of the Constitution; this was carried by one vote, and a dissolution followed.

II. THE CABINET [8]

Functions of the Cabinet

The Cabinet system, or system of Cabinet government, was generally agreed to prevail between the wars. The main functions of the Cabinet at the end of the first war were summarised in the following way: " (a) the final determination of the policy to be submitted to Parliament; (b) the supreme control of the national executive in accordance with the policy prescribed by Parliament; and (c) the continuous co-ordination and delimitation of the interests of the several Departments of State." [9]   The Cabinet, giving collective " advice " to the Sovereign through the Prime Minister, was said to exercise under Parliament supreme control over all departments of state, and to be the body which co-ordinated the work on the one hand of the executive and the legislature, and on the other hand of the organs of the executive among themselves. The concept of the " Cabinet system " or " system of Cabinet government " may now need to be revised in the light of more recent developments, such as the predominance of the Prime Minister, the greater use of Cabinet committees and the growing influence of senior civil servants.[10] And the expression " policy prescribed by Parliament " must be read subject to the government's control of its party in the Commons, so that Parliament prescribes what the government wants.

Most important matters of policy are discussed at Cabinet meetings. However, for security reasons specific Budget proposals (as distinct from the general Budget strategy) are disclosed orally to the Cabinet a few days before the Chancellor of the Exchequer is to introduce

---

[8] J. P. N. Mackintosh, *The British Cabinet* (2nd ed. 1968); Sir Ivor Jennings, *Cabinet Government* (3rd ed. 1959); P. Gordon Walker, *The Cabinet* (revised ed. 1972); Herbert Morrison, *Government and Parliament* (1954); L. S. Amery, *Thoughts on the Constitution* (2nd ed. 1953); A. Berriedale Keith, *The British Cabinet System* (2nd ed. Gibbs, 1952); R. H. S. Crossman, *Inside View* (1972); Hans Dealdor, *Cabinet Reform in Britain 1914–1963* (1964); D. N. Chester, " Development of the Cabinet, 1914–1949 " in *British Government since 1918*; *Parliamentary Reform 1933–1960* (Hansard Society, 2nd ed. 1967) pp. 132 *et seq.*; Ronald Butt, *The Power of Parliament* (2nd ed. 1969).
[9] *Report of the Machinery of Government Committee* (1918) Cd. 9230, p. 5.
[10] *Infra*, pp. 282–283.

them in the Commons, and for diplomatic reasons it is not always possible to consult the Cabinet before taking action in foreign affairs. Among matters not usually discussed by the Cabinet are the exercise by the Home Secretary of the prerogative of mercy (not of great importance since the abolition of the death penalty for murder),[11] the personnel of the Cabinet itself, the making of appointments and the conferment of honours, which are matters within the patronage of the Prime Minister. The dissolution of Parliament was formerly a matter for Cabinet decision from 1841 to 1918; but since Lloyd George's premiership the Prime Minister has kept the decision in his own hands, although he consults a few chosen colleagues and the head of his party organisation. The principle may be discussed by members of the Cabinet, but the details are left to the Prime Minister.[12] Mr. Harold Wilson has called it " a lonely responsibility," and said that the Prime Minister is wise to consult his senior colleagues.[13]

The Cabinet may meet anywhere, for example, in the Prime Minister's room in the House of Commons or at Chequers. Most often it meets at No. 10 Downing Street, usually once or twice a week. A summons to a Privy Council takes precedence. There is no quorum for a Cabinet. The agenda is determined by the Prime Minister. The regular items begin with parliamentary business and then foreign and Commonwealth affairs. These are followed by White Papers, which have been processed by committees; statistical reports on such subjects as unemployment and balance of payments. Finally there are current matters from committees, emergencies, etc. Elaborate precautions are taken to ensure secrecy: the Cabinet room has double doors, and a person waiting in attendance outside is brought in by a Cabinet Minister. Every attempt is made to promote unanimity by refraining where possible from formal voting. The Prime Minister " collects the voices " and announces the decision.[14]

Composition of the Cabinet

The Cabinet consists of a group of Ministers, normally about twenty in number, who are agreed to pursue a common policy and who are invited by the Prime Minister to attend Cabinet meetings.

---

11 But the decision not to exercise the prerogative of mercy in the case of Sir Roger Casement (1916) was made by the Cabinet for political reasons: Roy Jenkins, *Asquith*, pp. 403–404.
12 B. E. Carter, *The Office of Prime Minister* (1956) pp. 289–291. For a discussion of the request for, timing of, and reasons for dissolutions in the present century, see B. S. Markesinis, *The theory and practice of Dissolution of Parliament* (1972) Pt. II and App. I.
13 Harold Wilson, " Why I Chose June," *Observer*, March 21, 1971.
14 For descriptions of a Cabinet meeting, see Morrison, *op. cit.* pp. 4–6; Gordon Walker, *op. cit.* Chap. 6.

Most of them are heads of the chief government departments, for example, the Chancellor of the Exchequer, the Foreign Secretary and the Home Secretary, but a number of heads of departments will be outside the Cabinet, and the Cabinet will include some Ministers whose offices involve few or no departmental responsibilities. These last are free to carry out miscellaneous tasks, such as the co-ordination of policy and administration, responsibility for research, acting as chairmen of Cabinet committees and giving advice as elder statesmen. The " Ministry," " Government " or " Administration " is the name given to the whole body of about a hundred holders of ministerial office, all of whose offices are known to the law,[15] and who are appointed by the Sovereign on the advice of the Prime Minister. The Cabinet itself has been mentioned a few times in statutes. The Ministers of the Crown Act 1937, s. 3, provided " additional salaries to Cabinet Ministers who hold offices at salaries less than five thousand pounds a year." The additional salary was made payable " if and so long as any Minister of the Crown to whom this section applies is a member of the Cabinet." The date on which any such Minister ceased to be a member of the Cabinet was to be published in the *London Gazette*, and such notification was to be " conclusive evidence " for the purposes of the Act.[16] The Parliamentary Commissioner Act 1967 excludes Cabinet papers from the papers that may be called for by the Parliamentary Commissioner.

The Cabinet is, then, the nucleus of the Ministry. In choosing the Cabinet the Prime Minister has a number of factors to consider, such as the importance of the various offices, the influence of members in the country, the authority of members in the Commons and their value in debate, the value of members as advisers in Committee, and the representation of the government in the House of Lords.[17] They are not generally experts in the subject-matter of their departments. By custom Cabinet Ministers are made Privy Councillors if they are not so already.[18] Since 1951 the Chief Whip has been invited to attend, so that he may be asked what would be the probable attitude of the party.

---

[15] They (except the Lord Chancellor) are listed in the Second Schedule to the House of Commons Disqualification Act 1957, as amended.

[16] See now, Ministerial Salaries Consolidation Act 1965.

[17] See *The British Prime Minister* (ed. Anthony King, 1969) pp. 60–79 (Attlee, " The Making of a Cabinet ").

[18] Publication by a present or former Cabinet Minister of references to Cabinet discussions or papers requires the consent of the Sovereign expressed through the Prime Minister. Disclosure by a present or former Minister of confidential state or official papers or information requires the approval of the government for the time being, application being made to the Secretary of the Cabinet. Cabinet papers in the Public Record Office are now open to readers after thirty years.

Cabinet Ministers in the House of Lords

Convention requires that all Ministers must sit in one or other of the Houses of Parliament, in order that their activities may be subject to parliamentary supervision.[19] The House of Commons Disqualification Act 1957 limits the number of Ministers who may sit in the House of Commons: the rest must therefore be peers. The government in any case will want to be adequately represented in the House of Lords. As regards the House of Lords, the Lord Chancellor will be automatically included,[20] and in recent years the Lord Privy Seal has been Leader of the House. These two are in practice the minimum number of Cabinet Ministers in the upper House. It is inconceivable that the Chancellor of the Exchequer should be in the House of Lords, since the Commons have a monopoly of financial affairs. The only other office that has raised controversy (apart from Prime Minister [21]) is that of Foreign Secretary. The appointment of Lord Halifax as Foreign Secretary in 1938 provoked some comment.[22] Considerable controversy arose in 1960 when the Earl of Home (now Sir Alec Douglas-Home) was appointed Foreign Secretary. A Foreign Secretary has to do much travelling, but nowadays he deals only with his opposite numbers in foreign countries. The Prime Minister in modern times is the overseer of foreign policy, and communicates personally with the heads of foreign governments or states: he is the only person who could answer for foreign affairs in the House of Commons if the Foreign Secretary is in the other House. It may be better for the Foreign Secretary himself that he should be in the Lords, but is it politically satisfactory?

Size of the Cabinet

The size of the Cabinet varies from time to time. Between the wars there were " full " Cabinets of over twenty members. After the last war we had " medium " Cabinets of sixteen to eighteen, but Sir Alec Douglas-Home and Mr. Wilson had Cabinets of twenty-three. During the two world wars there were " small " Cabinets of from six to ten members, although other Ministers were often present, and Chiefs of Staff, Dominion Prime Ministers and others were in attend-

[19] A temporary exception to this convention was the appointment of Mr. R. G. Casey, an Australian, as Minister of State in 1942, which was presumably made under the Re-election of Ministers Act 1919, s. 2. And see as regards Asquith, *post*, p. 276; Sir Alec Douglas-Home, (1963) *post*, p. 281; Mr. Gordon Walker and Mr. Frank Cousins, (1964–65) *ante*, p. 86.

[20] It was wholly exceptional that in the " caretaker government " formed after the withdrawal of the Labour Party from the National Coalition in 1945, the Lord Chancellor—Viscount Simon, a National Liberal—was not a member of the Cabinet.

[21] *Post*, p. 281.

[22] He even remained a member of the Cabinet after being appointed Ambassador to the United States.

ance. It has been persuasively argued that the large volume of work assumed by the Cabinet is too great to be efficiently performed by a group of Ministers most of whom have heavy departmental responsibilities as well as the duty of constant attendance at the House. One suggestion is that there should be a small policy-making Cabinet of about six, whose members would not be departmental heads.[23] Another is that more use should be made of Standing Committees of the Cabinet to co-ordinate the work of groups of departments whose interests overlap.[24] Attlee thought sixteen the best number. There is difference of opinion on how many members of this supreme policy-making body should be free from departmental duties, the manner in which the work of the departmental (non-Cabinet) Ministers should be co-ordinated, and the way in which Parliament can call Ministers to account.

Churchill's experiment from 1951–1953 of having several Ministers as " Overlords " who without statutory authority supervised groups of other Ministers, was not successful, as it degraded the Ministers who were supervised and confused ministerial responsibility. Mr. Heath's Cabinet at the end of 1970 included several " super-Ministers " who were directly responsible for multiple departments formed by the merger of a number of previous departments—for example, the Secretary of State for the Environment included the former Ministries of Housing and Local Government, Public Building and Works, and Transport.

Ministers who are not members of the Cabinet may be called in if matters specially affecting their department are under discussion. Civil servants are rarely present, except in the Legislation Committee by permission of the Prime Minister or the chairman of the Committee, although the Permanent Secretary to the Treasury or the Permanent Under-Secretary of State of the Foreign Office may be summoned. Chiefs of Staff, on the other hand, may be present when military questions are being discussed.

---

[23] Amery, *op. cit.* pp. 87, 90–93. This would be something like the small war Cabinets in the two world wars, although these were reinforced from time to time by Commonwealth statesmen: Lord Hankey, *Government Control in War* (1945); Winston S. Churchill, *The Second World War*, II, Chap. 3; III, pp. 784–786; IV, Chap. 5 and App. G; V, App. G; VI, App. H; Jennings, *op. cit.* pp. 287–291; Keith, *op. cit.* pp. 136–141; *Memoirs of Lord Chandos* (1962) Chaps. 12–14. Several meetings were also held in the first war with Dominion Prime Ministers, and called the " Imperial War Cabinet "; D. Lloyd George, *War Memoirs*, Chaps. 38 and 55; *Report of the Machinery of Government Committee* (1918) Cd. 9230, pp. 4–6; *The War Cabinet, Report for the Year 1917* (1918) Cd. 9005, pp. 1–10.

[24] Sir John Anderson, *The Machinery of Government* (Romanes Lecture, 1946). See also (1918) Cd. 9230 (*supra*); Lord Samuel, " A Cabinet of Ten " *The Times*, September 9. 1947.

Mr. Heath's Cabinet in early 1973 consisted of nineteen members, including three peers.

Shadow Cabinet [25]

It has come to be an accepted part of the working of our Constitution that the Opposition should organise itself on parallel lines to the government. The idea emerged gradually, and the Shadow Cabinet in an informal and modified form came into existence by the 1860s. It may be said to have become a convention that there should be a Shadow Cabinet. Statutory salaries are now provided for the Leader of the Opposition and the Chief Opposition Whip in each House. The Shadow Cabinet constitutes an alternative team from which the prospective Prime Minister can choose his senior colleagues, and which provides the electorate with an alternative choice of government.

The Conservative Party's Shadow Cabinet is technically its Consultative Committee, and the Labour Party's is its Parliamentary Committee. The Labour Shadow Cabinet since 1923 has been elected annually by the parliamentary Labour Party in the Commons. The Conservative Shadow Cabinet is chosen by the Leader of the Opposition.

Cabinet Committees [26]

Committees of the Cabinet were set up *ad hoc* in the nineteenth century to expedite government business. An example was the War Committee (1855) at the time of the Crimean War. The first Standing Committee was the Committee of Imperial Defence set up by Balfour in 1903. This was not confined to Ministers, and it used the Privy Council secretariat. During the First World War a large number of committees were set up unsystematically by Asquith and Lloyd George. Between the wars committees came and went, there being on an average twenty *ad hoc* committees at any one time. A system of Cabinet committees was developed in the last war. Attlee (Deputy Prime Minister) gave an account of these to the House of Commons in 1940, as did Churchill (Prime Minister) in 1941. Herbert Morrison has also given a full written account of the committees during the last war.[27] The most important of these was the Home Affairs Committee, which was responsible for a major part of domestic policy, such as the Education Bill. A new principle developed that a Cabinet committee had equal authority to the Cabinet, subject to possible reference to the Cabinet.

[25] D. R. Turner, *The Shadow Cabinet in British Politics* (1969); Mackintosh, *op. cit.* pp. 259–261, 524–529; Jennings, *Parliament* (2nd ed.) pp. 81–83.
[26] Walker, *op. cit.* pp. 38–47; App. (List of Standing Committees, 1914–64); Mackintosh, *op. cit.* pp. 510–518; Jennings, *Cabinet Government*, pp. 255–261.
[27] Herbert Morrison, *op. cit.* pp. 19–26.

Attlee was the first Prime Minister to have a permanent committee structure in peace time. The pattern continued during the 1950s and 1960s, *ad hoc* committees continuing alongside Standing Committees. "The Prime Minister sets up and disbands committees, appoints the chairman and members and sets the terms of reference." [28]   Some committees are chaired by the Prime Minister at No. 10; some by other Ministers in the Cabinet Office or at the House of Commons. Mr. Wilson raised the authority of Cabinet committees by ruling that a member could only appeal from a committee to the Cabinet with the agreement of the chairman. The recommendations of a committee can be turned down by the Cabinet.

The existence of a Cabinet committee, the name of its chairman and the terms of reference are not usually disclosed during the lifetime of a government, because of the principle of the unity and collective responsibility of the Cabinet. Paradoxically, we have been told most about the Defence Committee from White Papers on Defence.[29]

The committee system has increased the efficiency of the Cabinet, and enables a great deal more work to be done by Ministers. The Cabinet itself is left free for more important decisions,[30] and its business is better prepared. The system also enables non-Cabinet and junior Ministers to be brought into discussions.

Cabinet committees change their name, and are sometimes difficult to classify. Modern Standing Committees include: Home Affairs [31]; Future Legislation (principles and provisional priority of government Bills); Legislation (drafting and settled priority of government Bills and important Statutory Instruments [32]); Defence [33]; Economic Policy; and Social Services. Recent *ad hoc* committees have included one on Rhodesia (1969). Mr. Wilson in 1968 announced the formation of a Parliamentary Committee to co-ordinate the work in Parliament, and to consider the broader aspects of the government's business. In his memoirs he speaks of a Management Committee to hold preliminary discussions on matters of policy, such as the Industrial Relations Bill, before putting the matter to the full Cabinet.[34]   Commentators regarded both these as an Inner Cabinet.

---

[28] Walker, *op. cit.* p. 45.
[29] *Central Organisation for Defence* (1946) Cmd. 6923; (1958) Cmnd. 576; (1963) Cmnd. 2097.
[30] Mr. Wilson thought the EEC too important for a committee.
[31] The Attorney-General often attends: see Sir Jocelyn Simon in (1965) 81 L.Q.R. 292–293.
[32] The Attorney-General is a member.
[33] Chiefs of Staff are in attendance: (1963) Cmnd. 2097.
[34] Harold Wilson, *The Labour Government, 1964–70: A Personal Record* (1971).

Inner Cabinet [35]

Prime Ministers in recent years are said to be in the habit of summoning an " Inner Cabinet." The practice has been ascribed to Neville Chamberlain, Churchill, Attlee and Eden. Mr. Wilson's Parliamentary Committee and Management Committee (*supra*) were described as an Inner Cabinet. An Inner Cabinet is supposed to be the efficient part that really directs the Cabinet's activities. Mr. Gordon Walker, however, calls it a misnomer. According to him it is not a Cabinet or a Cabinet committee. It has no organic or set place in the Cabinet structure. It is merely an informal, small group of friends or confidants of the Prime Minister drawn from members of the Cabinet.[36] It is not formally set up; it has no papers or records; it is not served by the Cabinet secretariat. An Inner Cabinet has as such no power. It does not predigest Cabinet business, although it may among other things discuss questions that are to come before the Cabinet. The practice of different Prime Ministers in this respect varies. The Inner Cabinet, says Mr. Walker, is " a loose and informal thing." [37]

In contrast, Mr. Walker talks of a *Partial Cabinet*, which can act for the Cabinet. This is a standing or *ad hoc* committee, presided over by the Prime Minister, but acting for a time as if they were the Cabinet. Examples are Attlee's group of Ministers who decided to make the atom bomb, and Eden's group who determined the Suez policy.[38]

The Cabinet Office [39]

Cabinet minutes were sometimes kept in the reigns of George II, III and IV, but the practice lapsed until the First World War Ministers were expected to remember what was decided and to carry out those decisions in their departments. The Sovereign was kept informed by a letter from the Prime Minister after each meeting, retailing the topics considered and the decisions taken. It was a confidential letter written in the Prime Minister's own hand, and not

---

[35] Walker, *op. cit.* pp. 37–38; Anthony King, *op. cit.* pp. 64, 91, 174, 185–186. Attendance at an Inner Cabinet was referred to in evidence in *Churchill (Randolph)* v. *Nabarro, The Times,* October 25–29, 1960.

[36] *Cf.* Churchill's " cronies " with whom he liked to talk late into the night: they were personal friends, not men of influence.

[37] Mr. Gordon Walker, together with Mr. George Brown and Mr. Callaghan, was a member of Mr. Wilson's Inner Cabinet that discussed such questions as devaluation and the Bank Rate.

[38] Walker, *op. cit.* pp. 87–91.

[39] R. K. Mosley, *The Story of the Cabinet Office* (1969); Walker, *op. cit.* pp. 48–57; Jennings, *op. cit.* pp. 242–245; Mackintosh, *op. cit.* pp. 508–510; Stephen Roskill, *Hankey, Man of Secrets* (1972).

shown to other members of the Cabinet.[40] Lloyd George, when Prime Minister, introduced a secretariat in 1916 by borrowing as Secretary of the War Cabinet Sir Maurice Hankey, at that time Secretary to the Committee of Imperial Defence.[41] Since then minutes of Cabinet meetings have been sent to the Sovereign and circulated to members of the Cabinet.

The secretariat serves the committees as well as the full Cabinet. It organises the agenda, circulates reports, and records the Cabinet "Conclusions." This record contains not only the actual "Conclusions" or decisions, but also the subjects discussed and the relevant Papers, and a summary of the discussion. The arguments of individual Ministers are not usually recorded, in the interest both of anonymity and secrecy. The Conclusions are circulated to the Cabinet, unless the matter is one of exceptional secrecy.

The Cabinet secretariat has always been on the Treasury vote: there is no Cabinet vote. The Secretary to the Cabinet formerly combined the post with that of Clerk to the Privy Council and/or (Joint) Permanent Secretary to the Treasury. More recently he no longer doubles these posts, but he is also Principal Private Secretary to the Prime Minister.

The Prime Minister does not need a department, although he has a small " No. 10 " office. He is not only briefed by the Cabinet Secretary, but he can call on the Permanent Secretaries of the various departments.

Ministerial responsibility

The responsibility of Ministers, as was indicated in Chapter 5, is both individual and collective. The individual responsibility of a Minister for the performance of his official duties is both legal and conventional: it is owed legally to the Sovereign, and also by convention to Parliament. " Responsible " here does not mean morally responsible or culpable, but accountable or answerable.[42] The responsible Minister is the one under whose authority an act was done, or who must take the constitutional consequences of what has

---

[40] The Public Record Office contains photographic copies of the 1,700 " Cabinet letters " written by Prime Ministers to the Sovereign from 1868 to 1916. The originals are at Windsor Castle. The letters constitute the only official record of decisions by the Cabinet in that period. There are also in the Public Record Office photographic copies of Cabinet memoranda from 1880 to 1914, and the Committee of Imperial Defence from 1902 to 1914.

[41] Lord Hankey, *Diplomacy by Conference*, Chaps. 2 and 3.

[42] It also connotes a state of mind that acts as may be thought right after weighing the consequences: Amery, *op. cit.* p. 30.

been done either by himself or in his department.[43]   A Minister must accept responsibility for the actions of the civil servants in his depart-ment, and he is expected to defend them from public criticism, unless they have done something reprehensible which he forbad, or of which he disapproves and of which he did not have and could not reasonably be expected to have had previous knowledge.   In the latter case, which is unusual, he may dismiss them.[44]

It has been argued that an examination of ministerial resignations in the past century shows that the doctrine of individual responsibility in practice has no punitive effect, because either: (i) the Minister who resigns is appointed to another post; (ii) a timely reshuffle of ministerial posts renders resignation unnecessary; or (iii) a Minister who is unpopular with the Opposition is protected by the solidarity of his colleagues.[45]   Rare though individual resignations may be, however, their rarity—together with the general public acceptance of the doctrine—suggests that the convention is very strong.   J. H. Thomas resigned in 1936 after a Tribunal of Inquiry had upheld allegations that he had disclosed Budget proposals, and Hugh Dalton resigned in 1947 after making similar improper disclosures.   The resignation of Sir Samuel Hoare over the Hoare-Laval Pact concern-ing Abyssinia may have been a case of a Minister being "thrown to the wolves."   In 1954 Sir Thomas Dugdale, Minister of Agricul-ture, resigned because he admitted maladministration in his depart-ment over the Crichel Down case, although he defended its policy. Mr. John Profumo resigned in 1963.[46]   It should be borne in mind that the Prime Minister may always advise the Sovereign to dismiss a Minister—all ministerial posts are regarded as being at his disposal; but it is seldom necessary to resort to this expedient, for it is usually sufficient if the Prime Minister invites a Minister to resign.

The collective responsibility is owed by convention both to the Sovereign and to Parliament.   To the Sovereign Ministers must tender unanimous advice.   To Parliament and the nation they must show a united front by vote and speech.   This is illustrated by the resignations of Eden in 1938 over the policy of appeasement, Aneurin Bevan in 1951 over National Health Service charges, and Lord Salisbury in 1957 over the release of Archbishop Makarios.   Mr. Frank Cousins

[43] See Marshall and Moodie, *Some Problems of the Constitution* (1964) pp. 47–49, and Chap. 4; G. K. Fry, " Thoughts on the Present State of the Convention of Ministerial Responsibility " (1969–70) XXIII *Parliamentary Affairs* 10.

[44] 520 H.C.Deb. cols. 1287 *et seq.*; following the *Report of the Crichel Down Enquiry* (1954) Cmd. 9176.

[45] S. E. Finer, " The Individual Responsibility of Ministers " (1956) *Public Administra-tion* 377.   *Cf.* R. K. Alderman and J. A. Cross, *The Tactics of Resignation* (1967).

[46] (1963) Cmnd. 2152 (Lord Denning's Report); P. J. Madgwick, " Resignations " (1966–67) XX *Parliamentary Affairs* 59.

resigned from his post of Minister of Science and Technology in 1966 because he disagreed with the Government's Prices and Incomes Bill: being a trade union leader he could not keep quiet about it. The principle of collective responsibility is not applied in its full rigour to non-Cabinet Ministers, for they are often not consulted in matters that do not affect their department. In their case the responsibility is passive rather than active. Sir Edward Boyle, one of the two junior Ministers who resigned from Sir Anthony Eden's Government in 1956 because they disagreed with the Government's intervention in the Suez Canal Crisis, joined the Government formed by Mr. Harold Macmillan early in 1957 although the new Ministry confirmed its support for Eden's Suez policy. Technically they were different Ministries, but the policy disapproved of was the same, although it was no longer possible to pursue it.

Influence of the Sovereign

Since the Sovereign acts on the advice of the Cabinet, tendered through the Prime Minister, and the government is carried on in the name of the Sovereign, the Cabinet is expected to keep the Sovereign informed of any departure in policy, of the general march of political events, and in particular of the deliberations of the Cabinet. The *power* of the Monarch in modern times is confined—in Bagehot's well-known words [47]—to " the right to be consulted, the right to encourage, the right to warn." The *influence* of a Sovereign who has been on the Throne for some years, however, is far from negligible, for his experience will be wider and more continuous than that of most or all of his Ministers. Queen Victoria cannot perhaps be taken as a model for the twentieth century, but George V's reign of a quarter of a century shows many examples of the influence exerted by the Throne. By his advice, warnings and encouragement the King helped to bring the parties together in negotiating the Anglo-Irish Treaty of 1921; but he left the conduct of the negotiations entirely to the Prime Minister, and refrained from any comment or intervention while the conference lasted.[48] In 1923 the King tried unsuccessfully to dissuade Baldwin from a dissolution,[49] and later in the same year he persuaded Baldwin not to resign before meeting Parliament when the Conservatives at a general election had lost their absolute majority but were still the largest party in the Commons.[50]

As the Sovereign's influence may be underestimated, so on the other hand it may be exaggerated. Thus Lord Attlee discounts certain

---

[47] Bagehot, *The English Constitution* (World's Classics ed.) p. 67.
[48] Harold Nicolson, *King George the Fifth*, p. 360.
[49] *Ibid.* pp. 379–380.
[50] *Ibid.* pp. 382–384.

incidents given in the official biography of George VI [51] as examples of interference by that King, notably the choice of Ernest Bevin as Foreign Secretary and the holding of a general election in 1951. Attlee later said that the reason for the first was that he, as Prime Minister, wanted to keep Ernest Bevin away from Herbert Morrison; and the reason for the second was that he did not want the King to worry about the precarious position of the Government (majority 6) while he was abroad.[52]

III. THE PRIME MINISTER [53]

His formal position

The creation of the position of Prime Minister in the modern sense begins with the Ministries of Sir Robert Walpole (1721–1742) and the younger Pitt (1783–1801; 1804–1806), although the former disclaimed the title. It was brought about by a combination of a number of factors, including royal confidence, pre-eminence among Ministers, patronage as First Lord of the Treasury, and especially control of the Commons (not necessarily as leader of the largest party). The authority of the Prime Minister was firmly established in the late nineteenth century by the outstanding personalities of Disraeli and Gladstone, making use of the effects brought about by the Representation of the People Acts and the development of the party system. As we have seen, the Prime Minister was until recently hardly known to the law: like the Cabinet, he was the creature of convention. He is mentioned in the Treaty of Berlin 1878; a royal warrant of 1905 which gives him precedence next after the Archbishop of York; the Schedule to the Chequers Estate Act 1917, in which Parliament gave effect to the gift of the Chequers estate as a country residence for the Prime Minister of the day; the Ministers of the Crown Act 1937; the Physical Training and Recreation Act 1937; the House of Commons Disqualification Act 1957 (" Prime Minister and First Lord of the Treasury "); and the Chevening Estate Act 1959, under which this Kent estate was given on certain trusts as regards occupation, including " any Minister of the Crown nominated by the Prime Minister."

The Prime Minister now invariably takes the office of First Lord of the Treasury,[54] and occasionally some other office as well, *e.g.* that

[51] Wheeler-Bennett, *King George VI.*

[52] " The Role of the Monarchy " *The Observer*, August 23, 1959.

[53] B. E. Carter, *The Office of Prime Minister* (1956); Anthony King (ed.) *The British Prime Minister* (1969); Mackintosh, *op. cit.*; Humphry Berkeley, *The Power of the Prime Minister* (1968); P. Gordon Walker, *op. cit.* Chap. 5; Jennings, *op. cit.*; Keith, *op. cit.*; Thomson, *Constitutional History of England, 1642–1801.*

[54] They were last separated when Balfour was First Lord of the Treasury in Lord Salisbury's administrations (1891–1892, 1895–1902).

of Chancellor of the Exchequer (Gladstone), War Office (Asquith),[55] Foreign Secretary (Ramsay MacDonald) or Minister of Defence (Winston Churchill). The office of First Lord of the Treasury provided him with a salary. It places him technically at the head of the most important government department, yet with departmental duties which (apart from patronage) are only nominal, as the working head of that department is the Chancellor of the Exchequer. In the eighteenth and early nineteenth centuries, before the reform of the Civil Service and the parliamentary franchise, the fact that the First Lord of the Treasury exercised a very extensive patronage over many kinds of official appointments meant that the Prime Minister could control departmental appointments, and this helped him to obtain a parliamentary majority for his party. The Ministers of the Crown Act 1937 provided for a salary to be paid to "the person who is Prime Minister and First Lord of the Treasury." The Ministerial Salaries Consolidation Act 1965 now provides a salary to the "Prime Minister and First Lord of the Treasury." It is therefore unlikely that these positions will be held separately in future, although the Act does not require them to be held together. The Act of 1937 also provided that every former Prime Minister who does not hold any paid office should receive a pension. The Ministerial Salaries Consolidation Act 1965 [56] now provides that "any person who has been Prime Minister and has as First Lord of the Treasury taken the official oath prescribed by section 5 of the Promissory Oaths Act 1868" shall be entitled to a pension charged on the Consolidated Fund.

Functions of the Prime Minister [57]

The primary functions of the Prime Minister are to form a government, and to choose and preside over the Cabinet. He gives advice to his ministerial colleagues on matters before they come to the Cabinet, and he is the main channel of communication between the Cabinet and the Sovereign.[58] He advises the Sovereign on a dissolution.[59]

---

[55] At that time (1914) a member accepting this office had to seek re-election, so that for a time Asquith was Prime Minister without a seat in the House.

[56] Amended by the Pensions (Increase) Act 1971.

[57] For a general first-hand account, see Harold Macmillan, *Pointing the Way, 1959–61* (1972) Chap. 2 (" A Prime Minister's Life ").

[58] Other Ministers may communicate with the Sovereign on matters concerning their department.

[59] Lord Beaverbrook recounts that the decision of Lloyd George and his colleagues in January 1922 not to hold a general election was induced by the intervention of a parrot: *Men and Power* (1956) pp. 340–341. And see *ante*, p. 265.

The Prime Minister is the leader of his party. He has either been chosen Prime Minister because he is the leader of the largest party, or he has been elected leader because he is Prime Minister. He is primarily responsible for the organisation of the business of the House, even if (as is now usual) this work is delegated to the Leader of the House. In the House he is expected to speak in debates, and to answer questions on general government policy, the future business of the House and any residual matters. A Prime Minister is willing to give confidential information to the Leader of the Opposition on such matters as defence, security, the EEC and Northern Ireland.

The Prime Minister sees that Cabinet decisions are carried out by the departments, although, as we have said, the extent to which he supervises the administration varies with different holders of the office. His contact with the affairs of the Foreign Office is often especially close. The Cabinet secretariat is under his control, and consults him in preparing the agenda. He communicates directly with the other Commonwealth Prime Ministers, and presides when they meet in this country.

Many Crown appointments, in addition to ministerial offices, are made on his advice. These include the Lords of Appeal in Ordinary, the Lords Justices of Appeal, bishops and deans of the Church of England, peerages, Privy Councillors and most honours.[60] As First Lord of the Treasury and Minister for the Civil Service he approves the senior appointments in the Civil Service.

Choice of Prime Minister

The Sovereign chooses the Prime Minister. Conventions ensure that in most cases the " choice " is formal, for the Sovereign is expected to send for the leader of the party or group of parties that has, or can control, a majority in the House of Commons. The choice became formal owing to the development of the party system. Thus in 1855 Queen Victoria, who preferred Derby, was constrained to appoint Palmerston; and in 1880 she reluctantly appointed Gladstone although she would have preferred Hartington. If the government is defeated at a general election the Prime Minister resigns (and with him the other Ministers), and the Sovereign on the advice of the resigning Prime Minister sends for the Leader of the Opposition. The Leader of the Opposition is known, because both the Labour Party and (since 1964) the Conservative Party in opposition select a leader by ballot, and he has a statutory salary. The Leader of

---

60 Recommendations for some honours and decorations are also made by the Foreign Secretary, the Defence Minister, Commonwealth Prime Ministers, and on the Queen's personal initiative.

the Opposition will accept office if his party commands a majority in the Commons, which it usually will if the government was defeated at a general election.[61]

If the Prime Minister dies in office or retires on *personal* grounds, such as ill health or old age, the Sovereign has really no discretion in the common case where the government has an absolute majority and one other Cabinet Minister in the Commons is obviously regarded as ranking next to the Prime Minister. In this way Neville Chamberlain succeeded Baldwin in 1937 and Mr. Eden succeeded Sir Winston Churchill in 1955. A *retiring* Prime Minister is probably not entitled to proffer advice as to his successor,[62] but he can make his views known beforehand, and anyway the Sovereign is free to consult him and other members of the government party.

There are exceptional circumstances when the Sovereign really has to exercise a personal discretion within limits; and this is perhaps the most important function of the Sovereign at the present day. There may be more than two parties in the House of Commons with no one party having an absolute majority, either as a result of a general election or on a defeat in the Commons of a government that has already been granted one dissolution; and the question arises whether one of the minority parties, and if so which, will be able to carry on the government with the support of one of the other parties, or whether a coalition shall be formed: or the government may break up owing to internal dissension. The Sovereign then may consult all interested parties with a view to the formation of a Ministry that can hold a majority in the House.

George V took the initiative in the formation of the National (coalition) Government under Ramsay MacDonald in 1931 when the "economic crisis" caused the minority Labour Government to break up. The King consulted the Conservative and Liberal leaders, each of whom had a considerable following in the House, and then entrusted MacDonald with the task of resuming office as head of a coalition and in spite of the defection of his own Labour Party.[63] On the other hand, when Baldwin's minority Conservative Government was defeated in the House in 1924 not long after a general

---

[61] The Leader of the Opposition is not bound to accept office. Disraeli in 1873, when the parties were very even, thought it would be more advantageous if Gladstone carried on for a while.

[62] In March 1955 Churchill said to Mr. Eden and Mr. Butler: " I am going and Anthony will succeed me. We can discuss details later ": Lord Butler, *The Art of the Possible* (1971) p. 176; but he refrained from mentioning to the Queen the question of his successor: J. Wheeler-Bennett (ed.) *Action This Day* (1968) p. 234.

[63] Nicolson, *King George the Fifth*, pp. 460–469; G. M. Young, *Stanley Baldwin*, Chap. 16; Keith Middlemas and John Barnes, *Baldwin* (1969) Chap. 23.

election, the King did not seek any advice before sending for Ramsay MacDonald, the leader of the second largest party.[64]

Neville Chamberlain, the Conservative Prime Minister, resigned in 1940 because, although he had not been defeated in the House (his normal majority of about 200 was reduced to 81, a number of Conservatives voting against him or abstaining) he realised that he had lost the confidence of his own party as well as of the Labour Party, which was supporting the Government in the conduct of the war. A coalition government was needed, and Labour members intimated that they would not serve under Chamberlain. The possible choice of a successor lay between Winston Churchill, First Lord of the Admiralty, and Lord Halifax, Foreign Secretary. The Labour Party were willing to serve under Churchill. Lord Halifax expressed the view, in a conference between the three statesmen, that it would be impracticable to try to lead the government from the Lords in wartime.[65] Chamberlain then tendered his resignation to George VI, who accepted it. In an informal discussion as to his successor the King suggested Lord Halifax, but Chamberlain told the King what Lord Halifax had said. " I asked Chamberlain his advice," the King recorded, " and he told me Winston was the man to send for . . . . I sent for Winston and asked him to form a Government." [66]

The most difficult case is where a Prime Minister dies in office or resigns on personal grounds, such as health or age, leaving no obvious successor. There may be no obvious successor because it has not been the practice for a Conservative Party in office to elect a deputy leader. The first time the Conservative Party in opposition has appointed a deputy leader was the appointment of Mr. Maudling in 1965. When the parliamentary Labour Party are in opposition they elect both a leader and a deputy leader annually.[67] It was wholly exceptional that twice during the last war George VI asked Churchill to advise him on his successor if the Prime Minister should die as a result of enemy action while abroad. George VI objected to Mr. Eden being described as Deputy Prime Minister in 1951, as it would imply a line of succession and so restrict the royal prerogative.[68] There have been appointments by both the main parties of Deputy Prime Minister, notably Attlee (Leader of the Labour

---

[64] Nicolson, op. cit. pp. 382–386; cf. Sidney Webb, " The First Labour Government " (1961) 32 Political Quarterly 6.

[65] Winston S. Churchill, Second World War, Vol. I, pp. 523–526; K. Feiling, The Life of Neville Chamberlain, pp. 439–441; Earl of Halifax, Fulness of Days, pp. 218–220; Earl of Birkenhead, Halifax (1965) pp. 453–455.

[66] Wheeler-Bennett, King George VI, pp. 438–445.

[67] See A. Howard and R. West, The Making of the Prime Minister (1965) for the election of Mr. Harold Wilson as party leader after the death of Gaitskell in 1963.

[68] Wheeler-Bennett, op. cit. p. 797.

Party) in the coalition Government during the last war. The title generally is not known to our Constitution, and it does not imply any right of succession to the Prime Minister.[69]

In 1923 Bonar Law, the Conservative Prime Minister, was so ill that he sent his resignation to George V. The choice of successor lay between Lord Curzon, Foreign Secretary and former Viceroy of India, a statesman of brilliant gifts and vast experience; and Mr. Baldwin who, although recently appointed Chancellor of the Exchequer, had little political experience and was not well known either inside or outside the House. After the King or his Private Secretary had consulted Lord Balfour (former Prime Minister) and Lord Salisbury (Lord President of the Council) and members of the government party, the King chose Baldwin both on personal grounds and because he was in the Commons, although the latter reason was emphasised in breaking the news to Curzon.[70]

When Sir Anthony Eden, Conservative Prime Minister, resigned in 1957 because of serious ill-health, the succession lay by common consent between Mr. R. A. Butler (Lord Privy Seal and Leader of the House of Commons) and Mr. Harold Macmillan (Chancellor of the Exchequer). All that was publicly known was that the Queen consulted two elder statesmen of the Conservative Party—Lord Salisbury (Lord President of the Council and son of the adviser of 1923) and Sir Winston Churchill, the former Prime Minister—and selected Mr. Macmillan. We now know that they both recommended Mr. Macmillan, and that only one member of the Cabinet supported Mr. Butler.[71]

In 1963 (after the Peerage Act had been passed) Mr. Macmillan became ill, entered hospital for an operation and announced his intention to resign. In accordance with the practice of the Conservatives at that time " soundings " were taken in the party. The result of these soundings was communicated by the Lord Chancellor to the Prime Minister, who then sent a letter of resignation to the Queen, presumably intimating that he had advice to give if requested. The Queen (who is not known to have sought any other advice) visited Mr. Macmillan in hospital, and immediately afterwards sent

[69] Butler, op. cit. p. 234.
[70] Robert Blake, The Unknown Prime Minister (1955) pp. 514–527; Winston S. Churchill, Great Contemporaries, pp. 215–220; L. S. Amery, op. cit. pp. 21–22; Harold Nicolson, King George the Fifth, pp. 375–379; Curzon, The Last Phase, pp. 353–355; G. M. Young, Stanley Baldwin, pp. 48–49; Keith Middlemas and John Barnes, Baldwin, Chap. 8.
[71] Mackintosh, op. cit. pp. 522–523. Lord Salisbury and Lord Kilmuir (Lord Chancellor) sounded the Cabinet Ministers. " What they wanted was a straight answer to the question: ' Who's best—Rab or Harold? ' They got it ": Lord Egremont, Wyndham and Children First (1968) pp. 158–159.

for Lord Home and invited him to form an Administration.[72] (She might have invested him with office straight away, as was done with Eden and Macmillan.) A day or two later Lord Home informed the Queen that he was able to form an Administration.[73]

In 1964 the Conservatives adopted a new method of selecting their party leader. A ballot is taken of the party in the Commons. The candidate so selected is then presented for election at a party meeting.[74] On Sir Alec Douglas-Home's resignation (out of office) this led to the election of Mr. Heath.

It ought to be possible, if a Prime Minister dies or resigns on personal grounds and the succession is not clear, for the government party to be allowed a few days in which to elect a new leader, without appearing to force the Sovereign's hand. This would keep the Crown out of politics in a delicate situation, and has been the practice in Australia and New Zealand.[75]

Should a Prime Minister be a peer?

The question whether it is constitutionally proper for a Prime Minister to be in the House of Lords in modern times has often been discussed, especially in connection with the resignation of Bonar Law in 1923. No peer has been Prime Minister since Lord Salisbury (1895–1902). Even in the nineteenth century Prime Ministers who were peers found it difficult to control the Commons; but as late as 1921 Cabinet colleagues seriously considered Lord Birkenhead (Lord Chancellor) as Prime Minister to succeed Lloyd George, and in 1922 they offered the position to Lord Derby.[76] Lord Halifax saw the difficulty in 1940, but neither he nor Neville Chamberlain acknowledged a convention. George VI suggested to Chamberlain that Lord Halifax's peerage could be " placed in abeyance for the time being," apparently meaning that legislation should be passed allowing Lord Halifax to speak in the House of Commons.[77] In 1957 Lords Salisbury and Kilmuir considered themselves excluded by virtue of their peerage.[78]

---

[72] " What is certain is that Macmillan . . . acted . . . with utter determination and dispatch, making a definite recommendation of Home ": Lord Butler, *The Art of the Possible* (1971) pp. 247–248.

[73] He forthwith renounced his peerage under the new Act, and (being a Knight of the Thistle) became known as Sir Alec Douglas-Home. He had then, of course, to fight a by-election to get into the House of Commons.
See A. Howard and R. West, *op. cit.* Chap. 4.

[74] See Humphry Berkeley, *Across the Floor* (1972).

[75] See E. M. McWhinney, " Constitutional Conventions " (1957) 35 Can.Bar Rev. 92, 242, 368, 369.

[76] Lord Beaverbrook, *The Decline and Fall of Lloyd George* (1963) pp. 68 *et seq.*; p. 181.   [77] Wheeler-Bennett, *op. cit.* p. 444.

[78] Mackintosh, *op. cit.* p. 523. *Cf.* Lord Moran, *Churchill: The Struggle for Survival, 1940–65*, where Lord Salisbury is said to have suggested in 1953 that Churchill,

The weight of opinion is in favour of the view that it is un-desirable and impracticable for the Prime Minister to have a seat in the Lords. The House of Commons is the centre of interest and influence; it has exclusive control over national finance and, although the office of First Lord of the Treasury is only nominally concerned with financial matters, it would be absurd for the holder of that office to sit in the upper House; it is in the elected Second Chamber that governments are made and defeated; and the Labour Party is sparsely represented in the Lords, so that the real opposition to a Conservative Government is in the lower House. The question has lost much of its importance since the Peerage Act 1963 allowed existing hereditary peers, and persons who later succeed to hereditary peerages, to renounce their peerages within a time limit.

Prime Ministerial government? [79]

Some writers say we no longer have Cabinet government as we used to know it, but that since the last war—if not before—we have had " Prime Ministerial government." Policy is not usually initiated by the Cabinet. Decisions tend to be taken either by the Prime Minister alone or by him after consulting one or two Ministers, or else by Cabinet committees or informal meetings of the Ministers concerned. To these factors may be added the unification and centralisation of an expanding Civil Service under the Prime Minister. Mr. Crossman, who thinks we have gone a long way towards Prime Ministerial government, emphasises the point that the Prime Minister is the only political master of the powerful trinity consisting of the Permanent Secretary of the Treasury, the head of the Civil Service, and the Secretary to the Cabinet.

In considering the relative positions of the Prime Minister and the Cabinet we have to take note of such factors as the moral autho-rity of his office as Leader in the eyes of the public and his standing in his party; the power of the Prime Minister to appoint and re-shuffle Ministers, to determine the scope of the various offices, to control the Cabinet agenda and to advise a dissolution. The Prime Minister has the advantage of knowing more than his colleagues what is going on. It is difficult to overthrow a Prime Minister, because the Cabinet must not only be united against him but agreed on his

who had had a stroke, ought to go to the Lords while remaining Prime Minister—an idea that commended itself to the Queen's Private Secretary but not to Churchill, who was 77.

[79] A. H. Brown, " Prime Ministerial Power " [1968] P.L. 28, 96; Harold Wilson, " Where the Power Lies " *Listener*, February 9, 1967. And see: Mackintosh, *op. cit.*; Crossman, *op. cit.*; Gordon Walker, *op. cit.*; King, *op. cit.*; Hood Phillips, *Reform of the Constitution*, pp. 42–47, 51–54.

successor, and backbenchers are not likely to want to precipitate a
general election in which many of them may lose their seats. On the
other hand, if the Cabinet does not often initiate policy, it co-ordinates.
The Cabinet " reconciles, records and authorises." [80] All important
matters must go before the Cabinet at some stage. Also, the Cabinet
have greater *legal* powers than the Prime Minister.

The relative positions of the Prime Minister and the Cabinet are
variable, depending on personalities, not only that of the Prime
Minister but also those of his colleagues. A Prime Minister cannot
ride roughshod over his Cabinet—even Churchill gave way on
occasion. Their positions may also vary in different aspects of policy
and administration. The main influence of the Prime Minister tends
to lie in foreign policy, defence and national security, and in emergencies like a general strike, abdication or the Rhodesian U.D.I.
His influence fluctuates in economic policy, and he does not usually
intervene in person in such matters as education and housing. Thus
the Prime Minister is more powerful than any other Minister, and
than most combinations of Ministers, but less powerful than the
Cabinet collectively. Mr. Harold Wilson sees the role of the Prime
Minister as " if not that of a managing director, as that of an executive chairman." According to Mr. Wilson power still lies in the
Cabinet, but as the Cabinet must keep the confidence of the House,
it is the Cabinet in Parliament. The power-base lies in his party in
Parliament. A similar conclusion is reached by Mr. Patrick Gordon
Walker, who finds " the Cabinet in Parliament " to be the central
feature of the British Constitution. The Prime Minister is not independent of the Cabinet: he cannot habitually or often commit it.
The Cabinet is the activating and leading part of Parliament, and
through its control of the majority party it controls Parliament.
Partial Cabinets [81] have become an accepted part of the Cabinet
system, and a partial Cabinet is the opposite of Prime Ministerial
government.

If we cannot say that we have Prime Ministerial government, still
less can we say that we have " Presidential government." [82] The
American Presidential or Congress system is so different from ours
that comparison is difficult. The American party system is looser,
the President has a fixed term of office and he is not immediately
dependent on Congress.

---

[80] Mackintosh, *op. cit.* p. 612.
[81] *Ante*, p. 271.
[82] See Berkeley, *The Power of the Prime Minister*; *cf.* Max Beloff, " Prime Minister
and President " (Hugh Gaitskell Memorial Lecture, University of Nottingham,
1966), who admits, however, that the pull of the American pattern is very strong.

CHAPTER 16

CENTRAL GOVERNMENT DEPARTMENTS AND CIVIL SERVICE

I. CENTRAL GOVERNMENT DEPARTMENTS

Offices of state

The origin of the great offices of state is to be found in the royal household of the Saxon and Norman Kings. The Saxon King had his chamberlain, steward, marshal and cupbearer, and the Norman King his Lord High Steward, Lord Great Chamberlain, Constable and Marshal. In the process of time these offices became hereditary and honorary. Their public, as distinct from purely personal, services came to be performed by others who duplicated the offices and were appointed from time to time on merit and received a salary.[1] Two of the original offices survive as non-political appointments, namely, the hereditary Earl Marshal (Duke of Norfolk) in charge of styles and precedence, and the Lord Great Chamberlain. Their " doubles," Master of the Horse and Lord Chamberlain (former censor of plays), and the Lord Steward of the Household (who was the " double " of the Lord High Steward who presided over the trial of peers) used to be political officers. The offices of Treasurer, Comptroller and Vice-Chamberlain of the Household are still often given to members of the House of Commons who, together with the Joint Parliamentary Secretaries and the Junior Lords of the Treasury, act as Government Whips.

As the work of government grew, it became necessary for the King to employ secretaries and other officers to transact state business as distinct from the administration of the affairs of the royal household. The earliest and most important of these was the Lord Chancellor, who, as the King's chaplain, was both an educated " clerk " and the Keeper of the King's Conscience. His name is derived, says Holdsworth,[2] from " the *cancelli* or screen behind which the secretarial work of the royal household was carried on." To him was entrusted the custody of the Great Seal, under which the most important state documents were issued. For more than 400

---

[1] Maitland, *Constitutional History*, pp. 390–394; S. B. Chrimes, *Introduction to the Administrative History of Medieval England* (1952), describes the origins and early history of the royal household; Randolph S. Churchill, *They Serve the Queen* (1953) is a popular account.

[2] Holdsworth, *History of English Law* (5th ed.) Vol. I, p. 37.

years the use of the Privy Seal, held by the Lord Privy Seal, was a necessary prerequisite before letters patent under the Great Seal could be passed. Other secretaries were appointed in Plantagenet times, and they also held royal seals for affixing to appropriate documents. There is strictly only one office of Secretary of State, although it may be held by several persons whose powers are, with certain statutory exceptions, equal and interchangeable. They are appointed by the delivery of three seals, namely, the signet, a lesser seal and a small seal called the *cachet*.[3]

For the functions of finance and defence the great officers of state were the Lord High Treasurer, the Lord High Admiral, the Lord High Constable and the Earl Marshal. The first office has for a long time been in commission, the work being carried on by the First Lord of the Treasury and the Chancellor of the Exchequer, the two most important members of the Treasury Board. Queen Elizabeth II assumed the title of Lord High Admiral in order to perpetuate the name of an office dating back 600 years, which would otherwise have been lost on the abolition of the Lords Commissioners of the Admiralty. The Constable and the Earl Marshal issued regulations for the army. A Lord High Constable is still appointed for the coronation ceremony. The courts in which the Constable and Earl Marshal enforced military discipline disappeared soon after the Bill of Rights, giving way to the courts martial which now function under statutory authority. The only vestige is the High Court of Chivalry presided over by the Earl Marshal to try complaints of usurpation of arms. The English law of arms is a civilian jurisdiction.[4] This court was revived in 1954 after a lapse of 223 years.[5]

The Lord President of the Council is in charge of the Privy Council Office, but his departmental duties are light. He is usually a member of the Cabinet entrusted by the Prime Minister with special duties.

The office of Lord Privy Seal was considered important in the Middle Ages, but under modern statutes the use of the Privy Seal is no longer necessary. The Lord Privy Seal has now no departmental duties. He is generally used by the Prime Minister for special duties, although he is not always in the Cabinet. The same applies to the Chancellor of the Duchy of Lancaster, whose department administers

---

3 For an account of these seals and their use, see Anson, *Law and Custom of the Constitution*, Vol. II (4th ed. Keith) Pt. I, pp. 182–184.

4 See G. D. Squibb Q.C., *The High Court of Chivalry*.

5 *Manchester Corporation* v. *Manchester Palace of Varieties* [1955] P. 133; verbatim report, The Heraldry Society, 1955. The Earl Marshal (Duke of Norfolk) was assisted by his Surrogate (Lord Goddard D.C.L.), who delivered judgment, and the officers of arms. Lord Goddard was Lord Chief Justice, but he sat as a Doctor of Civil Law, his robes including a scarlet D.C.L.(Oxon.) gown, white bow tie and bob wig.

the estates of the Duchy of Lancaster, and who appoints and removes county court judges and justices of the peace within the Duchy.

Until recent times some of our government departments were boards that were once committees of the Privy Council.[6] The last survival was the Board of Trade, dating from the seventeenth century. The post of President of the Board of Trade is now held by the Secretary of State for Trade and Industry.

The Sovereign can create Ministers by virtue of the prerogative; but statutory authority is requisite in most cases, first, because it will usually be necessary for the Minister and his staff to be paid out of money voted by Parliament, and, secondly, because of the statutory restrictions on the number of Ministers who may sit in the House of Commons. The Ministers of the Crown (Transfer of Functions) Act 1946 enables functions to be transferred from one Minister to another by Order in Council on the initiative of the Prime Minister.

The Ministry

As has been seen in connection with a discussion of the disqualification for membership of the House of Commons,[7] the number of holders of ministerial posts is now about one hundred, including Cabinet Ministers, Ministers not in the Cabinet and Junior Ministers. The Ministerial Salaries Consolidation Act 1965 provides a salary to the Chancellor of the Exchequer, the Secretaries of State and the holders of the senior ministerial posts mentioned in Schedule 1. Ministers of State are to be paid such an amount (within the maximum) " as the First Lord of the Treasury may determine." The same applies to the Lord President of the Council, the Lord Privy Seal, the Chancellor of the Duchy of Lancaster or the Paymaster-General " when not a member of the Cabinet." Parliamentary Secretaries are also provided with a salary.

Section 2 of the Act fixes a maximum number of paid Ministers in various classes, namely: holders of the office of Secretary of State; Ministers of State; Treasury Secretaries; Junior Lords of the Treasury; Assistant Government Whips in the House of Commons; Lords in Waiting; and Parliamentary Secretaries.

Organisation of Government Departments

Ministers

At the head of each political department or Ministry is the Secretary of State or Minister. He is, of course, a member of the

---

6 Anson, *op. cit.* p. 160.
7 *Ante*, Chap. 8.

government and changes with the Ministry of the day; he may also be a member of the Cabinet.

Parliamentary Secretaries [8]

Under the Secretary of State or Minister will be one or more Parliamentary Under-Secretaries of State or Parliamentary Secretaries. As their name implies, they are members of one or other of the Houses of Parliament; they are Junior Ministers [9] who change with the government of the day. They assist their chief in the parliamentary or political side of his work, as well as the administration of his department. In the past they were usually chosen from the House in which the Minister did not sit,[10] but since 1945 Junior Ministers, as well as the heads of departments, have been recruited mainly from the lower House.

The Treasury [11]

The Treasury is the department entrusted by the Crown and by Parliament with the supervision and control of national finance. It is regarded as the senior government department. The Treasury was an offshoot of the Exchequer, which in the twelfth century was the *Curia Regis* sitting for revenue purposes. The Upper Exchequer, which audited and managed the King's accounts, developed into the Court of Exchequer; while the Lower Exchequer, from which the Treasury emerged, was concerned with the receipt of the royal revenue. The office of Treasurer, which is described in the *Dialogus de Scaccario* (1177), has been in commission since 1714.[12]

The Treasury Board consists of the First Lord of the Treasury (nowadays invariably the Prime Minister), the Chancellor of the Exchequer (whose office dates from Henry III) and five Junior Lords. Meetings of the full Board became less frequent by the beginning of the nineteenth century, and were discontinued altogether in 1856. The Junior Lords (who act mainly as Government Whips) still have certain formal functions, such as signing Treasury warrants. The management of the department is in the hands of the Chancellor of the Exchequer, who is also Under-Treasurer. In addition to his traditional duties with regard to national finance, the Chancellor in

---

8 These are to be distinguished from Parliamentary Private Secretaries, whose office is unofficial and unpaid.

9 Junior Ministers include the Parliamentary Secretaries, Treasury Commissioners (Government Whips) and H.M. Household.

10 A Minister has not the right—as he has in some constitutions—to address both Houses of the legislature.

11 Heath, *The Treasury.*

12 Holdsworth, *History of English Law,* Vol. I (5th ed.) pp. 42–44.

recent times has acquired responsibilities relating to economic policy. Under him are the Chief Secretary, the Parliamentary Secretary, the Financial Secretary and the Ministers of State.

The Plowden Committee summarised the responsibilities of the Treasury in 1961 in the following terms: "(a) for allocating the amount of money and economic resources to be made available for each purpose to each department; (b) for assisting the departments on economic and financial matters, and for assisting them to maintain proper practice in the expenditure of public money; (c) for the over-all efficiency of the public service, and thus for seeing that the departments are staffed, particularly at the top levels, with the best available officers drawn from the service as a whole; (d) for the development of management services throughout the public service; for taking the initiative in the introduction of new management techniques; and for keeping an oversight over the management practice of all the departments; (e) for the settlement of pay and conditions of service, and grading of staff throughout the service." [13]

The Treasury Solicitor's Office, which is staffed by barristers and solicitors, is available to the departments for legal advice and conveyancing. The senior official of this department is H.M. Procurator-General and Treasury Solicitor, who in the latter capacity acts as solicitor to government departments in litigation. He is also appointed *Queen's Proctor* in connection with proceedings for Admiralty droits and matrimonial causes. The general practice is that departments whose work is primarily the administration of detailed legal rules have their own solicitor's department, while departments whose legal problems are likely to be involved with policy rely on the Treasury Solicitor, whose position is independent of department policy.

Lord Chancellor's Office

The Lord Chancellor's Office is usually classified under the Supreme Court rather than as a government department. The staff includes the Clerk of the Crown in Chancery and Permanent Secretary to the Lord Chancellor; the Deputy Clerk of the Crown in Chancery; the Secretary for Ecclesiastical Patronage (who is also the Prime Minister's Appointments Secretary); the Secretary of Commissions of the Peace; and solicitors and legal assistants.

[13] *Control of Public Expenditure* (1961) Cmnd. 1432. And see *Report of the Machinery of Government Committee* (1918) Cmd. 9230, pp. 18–19; S. H. Beer, *Treasury Control: The Co-Ordination of Financial and Economic Policy in Great Britain* (1956); Sir Ivor Jennings, *Cabinet Government* (3rd ed.) Chap. 7.

Law Officers' department [14]

The Law Officers are legal advisers to the Crown and the Houses of Parliament. They hold ministerial posts and therefore change with the government. The Law Officers consist of the Attorney-General and Solicitor-General for England, and the Lord Advocate and Solicitor-General for Scotland.[15] They are regarded as the heads of the Bar in their respective countries, and as such are referees on points of professional etiquette. They are consulted by the various departments on legal problems. Although they are responsible to Parliament, they should not be questioned on particular criminal cases until after the proceedings are ended.

The Attorney-General was so called in 1461. The Solicitor-General dates from 1515. Formerly the Law Officers were summoned to advise the House of Lords,[16] and there was some doubt whether the Attorney-General was entitled to sit in the Commons; but his attendance in the Lords is dispensed with except in peerage cases, and his right to sit in the Commons has not been seriously questioned since Bacon's time.[17] The Solicitor-General also became entitled to sit in the Commons during the seventeenth century, although strictly he need not be a member.

The Attorney-General represents the Crown in civil proceedings in which it is specially concerned. His consent is necessary for the prosecution of certain offences, e.g. under the Official Secrets Acts. In criminal proceedings he or the Solicitor-General, or their deputies, prosecute in important cases.[18] It is the practice for the Attorney-General to lead in treason and important constitutional cases. He may stop the trial of an indictment by entering a *nolle prosequi*. He may also take over certain proceedings on the relation of private individuals (relator actions), e.g. public nuisance. Owing to the increase in their ministerial work, the Law Officers appear less frequently in criminal cases nowadays. The Attorney-General advises the House of Lords Committee for Privileges in peerage claims, and is a member of the House of Commons Committee of Privileges. The Director of Public Prosecutions [19] is responsible to him for the exercise of his duties. Actions may be brought against the Attorney-

---

[14] J. Ll. J. Edwards, *The Law Officers of the Crown* (1964); and review by Sir Jocelyn Simon in (1965) 81 L.Q.R. 289; Sir Elwyn Jones, " Office of Attorney-General " (1969) 27 C.L.J. 43.

[15] Other Officers are the Attorney-General of the Duchy of Lancaster, the Attorney-General and Solicitor-General of the County Palatine of Durham, and the Attorney-General to the Prince of Wales in respect of the Duchy of Cornwall.

[16] They still are, but they attend for ceremonial purposes only.

[17] Lord Campbell, *Lives of the Chancellors*, III, Chap. 54.

[18] *R.* v. *Wilkes* (1768) Wilson 322; (1768) 4 Burr. 2829.

[19] See *post*, Chap. 19.

General under the Crown Proceedings Act 1947 if there is no appropriate department.[20] The Law Officers are forbidden by Treasury Minute to engage in private practice, but they receive a salary inclusive of fees.

The better opinion is that the Attorney-General should not be in the Cabinet because of his quasi-judicial functions with regard to prosecutions, and also because it is desirable to separate the giving of advice from those who decide whether to act on the advice. The Attorney-General (and sometimes the Solicitor-General) is a member of the Legislative Committee of the Cabinet, and he is sometimes a member of (and in any case frequently attends) the Home Affairs Committee.[21] As regards the decision whether or not to institute public prosecutions, the Attorney-General acts in a quasi-judicial capacity, and does not take orders from the government that he should or should not prosecute in particular cases.[22] In political cases, such as sedition, he may seek the views of the appropriate Ministers, but he should not receive instructions. He may consider broad questions of public policy, but he should not be influenced by party political factors. Ministers may not be questioned in the House as to what advice the Law Officers have given, although they may be asked whether they have sought such advice. The fact that the Attorney-General consults informally and selectively, emphasises that both the decision and the responsibility are his alone.[23] This makes his position anomalous in relation to the doctrine of collective ministerial responsibility.

The Solicitor-General is a subordinate of the Attorney-General, and often gives a joint opinion with him on legal matters. His duties are in general similar to those of the Attorney-General, and he usually succeeds to that post if it becomes vacant. He may deputise for the Attorney-General if the office becomes vacant, or if the latter is absent or ill or authorises him to do so.[24]

The Scottish Law Officers have analogous functions with regard to Scotland.

20 The Attorney-General may also demand a trial at Bar (*i.e.* now, before a divisional court); he has the right to choose the venue for any civil or criminal proceedings in which the Crown is concerned; and he may file an *ex officio* criminal information, although this procedure is now rarely used.

21 The Attorney-General is in the Cabinet in some Commonwealth countries, *e.g.* Australia. In other Commonwealth countries the corresponding office is not regarded as a political one.

22 (1959) 600 H.C.Deb. col. 58. And see Lord MacDermott, *Protection from Power under English Law*, pp. 25–40; Sir Patrick Devlin, *The Criminal Prosecution in England*, p. 18; Marshall and Moodie, *Some Problems of the Constitution*, pp. 172–180; Jennings, *op. cit.* pp. 236–257.

23 Sir Jocelyn Simon, *loc. cit.*

24 Law Officers Act 1944.

Home Office [25]

The work of the two Secretaries of State then existing was divided in 1782 into home affairs and foreign affairs. The Home Secretary collaborates with the Secretary of State for Scotland in certain matters affecting that country. He is the medium of communication between the British Government and Northern Ireland,[26] the Channel Islands and the Isle of Man.

The Home Secretary exercises the prerogative of the Queen's pleasure in many ways. He is the channel of communication between the subject and the Queen for addresses and petitions, and he authorises many of the royal commissions set up from time to time to examine various matters. He is also the medium of communication between the Church of England and the Queen, its Governor.

Matters connected with the administration of justice not dealt with by the Lord Chancellor or the Attorney-General come within the sphere of the Home Secretary. He is ultimately responsible for the maintenance of the Queen's peace, and in this capacity he is in direct control of the Metropolitan Police and indirectly supervises the local police forces, and provides for co-operation between magistrates, the police, special constables and the armed forces. He appoints the Director of Public Prosecutions, and has a general supervision over coroners. He exercises the prerogative of mercy. He is also responsible for prisons, Borstals, remand centres and detention centres; the treatment of offenders; the probation and after-care services; the organisation of magistrates' courts; and legislation on criminal justice.

The Home Secretary administers the law relating to naturalisation, supervision of aliens, immigration, deportation and extradition.

The Home Office, being the residuary department of state, is concerned with many other miscellaneous matters under various statutes, including the supervision of the fire service; civil defence; community relations; the law relating to parliamentary and local government elections; explosives; fire-arms; dangerous drugs; liquor licensing; by-laws; betting and gaming.

Foreign and Commonwealth Office [27]

The Foreign Office, diplomatic and consular services were

25 Sir Frank Newsam, *The Home Office* (1954); *Report of the Committee on the Machinery of Government* (1918) Cd. 9230, pp. 63–78.
26 During the emergency, however, a special Minister (Mr. Whitelaw) has been appointed to take charge of the Northern Ireland government.
27 Lord Strang, *The Foreign Office* (1955); Sir Charles Jeffries, *The Colonial Office* (1956); Sir George Fiddes, *The Dominions and Colonial Offices* (1926); J. A. Cross, *Whitehall and the Commonwealth* (1967).

amalgamated into the Foreign Service in 1943. The Foreign Office is concerned with the formulation and conduct of foreign policy, and controls the Foreign Service. The Foreign Office combined in 1968 with the Commonwealth Office which (as the Commonwealth Relations Office) had merged with the Colonial Office in 1966. The Secretary of State maintains direct contact with the diplomatic representatives of foreign and Commonwealth states, with foreign and Commonwealth governments, and with the British diplomatic representatives overseas. He is in constant communication with the Queen, the Prime Minister and the Cabinet on all important matters relating to foreign and Commonwealth affairs. The Passport Office is a subordinate directorate. The Permanent Under-Secretary is head of the Diplomatic Service.

The Secretary of State is ultimately responsible for the government of British dependent territories.

Privy Council Office

The Lord Privy Seal is often nowadays Leader of the House of Lords. The senior official is the Clerk of the Council.

Scottish Office

Scottish affairs were formerly conducted by the Home Secretary and various other departments. In 1885 a Secretary for Scotland, with a Scottish Office, was created by statute, and in 1926 he was made a Secretary of State. The department has offices in London and Edinburgh.

The Secretary of State for Scotland is the keeper of the Great Seal of Scotland, which the Act of Union requires to be used for Scottish matters. He exercises in Scotland the powers of a Secretary of State (especially the Home Secretary), except in certain matters such as aliens.

Welsh Office

A Minister for Welsh Affairs was appointed in 1951, but for some years this office was held by the Minister of another department, usually of Cabinet rank. Since 1964 there has been a Secretary of State for Wales, and he has acquired responsibility for primary and secondary education. The department has offices in London and Cardiff.

Ministry of Defence

Churchill assumed the title of Minister of Defence on becoming Prime Minister in 1940. The Ministry was constituted in 1946 to co-ordinate the policy of the three services and to allocate funds between them. Later its responsibility was extended to the defence programme and the administration and efficiency of the armed forces as a whole. The Ministry of Defence was reconstituted in 1964 as a unified department, absorbing the Admiralty, War Office and Air Ministry.[28] There is a Secretary of State for Defence, who is a Cabinet Minister, and Parliamentary Under-Secretaries for the Royal Navy, the Army and the Royal Air Force.

Department of the Environment

This Department was formed in 1970 by the merging of the Ministries of Housing and Local Government, Public Building and Works, and Transport. Its head is the Secretary of State for the Environment. The Minister for Local Government and Development is in this Department.

Civil Service Department

This Department was established in 1968 to take over from the Treasury responsibility for the management of the Civil Service. The Prime Minister is Minister for the Civil Service, and approves the appointment of the two senior posts in each department. The Lord Privy Seal controls the everyday management, and the Permanent Secretary is Head of the Home Civil Service. The selection of civil servants continues to be done by the Civil Service Commission set up in 1855.

Other government departments

The other government departments not specifically dealt with here are mainly the creation of twentieth-century statutes. Their powers are almost entirely statutory, and their functions are sufficiently indicated by their names. Some are subject to frequent transformation, amalgamation, division or mere change of name.[29] The most important at the time of writing are: the Department of Health and Social Security (formed out of the Ministry of Health and the Ministry of Social Security) under the Secretary of State for Social Services; the Department of Employment; the Department of Education and

---

[28] *Central Organisation for Defence* (1963) Cmnd. 2097; Defence (Transfer of Functions) Act 1964.
[29] *The Organisation of British Central Government 1914–1969* (ed. F. M. G. Willson, 2nd ed. 1968).

Science; the Ministry of Agriculture, Fisheries and Food; the Department of Trade and Industry; the Ministry of Posts and Telecommunications; and the Board of Inland Revenue (management and collection of direct taxes).

Advisory Committees

There are about 250 permanent bodies outside the Civil Service set up to give advice direct to senior Ministers.[30]

II. THE CIVIL SERVICE

The detailed administration of the work of a government department is carried out by civil servants. Although, like Ministers, they are servants of the Crown, civil servants are called " permanent " since their appointment is non-political and in practice lasts during good behaviour, as opposed to Ministers and Parliamentary Secretaries who are responsible to Parliament and change office with the government.

The backbone of the department or Ministry is the secretariat under the Permanent Under-Secretary of State or Permanent Secretary. There used to be a hierarchy of administrative, executive and clerical classes; but following the recommendation of the Fulton Report,[31] these classes (up to and including the level of assistant secretary) have been merged in one administrative group. Departments with technical functions will also require a number of inspectors, accountants, contract officers, production officers, scientific officers and others with professional or technical qualifications.[32]

Who is a civil servant?

A civil servant is one kind of Crown servant, and whether or not a person is a Crown servant depends on the facts of the case. There is no formal definition of " Crown servant," although we may say that generally he is appointed by or on behalf of the Crown to perform public duties which are ascribable to the Crown; usually, but not necessarily, he is paid by the Crown out of the Consolidated Fund or out of moneys voted by Parliament. Modifications must be made for servants of the Crown in overseas territories.[33]

---

30 *Advisory Committees in British Government* (P.E.P. 1965).
31 (1971) Cmnd. 3638.
32 The personnel of the royal household and the government departments in the United Kingdom is given in *The British Imperial Calendar and Civil Service List*, published annually by H.M.S.O.
33 H. H. Marshall, " The Legal Relationship between the State and its Servants in the Commonwealth " (1966) 15 I.C.L.Q. 150.

All civil servants are Crown servants, but not all Crown servants are civil servants, for the term is not applied to Ministers, their Parliamentary Secretaries and Parliamentary Private Secretaries, or other holders of political offices, nor to members of the armed forces.[34] Local government officers and the employees of public corporations are not civil servants, although the nature of their work and their conditions of employment bear many similarities.[35] A subordinate engaged by, or working under, a civil servant is himself a servant of the Crown and not of his superior.[36]

Civil servants may be established (*i.e.* entitled to statutory superannuation), non-established or temporary. In *Mulvenna* v. *The Admiralty* [37] it was held by a Scottish court that a civilian telephone attendant employed at a naval dockyard had the same immunity from the arrestment of wages as a Crown servant. Civil servants who may render the Crown liable in actions of tort by third parties are those appointed directly or indirectly by the Crown and paid wholly out of the Consolidated Fund or moneys provided by Parliament, or holding an office which would normally be so paid: Crown Proceedings Act 1947, s. 6 (6).[38]

Appointment and conditions of service

On taking up their appointment civil servants are required to sign a declaration that they have read extracts from, and will observe, the Official Secrets Acts. At common law they hold office, as do other Crown servants, at the pleasure of the Crown, but in practice established civil servants are not dismissed except for misconduct.

Security measures have been taken since the war in respect of civil servants engaged on work that is vital to the national security who are suspected of being sympathetic to Communism or Fascism. If after inquiry the Minister finds that a civil servant engaged on such work is politically unreliable he may (subject to an appeal to three advisers) either post him to non-secret work or dismiss him.[39] A Standing Commission on Security, under the chairmanship of a High Court judge, was set up in 1964. Its terms of reference are, if so requested by the Prime Minister, to investigate and report on the circumstances in which a breach of security is known to have

34 N. E. Mustoe, *Law and Organisation of the British Civil Service*, p. 26.
35 See *The British Civil Servant*, and *Public Enterprise* (ed. Robson); *The Civil Service in Britain and France* (ed. Robson).
36 *Lane* v. *Cotton* (1701) 1 Ld.Raym. 646; *Bainbridge* v. *Postmaster-General* [1906] 1 K.B. 178.
37 1926 S.C. 824.
38 *Post*, Chap. 32.
39 *Statement on the Findings of the Conference of Privy Councillors on Security* (1955) Cmd. 9715.

occurred in the public service, and on any related failure of departmental security arrangements or neglect of duty; and to advise whether any change of security arrangements is necessary or desirable. The Commission will, if necessary, be invested with the powers of a tribunal set up under the Tribunals of Inquiry (Evidence) Act 1921; but it will generally sit in private as an administrative tribunal.

The legal and other rules regulating the Civil Service are contained in statutes, law reports (*e.g.* common law relating to liability), prerogative Orders in Council and Regulations made thereunder, Treasury Minutes and Circulars. The Civil Service is governed mainly under prerogative powers through the Civil Service Department,[40] although maximum salaries and superannuation benefits are prescribed by statute.[41] The Civil Service Commission, established by Order in Council in 1855, conducts the examination of entrants to the Civil Service. The National " Whitley " Council was formed in 1919 to provide means of consultation and conciliation between members of the official side and the staff side. The Contracts of Employment Act 1963 does not apply to civil servants. The Prime Minister as Minister for the Civil Service approves the appointment of certain senior officers, including Permanent Secretaries.

At common law a civil servant was dismissible at pleasure,[42] even if he was engaged for a definite period that had not yet expired.[43] There was an implied term to this effect, resting on public policy and not on the incapacity of the Crown to bind itself.[44] In such cases no action for damages lies against a superior Crown servant[45]; nor, apparently, does an action lie for breach of warranty of authority.[46] The Industrial Relations Act 1971, s. 162, provides that the

---

[40] *Ante*, p. 293.
[41] It has been argued that the civil servant, like the soldier, has a status and is subject to a special kind of law contained in Royal Warrants, Treasury Minutes, etc.; and on the other hand that civil servants (unlike the armed forces) are not governed by prerogative: *cf.* L. Blair, " The Civil Servant—A Status Relationship? " (1958) 21 M.L.R. 265; " The Civil Servant—Political Reality and Legal Myth " [1958] P.L. 32; J. D. B. Mitchell, *The Contracts of Public Authorities,* pp. 32 *et seq.*; H. Street, *Governmental Liability,* pp. 111 *et seq.*; Margaret Cowan, " Contracts with the Crown " (1965) C.L.P. 153.
[42] *Shenton* v. *Smith* [1895] A.C. 229 (P.C.); *Gould* v. *Stuart* [1896] A.C. 575.
[43] *De Dohsé* v. *R.* (1886) 3 T.L.R. 114 (H.L.); *Dunn* v. *The Queen* [1896] 1 Q.B. 116 (C.A.); *Hales* v. *R.* (1918) 34 T.L.R. 589 (C.A.); *Denning* v. *Secretary of State for India* (1930) 37 T.L.R. 138 (Bailhache J.); *Terrell* v. *Secretary of State for the Colonies* [1953] 2 Q.B. 482.
[44] *Inland Revenue Commission* v. *Hambrook* [1956] 2 Q.B. 640; *Att.-Gen. for New South Wales* v. *Perpetual Trustee Co. Ltd.* [1955] A.C. 457 (P.C.); *Riordan* v. *War Office* [1961] 1 W.L.R. 210 (C.A.); *Denning* v. *Secretary of State for India* (1920) 37 T.L.R. 138; *Rodwell* v. *Thomas* [1944] K.B. 596.
[45] *Gidley* v. *Lord Palmerston* (1822) 3 Brod. & B. 275; *Worthington* v. *Robinson* (1897) 75 L.T. 446.
[46] *Dunn* v. *MacDonald* [1896] 1 Q.B. 555; see also *Riach* v. *Lord Advocate,* 1932 S.C. 138.

provisions of the Act shall apply, with certain modifications, to Crown employment and Crown employees. Thus the right not to be unfairly dismissed (s. 22) applies to civil servants. On a complaint to the Industrial Court of unfair industrial practice or breach of duty against a Minister or government department the only remedies available to the Industrial Court are an order determining rights or an award of compensation, and not an order to take or refrain from action. A Minister may issue a certificate that certain employment, or the employment of a certain person, requires to be excepted from the provisions of the Act for the purpose of safeguarding national security.

Can a civil servant recover arrears of pay for services rendered, either during the subsistence of his employment or after his employment has been terminated? It was held in an early case that no action lay against the East India Company to recover a non-statutory pension.[47] In *Mulvenna* v. *Admiralty* [48] it was held that the rule that members of the forces may only claim on the bounty of the Crown and not for a contractual debt applies also to civilians as an implied condition in the terms of their contract. The latter case was followed in *Lucas* v. *Lucas and High Commissioner for India*,[49] where Pilcher J. held that the salary due to a civil servant was not a debt for the purpose of garnishee proceedings. The decision was much criticised, and in any case it could have been based on another ground.[50] In *Sutton* v. *Att.-Gen.*,[51] on the other hand, the House of Lords assumed that a civil servant's pay was recoverable, and the only question in that case was, how much was due. The question was regarded as one of the interpretation of an enlistment circular for Post Office [52] telegraphists in the first war. None of the judgments raised the question whether the pay was legally recoverable at all, and counsel for the Crown do not seem to have argued the point. Lord Goddard C.J. expressed the opinion *obiter* in *Terrell* v.

---

[47] *Gibson* v. *East India Co.* (1839) 5 Bing.N.C. 262.

[48] 1926 S.C. 842.

[49] [1943] P. 68.

[50] D. W. Logan, " A Civil Servant and his Pay " (1945) 61 L.Q.R. 240. *Cf.* Crown Proceedings Act 1947, s. 27 (1). *Cf. Considine* v. *McInerney* [1916] 2 A.C. 162 (H.L.); *ex gratia* pension paid to civil servant should be taken into account in fixing the amount of compensation under Workmen's Compensation Acts.

[51] (1923) 39 T.L.R. 294. Considered by the Privy Council in *Kodeeswaran (Chelliah)* v. *Att.-Gen. of Ceylon* [1970] A.C. 1111, where dicta of Lord Blackburn in *Mulvenna* v. *The Admiralty*, *supra*, were strongly criticised as being a *non sequitur* from the Crown's right to terminate a contract of service at will. It was not necessary in *Dudfield* v. *Ministry of Works* and *Faithful* v. *Admiralty* (*The Times*, January 24, 1964) to decide whether industrial civil servants could have sued their departments for arrears of pay, because there was no contractual right to receive the negotiated increases that were postponed by a " pay pause."

[52] The Post Office was at that time a government department.

Secretary of State for the Colonies [53] that a civil servant who had been dismissed could recover arrears of salary up to the time of dismissal, and in *Inland Revenue Commissioners* v. *Hambrook* [54] that a civil servant (although not perhaps a soldier) could recover for services rendered on a *quantum meruit.*

On the question whether at common law there subsists between the Crown and a civil servant a contractual relationship, a contract of service the terms of which are enforceable, the decisions and dicta are conflicting. In *Sutton* v. *Att.-Gen.* (*supra*) all the judgments in the Court of Appeal and the House of Lords assumed that there was a contract of employment and that the terms as regards pay were enforceable. On the other hand, Pilcher J. in *Lucas* v. *Lucas* (*supra*) based his judgment on the ground that there was no contract the terms of which could be enforced by the civil servant.

As far as third parties are concerned, a contractual relationship may be said to exist between the Crown and a civil servant. The House of Lords in *Owners of S.S. Raphael* v. *Brandy*,[55] where a stoker on board a merchant ship was injured in an accident, held that the retainer he was paid as a member of the Royal Naval Reserve must be taken into account as earnings under a concurrent contract of service in assessing compensation under the Workmen's Compensation Act 1906. In *Picton* v. *Cullen* [56] the Irish Court of Appeal held that, where a judgment debt had been entered against a schoolteacher employed by the Board of National Education, the court could appoint a receiver over an instalment of salary that had actually become due, although there could be no attachment of such future income.

In *Reilly* v. *The King* [57] the appellant had been appointed a member of a statutory board in Canada for a term of five years, but after two years the board was abolished by a Canadian statute. His office was therefore terminated, and he brought a petition of right for breach of contract. It was held that further performance of the contract had become impossible by legislation, and the contract was therefore discharged. The case is notable for Lord Atkin's dicta [58] because, although they were *obiter*, he was delivering the opinion of a strong Judicial Committee. He said that " in some offices at least it is difficult to negative some contractual relations, whether it be as

53 [1953] 2 Q.B. 482, 499.
54 [1956] 2 Q.B. 641, 654.
55 [1911] A.C. 413. The Crown itself would have been expressly not liable under the Workmen's Compensation Act.
56 [1900] 2 I.R. 612.
57 [1934] A.C. 176 (P.C.).
58 *Ibid.* at pp. 179–180. And see *per* Denning J. in *Robertson* v. *Minister of Pensions* [1949] 1 K.B. 227, 231.

to salary or terms of employment on the one hand, and duty to serve faithfully and with reasonable care and skill on the other." Lord Atkin also said: " If the terms of the appointment definitely prescribe a term and expressly provide for a power to determine ' for cause ' it appears necessarily to follow that any implication of a power to dismiss at pleasure is excluded." This statement is difficult to reconcile with Lord Goddard's statement in *Terrell's* case [59] that, where the Crown has the right to dismiss at pleasure, it cannot be taken away by any contractual arrangement made by a Secretary of State or an executive officer or department of state.

The answer seems to be that a statute or letters patent creating an office may prescribe a definite term with power to determine " for cause " within that period, excluding the implication of a power to dismiss at will, but no such binding arrangement can be made *ad hoc* between an officer on behalf of the Crown and a prospective Crown servant. In *Riordan* v. *War Office* [60] Diplock J. gave reason for saying that the Crown might be held bound by other terms in the regulations than length of service or dismissal, and that the civil servant for his part would be bound by the express terms; but this also was *obiter*.

For the purposes of the Industrial Relations Act 1971, " Crown employment " is equated with other forms of employment so far as civil servants (but not members of the armed forces) are concerned (s. 162).

Political activities of civil servants

In determining the extent to which civil servants shall be free to take part in political activities, the government has to effect a compromise between two conflicting principles. On the one hand it is desirable in a democratic society " for all citizens to have a voice in the affairs of the state and for as many as possible to play an active part in public life ": on the other hand " the public interest demands the maintenance of political impartiality in the Civil Service and confidence in that impartiality as an essential part of the structure of government in this country." [61]

(i) As we have seen, civil servants are disqualified by statute from sitting in the House of Commons, and by the Servants of the Crown (Parliamentary Candidature) Order 1960 a civil servant must resign his office before standing as a candidate for a parliamentary election.

[59] *Terrell* v. *Secretary of State for the Colonies* [1953] 2 Q.B. 482, 497–500.
[60] [1959] 1 W.L.R. 1046; [1959] 3 All E.R. 552. And see note by C. Grunfeld in (1960) 23 M.L.R. 194.
[61] *Report of the Committee on the Political Activities of Civil Servants* (Masterman), (1949) Cmd. 7718.

(ii) With regard to other political activities, civil service regulations issued in 1953 distinguished, first, between three classes of civil servants and, secondly, between national and local politics.[62]

(a) The administrative and professional grades, and those members of the executive and clerical grades who work with them and come into contact with the public, are restricted from taking an active part in national politics. They may be permitted where possible to take part in local government, but most would probably not have time to do so.

(b) The remaining members of the executive and clerical grades may be permitted to take part in national as well as local politics (except parliamentary candidature), subject to a code of " discretion " with regard to the expression of views on governmental policy and national political issues.

(c) The minor, manipulative and industrial grades are free to engage in both national and local politics (other than parliamentary candidature), except when on duty or on official premises or while wearing uniform. They remain subject, of course, to the Official Secrets Acts.

---

62 *Political Activities of Civil Servants* (1953) Cmd. 8783. The merger of the administrative and executive classes following the Fulton report (*ante*, p. 294) has not affected these regulations.

CHAPTER 17

THE ARMED FORCES

I. The Armed Forces and the Constitution

History of the armed forces [1]

After the Norman Conquest came the feudal levy, which could be called upon to serve within England for forty days in the year. All military tenants served at their own expense. Henry I is reported to have invented scutage (shield money) whereby personal service was dispensed with, and the military tenant, instead of serving himself, had to equip and maintain a knight. Scutage was a subject of grievance in Magna Carta, and after 1215 it was supposed not to be levied without the consent of the Great Council and afterwards of Parliament. At the Restoration military tenures were abolished,[2] and with them scutage. The militia was retained by the Militia Act 1661.[3] James II raised an army by voluntary enlistment, which caused such apprehension that a standing army in time of peace was forbidden by the Bill of Rights 1688, which declares that " the raising or keeping a standing army within the Kingdom in time of peace, unless it be with consent of Parliament, is against law."

It was soon realised, however, that a standing army was necessary for the national safety. The solution was found in the Mutiny Act 1688, which authorised the keeping of an army for one year, and provided that the Act should not exempt any officer or soldier from the ordinary process of law. This force was maintained (except for short intervals) by annual Mutiny Acts down to 1879 and continued by the Army Act 1881, which formed to a large extent a military code. The Act of 1881 was annually renewed with amendments by short Army (Annual) Acts down to 1956. Meanwhile the Royal Air Force was established as a separate force by Parliament in 1917. Authority for this was renewed by Army and Air Force (Annual) Acts down to 1956.

Since 1955 Parliament, instead of passing annual Acts, has given the Army and Air Force Acts a maximum life of five years, but they

---

[1] Clode, *Military Forces of the Crown* (1869); Bl.Comm. I, Chap. 13; Anson, *Law and Custom of the Constitution*, II, ii (4th ed. Keith) pp. 199–222; *Manual of Military Law*, Part II, Section 1; Maitland, *Constitutional History*, pp. 275–280.

[2] Tenure Abolition Act 1660.

[3] Repealed by the Statute Law (Repeals) Act 1969, except sections 4 and 9.

301

would expire unless continued in operation annually by Order in Council. Such Orders in Council must be laid in draft before Parliament and are subject to an affirmative resolution by each House.

Legislation was necessary to legalise not only the raising of a standing army but also the enforcement of military discipline, which would infringe the common law, as well as to provide the money for its upkeep. The practice of authorising the keeping of an army for one year at a time was devised to ensure the observance of the convention that Parliament should be summoned at least once a year. The money is now provided by annual Appropriation Acts, which might be taken to imply the lawfulness of maintaining the forces for which funds are appropriated.

Public opinion has never feared the existence of a standing navy, so that the history of the Royal Navy has been free from constitutional problems.[4] It was the customary duty of the coastal towns, and especially the Cinque Ports, to provide ships and men in an emergency. The maintenance of the Navy has always been, and still is, within the royal prerogative; but terms of enlistment and naval discipline are now regulated by the Naval Discipline Act, and of course in modern times the money has to come from Parliament. The Naval Discipline Act is now subject to continuance in the same manner as the Army and Air Force Acts.[5]

Conscription, or compulsory military service, was introduced by statute in both world wars.[6]

Legal position of members of the armed forces

The control of the armed forces is part of the royal prerogative (*Chandler* v. *D.P.P.*).[7] The prerogative powers in relation to such matters as the training of the forces are preserved by the Crown Proceedings Act 1947. The provisions of the Industrial Relations Act 1971, relating to such matters as unfair dismissal, do not apply to members of the armed forces (s. 162).

Contract of service

Officers are commissioned by the Crown. They may be dismissed

---

[4] But *cf. The Case of Ship Money* (*R.* v. *Hampden*) (1637) 3 St.Tr. 825.

[5] Armed Forces Act 1971.

[6] The prerogative of " impressment " or " pressing " mariners into the Navy whenever the public safety requires, has never been abolished by statute although in practice it is obsolete: *R.* v. *Broadfoot* (1743) 18 St.Tr. 1323; Foster, *Crown Law*, p. 154; *R.* v. *Tubbs* (1776) Cowp. 512, *per* Lord Mansfield; *Ex p. Fox* (1793) 5 St.Tr. 276, *per* Lord Kenyon; *Barrow's Case* (1811) 14 East 346; Foster, 158.

[7] [1964] A.C. 763 (H.L.).

at the pleasure of the Crown, but may not resign their commission without leave.[8]

Other ranks are recruited—apart from statutory conscription or compulsory national service—by voluntary enlistment by attestation before a recruiting officer. Enlistment being a civil contract, its terms cannot be varied without the consent of the soldier, but he can be discharged at the pleasure of the Crown.

No action lies against the Crown to enforce the terms of service, for damages for wrongful dismissal or to recover arrears of pay.[9]

Subject to ordinary law

A soldier becomes subject to military law, but he also remains bound by the ordinary civil and criminal law.[10] It is hardly correct to say that he is governed by two systems of law, for military law is part of the law of the land.[11] Statutory exceptions include the right to make an informal will on actual military service[12] or at sea, exemption from estate duty if killed in action, exemption from jury service, and the right to be put on the absent voters' list.[13]

Superior orders as a defence

A member of the armed forces is primarily bound to obey the civil (*i.e.* non-military) law, even though such obedience may render him liable to be tried by court-martial. "A soldier for the purpose of establishing civil order," it has been said,[14] "is only a citizen armed in a particular manner." Although military regulations forbid the firing on rioters except under an order from a magistrate who is present, the existence or absence of a magistrate's order neither justifies what is done nor excuses what is not done in the eyes of the civil law. The soldier may therefore sometimes find himself in a dilemma if he is ordered by a superior officer to do something which is unlawful; and the question has arisen how far, if at all, he can plead obedience to superior orders—one of the first duties of a soldier—as a defence. In *R.* v. *Smith* (1900),[15] a case heard by a

---

8 *Vertue* v. *Lord Clive* (1769) 4 Burr. 2472; *R.* v. *Cuming, ex p. Hall* (1887) 19 Q.B.D. 13; *Hearson* v. *Churchill* [1892] 2 Q.B. 144; *Marks* v. *Commonwealth of Australia* (1964) 111 C.L.R. 548.
9 *Grant* v. *Secretary of State for India* (1877) 2 C.P.D. 445; *Mitchell* v. *R.* [1896] 1 Q.B. 121; *Leaman* v. *R.* [1920] 3 K.B. 663. See Z. Cowen, "The Armed Forces of the Crown" (1950) 66 L.Q.R. 478.
10 The subjection of the soldier to English law is indeed wider than that of a civilian in that the soldier takes English law with him wherever he goes.
11 *Burdett* v. *Abbot* (1812) 4 Taunt. 401, *per* Mansfield C.J.; *Grant* v. *Gould* (1792) 2 H.Bl. 98, *per* Lord Loughborough.
12 *Re Wingham* [1949] P. 187.
13 And see Crown Proceedings Act 1947, s. 10; *post*, Chap. 32.
14 *Report of the Commission on the Featherstone Riots* (1893) C. 7234.
15 [1900] Cape of Good Hope S.C. 561.

special tribunal of three civilian judges set up in the Cape of Good Hope during the Boer War, Solomon J. said: " I think it is a safe rule to lay down that if a soldier honestly believes he is doing his duty in obeying the commands of his superior, and if the orders are not so manifestly illegal that he must or ought to have known that they were unlawful, the private soldier would be protected by the orders of his superior officer." In that case it was held that the order to shoot an African if he did not fetch a bridle was not so plainly illegal that the accused would have been justified in the circumstances in refusing to obey it, and it was therefore not necessary to decide whether in the circumstances the order was unreasonable or unnecessary. The accused was therefore not guilty of murder.

In *Keighley* v. *Bell* (1866),[16] Willes J., a great authority on the common law, said *obiter*: " I hope I may never have to determine that difficult question, how far the orders of a superior officer are a justification. Were I compelled to determine that question, I should probably hold that the orders are an absolute justification in time of actual war—at all events, as regards enemies or foreigners—and I should think, even with regard to English-born subjects of the Crown, unless the orders were such as could not legally be given. I believe that the better opinion is, that an officer or soldier acting under the orders of his superior—not being necessarily or manifestly illegal— would be justified by his orders." If modified to the extent that the soldier's belief in the lawfulness of the order must be reasonable, Willes J.'s opinion would probably be accepted by the legal profession.

The soldier's obligation is to obey any *lawful* command. " Lawful command " is described in the *Manual of Military Law* [17] as a command which is not contrary to English or international law and is justified by military law. " A superior has the right," says the *Manual*, " to give a command for the purpose of maintaining good order or suppressing a disturbance or for the execution of a military duty or regulation or for a purpose connected with the welfare of troops. . . . If a command is manifestly illegal the person to whom it is given would be justified in questioning and even refusing to execute it." With regard to a soldier's responsibility for carrying out an order which is not manifestly illegal, on the other hand, the *Manual* disagrees with the dictum in *Keighley* v. *Bell* (*supra*), but says that " it may give rise to a defence on other grounds, *e.g.* by establishing a claim of right made in good faith in answer to a charge of larceny, or by negativing a particular intent which may be a com-

16 4 F. & F. 763, 790.
17 Part I (12th ed. 1972). The *Manual* is not authoritative: *R.* v. *Tucker* [1952] 2 All E.R. 1074; 36 Cr.App.R. 192.

plete defence or reduce the crime to one of a less serious nature, or by excusing what appears to be culpable negligence.[18]

Whichever view is accepted it is obvious that a soldier may be placed in a serious dilemma, with the prospect of being proceeded against in the ordinary courts if he commits a crime or tort and of being court-martialled if he refuses to obey the command. So far as criminal liability is concerned, the soldier's position is somewhat mitigated by the power of the Crown to enter a *nolle prosequi* or to pardon after conviction, and the existence of the Courts-Martial Appeal Court (which is substantially the same body as the criminal division of the Court of Appeal) to hear appeals from courts-martial provides a forum for resolving any conflict of jurisdictions. Ultimately, the House of Lords could dispose of the problems as regards liability in tort as well.

With regard to liability for war crimes, *i.e.* violations of the principles of international law relating to warfare, the edition of the *Manual of Military Law* still issued at the beginning of the Second World War allowed superior orders as a valid defence. An amendment drafted by the Law Officers of the Crown was made in 1944 so as to read: " Obedience to the orders of a government or of a superior, whether military or civil, or to a national law or regulation, affords no defence to a charge of committing a war crime but may be considered in mitigation of punishment."[19] The Nuremberg Charter similarly provided that: " The fact that the defendant acted pursuant to orders of his government or of a superior shall not free him from responsibility, but may be considered in mitigation of punishment " (Art. 8). The true test, said the International Military Tribunal, is not the existence of the order, but whether moral choice is in fact possible.[20]

II. MILITARY LAW AND COURTS-MARTIAL

Military law [21]

We have said that when a person joins the armed forces he becomes subject to the special code of military law in addition to the ordinary law. The objects of military law are disciplinary and administrative. It provides in the first place for the maintenance of discipline and good order among the troops, and secondly, for

---

[18] Citing *R.* v. *James* (1839) 8 C. & P. 131; *R.* v. *Trainer* (1864) 4 F. & F. 105.

[19] Part III, p. 176. *Cf.* Shakespeare, *Henry V*, Act IV, sc. 1, ll. 138–140.

[20] See Viscount Kilmuir, *Nuremberg in Retrospect* (Holdsworth Club, University of Birmingham, 1956) pp. 14–17.

[21] It is convenient here to speak of " military law," which is the law of the Army; but similar considerations apply to Air Force law and Naval discipline.

administrative matters such as terms of service, enlistment, discharge
and billeting.

The sources of military law are the Army Act, the Acts relating
to the Reserve and Auxiliary forces, and certain other Acts applying
to the Army (e.g. the Official Secrets Acts and the Emergency Powers
Act 1920), supplemented by the Rules of Procedure, the Queen's
Regulations and royal warrants. The laws and customs of war
established by international conventions (i.e. multilateral treaties) are
also required to be observed by members of the forces. It was
argued in *R.* v. *Durkin* [22] that there is also a "common law of the
army," and the Courts-Martial Appeal Court did not reject it, but
the existence of such a common law is doubtful. In addition to
legally binding rules, there is "the custom of the service and military
usage."

Employed civilians and followers with the Regular forces anywhere when on active service are subject (with modifications) to
Part II of the Army Act, which deals with discipline and the trial
and punishment of military offences. All civilians listed in the Fifth
Schedule to the Army Act are subject to the "civil offences" and
certain specific offences within the jurisdiction of the Act, when in the
command area of any part of the Regular forces abroad at any time.
These include employed persons, persons attached to the forces for
the purposes of their profession, and resident families. Civilians
may be awarded a fine or any punishment less than imprisonment
by court-martial, and a fine not over £10 if dealt with summarily by
"the appropriate superior authority." [23]

The civil courts have jurisdiction to determine in proceedings
brought before them, i.e. in the exercise of their supervisory jurisdiction by way of prerogative orders and in actions for damages in
tort, whether a person is subject to military law.

Courts-martial

The King's troops in medieval times were governed by regulations
or articles of war issued by the King and administered in the Court
of the Constable and the Marshal, two hereditary officers of state. [24]
The office of Constable became extinct in the reign of Henry VIII,
but the Court of the Constable and the Marshal continued to exist.

22 [1953] 2 Q.B. 364 (C.-M.A.C.).
23 See G. J. Borrie, " Courts-martial, civilians, and civil liberties " (1969) 32 M.L.R.
   35.
24 For the history of this Court, see Holdsworth, *History of English Law* (5th ed.)
   Vol. I, pp. 573–580. See also Clode, *Military Forces of the Crown*, Vol. I, pp.
   76–77; Richard O'Sullivan, *Military Law and the Supremacy of the Civil Courts*
   (1921) pp. 1–12.

During the early eighteenth century the Court ceased to function although it was never formally abolished.[25] From that time articles of war governing Army discipline were issued under parliamentary authority. The modern system of courts-martial for the trial of persons subject to *military law* was established by the Mutiny Act 1688, and the Army Act 1881 combined it with the statutory articles of war.

The courts-martial that exist today enforce military law, Air Force law and Naval discipline, but do not administer martial law, although there has inevitably been some confusion on the point. " As a matter of etymology," says Maitland,[26] " *marshall* has nothing whatever to do with *martial*—the marshall is the master of the horse—he is marescallus, mareschalk, a stable servant—while of course Martial has to do with Mars, the God of war. Still, when first we hear of martial law in England, it is spelt indifferently *marshall* and *martial*, and it is quite clear that the two words were confused in the popular mind. . . ." Courts-martial have jurisdiction to try and to punish persons subject to military law for two classes of offences: first, military offences created by Part II of the Army Act, as to which their jurisdiction is exclusive; and secondly, under certain conditions, civil offences (*i.e.* criminal offences under non-military law), as to which their jurisdiction in this country is concurrent with the civil (*i.e.* non-military) courts.[27] Courts-martial have no jurisdiction, however, to try cases of treason, murder, manslaughter, treason-felony or rape committed in the United Kingdom.

The members of a court-martial are judges of both fact and law. Counsel may appear for either side. Courts-martial must observe the rules of English criminal law relating to the admissibility of evidence, although these were largely designed for use in jury trial. Witnesses and other persons whose duty it is to attend a court-martial are entitled to the same immunities and privileges as in the High Court, in particular, immunity from being sued for defamation.

The Army Act does not restrict the offences for which persons may be tried in the civil courts, or the jurisdiction of the civil courts to try a person subject to military law for any offence; but where a person is tried by a civil court the fact that he has been punished by a court-martial must be taken into consideration in awarding

---

[25] The last case tried by the Court of the Marshal appears to be *Sir H. Blount's Case* (1737) 1 Atk. 296. *Cf.* Court of Chivalry, *ante*, p. 285.

[26] *Constitutional History*, p. 266. For martial law, see *post*, Chap. 18.

[27] See *e.g. R.* v. *Gordon-Finlayson* [1941] 1 K.B. 171; *Cox* v. *Army Council* [1963] A.C. 48 (H.L., on appeal from C.-M.A.C.). With regard to murder committed abroad, see *R.* v. *Page* [1954] 1 Q.B. 170 (C.-M.A.C.); *cf.* M. J. Prichard, " The Army Act and Murder Abroad " (1954) C.L.J. 232.

punishment. On the other hand, a person subject to military law who has been tried by a civil court may not subsequently be tried by court-martial for the same offence.

A judge-advocate must be appointed to sit on a general court-martial, and may be appointed to sit on a field general court-martial or a district court-martial. The prosecutor and the accused are entitled to the opinion of the judge-advocate on any question of law or procedure, and during the trial he must advise the court on any questions of law or procedure. The judge-advocate advises the court on the law before the court deliberates on its findings. The Judge-Advocate-General advises on the confirmation of the findings and sentences of all court-martial proceedings which are referred to him. His advice is given on the legal aspects, not on the merits of the case.

The Courts-Martial (Appeals) Act 1951 established a Courts-Martial Appeal Court to hear appeals from persons convicted by a Naval, Army or Air Force court-martial.[28] The composition of the Courts-Martial Appeal Court in English cases is similar to that of the criminal division of the Court of Appeal. In appeals from Scotland or Northern Ireland, members of the High Court of Justiciary or the Supreme Court in Northern Ireland may sit.

Appeal lies from the Courts-Martial Appeal Court to the House of Lords.[29]

Visiting forces

The Visiting Forces Act 1952 provides that visiting forces belonging to the member states of the Commonwealth and other countries specified by Order in Council under arrangements for common defence (e.g. NATO),[30] may be tried in the United Kingdom by the service courts of their own country according to their own service law; but a death sentence may not be carried out in the United Kingdom unless the law of the United Kingdom provides for the death sentence in such a case.

This jurisdiction does not oust the jurisdiction of British criminal courts over such visiting forces except in relation to offences arising in the course of service duty, offences against the person of a member of the same or another visiting force, and offences against the property of the visiting force or of a member of such force; and in these cases the appropriate authority may waive its jurisdiction. British courts may not try a member of a visiting force for an offence for which he has already been tried by his service court.

---

28 See e.g. R. v. Tucker [1952] 2 All E.R. 1074; 36 Cr.App.R. 192.
29 Courts-Martial (Appeals) Act 1968.
30 See G. I. A. D Draper, Civilians and the Nato Status of Forces Agreement (1966).

Civil actions may be brought in the ordinary courts against members of visiting forces; but the Secretary of State for Defence may arrange, under regulations issued by the Lord Chancellor's department, for the settlement of claims in tort.

Supervisory jurisdiction of the High Court

Courts-martial are inferior courts over which the High Court exercises a supervisory jurisdiction, distinct from the system of appeals to the Courts-Martial Appeal Court. This supervisory jurisdiction is exercisable by means of the prerogative writ of habeas corpus and the orders of certiorari, prohibition and mandamus.[31] Civil actions may be brought against individual officers for damages for false imprisonment, assault, malicious prosecution, defamation, etc. Criminal proceedings against officers may take the form of a prosecution for e.g. murder, manslaughter or assault.

Actions for damages

As regards actions in tort the true principles are probably those stated by McCardie J. in *Heddon* v. *Evans* (1919),[32] an action brought by a private soldier against his commanding officer for false imprisonment and malicious prosecution in confining him to barracks on charges of making a frivolous complaint and conduct to the prejudice of good order and military discipline. His Lordship stated that: (1) an action lies if the court-martial or officer commits what would be a wrong at common law while acting without or in excess of jurisdiction[33]; but (2) no action lies if the court-martial or officer commits what would be a common law wrong while acting within its or his jurisdiction, even if the act was done maliciously[34] or without reasonable and probable cause.[35] Proposition (1) His Lordship thought was clear from the authorities as well as on principle. Proposition (2) he based on five cases, two of them in the Court of Appeal.[36] Only the House of Lords is free to hold that an action will lie for malicious abuse of military authority (within jurisdiction) without reasonable and probable cause.

[31] See also *post*, Chap. 31.
[32] 35 T.L.R. 642. McCardie J. went on to hold (although he did not consider it necessary for the decision) that the plaintiff had not established that the defendant did act maliciously or without reasonable and probable cause. A verbatim report is given in R. O'Sullivan, *Military Law and the Supremacy of the Civil Courts* (1921) pp. 43 *et seq.*
[33] *Grant* v. *Gould* (1792) 2 H.Bl. 100.
[34] *Dawkins* v. *Lord F. Paulet* (1869) L.R. 5 Q.B. 94.
[35] *Johnstone* v. *Sutton* (1786) 1 T.R. 493, 510, 784.
[36] *Dawkins* v. *Lord F. Paulet* (*supra*); *Dawkins* v. *Lord Rokeby* (1866) 4 F. & F. 806; *Marks* v. *Frogley* [1898] 1 Q.B. 888; *Fraser* v. *Hamilton* (1917) 33 T.L.R. 431; *Fraser* v. *Balfour* (1918) 34 T.L.R. 502.

In *Dawkins* v. *Lord F. Paulet* (1869) [37] an officer sued a superior officer for libels contained in letters written by the superior to the Adjutant-General in the course of his duty. The majority of the Court of Queen's Bench (Cockburn C.J. dissenting) held that the civil courts would not interfere in such cases even if the superior officer acted maliciously,[38] first, because the alleged wrong was done in the course of duty, and motive is therefore irrelevant; secondly, on grounds of convenience and public policy, as otherwise a superior officer would be unduly hampered in the performance of his duty; and, thirdly, because the party complaining of injustice has his remedy under military law. The opinion of Lord Mansfield and Lord Loughborough in the Court of Exchequer Chamber in *Johnstone* v. *Sutton* (1786) [39] may be cited for the same principle where a superior officer abuses his authority without reasonable and probable cause. In that case a naval captain sued an admiral for malicious prosecution in having him tried by court-martial for disobedience to orders. The opinion, however, was *obiter*, as the Exchequer Chamber held that the admiral had reasonable and probable cause.

A court-martial would act without jurisdiction if it proceeded against a person who was not subject to military law,[40] or if it was not properly convened or properly constituted in accordance with the Army Act, or if it convicted a man of an offence which is not an offence under the Act. It would exceed its jurisdiction if it awarded a heavier punishment than it has authority to award.

Prerogative writs and orders

As regards the issue of prerogative writs and orders against courts-martial, post-war cases such as *Martyn's* case [41] and *Elliott's* case [42] indicate that the High Court has gone a long way towards relinquishing its control, by ascribing jurisdiction to a court-martial merely because the applicant was a soldier, by requiring the infringement of some ill-defined " civil right " instead of some right (whether of life, liberty or property) recognised by the law, by refusing relief if there is a remedy provided by military law, and by declining to deal with matters of " military procedure." It has been persuasively argued [43] that in this respect the same general rule should apply to courts-martial as to other inferior courts, namely, that prerogative

[37] L.R. 5 Q.B. 94.
[38] The occasion was privileged; see *Dawkins* v. *Lord Rokeby* (1875) L.R. 7 H.L. 744.
[39] 1 T.R. 493, 510, 784.
[40] *R.* v. *Wormwood Scrubs Prison (Governor), ex p. Boydell* [1948] 2 K.B. 193.
[41] *R.* v. *Secretary of State for War, ex p. Martyn* [1949] 1 All E.R. 242.
[42] *R.* v. *O.C. Depot Battalion, R.A.S.C. Colchester, ex p. Elliott* [1949] 1 All E.R. 373.
[43] D. C Holland, " The Law of Courts-Martial " (1950) CL.P. 173, 174–192.

writs and orders may be issued to prevent a court-martial from exceeding its jurisdiction (see *per* Lord Loughborough in *Grant* v. *Gould* (1792) [44]), with the proviso that some right recognised by the civil law is involved and not merely dismissal from the service of the Crown (see *per* Cockburn C.J. in *Re Mansergh* (1861) [45]).

Since the courts will not interfere with the administration of military law by the properly constituted tribunals acting within their jurisdiction, the cases in which a soldier has applied to the civil courts successfully have been very rare. It does not appear that mandamus has ever been issued.[46] Prohibition [47] and certiorari [48] have generally been refused.

Habeas corpus, on the other hand, has occasionally been granted.[49] Habeas corpus may be issued, even though the court-martial would be acting within its jurisdiction, if it oppressively delays the trial, but this would not prevent the court-martial from subsequently trying the case.[50]

---

[44] 2 H.Bl. 69, 100.
[45] 1 B. & S. 400.
[46] Mandamus was refused in *R.* v. *Secretary of State for War* [1891] 2 Q.B. 326; *R.* v. *Army Council, ex p. Ravenscroft* [1917] 2 K.B. 504; and *R.* v. *Army Council, ex p. Sandford* [1940] 1 K.B. 719.
[47] Prohibition was refused in *Grant* v. *Gould* (1792) 2 H.Bl. 69; *R.* v. *Gordon-Finlayson* [1941] 1 K.B. 171.
[48] *Re Mansergh* (1861) 1 B. & S. 400.
[49] *e.g. Re Porrett* (1844) Perry's *Oriental Cases* 414.
[50] *R.* v. *O.C. Depot Battalion, R.A.S.C. Colchester, ex p. Elliott* [1949] 1 All E.R. 373, *per* Lord Goddard C.J.

CHAPTER 18

EMERGENCY POWERS OF THE EXECUTIVE

I. COMMON LAW POWERS TO DEAL WITH AN EMERGENCY

Use of force to maintain public order

Before the development of statutory professional police forces during the nineteenth century, the duty of maintaining internal order rested mainly on the sheriffs, mayors of boroughs and county magistrates, who were charged with the duty of suppressing riots and dispersing unlawful assemblies. This duty has never been expressly abrogated, but in practice the function of maintaining order is now the responsibility of the local chief constable.[1] Force must not be used unless necessary, and then only in a degree proportionate to the necessity. Those who adopt excessive or cruel measures will be criminally liable (*Wright* v. *Fitzgerald*, 1799 [2]), but if the right amount of force is applied, incidental assaults or trespasses will be justified. It is only as a last expedient that the civil authority should invoke the assistance of the military.

At the time of the Gordon Riots in 1780 Wedderburn, the Attorney-General, advised that as soldiers are also citizens they may lawfully be used to prevent felony, even without the Riot Act proclamation being read. The military, if invoked, should act under the direction of the civil authority (usually a magistrate): they should not, in ordinary cases, fire without his orders, nor fail to fire when ordered by him. Exceptional circumstances may exist which make it the duty of the troops to ignore or act in independence of the orders of the magistrate. In *R.* v. *Kennett* (1781) [3] Lord Mansfield laid it down that magistrates who neglected their duty of " reading the Riot Act " were guilty of misdemeanour. Alderman Kennett, Lord Mayor of London, was convicted of neglect of duty in failing to act during the Riots and releasing some prisoners, but he died before sentence was passed.

In *R.* v. *Pinney* (1832) [4] the Mayor of Bristol was charged with

---

[1] *Post*, Chap. 20, and see *ante*, pp. 237–238.
[2] 27 St.Tr. 759; Forsyth, *Cases and Opinions on Constitutional Law*, p. 557; and *cf. Wolfe Tone's Case* (1799) 27 St.Tr. 613, 624–625.
[3] 5 C. & P. 282. The Riot Act 1714 was repealed by the Criminal Law Act 1967; *post*, Chap. 25.
[4] B. & Ad. 947. And see the charge of Tindal C.J. to the Bristol grand jury, as reported in 3 St.Tr(N.S.) 11. Mayors were formerly *ex officio* magistrates.

neglect of duty in failing to suppress a serious riot, directed in the first instance against the Recorder who had expressed unpopular views in Parliament about parliamentary reform. " A person, whether a magistrate or peace officer, who has the duty of suppressing a riot," Littledale J. told the jury, " is placed in a very difficult situation; for if, by his acts, he causes death, he is liable to be indicted for murder, or manslaughter, and if he does not act he is liable to an indictment on an information for neglect. He is, therefore, bound to hit the exact line between excess and failure of duty." The jury found that the Mayor had acted " according to the best of his judgment, with zeal and personal courage," and acquitted him. A prosecution for such neglect of duty is in fact extremely rare.

The common law principles, particularly in relation to the use of military force, were explained in the report of the commission appointed to report on the disturbances at Featherstone Colliery, near Wakefield, during a coal strike in 1893. All the available Yorkshire constables were concentrated at Doncaster, and the Home Secretary (Asquith) at the request of the local magistrates approved the sending of an infantry platoon. A magistrate, who was present with the troops, appealed repeatedly to the crowd to cease destroying property; the proclamation in the Riot Act was read; a bayonet charge proved unavailing; and as the defensive position held by the soldiers was becoming untenable and the complete destruction of the colliery was imminent, the magistrate gave orders to the commander to fire. Two men on the fringe of the crowd were killed. The coroners' juries disagreed on whether there had been sufficient reason for the troops to fire. Asquith appointed a Special Commission consisting of Lord Justice Bowen (afterwards Lord Bowen), Haldane (later Lord Chancellor), and Sir Albert Rollitt, M.P., a solicitor.[5] " Officers and soldiers," said the Commissioners in their Report,[6] " are under no special privileges and subject to no special responsibilities as regards this principle of the law. A soldier for the purpose of establishing civil order is only a citizen armed in a particular manner. . . . One salutary practice is that a magistrate should accompany the troops. The presence of a magistrate on such occasions, although not a legal obligation, is a matter of the highest importance. . . . The question whether, on any occasion, the moment has come for firing on a mob of rioters, depends, as we have said, on the necessities of the case. . . . An order from the magistrate who is present is required by military regulations . . . but the order of the magistrate has at law no legal effect. Its presence does not

---

5 H. H. Asquith, *Memories and Reflections*, I, p. 130.
6 (1893) C. 7234. See also *Lynch* v. *Fitzgerald* [1938] I.R. 382, *per* Hanna J.

justify the firing if the magistrate is wrong. Its absence does not excuse the officer for declining to fire when the necessity exists. . . . The justification of Captain Barber and his men must stand or fall entirely by the common law [*i.e.* it was not affected by the Riot Act]. Was what they did necessary, and no more than was necessary, to put a stop to or prevent felonious crime? In doing so, did they exercise all ordinary skill and caution, so as to do no more harm than could reasonably be avoided? " The Commission exonerated the magistrates, officers and troops from blame.

Every citizen may, and in the last resort must, help to preserve the Queen's peace by the exercise of any degree of necessary force in time of riot or insurrection. The degree of force that may properly be exercised for this purpose may extend to the destruction of life or property.[7] In *R*. v. *Brown* (1841)[8] it was held to be an indictable misdemeanour for a bystander to refuse to aid a police officer in suppressing a riot, if reasonably called upon by him to do so. Alderson B. said that liability for this offence requires three conditions: (i) the constable must actually see a breach of the peace committed by two or more persons; (ii) there must be a reasonable necessity for the constable to call on other persons for assistance; and (iii) the defendant must have refused to render assistance without any physical impossibility or lawful excuse. It is immaterial whether the help the defendant could have given would have proved sufficient or useful. Prosecutions for failing to assist the police are very rare.

If a chief constable was unable to cope with serious civil disturbance even with the help of men from other police forces[8] it is probable that in this age of instant telecommunications the decision to use troops would be made between the Home Secretary and the Secretary of State for Defence at Cabinet level.

Martial law

Uses of the term " martial law "

The question is often raised, whether the Crown has a prerogative power to declare martial law. The term " martial law " is sometimes incorrectly used to cover any one or more of the following:

(i) Military law, *i.e.* the codes governing the armed forces at home and abroad, in war and in peace. In former times, what we now call military law was sometimes referred to as martial law.

---

[7] The common law on this topic may be modified by the Criminal Law Act 1967. s. 2 (arrest without warrant in cases of arrestable offences) and s. 3 (use of force in the prevention of crime or in making arrest).

[8] Police Act 1964, s. 14.

[9] P. O'Higgins, " *Wright* v. *Fitzgerald* Revisited " (1962) 25 M.L.R. 413.

(ii) The law administered by a military commander in occupied enemy territory in time of war. This is sometimes called martial law by international lawyers. It is unnecessary to say more than that the law so administered amounts to arbitrary government by the military, tempered by international custom (*e.g.* the Hague Conventions), and such disciplinary control as the British Government think fit to exercise.

(iii) The common law right and duty to maintain public order by the exercise of any degree of necessary force in time of invasion, rebellion, insurrection or riot (*supra*).

Martial law in the strict sense means the suspension of the ordinary law, and the substitution therefor of discretionary government by the executive exercised through the military. In France a state of siege (*état de siège*) may be decreed in the Council of Ministers, but only Parliament may authorise its extension beyond twelve days.[10] It involves the temporary and partial transfer of powers from the civil to the military authorities.[11] The purpose of a state of siege in France is merely to maintain public order: for the conduct of a war it is necessary, as in England, for emergency powers to be conferred on the executive by legislation.[12]

Is martial law known to English law?

Dicey asserted that martial law in this last sense is unknown to our Constitution.[13] Other writers have drawn a distinction between martial law in time of peace and in time of war, and contend that while the Petition of Right (1628) declared it illegal in the former case, it may still validly be proclaimed in the latter. The Petition of Right complained that commissions had been issued to certain persons giving them power to proceed " within the land " against such soldiers or mariners or other dissolute persons joining with them as should commit crimes, and to try them by such summary course " as is agreeable to martial law and as is used in armies in time of war "; and it prayed that no such commissions should thereafter issue. Cockburn C.J. in his charge to the grand jury in *R. v. Nelson and Brand* (1867)[14] pointed out that no distinction was made until after the time of Blackstone between " martial law " in the modern sense and what is now called " military law." In Great Britain, at any rate, the

---

10 *Constitution of the Fifth Republic*, Art. 36.

11 Duguit emphasises that the powers of the military remain limited by law: *Traité de Droit Constitutionnel* (3rd ed.) Vol. V, Chap. 1, s. 7.

12 Hauriou, *Précis de Droit Constitutionnel* (2nd ed.) pp. 448–453, 709.

13 Dicey, *Law of the Constitution* (10th ed.) p. 293.

14 *Special Report*, pp. 99–100.

Crown cannot proclaim martial law by prerogative in time of peace. Nor has the Crown purported to proclaim it in time of war since the reign of Charles I, and it makes no difference whether or not a state of war has been proclaimed.

What on rare occasions has been called " martial law " since 1628 by British constitutional writers has been a state of affairs outside Great Britain in which, owing to civil commotion, the ordinary courts were unable to function, and it was therefore necessary to establish military tribunals. It is merely an extended application of the principle, discussed above, that the executive has such powers as are necessary for the preservation of public order. Even then specific powers have usually been obtained from Parliament, as in Ireland in 1799 and Jamaica in 1865.

Some authorities hold, nevertheless, that martial law may validly be called into operation in time of war both in Great Britain and outside, and that when this has been done the civil courts have no authority to call in question the actions of the military authorities. They rely on the preamble to certain Irish Acts of Parliament, e.g. (1799) 39 Geo. 3, c. 11, which referred to " the wise and salutary exercise of His Majesty's undoubted prerogative in executing martial law." They also pray in aid language used by Lord Halsbury in *Ex p. D. F. Marais* [15]: " The framers of the Petition of Right well knew what they meant when they made a condition of peace the ground of the illegality of unconstitutional procedure." One answer to this line of reasoning was anticipated by Lord Blackburn when he said in his charge in *R. v. Eyre* (1868) [16]: " It would be an exceedingly wrong presumption to say that the Petition of Right, in not condemning martial law in time of war, sanctioned it." Another answer is afforded by the fact that when martial law has been proclaimed, the Crown has almost invariably protected its servants after the event by obtaining the passing of Acts of Indemnity.[17]

It is sometimes difficult to determine when a state of war exists in a particular district. Coke, Rolle and Hale were of the opinion that time of peace is when the civil courts are open, and that when they are closed it is time of war. The decision of the Privy Council in *Ex p. D. F. Marais*,[18] however, shows that this test is not conclusive and that the existence of a state of war in a given district is compatible with the continued functioning for some purposes of the civil courts

---

15 [1902] A.C. 109. This decision gave rise to four articles on martial law in (1902) 18 L.Q.R. 117, 133, 143 and 152.
16 Finlayson, 73.
17 See *R. v. Nelson and Brand* (1867) F. Cockburn's Reports, 59, 79; Forsyth, *Cases and Opinions on Constitutional Law*, pp. 198, 199, 553, 556–557; Holdsworth *History of English Law*, Vol. X, pp. 705–713.
18 [1902] A.C. 109; and see *Elphinstone v. Bedreechund* (1830) 1 Knapp 316.

within that district. To exclude the legality of martial law, says Holdsworth,[19] " the courts must be sitting in their own right and not merely as licensees of the military authorities."

The judicial decisions are few and inconclusive and mostly Irish, but the following seem to be the general principles:

(i) The ordinary courts have jurisdiction to determine as a question of fact whether a state of war exists, or did exist at the relevant time, in a given area so as to justify the setting up of a military tribunal (*R*. v. *Allen* [20]; *R*. (*Garde*) v. *Strickland* [21]).

(ii) If it is held that a state of war does or did exist, then the military tribunal—not being a court but merely a body of military officers to advise the military commander—would not be bound by the ordinary law or procedure. In *Re Clifford and O'Sullivan* [22] the appellants had been sentenced to death for being in possession of firearms by a military tribunal constituted under the authority of the Commander-in-Chief in Ireland, and they applied for a writ of prohibition. The House of Lords held that if in fact a state of war exists or existed at the time in question, a military tribunal is not a court in the ordinary sense, but merely a body of military officers advising their commander; such a tribunal is not bound by the ordinary law of procedure, and therefore prohibition would not lie. Further, in this case the military " court " had concluded its business, so that prohibition was too late anyway: relief might be sought by habeas corpus when order was restored if the appellants were still alive. There is no remedy during the state of war (*Ex p. D. F. Marais, supra*). During the disturbances in Ireland that followed the passing of the Irish Free State Constitution Act 1922, many persons were sentenced to death by courts-martial, among them Erskine Childers. He applied for a writ of habeas corpus, which was refused on the ground that a state of war existed in Ireland at the time, and that the civil courts were unable to discharge their duties (*R*. v. *Portobello Barracks Commanding Officer, ex p. Erskine Childers* [23]). Nor is there any remedy after the war is over, if what was done was done in good faith or at least was dictated by necessity (*Wright* v. *Fitzgerald*, 1799 [24]).

(iii) If on the other hand it is held that a state of war does not or did not exist at the relevant time, the person injured has his remedy

19 Holdsworth, *History of English Law*, Vol. I, p. 576.
20 [1921] 2 I.R. 241.
21 [1921] 2 I.R. 313. And see *R*. (*O'Brien*) v. *Military Governor, N.D.U. Internment Camp* [1924] 1 I.R. 32.
22 [1921] 2 A.C. 570.
23 [1923] I.R. 5.
24 27 St.Tr. 759; P. O'Higgins, " *Wright* v. *Fitzgerald* Revisited " (1962) 25 M.L.R. 413.

by habeas corpus (*Wolfe Tone's Case*, 1798 [25]) or otherwise for injury done to him, subject to the terms of an Act of Indemnity which will probably have been passed in the meanwhile (*Tilonko* v. *Att.-Gen. for Natal* [26]).

II. STATUTORY POWERS TO DEAL WITH AN EMERGENCY

1. *In Time of Peace*

The Emergency Powers Act 1920

This is a *permanent* statute, and was designed to meet emergencies such as the coal strike of 1921 or the General Strike of 1926. The Act, as amended in 1964,[27] provides that Her Majesty may by proclamation declare a state of emergency if at any time it appears that there have occurred, or are about to occur, events of such a nature as to be calculated, by interfering with the supply and distribution of food, water, fuel or light, or with the means of locomotion, to deprive the community, or any substantial portion of the community, of the essentials of life. No such proclamation remains in force for more than a month, without prejudice to the issue of a fresh proclamation during that period (s. 1 (1)). Where a proclamation of emergency has been made Parliament is to be informed thereof forthwith, and if the Houses be then adjourned or prorogued they are to be summoned to meet within five days (s. 1 (2)).

Where a proclamation of emergency has been made, and so long as it is in force, Her Majesty in Council may make regulations for securing the essentials of life to the community; and those regulations may confer on a Secretary of State or other government department, or any other persons in Her Majesty's service or acting on Her Majesty's behalf, such powers and duties as Her Majesty may deem necessary for preserving the peace, securing to the public the necessaries of life, the means of locomotion and the general safety. Nothing in the Act authorises the making of regulations imposing military or industrial conscription, the alteration of the rules of criminal procedure, or making it an offence to take part in a strike or peacefully to persuade other persons to take part in a strike (s. 2 (1)).

All regulations so made must be laid before Parliament as soon as may be after they are made, and cease to remain in force after the expiration of seven days from the time they were laid before Parliament unless a resolution is passed by both Houses providing for

[25] 27 St.Tr. 613.
[26] [1907] A.C. 93.
[27] Emergency Powers Act 1964.

their continuance (s. 2 (2)). Regulations may provide for the trial by courts of summary jurisdiction of persons offending against the regulations. The maximum penalty for breach of the regulations is imprisonment for three months or a fine of £100 or both, together with the forfeiture of any goods or money in respect of which the offence has been committed. Regulations may not alter criminal procedure or confer any right to punish without trial (s. 2 (3)).

The Act was fully invoked during the General Strike of 1926. Proclamations of a state of emergency have been issued during strikes a number of times since. On some occasions regulations have been laid before Parliament, but they are usually dormant until put into force by orders, and they have not often needed to come into operation as most strikes are not sufficiently serious or are settled before the need arises. A proclamation of emergency was issued at the time of the seamen's strike in 1966. Regulations were then laid before Parliament making provision for control over maximum prices for such foods as might be specified; control of ports and dock labour; direction of the supply of fuel, food and animal food-stuffs, restriction of postal services, and control of home trade, shipping and cargoes; and the requisitioning of land, including houses and buildings. At the time of a miners' strike in February 1972, which cut off supplies of coal to power stations, emergency regulations came into force authorising electric power cuts and restricting the use of electricity in advertising and display-lighting.

2. In Time of War

Defence of the Realm Acts 1914–15

The experience of the two great wars of the present century shows that the executive rely in time of war almost exclusively on statutory powers. Shortly after the outbreak of war in 1914, the United Kingdom was in effect placed under military law by the Defence of the Realm Act 1914, and British subjects and aliens were triable by courts-martial in connection with certain offences for some months. Subsequent Defence of the Realm Acts allowed British subjects to claim a civil trial on taking the prescribed steps, and gave to the King in Council such powers as were necessary for the efficient prosecution of the war. The doctrine of *ultra vires*, of course, still applied (*Chester* v. *Bateson* [28]; *Att.-Gen.* v. *Wilts. United Dairies* (1922) [29]). But as Scrutton L.J. is reported to have said in *Ronnfeldt* v. *Phillips* [30]:

28 [1920] 1 K.B. 829.
29 91 L.J.K.B. 897. *Cf. Yoxford and Darsham Farmers' Association Ltd.* v. *Llewellin* (1946) 62 T.L.R. 347.
30 (1918) 35 T.L.R. 46, 47 (confirming Darling J. at (1917) 34 T.L.R. 556).

" It had been said that a war could not be conducted on the principles of the Sermon on the Mount. It might also be said that a war could not be carried on according to the principles of Magna Carta. Very wide powers had been given to the Executive to act on suspicion on matters affecting the interests of the State."

The Indemnity Act 1920

The liability of the executive for action taken to put down grave civil disturbances, and acts done in the prosecution of a war, may be greatly limited by Acts of Indemnity. These may be quite narrow in scope, or they may be framed in such general terms as the Indemnity Act 1920. This provided that no civil or criminal proceedings should be instituted for anything done in or outside British territory during the war before the passing of the Act, if done in good faith, and done or purported to be done in the execution of duty or for the defence of the realm or the public safety, or for the enforcement of discipline or otherwise in the public interest, by any servant of the Crown, military or civil, or any person acting under his authority.

The Emergency Powers (Defence) Acts 1939 and 1940

The main provisions of the Emergency Powers (Defence) Act 1939, which was passed a week before the outbreak of war with Germany, were as follows: section 1 gave a general power to His Majesty by Order in Council to make such Regulations " as appear to him to be necessary or expedient for securing the public safety, the defence of the realm, the maintenance of public order and the efficient prosecution of any war in which His Majesty may be engaged, and for maintaining supplies and services essential to the life of the community." Without prejudice to the generality of the preceding powers, it specified certain particular matters which might be the subject of Defence Regulations, *viz.*: the apprehension, trial and punishment of persons offending against the Regulations; the detention of persons whose detention appeared to the Secretary of State to be expedient in the interests of public safety or the defence of the realm; the taking of possession or control of any property or undertaking; the acquisition of any property other than land; the entering and searching of any premises; and the amendment, suspension or modification of any enactment.[31]

Section 2 of the Act of 1939 authorised the Treasury to impose charges in connection with any scheme of control authorised by Defence Regulations, *e.g.* the grant of licences or permits (*cf. Att.-Gen.*

---

[31] This meant any enactment passed before the Emergency Powers (Defence) Act 1940.

v. *Wilts. United Dairies, supra*); but any such order had to be laid
before the Commons and would cease to have effect unless approved
within twenty-eight days by a resolution of the House.

Every Order in Council containing Defence Regulations had to be
laid before Parliament, subject to amendment by either House within
twenty-eight days.

The Emergency Powers (Defence) Act 1940, passed at a time when
invasion seemed to be imminent, allowed Defence Regulations, issued
for the purposes prescribed by the Act of 1939, to make provision
" *for requiring persons to place themselves, their services, and their
property at the disposal of His Majesty.*" This very remarkable piece
of legislation, which was passed through all its stages in both Houses
and received the Royal Assent in one day, described itself as an
extension of powers, but it is doubtful whether it did extend the
powers already contained in the earlier Act.[32] The Emergency
Powers (Defence) (No. 2) Act 1940, which was passed a few months
later in order to remove doubts, declared that provision might be
made by Defence Regulations " for securing that, where by reason of
recent or immediately apprehended enemy action the military situation
is such as to require that criminal justice should be administered more
speedily than would be practicable by the ordinary Courts, persons,
whether or not subject to the Naval Discipline Act, to military law,
or to the Air Force Act, may . . . be tried by such special courts,
not being courts-martial, as may be so provided."

The Emergency Powers Act 1964, s. 2, made permanent the
Defence (Armed Forces) Regulations 1939, which authorise the
temporary employment of members of the armed forces in agricultural work or other urgent work of national importance. Otherwise,
the Emergency Laws (Re-enactments and Repeals) Act 1964 repealed
the remaining Defence Regulations, re-enacting some of them with
modifications.

Emergency powers and personal freedom

In *R. v. Halliday, ex p. Zadig,*[33] Zadig, a naturalised British subject
of German birth, was interned by order of the Home Secretary under
a Regulation made under the Defence of the Realm Consolidation
Act 1914. The Act gave power to the King in Council " during the
continuance of the present war to issue regulations for securing the
public safety and the defence of the realm," and went on to make

---

2 Sir Ivor Jennings suggested that it was rather an act of defiance to the all-conquering
  Germans, which " put into a legal formula the ' blood and tears and sweat ' that
  Mr. Churchill had promised as the British contribution to the war effort ": *Law
  and the Constitution* (3rd ed.) pp. xxv–xxvi.
3 [1917] A.C. 260.

detailed provisions for the trial and punishment of offences against the Regulations. The Regulation provided that where, on the recommendation of a competent naval or military authority or of one of the advisory committees set up by the Home Secretary to advise him on the internment and deportation of aliens, it appeared to the Home Secretary that for securing the public safety or the defence of the realm it was expedient in view of the hostile origin or associations of any person that he should be subjected to restriction of movement or internment, the Home Secretary might issue an order accordingly; failure to comply with such order would be an offence. Zadig commenced habeas corpus proceedings, contending that the Regulation was *ultra vires*, but its validity was upheld by a Divisional Court of five judges, by the Court of Appeal, and by the House of Lords (Lord Finlay L.C. and Lords Dunedin, Atkinson and Wrenbury, with Lord Shaw dissenting). " It is beyond dispute," said Lord Finlay L.C., " that Parliament has power to authorise the making of such a regulation. The only question is whether on a true construction of the Act it has done so." Lord Shaw in his dissenting judgment said: " if Parliament had really meant to sanction internment without trial for the cause assigned it could have said so without the slightest difficulty, and not left a point which, I think, is so fundamental to be reached by inference." Zadig was in fact released shortly afterwards.

In *Liversidge* v. *Anderson* [34] Regulation 18B (1) of the Defence (General) Regulations issued under the Emergency Powers (Defence) Act 1939 provided that: " If the Secretary of State *has reasonable cause to believe* any person to be of hostile origin or associations . . . and that by reason thereof it is necessary to exercise control over him, he may make an order against that person directing that he be detained." Persons aggrieved by a detention order might make objections to an advisory committee, and it was the duty of the chairman to inform the objector of the grounds on which the order had been made against him. A detention order was made by the Home Secretary against Liversidge (alias Perlzweig) on the ground that he had reasonable cause to believe that Liversidge was a person of hostile associations, and that by reason thereof it was necessary to exercise control over him. Liversidge was accordingly detained in Brixton Prison, and next year he issued a writ against the Home Secretary claiming a declaration that his detention was unlawful and damages for false imprisonment. The Home Secretary did not make any affidavit showing why, or on what information, he had reached his

[34] [1942] A.C. 206. See R. F. V. Heuston, " *Liversidge* v. *Anderson* in retrospect " (1970) 86 L.Q.R. 331, and note in (1971) 87 L.Q.R. 161.

decision, but merely produced the order purporting to be made under Regulation 18B (1).[35]   The action proceeded on a claim for particulars of defence: there was no suggestion that the Home Secretary had not acted in good faith; and the House of Lords (Lord Maugham L.C. and Lords Macmillan, Wright and Romer, with Lord Atkin dissenting) held that the order was valid and the Home Secretary's answer sufficient.

Lord Maugham L.C. emphasised the points that this was a matter for executive discretion; the Home Secretary was not acting judicially, his decision must necessarily be based on confidential information, and he was responsible to Parliament.   It may be noticed that this last point was not merely a constitutional convention, for the Regulation required the Home Secretary to make a monthly report to Parliament of his exercise of this power.   His Lordship further said that the words " if he has reasonable cause to believe " drew the attention of the Home Secretary to the fact that he should personally consider the matter himself: the only requirement was that he must have acted in good faith.   The other majority opinions emphasised the facts that these were emergency executive powers, conferred at a time of great national danger on a responsible Minister who was answerable to Parliament, and whose sources of information were confidential on security grounds.

Lord Atkin, in his spirited dissenting judgment,[36] contended that the words " if he has reasonable cause " to believe did not mean " if he *thinks* he has reasonable cause ": they have an objective meaning and give rise to a justiciable issue.   He supported his argument by references to the common law and statutory power of arrest, statutes dealing with other criminal matters, and actions at common law for malicious prosecution.   His Lordship did not consider that the case of *R.* v. *Halliday* (*supra*) was relevant, as in that case (on which he had sat as a member of the Divisional Court) the appellant's contention was that the Regulation was *ultra vires*.   Nor was he suggesting that the courts should substitute their opinion for that of the Home Secretary as to whether, for example, a person is of hostile origin: the question was, whether the Home Secretary had reasonable cause to believe that he was of hostile origin.

In *Greene* v. *Home Secretary* [37] the House of Lords dismissed an appeal on an application for habeas corpus arising out of the same Regulation.   Lord Atkin in this case agreed with his colleagues,

---

5 *Cf. R.* v. *Home Secretary, ex p. Lees* [1941] 1 K.B. 72 (application for habeas corpus; Court of Appeal held Home Secretary's affidavit sufficient answer).

6 *Ibid.* at pp. 225–247.

7 [1942] A.C. 284.   See R. F. V. Heuston in (1971) 87 L.Q.R. 163.   The Court of Appeal refused habeas corpus in *R.* v. *Home Secretary, ex p. Lees* [1941] 1 K.B. 72, in a case arising under Regulation 18B (1A).

as the Home Secretary had filed an affidavit setting out a number of particulars and stating that he had acted on information from responsible and experienced persons.

Both Liversidge and Greene were, in fact, released shortly after these decisions.

Liversidge v. *Anderson* and *Greene* v. *Home Secretary* were applied by Asquith J. in *Budd* v. *Anderson*,[38] a case arising out of Regulation 18B (1A). The decision in *Liversidge* v. *Anderson*, however, met with a mixed reception outside the courts,[39] and we cannot do better than adopt the conclusion of the late Professor Berriedale Keith: " The question is one of great difficulty, but the concurrent view of so many judges leaves little doubt that the decision has been rightly taken on the wording of the regulation." [40]

In *Nakkuda Ali* v. *Jayaratne* [41] a strong Privy Council held that *Liversidge* v. *Anderson* must not be taken to lay down any general rule on the construction of the expression " has reasonable cause to believe." The Board adopted the contrary construction on a similar phrase in the Ceylon Defence Regulations concerning the revocation by the Government Controller of Textiles of a licence to trade. The distinction may turn on the difference between a senior Minister of the Crown responsible to Parliament and a comparatively junior official. The fact that the emergency was already over in *Nakkuda's* case may also have made some difference. But this part of the Board's opinion should perhaps be regarded as *obiter*, since the Controller's function was held to be executive and therefore not subject to review by the courts. *Liversidge* v. *Anderson* was described by Lord Reid in *Ridge* v. *Baldwin* [42] as a " very peculiar decision."

Other war legislation

Legislation for the purposes of the last war was mostly carried out by means of Defence Regulations, but Acts of Parliament were

---

38 [1943] K.B. 642. *Cf. R.* v. *Home Secretary, ex p. Budd* [1942] 2 K.B. 14, where the Court of Appeal held that the Home Secretary must apply himself to each case under the Regulation, and sign the detention order, otherwise the person detained was entitled to release under habeas corpus; but if the procedure is regularised after release, the person may be detained again for the same cause.

Liversidge v. *Anderson* has also been followed in the courts of India and Pakistan in cases of preventive detention. See also *Ross-Clunis* v. *Papadopoullos* [1958] 1 W.L.R. 546 (P.C.).

39 For: Keith, *Journal of Comparative Legislation* (1942) 3rd Ser., Vol. XXIV, Pt. I, pp. 63–64; Holdsworth (1942) 58 L.Q.R. 1–3; Goodhart, *ibid.* pp. 3–8 and 243–246. Against: Allen, *ibid.* pp. 232–242; Keeton (1942) 5 M.L.R. 162–173; Allen *Law and Orders* (2nd ed.), App. 1. Neutral: Jennings, *The Law and the Constitution* (3rd ed.) pp. xxx–xxxi.

40 *The Constitution under Strain* (1942) p. 51.

41 [1951] A.C. 66. The application for certiorari failed on the ground that the Controller's function was executive and not judicial.   42 [1964] A.C. 40

necessary where: (i) what was wanted to be done was outside the scope of the Emergency Powers (Defence) Acts 1939 and 1940, or (ii) the provisions were not to be limited to the war period, or (iii) it was necessary to raise money. The practice with regard to the last was for the Government to ask Parliament periodically for votes of £1,000,000,000, while for security reasons the estimates for each of the service and supply departments were put at the nominal figure of £100.

Many of the emergency Acts [43] passed on account of the war contained a provision to the effect that they were to continue in force until such date as His Majesty might by Order in Council declare to be the date on which the emergency which was the occasion of the passing of the Act should have ended. In *Willcock* v. *Muckle* (1951) [44] it was held that there must be an Order in Council declaring the end of the emergency in relation to the particular Act.

The dearth of judicial decisions after 1939 on the nature and extent of the prerogative in time of war is due to the fact that the Emergency Powers (Defence) Acts and the other emergency statutes mentioned covered practically everything that the Government would want to do, except for taxation and the acquisition (as distinct from the taking possession) of land.[45]

---

[43] See Carr, *Concerning English Administrative Law*, Chap. 3, for the spate of legislative activity in the first week of the war.
[44] [1951] 2 K.B. 844.
[45] *Cf.* Requisitioned Land and War Works Acts 1945 and 1948; Land Powers (Defence) Act 1958. And *cf. Burmah Oil Co.* case, *ante*, p. 238.

Part IV

JUSTICE AND POLICE

CHAPTER 19

THE ADMINISTRATION OF JUSTICE

Prerogative and administration of justice

The administration of justice is one of the prerogatives of the Crown, but it is a prerogative that has long been exercisable only through duly appointed courts and judges.[1] The various courts and their jurisdictions are now almost entirely on a statutory basis.[2] The Sovereign is " the fountain of justice " and general conservator of the peace. " By the fountain of justice," Blackstone explains,[3] " the law does not mean the *author* or *original*, but only the *distributor* . . . . He is not the spring, but the reservoir; from whence right and equity are conducted, by a thousand channels, to every individual." In the contemplation of the law the Sovereign is always present in court and therefore cannot be non-suited. Instances are recorded of Plantagenet Kings personally dealing with criminal cases, and Edward IV sat with his judges for three days to see how they did their work; but the personal interference of the Sovereign with the judges was infrequent, and Coke told James I that although he might be present in court he could not give an opinion *(Prohibitions del Roy,* 1607 [4]). Criminal proceedings, whether initiated by the Crown or a private individual, are conducted on behalf of the Crown and indictments are in the Queen's name. Writs commencing civil actions are issued in the Queen's name, and in her name judgment is executed, but the Crown has no control over the conduct of civil cases. The prerogative power to create courts is now virtually useless, because, first (if Coke was right), such courts could not administer equity or any other system except the common law; and secondly, the expense of maintaining such courts would require parliamentary authority. For practical purposes, then, the following may be regarded as the most significant of the existing prerogatives relating to the administration of justice.

The maxim " the King can do no wrong " extended to the Sovereign in his public capacity and in effect to the government

---

[1] *Prohibitions del Roy* (1607) 12 Co.Rep. 63.

[2] *e.g.* Supreme Court of Judicature (Consolidation) Act 1925; Appellate Jurisdiction Act 1876; Courts Act 1971; County Courts Act 1959; Magistrates' Courts Act 1952.

[3] Bl.Comm. I, 266.

[4] 12 Co.Rep. 63, 64. And see Holdsworth, *History of English Law*, Vol. I (5th ed.) pp. 194, 207.

generally. The common law rule that no civil action might be brought against the Crown must now be read subject to the important exceptions contained in the Crown Proceedings Act 1947; although even then there are savings with regard to prerogative powers, such as defence and the training of the forces. The Crown still has procedural privileges with regard to discovery and interrogatories, and no execution may be levied against the Crown.[5]

Time does not run against the Crown at common law. *Nullum tempus occurrit regi.*[6] But there are numerous statutes providing that specified criminal proceedings must be taken within a limited period; and the Crown Proceedings Act 1947 expressly makes the Crown bound by statutes limiting the time within which civil proceedings must be commenced, *e.g.* Limitation Acts.

The Attorney-General has a discretion by his fiat (*nolle prosequi*) to discontinue any criminal proceedings on indictment, whether the proceedings were initiated by the Crown or a private prosecutor.[7] He is answerable *ex post facto* to Parliament for the exercise of this power, although it is seldom questioned. This power does not extend to summary proceedings in a magistrates' court, where the leave of the court for the withdrawal of a prosecution is required. A *nolle prosequi* does not have the effect of an acquittal, although if further proceedings were brought the Attorney-General could enter a *nolle prosequi* again. An alternative course in appropriate cases, therefore, is for the Crown to offer no evidence, so that the jury can formally acquit the accused.

The prerogative of mercy

The Sovereign, acting in this country by the Home Secretary, may pardon offences of a public nature which are prosecuted by the Crown.[8] A pardon may generally be granted before or after a conviction, but no pardon may be pleaded as a bar to impeachment (Act of Settlement 1700),[9] nor may the Crown remit the penalties prescribed by the Habeas Corpus Act 1679 for sending a prisoner out of the realm. The Crown cannot by a pardon deprive a third party of his rights.[10]

The Crown may grant a reprieve, which temporarily suspends the

---

5 *Post*, Chap. 32.
6 *Magdalen College Case* (1615) 11 Co.Rep. 66b.
7 *R.* v. *Allen* (1862) 1 B. & S. 850. See J. Ll. J. Edwards, *The Law Officers of the Crown* (1964) pp. 227–237.
8 *Hanratty* v. *Lord Butler of Saffron Walden, The Times*, May 13, 1971 (C.A.): it is outside the competence of the courts to inquire whether a former Home Secretary was negligent in the exercise of this prerogative.
9 *Cf. Danby's Case* (1679) 11 St.Tr. 599.
10 *Thomas* v. *Sorrell* (1674) Vaughan 330.

execution of sentence; or (within statutory limits) may remit the whole or part of a penalty.

Anyone may commence a civil action, subject to losing money if he has no case and subject to the law against frivolous and vexatious litigation; and in general anyone may commence criminal proceedings, subject to the risk of damages for malicious prosecution. Statutes require that certain prosecutions shall be brought by the Director of Public Prosecutions or with the consent of the Attorney-General. The office of Director of Public Prosecutions was established in 1879.[11] Besides being required to take charge of certain prosecutions, he may take over any prosecution, whether indictable or summary. He is appointed by the Home Secretary, but is responsible to the Attorney-General for the exercise of his powers. The Director of Public Prosecutions also gives advice, either on application or on his own initiative, to government departments, clerks to justices and chief officers of police in important or difficult criminal matters. He is not what is regarded on the Continent as a " Public Prosecutor "; if anyone deserved that title it would be the Attorney-General. Many prosecutions for offences against regulations are brought by government departments and local authorities; but most prosecutions are brought by the police, and these are in theory private prosecutions.[12]

Legal aid in defending criminal proceedings was introduced in 1903[13] and has been gradually extended. A defence certificate or legal aid certificate is granted by the court or the justices in proper cases, subject to a means test, whether on indictment, summary trial, preliminary examination or appeal. Legal aid was introduced for civil cases by the Legal Aid and Advice Act 1949, the amounts having been increased from time to time since then.

Justices of the peace [14]

Statutes of Edward I (Statute of Winchester 1285) and Edward III confirmed and extended the practice of commissioning conservators, custodians or guardians of the peace. In 1344 the custodians of the peace were given judicial powers to hear and determine felonies

---

[11] Prosecution of Offences Act 1879. See J. Ll. J. Edwards, *Law Officers of the Crown* (1964) Chaps. 16 and 17; Sir Theobald Mathew, *The Office and Duties of the Director of Public Prosecutions.*

[12] Sir Patrick Devlin, *The Criminal Prosecution in England* (1960) p. 17. It is desirable that police prosecutions should be conducted by prosecuting solicitors, and not by police officers. (Police prosecutors give evidence under oath.)

[13] Poor Prisoners' Defence Act 1903.

[14] Sir Carleton Allen, *The Queen's Peace* (1953) Chap. 5; R. M. Jackson, *The Machinery of Justice in England* (6th ed. 1972) Chap. 3, para. 6; Glanville Williams, *The Proof of Guilt*, Chap. 11; Maitland, *Justice and Police* (1885) Chaps. 8 and 9; Leo Page, *Justice of the Peace* (3rd ed.); B. Osborne, *Justices of the Peace, 1361–1848* (1960); " Magistrates 1361–1961 " [1961] Crim.L.R. 653–736.

and trespasses. They were first called justices of the peace in the Justices of the Peace Act 1361. Each county had a separate Commission of the Peace. Boroughs later came to have their own justices.

One of the most remarkable features of the English system of the administration of justice is the large part played by laymen, either as lay magistrates or as jurymen.[15] The county and borough justices were the forerunners of the old Courts of Quarter Sessions and Petty Sessions, the former being now absorbed in the new Crown Court system, the latter becoming the magistrates' courts. Lay magistrates are supplemented in London and some other cities by stipendiary magistrates; but the system they represent—involving the trial of 95 per cent. of all criminal cases, and the preliminary examination of the rest—is perhaps an even more remarkable feature of our judicial system than the jury system as it now survives. Lay magistrates must now undertake on appointment to attend a course of instruction. They are entitled to travel and limited subsistence and financial loss allowances.

The Courts Act 1971, s. 5, provides that in appeals from magistrates' courts and in proceedings on committal for sentence the judge of the Crown Court shall sit with not fewer than two or more than four justices of the peace; and the Lord Chief Justice may make directions for justices of the peace to sit with the Crown Court judge in other suitable cases, such as pleas of " guilty " and short trials on indictment. These are roughly the cases in which county justices sat at Quarter Sessions before the Act.[16] The requirement may be waived if justices are not available, and proceedings may continue even though one or more justices have left.

Appointment of judges

The Queen appoints the Lord Chancellor, the Lord Chief Justice, the Master of the Rolls, the President of the Family Division, the Lords of Appeal in Ordinary and the Lords Justices of Appeal, by convention on the advice of the Prime Minister, who presumably consults the Lord Chancellor. The Queen appoints the puisne judges of the High Court, by convention on the advice of the Lord Chancellor, who no doubt consults the Prime Minister. The Queen on the recommendation of the Lord Chancellor also appoints Circuit judges to serve in the Crown Court and county courts, and Recorders to act as part-time judges of the Crown Court.[17] Stipendiary magi-

---

[15] Sir Carleton Allen, " The Layman and the Law in England " (1959) 2 *Journal of International Commission of Jurists* 57.

[16] Borough Quarter Sessions were taken by the Recorder alone.

[17] Courts Act 1971, ss. 16, 21.

strates are appointed by the Crown on the advice of the Lord Chancellor. Lay justices are appointed to the Commission of the Peace in the name of the Queen, but on the nomination of the Lord Chancellor or the Chancellor of the Duchy of Lancaster.

Judges and magistrates on appointment take the judicial oath, by which they promise " to do right to all manner of people after the laws and usages of this realm, without fear or favour, affection or ill-will." [18]

Functions of the courts

The work of the courts is, of course, mainly judicial, and involves the interpretation of the common law and statute law, and its application, according to the rules of procedure and evidence, to the cases that come before them. The courts have also certain subsidiary executive or administrative functions, especially the magistrates in relation to licensing. The superior courts supervise such matters as the affairs of infants and persons of unsound mind, the administration of trusts and insolvent estates and the liquidation of companies, and they issue declarations of legitimacy or legitimation and nullity of marriage.

The Supreme Court also has powers of delegated legislation, namely, to make Rules of Court. This power it exercises through its Rule Committee, which consists of the Lord Chancellor, the Lord Chief Justice, the Master of the Rolls, four judges, two barristers and two solicitors. The rules are required to be laid before Parliament.[19]

Judicial independence

The independence of the judiciary from interference by the executive has been mentioned in Chapter 2 as one of the most important principles of British constitutional law. Here we will say something more about the means by which this independence is secured. The main topics under this heading are the tenure of the judicial office and the manner in which judges may be removed.

Judges of superior British courts

Down to the reigns of James I and Charles I, judges (other than the Barons of the Exchequer) usually held office *durante bene placito nostro* (during the King's pleasure). Like other Crown servants, they could be dismissed by the King at will, although they seldom were.

---

[18] Promissory Oaths Act 1868.
[19] Judicature (Consolidation) Act 1925.

The fact that office was held during pleasure had a certain effect on some of the decisions of the courts in those reigns. Coke was dismissed by writ of *supersedeas* in 1616 for the attitude he adopted in the *Case of Commendams* concerning the staying of suits *Rege inconsulto*.[20] In the Commonwealth period judges were appointed to hold office *quamdiu se bene gesserint* (during good behaviour), but Charles II and James II in many cases revived the former practice.[21] William III's judges held office during good behaviour, but when Parliament in 1691 wanted to put the matter on a statutory basis owing to the doubt whether at common law " good behaviour " meant only good behaviour in relation to the Crown, William refused his consent because the Bill charged their salaries on the hereditary revenues.[22] At last the Act of Settlement (1700), which was to come into force when the Hanoverians ascended the throne, provided " that . . . judges' commissions be made *quamdiu se bene gesserint*, and their salaries ascertained and established, but upon the address of both Houses of Parliament it may be lawful to remove them."

The statutory provisions now in force are the Supreme Court of Judicature (Consolidation) Act 1925, s. 12 (1): " All the Judges of the High Court and the Court of Appeal, with the exception of the Lord Chancellor, shall hold their offices during good behaviour subject to a power of removal by His Majesty on an address presented to His Majesty by both Houses of Parliament," [23] and the Appellate Jurisdiction Act 1876, s. 6: " Every Lord of Appeal in Ordinary shall hold his office during good behaviour . . . but he may be removed from such office on the address of both Houses of Parliament." Such an address must be introduced in the House of Commons. Most Commonwealth countries prescribe a more judicial procedure for the removal of judges, in some cases involving a reference to the Judicial Committee of the Privy Council.

It is commonly but erroneously stated that since the Act of Settlement judges can be dismissed by the Crown *only* on an address from both Houses of Parliament.[24] The true position, however, is stated by Anson: " the words mean simply that if, in consequence of misbehaviour in respect of his office or from any other cause, an

---

20 *Colt and Glover* v. *Bishop of Coventry* (1616) Hob. 140; see Maitland, *Constitutional History*, pp. 270–271. It was admitted that a charge of misconduct was required for the removal of a judge: *Earl of Shrewsbury's Case* (1611) 9 Co.Rep. 42a, 50. In the case of Coke this was difficult. The charge eventually brought was that he had introduced into his Reports statements in derogation of the royal prerogative. Coke was ordered to correct his Reports, and he declared that in the eleven volumes, containing 500 cases, there were only four errors.
21 Holdsworth, *History of English Law* (5th ed.) Vol. I, p. 195.
22 Holdsworth, *op. cit.* Vol. VI, p. 234.
23 Re-enacting Judicature Act 1875, s. 5.
24 This is the position in some Commonwealth countries.

officer of state holding on this tenure has forfeited the confidence of the two Houses, he may be removed, although the Crown would not otherwise have been disposed or entitled to remove him. Such officers hold, as regards the Crown, *during good behaviour*; as regards Parliament, also during good behaviour, though the two Houses may extend the term so as to cover any form of misconduct which would destroy public confidence in the holder of the office." [25] The Crown could remove without an address for official misconduct, neglect of official duties, or (probably) conviction for a serious offence (*Earl of Shrewsbury's Case*, 1611 [26]). The Queen would be bound by convention to act on an address from both Houses.[27] The first case in which Parliament initiated proceedings for the removal of a judge under the Act of Settlement was that of Mr. Justice Fox, of the Irish Bench, in 1805; but it was abandoned on the ground that the proceedings should have commenced in the Commons instead of in the Lords. The only case which has resulted in removal under the Act of Settlement procedure was that of Sir Jonah Barrington, another Irish judge, in 1830. Most of the cases—and they are few—have concerned colonial judges, or judges accused of partiality in hearing election petitions.[28]

Judges of the Supreme Court are appointed by letters patent, and the writ of *scire facias* appears to have been the method of enforcing forfeiture of an office held by letters patent for breach of a condition of tenure. *Scire facias* in civil proceedings was abolished by the Crown Proceedings Act 1947; this would include *scire facias* on the Revenue side of the Queen's Bench Division but not on Crown side.[29] Criminal information at the suit of the Attorney-General could perhaps be used, and it has been suggested that the Crown would take proceedings by way of motion in the Queen's Bench

---

[25] Anson, *Law and Custom of the Constitution* (4th ed. Keith) Vol. II, Part I, pp. 234–235.

[26] 9 Co.Rep. 42a, 50.

[27] As to what amounts to misbehaviour in a public office, and the methods by which an office in which a person has a life interest may be forfeited, see Todd, *Parliamentary Government in England* (2nd ed.) Vol. II, pp. 857–859; Anson, *ibid.* at pp. 235–236. But all judges (except the Lord Chancellor) are now subject to a statutory age of retirement.

[28] For an account of a number of cases, and the principles and proceedings established, see Todd, *ibid.* at pp. 86 *et seq.*; Hearn, *The Government of England* (2nd ed.) pp. 82–89; Keith, *Responsible Government in the Dominions*, II, pp. 1073–1074. The last address in the Houses in relation to an English judge seems to have been the case of Wright C.J., the predecessor of Holt C.J.; see Veeder, *Select Essays in Anglo-American Legal History*, Vol. II, p. 141.

[29] *Att.-Gen.* v. *Colchester Corporation* [1955] 2 All E.R. 124, 127, *per* Lord Goddard C.J. And see Bickford Smith, *The Crown Proceedings Act 1947*, p. 108; Glanville L. Williams, *Crown Proceedings*, p. 114.

Division for the cancellation of the letters patent on the ground of misbehaviour.[30]

There is now a compulsory retiring age of seventy-five for Lords of Appeal in Ordinary and judges of the Supreme Court appointed after 1959.[31] It is hardly necessary to add that judges could be removed by Act of Parliament, although there seems to be no point in adopting that form except to circumvent the House of Lords under the provisions of the Parliament Acts 1911 and 1949 in a case where the Crown was not justified in dismissing by itself.[32]

Judges' salaries are charged by statute on the Consolidated Fund, so that they do not come up for review by the Commons every year as do most estimates of national expenditure. They may now be increased, though not reduced, by Order in Council.[33]

Other judicial officers

Circuit judges may be removed by the Lord Chancellor " on the ground of incapacity or misbehaviour." They are subject to a retiring age of seventy-two, except that the Lord Chancellor may in the public interest continue them in office up to the age of seventy-five.[34] The Lord Chancellor may terminate the appointment of a Recorder on the ground of incapacity or misbehaviour or of failure to comply with the terms of his appointment.[35]

Justices of the peace may be removed from the Commission of the Peace by the Lord Chancellor [36] if he thinks fit, although by convention he does not remove them except for good cause, such as refusal to administer the law because the justice does not agree with it. The Justices of the Peace Act 1949 also requires the Lord Chancellor to keep a Supplemental List of justices who are no longer entitled to exercise judicial functions. The Lord Chancellor may direct that the name of a justice be put on the Supplemental List on the ground of " age or infirmity or other like cause," or if he " declines

---

[30] R. M. Jackson, *op. cit.* p. 368n. Sir Kenneth Roberts-Wray, *Commonwealth and Colonial Law* (1966) pp. 489–490, mentions impeachment, but this is a parliamentary and not a royal method, and does not appear to have any advantage over an Address under the statute; and also " the exercise of the inquisitorial and judicial jurisdiction of the House of Lords." The latter expression is obscure, unless it refers to the trial of peers, which has been abolished. The House of Lords might have some privilege jurisdiction over Lords of Appeal.

[31] Judicial Pensions Act 1959.

[32] The tenure of judicial office is no longer affected by the demise of the Crown: Commissions and Salaries of Judges Act 1760; Demise of the Crown Act 1901.

[33] Judges' Remuneration Act 1965.

[34] Courts Act 1971, s. 17.

[35] Courts Act 1971, s. 21 (6). Section 21 (3) provides that a Recorder's appointment shall specify the frequency and duration of the occasions on which he must be available to perform his duties.

[36] Or the Chancellor of the Duchy of Lancaster; *Ex p. Ramshey* (1852) 18 Q.B. 173.

or neglects " his judicial functions, and his name must be put on this List when he reaches the age of seventy. A justice of the peace whose name has been put on the Supplemental List may authenticate signatures, e.g. on passport applications, but he may not sign any information, complaint, summons or warrant.

The Act of Settlement does not apply to judges of colonial courts, who therefore—subject to the colonial constitution or any local statute—hold office at the pleasure of the Crown (Terrell v. Secretary of State for the Colonies [37]).

Are judges " Crown servants "?

A great stir was caused in 1931 when the Commissioners of Inland Revenue reduced the salaries of the judges of the Supreme Court, purporting to act under the authority of an Order in Council made under the National Economy Act of that year. The Act provided that, in order to effect economies at a time of economic crisis, the remuneration " of persons in His Majesty's Service " might be reduced, even though the amount of the remuneration " in respect of certain officers in the service of His Majesty " was specified in statutes. It was widely thought that the Inland Revenue were not justified in making the deductions, as judges are not properly regarded as servants of the Crown. There was no tribunal which could determine the question, because a judge cannot be judge in his own cause. It should be added that the judges themselves were willing to make the same sacrifices as many other members of the community, but it was considered that if Parliament had intended the Act to apply to them they should have been specifically mentioned. Holdsworth [38] argued that the judges are not properly called " servants " of the Crown because they are not subject to the orders of the Crown as to the manner in which they shall discharge their duties. On the contrary, such eminent authorities as Bracton, Fortescue and Coke could be cited —against Bacon—to the effect that the Sovereign is subject to the law, and the judges enforce the law even against the Sovereign. It was not relevant to the question to consider whether judges were paid or dismissed by the Crown. " It is a nice problem," Holdsworth added, " but the difficulty is to find out who is to solve it."

As theory, the question was not solved; but it was solved in practice soon afterwards by the Inland Revenue restoring the cuts in deference to public opinion.

[37] [1953] 2 A.C. 482; post, Chap. 34. Service regulations now give greater security of tenure.
[38] Holdsworth, " The Constitutional Position of the Judges " (1932) 48 L.Q.R. 25–36. The story is now more fully told, with the Memorandum of Lord Sankey, the Lord Chancellor, in R. F. V. Heuston, Lives of the Lord Chancellors 1885–1940 (1964) pp. 513–519.

No general duty to advise the executive

It is often said that one of the hallmarks of the independence of the English judiciary is that they have no duty to advise the executive on cases that do not come before the courts in the ordinary course of litigation. That such a duty does not necessarily impair the independence of the courts is shown by the fact that it exists in many constitutions, including some in the Commonwealth, and also in our judicial system in the case of the Judicial Committee and the Courts-Martial Appeal Court. Further, where a person has been convicted on indictment, or been tried on indictment and found not guilty by reason of insanity, the Home Secretary may at any time either refer the whole case to the Court of Appeal, and the case is then to be treated as an appeal to the court by that person; or refer any point to the court for their opinion.[39] But in 1925 a great outcry was raised in the House of Lords when it was proposed in the Rating and Valuation Bill that advisory judgments should be allowed on rating questions.[40]

Such advisory functions should be distinguished from the ancient duty of the judges to advise the House of Lords in its judicial capacity, and from the binding declaratory judgments that may be given in certain cases.[41]

Judicial impartiality

Exclusion from the House of Commons

The exclusion of the holders of judicial office (other than lay magistrates) from sitting in the House of Commons [42] is now based on the modern constitutional doctrine that judges should not take part in political and party controversy.[43] Formerly the exclusion of judges from the House of Commons was based on different principles. When the Commons asserted their right to exclude James I's judges they did so on the ground of parliamentary privilege, because the judges of the common law courts were advisers of the House of Lords. For the same reason the Law Officers of the Crown should have

---

39 Criminal Appeal Act 1968, s. 17; replacing Criminal Appeal Act 1907, s. 19, as amended by the Administration of Justice Act 1960. See *e.g. R.* v. *Pedrini, The Times,* July 29, 1964: defendants convicted on evidence of detective officer later found to be insane, and probably (at the time of the trial) suffering from paranoid schizophrenia.

40 See E. C. S. Wade, " Consultation of the Judiciary by the Executive " (1930) 46 L.Q.R. 169.

41 *Dyson* v. *Att.-Gen.* [1911] 1 K.B. 410.

42 House of Commons Disqualification Act 1957.

43 The Lord Chancellor as a member of the government is to some extent an exception.

been disqualified, but in this case the disqualification was eventually waived.[44]

Natural justice

The principles of natural justice, which are to be discussed in Chapter 30 in relation to the judicial control of public authorities, apply *a fortiori* to the courts, which are in addition governed as to procedure by Rules of Court. In *Bridgman* v. *Holt* (1693),[45] when the puisne judges of the King's Bench were determining the question whether the valuable sinecure office of Chief Clerk of the King's Bench was in the gift of the Chief Justice, the latter took no part in the decision but sat " near the defendant's counsel upon a chair uncovered."

Publicity of proceedings

One of the chief safeguards of the impartial administration of justice lies in the common law right of the public, including the Press, to be present and to publish accurate reports and fair comments on the proceedings. This is embodied, too, in the maxim that it is not sufficient that justice be done, but it must be seen to be done (*Scott* v. *Scott* [46]). In *McPherson* v. *McPherson* [47] a decree was held voidable on the ground that the public had been unintentionally excluded from the hearing of a matrimonial cause.

The courts have a discretion, which must be carefully exercised, to hear proceedings *in camera* on grounds of public policy, *e.g.* where secret information that might endanger the safety of the state is to be divulged, or to clear the court for the suppression of disorder. Statutory limitations on grounds of public morality are imposed in certain cases on the details that may be published, *e.g.* under the Judicial Proceedings (Regulation of Reports) Act 1926 and various statutes relating to children and young persons, divorce, nullity, and domestic proceedings in magistrates' courts.

Fair reports of contemporary judicial proceedings are privileged (*Kimber* v. *The Press Association* (1893) [48]).

---

[44] *Report and Minutes of Evidence of the Select Committee on Offices or Places of Profit under the Crown* (1941) H.C.Pap. 120, 147.
[45] Shower P.C. 111. And see *Dimes* v. *Grand Junction Canal* (1852) 3 H.L.C. 759, *post*, Chap. 30. The Lord Chancellor may, however, sit in the House of Lords or the Judicial Committee in a case involving political questions in which the government of which he is a member, is interested. See *e.g. Marais* v. *G.O.C., ex p. Marais* [1902] A.C. 109.
[46] [1913] A.C. 417.
[47] [1936] A.C. 177 (P.C.).
[48] 62 L.J.Q.B. 152.

Judicial immunity [49]

The absolute privilege accorded by the law of defamation to those taking part in judicial proceedings extends to magistrates as well as judges (*Law* v. *Llewellyn* [50]). With regard to torts other than defamation the law is not altogether clear. The distinction usually taken is that between superior courts and inferior courts,[51] other than magistrates who are in a special position.

Judges are exempt from civil or criminal liability for things done or said while acting within their jurisdiction, even if done maliciously and without reasonable or probable cause (*Anderson* v. *Gorrie* (1895) [52]). Judges of *superior* courts are apparently not liable for judicial [53] acts done outside their jurisdiction (*Hammond* v. *Howell* (1677) [54], *Anderson* v. *Gorrie, supra*), and the acts of a superior court are presumed to be within their jurisdiction (*Peacock* v. *Bell* (1666) [55]). Anyway, there is no tribunal to enforce such liability.

Judges of *inferior* courts, including county courts,[56] courts-martial [57] and consular courts,[58] are liable for judicial acts done without, or in excess of, their jurisdiction (*Peacock* v. *Bell, supra*). The judge of an inferior court will not be deemed to have acted without jurisdiction, however, if he was induced to act by some false allegation of fact which, if true, would have given him jurisdiction (*Houlden* v. *Smith* [59]; *Calder* v. *Halket* (1839) [60]). The distinction between superior and inferior courts began to develop in the seventeenth century, and was the product of two principles: first, the jurisdiction of inferior courts is limited by subject-matter, persons or place, while superior courts are not so limited; and, secondly, inferior courts are answerable to the superior courts if they exceed their jurisdiction, while superior courts are answerable only to God and the King.[61]

---

[49] Winfield, *The Present Law of Abuse of Legal Procedure* (1921) Chap. 7; *cf.* D. Thompson, " Judicial Immunity and the Protection of Justices " (1958) 21 M.L.R. 517; L. A. Sheridan, " The Protection of Justices " (1951) 14 M.L.R. 267; A. Rubinstein, " Liability in Tort of Judicial Officers " (1963) 15 U.T.L.J. 317.

[50] [1906] 1 K.B. 487.

[51] Thompson, *op. cit.*, however, argues that the distinction in English law between courts of record and courts not of record ought also to be taken into account. This distinction is admittedly not applicable to Scottish or Colonial courts.

[52] [1895] 1 Q.B. 668 (colonial court); see also *Scott* v. *Stansfield* (1868) L.R. 3 Ex. 220 (county court).

[53] *Cf.* ministerial acts; *Ferguson* v. *Earl of Kinnoull* (1842) 9 Cl. & F. 251, 311 (H.L.).

[54] 2 Mod. 219.

[55] 1 Wms.Saund. 74.

[56] *Houlden* v. *Smith* (1850) 14 Q.B. 841.

[57] *Dawkins* v. *Lord F. Paulet* (1869) L.R. 5 Q.B. 94; *Dawkins* v. *Lord Rokeby* (1873) L.R. 8 Q.B. 255; *Heddon* v. *Evans* (1919) 35 T.L.R. 642.

[58] *Haggard* v. *Pelisier Frères* [1892] A.C. 61.

[59] *Supra.*

[60] 3 Moo.P.C. 28.

[61] Holdsworth, *op. cit.*, Vol. VI, pp. 234–240.

The liability of justices of the peace, apart from defamation (*Law* v. *Llewellyn, supra*), is laid down in the somewhat obscure provisions of the Justices' Protection Act 1848. Section 1 provides that an action against a justice of the peace for any act done by him within his jurisdiction shall be an action on the case, and the action will fail unless the plaintiff proves that the act was done maliciously and without reasonable and probable cause.[62] Section 2 provides that if a person is injured by an act done by a justice of the peace [63] acting without or in excess of jurisdiction, it is not necessary to allege that the act was done maliciously and without probable cause; but no such action may be brought in respect of a conviction until after the conviction has been quashed. The Administration of Justice Act 1964, s. 27, now provides a scheme of indemnification covering justices and justices' clerks in respect of proceedings against them arising out of the performance of their duties.

In order to protect the fair administration of justice, immunity from suit also attaches to words spoken in the course of judicial proceedings by the parties (*Astley* v. *Younge* (1759) [64]), witnesses (*Seaman* v. *Netherclift* (1876) [65]), and counsel (*Munster* v. *Lamb* (1883) [66]), and to the verdicts of juries (*Bushell's Case* (1670) [67]). In *Rondel* v. *Worsley* [68] the House of Lords held that barristers are immune—for reasons of public policy, and not inability to sue for fees—from actions for negligence in respect of their professional work in conducting litigation. A majority of their Lordships also expressed the opinion *obiter* that this immunity should not extend to a barrister's non-litigious advisory work, but that it should extend to solicitors appearing as advocates in court.

Immunity from suit for things done or words spoken in a judicial capacity extends not only to the ordinary courts but also to other persons and bodies exercising judicial functions, such as military courts of inquiry,[69] the Solicitors' Disciplinary Committee [70] and a statutory ecclesiastical commission of inquiry [71]; but not to a local

---

[62] Thompson, *op. cit.*, would distinguish between the judicial and the ministerial functions of justices. In exercising judicial functions, *e.g.* the trial of summary offences, magistrates' courts are probably courts of record. Ministerial functions, *e.g.* issuing warrants or refusing bail, on the other hand, ought to be protected only if exercised in good faith.

[63] *Cf. O'Connor* v. *Isaacs* [1956] 2 Q.B. 288.

[64] 2 Burr. 807. See also *Re Hunt* [1959] 2 Q.B. 69 (C.A.).

[65] 2 C.P.D. 53.

[66] 11 Q.B.D. 588.

[67] 6 St.Tr. 999; (1677) Vaughan 135. The practice of punishing jurors for finding against the evidence or direction of the judge was finally stopped by this case.

[68] [1969] 1 A.C. 191.

[69] *Dawkins* v. *Lord Rokeby* (1873) L.R. 8 Q.B. 255.

[70] *Addis* v. *Crocker* [1961] 1 Q.B. 11 (C.A.).

[71] *Barratt* v. *Kearns* [1905] 1 K.B. 504.

authority when licensing music and dancing,[72] and probably not a Ministry inspector holding a public local inquiry.[73]

Contempt of court [74]

Judges have no general immunity from criticism of their judicial conduct, provided it is made in good faith and does not impute improper motives to those taking part in the administration of justice: it must be genuine criticism, and not malicious or an attempt to impair the administration of justice. "Justice is not a cloistered virtue," said Lord Atkin,[75] " she must be allowed to suffer the scrutiny and respectful, though outspoken, comments of ordinary men." It is a convention, however, that the judicial conduct of judges of the Supreme Court should not be reflected on in Parliament by a question, or by way of amendment or in debate, unless the discussion is based on a substantive motion in proper terms. When criticism steps beyond the proper bounds, the courts have power to punish the offender for contempt. Contempt of court may be either civil or criminal.

Civil contempt of court consists of disobedience to an order of the court made in civil proceedings. Although punishable by imprisonment, this is a form of civil process.[76] Imprisonment is usually until the prisoner has " purged " his contempt by a complete apology. It may be imposed for a definite term, but not so as to bar the prisoner from access to the courts meanwhile.[77]

Criminal contempt of court, a non-arrestable common law offence, may take such form as: (a) contempt committed in face of the court, such as directly insulting the judge; (b) interference with jurors, parties or witnesses; (c) the publication of comments on a pending case that are calculated to prejudice a fair trial and so to interfere with the course of justice; (d) the publication of matter scandalising the court, e.g. scurrilous abuse of a judge with reference to remarks made by him in a judicial proceeding.

Thus in *Morris* v. *Crown Office*,[78] where a number of Welsh students interrupted civil proceedings in the High Court by way of a demonstration—shouting slogans, singing songs and breaking up the hearing—some who apologised were fined and bound over to keep

---

[72] *Royal Aquarium and Summer and Winter Garden Society Ltd.* v. *Parkinson* [1892] 1 Q.B. 431; see *per* Fry L.J. *Cf. R.* v. *London County Council, ex p. Entertainments Protection Association Ltd.* [1931] 2 K.B. 215 (certiorari granted).

[73] *Cf.* Crown Proceedings Act 1947, s. 2 (5), giving immunity to Crown appointees discharging " responsibilities of a judicial nature."

[74] Sir John C. Fox, *The History of Contempt of Court* (1927).

[75] *Ambard* v. *Att.-Gen. for Trinidad and Tobago* [1936] A.C. 323, 335.

[76] *Scott* v. *Scott* [1913] A.C. 417.

[77] *Yager* v. *Musa* [1961] 2 Q.B. 214 (C.A.).

[78] [1970] 2 Q.B. 114 (C.A.).

the peace; the others were sentenced to three months' imprisonment, although the Court of Appeal in the special circumstances allowed them to be released provided they were bound over to be of good behaviour, to keep the peace and to come up for judgment if called upon within twelve months. In *R.* v. *Bolam, ex p. Haigh*,[79] the editor of the *Daily Mirror* was sentenced to three months' imprisonment and the proprietors were fined £10,000, for comments made before a murder trial; and in *R.* v. *Thompson Newspapers, ex p. Attorney-General*[80] the publishers of a newspaper were fined £5,000 for publishing certain matter about a person pending his trial: the editor was not punished because, although he was responsible, he was not in the circumstances culpable. On the other hand in *R.* v. *Commissioner of Police of the Metropolis, ex p. Blackburn (No. 2)*,[81] where Mr. Quintin Hogg, Q.C., M.P., had published an article in *Punch* criticising the decisions of the Court of Appeal on the Gaming Acts, the court held that criticisms of a court's decisions do not amount to contempt of court, even though they are in bad taste and contain inaccuracies of fact, provided they are in good faith and do not impute improper motives to those taking part in the administration of justice.

A person is no longer guilty of contempt of court on the ground that: (1) he has published any matter calculated to interfere with the course of justice in connection with proceedings pending or imminent at the time of publication, if at that time (having taken all reasonable care) he did not know and had no reason to suspect that proceedings were imminent or pending; or (2) he has distributed a publication containing such matter, if at that time (having taken all reasonable care) he did not know that it contained such matter and had no reason to suspect that it was likely to do so.[82] The publication of any information relating to proceedings before a court sitting in private (including a judge sitting *in camera*) is not of itself contempt of court, with certain exceptions including cases involving national security and information relating to a secret process, and where the court exercises a specific power to prohibit publication.[83]

Criminal contempt of court is punishable by fine or imprisonment. Power to commit for contempt is now exercisable only by order of committal, attachment for this purpose having been abolished. Even if the proceeding is *in camera* the order must be made in open court. A court of record can punish contempt committed in face of the court by immediate fine and imprisonment. A county court, like the

[79] (1949) 93 S.J. 220.
[80] [1968] 1 W.L.R. 1 (D.C.).
[81] [1968] 2 Q.B. 150 (C.A.).
[82] Administration of Justice Act 1960, s. 11.
[83] *Ibid.* s. 12.

High Court, has full power to imprison for past contempts.[84] The Queen's Bench Division has power to protect inferior courts against contempt to the extent that they cannot protect themselves.[85]

The Administration of Justice Act 1960, s. 13, provides that an appeal lies from any order or decision of a court punishing for contempt of court, including criminal contempt.[86]

Trial by jury [87]

The belief was strongly held in the eighteenth century, and it has since become an accepted tradition, that trial by jury is one of the chief protections of the rights of the citizen and a bulwark of the Constitution. Thus Blackstone, after discoursing upon the " antiquity and excellence of this trial " in civil cases,[88] says that his remarks " will hold much stronger in criminal cases; since, in times of difficulty and danger, more is to be apprehended from the violence and partiality of judges appointed by the Crown, in suits between the King and the subject, than in disputes between one individual and another.
. . . Our law has therefore wisely placed this strong and twofold barrier, of a presentment [89] and a trial by jury, between the liberties of the people and the prerogative of the Crown. . . . So that the liberties of England cannot but subsist so long as this *palladium* remains sacred and inviolate." [90] So Lord Camden said: " Trial by jury is indeed the foundation of our free constitution; take that away, and the whole fabric will soon moulder into dust "; and Lord Eldon is stated when Solicitor-General to have professed " a most religious regard " for the institution of juries. The right of trial by jury was enshrined in the Constitution of the United States, where much greater use is made of juries (both civil and criminal) than here.

Professor R. M. Jackson after examining the matter concludes that juries have in fact played " an insignificant part " in disputes between the citizen and the state, that is, in political rather than purely criminal trials. The court most actively concerned, the Queen's Bench Division (formerly the King's Bench) has exercised jurisdiction in relation to prerogative writs or orders, appeals from Quarter Sessions,

---

84 *Jennison* v. *Baker* [1972] 2 Q.B. 52 (C.A.).
85 *R.* v. *Judge* [1931] 2 K.B. 442; *R.* v. *Daily Herald, ex p. Bishop of Norwich* [1932] 2 K.B. 402 (consistory court); *cf. R.* v. *Duffy, ex p. Nash* [1960] 2 Q.B. 188 (D.C.).
86 The first such appeal was *Morris* v. *Crown Office, supra.*
87 See Sir Patrick Devlin, *Trial by Jury* (revised ed. 1966); R. M. Jackson, *The Machinery of Justice in England* (6th ed.) Chap. 4, para. 6; Glanville Williams, *The Proof of Guilt* (3rd ed.) Chap. 10; W. R. Cornish, *The Jury* (1968).
88 Bl.Comm. III, 379.
89 The jury of presentment, or grand jury, has been abolished.
90 Bl.Comm. IV, 349.

and appeals by case stated from magistrates' courts, without juries.
Where a jury has been used in cases reported for their legal interest,
it " either (a) answered questions so put that the jury cannot have
known in whose favour they were finding, or (b) followed the judge's
opinion." In reading Howell's *State Trials*—a series of political trials,
including sedition, reported for their political interest regardless of
whether an important point of law was involved—it will be found
impossible to predict what the jury is going to do. This fact may be
attributed largely to the restricted qualification of jurors and the mode
of selecting juries.

A prisoner who is indicted is tried by a petty jury, except that
some indictable offences may be dealt with summarily by the magistrates with the consent of the accused. Summary offences are triable
on information by magistrates' courts without formal indictment or
jury; but a person charged with certain offences punishable on summary conviction may claim to be tried by jury in the Crown Court.
At the present day about 85 per cent. of *indictable* offences are in fact
tried summarily. Of the 15 per cent. sent for trial by jury, about
two-thirds plead " guilty." Thus only about 5 per cent. even of
indictable offences are actually tried by jury. A majority verdict may
be accepted in criminal proceedings where not fewer than ten out of
twelve (or nine out of eleven) jurors agree, provided that the jury have
had at least two hours for deliberation.[91]

A coroner must summon a jury (of seven to eleven jurors) in
certain cases, and may accept a majority verdict if the dissentients are
not more than two.[92]

The use of the jury in civil cases has declined greatly since the
first war. The High Court has a discretion whether or not a jury shall
be summoned, except that a jury must generally be ordered on the
application of either party in certain cases, including defamation,
malicious prosecution and false imprisonment, or on the application
of a party against whom fraud is charged.[93] The number of jury
trials in civil cases in the Queen's Bench Division is not likely to be
much more than 1 per cent. in the near future. The power to summon
juries in the Chancery Division [94] has been practically neglected.
Juries are occasionally applied for in defended divorce petitions and
contested probate causes. The right to apply for a jury in the county
courts is very rarely exercised. Majority verdicts may now be accepted

91 Criminal Justice Act 1967; *Practice Direction (C.A.) (Crime: Majority Verdicts)*
   [1967] 1 W.L.R. 1198; [1967] 3 All E.R. 137.
92 Coroners Acts 1887–1954.
93 Administration of Justice (Miscellaneous Provisions) Act 1933.
94 Judicature Acts 1873–1925.

in civil proceedings in the High Court if ten out of twelve (or nine out of eleven) jurors agree, and in a county court if seven (out of eight) jurors agree; provided that it appears to the court that the jury have had a reasonable time for their deliberations having regard to the nature and complexity of the case.[95]

Jury service

Persons between the ages of eighteen and sixty-five are liable to jury service if they have been resident for five years in the United Kingdom.[96] Jurors are now entitled to travelling and subsistence allowances, and compensation for loss of earnings.[97] The jury list is based on the Electoral Register, those who are liable for jury service being marked " J." There is an opportunity to claim exemption while the electoral lists are on view. Various classes of person are exempt, or may claim exemption from jury service, including peers, Members of Parliament, councillors, clergymen, practising barristers, solicitors, police and prison officers, medical practitioners, members of the armed forces, and justices of the peace.[98]

The Morris Committee on Jury Service (1965) [99] recommended that an understanding of English should be required; and that the miscellaneous " exemptions " should be replaced by categories of those who are ineligible (e.g. lawyers and clergy), disqualified (e.g. ex-prisoners), or entitled to excusal as of right (e.g. Members of Parliament, the forces and the medical profession). The Criminal Justice Act 1967 disqualifies from serving on criminal juries anyone who during the last ten years has served any part of a sentence of imprisonment or detention for a term of three months or more, and anyone who has at any time been sentenced to imprisonment for life or for a term of five years or more.

The Courts Act 1971 transferred to the Lord Chancellor the responsibility for summoning and preparing panels of jurors, and making arrangements for payments in respect of jury service. A person may be excused if he can show that he has served on a jury within the previous two years. Failure to attend without excuse, or serving on a jury while disqualified, is punishable by a fine within a maximum of £400.[1]

---

95 Courts Act 1971, s. 39. And see (1968) Cmnd. 3750, *Tenth Report of Criminal Law Division Committee: Secrecy of Jury Room.*
96 Criminal Justice Act 1972, increasing the age range at both ends and abolishing property qualifications that were fixed in 1825.
97 Juries Act 1949.
98 Justices of the peace are exempted by Courts Act 1971, Sched. 8.
99 Cmnd. 2627.
1 Criminal Justice Act 1972.

System of appeals

Criminal cases

A person who has been convicted by a magistrates' court has the right of appeal to the Crown Court (formerly Quarter Sessions) against conviction or sentence, on a question of law or fact. Either the defendant or the prosecutor may require the magistrates to state a case for the opinion of a Divisional Court of the Queen's Bench Division on the ground that a proceeding of a magistrates' court is wrong in law or is in excess of jurisdiction.[2]

A person convicted on indictment has a right of appeal to the Court of Appeal (Criminal Division) against conviction on a question of law alone, or (with leave of the Court of Appeal or on a certificate of the trial judge) on a question of fact alone or a mixed question of law and fact. The Court of Appeal must allow an appeal against conviction if they think: (a) that the verdict is unsafe or unsatisfactory; or (b) that the judgment was a wrong decision on a question of law; or (c) that there was a material irregularity in the trial; provided that the Court of Appeal may dismiss the appeal if they consider that no miscarriage of justice has actually occurred. A person who has been convicted on indictment may, with the leave of the Court of Appeal, appeal against sentence, not being a sentence fixed by law.[3]

Either the defendant or the prosecutor may appeal to the House of Lords from the Court of Appeal or a Divisional Court of the Queen's Bench Division in a criminal case, with the leave either of the court below or of the House of Lords, but such leave must not be granted unless the court below certifies that a point of law of general public importance is involved, and it appears to that court or to the House of Lords that the point is one which ought to be considered by that House.[4] The certificate is not required in appeals from a Divisional Court in habeas corpus cases.

Civil cases

Appeal from county courts lies to the Court of Appeal (Civil Division) on a question of law or the admission or rejection of evidence, but the leave of the judge is generally required in actions of contract or tort if the claim does not exceed a small amount.[5] There is also a right of appeal on questions of fact in the more important cases.[6]

---

[2] Magistrates' Courts Act 1952.
[3] Criminal Appeal Act 1968.
[4] Ibid. Appeal also lies to the House of Lords under similar conditions from the Court of Criminal Appeal in Northern Ireland (Criminal Appeal (Northern Ireland) Act 1968), and from the Courts-Martial Appeal Court (Courts-Martial (Appeals) Act 1968); but there is no appeal to the House of Lords in criminal cases from Scottish courts.   [5] Administration of Justice (Appeals) Act 1934.
[6] County Courts Act 1959.

There is a general right of appeal to the Court of Appeal (Civil Division) from final orders of the High Court in civil matters on a question of law or fact; and from a Divisional Court in applications for habeas corpus or one of the prerogative orders in non-criminal matters.[7]

Appeal lies from the Court of Appeal (Civil Division) to the House of Lords, with the leave either of the Court of Appeal or of the Appeals Committee of the House of Lords, except in cases where the decision of the Court of Appeal is declared by statute to be final,[8] e.g. appeals from an election court.[9] Appeals are nearly always, although they need not be, on questions of law. In order to save costs, appeals may in certain cases go direct from the High Court to the House of Lords (" leap-frogging ").[10]

7 Judicature Act 1925.
8 Administration of Justice (Appeals) Act 1934.
9 Representation of the People Act 1949.
10 Administration of Justice Act 1969.

CHAPTER 20

THE POLICE [1]

ALTHOUGH the preservation of the peace, which is a royal prerogative, is one of the primary functions of any state, the administration of the police has always been on a local basis in this country. That there is still no national police force today is partly a historical accident. In the sixteenth and seventeenth centuries constables were controlled both administratively and judicially by the justices of the peace, and they in their turn were controlled by the Council. The Long Parliament put an end to conciliar government by abolishing in 1642 the Star Chamber, through which this control was exercised. The Revolution Parliament had an equally strong fear of government by means of a standing army as is witnessed by the famous declaration in the Bill of Rights 1688, and this traditional fear has since then been sufficient to prevent the formation of a national police force. One incidental disadvantage has been to limit the questions that the Home Secretary can be asked in the House about provincial police forces.

History of the police [2]

In early English law the duty of seeing that the peace was preserved and of apprehending malefactors lay on the local communities of township and hundred. These duties—represented by such terms as frankpledge, hue and cry and sheriff's tourn—were reinforced by the Assize of Arms 1181, an ordinance of 1252 which first mentions constables, and the Statute of Westminster 1285. Under this legislation a high constable was appointed for each hundred,[3] and one or more petty constables in each township. The office of constable was an annual duty and unpaid. The constables gradually came under the control of the justices of the peace, who were introduced

---

[1] Practical manuals are J. D. Devlin, *Police Procedure, Administration and Organisation* (1966) and *Moriarty's Police Law* (ed. Sir William J. Williams, 21st ed. 1972). The word " police " was not used in English in the modern sense before the latter part of the eighteenth century.

[2] L. Radzinowicz, *History of English Criminal Law and its Administration*, Vol. III (1956), Vol. IV (1968) Chap. 7; Sir Carleton Allen, *The Queen's Peace* (1953) Chap. 4; Sir Frank Newsam, *The Home Office* (1954) Chap. 4; Sir Harold Scott, *Scotland Yard* (1954); Holdsworth, *History of English Law*, Vol. IV, pp. 122–126; W. L. M. Lee, *History of the Police in England* (1905); Maitland, *Constitutional History*, pp. 235–236, 486–489; *Justice and Police* (1885) Chap. 10; Sir William O. Hart, *Introduction to the Law of Local Government and Administration* (8th ed. 1968) Chap. 24.

[3] High constables were abolished by the High Constables Act 1869.

in the fourteenth century. In the latter part of the seventeenth century the petty constables, now appointed and dismissed by the local justices, came to be identified with the parish.[4] Towns had also an inefficient system of watch by night and ward by day.

No one did more to rouse public opinion in the eighteenth century on the necessity for efficient organisation for the prevention of crime than Henry Fielding, both as author and magistrate. Sir Robert Peel, when Home Secretary, laid the foundation of a permanent professional police force for the metropolis. Nineteenth-century legislation made away with the ancient arrangements for trying to preserve the peace. Following on Peel's Metropolitan Police Act 1829,[5] the Municipal Corporations Act 1835 required boroughs to maintain a paid police force. Every borough at one time maintained its own police force, but many of these were too small for efficiency and a series of statutes pursued a general policy of reducing their number. The borough police were administered by a Watch Committee of the Council, consisting of not more than one-third of the councillors. Meanwhile the City of London had obtained similar powers under a local Act, the City of London Police Act 1829. Optional powers were conferred on county Quarter Sessions by the Rural Police Act 1839. Not all counties availed themselves of these powers, and eventually the Rural Police Act 1856 extended the metropolitan scheme with modifications to all counties in England and Wales.[6] When county councils were created by the Local Government Act 1888, the control of county police was transferred by way of compromise to a Joint Standing Committee of county councillors and justices.

By 1964, then, there were in London the Metropolitan Police Force under the direct control of the Home Secretary, who appoints the Commissioner, and the City of London Police, the appointment of whose Commissioner requires the approval of the Home Secretary; and in the rest of England and Wales there were three groups of police forces, all under the indirect supervision of the Home Secretary— county, county borough, and combined (county and county borough). In Scotland the local government areas are somewhat different, and the indirect supervision is by the Secretary of State for Scotland.

Main functions of the police

The Royal Commission on the Police (1962) outlined the main functions of the police at the present day as follows[7]:

---

[4] Parish constables were abolished by the Police Act 1964.
[5] Modern statutory police forces may be traced back to the Dublin Police Act passed by the Irish Parliament in 1786, which established the Royal Irish Constabulary.
[6] H. Parris, " The Home Office and the Provincial Police in England and Wales: 1856–1870 " [1961] P.L. 230.   [7] Cmnd. 1728, pp. 157 et seq.

(i) The duty to maintain law and order, and to protect persons and property.

(ii) The duty to prevent crime.

(iii) Responsibility for the detection of criminals. In the course of interrogating suspected persons, they have a part to play in the judicial stages of the judicial process, acting under judicial restraint.[8]

(iv) Responsibility in England and Wales (though not in Scotland) of deciding whether to prosecute suspected criminals.[9]

(v) The duty of controlling road traffic, and advising local authorities on traffic questions.

In *R.* v. *Commissioner of Police of the Metropolis, ex p. Blackburn*,[10] where a private citizen applied for mandamus to require the Commissioner of the Metropolitan Police to enforce the Betting, Gaming and Lotteries Act 1963 against gaming clubs, it was held that the Commissioner owed a duty to the public to enforce the law, which he could be compelled to perform either by action at the suit of the Attorney-General or by mandamus; and that, although he had a discretion not to prosecute in particular cases, his general discretion was not absolute.

In 1960 [11] a " ticket " system of fixed penalties payable on the spot was introduced to save the time of going to court, police witnesses and so on. Police constables operate this system of punishment without prosecution [12] of certain lighting offences, the violation of certain parking regulations and failure to display a valid excise licence. The Act of 1960 also introduced traffic wardens to assist the police in the control and regulation of road traffic. They are appointed by the police authority, and act under the direction of the chief officer of police. They perform such functions as may be prescribed, including the control of parking meters and the operation of the " ticket " system.

Legal status of police officers

The Queen's peace is part of the prerogative.[13] Although police

---

[8] *e.g.* the Judges' Rules as to the admissibility in evidence of statements or confessions.

[9] In some cases prosecution depends on the Attorney-General or the Director of Public Prosecutions.

[10] [1968] 2 Q.B. 118 (C.A.); *cf. R.* v. *Commissioner of Police of the Metropolis, ex p. Blackburn (No. 3)* [1973] 2 W.L.R. 43 (C.A.) (pornography); D. G. T. Williams, " The Police and Law Enforcement " [1968] Crim.L.R. 351.

[11] Road Traffic and Roads Improvement Act 1960. Extended by order of the Secretary of State under the Road Traffic Regulation Act 1967 and the Transport Act 1968, etc.

[12] If the penalty specified on the ticket is duly paid, the offender is not liable to be convicted: if the penalty is not paid he is liable to be prosecuted in the ordinary way.

[13] *Coomber* v. *Berks. Justices* (1883) 9 App.Cas. 61, 67 *et seq.*, *per* Lord Blackburn.

officers are not Crown servants, the Home Secretary on behalf of the police in the course of litigation may claim " Crown privilege " in respect of documents that may be used in a criminal prosecution [14]; and a letter written by a police officer may be protected by Crown privilege, although it does not emanate from a government department and is not in the possession of a civil servant.[15]

A constable is an officer of the peace, and as such has common law powers and duties.[16] The office is very ancient, older than that of justice of the peace, and was originally associated with the village.[17] These powers are exercised by a constable by virtue of his office, and not on the responsibility of anyone else, nor as a delegate or agent.[18] The status of a Chief Constable in relation to the police authority was uncertain before 1964, although it was agreed that the police authority could not interfere in criminal matters in particular cases.[19] Although a constable exercised original, not delegated, discretionary powers, this was not incompatible with his being a member of a disciplined body subject to the lawful orders of his superior officers. The Royal Commission on Police Powers and Procedure 1929 [20] said that a policeman in the view of the common law is only " a person paid to perform, as a matter of duty, acts which if he were so minded he might have done voluntarily." " Indeed," they added, " a policeman possesses few powers not enjoyed by the ordinary citizen." This statement may have been true at common law but it gives a dangerously misleading picture of the position at the present day, when the policeman has many statutory powers and duties. A constable also exercises statutory powers and duties on behalf of his police authority. One may imagine the " ordinary citizen " trying to identify the finger-prints of a gang of train robbers, or to control the traffic in Piccadilly Circus.[21] The constable's main power is the power of arrest and search, and his main duty the

---

[14] *Conway* v. *Rimmer* [1968] A.C. 910 (H.L.); see *per* Lord Reid.

[15] *R.* v. *Lewes Justices, ex p. Home Secretary, The Times,* May 24, 1971 (D.C.).

[16] *Lewis* v. *Cattle* [1938] 2 K.B. 454 (D.C.). Before the establishment of a professional police force petty constables were equated with servants of the Crown, such as sheriffs and justices of the peace, in *Mackalley's Case* (1612) 9 Co.Rep. 68a–b.

[17] H. B. Simpson, " The Office of Constable " (1895) *English Historical Review* 625.

[18] *Enever* v. *The King* (1906) 3 C.L.R. 969, *per* Griffiths C.J. at p. 977; approved in *Fisher* v. *Oldham Corporation* [1930] 2 K.B. 364, and *Att.-Gen. for New South Wales* v. *Perpetual Trustee Co.* [1955] A.C. 457 (P.C.).

[19] B. Keith-Lucas and D. N. Chester, " The Independence of Chief Constables " (1960) 38 *Public Administration* 1. And see *Nelms* v. *Roe* [1970] 1 W.L.R. 4; [1969] 3 All E.R. 1379 (D.C.); a Chief Constable may orally delegate some of his powers.

[20] Cmd. 3297.

[21] *Cf.* Dr. A. L. Goodhart: " To say that a constable is a citizen in uniform is no more accurate than it would be to say that all citizens are constables in plain clothes " (1962) Cmnd. 1728, p. 162.

execution of the justices' warrants.[22] Special powers of arrest or search without warrant are conferred on a constable.[23] Further, he is protected if he acts on a justice's warrant which is beyond the latter's jurisdiction (Constables Protection Act 1750). He also has certain statutory powers of entry and inspection,[24] and extensive duties in connection with traffic control.

Nineteenth-century legislation preserved the traditional obligation of a constable to obey the legal orders of a justice of the peace. This form of control, although unrepealed by Parliament, has now fallen into virtual disuse and is today little more than a theoretical survival. The Royal Commission on the Police in 1962 found no evidence that justices of the peace nowadays ever exercise their powers over the police except in the normal course of their judicial business, e.g. in issuing warrants for the arrest of suspected criminals.[25] In times of riot or serious civil disturbance, however, there may still be some ultimate responsibility laid on justices to see that order is restored,[26] or, more likely, on the police authority which now consists as to one-third of justices.

A police officer who exceeds or abuses his powers to the injury of another may make himself personally liable in tort. Thus in Christie v. Leachinsky[27] two police officers were held liable by the House of Lords for damages for false imprisonment because in arresting the plaintiff without a warrant and detaining him overnight they misinformed him of the nature of the charge. An engaged couple have been awarded £5,200 damages against two police constables for malicious prosecution and false imprisonment.[28]

Police vehicles, like fire engines and ambulances, are exempt from statutory speed limits. This exemption of police drivers does not affect their criminal liability for dangerous driving, or their civil liability for negligence if they do not exercise a degree of care and skill proportionate to the speed at which they are driving.[29] They are not

---

[22] Warrants are mostly applied for by the police themselves.

[23] Criminal Law Act 1967, s. 2. See D. C. Holland, " Police Powers and the Citizen " (1967) C.L.P. 104; and post, Chap. 23. [24] Post, Chap. 23.

[25] Report of the Royal Commission on the Police 1962, Cmnd. 1728, paras. 82–84.

[26] See O'Kelly v. Harvey (1883) 14 L.R.Ir. 105. In R. v. Pinney (1832) 5 C. & P. 254; (1832) 3 St.Tr.(N.S.) 11, this duty was held to be that of the mayor, but mayors are no longer ex officio magistrates. The Lord Mayor of Birmingham until recently had a consultative committee of three J.P.s to confer with him in time of public tumult or riot or other exceptional circumstances, and there was a rota of five J.P.s to act in times of tumult or riot.

[27] [1947] A.C. 573.

[28] Selby v. Maclennan, The Times, May 9, 1961. See also Allum and Hislop v. Heller and Jackson, The Times, February 25, 1966 (£8,057 damages against two constables). Cf. Glinski v. McIver [1962] A.C. 726 (H.L.).

[29] Gaynor v. Allen [1959] 2 Q.B. 403; Dyer v. Bannell (1965) 109 S.J. 216. Driving to court to give evidence is a " public purpose " conferring exemption: Aitken v. Yarwood [1965] 1 Q.B. 327 (D.C.).

expressly exempted from other traffic regulations, *e.g.* traffic lights, although they might be excused from the latter on the ground of necessity if in the particular case there was clearly no danger to the public.[30]

Police Act 1964

The organisation of police administration and the legal status of the police officer grew up piecemeal and shared many anomalies. A Royal Commission was set up in 1960 to consider the constitutions and functions of local police authorities; the status and accountability of members of police forces, including chief officers of police; the relationship of the police with the public, and the means of ensuring that complaints by the public against the police are effectively dealt with. In their Report published in 1962,[31] the Royal Commission rejected the case for creating a national police system, although many of the members thought a national police service would be more effective in fighting crime and handling road traffic, and the Commission did not think it would be constitutionally objectionable or politically dangerous. While recommending the continuance of the system of separate local police forces, they advocated better liaison between them, and also greater responsibilities being transferred to the Secretaries of State. Although the Police Act 1964 accepted in general the majority recommendations of the Royal Commission, and did confer greater responsibility on the Home Secretary, the primary duty of ensuring the efficient policing of an area rests not (as the Commission appear to have intended) on the Home Secretary, but on the Chief Constable.

The Royal Commission also recommended that there should be further amalgamations of small police forces, the optimum size being over 500 men; that the appointment and continuance in office of all Chief Constables should require the approval of the Secretary of State; that a Chief Inspector of Constabulary for Great Britain should be appointed, who would be responsible for research and planning; and that justices of the peace should compose a third of the members of the Police Committees in boroughs as well as counties. The Commission would clarify relations between Chief Constables and police authorities, but they did not favour a separate corps of traffic police

---

[30] Glanville Williams, *Criminal Law*, I, para. 201.
[31] *Final Report* (1962) Cmnd. 1728. *Cf.* Dr. A. L. Goodhart's *Memorandum of Dissent*, pp. 157 *et seq.* For a somewhat intemperate criticism of the Report, see Jennifer Hart, " Some Reflections on the Report of the Royal Commission on the Police " [1963] P.L. 283.

The Police Act 1964 [32] re-enacted certain previous statutes, with modifications which implement to a greater or less degree the recommendations of the Royal Commission. The main provisions are dealt with in the following paragraphs.

Organisation of police forces

Police areas outside London after the Police Act 1964 came into force were counties, county boroughs and combined areas. The police authority for a county was the Police Committee, and for a county borough the Watch Committee. In each case the Committee consisted of two-thirds councillors and one-third magistrates. The police authority for a combined area was similarly composed of two-thirds members of the constituent councils and one-third magistrates for the constituent areas. Under the Local Government Act 1972 the police authorities outside London are metropolitan counties and the other counties or amalgamated counties.

Functions of police authorities

It is the duty of every police authority to secure the maintenance of an adequate and efficient police force for the area (Police Act 1964, s. 4 (1)). The police authority, subject to the approval of the Home Secretary, appoints the Chief Constable and determines the number of members of the force; after consulting the Chief Constable and with the approval of the Home Secretary, it appoints the Deputy Chief Constable and Assistant Chief Constable; with the consent of the Home Secretary it provides buildings, and subject to any regulations it provides vehicles and equipment.

The Chief Constable has direction and control of his force (s. 5). The police authority does not control the policy of the force with regard to such matters as law enforcement or traffic control. The police authority, with the approval of the Home Secretary, may call on the Chief Constable, Deputy Chief Constable or Assistant Chief Constable to retire in the interests of efficiency. (This does not necessarily imply the inefficiency of the officer himself.) Before seeking the approval of the Home Secretary, the police authority is required to give the Chief Constable or other officer an opportunity to make representations, and to consider any representations so made (Police Act 1964, s. 5 (5); s. 6 (5)). This provision replaces the decision in *Ridge* v. *Baldwin* [33] under the previous law. In that case the House

---

[32] See Geoffrey Marshall, *Police and Government* (1965); D. W. Pollard, " The Police Act 1964 " [1966] P.L. 35; D. E. Regan, " The Public Service : Central Control over Local Authorities," *op. cit.* p. 13.

[33] [1964] A.C. 40; *post*, Chap. 30. See A. L. Goodhart, " *Ridge* v. *Baldwin* : Administrators and Natural Justice " (1964) 80 L.Q.R. 105.

of Lords by a majority over-ruled a unanimous Court of Appeal in
deciding that the Brighton Watch Committee, in dismissing the Chief
Constable, ought to have observed the principles of natural justice by
informing him of the charges and giving him an opportunity to be
heard. The decision may have been wrong on the interpretation of
the relevant legislation, but in any event, in view of the new provision
of the Police Act, the remaining importance of the case lies among
the general principles of administrative law.

Appointments and promotions below the rank of Assistant Chief
Constable are made by the Chief Constable, subject to regulations
made by the Home Secretary (s. 7).

The police fund for each area is under the general control of the
county council, and police accounts are subject to audit by the district
auditor (s. 18). Arrangements are to be made for questions to be
asked in the local council concerning the exercise of the police
authority's functions (s. 11). The Chief Constable must submit an
annual report to the police authority, and the latter may require him
to report on specific matters from time to time (s. 4).

Provision is made in the Police Act for collaboration and mutual
aid between police forces, to be arranged by Chief Constables with
the approval of their police authorities (ss. 13 and 14). Provincial
forces may seek the assistance of the Criminal Investigation Department of the Metropolitan Police Force (" Scotland Yard "). The
Chief Constable may agree to provide special police services at any
premises in his area, e.g. at demonstrations on private premises:
charges are payable to the police authority on such a scale as may be
determined by that authority (s. 15). The Chief Constable may
appoint special constables for his area, who are under his direction
and control and dismissible by him (s. 16).

The Home Secretary may order the amalgamation of police forces
if he considers it expedient in the interests of efficiency (s. 21). Police
authorities may propose amalgamation, in which case the proposals
must be submitted to the Home Secretary for his approval.[34]

Every member of a police force must be attested as a constable
before a justice of the peace. In this he promises to serve the Queen
in the office of constable, without favour or affection, malice or ill
will; and that he will to the best of his power cause the peace to be
kept and preserved, and prevent all offences against the persons and
properties of Her Majesty's subjects (s. 18, Sched. 2). A member
of the police force now has all the powers and privileges of a constable
throughout England and Wales (s. 19); but the powers of a special
constable are limited to the area for which he is appointed.

---

[34] The Home Secretary announced in May 1966 that the number of police forces in
England and Wales was to be reduced from 117 to 49.

Functions of the Secretary of State

The Home Secretary has a general duty to exercise his powers under the Act in such manner and to such extent as appears to him to be best calculated to promote the efficiency of the police (s. 28). This gives the Home Secretary a wider responsibility outside London than he had before, and so extends the range of questions he may be asked in Parliament. He may be asked, for example, whether he intends to call for a report from, or to require the removal of, a Chief Constable. The Home Secretary may require a police authority to exercise its power to call on a Chief Constable to retire in the interests of efficiency, after hearing his representations and holding a local inquiry (s. 29).[35] He may require a Chief Constable to submit a report on specific matters, and a copy of the Chief Constable's annual report to the police authority must be sent to him (s. 30).

The Home Secretary may make grants to police authorities of such amounts, and subject to such conditions, as he may with the approval of the Treasury determine (s. 31). The police grant has for some years amounted to 50 per cent. of police expenditure. The Home Secretary may withhold, or threaten to withhold, the whole or part of this grant if, for example, a police authority tries to appoint or declines to dismiss a Chief Constable contrary to his wishes.

The Home Secretary may cause local inquiries to be held into local police matters, either in public or in private (s. 32). He has power to make regulations concerning the government, administration and conditions of service generally. These have been consolidated in the Police Regulations 1965. In particular, he may make regulations concerning discipline (s. 33). The police authority is the disciplinary authority with regard to the Chief Constable, his Deputy and his Assistant. The Chief Constable is the disciplinary authority for other ranks. The investigation of an alleged disciplinary offence must normally be carried out by an officer from a different division or branch. A member of the public who is a complainant may attend the hearing of the charge.[36] Appeal lies to the Home Secretary in disciplinary cases. He must normally set up an inquiry. The appellant is entitled to legal representation, and the complainant may attend the hearing.[37]

The Home Secretary determines the number of Inspectors of Constabulary who are appointed by the Crown to inspect and report on the efficiency of police forces (s. 38). He may appoint a Chief Inspector of Constabulary. The latter, who is concerned with research and planning, must report annually to the Home Secretary, and his report is to be laid before Parliament.

---

[35] Cf. Ridge v. Baldwin, ante, pp. 355–356.
[36] Police (Discipline) Regulations 1965. [37] Police (Appeals) Rules 1965.

Police representative institutions

A member of a police force may not be a member of any trade union, or of any association having for its objects to influence pay or conditions of service (s. 47). There continues to be a Police Federation representing the police forces,[38] which negotiates concerning pay and conditions of service with the Police Council,[39] a body containing both an official side and a staff side. Police advisory boards for England and Scotland are also set up, which must be consulted by the Secretary of State before issuing certain regulations, *e.g.* concerning promotion and discipline (s. 46).

Liability for wrongful acts of constables

Before 1964, where a police officer committed a tort the position was anomalous. He himself was personally liable (*Christie* v. *Leachinsky* [40]) but the police authority could not be made vicariously liable, at least in connection with such matters as arrest and detention. This was decided by McCardie J. in *Fisher* v. *Oldham Corporation*,[41] where the corporation was held not liable through its Watch Committee for false imprisonment on account of the arrest and detention of the plaintiff by one of its police inspectors through mistaken identity. A police officer, said McCardie J., was not a servant or agent of the police authority in exercising his powers of arrest and detention. Nor, on the other hand, could the Crown be made vicariously liable in such cases under the Crown Proceedings Act 1947, because police officers (at least, outside London) are not appointed directly or indirectly by the Crown, nor are they anywhere paid wholly out of parliamentary grant.[42] It was the practice of police authorities to compensate police officers who had incurred such liability in appropriate cases.[43] The Police Act provides that the Chief Constable should be liable for torts committed by constables under his direction and control in the performance or purported performance of their functions, in the same way as a master is liable for the torts of his servants.[44] Damages and costs are payable out of the local police

---

38 The Police Act 1972 relaxes (subject to restrictions) the prohibition in s. 44, Police Act 1964 prohibiting the Police Federation from being associated with any person or body outside the police service.
39 The Police Act 1969 established a Police Council of the United Kingdom, in place of the Police Council for Great Britain. The Act also enabled assistance to be given by home forces to the Royal Irish Constabulary, and empowered the Parliament of Northern Ireland to enable reciprocal assistance to be given.
40 [1947] A.C. 573; *ante*, p. 353.
41 [1930] 2 K.B. 364.   42 *Cf.* Crown Proceedings Act 1947, s. 2 (6).
43 Mary Bell Cairns, " Liability of the Police-Constable in Tort " (1959) 103 S.J. 1013, 1036.
44 That is, the Chief Constable and the constable concerned are regarded as joint tortfeasors, and as such are jointly and severally liable.

fund. The police authority has also a discretion to pay similar expenses incurred personally by a police officer (s. 48).

It may be noticed that no Minister is politically responsible to Parliament for the negligence or other misconduct (not amounting to illegality) of a police constable. The latter can be reprimanded by a senior police officer, and may consider it expedient to resign.

Investigation of complaints

The Chief Constable is required to record a complaint made against a police officer and (unless the officer has been charged with an offence) to cause it to be investigated. He may call upon another police force to provide an officer to carry out the investigation. The Home Secretary may require an officer from another force to be called in to investigate the complaint. The report of the investigation must be sent to the Director of Public Prosecutions, unless the Chief Constable is satisfied that no criminal offence has been committed. Even if there is no need to send the report to the Director of Public Prosecutions a disciplinary charge may be made, and the Home Secretary has an overriding power to order a local inquiry (s. 49). The police authority is required to keep itself informed as to the manner in which complaints from members of the public against members of its force are dealt with by the Chief Constable (s. 50).

A common criticism of these arrangements is that the police appear to be judging their own cause, and that there ought to be some kind of independent inquiry. One suggestion is the establishment of a separate legal department staffed by lawyers responsible to the Lord Chancellor. If the complainant asked for a formal hearing, the preliminary examination would be conducted by a lawyer; and if this disclosed that a trial ought to be held, then a Judge Advocate of Police would be appointed to act as legal adviser to the tribunal. The difficulty about an independent inquiry, however, is that most complaints involve the alleged commission of a crime, such as assault or false evidence, and that necessitates investigation by the police. If there were two inquiries—the first independent and the second by the police—the officer complained against would be in double jeopardy. Further, too many complaints are made (of which fewer than 10 per cent. are found to have any substance) for a double procedure. Each police force could perhaps have its own ombudsman.

The Home Secretary announced in December 1971 the introduction of an element of independent inquiry into the handling of complaints against the police. He issued a circular recommending police authorities to develop their supervisory role under the Police Act; encouraging chief officers to borrow officers from other forces to conduct investigations of serious complaints, and advising them to take greater trouble in explaining to complainants what action had been taken on their complaints. As police authority for the Metropolitan Police District, the Home Secretary has himself agreed with the Commissioner for Police that serious complaints against his officers will be investigated by officers from other forces. Complaints are handled in a single unit directly responsible to the Deputy Commissioner. With regard to complaints involving crime, the Director of Public Prosecutions himself informs the complainant direct of his decision whether or not the police officer complained of will be prosecuted.[45]

Assaults on, and obstruction of, constables

Section 51 of the Police Act re-enacts the statutory offence of assaulting a constable (or a person assisting him) in the execution of his duty,[46] and the offence of resisting or wilfully obstructing a constable (or a person assisting him) in the execution of his duty,[47] and regularises the penalties.

Section 52 imposes penalties on a person who: (1) impersonates a police officer with intent to deceive, or makes any statement or does any act calculated falsely to suggest that he is a police officer; or (2) (not being a constable) wears a police-style uniform in circumstances that are likely to deceive.[48]

It is also an offence to cause or attempt to cause, disaffection amongst the members of any police force; or to induce, or attempt to induce, any member of a police force to withhold his services or to commit breaches of discipline (s. 53).

---

[45] And see Preface.
[46] A. Zuckerman, " Assault or Not Assault " (1972) 88 L.Q.R. 246. See *Duncan* v. *Jones* [1963] 1 K.B. 218; *post*, Chap. 25; *Fagan* v. *Metropolitan Police Commissioner* [1969] 1 Q.B. 439 (D.C.) (leaving car wheel on constable's foot); *Donnelly* v. *Jackman* [1970] 1 W.L.R. 562 (D.C.); *R.* v. *Fennell* [1971] 1 Q.B. 428 (C.A.); *cf. Bailey* v. *Wilson* [1968] Crim.L.R. 617 (constable trespassing); *Kenlin* v. *Gardiner* [1967] 2 Q.B. 510 (D.C.); *R.* v. *Woolwich Justices, ex p. Toohey* [1967] 2 A.C. 1 (D.C.) (no right to be tried by jury).
[47] See *Rice* v. *Connolly* [1966] 2 Q.B. 414 (D.C.) as to " obstruct " and " wilful " (no legal duty to answer questions); *Gelberg* v. *Miller* [1961] 1 W.L.R. 153 (refusing to move car). As to warning motorists of speed trap, see *Betts* v. *Stevens* [1910] 1 K.B. 1 (D.C.); *cf. Bastable* v. *Little* [1907] 1 K.B. 59 (D.C.).
[48] *Turner* v. *Shearer* [1972] 1 W.L.R. 1387 (D.C.).

Part V

RIGHTS AND DUTIES OF THE INDIVIDUAL

CHAPTER 21

NATIONALITY, IMMIGRATION AND EXTRADITION

I. BRITISH NATIONALITY [1]

Nationality and allegiance

Nationality is a nineteenth-century concept. It is important in international law as well as constitutional law in connection with such matters as diplomatic protection abroad, immigration, deportation and the negotiation of treaties. In constitutional law the distinction between nationals and aliens is also important because the latter are subject to certain disabilities, especially as regards public or political rights.

Until 1948, British nationality law, which had been put on a statutory basis in 1914, was founded on the common law doctrine of allegiance. Allegiance was defined by Blackstone as "the tie, or *ligamen*, which binds the subject to the King, in return for that protection which the King affords the subject." [2] A natural or permanent allegiance was owed by subjects, who at common law were persons born within the King's dominions: while aliens within the King's dominions owed the Sovereign a local or temporary allegiance. No one could relinquish his nationality ("*nemo potest exuere patriam*"). Conversely, a special Act of Parliament was necessary to give an alien English or British nationality. All these matters were discussed in the famous but now obsolete *Calvin's Case* (1608), [3] where it was decided that "*postnati*," *i.e.* persons born in Scotland after the accession of James VI of Scotland to the English throne as James I, were not aliens in England.

The distinction between natural-born subjects and others (including naturalised aliens) was in earlier times more important than that between subjects and aliens. [4] General provision was made

---

[1] Clive Parry, *Nationality and Citizenship Laws of the Commonwealth* (2 vols. 1957–60); Mervyn Jones, *British Nationality Law* (2nd ed. 1956). For the history, see Holdsworth, *History of English Law*, Vol. IX, pp. 72–104.

[2] Bl.Comm. I, 366.

[3] 7 Co.Rep. 1a. *Cf. Isaacson* v. *Durant* (1886) 17 Q.B.D. 54 (Hanoverian born before accession of Queen Victoria).

[4] An Act of 1705 provided that the lineal descendants of Princess Sophia should be deemed to be natural-born British subjects: see *Att.-Gen.* v. *Prince Ernest Augustus of Hanover* [1957] A.C. 436; Clive Parry, "Further Considerations upon the Prince of Hanover's Case" (1956) 5 I.C.L.Q. 61; note by C. d'O. Farran in (1956) 19 M.L.R. 289. And see *Duke of Brunswick* v. *King of Hanover* (1844) 6 Beav. 1, 19, 34.

by the Naturalisation Act 1870 to enable aliens to acquire British nationality by executive grant of the Home Secretary instead of by private Act of Parliament.

The common law doctrine of allegiance plays no part in the new concept of nationality. Allegiance is no longer a source of British nationality, although it may be a consequence of it. It must be regarded henceforth as relevant to the law of treason rather than nationality, and perhaps also to "acts of state." [5]

The Act of 1914

The British Nationality and Status of Aliens Act 1914 repealed the Naturalisation Act 1870 (except as regards persons born before 1915) and provided a comprehensive code for the acquisition and loss of British nationality. Part I, relating to natural-born British subjects, applied throughout the British Empire. The general principles governing the status of natural-born British subjects were: (a) birth in British territory; or (b) birth abroad of a father who was a British subject; and (c) a married woman acquired British nationality if she married a British subject, and she lost British nationality if she married an alien. Part II related to naturalisation.

Further Acts were passed dealing notably with the status of married women, and this legislation was known as the British Nationality and Status of Aliens Acts 1914–1943. These Acts were almost entirely repealed by the British Nationality Act 1948, but they are still of practical importance for they determine whether any person born before 1949 was a British subject, so as to retain British nationality under the transitional provisions of the Act of 1948.

British Nationality Act 1948 [6]

Before 1948 British nationality was based on the common law doctrine that (with certain exceptions) every person born in British territory was a natural-born British subject. The pre-1948 statutes embodied this doctrine, but also laid down conditions on which persons born outside British territory might become natural-born British subjects, and made rules regarding naturalisation, the status of married women and children, and loss of British nationality. The combination of United Kingdom legislation and Dominion legislation along similar lines would constitute, it was hoped, a common code of British nationality for the British Commonwealth.

[5] *Ante*, Chap. 13.
[6] See E. C. S. Wade, " British Nationality Act, 1948 " (1948) xxx *Journ. Comp. Leg.* 67.

In the course of time divergencies began to appear between the laws of various members of the Commonwealth, in particular in relation to married women. In 1946 Canada enacted a Citizenship Act which defined Canadian *citizens*, provided that all Canadian citizens were British subjects, and further provided that all persons who were British subjects under the law of any other Commonwealth country would be recognised by Canada as British subjects. The Act thus retained the common status of British subjects, but abandoned the common code of nationality. A Commonwealth legal conference was held in London in 1947, and it was decided to accept the principles of the Canadian Citizenship Act 1946 for general application throughout the Commonwealth. The British Nationality Act 1948, as amended from time to time, gave effect to these principles so far as the United Kingdom and British colonies are concerned. It provided a new method of giving effect to the principle that the people of each of the self-governing countries within the Commonwealth have both a particular status as citizens of their own country and a common status as members of the wider association of peoples comprising the Commonwealth. The Act is divided into two main parts: Part I deals with British nationality, Part II with citizenship of the United Kingdom and colonies.

British Nationality

Under the British Nationality and Status of Aliens Acts 1914–1943 the following persons born after 1914 were natural-born British subjects:

(a) Any person born within His Majesty's dominions and allegiance; and

(b) Any person born out of His Majesty's dominions whose father was, at the time of that person's birth, a British subject and fulfilled one of a number of conditions; and

(c) Any person born on board a British ship.

Section I of the British Nationality Act 1948 provides that:

" (1) Every person who under this Act is a citizen of the United Kingdom and Colonies,[7] or who under any enactment for the time being in force in any country mentioned in subsection (3) of this section is a citizen of that country, shall by virtue of that citizenship have the status of a British subject.

(2) Any person having the status aforesaid may be known either as a British subject or as a Commonwealth citizen; and accordingly in this Act and in any other enactment or instrument whatever, whether passed or made before or after the commencement of this

---

[7] *Post,* pp. 368 *et seq.*

Act, the expression ' British subject ' and the expression ' Commonwealth citizen ' shall have the same meaning."

Subsection (3), specifying the Commonwealth countries concerned, has been amended from time to time so as to include all independent members of the Commonwealth, Southern Rhodesia and any other Commonwealth country that may have been granted power to enact its own citizenship laws. Each of the countries mentioned in subsection (3), as amended, is a legislative unit for nationality or citizenship purposes. It was intended that each of them should enact a citizenship law containing the principle of section 1 (1), *supra*, by which mutual recognition as British subjects would be given to the citizens of other Commonwealth countries. The result would be that " British subjects," instead of being ascertained by a common code, would simply comprise the citizens of all Commonwealth countries, as is shown by the alternative title " Commonwealth citizens."

In the United Kingdom, therefore, there are now five classes of person:

1. Citizens of the United Kingdom and Colonies (*infra*).[8]

2. Citizens of other Commonwealth countries or associated states.

3. Citizens of the Republic of Ireland, who by the Ireland Act 1949, s. 2, are not to be regarded as aliens.[9]

4. British protected persons, *i.e.* (roughly) persons born in British protectorates, protected states or trust territories.[10]

5. Aliens.

Status of aliens

Under the medieval common law aliens had practically no public or private rights. The rules were gradually relaxed by statute and a more liberal attitude on the part of the common law courts. By the end of the sixteenth century it was recognised that aliens in the King's dominions owed a temporary and local allegiance. Friendly aliens could now bring personal actions such as trespass and debt, and could own personal property, including leaseholds.

Friendly aliens, i.e. citizens of countries with which the Crown is

8 Those connected with the Channel Islands and the Isle of Man may, if they so desire, be known as " citizens of the United Kingdom, Islands and Colonies ": s. 33.

9 The Ireland Act, s. 5 (1), provided for the retention of British nationality (with certain exceptions) by persons born in Eire, or the Irish Free State, before 1922 (the date of the Anglo-Irish Treaty) who were British subjects immediately before 1949.

10 Before 1949 they were regarded as aliens while in this country: *R. v. Ketter* [1940] 1 K.B. 787.

not at war,[11] have long had the right to contract, to own and dispose of personal property, and to bring and defend actions. They may now own and dispose of real property. Resident aliens owe allegiance to the Crown, and are subject to the general civil and criminal law.[12] They do not enjoy the parliamentary or local government franchise [13]; they may not sit in either House of Parliament [14] or hold any public office; but they may be employed in any civil capacity under the Crown (a) outside the United Kingdom, or (b) under a certificate issued by a Minister with Treasury approval.[15] Aliens are subject to restrictions with regard to employment in the armed forces, the Civil Service in this country, and the merchant navy; jury service; the ownership of British ships; holding a pilot's certificate; change of name; and taking part in certain industrial activities.

Enemy aliens [16]

Enemy aliens, *i.e.* nationals of countries with which the Crown is at war, were at one time virtually rightless, unless exceptionally they were here with the licence of the King. In course of time it came to be seen that what mattered so far as commerce was concerned was to prevent any trade with the enemy country, regardless of what persons were carrying it on. And so an " enemy " came to mean any person (whether a British subject or not) who voluntarily resided or carried on business in an enemy country.[17] An enemy alien in this sense cannot enter into contracts by English law, and contracts entered into with him before the war are suspended for the duration of the war. " Enemy character " is largely of importance in relation to corporations, and in relation to offences under the Trading with the Enemy Acts.

An enemy alien cannot bring an action in the British courts; nor, if he was plaintiff in an action begun before the war, can he appeal during the war: for the enemy cannot be given the advantage of

---

11 " Friendly " aliens may in some contexts include nationals of countries with which the Crown is at war, but who have come to reside or are allowed to remain here by the Sovereign's licence: *Wells* v. *Williams* (1697) 1 Ld.Raym. 282. The Sovereign's licence, express or implied, gives the protection of the law and the courts: *Sylvester's Case* (1702) 7 Mod. 150. A licence is commonly implied by the fact that an alien has registered and has been allowed to remain: *Thurn and Taxis (Princess)* v. *Moffitt* [1915] 1 Ch. 58; *Schaffenius* v. *Goldberg* [1916] 1 K.B. 284. See further, W. E. Davies, *The English Law relating to Aliens* (1931) Chap. 1.
12 *Cf.* Visiting Forces Act 1952.
13 Representation of the People Act 1949.   14 Act of Settlement 1700
15 Aliens' Employment Act 1955.   16 See McNair, *Legal Effects of War* (3rd ed.).
17 *Wells* v. *Williams* (1697) 1 Ld.Raym. 282; *The Hoop* (1799) 1 C.Rob. 196; *Janson* v. *Driefontein Consolidated Mines* [1902] A.C. 484. For the position of corporations, see *Daimler Co.* v. *Continental Tyre and Rubber Co.* [1916] 2 A.C. 307; as to firms, see *Rodriguez* v. *Speyer Bros.* [1919] A.C. 59. Territory occupied by the enemy is regarded as enemy territory: *Sovfracht (V.O.)* v. *Van Udens Scheepvaart en Agentur Maatschappij (N.V.Babr.)* [1943] A.C. 203.

enforcing his rights by the assistance of the Sovereign with whom he is at war. On the other hand an enemy alien can be sued during the war, as that permits British subjects or friendly aliens to enforce their rights with the assistance of the Sovereign against the enemy; and if he is sued justice demands that he be allowed to appear and defend. Further, if he is unsuccessful as defendant he may appeal, for he is entitled to have the case decided according to law and therefore to have the error of a court of first instance rectified (*Porter* v. *Freudenberg* [18]). The Crown has the prerogative of confiscating enemy property, but if it is taken it is usually handed over to a Custodian during the war.[19]

With regard to the control of aliens for the security of the realm in time of war, the original distinction between enemy and friendly aliens is commonly used. Wartime legislation and emergency powers during both the two world wars gave the Crown very extensive powers of control over enemy aliens in this sense. The legislation expressly preserved the Crown's prerogative in relation to enemy aliens. At common law their licence to remain at large may be revoked at any time at the complete discretion of the Crown, and they can be interned [20] or deported.[21] The internment of an enemy alien is an act of state, and he has no right to apply for a writ of habeas corpus against the executive to challenge the Crown's power to intern or deport (*R.* v. *Bottrill, ex p. Kuechenmeister* [22]). In the last case it was discussed, but not decided, whether an interned enemy alien is in the position of a prisoner of war. Internment, however, does not revoke the licence to bring civil actions in the courts, or, probably, to commence habeas corpus proceedings against private persons.[23]

II. CITIZENSHIP OF THE UNITED KINGDOM AND COLONIES

1. Citizenship by birth or descent

The British Nationality Act 1948, s. 4, provides that every person born within the United Kingdom and Colonies on or after January 1,

---

[18] [1915] 1 K.B. 857 (C.A.) *per* Lord Reading C.J. See also *Eichengruen* v. *Mond* [1940] 1 Ch. 785; *cf. Weber's Trustees* v. *Riemer*, 1947 S.L.T. 295 (counterclaim not permissible).

[19] See *e.g. Administrator of Austrian Property* v. *Russian Bank for Foreign Trade* (1931) 48 T.L.R. 37; *Bank voor Handel en Scheepvaart N.V.* v. *Administrator of Hungarian Property* [1954] A.C. 584.

[20] *R.* v. *Commandant of Knockaloe Camp* (1917) 117 L.T. 627; *Ex p. Liebmann* [1916] 1 K.B. 268; *Ex p. Weber* [1916] A.C. 421.

[21] *Netz* v. *Chuter Ede* [1946] Ch. 224; *Att.-Gen. for Canada* v. *Cain* [1906] A.C. 542 (P.C.).

[22] [1947] K.B. 41 (C.A.).   [23] *Ibid. per* Asquith L.J.

1949, shall be a citizen of the United Kingdom and Colonies by *birth*, unless (a) his father enjoys diplomatic immunity and is not a citizen of the United Kingdom and Colonies, or (b) his father is an enemy alien and the birth occurs in a place then under enemy occupation.[24]

Section 5 enacts that a person born on or after January 1, 1949, shall be a citizen of the United Kingdom and Colonies by *descent* if his father is a citizen of the United Kingdom and Colonies at the time of that person's birth, with the proviso that if the father is a citizen by descent only, one of a number of other conditions must be satisfied.

Section 12 provides that any person who was a British subject immediately before January 1, 1949, became a citizen of the United Kingdom and Colonies if: (a) he was born in the United Kingdom and Colonies; or (b) he was naturalised in the United Kingdom and Colonies; or (c) he became a British subject by annexation of territory to the United Kingdom and Colonies; or (d) his father was a British subject and fulfilled any of the above conditions; or (e) he was born in a British protectorate, protected state or trust territory.

2. Citizenship by naturalisation

Naturalisation is now governed by section 10 of the British Nationality Act 1948 and Regulations made thereunder. On the application of any alien or British protected person [25] of full age and capacity, the Home Secretary [26] may grant a certificate of naturalisation; and the applicant, on taking the oath of allegiance specified in the Act, becomes a citizen of the United Kingdom and Colonies from the date of the certificate. Before granting a certificate the Home Secretary must be satisfied that the applicant: (a) has either resided in the United Kingdom or been in Crown service under the United Kingdom Government throughout the preceding twelve months; and (b) has either resided in the United Kingdom or any colony or dependency or been in Crown service under the United Kingdom Government for periods amounting to not less than four years during the seven years preceding the twelve months; and (c) is of good character; and (d) has sufficient knowledge of the English language [27];

---

[24] And see British Nationality (No. 2) Act 1964, s. 2.

[25] Previously the term "naturalisation" was applied only to aliens, but under this Act British protected persons are not aliens.

[26] Or the Governor in the Isle of Man or the Channel Islands, or (with the approval of the Home Secretary) in a colony or dependency.

[27] Where application for naturalisation is made by a person resident in a colony or dependency, a British protected person may show alternatively that he has a sufficient knowledge of any other language in current use in that territory; and an alien may show alternatively that he has a sufficient knowledge of any language recognised in that territory as being on an equality with the English language.

and (e) intends (i) to reside in the United Kingdom or in any colony or dependency, or (ii) to enter into or continue in Crown service under the United Kingdom Government, or service under an international organisation of which the United Kingdom Government is a member, or service in the employment of a society or company established in the United Kingdom or any colony or dependency (Schedule 2).

A British protected person may be naturalised on easier terms than an alien: for instead of conditions (a) and (b) *supra*, it is sufficient if he has been ordinarily resident in the United Kingdom or in government service in the United Kingdom throughout the preceding five years.[28]

A citizen by naturalisation has all the political and legal rights of a citizen by birth or descent, except that his certificate of naturalisation is revocable.[29]

The Home Secretary may by order deprive a naturalised person of his citizenship if the certificate was obtained by fraud, false representation or concealment of any material fact; or if he is satisfied that that person has shown himself disloyal to Her Majesty, or has traded with the enemy during any war, or (unless the effect of deprivation would be to render that person stateless) [30] has been sentenced to not less than twelve months' imprisonment within five years of naturalisation. A naturalised person is not to be deprived of citizenship unless the Home Secretary is satisfied that it is not conducive to the public good that that person should continue to be a citizen of the United Kingdom and Colonies; and except in the case of continuous residence abroad, a person against whom an order is proposed to be made may require that the case be referred to a committee of inquiry (s. 20).

3. Citizenship by registration

On application to the Home Secretary [31] certain persons are entitled as of right to be *registered* as citizens of the United Kingdom and Colonies: others may be so registered at his discretion. Those entitled to registration are:

(i) A citizen of a Commonwealth country who is patrial,[32] and

---

[28] This period was extended from twelve months to five years by the Commonwealth Immigrants Act 1962.

[29] After the Naturalisation Act 1870 a naturalised British subject could, for example, be a member of the Privy Council: *R.* v. *Speyer* [1916] 2 K.B. 858; *cf.* Act of Settlement 1700, s. 3. Before 1914 a certificate of naturalisation was irrevocable.

[30] British Nationality (No. 2) Act 1964, s. 4.

[31] Or the Governor in the Isle of Man, the Channel Islands, a colony or dependency, or (by arrangement with the Home Secretary) by the United Kingdom High Commissioner in a Commonwealth country.

[32] *i.e.* has the right of abode; see *post*, p. 375.

who for the previous five years has been ordinarily resident in the United Kingdom or engaged in relevant employment, *i.e.* Crown service under the United Kingdom Government or an international organisation of which the United Kingdom Government is a member, or employed by a society or company established in the United Kingdom (s. 5A).[33]

(ii) A woman who has been married to a citizen of the United Kingdom and Colonies (s. 6).

The Home Secretary has a discretion to register as a citizen of the United Kingdom and Colonies, on application made to him, any citizen of a Commonwealth country who satisfies the Home Secretary that he is of good character and has a sufficient knowledge of the English or Welsh language, and that he intends to reside in the United Kingdom or a colony, or to enter into or continue in " relevant employment " (*supra*), provided that for the previous five years he has been ordinarily resident in the United Kingdom, or engaged in relevant employment (s. 5A).[33]

A citizen by registration may be deprived of citizenship by order of the Home Secretary if he is satisfied that the registration was obtained by means of fraud, false representation or the concealment of any material fact, and it is not conducive to the public good that that person should continue to be a citizen. The person concerned is entitled to have the case referred to a committee of inquiry called the Deprivation of Citizenship Committee (s. 20).

4. Citizenship by incorporation of territory

The British Nationality Act 1948 provides: " If any territory becomes a part of the United Kingdom and Colonies, His Majesty may by Order in Council specify the persons who shall be citizens of the United Kingdom and Colonies by reason of their connection with that territory; and those persons shall be citizens of the United Kingdom and Colonies as from a date to be specified in the Order " (s. 11). This provision is designed to avoid the difficulties and uncertainties of the common law as regards the effect on nationality of annexation and acquisition by cession.

Loss of citizenship

We have seen that citizenship may be lost by *deprivation* in the case of naturalised citizens and citizens by registration. The British Nationality Act 1948 also provides for loss by *renunciation*. At common law a British subject could not become naturalised in a

[33] Immigration Act 1971, s. 2 and Sched. 1.

foreign country.[34] The Naturalisation Act 1870 provided that if he did so he should be deemed to have ceased to be a British subject and be regarded as an alien.[35] The 1948 Act in order to prevent statelessness provides that the acquisition of a foreign nationality or of another Commonwealth citizenship, instead of involving automatic forfeiture, shall entitle a person to renounce his citizenship of the United Kingdom and Colonies if he so desires.

Any citizen of the United Kingdom and Colonies of full age and capacity (including a married woman under eighteen), who is also (a) a citizen of a Commonwealth country or Irish citizen, or (b) a national of a foreign country, may make a declaration of renunciation of citizenship of the United Kingdom and Colonies, which the Home Secretary shall cause to be registered: and on registration that person ceases to be a citizen of the United Kingdom and Colonies (s. 19). It is provided, however, that the Home Secretary may withhold registration of any such declaration if made during any war in which Her Majesty may be engaged by a person who is a national of a foreign country.

Provisions are now made for the resumption of citizenship by re-registration in certain cases, and for the prevention of a person's becoming stateless by renunciation of citizenship.[36]

Married women

Under the Act of 1914 a British woman lost her British nationality if she married an alien, or if her husband became an alien after the marriage. Later amendments provided that she would retain her British nationality: (i) if on marrying an alien she did not acquire his nationality, and (ii) if on her husband's becoming an alien she made a declaration of retention of British nationality or did not acquire her husband's nationality. "Citizenship," however, was a new concept introduced by the British Nationality Act 1948; and under that Act married women are generally (as they were at common law) in the same position as single women and men.

The position now is, therefore, that a British woman who marries an alien retains her British nationality unless she chooses to renounce it: on the other hand an alien woman who marries a United Kingdom citizen does not *ipso facto* acquire British nationality, but may do so by registration.

---

[34] *Ante*, p. 363.
[35] In *R.* v. *Lynch* [1903] 1 K.B. 444, however, it was held that naturalisation in a country with which Britain was at war not only amounted to treason, but was probably null and void.
[36] British Nationality (No. 1) Act 1964, ss. 1 and 2.

III. IMMIGRATION AND DEPORTATION

Introduction

Aliens

At common law an alien had no right to enter this country.[37] The Crown probably had no prerogative power to send an alien (other than an enemy alien) compulsorily out of the realm,[38] but since the eighteenth century the government has sought statutory powers to do so.

The Aliens Restriction Act 1914 gave wide powers to the executive to make orders concerning aliens in time of war or emergency. Some of these powers were perpetuated by the Aliens Restriction Amendment Act 1919. Statutory regulations covered the admission, supervision and deportation of aliens. The Home Secretary might order the deportation of an alien not only when he had been recommended to do so by a court that had sentenced him to imprisonment, but also where the Home Secretary deemed it to be " conducive to the public good."

Commonwealth citizens

British subjects were free at common law to come into or leave the " mother country." The British Nationality Act 1948, which created citizenship of the United Kingdom and Colonies, retained the old term " British subject " as an alternative to the new term " Commonwealth citizen " for the citizens of other independent Commonwealth countries. It was not until 1962 that Parliament found it desirable by the Commonwealth Immigrants Act 1962 [39] to give some power to control immigration into the United Kingdom by citizens of Commonwealth countries. All other Commonwealth countries had power to control such immigration.[40] The power of control conferred in 1962 applied to all Commonwealth citizens except those born in the United Kingdom and those holding United Kingdom passports,[41] and also to British protected persons and Irish citizens. It was found expedient in 1965 to exercise a rather stricter control over such

---

[37] Schmidt v. Secretary of State for Home Affairs [1969] 2 Ch. 149, 168, per Lord Denning M.R.; Musgrove v. Chun Teeong Toy [1891] A.C. 272.

[38] Forsyth, Cases and Opinions on Constitutional Law (1869) p. 181; Holdsworth, History of English Law, Vol. X, pp. 393–400. Cf. dictum of Lord Atkinson in Johnstone v. Pedlar [1921] A.C. 262, 283.

[39] See C. Thornberry, " Law, Opinion, and the Immigrant " (1962) 25 M.L.R. 654.

[40] Colonies also can restrict the immigration of citizens of the United Kingdom and colonies; see Thornton v. The Police [1962] A.C. 339 (P.C.).

[41] Cf. Commonwealth Immigrants Act 1968, by which the exemption of persons holding United Kingdom passports was restricted to those who had specified connections with the United Kingdom. Cf. R. v. Secretary of State for Home Department, ex p. Bhurosah [1968] 1 Q.B. 266.

immigration on the grounds of housing and employment. Control over Irish citizens has not in fact been exercised so far as that can be avoided. Apart from the fact that many Irish workers come for seasonal employment, it is difficult to close the Irish border and it has not been thought desirable to exercise such control against the people of Northern Ireland as well.

The Home Secretary was also given for the first time a limited power to deport from the United Kingdom Commonwealth citizens,[42] British protected persons and Irish citizens on the recommendation of a court that had sentenced them to imprisonment. The power to deport in such cases was possessed by practically every other territory in the Commonwealth.

The Commonwealth Immigrants Act 1968 amended the Act of 1962 with regard to (inter alia) exemption from control enjoyed by citizens of the United Kingdom and Colonies holding United Kingdom passports [43]; made it an offence to land otherwise than in accordance with immigration regulations; and extended the period for the examination of persons landing in the United Kingdom.[44]

There was no system of appeals before 1969 from the Home Secretary's decision to exclude a person from the United Kingdom or to deport him, although since 1956 the Home Secretary had allowed aliens whom he proposed to deport in the interest of the public good to make representations to the Bow Street magistrate, whose advice the Home Secretary usually accepted. European Conventions apparently required more than this, and in 1969 an Immigration Appeals Act was passed, giving a right of appeal to Commonwealth citizens subject to immigration control or liable to deportation under the Commonwealth Immigrants Act 1962, and allowing provision to be made for appeals by aliens.[45] Commonwealth citizens had a right to appeal to an adjudicator against exclusion from the United Kingdom, conditions of admission, deportation orders and directions for removal from the United Kingdom. Determinations of adjudicators were subject to review by an Immigration Appeal Tribunal. Aliens were given a limited right of appeal by order. The Home

---

[42] Cf. R. v. Sabri, The Times, November 10, 1964 (C.C.A.). Before 1962 a deportation order against any British subject would be quashed: R. v. Home Secretary, ex p. Château Thierry (Duke) [1917] 1 K.B. 922, 930, per Swinfen Eady L.J.

[43] R. C. B. Forman, " British immigrant applications: the European Commission on Human Rights," 1970 S.L.T. 157.

[44] Cf. R. v. Governor of Brixton Prison, ex p. Ahsan [1969] 2 Q.B. 222 (D.C.), the case of the eleven smuggled Pakistanis.

[45] Cmnd. 3387. See B. A. Hepple, " Immigration Appeals Act 1969 " (1969) 32 M.L.R. 668.

Secretary retained his discretion where the interests of national security were involved.[40]

The Aliens Restriction Act 1914, the Commonwealth Immigrants Act 1962,[47] the Commonwealth Immigrants Act 1968 and the Immigration Appeals Act 1969 were repealed and replaced by the Immigration Act 1971.

Immigration Act 1971

General principles

The Immigration Act 1971 deals with regulation of entry and stay in the United Kingdom, of Commonwealth citizens as well as aliens. Section 1 sets out the general principles. All persons who have the "right of abode" under section 2 (they are called "patrial," *infra*) are free to live in, and to come and go into and from, the United Kingdom. Persons not having that right may live, work and settle in the United Kingdom by permission and subject to regulation and control; and those who were settled here when the Act came into force are treated as if they had been given indefinite leave to enter or remain. The Act does not control local journeys between the United Kingdom, the Isle of Man, the Channel Islands and the Republic of Ireland (" the common travel area "). The Home Secretary is to make rules for the admission of students,[48] visitors and dependants, but such rules do not affect the freedom of Commonwealth citizens already settled here.

Right of abode

Section 2 provides that a person has the right of abode in the United Kingdom if he is a citizen of the United Kingdom and Colonies who acquired that citizenship by birth, adoption, naturalisation or registration; or has a parent with such connection; or has been settled in the United Kingdom and been ordinarily resident [49] here for the last five years; or if he is a Commonwealth citizen having a parent who at the time of that person's birth was a citizen of the United Kingdom and Colonies by birth in the United Kingdom. A woman who

---

[46] *e.g.* in the case of Dutschke, a German who wished to extend the period for which he had been admitted into this country as a student: *The Times,* December 24, 1970; B. A. Hepple, " Aliens and Administrative Justice: the Dutschke case " (1971) 34 M.L.R. 501.

[47] Except section 12 (2) which extended to five years the periods of residence, etc. required for the registration of Commonwealth citizens as citizens of the United Kingdom and Colonies.

[48] See *R.* v. *Chief Immigration Officer, Bradford Airport, ex p. Hussain* [1970] 1 W.L.R. 9; *R.* v. *Baidoo* (1971) 55 Cr.App.R. 253 (C.A.).

[49] *Levine* v. *I.R.C.* [1928] A.C. 217 (some degree of continuity); *I.R.C.* v. *Lysaght* [1928] A.C. 234 (not casual or extraordinary); *R.* v. *Hussain, The Times,* November 13, 1971 (C.A.) (interruption by prolonged absence).

is a Commonwealth citizen has the right of abode if she is the wife of any of the persons mentioned above. Persons having the right of abode are called " patrial." [50]

Regulation and control

Section 3 makes general provisions for regulation and control. Persons who are not patrial require leave to enter, which may be given for a limited or indefinite period, and may be subject to conditions restricting employment and occupation [51] and/or requiring registration with the police.[52] Immigration rules [53] are to be laid before Parliament, and if they are disapproved by either House the Home Secretary is to make such changes as appear to him to be required. Crews of ships [54] or aircraft may enter for limited periods without leave. Diplomats and their families and members of home, Commonwealth and visiting forces are exempt from control (s. 8). Provision may be made by Order in Council with regard to persons entering otherwise than by ship or aircraft,[55] e.g. by land from the Republic of Ireland or by swimming the Channel; and such provisions may exclude the Republic of Ireland from the common travel area (s. 10).

Deportation

Section 3 (5) and (6) provides that a non-patrial is liable to deportation if: (i) he does not observe a condition or remains beyond the time limit; or (ii) the Home Secretary deems his deportation to be conducive to the public good [56]; or (iii) another person to whose family he belongs is deported; or (iv) being seventeen or over he is convicted of an offence punishable with imprisonment and the court recommends him for deportation.[57] A deportation order is an order requiring a person to leave and prohibiting him from entering the United Kingdom (s. 5). The Home Secretary has a discretionary

---

[50] A seventeenth-century word meaning " of or belonging to one's native country." The first a may be pronounced long or short.
[51] R. v. Immigration Appeal Tribunal, ex p. Martin, The Times, July 20, 1972 (D.C.).
[52] The Home Office have given an assurance that Commonwealth citizens will not be required to register with the police, but with the Department of Social Security.
[53] Immigration Rules, Cmnd. 4295.
[54] Cf. Re Sirazul Hoque, The Times, July 26, 1968 (C.A.).
[55] Cf. R. v. Bhagwan [1972] A.C. 60 (H.L.) (landing on lonely beach).
[56] This power is new as regards Commonwealth citizens.
[57] It is not necessary that he shall have been sentenced to imprisonment; he might, for example, be a teenager given an absolute discharge. Magistrates have no power to bind a person over to leave the country: R. v. East Grinstead Justices, ex p. Doeve [1969] 1 Q.B. 136 (scientologist).

executive power to make such an order.[58] and is not bound to afford the deportee a hearing.[59]

The Home Secretary may give directions for the removal of a deportee to a country of which he is a national or citizen, or to which there is reason to believe that he will be admitted.[60] Such directions may be given to the captain or owners of a ship or aircraft,[61] or arrangements may be made by the Home Secretary. A bona fide order of deportation for the public good may be made to send an alien back to his own country, even though that country has requested his surrender for a criminal offence that is not extraditable (Ex p. Soblen[62]). Where a court has recommended deportation and the person is neither detained under sentence or order of the court nor released on bail, he may be either detained or released by order of the Home Secretary pending the making of a deportation order.

Section 6 deals with recommendations by a court for deportation. A court may not make such recommendation unless the person has been given seven days' notice of his rights and liability. The validity of a recommendation by a court may only be questioned in an appeal against the recommendation or against conviction.[63] Commonwealth citizens or citizens of the Republic of Ireland who, when the Act came into force, were ordinarily resident in the United Kingdom, are not liable to be deported if they had been ordinarily resident for five years at the time of the Home Secretary's decision or at the time of conviction; and such a person is not liable to deportation on the ground that the Home Secretary deems his deportation to be conducive to the public good if at the time of the Home Secretary's decision he had at all times since the Act came into force been ordinarily resident (s. 7).

Appeals

Part II of the Immigration Act deals with appeals. Section 12 continues the Immigration Appeal Tribunal and adjudicators provided

58 Ex p. Venicoff [1920] 3 K.B. 72. Cf. R. v. Chiswick Police Superintendent, ex p. Sachsteder [1918] 1 K.B. 578.
59 R. v. Governor of Brixton Prison, ex p. Soblen [1963] 2 Q.B. 243 (C.A.), per Lord Denning M.R. Cf. appeal, infra.
60 Cf. R. v. Home Secretary, ex p. Duke of Château Thierry [1917] 1 K.B. 922; R. v. Governor of Brixton Prison, ex p. Sliwa [1952] 1 K.B. 169 (C.A.).
61 Cf. R. v. Governor of Richmond Remand Centre, ex p. Ashgar [1971] 1 W.L.R. 129 (D.C.).
62 R. v. Governor of Brixton Prison, ex p. Soblen [1963] 2 Q.B. 243 (C.A.). The action of the Home Secretary was criticised as " disguised extradition ": P. O'Higgins, " Disguised Extradition: the Soblen case " (1964) 27 M.L.R. 521; and see C. H. R. Thornberry, " Dr. Soblen and the Alien Law of the United Kingdom " (1963) 12 I.C.L.Q. 414. Legally and politically, however, Soblen's case was without merit.
63 For this purpose such recommendation is treated in England as a sentence, and in Scotland in the same manner as a conviction.

for by the Immigration Appeals Act 1969.   Members of the Tribunal
are appointed by the Lord Chancellor, the President and some of the
other members being legally qualified.   Adjudicators are appointed by
the Home Secretary.   There is a right of appeal to an adjudicator (or
direct to the Tribunal in respect of a deportation order otherwise than
on the recommendation of a court) against refusal of leave to enter and
refusal of certificate of patriality, entry certificate or visa, against
certain conditions of entry, a deportation order made otherwise than
on the recommendation of a court, or the destination to which it is
proposed to remove him (ss. 13–17).

There is no appeal against a decision of a Home Secretary that
refusal of entry is conducive to the public good (s. 13 (5)), or that deportation is conducive to the public good as being in the interests of
national security or foreign relations or for other reasons of a political
nature (s. 15 (3)).

An appeal is to be allowed by an adjudicator (or the Tribunal
where appeal is to the Tribunal in the first instance) if the adjudicator or Tribunal considers that the decision was contrary to law or
to the immigration rules, or that a discretion should have been
exercised differently.

Appeal lies to the Immigration Appeal Tribunal from the determination of an adjudicator, subject to any requirement about leave
to appeal.   The Home Secretary, after an appeal has been dismissed,
may refer a case back to an adjudicator or the Tribunal for an opinion
on any matter that was not before them in the earlier proceedings.

Criminal proceedings, etc.

It is an offence to contravene restrictions imposed by the Act on
entry, to overstay a limited leave to enter or remain, or to fail to
observe conditions attached to such leave (s. 24).   Section 25 deals
with certain offences relating to assisting illegal entry and harbouring.
and creates the serious new offence of " being knowingly concerned
in illegal entry." [63a]   There are also miscellaneous offences connected
with the administration of immigration control.

Section 29 empowers the Home Secretary to make payments
from public funds towards the expenses incurred by persons who are
not patrial in leaving the United Kingdom, with their families, to
live permanently abroad.

The Act may be extended to the Channel Islands and the Isle of
Man.

[63a] R. v. Singh (Amar Jit) [1972] 1 W.L.R. 1600 (C.A.).

The Act states that it shall not be taken to supersede or impair any power exercisable by Her Majesty in relation to aliens by virtue of her prerogative. This would include a prerogative to refuse them admission,[64] and perhaps to deport them.[65]

IV. EXTRADITION AND FUGITIVE OFFENDERS

Extradition Acts

The Extradition Acts 1870 to 1935, as amended, provide that the Crown may, subject to certain restrictions and formalities, hand over to any state with which a reciprocal treaty has been made any persons (whether British subjects or aliens) who have been found guilty of committing in that state any offence covered by the Extradition Acts.[66] The foreign state in return undertakes to surrender to the United Kingdom persons who have committed extraditable crimes in British territory. The Act of 1870 enables the Crown to make an Order in Council directing that the Extradition Acts shall apply to any given state.[67]

When extradition is requested through diplomatic channels, the accused can be arrested either by warrant of the Chief Metropolitan Magistrate at Bow Street issued on order of the Home Secretary, or by warrant of a justice of the peace issued on information, which warrant may be cancelled by the Home Secretary. The Chief Magistrate or another metropolitan magistrate at Bow Street receives the extradition order and documents from the Home Office, and decides whether there is a prima facie case.[68] The alleged offence must be one that is included in the Order in Council applying to the state concerned, construed according to English law at the date of the alleged crime; and there must be sufficient evidence of the identity of the accused. If the magistrate does not commit him he is discharged. The Home Secretary has a discretion not to surrender a

---

[64] *Ante*, p. 373.

[65] *Att.-Gen.* v. *Cain* [1906] A.C. 542; and see Thornberry (1963) 12 I.C.L.Q. 422–428.

[66] There is no prerogative power to seize an alien in this country and hand him over to a foreign state: Forsyth, *Cases and Opinions on Constitutional Law*, pp. 369–370; *cf. East India Co.* v. *Campbell* (1749) 1 Ves.Sen. 246; *Mure* v. *Kaye* (1811) 4 Taunt. 43.

[67] *Cf.* Backing of Warrants (Republic of Ireland) Act 1965; see *e.g. R.* v. *Brixton Prison Governor, ex p. Keane* [1972] A.C. 204 (H.L.); Paul Jackson, " Anglo-Irish Extradition " (1967) 2 *Irish Jurist* 43.

[68] *R.* v. *Metropolitan Police Commissioner, ex p. Savundranayan* [1955] Crim.L.R. 309 (D.C.); *R.* v. *Brixton Prison Governor, ex p. Frenette, The Times*, March 19, 1952 (D.C.). To the list of extraditable offences have been added genocide (Genocide Act 1969) and hijacking (Hijacking Act 1971).

fugitive criminal if he thinks it would be unjust or oppressive to do so.[69]

Section 3 of the Act of 1870 provides that a person is not to be surrendered for " an offence of a political character." Thus in *Re Castioni*,[70] where a native of the Swiss canton of Ticino had committed murder during an insurrection and escaped to England, he was not surrendered. An offence is political only when there are two parties in the state each trying to impose its own government on the other. The mere fact that the prisoner is accused of murder in a political disturbance does not in itself justify the refusal of an order for his extradition, and an explosion caused by an anarchist is not a political offence within the Act.[71] In *Schtraks* v. *Government of Israel*,[72] where the charges involved were perjury and child-stealing, the case had become a political issue in Israel but that did not make it an offence of a political character. The idea behind the latter phrase, said Viscount Radcliffe, is that the fugitive is at odds with the state that applies for his extradition on some issue connected with the political control or government of the country. On the other hand in *Ex p. Kolczynski*,[73] where the members of a Polish trawler had taken charge of the ship, putting the master under restraint, and steered her into an English port because they feared they would be punished for their political opinions if they returned to Poland, they were successful in their application for habeas corpus, the Divisional Court holding that the offences were committed in order to escape from political tyranny.

If the magistrate commits a prisoner for surrender, he must be informed of his right to apply for habeas corpus. He may not be surrendered within fifteen days of the committal order, nor until a final decision on habeas corpus proceedings has been made (Extradition Act 1870, s. 11). If he is not conveyed out of the Kingdom within two months after committal, or if a writ of habeas corpus is issued after the decision thereon, any judge of a superior court may, on the prisoner's application and on proof that the Home Secretary has had reasonable notice of such application, order the discharge of the prisoner unless sufficient cause is shown to the contrary (s. 12). If the prisoner is not discharged, he is surrendered under the warrant of the Home Secretary.

---

69 *Atkinson* v. *United States Government* [1971] A.C. 197 (H.L.); *Royal Government of Greece* v. *Brixton Prison Governor* [1971] A.C. 250 (H.L.).
70 [1891] 1 Q.B. 149.
71 *Re Meunier* [1894] 2 Q.B. 415.
72 [1964] A.C. 556 (H.L.). See C. F. Amerasinghe, " The *Schtraks* Case, defining Political Offences and Extradition " (1965) 28 M.L.R. 27.
73 *R.* v. *Brixton Prison Governor, ex p. Kolczynski* [1955] 1 Q.B. 540.

Fugitive Offenders Acts

The Fugitive Offenders Act 1881 [74] made provision for the arrest and surrender of persons of any nationality accused of crimes to which the Act applied, when they fled from one part of Her Majesty's dominions to another part. The Act was a relic of the time when the Crown was indivisible throughout the Empire. It continued to apply not only between the United Kingdom (which for this purpose includes the Channel Islands and the Isle of Man) and colonies and other British dependencies,[75] but also between them and independent Commonwealth countries.[76] The Act did not exclude political offences (*Ex p. Enahoro* [77]), but a superior court might discharge a fugitive for various reasons.[78]

The Fugitive Offenders Act 1967,[79] based on an agreement among the Law Ministers of twenty Commonwealth countries that reciprocal and uniform arrangements should be made for offenders who flee from one part of the Commonwealth to another, replaces the Act of 1881. The new Act applies to the United Kingdom, the Channel Islands, the Isle of Man and (with modifications) to British dependencies. With regard to arrest, proceedings before the Bow Street Magistrate and applications to the High Court for habeas corpus, the Act is similar to the Extradition Act, but in other respects it is an improvement.

A person is not liable to be returned to another Commonwealth country unless the offence not only falls within the list of offences in Schedule 1 to the Act, but is punishable by the law of that country

---

74 Sir Kenneth Roberts-Wray, *Commonwealth and Colonial Law*, pp. 604–611; Paul O'Higgins, " Extradition within the Commonwealth " (1960) 9 I.C.L.Q. 486; Note on " The Enahoro Case " (1963) 12 I.C.L.Q. 1364; " Recent Practice under the Fugitive Offenders Acts " [1965] Crim.L.R. 133; S. A. de Smith, " Political Asylum and the Commonwealth " (1963) 16 *Parliamentary Affairs* 396.

75 The Act might be extended to protectorates and protected states by Order in Council under the Foreign Jurisdiction Act 1890; R. v. *Secretary of State for Home Affairs, ex p. Demetrious* [1966] 2 Q.B. 194.

76 As to the Republic of Ireland, see Paul O'Higgins, " Irish Extradition Law and Practice " (1958) B.Y.I.L. 274; *cf.* Backing of Warrants (Republic of Ireland) Act 1965, passed as a consequence of R. v. *Metropolitan Police Commissioner, ex p. Hammond* [1965] A.C. 810 (H.L.).

77 R. v. *Brixton Prison Governor, ex p. Enahoro (No. 2)* [1963] 2 Q.B. 455 (D.C.).

78 R. v. *Brixton Prison Governor, ex p. Naranjan Singh* [1962] 1 Q.B. 211; *cf. Zacharia* v. *Republic of Cyprus* [1963] A.C. 634 (H.L.), where the Home Secretary exercised his discretion not to hand the appellant over to Cyprus. And see *Armah* v. *Government of Ghana* [1968] A.C. 192 (H.L.).

79 See *Scheme Relating to the Rendition of Fugitive Offenders within the Commonwealth* (1966) Cmnd. 3008; Paul O'Higgins, " The Reform of Intra-Commonwealth Extradition " [1966] Crim.L.R. 361; Alec Samuels, " English Fugitive Offenders Act 1967 " (1968) 18 U.T.L.J. 198.

with imprisonment for twelve months, and also would be an offence against the law of the United Kingdom if it took place here (s. 3).[80] The Fugitive Offenders Act 1967 excludes offences of a political character, though not offences against the life or person of the Head of the Commonwealth. Further, a person may not be returned if the request for his return is in fact made in order to try him on account of his race, religion, nationality or political opinions; or if he might be prejudiced at his trial on account of his race, etc.[81]; or unless arrangements secure that he is not tried for a different (and not lesser) offence (s. 4).[82]

The High Court on an application for habeas corpus may discharge a person from custody if it appears that it would be unjust or oppressive to return him, because: (a) the offence is trivial; or (b) of the length of time since the offence is alleged to have been committed [83]; or (c) the accusation is not made in good faith in the interests of justice [84] (s. 8 (3)).

The Home Secretary may not make an order for return if it appears to him that it would be unjust or oppressive to do so, on the same grounds as section 8 (3) above; and he has a discretion not to order a person's return if he would be liable to the death penalty (s. 9).

---

[80] R. v. Brixton Prison Governor, ex p. Gardner [1968] 2 Q.B. 399 (D.C.); cf. R. v. Brixton Prison Governor, ex p. Rush [1969] 1 W.L.R. 165 (D.C.) (conspiracy completed outside Canada).

[81] Fernandez v. Singapore Government [1971] 1 W.L.R. 987 (H.L.).

[82] The Home Secretary has a discretion under section 4 with regard to dependencies.

[83] R. v. Brixton Prison Governor, ex p. Cook (1970) 114 S.J. 827 (D.C.) (eighteen months).

[84] R. v. Pentonville Prison Governor, ex p. Teja [1971] 2 Q.B. 274 (D.C.); [1971] 1 W.L.R. 678 (H.L.).

CHAPTER 22

OFFENCES AGAINST THE STATE

IN a wide sense, all crimes are offences against the state. The object of this chapter is to consider the more important of those criminal offences that have a political aspect and overlap the field of constitutional law, in so far as they are not dealt with in later chapters.[1]

Classification of offences against the State

Offences of a public nature are usually classified in the following manner:

(i) *Offences against the Crown and government.* These include treason, misprision of treason, treason-felony, incitement to mutiny, sedition and disclosure of official secrets, which are described below; as well as illegal training and drilling, illegal wearing of uniforms, associating with military organisations and incitement to disaffection.

(ii) *Offences against public peace and morals.* These include blasphemy, obscene and defamatory libels, unlawful assembly, riot and public nuisance.

(iii) *Offences against public justice.* These include perjury, bribery, embracery and interference with witnesses, contempt of court, obstructing or resisting the police, and corrupt or illegal practices at elections.

(iv) *Offences connected with trade and commerce.* These include trading with the enemy, coinage offences and smuggling.

Treason

Treason is a betrayal (*trahison*) or breach of the faith and allegiance due to the Sovereign. Allegiance, as we have seen in the previous chapter, is correlative to protection. It is owed to the Crown by citizens of the United Kingdom and Colonies wherever they may be; by citizens of other Commonwealth countries and Irish citizens while they are in the United Kingdom[2]; and by aliens[3] while they are in

---

[1] See also Chaps. 24 and 25.

[2] Citizens of other Commonwealth countries which owe allegiance to the Queen as Queen also owe allegiance by the law of their respective countries. And see British Nationality Act 1948, s. 3.

[3] *Semble*, including civilian enemy aliens who remain at large within the realm by licence, and internees; *cf.* prisoners of war.

British territory by the Sovereign's licence, express or tacit. Foreign diplomatic representatives and members of foreign invading or occupying forces, however, do not owe allegiance. Although treason is still described in feudal language, the essence of the crime now is disloyalty to the state as a political entity rather than to the Sovereign as a person. Protection, as we have also seen, is not legally enforceable, and it has been held that aliens resident in the Sovereign's dominions may continue to owe allegiance even after protection is withdrawn.[4]

The earliest statute on the subject is the Treason Act 1351, which was supposed to be declaratory of the common law.[5] The statute is still in force with amendments, and constitutes the following offences high treason[6]: (i) compassing or imagining the death of the King,[7] Queen Consort,[8] or their eldest son and heir; or (ii) violating the King's consort or the King's eldest daughter unmarried or the wife of the King's eldest son and heir; or (iii) levying war against the King in his realm; or (iv) adhering to the King's enemies in his realm, giving them aid or comfort in the realm or elsewhere; or (v) slaying the Chancellor, Treasurer or the King's justices assigned to hear and determine, being in their places doing their offices.

Compassing or imagining the death of the Sovereign

The words " compass or imagine " import design, which must be manifested by an overt act. The following are overt acts according to Blackstone[9]: providing weapons, conspiring to imprison the King though not intending his death, or assembling and consulting to kill the King.

Levying of war in the realm

This has been held to include not only levying of war to dethrone the King, but also levying war to reform religion, remove councillors or redress grievances. Resistance to the royal forces by defending a castle against them is levying war, and so is an insurrection with an avowed design to pull down all chapels and the like. In *Damaree's*

---

[4] *De Jager* v. *Att.-Gen. of Natal* [1907] A.C. 326.

[5] See J. G. Bellamy, *The Law of Treason in England in the Later Middle Ages* (1970); G. P. Bodet, " Sir Edward Coke's *Third Institute*: a primer for treason defendants " (1971) 20 U.T.L.J. 469.

[6] Petit treason under this statute consisted of: (a) the killing of a master by his servant, (b) the killing of a husband by his wife, and (c) the killing of a prelate by his ecclesiastical inferior. Since 1828 these offences have been regarded as ordinary murder.

[7] A Queen Regnant, where the context so admits, is in the same position as a King.

[8] The consort of a Queen Regnant is not protected by the law of treason.

[9] Bl.Comm. IV, 74 *et seq.*

Case (1709) [10] Damaree and Purchas were convicted of treason for burning Nonconformist meeting-houses, the court being of opinion that the design was a general one against the state, and therefore a levying of war. Blackstone says that merely conspiring to levy war is not a treasonable levying of war, but that it constitutes compassing the King's death where it is pointed at the royal person or government. To enlist men in the realm to go to the aid of the King's enemies abroad is not levying war in the realm, but it may be brought under compassing the King's death and adhering to the King's enemies.

Adhering to the King's enemies

It is an offence under (iv) above either to give the King's enemies in his realm aid and comfort in his realm, or to give aid and comfort elsewhere to the King's enemies elsewhere. " Enemies " here means public belligerents as understood in international law, and not mere pirates or British rebels; but to aid the latter in the realm would constitute levying of war. Persons acting under duress as regards life or person cannot be convicted as traitors, provided that they leave the King's enemies at the first opportunity.

In *R.* v. *Lynch*,[11] where a British subject commanded an Irish brigade on the side of the Boers against the British forces, the court held that the words " adhering to the King's enemies in his realm " did not mean that the " accused person *being in the realm* has been adherent to the King's enemies *wherever they were*," to the exclusion of such a case as that before the court. So narrow a construction not only would enable an Englishman to engage with a foreign hostile power against his own country, so long as he took care to remain abroad, but also ignores the words " or elsewhere " in the same sentence of the section. *R.* v. *Lynch* also decided that section 6 of the Naturalisation Act 1870 did not enable a British subject to become naturalised in an enemy state in time of war, and, further, that the very act of purporting to become naturalised in those circumstances constituted an overt act of treason.

In *R.* v. *Casement* (1917) [12] it was decided that a subject may " adhere to the King's enemies in his realm " and so be found guilty of treason under the statute of 1351, whether the act complained of was committed within or outside the realm. In that case Sir Roger Casement, a British subject,[13] was found guilty on the ground that he went to Germany when the United Kingdom was at war with that

10 *R.* v. *Damaree* (1709) 15 St.Tr. 521.
11 [1903] 1 K.B. 444.
12 [1917] 1 K.B. 98.
13 An Irishman by birth: at that time the whole of Ireland was part of the United Kingdom.

country, and while there endeavoured to persuade Irish prisoners of war (who were British subjects) to join the enemy's forces and thus to assist the liberation of Ireland. The Court of Criminal Appeal had to interpret the statute of Edward III, which was written without punctuation, according to its meaning when it was passed.

It was resolved by the judges in 1707 [14] that a resident alien, who during a war with his native country returned there and adhered to the King's enemies, leaving his family and effects here, might be dealt with as a traitor: " For he came and settled here under the protection of the Crown; and though his person was removed for a time, his effects and family continued still under the same protection." The principle of this rule was extended by the House of Lords in *Joyce* v. *Director of Public Prosecutions* [15] to an alien who departed entirely from this country, but who was held in the particular circumstances to have remained under the protection of the Crown. William Joyce (popularly known as " Lord Haw-Haw ") was brought back from Germany at the end of the last war and charged with high treason in that he, while owing allegiance to the Crown, adhered to the King's enemies elsewhere than in the realm by broadcasting Nazi propaganda. It transpired that although he had obtained a British passport by falsely declaring himself to be a British subject, he was in fact a citizen of the United States. The House of Lords held that his possession of a British passport extended to him outside the realm that protection of the Crown which is the counterpart of the duty of allegiance; and that having continued to avail himself of that protection he continued to owe allegiance, and was properly convicted of treason. Treason is not confined—as had often been stated—to British subjects and to aliens within the realm, but it may be committed by anyone who, at the material time, owes allegiance to the Crown. The decision certainly stretched the doctrine of protection to extreme limits, and Joyce's allegiance was deduced as a consequence of that protection.[16]

On the other hand, *mens rea* is required for treason as for other crimes. In *R.* v. *Ahlers* (1915) [17] the accused was German Consul at Sunderland, and it was therefore part of his ordinary duty to give his compatriots assistance, monetary and otherwise. He took steps on the outbreak of war in 1914 to assist German subjects of military age to return home to fight in the German army. A statutory Order in Council limited the time for the departure of alien enemies: of

---

14 Foster's *Crown Cases* (3rd ed.) p. 185.
15 [1946] A.C. 347.
16 For criticisms of the decision, see Cobbett's *Cases on International Law* (6th ed. W. L. Walker), i, p. 199; Glanville L. Williams, " The Correlation of Allegiance and Protection " (1948) 10 C.L.J. 54; S. C. Briggs, " Treason and the Trial of William Joyce " (1947) 7 U.T.L.J. 162.
17 [1915] 1 K.B. 616 (C.C.A.).

this the accused knew nothing, but he believed he was acting in accordance with international law. His conviction for treason by adhering to the King's enemies was quashed for lack of proof that he was aware that he was assisting the King's enemies.

Slaying the Chancellor, etc.

As the Lord Chancellor and judges represent the Sovereign in court, Blackstone considered them entitled to equal protection and justified this section of the statute accordingly. However, attempted murder of the Chancellor and judges in court is, according to the same authority, not treason. These technical treasons could conveniently be abolished and dealt with as murder.

Treason Acts subsequent to 1351

The Treason Act 1495 provided that a subject who obeyed a usurper while he was occupying the throne would not later be charged with treason after the lawful King had regained the throne, but no protection was given to any person who thereafter declined from his allegiance.[18]

Under the Treason Act 1702, endeavouring to deprive or hinder any person next in succession to the Throne under the Act of Settlement from succeeding thereto, and maliciously and directly attempting the same by any overt act, is treason. The Succession to the Crown Act 1707 made it treason maliciously and directly by writing or print to maintain and affirm that any other person has any right to the Crown other than in accordance with the Act of Settlement, or that Parliament has not power to make laws to bind the Crown and the descent thereof.

Judicial interpretation of the statute of 1351 relating to compassing the King's death led to a number of " constructive treasons." [19] Some of these were enacted as treasons by the Treason Act 1795 [20] which covered compassing, imagining, devising or intending the death, wounding or imprisonment of the King, whether within the realm or without, provided such compassing, etc. was expressed in writing or by any overt act.

[18] *Madzimbamuto* v. *Lardner-Burke* [1969] 1 A.C. 645 (P.C.); A. M. Honoré, " Allegiance and the Usurper " (1967) C.L.J. 214; *cf.* Taswell-Langmead, *English Constitutional History* (11th ed. Plucknett) pp. 224–225, 446–447.

[19] *e.g.* R. v. *Hardy* (1794) 24 St.Tr. 199; R. v. *Horne Tooke* (1794) 25 St.Tr. 1. See further, Stephen, *History of the Criminal Law*, Vol. II; Holdsworth, *History of English Law*, Vol. VIII, pp. 309–322.

[20] A temporary Act made permanent by the Treason Act 1817.

Trial and punishment

The punishment prescribed for treason is now death by hanging or, under royal warrant, by beheading.[21] Formerly a male traitor was hanged and quartered, after being drawn on a hurdle to the place of execution [22]; a female traitor was burnt. Until the Forfeiture Act 1870 conviction was followed by forfeiture and corruption of blood.

Treason or misprision of treason committed abroad is triable in England.[23]

Treason committed within the realm must be prosecuted within three years after its commission, except in the case of designing or attempting the assassination of the Queen.[24] Bail cannot be granted by magistrates, but only by a Secretary of State or a judge of the Queen's Bench Division.

The procedure in all cases of treason and misprision of treason has been assimilated—except for the time limit and the sentence—to the procedure in cases of murder.[25]

Misprision of treason

Misprision of treason is the bare knowledge and concealment of treason, without the assent thereto which is necessary to constitute the crime of treason (Treason Act 1554). At common law mere concealment of treason was deemed to constitute assent, and there was no distinction in treason between principles and accessories, so that misprision itself amounted to treason. Misprision under the Act of 1554 consists in knowing of the treasonable design, its nature and would-be perpetrators, and failing to disclose the information to some responsible public officer such as a High Court judge or justice of the peace. Misprision of treason is a non-arrestable offence punishable by imprisonment for life.

Treason-felony

By the Treason Felony Act 1848 a person is guilty of an arrestable offence if, by writing or overt act within or without the United Kingdom, he compasses, imagines, devises or intends to deprive or depose the Queen from the style, honour or royal name of the imperial crown of the United Kingdom, or of any other of Her Majesty's

---

21 Treason Act 1814. Beheading is in practice obsolete. Among other offences for which civilians are punishable with death are piracy accompanied by any act that may endanger life (Piracy Act 1837), and arson of H.M. ships or dockyards (Dockyards Protection Act 1772).

22 These barbarous practices were gradually discarded and were finally abolished by the Forfeiture Act 1870.

23 Treason Act 1543.

24 Treason Act 1695.

25 Treason Act 1945; Criminal Law Act 1967, s. 12.

dominions and countries; or to levy war against Her Majesty within any part of the United Kingdom, in order to compel her to change her measures or counsels, or in order to intimidate or overcome both Houses or either House of Parliament; or to move any foreigner with force to invade the United Kingdom or any other of Her Majesty's dominions. Some of these offences had been enacted as treason by the Treason Act 1795 (*supra*). The Treason Felony Act does not affect the Act of 1795, but provides an alternative remedy in some cases. Its object was partly to cover Ireland, and partly to encourage juries to convict, which they had been loath to do in recent treason trials.

The maximum punishment under the Act of 1848 is imprisonment for life. If a person is indicted for treason-felony and the offence turns out to be treason, he may be convicted of treason-felony.

Attempt to alarm or injure the Sovereign

An attempt to alarm or injure the Sovereign by discharging or aiming or producing a gun, whether loaded or not, at or near the person of Her Majesty was made an offence punishable by imprisonment for seven years by the Treason Act 1842, after an incident involving Queen Victoria.

Sedition

The word " sedition " covers three indictable but non-arrestable common law offences: the publication of a seditious libel, the uttering of seditious words, and conspiracy to do an act in furtherance of a seditious intention.[26] A seditious intention is necessary for all three offences. It is an intention to bring into hatred or contempt, or to excite disaffection against, the person of the Sovereign, or the government and Constitution of the United Kingdom as by law established, or either House of Parliament or the administration of justice, or to excite Her Majesty's subjects to attempt, otherwise than by lawful means, the alteration of any matter in Church or state by law established, or to raise discontent or disaffection among Her Majesty's subjects, or to promote feelings of ill will or hostility between different classes of her subjects (*R. v. Burns, per* Cave J.[27]). On the other hand, it is not seditious to show that the government has been mistaken, or to point out defects in the Constitution, or to excite people to attempt by lawful means the alteration of the law relating to Church or state, or to point out (with a view to their removal)

---

[26] Stephen, *History of the Criminal Law*, Vol. II, Chap. 24.
[27] 16 Cox 355; approving Stephen, *Digest of the Criminal Law* (see 8th ed. art. 114).

matters which produce feelings of hatred or ill will between classes of Her Majesty's subjects (*ibid.*).

Seditious libel is the publication in permanent form of matter which is of a seditious nature. The truth of a statement is no defence to a criminal charge if it is seditious.[28] More will be said about seditious libel in Chapter 24.

A conspiracy is formed when two or more persons combine to do an unlawful act, or to do a lawful act by unlawful means. A seditious conspiracy is a conspiracy having a seditious object.[29]

Official Secrets [30]

The Official Secrets Act 1911, s. 1 (1), makes it an arrestable offence if any person, for any purpose prejudicial to the safety or interests of the state: (a) approaches or enters a prohibited place; (b) makes a sketch or plan, etc. calculated or intended to be, or which might be, useful to an enemy; or (c) obtains or communicates to any other person any sketch, document, or information, etc. calculated or intended to be, or which might be, useful to an enemy.[31] A purpose prejudicial to the safety or interests of the state may be inferred from the circumstances (s. 1 (2)). In *Chandler* v. *Director of Public Prosecutions* [32] members of the Committee of 100 were convicted under section 1 for entering an RAF station, which was a prohibited place. Their intention was to sit in front of aircraft so as to prevent them from taking off; their ultimate object was to bring about nuclear disarmament, which they considered would be beneficial to this country. The House of Lords, upholding the convictions, held: first, that the section (in spite of the marginal note: " Penalties for spying ") covered sabotage; secondly, that the question whether the purpose of the accused was " prejudicial to the safety or interests of the state " was a question for the court on hearing evidence from the Crown as to what were the interests of the government, and not a question for the jury on which the accused could give evidence of their ultimate object.

A person commits an offence under the 1911 Act if he communicates a sketch, etc. of a prohibited place to an unauthorised

---

28 *R.* v. *Burdett* (1821) 4 B. & Ald. 314.
29 *R.* v. *Hunt* (1820) 3 B. & Ald. 566; *O'Connell* v. *R.* (1844) 11 Cl. & Fin. 155.
30 See D. G. T. Williams, *Not in the Public Interest* (1965).
31 *R.* v. *Britten* [1969] 1 W.L.R. 151 (C.A.); deterrent sentences may be appropriate.
32 [1964] A.C. 763. The decision was clearly right according to the method of interpretation used by the courts; but it has been pointed out that this interpretation of section 1 is inconsistent with statements made by Lord Chancellors and Attorneys-General in parliamentary debates on Official Secrets Bills: Donald Thompson, " The Committee of 100 and the Official Secrets Act 1911 " [1963] P.L. 201.

person, or retains it after he should have handed it over (s. 2 (1)). This suggests carelessness rather than guilty intent. It is also an offence for a person to receive any such sketch, etc. knowing or having reasonable grounds to believe that it is communicated in contravention of the Act, unless he proves that the communication was contrary to his choice (s. 2 (2)). The burden of proof is on a passive receiver. A " prohibited place " includes any defence works, arsenal, naval or air force station, camp, ship or aircraft belonging to or occupied by the Crown (s. 3). It is also an offence to harbour spies (s. 7). Prosecution under the Acts is by or with the consent of the Attorney-General (s. 8). The Acts apply to offences committed in any part of Her Majesty's dominions, and to offences committed anywhere by British officers or subjects (s. 10). A chief officer of police may, with the permission of a Secretary of State, authorise a police officer not below the rank of inspector to require a suspect to give information (Official Secrets Act 1939).[33]

The Official Secrets Act 1920, s. 1 (1), provides that it is an offence to wear an unauthorised uniform, make a false declaration, forge a permit or impersonate a government official for the purpose of gaining admission to a prohibited place, or for any other purpose prejudicial to the safety or interests of the state. It is also an offence for a person to retain an official document for a purpose prejudicial to the safety or interests of the state, or to allow any other person to have possession of an official document issued for his use alone (s. 1 (2)). Section 2 provides that communication with a foreign agent is evidence of obtaining, or attempting to obtain, information calculated or intended to be useful to an enemy contrary to section 1 of the Act of 1911.[34] Thus preparatory acts, which are not even attempts, may be punishable. Section 3 provides that no person " in the vicinity of " a prohibited place shall obstruct or interfere with a military or police guard. In *Adler* v. *George* [35] it was held that such obstruction *in* a prohibited place, *viz.* an RAF airfield, was an offence.

A common objection to the Official Secrets Acts is that " interests of the state " may be interpreted by the prosecution to mean the interests of the Civil Service, and it has been suggested that " official secrets " should be confined to state security. A Departmental Committee has recommended that section 2 of the 1911 Act should be repealed and replaced by an Official Information Act, which would

---

[33] *Cf. Lewis* v. *Cattle* [1938] 2 K.B. 454 (official secret, but no question of state security), decided under the previous Acts.
[34] The archives of a foreign embassy in London can be the subject-matter of a charge under the Acts: *R.* v. *A.B.* [1941] 1 K.B. 455.
[35] [1964] 2 Q.B. 7 (D.C.).

make it an offence to leak *classified* information whose disclosure would affect such matters as defence, internal security, criminal activities and law enforcement.[36]

Offensive weapons

The law relating to the possession, handling and distribution of firearms was consolidated by the Firearms Act 1968, although penalties have since been increased. It is an offence to possess any firearm or ammunition without a certificate from a chief constable of police; to be in possession of any firearm or ammunition with intent by means thereof to endanger life or to cause serious injury to property; to use or attempt to use a firearm or imitation firearm with intent to resist or prevent lawful arrest; to be in possession of such weapon when committing, aiding or attempting to commit a number of offences under various other Acts, *e.g.* criminal damage, theft and offences against the person; and also to carry firearms with intent to commit a serious offence or to resist or prevent arrest, to carry firearms in a public place, and to trespass with firearms in a building or on land.

The manufacture, possession and use of explosives are controlled by the Explosives Acts 1883–1923.

By the Prevention of Crime Act 1953, which was passed to cope with " cosh-boys," it is an offence to carry an offensive weapon in a public place without lawful authority or reasonable excuse, the burden of proof of the latter lying on the accused.[37] Constables may arrest for this offence without warrant.

The Restriction of Offensive Weapons Acts 1959 and 1961 make it an offence to manufacture, sell, hire or give, or to offer or expose for sale or hire, a flick knife or gravity knife.

Public mischief [38]

The Criminal Law Act 1967, s. 5 (2), makes it an offence to cause a wasteful employment of the police by knowingly making to any person a false report tending to show that an offence has been committed, or to give rise to apprehension for the safety of any person or property, or tending to show that he has information material to

---

[36] *Departmental Committee on Section 2 of the Official Secrets Act 1911* (Franks), (1972) Cmnd. 5104.

[37] See *R.* v. *Jura* [1954] 1 Q.B. 503 (C.C.A.). *Cf. R.* v. *Petrie* [1961] 1 W.L.R. 358 (C.C.A.), weapon not offensive *per se*; *R.* v. *Cugullere* [1961] 1 W.L.R. 858 (C.C.A.), knowledge of having.

[38] W. T. S. Stallybrass, " Public Mischief " (1933) 49 L.Q.R. 183–191; Sir Alfred Denning, *Freedom under the Law* (1949) pp. 40–43; Glanville Williams, " Public Mischief and Conspiracy " *The Law in Action*, I, p. 67; G. McCarthy, " Public Mischief and the Crank " (1956) 30 A.L.J. 389.

a police inquiry. Proceedings may be instituted only by or with the consent of the Director of Public Prosecutions. This provision covers the most obvious example of the common law offence of causing a public mischief, as in *R. v. Manley*,[39] where a woman was convicted of effecting a public mischief because she made false statements to the police to the effect that she had been the victim of a robbery, thus causing them to waste their time in futile investigations. Liability of individuals for effecting a public mischief at common law was probably limited to interfering with the course of justice, including the investigation of crime by the police, and defrauding the public revenue.[40] There are undoubtedly kinds of conduct like that in *R. v. Manley* which ought to be punishable, but it is to be preferred that both the conduct and the punishment should be specified by statute, as was done in the case of false fire alarms and false telephone messages,[41] and now by the Criminal Law Act 1967.

Most of the convictions for " public mischief " have been cases of conspiracy. Thus in *R. v. Bassey* (1931) [42] the Court of Criminal Appeal upheld a conviction for conspiracy to effect a public mischief by attempting to obtain admission to an Inn of Court as a student although not qualified for admission; and in *R. v. Newland* [43] the court upheld a conviction for conspiracy to effect a public mischief by conspiring to distribute on the home market decorated pottery which was intended by statutory order for export. Lord Goddard C.J. said that *R. v. Manley* was wrongly decided, and the safe course was no longer to follow it : public mischief should be regarded, he said, as part of the law of conspiracy.

In *Shaw* v. *D.P.P.*[44] the House of Lords held that a conspiracy to corrupt public morals by the publication of *The Ladies' Directory* was a common law misdemeanour. In *R. v. Bhagwan* [45] where a Commonwealth citizen landed on a lonely beach, the House of Lords held that there was no duty under the Commonwealth Immigrants Act 1962 [46] to present oneself to an immigration officer for examina-

---

39 [1933] 1 K.B. 529 (C.C.A.).
40 *R. v. Hudson* [1956] 2 Q.B. 252 (making false statements to the prejudice of the Crown and public revenue with intent to defraud). *Cf. R. v. Leese, The Times,* September 19 and 22, 1936 (C.C.A.), where the printers and publishers were convicted of a public mischief in publishing statements reflecting on the Jewish community.
41 False Alarms of Fire Act 1895; Post Office Act 1953; *Police v. Brown* [1956] Crim.L.R. 568.
42 22 Cr.App.R. 160.
43 [1954] 1 Q.B. 158. The accused fell within the spirit but not the letter of the order.
44 [1962] A.C. 220. See A. L. Goodhart, " The Shaw Case: The Law and Public Morals " (1961) 77 L.Q.R. 560.
45 [1972] A.C. 60. And see *Joshua* v. *The Queen* [1955] A.C. 121 (P.C.).
46 The law in this respect was altered by the Commonwealth Immigrants Act 1968.

tion unless required by such officer to do so. It was no offence to do, or to agree with others to do, acts which—though not prohibited by statute or criminal or tortious—are calculated to evade the purpose of the Act. There was no criminal conspiracy in this case. Their Lordships criticised the dictum of Lord Goddard in *R.* v. *Newland* (*supra*). The House of Lords applied *Shaw* v. *D.P.P.* in *R.* v. *Knuller*,[47] but disclaimed any doctrine that the courts have a general or residual power to create new offences or to widen existing ones. There are *dicta* suggesting that conspiracy to corrupt public morals is one kind of, or similar to, conspiracy to effect a public mischief. In *R.* v. *Foy*[48] the Court of Appeal said that a judge may direct the jury that conspiracy to indemnify a person of his bail is a public mischief, but that on other charges where questions of morality arise, it may be necessary to ask the jury whether conduct amounts to a public mischief.

Racial hatred and discrimination [49]

The Race Relations Act 1965, s. 6, created the offence of incitement of racial hatred by publishing or distributing [50] written matter, or using words in a public place, or at a public meeting, which are threatening, abusive or insulting. There must be the intention and likelihood of stirring up hatred against any section of the public distinguished by colour, race, or ethnic or national origins. Prosecution in England and Wales is only by or with the consent of the Attorney-General.[51] The various forms of sedition would cover much of the ground, but sedition is indictable only and might require incitement to violence. It was hoped that in practice the conciliation provisions (*infra*) would be the more important.

Sections 1–5 of the 1965 Act make provisions to *prevent* racial discrimination. It is declared unlawful for a proprietor or manager of specified places of public resort (*e.g.* eating places, places of enter-

---

[47] *R.* v. *Knuller (Publishing, Printing and Promotions) Ltd.* [1972] 2 Q.B. 179 (publication of advertisements inviting readers to meet the advertisers for the purpose of homosexual practices); conspiracy to corrupt public morals not affected by Sexual Offences Act 1967, s. 1.

[48] *The Times*, June 1, 1972.

[49] G. Bindman and A. Lester, *Race and Law* (1972); D. G. T. Williams, " Racial Incitement and Public Order " [1966] Crim.L.R. 320; A. Dickey, " Prosecution under the Race Relations Act 1965, s. 6 " [1968] Crim.L.R. 489; A. Avins, " Freedom of Choice in Public and Private Accommodations in British Commonwealth Law " (1968) Jur.Rev. 254; B. A. Hepple, " Race Relations Act 1968 " (1969) 32 M.L.R. 186.

[50] *R.* v. *Britton* [1967] 2 Q.B. 51 (C.A.).

[51] *R.* v. *Jordan* [1967] Crim.L.R. 483 (D.C.); *Thorne* v. *BBC* [1967] Crim.L.R. 1104 (C.A.); *R.* v. *Malik* [1968] 1 W.L.R. 353 (C.A.).

tainment and public transport) to practise discrimination on the ground
of colour, race, or ethnic or national origins, by refusing or neglecting
to afford access to the place or the same facilities or services as are
offered to other persons (s. 1). A *Race Relations Board* is constituted,
which is in turn to constitute *Local Conciliation Committees* to consider complaints, and to try to settle differences and secure that contra-
ventions shall not be repeated. If the committee cannot secure a
settlement or if the assurances are not complied with, the committee
is to report to the Race Relations Board, which may in turn report
to the Attorney-General.[52] The Attorney-General may bring proceedings in a county court for an injunction against infringements
of section 1. Breach of injunction would be contempt of court.
Section 5 deals with discriminatory restrictions on the disposal of
tenancies.

The Race Relations Act 1968 declares that discrimination is unlawful on grounds of colour, race, or ethnic or national origins in
the provision of goods, facilities or services; employment; trade unions,
employers' or trade organisations; or the disposal of housing accommodation, and business or other premises (ss. 1–5).[53] There are
exceptions for the occupiers of small houses and small firms (ss. 7
and 8). Section 6 makes it unlawful to publish or display any
advertisement or notice indicating an intention to discriminate, whether
or not the act to which the advertisement or notice refers would be
unlawful under any of the other sections. Thus a landlady may
discriminate in the house where she lives against taking coloured
lodgers, but she must not advertise her intention to do so. It might
be an offence to advertise for a Scottish cook to make porridge, an
Indian cook to make curry or a Moorish actor to play Othello.[54]

Under the 1968 Act the Race Relations Board may bring proceedings in a county court for an injunction, declaration and/or
damages.[55] The Secretary of State or the Race Relations Board will
not proceed with a complaint if it is or could be the subject of a
complaint to an industrial tribunal; but when an industrial tribunal
has found that action taken against the complainant constitutes an
unfair industrial practice, such as unfair dismissal, and was taken by
reason of the complainant's colour, etc., then the Secretary of State

52 Or the Lord Advocate in Scotland.
53 *Ealing London Borough Council* v. *Race Relations Board* [1972] A.C. 342 (H.L.),
housing, British nationality not " national origins "; *R.R.B.* v. *Charter* [1973] 2
W.L.R. 299 (H.L.), discrimination by private club not unlawful.
54 See A. Dickey, " ' Scottish cook ' Affair " (1969) 119 New L.J. 1097.
55 The Board, in its first successful action in Birmingham county court, obtained a
declaration that a working men's club acted unlawfully in barring Mrs. Floribel
Apparicio, a Jamaican, from a Christmas party: *The Times*, April 10, 1970.

or the Board may take certain steps under the 1968 Act.[56]   The
1968 Act binds the Crown, although no injunction may be issued
against it; and police constables are treated for the purposes of the
Act as if they were employed by the police authority (s. 27).   A
Community Relations Commission is established to encourage har-
monious community relations, and to advise the Secretary of State
(s. 25).

[56] Industrial Relations Act 1971, s. 149.

CHAPTER 23

FREEDOM OF PERSON AND PROPERTY

Individual rights generally [1]

As has been seen in Chapter Two, there are no strictly "fundamental" rights in English law, owing to the supremacy of Parliament and the absence of a written constitution with entrenched provisions. Most of the "rights" of individuals that are of constitutional importance are more strictly liberties and immunities. The liberties of the individual in English law are residual: they represent the freedom left over when we have subtracted the limitations imposed by statute, common law and local by-laws. No legal system can allow absolute rights. There must be a balance—a compromise—between the interests of an individual and the interests of other individuals and society as a whole. The difference between liberty and licence is crucial. The strength of English law lies in its provision of adequate remedies for most [2] infringements of legitimate interests, notably habeas corpus, injunction and damages.

The motives behind the current call for a new Bill of Rights are largely emotional or political, rather than legal. On the one hand some people want there to be practically no restrictions on, for example, the Press or demonstrations. On the other hand, others resent government "interference," such as planning restrictions on property. Two difficulties in drawing up a Bill of Rights are selection of the rights to be included, and the drafting of the principles, their limitations and exceptions. More fundamental in our system is the problem of how (if at all) such a declaration could impose restrictions on the legislature, in view of the generally accepted doctrine that Parliament cannot bind itself.

I. FREEDOM OF THE PERSON [3]

"The right to personal liberty as understood in England," says Dicey,[4] "means in substance a person's right not to be subjected to

---

[1] O. Hood Phillips, *Reform of the Constitution* (1970) Chaps. 6 and 7; *Human Rights in the United Kingdom* (Central Office of Information, 1967).

[2] But English law does not recognise a right of "privacy," although the ground is partly covered by trespass, nuisance, defamation, breach of confidence (*Gee* v. *Pritchard* (1818) 2 Swan. 402), and self-help. See *Report of the Committee on Privacy* (1972) Cmnd. 5012; "Report on Privacy" *Justice* (1970); G. D. S. Taylor, "Privacy and the Public" (1971) 34 M.L.R. 288; J. Jacob, "Right of Privacy" (1969) 119 New L.J. 205.

For footnotes 3 and 4 please see p. 398.

imprisonment, arrest, or other physical coercion in any manner that does not admit of legal justification." It is " one of the pillars of liberty," said Lord Atkin in *Liversidge* v. *Anderson*,[5] that " in English law every imprisonment is prima facie unlawful, and that it is for a person directing imprisonment to justify his act." The justification is usually that the person is arrested and detained without bail pending trial in court on a charge of crime, or that after trial by a court of competent jurisdiction he has been convicted and sentenced to imprisonment or some other kind of detention provided by statute. Other kinds of lawful detention [6] are committal for contempt of court or Parliament, custody pending deportation or extradition, children in need of care and protection, and imprisonment for failing to make certain payments in spite of having had the means to do so.[7] There is no preventive detention in English law, except under statutory war regulations.[8]

Redress for wrongful deprivation of liberty

For wrongful deprivation of liberty the following remedies are available: (i) civil proceedings for damages in respect of malicious prosecution, false imprisonment or assault; (ii) criminal prosecution for assault, battery, or in respect of false imprisonment itself; (iii) application for a writ of habeas corpus to obtain release; (iv) appeal against conviction or sentence to a higher court; (v) in appropriate cases an order of certiorari or prohibition.

The common law allows a person to use a reasonable amount of force in self-defence to resist unlawful arrest without warrant, whether by a police constable or private citizen; but it is inadvisable to resist arrest by a police constable as the arrest may well turn out to be lawful.

The police have power at common law without warrant to search the person of someone who is arrested.

---

[3] Dicey, *Law of the Constitution* (10th ed. E. C. S. Wade) Chap. 5; Sir Alfred Denning, *Freedom under the Law*, Chap. 1; R. F. V. Heuston, *Essays in Constitutional Law* (2nd ed. 1964) Chaps. 5 and 6; H. Street, *Freedom, the Individual and the Law* (3rd ed. 1972) Chap. 1.
[4] Dicey, *op. cit.* pp. 207–208.
[5] [1942] A.C. 206 (H.L.).
[6] The Ecclesiastical Jurisdiction Measure 1963, s. 82 (4), provides that " No person shall be liable to suffer imprisonment in consequence of being excommunicated."
[7] The Debtors Act 1869 abolished imprisonment for debt with certain exceptions, *e.g.* non-contractual penalties, sums recoverable summarily before magistrates, and certain defaults by trustees, solicitors and bankrupts, provided that the debtor has had the means to pay. The Administration of Justice Act 1970 attempts to do away with such " imprisonment for debt " by extending the use of attachment of earnings orders.
[8] And statutory emergency regulations in Northern Ireland.

Arrest

(a) *By warrant*

No man may be arrested or imprisoned except under due process of law (Petition of Right 1628 [9]). Where a person is suspected of serious crime, the usual course is for the police to apply to a magistrate for a warrant for his arrest. That warrant can only be granted on sworn information. Sufficient particulars of the charge must be specified in the warrant in non-technical language. A " general warrant," *i.e.* one which does not name the person to be arrested, is illegal. In *Leach* v. *Money* (1765) [10] a Secretary of State (Lord Halifax) had issued a warrant to search for the authors, printers and publishers of No. 45 of the *North Briton*, alleged to contain seditious libels, and to apprehend them together with their papers. Leach, who was arrested but released as he was not the printer, obtained damages against the King's messenger for trespass and false imprisonment. " There is no case for these uncertain warrants," said Lord Mansfield C.J.; " . . . The magistrates ought to judge and give definite directions to the officer as to the person to be arrested." In *Wilkes* v. *Lord Halifax* (1769) [11] John Wilkes, a Member of Parliament and the author of No. 45 of the *North Briton* which strongly criticised the King's speech on the prorogation of Parliament and the recent Peace of Paris, eventually obtained £4,000 damages against Lord Halifax, the Secretary of State under whose general warrant he was arrested and his papers seized.

In minor cases a summons is usually applied for, and if the person summoned does not appear a warrant for his arrest can then be issued. Otherwise, for minor offences a warrant for arrest may not be issued unless the offence is indictable or punishable with imprisonment, or the defendant's address is not sufficiently established for a summons to be issued on him. [12]

(b) *Without warrant*

The Criminal Law Act 1967, s. 2 [13] provides that: (a) Any person may arrest without warrant anyone who is, or whom he with reasonable cause suspects to be, in the act of committing an arrestable offence. [14]

---

[9] Relying on Magna Carta (9 Hen. III, c .29).

[10] 3 Burr. 1692, 1742; 19 St.Tr. 1001; Holdsworth, *History of English Law*, Vol. X, pp. 659 *et seq.*

[11] 19 St.Tr. 1407, summing-up by Wilmot C.J.

[12] Criminal Justice Act 1967, s. 24.

[13] This Act was based on *Felonies and Misdemeanours*: Criminal Law Revision Committee, 7th Report, (1965) Cmnd. 2659. Section 2 clarified, and in some respects amended, the law, but it does not provide a comprehensive code of arrest.

[14] *i.e.* an offence for which the sentence is fixed by law (*e.g.* treason, murder), or for which a person is liable by statute on first conviction to imprisonment for five years, and an attempt to commit such offence.

(b) Where an arrestable offence has been committed, any person may arrest without warrant anyone who is, or whom he with reasonable cause suspects to be, guilty of the offence. (c) When a constable [15] with reasonable cause suspects that an arrestable offence has been committed, he may arrest without warrant anyone whom he with reasonable cause suspects to be guilty of the offence. (d) A constable may arrest without warrant any person who is, or whom he with reasonable cause suspects to be, about to commit an arrestable offence. This section does not prejudice any power of arrest conferred otherwise by law, e.g. the power to arrest without warrant a person who causes a breach of the peace (formerly a common law misdemeanour).

Section 3 of the Criminal Law Act 1967 provides that a person may use such force as is reasonable in the circumstances in the prevention of crime,[16] or in effecting or assisting in the lawful arrest of offenders or suspected offenders. This provision replaces the relevant rules of common law, and is not restricted to arrestable offences.

There are also a number of statutes giving power, usually to constables but sometimes to members of the public generally or to specified persons, to arrest without warrant for particular offences.[17]

Where a person exercises a power of arrest without warrant, he should take the arrested person before a justice of the peace or a police officer as soon as reasonably possible. It was held in *John Lewis & Co. Ltd.* v. *Tims* [18] that where the appellant company's private detectives took the respondent to its office in order that the circumstances of her arrest might be explained to the managing director and to obtain authority to prosecute for theft, that was not an unreasonable delay before handing her over to the police, and the appellants were therefore not liable for false imprisonment.

A person who is arrested without a warrant must be informed of the true ground of the arrest, although the information need not be given in technical language, nor indeed is any such information necessary if in the circumstances the reason for the arrest is obvious. Every person is prima facie entitled to his freedom, and is only bound to submit to restraint if he knows why it is claimed to impose restraint upon him (*Christie* v. *Leachinsky* [19]).

---

[15] A justice of the peace probably had the same common law powers of arrest as a constable.

[16] It may be that no force by a private individual would be reasonable unless it was an arrestable offence or breach of the peace or in defence of person or property.

[17] e.g. Official Secrets Act 1911; Prevention of Crimes Act 1953; Sexual Offences Act 1956; Dangerous Drugs Act 1965; Theft Act 1968; Criminal Damage Act 1971. Power to arrest without warrant may also be given by local Acts.

[18] [1952] A.C. 676 (H.L.).

[19] [1947] A.C. 573 (H.L.); cf. R. v. *Kulynycz* [1971] 1 Q.B. 367 (C.A.).

Bail [20]

In many cases a person who is arrested on a criminal charge is released by the court [21] on bail pending the trial, that is to say, he enters into recognisances (a written promise binding him under penalty) to appear in court on a certain day, and he may also be required to find other persons as sureties for his appearance.[22] Magistrates have generally a discretion whether to grant bail to a person committed for trial; but they may not grant bail in cases of treason.[23] A magistrates' court must grant bail to a person charged with a summary offence punishable with not more than six months' imprisonment if it adjourns the trial or remands him for further inquiries, unless he is unable to provide recognisances or acceptable sureties.[24] A person refused bail may apply to a High Court judge, and he must be informed of this right. Bail may also be granted by the higher courts in the course of their proceedings or pending an appeal.

Bail can be fixed at any amount, but the Bill of Rights provides that bail shall not be " excessive." In such cases as theft, fraud or smuggling, the amount of money involved may be very large, with a corresponding danger that the accused may leave the country. If the accused objects to the amount of bail he may appeal to a judge in chambers, or in appropriate cases may apply for a writ of habeas corpus.[25]

Writ of habeas corpus [26]

In origin this writ, which is found in Edward I's reign, was merely a command by the court to someone to bring before itself persons whose presence was necessary to some judicial proceeding. In other words, it was " originally intended not to get people out of prison, but

20 A. M. Qasem, " Bail and Personal Liberty " (1952) 30 Can.Bar Rev. 378; A. Samuels, " Bail Principles " (1966) 116 New L.J. 1269; M. Zander, " Bail : A Re-Appraisal " [1967] Crim.L.R. 25, 100, 128.
21 A police officer may grant bail to appear at a police station where a person has been taken into custody without a warrant and inquiries cannot be completed forthwith; Magistrates' Courts Act 1952, s. 38; see R. v. Jones, ex p. Moore (1965) 109 S.J. 175; The Times, January 29, 1965 (D.C.).
22 The bailment originally consisted in the accused being handed over into the custody of his sureties.
23 Magistrates' Courts Act 1952.
24 Criminal Justice Act 1967, s. 18.
25 Ex p. Thomas [1956] Crim.L.R. 119 (D.C.). Cf. R. v. Governor of Brixton Prison, ex p. Goswani, The Times, December 22, 1966; Ex p. Goswami (1966) 111 S.J. 17 (D.C.): bail of £50,000 not too high, although the defendant could not find sureties.
26 For the history of the writ, see Blackstone, Comm. III, pp. 121 et seq.; Holdsworth, History of English Law, Vol. IX, pp. 104–125; E. Jenks, " The Story of Habeas Corpus " (1902) 18 L.Q.R. 64; Maxwell Cohen, " Some Considerations on the Origins of Habeas Corpus " (1938) 16 Can.Bar Rev. 92.

to put them in it." [27]   Habeas corpus [28] was a "prerogative" writ, that is, one issued by the King against his officers to compel them to exercise their functions properly.   In the form *habeas corpus ad subjiciendum* it came to be available, under certain conditions, to private individuals.   In the seventeenth century members of the parliamentary opposition imprisoned by command of the King availed themselves of the writ to seek release (*e.g. Darnel's Case,* 1627),[29] and it is from this application that originated its constitutional importance as the classic British guarantee of personal liberty.   The Petition of Right 1628 declared that the orders of the Sovereign were not to be sufficient justification for the imprisonment of his subjects.

Habeas corpus is available against any person who is suspected of detaining another unlawfully, and not merely against prison governors, the police or other public officers whose duties normally include arrest and detention.   It is applicable where a tribunal has no jurisdiction to detain the petitioner, but not where the detention is the result of a wrong decision made in exercise of jurisdiction: in the latter case there may be an appeal to a higher court.[30]   Habeas corpus was used in the eighteenth and early nineteenth centuries to set free slaves brought into this country by their owners, or who had escaped for protection to British warships, during the period when slavery was still lawful in parts of the British Empire and in other countries.[31]

Habeas corpus has been used to test the validity of detention by order of a court-martial.[32]   Since the seventeenth century, and before a system of criminal appeals was established, habeas corpus was the normal method of applying for bail.[33]   The writ is available to question detention pending deportation [34] and for breach of immigration regulations,[35] and also during proceedings under the Extradition

---

[27] Jenks, *op. cit.* p. 65.
[28] Habeas corpus=have (*i.e.* bring) the body [of X before the court].
[29] *The Five Knights' Case*, 3 St.Tr. 1; Holdsworth, *History of English Law*, Vol. VI, pp. 32–37.
[30] *Cf.* A. Rubinstein, "Habeas Corpus as a means of Review" (1964) 27 M.L.R. 322.
[31] *Somersett* v. *Stewart* (1772) 20 St.Tr. 1 (Lord Mansfield C.J.): Somersett was later appointed wharf-master of the new settlement of Sierra Leone (E. Fiddes in (1934) 50 L.Q.R. 1, 459); *Forbes* v. *Cochrane* (1824) 2 B. & C. 448; *The Slave Grace* (1827) 2 Hag.Adm. 94 (Lord Stowell); *cf. Hottentot Venus' Case* (1810) 13 East 195.
[32] *Re Porrett* (1844) Perry's *Oriental Cases* 414.   *Cf. Re Clifford and O'Sullivan* [1921] A.C. 570 (no prohibition to military tribunal administering martial law; ?habeas corpus).
[33] *Re Kray* [1965] Ch. 736 (Lord Gardiner L.C.).
[34] *R.* v. *Home Secretary, ex p. Soblen* [1963] 1 Q.B. 829 (C.A.).
[35] *R.* v. *Governor of Brixton Prison, ex p. Ahsan* [1969] 2 Q.B. 222 (D.C.); *R.* v. *Governor of Richmond Remand Centre, ex p. Ashgar* [1971] 1 W.L.R. 129 (D.C.).

Acts [36] and Fugitive Offenders Acts.[37] For detention by order of the House of Commons, reference should be made to the *Case of the Sheriff of Middlesex* (1840).[38] English courts have no jurisdiction to issue habeas corpus on behalf of persons detained in Northern Ireland.[39]

For constitutional purposes the special significance of this remedy is that it is available against Crown servants acting in the name of the Crown. Thus in *Home Secretary* v. *O'Brien* [40] the writ was issued against the Home Secretary, who had ordered the detention of an Irishman in England during the Irish "troubles." On the other hand it was held in *Re Ning Yi-Ching* (1939) [41] that habeas corpus would not lie for Chinese subjects on foreign territory, and that in any event the writ would not issue against the Foreign Secretary acting merely in an advisory capacity.

Habeas Corpus Act 1679 [42]

The passing of this Act followed the case of *Jenkes* (1676),[43] who, after being arrested for delivering a speech urging the summoning of Parliament, was kept in prison for several months without bail. The Act applied only to persons imprisoned (not after conviction by a court) for " criminal or supposed criminal matters." If the applicant showed that there was any ground for supposing that the prisoner was wrongfully imprisoned, the writ would be issued requiring the person detaining the prisoner to bring him before the court and to inform it of the grounds of his detention. If it appeared that the prisoner was confined without lawful authority, the court would release him: otherwise it would release him on bail, or make provision for his speedy trial.

Habeas corpus cannot be granted to a person who is serving a

---

[36] *Re Castioni* [1891] 1 Q.B. 149; *R.* v. *Governor of Brixton Prison, ex p. Cabon-Waterfield* [1960] 2 Q.B. 498 (D.C.).

[37] *R.* v. *Brixton Prison Governor, ex p. Naranjan Singh* [1962] 1 Q.B. 211 (D.C.); *R.* v. *Brixton Prison Governor, ex p. Sadri* [1962] 1 W.L.R. 1304 (D.C.); *Zacharia* v. *Republic of Cyprus* [1963] A.C. 634 (H.L.).

[38] 11 Ad. & E. 273; *ante*, Chap. 11.

[39] *Re Keenan* [1972] 1 Q.B. 533 (C.A.). See D. E. C. Yale, " Habeas Corpus—Ireland—jurisdiction " (1972) 30 C.L.J. 4, considering legislation of 1782 and 1783.

[40] [1923] A.C. 603 (H.L.).

[41] 56 T.L.R. 3.

[42] The Habeas Corpus Acts do not apply to Scotland, but there are other remedies: Fraser, *Outline of Constitutional Law* (2nd ed.) Chap. 17; Mitchell, *Constitutional Law* (2nd ed.) pp. 339–341.

[43] 6 St.Tr. 1190. For an account of the passing of this Act, see Holdsworth, *History of English Law*, Vol. IX, pp. 112–117. The Bill is said by Bishop Burnett to have been saved at one stage by a teller counting one fat peer as ten.

sentence passed by a court of competent jurisdiction,[44] unless, probably, the Divisional Court is satisfied that the prisoner is being detained after the term of his sentence has expired.[45] The Divisional Court does not sit as a court of appeal on an application for habeas corpus, and it will not rehear matters decided by the judicial authority,[46] but it may consider whether that judicial authority had any evidence which would justify its assumption of jurisdiction.[47]

The Habeas Corpus Act 1679 imposed heavy penalties for not making due returns to the writ, not delivering to the prisoner promptly a true copy of the warrant of commitment, or shifting the custody of the prisoner from one place to another, or sending prisoners out of England. The obligation to hear applications for habeas corpus was laid on the Lord Chancellor and judges of the King's Bench, Common Pleas, Exchequer and Chancery. It appears that under section 10, judges of the Supreme Court are still liable to a penalty of £500 for wrongfully refusing to issue a writ of habeas corpus in the case of a person in custody on a criminal charge, but it is uncertain whether this applies only in vacation.[48]

The defects of the 1679 Act were that:

(i) there was no protection where bail was fixed too high: this was met by the Bill of Rights (*supra*);

(ii) the return to the writ might not be truthful: the cause of commitment expressed in the return to the writ is assumed to be true, the question for the court at this stage being whether the cause stated is sufficient in law. There are other and separate remedies for making a false return;

(iii) it did not apply to civil detention. Before 1679 the main problem had been detention by Crown officers for supposed offences, but during the eighteenth century the common law procedure of habeas corpus was becoming inadequate to deal with such cases as impressment and the unjust committal of bankrupts.

Habeas Corpus Act 1816

This Act provided that the Act of 1679 (with certain improvements) should extend to detention otherwise than on a charge of crime.[49]

---

44 *Re Wring, Re Cook (Practice Note)* [1960] 1 W.L.R. 138 (D.C.). For the practice where a prisoner persists in his desire to apply for habeas corpus, see *Re Greene* (1941) 57 T.L.R. 533.
45 *Re Featherstone* (1953) 37 Cr.App.R. 146, *per* Lord Goddard C.J.
46 *Ex p. Hinds* [1961] 1 W.L.R. 325 (D.C.); affirmed by the House of Lords in *Re Hinds, The Times,* February 15, 1961.
47 *R. v. Board of Control, ex p. Rutty* [1956] 2 Q.B. 109.
48 It has been questioned whether by s. 2 of the Act of 1679 habeas corpus was grantable as of course by a judge in vacation.
49 Except in the case of persons imprisoned for debt or on process in a civil action. These kinds of imprisonment (except for certain debts due to the Crown and

The judges were required, on complaint made to them by or on behalf of the person in custody showing a prima facie ground for the complaint, to issue a writ of *habeas corpus ad subjiciendum;* and in civil cases they might inquire into the truth of the return to the writ. If the return is good on its face, the custodian must justify the detention.[50] Any person disobeying a writ sued out under this Act is guilty of contempt of court and becomes liable to imprisonment.

Modern procedure on habeas corpus

Habeas corpus is a writ of right, but not of course. A prima facie case must be shown, otherwise all the prisoners of England could delay or even defeat justice.[51] No application will be heard in person save for some exceptional reason.[52] The present procedure is governed by Rules of the Supreme Court.

Proceedings are generally to be heard by a Divisional Court of the Queen's Bench Division. Exceptionally, application may be made to a single judge of any division in court. In vacation, or at any time when no judge is sitting in court (*e.g.* at weekends or at night), application may be made to a judge sitting otherwise than in court, *e.g.* in vacation to a judge in chambers; at other times in an emergency, anywhere.[53] Application is to be *ex parte* in the first instance, and on affidavit. The affidavit is made by the person restrained, or by someone on his behalf if he is incapable, setting out the nature of the restraint. The application is usually adjourned in order that notice may be given to the respondent. On the hearing of the application the court or judge may order that the person restrained be released. Such order is a sufficient warrant for his release, so that there is no need to issue the actual writ.

There is power to order the immediate issue of the writ, though this is rarely done. Argument then takes place on the return to the writ. Where the writ is issued it is accompanied by a notice that in default of obedience proceedings for contempt of court against the party disobeying will be taken. The return to the writ must contain a copy of all the causes of the prisoner's detention.

The Administration of Justice Act 1960, s. 14, provides that on a criminal application for habeas corpus an order for release shall

judgment debts where the debtor has had the money to pay) were abolished by the Debtors Act 1869; *ante,* p. 398.
[50] R. v. *Brixton Prison Governor, ex p. Ahsan* [1969] 2 Q.B. 222 (D.C.).
[51] *Re Corke* [1954] 1 W.L.R. 899; [1954] 2 All E.R. 440, *per* Lord Goddard C.J.
[52] *Re Greene* (1941) 57 T.L.R. 533.
[53] In the *Soblen* case, *ante,* p. 377, application was made to the chambers judge at his home in the middle of the night, and the order signed on the dining-room table: R. v. *Home Secretary, ex p. Soblen, The Times,* July 27, 1962.
Custody of children cases are decided by a judge in chambers.

be refused only by a Divisional Court of the Queen's Bench Division, even where the original application is made to a single judge, *e.g.* in vacation.

Successive applications

Before 1876 an application for habeas corpus could be made to each of the Courts of Queen's Bench, Common Pleas, Exchequer and Chancery. The judges of the common law courts available in London sat together *in banc*, and each court was bound to hear the case *de novo* on its merits, because the refusal of the writ was not regarded as a judgment and therefore the matter was not *res judicata*.[54] After the Judicature Acts 1873–75 had amalgamated these courts into one High Court, there were dicta in the House of Lords and the Privy Council to the effect that Parliament could not have intended impliedly to restrict the rights of the subject in the vital matter of personal liberty, and that there was therefore a right to apply not only to each Division of the High Court but to each High Court judge individually.[55]   In *Re Hastings*,[56] however, a series of decisions showed that two differently constituted Queen's Bench Divisional Courts, as well as the Chancery Division, were all parts of the same High Court for this as for other purposes, and therefore the decision of any one Division was the decision of the whole court. Further, Rules of Court did not permit application to be made to a single judge in term time.[57]

The Administration of Justice Act 1960, s. 14, now provides that no *second* criminal or civil application may be made on the same grounds, whether to the same or any other court or judge, unless fresh evidence is adduced; and no such application may be made in any case to the Lord Chancellor.[58]   Whether successive applications may be made in vacation is still not certain.[59]

---

[54] Lord Goddard, " A Note on Habeas Corpus " (1949) 65 L.Q.R. 30. *Cf.* D. M. Gordon, " The Unruly Writ of Habeas Corpus " (1963) 26 M.L.R. 520.

[55] *Cox* v. *Hakes* (1890) 15 App.Cas. 506 (H.L.), *per* Lord Halsbury L.C.; *Eshugbayi (Eleko)* v. *Government of Nigeria (Officer Administering)* [1928] A.C. 459 (P.C.), *per* Lord Hailsham L.C.; and see [1931] A.C. 662; *Home Secretary* v. *O'Brien* [1923] A.C. 603 (H.L.), *per* Lord Birkenhead L.C. These dicta were disapproved *obiter* by the Irish Supreme Court in *The State (Dowling)* v. *Kingston (No. 2)* [1937] I.R. 699; see R. F. V. Heuston, " Habeas Corpus Procedure " (1950) 66 L.Q.R. 79.

[56] *Re Hastings (No. 1)* [1958] 1 W.L.R. 372 (D.C.); *(No. 2)* [1959] 1 Q.B. 358 (D.C.); *(No. 3)* [1959] 2 W.L.R. 454; [1959] 1 All E.R. 698 (D.C.); [1959] Ch. 368 (C.A.).

[57] See *Ex p. Le Gros* (1914) 30 T.L.R. 249 for an unsuccessful attempt to apply to the Lord Chief Justice alone.

[58] In effect, application for habeas corpus can no longer be made to the Lord Chancellor as he is not liable to serve as vacation judge: *Re Kray* [1965] Ch. 736 (Lord Gardiner L.C.).

[59] Heuston, *Essays in Constitutional Law* (2nd ed.) p. 127.

Appeal

An incidental effect of the Judicature Acts 1873–75 was that in non-criminal matters the persons detained might appeal to the Court of Appeal and thence to the House of Lords against a refusal to issue the writ or to discharge him under the writ.[60] On the other hand, a prisoner had no appeal against refusal to issue the writ in a criminal cause or matter, i.e. a matter of which the direct outcome might be his trial and possible punishment for an illegal act by a court claiming jurisdiction in that regard (*Amand* v. *Home Secretary and Minister of Defence of the Royal Netherlands Government*[61]). There never was an appeal before the Judicature Acts. Those Acts excluded criminal matters from the jurisdiction of the Court of Appeal, and no appeal to the Court of Criminal Appeal was given in such cases by the Criminal Appeal Act 1907. Another rule before 1960 was that the person detaining had no appeal against an order of the High Court discharging a prisoner from custody under the writ of habeas corpus (*Cox* v. *Hakes* (1890)[62]). Before the Judicature Acts error did not lie in the case of prerogative writs, and no appeal in this event was granted by statute.

The Administration of Justice Act 1960, s. 15, provides that an appeal shall lie in criminal as well as civil applications for habeas corpus, and that the appeal may be brought against an order for release as well as against the refusal of such an order.[63] In civil cases appeal lies through the Court of Appeal to the House of Lords. In criminal cases the appeal lies direct from the Divisional Court to the House of Lords.[64] It is not necessary to obtain a certificate that a point of law of general public importance is involved. Proceedings under Extradition Acts and Fugitive Offenders Acts, and for breaches of regulations under the Immigration Act 1971, are classed as criminal.[65] Deportation cases generally are classed as civil.

A Divisional Court which has granted an application for habeas corpus in a criminal case can order the applicant's detention or release on bail pending an appeal; but if no such order is made (i.e. if he has been released without bail) he may not be detained again if the appeal in the House of Lords goes against him. Where an application for habeas corpus has been granted in a civil case, the

---

[60] *Ex p. Woodhall* (1888) 20 Q.B.D. 832 (C.A.); see *per* Lindley L.J. at p. 838.
[61] [1943] A.C. 147 (H.L.), *per* Viscount Simon L.C.
[62] 15 App.Cas. 506 (H.L.).
[63] See *e.g. R.* v. *Metropolitan Police Commissioner, ex p. Hammond* [1965] A.C. 810 (H.L.).
[64] Administration of Justice Act 1960, s. 1.
[65] *Ex p. Woodhall*; *Amand* v. *Home Secretary and Minister of Defence of the Royal Netherlands Government, supra.*

applicant may not in any event be detained again if the appeal goes against him, the right of appeal in such cases being to enable questions of law to be settled by the House of Lords.

Habeas Corpus to places overseas

The old rule was that a writ of habeas corpus could be issued out of England to any part of the dominions of the King of England, but not to Scotland or Hanover.[66] In *Ex p. Anderson* (1861) [67] the Aborigines Protection Society applied to the Court of Queen's Bench for habeas corpus on behalf of Anderson, a negro slave who, after killing Seneca T. P. Diggs in defence of his freedom, had escaped from the United States into the colony of Upper Canada where he was arrested. It was held that there was no evidence for a charge of murder according to the law in Canada, and therefore Anderson was not extraditable; otherwise habeas corpus could have been issued out of England into Upper Canada. The court added, however, that the issue of the writ to a self-governing colony was inconvenient, unnecessary and *infra dignitatem*. The Habeas Corpus Act 1862 was therefore passed, which provides that no writ of habeas corpus shall issue out of England into any " colony or foreign dominion of the Crown " where a court has been established with authority to issue the writ and to ensure due execution thereof. The expression " foreign dominion of the Crown " is obscure. There were no protectorates at that time. Cockburn C.J.[68] suggested that it meant a country which had once formed part of the dominions of a foreign state but which had been acquired by the Crown by conquest or cession.

In *Ex p. Mwenya* [69] the applicant, who was assumed to be a British subject by virtue of citizenship of Rhodesia and Nyasaland applied to a Divisional Court in England for a writ of habeas corpus against the Secretary of State for the Colonies,[70] the Governor and the District Commissioner on the ground that he was unlawfully confined to the Mporokoso district in Northern Rhodesia, then a British protectorate. His contentions that the Order in Council setting up a High Court in Northern Rhodesia was invalid and that his confine

---

66 *R.* v. *Cowle* (1759) 2 Burr. 855–856. Scotland had a different, though somewhat similar, remedy.

67 3 El. & El. 487, 494. For a full account of the facts see *Annual Register*, 1861 pp. 520–528.

68 *Ex p. Brown* (1864) 5 B. & S. 280.

69 [1960] 1 Q.B. 241. See notes by E. C. S. Wade in [1960] C.L.J. 1; L. J. Blom Cooper in (1960) 23 M.L.R. 73; R. F. V. Heuston in (1960) 75 L.Q.R. 25; and G. I. A. D. Draper in (1960) 76 L.Q.R. 211 And *cf. R.* v. *Earl of Crewe, ex p Sekgome* [1910] 2 K.B. 576 (C.A.).

70 The Court of Appeal did not decide whether the Secretary of State had " control " over Mwenya.

ment was sufficient for the application, were accepted for the sake of argument. The Court of Appeal held that the jurisdiction of the English court to issue the writ of habeas corpus to territories outside England was not limited to " colonies or foreign dominions " strictly so called, but extended to territories which, having regard to the extent of the dominion in fact exercised, could be said to be " under the subjection of the Crown " and in which the issue of the writ would be regarded as " proper and efficient." This did not necessarily mean that the writ would run in *any* protectorate. The case was inconclusive, because Mwenya was in fact released.

It is doubtful whether habeas corpus can be issued to bring before the Queen's Bench Division an alien in a British ship on the high seas.[71]

II. FREEDOM OF PROPERTY

The Englishman's castle

" The house of every one is to him as is his castle and fortress, as well for his defence aaginst injury and violence, as for his repose," it was said in *Semayne's Case* (1603) [72]: " if thieves come to a man's house to rob him, or murder, and the owner or his servants kill any of the thieves in defence of himself and his house, it is not felony, and he shall lose nothing. So it is held every one may assemble his friends and neighbours to defend his house against violence . . . because *domus sua cuique est tutissimum refugium.*" " By the laws of England." said Lord Camden C.J. in *Entick* v. *Carrington* (1765),[73] " every invasion of private property, be it ever so minute, is a trespass. No man can set his foot upon my ground without my licence . . . . If he admits the fact, he is bound to show by way of justification, that some positive law has empowered or excused him." The owner is protected against unjustifiable interference with his property by actions for damages or injunction or for the recovery of the property, or by declaration or order of certiorari.

Various kinds of damage to property which the law makes criminal have been revised and collected together in the Criminal Damage Act 1971. Trespass, otherwise than with firearms,[74] is not a crime in English law,[75] but it may involve other offences such as burglary,

---

[71] R. v. *Secretary of State for Foreign Affairs, ex p. Greenberg* [1947] 2 All E.R. 550.
[72] 5 Co.Rep. 91, 91b. The maxim was anticipated by Staunford, *Plees del Coron* (1567): " *ma meason est a moy come mon castel.*" Cf. D.2.4.21 : *de domo sua nemo extrahi debet.*
[73] 19 St.Tr. 1029, 1066.
[74] Firearms Act 1968, s. 20.
[75] But conspiracy to trespass is: R. v. *Kamara* [1973] 2 W.L.R. 126 (C.A.).

criminal damage or conspiracy. Where squatters have taken possession of an unoccupied building, the owner may apply to the court for an order for possession; if this is not complied with, a writ of possession may be issued authorising the sheriff or his officers to eject the squatters, if necessary with the help of the police. The last few years have seen organised multiple squatting by way of demonstration against the housing shortage. Difficulty was caused where the identity of the squatters or trespassers was not known, and a special form of originating summons was provided by Rules of Court in 1970 to meet such cases.[76]

Forcible entry, as by violence or breaking open doors or windows, and forcible retainer were probably common law offences. They were made indictable by the Forcible Entry Acts 1381 (forcible entry), 1391 (forcible entry followed by forcible retainer), 1429 (forcible retainer after peaceable entry) and 1623 (estates for years), all of which are still in force. It is no defence that the person charged was entitled to possession or had a legal right of entry, for the purpose of the statutes is to prevent breaches of the peace (*R.* v. *Mountford*[77]; *R.* v. *Brittain*[78]). Summary proceedings may also be brought under the Acts.[79] Squatters may be liable for conspiracy to contravene the Forcible Entry Acts.[80]

Power of entry and search [81]

Entry of premises under criminal process requires a magistrate's warrant for arrest and search at common law, with certain exceptions. A constable may enter private premises to prevent an arrestable offence, to prevent or suppress a breach of the peace or to recapture someone who has escaped from lawful arrest. The police before 1935 had been in the habit of entering private premises at the owner's request to deal with actual breaches of the peace, but in *Thomas* v. *Sawkins*[82] the Divisional Court went considerably further and held that the police may, without warrant or licence, enter private premises —at least if a public meeting is being held there—in which they have reasonable grounds for believing that an offence (or, at least, a breach

---

[76] *Greater London Council* v. *Lewis, The Times*, August 6, 1970; *Re 9 Orpen Road, Stoke Newington* [1971] 1 W.L.R. 166; *cf. Re Wykeham Terrace, Brighton, ex p. Territorial etc. Association* v. *Hales* [1971] Ch. 204.

[77] [1972] 1 Q.B. 28 (C.A.).

[78] [1972] 1 Q.B. 357 (C.A.).

[79] *R.* v. *Beacontree Justices, ex p. Mercer, The Times*, December 3, 1969 (C.A.).

[80] *Ex p. London Diocesan Board of Education, The Times*, September 25, 1969; *R.* v. *Robinson (Robert)* [1970] 1 W.L.R. 15 (C.A.); *R.* v. *Robinson (Michael)* [1971] 1 Q.B. 156 (C.A.).

[81] L. H. Leigh, " Recent Developments in the Law of Search and Seizure " (1970) 33 M.L.R. 208.

[82] [1935] 2 K.B. 249.

of the peace) is likely to be committed. The case is unsatisfactory because the police attended in plain clothes as members of the public, after the licence to the police had been withdrawn. In *Davis* v. *Lisle* [83] a Divisional Court held that the police have no right without a warrant, in connection with a summary offence not involving a breach of the peace (in this case, a car obstructing the highway), to enter private premises, or to remain against the owner's wishes on premises into which they are invited to enter.

It is a principle of the common law that a " *general warrant* " to search premises, *i.e.* one in which either the person or the property is not specified, is illegal. Thus in *Wilkes* v. *Wood* (1763) [84] John Wilkes recovered £1,000 damages for trespass against Wood, an Under-Secretary of State, for entering his house and seizing his papers under a warrant to arrest the (unnamed) authors, printers and publishers of No. 45 of the *North Briton*. In *Entick* v. *Carrington* (1765) [85] Entick, suspected to be the author of the *Monitor, or British Freeholder*, obtained £300 damages for trespass against Carrington and other King's messengers for breaking and entering his house and seizing his books and papers under a general search warrant from the Secretary of State. Lord Camden C.J. delivered a powerful judgment against the legality of such general warrants.

Entry or search usually requires arrest, and arrest (as we have seen) usually requires a warrant. A number of statutes authorise the issue by magistrates of search warrants on sworn information, concerning *e.g.* stolen goods, offences against the person, coinage, official secrets, criminal damage, obscene publications and dangerous drugs. For certain cases under the Public Order Act 1936 and the Incitement to Disaffection Act 1934 a High Court judge may issue a warrant to enter and seize documents, etc. The Criminal Law Act 1967, s. 2 (6), provides that, for the purpose of arresting a person for an arrestable offence, a constable may enter (if need be by force) and search any place where that person is, or where the constable with reasonable cause suspects him to be. A very few other statutes allow entry and seizure without warrant, *e.g.* certain cases of stolen goods (authority of Chief Constable), and emergencies connected with explosions and official secrets (authority of superintendent).

In *Elias* v. *Pasmore* [86] Horridge J. held that the police had power

---

[83] [1936] 2 K.B. 434; approving *Great Central Ry.* v. *Bates* [1921] 3 K.B. 578, *per* Atkin L.J. at p. 582: " nobody has a right to enter premises except strictly in accordance with authority " (L.R. headnote to *Great Central Ry.* v. *Bates* corrected by du Parcq J. at [1936] 2 K.B. 439–440). *Cf. Robson* v. *Hallett* [1967] 2 Q.B. 939 (D.C.).
[84] 19 St.Tr. 1153.
[85] 19 St.Tr. 1029.
[86] [1934] 2 K.B. 164.

at common law to seize any documents found on the premises where a person is lawfully arrested and which would form material evidence on any criminal charge committed by anyone. In *Ghani* v. *Jones* [87] the police searched without warrant the house of the father-in-law of a murdered Pakistani immigrant woman. At their request he handed over certain documents, including the Pakistani passports of himself and his family. The plaintiffs, who did not claim that the search was illegal, later asked for the return of the documents. The police, who had not arrested anyone in connection with the suspected murder, refused on the ground that there would be a serious risk that the plaintiffs would leave the country. The Court of Appeal, disapproving the dictum of Horridge J. in *Elias* v. *Pasmore* (*supra*), held that, although the police might have reasonable grounds for believing that a serious offence had been committed, the passports and other documents ought to be returned. Lord Denning M.R. said the police may seize: (a) the fruit of the crime; (b) the instrument of the crime, or (c) material evidence of the commission of the crime for which a person is arrested or for which they enter: the person in possession must be reasonably believed to have committed the crime or to be implicated in it, or accessory, or his refusal must be quite unreasonable.[88]

Entry in administrative law

Modern statutes give power of entry and search to many thousands of civil servants, local government officers and officials of public corporations, *e.g.* inspectors of food and drugs and weights and measures, factory inspectors, public health inspectors, town planning officers and inspectors of the gas and electricity boards.[89] There is no consistency with regard to the persons authorised, the nature of the authorising document, length of notice, or whether notice is to be given to the owner or the occupier.[90] The statute usually prescribes that the official must produce his written authority to any person who reasonably requires to see it.[91] If the conditions of entry prescribed by statute are not strictly fulfilled the owner is entitled to oppose entry. " When the sanitary inspector of the council arrived,"

---

[87] [1970] 1 Q.B. 693 (C.A.). And see *Chic Fashions (West Wales)* v. *Jones* [1968] 2 Q.B. 299 (C.A.) (stolen goods). *Cf. R.* v. *Waterfield* [1964] 1 Q.B. 164 (refused to let police inspect car).

[88] The words " or his refusal must be quite unreasonable " are said to have been added to the draft report: (1970) 120 New L.J. 423; [1970] C.L.J. 1; *cf.* (1969) 119 New L.J. 1011.

[89] The number of officials who could exercise statutory powers to enter *private houses* was stated on July 18, 1950, to be 4,170, including 3,154 officers of the Inland Revenue (*Hansard*, cols. 2044–2045).

[90] See D. Waters, " Public Right of Entry " [1958] C.L.P. 132.

[91] *Grove* v. *Eastern Gas Board* [1952] 1 K.B. 77 (C.A.), *re* Gas Act 1948.

said Lord Goddard C.J. in *Stroud* v. *Bradbury*,[92] " the appellant obstructed him with all the rights of a free-born Englishman whose premises are being invaded and defied him with a clothes prop and a spade. He was entitled to do that unless the sanitary inspector had a right to enter." An abuse of the power of entry would amount to trespass *ab initio*.[93] The Rights of Entry (Gas and Electricity Boards) Act 1954 regulated the exercise of the statutory right of entry on behalf of gas boards and electricity boards. Except in certain emergencies, such statutory right of entry is exercisable only with the consent of the occupier of the premises or under authority of a warrant issued by a justice of the peace.

Liability to taxation

Since the Bill of Rights (1688) it has been firmly established that taxation may only be imposed by authority of an Act of Parliament (*Att.-Gen.* v. *Wilts United Dairies* (1921)[94]). This is done by Parliament either directly, as in the case of income tax, customs and excise duties, estate duties and stamp duties, or indirectly, through the delegation of power to local authorities to levy rates. Inland Revenue officials have an extensive power to " discover " what is not there and to assess taxpayers on that, in order to induce the latter to disclose what *is* there. The illegal conduct of the Postmaster-General in charging fees for wireless licences without complying with the requirements of the Wireless Telegraphy Act 1904 was pointed out in the case of *Davey Paxman & Co. Ltd.* v. *Post Office*,[95] and the position was regularised retrospectively by the Wireless Telegraphy (Validation of Charges) Act 1954.

Statutory restrictions on freedom of property

Parliament authorises and controls the compulsory acquisition of land by the Crown for defence purposes [96]; and by various Ministers, local authorities and public corporations under a great variety of statutes. A compulsory purchase by a local authority or public corporation must be confirmed by a Minister. Statutes prescribe both the procedure of compulsory acquisition and the method of assessing compensation.

The process of compulsory acquisition, with compensation, has undergone a rapid expansion into the field of movable property with

---

92 [1952] W.N. 306; [1952] 2 All E.R. 76 (D.C.), *re* Public Health Act 1936.
93 *Six Carpenters' Case* (1610) 8 Co.Rep. 146a. See Denning, *Freedom under the Law*, pp. 107–110.
94 91 L.J.K.B. 897; (1921) 37 T.L.R. 884.
95 *The Times*, November 16, 1954.
96 *Cf. Att.-Gen.* v. *De Keyser's Royal Hotel Ltd.* [1920] A.C. 508 (H.L.).

the passing of the nationalisation Acts, which since 1945 have taken a considerable part of the industrial resources of the country out of private ownership. There is a strong presumption that if a statute authorises the compulsory acquisition of property, the owner is entitled to reasonable compensation (*Newcastle Breweries* v. *The King* [97]).

Restrictions on the use or enjoyment of property have been increasingly imposed by such statutes as the Town and Country Planning Acts, Agriculture Acts and Rent Acts.

" Freedom of property," then, like personal freedom, is residual.

[97] [1920] 1 K.B. 584. *Cf. Hudson's Bay Co.* v. *Maclay* (1920) 36 T.L.R. 469.

CHAPTER 24

FREEDOM OF SPEECH [1]

General principles

Under this heading we include freedom of opinion and expression in speech, writing or printing, even though it is critical of the government or the political system. This freedom, like the others, is residual and subject to limitation by common law and statute.

It includes freedom to hold opinions without interference; and to seek, receive and impart information and ideas through any media and regardless of frontiers. It covers the import of foreign papers, whatever their political or social views, and the reception of foreign broadcasts. In English law there was never any attempt to control the right to hold opinions. Limitations are on expression or communication, and are concerned mainly with the public welfare and the preservation of public order. Freedom of thought includes freedom of conscience and religion or belief, and the freedom—whether in public or in private—to manifest one's religion or belief in teaching, practice, worship and observance. Religious toleration has existed in English law since the eighteenth century: religious disabilities for public office, education and so on were abolished during the nineteenth century.

Limitations on this freedom include treason [2]; official secrets [2]; sedition; contempt of court [3] or Parliament [4]; defamation (civil libel and slander; criminal libel); incitement to mutiny or disaffection among the forces or police; obscene publication; blasphemy; incitement to any criminal offence; provoking public disorder; and incitement to racial hatred. [2]

Defamation

Defamatory matter is matter which exposes the person about whom it is published to hatred, ridicule or contempt, or which causes him to be shunned or avoided. [5] Such matter if in writing, printing

---

[1] Dicey, *Law of the Constitution* (10th ed.) Chap. 6. See also Denning, *Freedom under the Law*, Chap. 2; Holdsworth, *History of English Law*, Vol. X, pp. 672 et seq.; H. Street, *Freedom, the Individual and the Law* (3rd ed. 1972) Chaps. 3–7, 10; D. G. T. Williams, *Not in the Public Interest.*
[2] *Ante*, Chap. 22.
[3] *Ante*, Chap. 19.
[4] *Ante*, Chap. 11.
[5] *Capital and Counties Bank* v. *Henty* (1882) 7 App.Cas. 741, 771, *per* Lord Blackburn; *cf. Sim* v. *Stretch* (1936) 53 T.L.R. 669.

or some other permanent medium,[6] is a libel; if in spoken words or significant gestures, a slander. Where the defendant had no intention of referring to the plaintiff, he may make an offer of amends involving the publication of a correction and apology, which (if accepted) stays the action (Defamation Act 1952, s. 4).

Communications made on certain occasions enjoy *absolute privilege*, either at common law or by statute, that is to say, no proceedings can be brought in respect of them. These occasions include: judicial proceedings and statements made in the course of litigation by judges, counsel and witnesses [7]; words uttered in either House of Parliament by members [8]; state communications, which include communications about state business made by persons in government service [9]; proceedings at a court-martial, and reports made in pursuance of military duty [10]; fair and accurate reports in *newspapers* or *broadcasts* from the United Kingdom of proceedings publicly heard before a court in the United Kingdom exercising judicial authority,[11] if published contemporaneously and neither blasphemous nor indecent [12]; reports and other documents published *by order* of either House of Parliament [13]; the Parliamentary Commissioner's report to Parliament, communications between the Parliamentary Commissioner and M.P.s, and communications by the Commissioner or M.P.s to complainants.[14]

Communications on certain other occasions enjoy *qualified privilege*, that is to say, they are protected in the absence of actual malice or " malice in fact," *i.e.* spite, fraud or some other indict motive of which the law disapproves. These occasions include the following: fair and accurate reports (whether in newspapers or not) [15] of judicial proceedings not covered by section 3 of the Law of Libel Amendment Act 1888 (*supra*), published in good faith and not blasphemous or indecent, and not prohibited by order of the court [16] or by statute [17]; the printing or broadcasting of (unauthorised) extracts from, or

---

[6] A defamatory talking film is libel: *Youssoupoff* v. *Metro-Goldwyn-Mayer Pictures Ltd.* (1934) 50 T.L.R. 581; so is a defamatory radio broadcast: Defamation Act 1952, s. 1.

[7] *Royal Aquarium Society* v. *Parkinson* [1892] 1 Q.B. 431.

[8] *R.* v. *Creevey* (1813) 1 M. & S. 273:

[9] *Isaacs & Sons* v. *Cook* [1925] 2 K.B. 391; but see *Szalatnay-Stacho* v. *Fink* [1947] K.B. 1.

[10] *Dawkins* v. *Lord Rokeby* (1875) L.R. 7 H.L. 744.

[11] *Cf.* an administrative tribunal, *Collins* v. *H. Whiteway & Co.* [1927] 2 K.B. 378.

[12] Law of Libel Amendment Act 1888, s. 3; Defamation Act 1952, ss. 8, 9; *Kimber* v. *Press Association* (1893) 62 L.J.Q.B. 152; *Ponsford* v. *Financial Times* (1900) 16 T.L.R. 248.

[13] Parliamentary Papers Act 1840, ss. 1, 2.

[14] Parliamentary Commissioner Act 1967, s. 10.

[15] *Steele* v. *Brannan* (1872) L.R. 7 C.P. 261.

[16] *R.* v. *Clement* (1821) 4 B. & Ald. 218.

[17] *e.g.* the Judicial Proceedings (Regulation of Reports) Act 1926.

abstracts of, parliamentary papers[18]; fair and accurate (unauthorised) reports of parliamentary debates[19]; fair and accurate reports in any *newspaper* of the proceedings of a public meeting, or (except where neither the public nor newspaper reporters are admitted) of a meeting of any public body specified in the Public Bodies (Admission to Meetings) Act 1960; and the agenda of meetings of local authorities and other bodies specified in the Act of 1960, except meetings from which the public and the Press are excluded.

An election address does not enjoy qualified privilege.[20]

Defamation is usually treated as a civil wrong, and as such it belongs to the law of tort. *Slander* is not a crime merely as defamation, but is only a crime if the words are also treasonable or seditious, etc. *Libel* may always have been a common law misdemeanour, but the gist of the offence is its tendency to cause a breach of the peace, and in practice a non-seditious libel is not proceeded against criminally unless it is likely to cause a breach of the peace.[21]

Truth is a defence to a *civil* action for libel, for a person cannot lose a reputation which he has not got or does not deserve; but in *criminal* libel truth is not a defence at common law, since a breach of the peace is as likely, or more likely, to occur if the statement is true. By section 6 of the Libel Act 1843 (" Lord Campbell's Act "), however, it is a defence to a prosecution for criminal libel if the accused can prove not only that the matter published was true in substance but also that the publication was for the public good. Truth, of course, is no defence if the matter is also seditious, etc.

Seditious libel[22]

Prosecutions for seditious libel were frequent during the reign of George III, at the instance either of the government or the House of Commons. The growth of political parties, the development of periodical publications, and fear of the consequences of the French Revolution all contributed at various periods to this result. The prosecution of Wilkes in 1765 for his criticism of the Government in No. 45 of the *North Briton*[23] gave rise to the cases of *Wilkes* v. *Wood* (1763)[24] and *Leach* v. *Money* (1765)[25]; and it was the seizure

---

[18] Parliamentary Papers Act 1840, s. 3; Defamation Act 1952, s. 9.
[19] *Wason* v. *Walter* (1868) L.R. 4 Q.B. 73. Strictly, the defence of fair comment does not come under the heading of qualified privilege; but space does not permit a scientific classification.
[20] Defamation Act 1952, s. 10; *cf. Plummer* v. *Charman* [1962] 1 W.L.R. 1469 (C.A.).
[21] *Wood* v. *Cox* (1887) 4 T.L.R. 264; *R.* v. *Wicks* (1935) 52 T.L.R. 253.
[22] See also *ante*, pp. 389–390.
[23] *R.* v. *Wilkes* (1770) 4 Burr. 2527, 2574.
[24] 19 St.Tr. 1153; and see *ante*, p. 399.   [25] 3 Burr. 1692, 1742; 19 St.Tr. 1001.

in the same year of the books and papers of Entick, who was suspected of being the author of the *Monitor or British Freeholder*, that led to the case of *Entick* v. *Carrington* (1765).[26]

Fox's Libel Act 1792

At common law a jury in a prosecution for criminal libel could not give a verdict on the general issue (*i.e.* " liable " or " not liable "). In *R.* v. *Almon* (1770),[27] where a bookseller was charged with selling a reprint of Junius's " Letter to the King " from the *Morning Advertiser*, Lord Mansfield C.J. said it was for the judge to decide whether the libel was seditious: the jury could only determine the fact of publication and whether the libel had the meaning alleged in the indictment. When in *R.* v. *Woodfall* (1770) [28] the publisher of Junius's letter was prosecuted, the jury found him guilty of " printing and publishing only," but the court refused to accept the verdict and ordered a new trial; and so when the printer of the letter came to trial (*R.* v. *Miller*, 1770) [29] the jury bravely found him " not guilty." In *R.* v. *Shipley* (*Dean of St. Asaph's Case*, 1783 [30]) Lord Mansfield C.J. rejected Erskine's eloquent argument in defence of the Dean of St. Asaph, who was charged with seditious libel in publishing a political pamphlet entitled " A dialogue between a Gentleman and a Farmer," Lord Mansfield holding that the jury could only determine the fact of publication and the meaning of innuendos. This may have been a correct statement of the law, but it was not in keeping with the public opinion of the time. Erskine made a similarly eloquent defence in *R.* v. *Stockdale* (1789),[31] where criticism of the Commons' conduct of the impeachment of Warren Hastings was alleged to be " a scandalous and seditious libel." The law was changed by the Libel Act 1792 (" Fox's Libel Act ").

" This celebrated Act, and the discussions which led to it," said Stephen,[32] " are perhaps the most interesting and characteristic passages in the whole history of the criminal law." The Act provides that the jury may give a general verdict of " guilty " or " not guilty " on the whole matter in issue, and may not be directed by the court to find the defendant guilty merely on proof of the publication by him of the paper charged to be libel and of the sense ascribed to it in the indictment. In other words, whereas formerly it was only

26 19 St.Tr. 1030.
27 20 St.Tr. 803.
28 20 St.Tr. 870.
29 20 St.Tr. 895.
30 4 Doug. 73, 162; (1783) 21 St.Tr. 847, 1033.   31 22 St.Tr. 237.
32 *History of the Criminal Law*, II, p. 347. For an historical account of the passing of the Act, see *ibid.* Chap. 24; Holdsworth, *History of English Law*, Vol. X, pp. 673–695. And see *R.* v. *Burdett* (1820) 4 B. & Ald. 95

necessary that there should be intention to publish matter that was seditious, since the Act the intention must be seditious. The judge may give his opinion and directions to the jury on the matter in issue, and the Act does not prevent the jury in its discretion from finding a special verdict as in other criminal cases. It is still for the judge to say, as questions of law, whether the words are capable of a defamatory meaning and whether they amount to criminal libel, so that he can direct the jury to give a verdict of " *not* guilty."

Charges of seditious libel continued to be brought, although not always so successfully for the prosecution. One of the latest cases of the old type—though here the accused was ultra conservative—was that of John Reeves,[33] the author of a well-known *History of English Law*. The Commons put pressure on the Government to prosecute him in 1796 for seditious libel for expressing opinions in a pamphlet based on his reading of legal history—exalting the prerogative of the Crown in relation to the authority of the Commons. He had likened the Crown, the source of all legal power, to the timber of a tree, and the other parts of the Constitution to the branches and leaves. The jury found him " not guilty " as the pamphlet showed no seditious intent.

After the Reform Act 1832 prosecution for seditious libel ceased to be a political weapon. Henceforth, as governments came to rely more and more on popular suffrage, they realised that criticism of the government at least showed an interest in politics and was better than apathy. The mid-nineteenth century conception of seditious intent formulated by Stephen [34] is still regarded as good law. Prosecutions nowadays for seditious libel are rare, and in practice they are not instituted unless there is incitement to violence.[35] In R. v. *Caunt* (1947) [36] a newspaper proprietor was prosecuted for seditious libel for writing an avowedly anti-Semitic article, in terms which could scarcely fail to " promote feelings of illwill and hostility between different classes." Birkett J. in his summing-up said it must be proved that the accused published the libel " with the intention of promoting violence." The jury acquitted.

Liberty of the Press

" The Press " generally covers printed matter of all kinds, and not merely newspapers and periodicals. " The liberty of the press,"

---

[33] 29 St.Tr. 530. For John Reeves see Holdsworth, *History of English Law*, Vol. XII, pp. 412–415. Holdsworth describes his predecessor's *History of English Law* as uninteresting, but not unreadable.   [34] *Ante*, p. 389.
[35] *The King* v. *Aldred* (1909) 22 Cox C.C. 1, *per* Coleridge J.
[36] *The Times*, November 18, 1947. An account of the trial is given in H. Montgomery Hyde, *Norman Birkett* (1964) pp. 532–535. See note by E. C. S. Wade in

says Blackstone,[37] " consists in laying no *previous* restraints upon publications, and not in freedom from censure for criminal matter when published." This liberty, said Lord Mansfield in *Dean of St. Asaph's Case*,[38] consists in " printing without any previous licence, subject to the consequences of law." " The liberty of the press," said Alexander Hamilton,[39] " is the right to publish with impunity, truth, with good motives, for justifiable ends though reflecting on government, magistracy, or individuals." It has existed in this country since the end of the seventeenth century.

Soon after the introduction of the art of printing in the fifteenth century, a series of proclamations began to be issued to restrict and control printing, in addition to the law of treason, sedition, heresy and blasphemy. Throughout most of the sixteenth and seventeenth centuries all printing required a licence. By an assumption of the prerogative of the Crown as *custos morum*[40] in the late Tudor and early Stuart periods, secular printing was controlled by the Star Chamber and theological printing by the High Commission. Soon after the abolition of these bodies in 1641, a licence to print was required by the Licensing Act 1662. Several Licensing Acts followed, but the last expired in 1695. The Commons refused to renew it, not so much out of respect for freedom of expression but rather because experience showed that licensing did not succeed in its object. In England the printing of books in the early period was confined to the members of the Stationer's Company in London and to the Universities of Oxford and Cambridge.[41] Since 1695, then, the Press has been governed by the ordinary law of sedition and libel.

The Press has no privilege to obtain information by methods that would be wrongful in the ordinary person. There is no doubt that " freedom of the Press " is a maxim often distorted in order to justify freedom in the methods of collecting news.[42] But English law does not recognise a right of privacy, as do some of the American states,

---

(1948) 64 L.Q.R. 203; and see *Boucher* v. *R.* [1951] 2 D.L.R. 369. *Cf. R.* v. *Leese, The Times,* September 19 and 20, 1936.

[37] Bl.Comm. IV, 151. He adds that " to censure the licentiousness, is to maintain the liberty, of the press ": *ibid.* p. 153. And see *R.* v. *Burdett* (1820) 4 B. & Ald. 95, *per* Best J.: " Where vituperation begins, the liberty of the press ends."

[38] *R.* v. *Shipley* (1783) 21 St.Tr. 847, 1040; *ante,* p. 418.

[39] In *People* v. *Croswell* (1804) 3 Johns (N.Y.) 337.

[40] For a recent exercise of jurisdiction by the court as *custos morum* see *Shaw* v. *Director of Public Prosecutions* [1962] A.C. 220 (H.L.), conspiracy to corrupt public morals; *ante,* p. 393.

[41] For the history of the law of the Press, see Holdsworth, *History of English Law* Vol. VI, pp. 360–378.

[42] Street, *op. cit.* pp. 251–253.

and members of the public are inadequately protected by the law of libel, trespass and other specific wrongs.[43]

The Press has no privilege not to disclose the sources of its information in judicial proceedings or in a statutory inquiry having the same status as a court. At the Vassall Tribunal of Inquiry in 1963 three journalists were sentenced to imprisonment for refusing to answer questions about the sources of their information (or mis-information), which questions were relevant to the inquiry concerning a matter of state security and were, in the opinion of the judge, proper for them to be asked.[44] The court has a discretion whether to require the information to be given, and usually will not insist on an answer if it is not essential to the case.

" D " notices [45]

" D " (Defence) notices are sometimes thought to be a form of censorship, but granted the wide scope of the Official Secrets Acts [46] they are actually the opposite of censorship and operate as a safety valve against the rigour of the Acts. Since 1912 there has been an official Services, Press and Broadcasting Committee of civil servants in defence departments and representatives of the press and broadcasting, whose purpose is to indicate to the press and broadcasting authorities when they may safely commit an offence against the Official Secrets Acts without risk of being prosecuted. A " D " notice asks editors and publishers not to publish certain specified items of defence information, the publication of which would be pre-judicial to the national interest. It is true that some of these items might not be covered by the Acts, but on the other hand much defence information that is strictly speaking secret is communicated to the Press for background knowledge, and no prosecution follows if it was not in a " D " notice.

Posts and telecommunications

Letters in the post may not be opened without a warrant from the Home Secretary.[47] Postal packets are inviolable, except under statutes relating to such matters as customs and excise,[48] and there is an obligation of secrecy with regard to information obtained in the course of data processing under the Post Office Act 1969.[49]

---

[43] See, e.g. Privacy and the Press (ed. H. Montgomery Hyde, 1947); and see ante, p. 397n.
[44] Att.-Gen. v. Clough [1963] 1 Q.B. 773 (Lord Parker C.J.); Att.-Gen. v. Mul-holland; Att.-Gen. v. Foster [1963] 2 Q.B. 477 (C.A.). Clough never served his sentence of imprisonment as the source revealed itself and he confirmed it.
[45] Street, op. cit. pp. 217–221; Williams, op. cit. pp. 80–88.
[46] Ante, Chap. 22.
[47] Post Office Act 1953, s. 58.
[48] Post Office Act 1969, s. 64.
[49] Section 65.

It is not a breach of any legal right for officials to " tap " telephone conversations, but the practice requires a warrant from the Home Secretary. A report by a committee of Privy Councillors on the question of telephone-tapping [50] recommended that communications should only be intercepted either to detect serious crime or to safeguard the security of the state, and that material obtained by interception should not be made available to anyone outside the public service. The Committee also recommended certain other safeguards which were accepted by the Government, namely, that such warrants should be individual, specific and temporary, that a regular review should be made and that full records should be kept at the Home Office. In other countries where telephone tapping is lawful, it usually requires the order of a judge.

The authority of the Minister of Posts and Telecommunications is required before any wireless transmitting station or apparatus may be set up in this country. The British Broadcasting Corporation has full control over the content of its programmes both in sound and television, although it is answerable on broad questions of policy to the Minister, who in turn is responsible to Parliament. The commercial companies that provide television programmes transmitted from stations of the Independent Television Authority have a similar control over their own programmes, subject to the approval of the Independent Television Authority as regards the balance of programmes.

The rules governing political broadcasts in sound and television are designed to ensure a fair hearing for members of all the major political parties, and broadcast discussions about industrial and other controversial issues are similarly expected to be impartial.

There is no official control over the reception of foreign broadcasts by members of the public, even in wartime.

The theatre

Under the Theatres Act 1843 there was a censorship by the Lord Chamberlain of the public performance of stage plays written after 1843. The Theatres Act 1968 abolished this censorship and repealed the Act of 1843. The 1968 Act prohibits the presentation of obscene performances of plays; exempts performances that are justified as being for the public good in the interests of the arts, literature or learning; treats the publication of words, gestures, etc. in the

---

[50] *Report of the Committee of Privy Councillors appointed to enquire into the interception of Communications* (1957) Cmnd. 283.

The Committee criticised the conduct of the Home Secretary in disclosing intercepted information to the Bar Council and the Benchers of Lincoln's Inn in connection with the case of *Re Marrinan, The Times,* June 28, 29; July 1, 4; October 3, 1957.

course of the performance of a play as publication in permanent form; and prohibits incitement to racial hatred or provocation of a breach of the peace by means of the public performance of a play. Magistrates may issue warrants to the police to enter and inspect. Prosecution requires the consent of the Attorney-General. Premises must be licensed for the public performance of plays, the licensing authorities in England and Wales being the Greater London Council and metropolitan and other county councils.

The cinema

The Cinematograph Act 1909 required a licence from the county council or the county borough council for the exhibition of inflammable films. This was a safety measure, but local authorities soon began to refuse to license films which they thought offended public morals, a practice that was declared to be lawful.[51] The film industry thereupon set up its own unofficial British Board of Film Censors, which certifies and classifies films intended for public exhibition. The Cinematograph Act 1952 extended the power of licensing authorities to non-inflammable films. The licensing of cinemas by local authorities is usually done on condition that the films to be shown there will conform to the Board's ruling. The licensing function may be delegated to the local justices.

Blasphemy

" Every publication is said to be blasphemous which contains any contemptuous, reviling, scurrilous or ludicrous matter relating to God, Jesus Christ or the Bible, or the formularies of the Church of England as by law established. It is not blasphemous to speak or publish opinions hostile to the Christian religion, or to deny the existence of God, if the publication is couched in decent and temperate language. The test to be applied is as to the manner in which the doctrines are advocated and not as to the substance of the doctrines themselves." [52] The common law misdemeanour of blasphemous words or writing seems to have been first recognised by the King's Bench in *R.* v. *Attwood* (1617).[53] In the earlier cases blasphemy was virtually equivalent to a kind of seditious libel.

Prosecutions for blasphemy are now rare, as the gist of the offence

---

[51] *London County Council* v. *Bermondsey Bioscope Ltd.* [1911] 1 K.B. 44.
[52] Sir J. F. Stephen, *Digest of Criminal Law* (9th ed.) p. 163.
[53] Cro.Jac. 421. See G. D. Nokes, *History of the Crime of Blasphemy* (1928) pp. 21 et seq.

is a tendency to cause a breach of the peace.[54] A sober and reverent inquiry into the truth of Christian doctrines is no longer against the policy of the law (*Bowman* v. *Secular Society*[55]).

Obscene publications

In early times jurisdiction over obscenity was exercised by the ecclesiastical courts as a matter of morals; but this jurisdiction was taken over by the common law courts in *Curl's Case* (1727),[56] where the misdemeanour of obscene libel was recognised. Of the three " public libels "—seditious libel, blasphemous libel and obscene libel—the last is the only one that is prosecuted with any frequency in modern times. The Obscene Publications Act 1857 also empowered magistrates to authorise the seizure and destruction of obscene articles kept for sale or other purpose of gain. The test of obscenity for the purpose of both the misdemeanour and a destruction order was that laid down by Cockburn C.J. in *R.* v. *Hicklin* (1868),[57] but there was much criticism of that definition and of the manner in which the courts applied it.[58]

The Obscene Publications Act 1959 [59] created the statutory offence of publishing obscene matter, which superseded the common law misdemeanour, and repealed and replaced the Act of 1857 as regards the seizure and forfeiture of obscene matter. A person who, whether for gain or not, publishes [60] an obscene article is liable to be punished by fine or imprisonment on indictment or summary conviction. An " article " includes matter to be read or looked at, a sound record or film, or thing intended to be used for the reproduction or manufacture of obscene articles, *e.g.* a photographic negative [61]; but not a cinematograph exhibition. The test of obscenity for the purposes of the Act is whether the effect " is, if taken as a whole, such as to tend to deprave and corrupt persons who are likely, having regard to all relevant circumstances, to read, see or hear the matter contained or embodied in it." The tendency to deprave and corrupt, instead of

---

54 *R.* v. *Gott* (1922) 16 Cr.App.R. 87 (C.C.A.), in which Gott was convicted of blasphemy. See Courtney Kenny, " The Evolution of the Law of Blasphemy " (1922) 1 C.L.J. 127.
55 [1917] A.C. 406 (H.L.).
56 2 Stra. 788.
57 L.R. 3 Q.B. 360.
58 See N. St. John-Stevas, *Obscenity and the Law* (1956).
59 Based on *Report from the Select Committee on Obscene Publications* (1958) H.C. No. 123. See A. Samuels, " Obscenity and the Law " (1959) 20 N.I.L.Q. 231.
60 Under the Obscene Publications Act 1964 it is also an offence to possess an obscene article for the purpose of publication for gain by anyone; *cf. Mella* v. *Monahan* [1961] Crim.L.R. 175 (exposure of article in shop window).
61 Obscene Publications Act 1964; *cf. Straker* v. *Director of Public Prosecutions* [1963] 1 Q.B. 926.

being a presumed consequence of obscenity, has become the test of obscenity and what has to be proved.[62] The Obscene Publications Act 1964 provides that obscenity is to be determined by reference to the circumstances of intended publication that the defendant may reasonably be inferred to have contemplated.[63] It is now a defence to prove that publication " is justified as being for the public good on the ground that it is in the interests of science, literature, art or learning, or of other objects of general concern." The Act of 1959 also declares that, contrary to the former practice, the opinion of experts may be admitted either to establish or to negative this defence.

In *R.* v. *Oz Publications Ink Ltd.*[64] the Court of Appeal held that " obscene " under the 1959 Act (" tendency to deprave and corrupt ") does not mean shocking, repulsive or lewd. This is a question for the jury, not for expert witnesses. The defence of " public good," although expert witnesses are allowed, is also a question for the jury. A novel is to be read as a whole, but a magazine is to be judged item by item. In this case the publishers of a magazine called *Oz*, containing matter that most people would consider to be repulsive and lewd, were acquitted under the Act of 1959; but they were convicted of sending an indecent or obscene article through the post, contrary to the Post Office Act 1953, s. 11, under which " obscene " has the ordinary meaning. Whether an article sent by post is indecent or obscene is a question for the jury, without evidence of the opinions of witnesses.[65]

Under the Obscene Publications Act 1959 a justice of the peace may issue a warrant empowering a constable to enter and search any premises, stall or vehicle, and to seize and remove any articles which he has reason to believe to be obscene articles kept for publication for gain. When the owner of the premises or user of the stall or vehicle has been summoned to appear to show cause why the articles should not be forfeited, the magistrates' court may order the articles to be forfeited if it is satisfied that they were obscene articles kept for publication for gain. The owner, author or maker may also appear to show cause against forfeiture. The defence of " public good " may be set up, and the opinion of experts may be

---

[62] *D.P.P.* v. *Whyte* [1972] A.C. 849, in which the House of Lords held that middle-aged men who are already addicts of pornography are capable of being further depraved and corrupted. *Cf.* Mark, Chap. 7, v. 15.

[63] *Cf. R.* v. *Clayton and Halsey* [1963] 1 Q.B. 163 (the case of the incorruptible police officers).

[64] *R.* v. *Anderson*; *R.* v. *Oz Publications Ink Ltd.* [1972] 1 Q.B. 304 (C.A.). And see *R.* v. *Calder and Boyars* [1969] 1 Q.B. 151 (C.A.) " Last Exit from Brooklyn." *Cf. D.P.P.* v. *A. and B.C. Chewing Gum Ltd.* [1968] 1 Q.B. 159 (D.C.), evidence of psychiatrists about effect on children.

[65] *R.* v. *Stamford* [1972] 2 Q.B. 39 (C.A.). And see now, Post Office Act 1969, s. 76.

admitted on either side. Appeal against a forfeiture order lies to the Crown Court or by case stated to the High Court.[65a]

Other statutes governing related offences are the Indecent Advertisements Act 1889, the Judicial Proceedings (Regulation of Reports) Act 1926, the Children and Young Persons (Harmful Publications) Act 1955, Customs Acts and Race Relations Acts.[66]

Provoking public disorder

The Public Order Act 1936, s. 5, as amended by the Race Relations Act 1965, s. 7, makes it an offence in any public place or at any public meeting (a) to use threatening, abusive or insulting words or behaviour, (b) to distribute or display any writing or sign that is threatening, abusive or insulting,[67] with intent to provoke a breach of the peace or whereby a breach of the peace is likely to be caused. Following the case of *Jordan* v. *Burgoyne*,[68] the first reported case on this section, the Public Order Act 1963 increased the penalties. A person guilty of such offence is liable on indictment or summary conviction to imprisonment or fine, or both. A constable may arrest without warrant any person reasonably suspected by him to be committing such offence.

65a For the discretion whether to prosecute, see R. v. *Commissioner of Police of Metropolis, ex p. Blackburn (No. 3)* [1973] 2 W.L.R. 43 (C.A.).
66 *Ante,* Chap. 22.
67 See *Williams* v. *D.P.P.* (1968) 112 S.J. 899 (D.C.).
68 [1963] 2 Q.B. 744 (D.C.); *post,* p. 430.

CHAPTER 25

FREEDOM OF ASSEMBLY AND ASSOCIATION [1]

Introduction

These freedoms include: (a) taking part in public meetings, processions and demonstrations; and (b) forming and belonging to political parties, trade unions, societies and other organisations. They are liberties rather than rights in the strict sense, and (like the other liberties of the individual) they are residual.

Freedom to assemble means that there is no law forbidding people to assemble. If a number of people choose to go to the same place at the same time this is not unlawful, provided that they keep within the limits of the law, individually and collectively. An assembly convened for the purpose of effecting a breach of the peace is unlawful at common law; and there are various statutory offences, notably under Public Order Acts, Highways Acts, the Police Act 1964 and local by-laws.

Similarly there is liberty to join an association, provided that it is not a criminal conspiracy (i.e. an agreement to do an unlawful act or a lawful act by unlawful means), or a civil conspiracy (which is a tort), and provided that the association is not organised to usurp the functions of the police or armed forces, or for the purpose of using force for a political object. It is important to notice that "force" does not necessarily mean armed force.

Conversely, no one is obliged by law to join any association against his will, although in practice it may be impracticable for a person to get a certain kind of employment or to engage in a particular occupation or trade unless he joins a trade union or professional association. The United Kingdom has ratified the International Labour Office Convention on Freedom of Association.

[1] Dicey, *Law of the Constitution* (10th ed.) Chap. 7; David Williams, *Keeping the Peace: The Police and Public Order* (1967); Ian Brownlie, *The Law relating to Public Order* (1968); H. Street, *Freedom, the Individual and the Law* (3rd ed. 1972); R. F. V. Heuston, *Essays in Constitutional Law* (2nd ed. 1964); L. Radzinowicz, *History of English Criminal Law*, Vol. 4 (1968) especially Chap. 4; D. G. T. Williams, " Protest and Public Order " [1970] C.L.J. 96; P. E. Kilbride and P. T. Burns, " Freedom of Movement and Assembly in Public Places " (1966) 2 N.Z.L.R. 1.

I. PUBLIC MEETINGS AND PROCESSIONS

Some statutory offences

The Tumultuous Petitioning Act 1661 provides that not more than ten persons may present a petition to the Queen or either House of Parliament; and not more than twenty persons may solicit signatures for such a petition without the consent of certain authorities. The Seditious Meetings Act 1817 provides that not more than fifty persons may assemble within one mile of Parliament when it is sitting, in order to consider a petition; and there is a similar provision in the Judicature Acts with regard to the law courts when they are sitting. These provisions are regarded as obsolescent.

Under the Public Meeting Act 1908, as amended by the Public Order Act 1936, disorderly conduct designed to break up a lawful public meeting is punishable summarily or on indictment. In the case of a political meeting held between the issue of a writ for the return of a Member of Parliament and the return, the offence is an illegal practice under the Representation of the People Act 1949. Under the Act of 1908, as amended, if a constable reasonably suspects any person of committing an offence under that Act he may, if requested by the chairman of the meeting, require the person to give his name and address. If the person refuses to give his name and address, or gives a false name and address, he is guilty of an offence. The constable may arrest without warrant if the person refuses to give his name and address, or if the constable reasonably suspects him of giving a false name and address.

There are offences of wilfully obstructing the highway,[2] wilfully obstructing or assaulting a police officer in the execution of his duty,[3] and incitement to racial hatred.[4]

The Public Order Act 1936, as amended (infra), is aimed at the wearing of political uniforms, the training of para-military organisations, provocative processions, the carrying of offensive weapons at public meetings or processions, and the use of threatening, abusive or insulting words or behaviour on such occasions. General laws governing criminal damage[5] and the possession of firearms, explosives and offensive weapons[6] have already been mentioned.

There may be local Acts creating special offences or imposing special penalties in particular local government areas. Finally, local authorities have power to make by-laws for the good order and gov-

---

[2] Highways Act 1959, post, p. 433.
[3] Police Act 1964, ante, p. 360.
[4] Race Relations Act 1965, ante, p. 394.
[5] Ante, Chap. 23.
[6] Ante, Chap. 22.

ernment of their areas, and these also may create minor offences, which are triable summarily in the magistrates' courts. A meeting on ground belonging to a local authority, such as a square or park, usually requires the written permission of the council; and permission may be refused if a breach of the peace is apprehended. A procession on a highway or other public place, which is liable to obstruct traffic if it causes no other public nuisance, generally requires an arrangement of time and route with the chief constable.

Public Order Acts 1936 and 1963

It is an offence to wear in any public place or at any public meeting a *uniform* signifying association with any *political* organisation or with the promotion of any political object. The Home Secretary may give permission for the wearing of such uniform on a ceremonial or other special occasion. The consent of the Attorney-General is necessary for the continuance of a prosecution after a person has been charged in court (section 1).

The statutes against liveries and maintenance passed in Tudor times were repealed in the nineteenth century as being no longer necessary. In the years between the wars, however, the growth of militant fascist, communist and other extreme organisations led, or threatened to lead, to serious public disorder. Section 2 of the Public Order Act 1936 therefore enacted that if members or adherents of any association of persons are: " (a) organised or trained or equipped for the purpose of enabling them to be employed in usurping the functions of the police or of the armed forces of the Crown; or (b) organised and trained or organised and equipped either for the purpose of enabling them to be employed for the use or display of physical force in promoting any political object or in such manner as to arouse reasonable apprehension that they are organised and either trained or equipped for that purpose," then any person who takes part in the control or management of the association or in so organising or training its members or adherents, is guilty of an offence punishable by fine and imprisonment. The consent of the Attorney-General is necessary before initiating a prosecution under this section. A person charged with taking part in the control or management of such an association may plead that he neither consented to nor connived at the unlawful organisation, training or equipment. The first conviction under section 2 was *R.* v. *Jordan and Tyndall* [7] for organising and equipping an association called "Spearhead" in such a manner as to arouse reasonable apprehension that they would be used for the use or display of physical force in promoting a political object. The Court

[7] *The Times*, November 10, 1962; [1963] Crim.L.R. 124.

of Criminal Appeal, upholding sentences of nine months' and six months' imprisonment as being appropriate deterrents, held that it was not necessary that there should be evidence of actual attacks or plans for attacks on opponents.

It is an offence under section 4 to carry any *offensive weapon*, otherwise than in pursuance of lawful authority, at a public meeting or procession. " Lawful authority " is confined to servants of the Crown or of either House of Parliament or of a local authority or a constable or a member of a recognised corps or a member of a fire brigade.

Under section 5, as extended by the Race Relations Act 1965, s. 7, it is an offence, in any public place or at a public meeting, (a) to use threatening, abusive or insulting words or behaviour, or (b) to distribute or display any writing, sign or visible representation which is threatening, abusive or insulting, with intent to provoke a breach of the peace or whereby a breach of the peace is likely to be occasioned. " Public place " is defined for this purpose by the Criminal Justice Act 1972 to include any highway and any other premises or place to which at the material time the public have or are permitted to have access, whether on payment or otherwise.[8] The maximum penalties under section 5 were increased by the Public Order Act 1963 to three months' imprisonment and/or a fine of £100 on summary conviction, and twelve months' imprisonment and/or a fine of £500 on conviction on indictment. A constable may arrest without warrant any person reasonably suspected by him of committing an offence under section 1, 4 or 5.

The Act is intended to preserve order, not only where many persons are involved, but also order in a public place; and it has therefore been held not to be confined to political meetings.[9] To use insulting words and behaviour in the same incident is not two separate offences, and one summons may cover them both.[10] The word " insulting " must be given its ordinary meaning: it is a question of fact in each case and not a question of law.[11] Where a person is charged under section 5 the test is whether he used such words, behaviour or writing, and not whether the audience consisted of ordinary reasonable men. In *Jordan* v. *Burgoyne*[12] Jordan, the leader of the British fascists, held a meeting of several thousand people in Trafalgar Square. A group of two or three hundred young people—Jews, sup-

---

[8] *Cf. Cooper* v. *Shield* [1971] 2 Q.B. 334 (D.C.): the definition in s. 9 of the Public Order Act 1936 did not include buildings, such as a railway station platform.
[9] *Ward* v. *Holman* [1964] 2 Q.B. 580 (D.C.)
[10] *Vernon* v. *Paddon, The Times*, February 12, 1972.
[11] *Cozens* v. *Brutus* [1972] 3 W.L.R. 521 (H.L.) anti-apartheid demonstration on Wimbledon tennis court.
[12] [1963] 2 Q.B. 744 (D.C.).

porters of the Campaign for Nuclear Disarmament and Communists—placed themselves in front, intending to prevent the meeting being held. There was much disorder during Jordan's speech, twenty people were arrested for breaches of the peace, and Burgoyne (a police superintendent) eventually stopped the meeting. Jordan was convicted of using insulting words under this section, it being held that his words were intended to be deliberately insulting to a certain section of the crowd. A person is entitled, said Lord Parker C.J., to express his views as strongly as he likes, to criticise and to say disagreeable things about his opponents; but he must not threaten, abuse or insult by " hitting with words."

Public meetings at common law

The common practice of holding public meetings dates from the habit of promoting meetings to discuss and present petitions to Parliament in the late eighteenth and early nineteenth centuries, the popular interest in parliamentary affairs being no doubt stimulated, first, by a more widespread dissemination of newspapers, and then by the extension of the franchise. The restrictive legislation of that period shows that the executive was concerned with criticism of the government, whereas the later statutes are intended mainly to prevent outbreaks of disorder. Public meetings and processions have engaged the attention of Parliament and the courts a good deal in the past; and although the old election meeting, or meeting held to advocate or criticise some projected legislation or government action, has largely given way to the radio or television talk, this topic has received a revived importance in the last few years as a result of the modern " demonstration " against nuclear armament, apartheid and other objects of popular protest.

A " public meeting " may be defined as a meeting held for the purpose of discussing or expressing views on matters of public interest, and which the public or any section thereof is invited to attend. A public meeting may be held either on private premises or in a public place. " Private premises " are premises to which the public have access only by permission of the owner or occupier. A " public place " includes any highway or any other premises or place (such as a public park, sea beach or public road) to which the public have or are permitted to have access, whether on payment or otherwise.[13]

There is a general liberty to promote or take part in a public meeting on private premises, subject to infringement of particular legal rules. It is doubtful whether there is such a general liberty to promote or take part in a public meeting in a public place without the licence

13 Definitions adapted from Public Order Acts and Criminal Justice Act 1972.

of the owners (often the local authority), since this will almost invariably involve trespass to land as well as in many cases an obstruction or a public nuisance, although a public meeting in a public place is not necessarily unlawful.[14]

Among the common law rules that may be infringed by the holding of a public meeting are those relating to sedition,[15] unlawful assembly, rout and riot which are discussed below; public nuisance, which may be proceeded against by indictment; assault, and trespass to land, which by itself in English law is a tort.[16]   A meeting that would otherwise be lawful will not be so if there is intention or provocation or incitement of others to cause a disturbance or to commit other unlawful acts.   Most of the reported cases relating to public disorder have been decided by a Divisional Court on appeal on a case stated from the magistrates, and there is a certain amount of vagueness or inconsistency that needs to be tidied up.   Opportunities for this may arise since the Administration of Justice Act 1960 gave an appeal in criminal cases from a Divisional Court direct to the House of Lords where the Divisional Court certifies that there is a point of law of general public importance.   Recently there have been some appeals from assizes to the Court of Appeal.[17]

Public meetings in private premises

The owner or occupier of private premises, for example, the hirer of a hall, may hold a public meeting there or licence others to do so. The organiser of the meeting may exclude or eject trespassers, after first asking them to leave; if they refuse he may use reasonable force, although he may not arrest or detain them.   The exercise of this right by the occupier or licensee may be embarrassed by the decision in *Thomas* v. *Sawkins*[18] that the police may enter the premises if they have reasonable grounds for believing that, if they were not present, seditious speeches would be made or breaches of the peace would occur.   In that case the meeting was held to protest against the Incitement to Disaffection Bill, and to demand the dismissal of the Chief Constable of Glamorgan.   The scope of the decision is uncertain.   Lord Hewart L.C.J. said the police had a right to enter if they had reasonable grounds for believing that " an offence is

---

14 *Cf.* A. L. Goodhart, " Public Meetings and Processions " (1937) 6 C.L.J. 161.   See also E. C. S. Wade, " The Law of Public Meetings " (1938) 2 M.L.R. 177; E. R. Ivamy, " The Right of Public Meeting " (1949) C.L.P. 183.
15 *Ante,* Chap. 22.
16 *Cf.* Trespass (Scotland) Act 1865, under which lodging in premises or camping on land without the owner's permission is a criminal offence.   And *cf.* trespassing with firearms, *ante,* p. 409.
17 *e.g. R.* v. *Caird*; *post,* p. 442.
18 [1935] 2 K.B. 434.

imminent or is likely to be committed," while Avory J. said they had this right if " seditious speeches would be made and/or . . . a breach of the peace would take place." Lawrence J. did not express an opinion on this point. Stress was laid in the judgments on the fact that, as the public were invited, the police could attend as members of the public; but the conveners can withdraw an invitation from particular persons or sections of the public, and in this case they did in fact ask the police to leave. The police may have been trespassers, but Avory J. seems to have thought that the revocation of the licence to the police was ineffective. If the licence to the police as members of the public was effectively revoked, the decision in *Thomas* v. *Sawkins* may apply also to private meetings. Shortly after that case it was held in *Davis* v. *Lisle* [19] that the police have no right to enter private premises without a warrant in connection with a summary offence not involving a breach of the peace.

Public meetings in public places

The highway is in a special category, because members of the public have a right to pass and repass on their lawful occasions, with such reasonable extensions as looking at shop windows, talking to one's friends and parking cars.[20] To exceed this right is technically the tort of trespass against the owner of the surface of the highway, which is usually the local highway authority.[21] If repeated, such abuse might amount to nuisance, public or private. Public nuisance in relation to the highway is indictable, or there may be a prosecution for incitement to commit a public nuisance. Wilful obstruction of the highway is a summary offence under the Highways Act 1959, s. 121,[22] and a constable may arrest without warrant a person whom he sees committing the offence. It is not necessary on a prosecution to prove that anyone was actually obstructed,[23] nor is it a good defence that there was a way round the obstruction,[24] although these facts may go to mitigation.

In *Arrowsmith* v. *Jenkins* [25] Miss A held a CND meeting on a part of the highway where meetings had often been held before, and she complied with a police request to get her audience to draw in closer; traffic was partially obstructed, and she was convicted of wilful

[10] [1936] 2 K.B. 434 (D.C.).
[20] Parking is a liberty only where there are no parking regulations. Adjacent houseowners have no *right* to park in the highway, but they may in some areas obtain a licence from the local authority.
[21] *Tunbridge Wells Corporation* v. *Baird* [1896] A.C. 434; *Llandudno U.D.C.* v. *Woods* [1899] 2 Ch. 705.
[22] Replacing the Highways Act 1835.
[23] *Gill* v. *Carson and Nield* [1917] 2 K.B. 674.
[24] *Homer* v. *Cadman* (1888) Cox C.C. 51.
[25] [1963] 2 Q.B. 561 (D.C.).

obstruction of the highway. It was no defence that she did not intend
to obstruct: it was sufficient that she intended to do the thing that
obstructed. The " why pick on me? " argument was turned down.
On the other hand, the fact that a meeting is held on the highway is
not enough in itself to make the meeting unlawful for the purposes
of the Public Meeting Act 1908,[26] in the absence of some other
unlawful element such as obstruction. Thus in *Burden* v. *Rigler* [27]
a political meeting was held on the highway, after being advertised
in advance; the police were present and did not object. B tried to
make a speech in favour of tariff reform, but R and others created a
disturbance. B charged R and others under the Public Meeting Act,
and it was held that the defendants could be convicted of disorderly
conduct at a lawful public meeting. In *Papworth* v. *Coventry* [28] a
peaceful stationary demonstration was held on the footpath in Whitehall at each corner of Downing Street against the Vietnam war,
previous notice having been given to the police superintendent. The
Commissioner of Metropolitan Police may direct that certain streets
in London should be kept clear of crowds under the Metropolitan
Police Act 1839, s. 52. It was held that this power was limited to
such assemblies and processions as are capable of obstructing M.P.s,
or creating a disturbance or annoyance about Parliament, and the
case was remitted to the magistrates to consider whether the assembly
fell within that category.

Rather more latitude is allowed in public parks and gardens, which
are intended for recreation and exercise rather than merely passing
up and down. Yet there is no common law right in the strict sense
to hold public meetings on a common,[29] on the foreshore,[30] in Hyde
Park [31] or Trafalgar Square (*R.* v. *Cunninghame Graham and Burns*
(1888) [32]). Public meetings may take place in Trafalgar Square, and
perhaps Hyde Park, only with the permission of the Minister of Public
Building and Works, under regulations made by the Home Secretary.
The general regulations restrict the holding of public meetings in
Trafalgar Square to daylight on Saturday afternoons, Sundays and
bank holidays, and require previous notice to be given to the police
and their directions as to the approach route of any procession to be
accepted.[33]

---

26 *Ante*, p. 428.
27 [1911] 1 K.B. 337 (D.C.).
28 [1967] 1 W.L.R. 663 (D.C.).
29 *De Morgan* v. *Metropolitan Board of Works* (1880) 5 Q.B.D. 155.
30 *Brighton Corporation* v. *Packham* (1908) 72 J.P. 318.
31 *Bailey* v. *Williamson* (1873) L.R. 8 Q.B. 118.
32 16 Cox C.C. 420; *post*, p. 436. And see *Ex p. Lewis* (1888) 21 Q.B.D. 191.
33 These regulations were issued in 1892 by Asquith (Home Secretary), who had
   defended Cunninghame Graham when at the Bar: Roy Jenkins, *Asquith*, pp. 64–
   65.

Public processions

A public procession is defined by the Public Order Act 1936 as a procession in a public place. Many of the general common law principles mentioned in connection with public meetings are applicable also to public processions. Indeed, a procession has been described as a meeting on the move, and many processions are in fact preliminary to the holding of a meeting. Since the right to use the highway is for passing and repassing, however, a procession on the highway is prima facie lawful.[34] Apart from actual obstruction or causing a breach of the peace or constituting an unlawful assembly or riot, which are discussed below, a public procession may easily involve a public nuisance.

A public nuisance will be caused if the user of the highway, although reasonable from the point of view of those taking part in the procession, is not reasonable from the point of view of the public. This question depends on the circumstances of the case, and may be affected by the numbers taking part.[35] The occasion, duration, place and hour must be considered, and also whether the obstruction is trivial, casual, temporary and without wrongful intent (*Lowdens* v. *Keaveney*[36]). Thus in *R.* v. *Clark*[37] a conviction for inciting persons to commit a nuisance by obstructing the highway, after taking part in a demonstration during a visit of Greek royalty, was quashed on the ground that a procession is lawful if there is a reasonable use of the highway, even though the highway is temporarily obstructed.

The same principles apply whether the obstruction is caused by the procession itself or by onlookers.[38] Thus in *Lowdens* v. *Keaveney* (*supra*) it was held that a band which marched through Belfast playing party airs, with the result that a crowd of several hundreds collected, was not liable for causing a material obstruction. In *Beatty* v. *Glenister* (1884)[39] a member of the Salvation Army who marched down the street playing a cornet, with the result that persons in the neighbourhood were disturbed by the hostile crowd, was held not liable for causing a breach of the peace, although in a case of this kind the result might be different if the charge were that of causing a public nuisance. It has been suggested that, because of the increase of motor traffic and also the existence of section 3 of the Public Order Act 1936,[40] the courts should now treat alleged obstructions by stationary meetings and by processions in the same way.[41]

[34] Goodhart, " Public Meetings and Processions," *loc. cit.* pp. 169–174.
[35] *Att.-Gen.* v. *Brighton and Hove Co-operative Supply Association* [1900] 1 Ch. 276.
[36] [1903] Ir.R. 82.   [37] [1964] 2 Q.B. 315 (C.C.A.).
[38] *Bellamy* v. *Wells* (1890) 7 T.L.R. 135.
[39] 51 L.T. 304.
[40] *Post,* p. 440.
[41] Williams, *op. cit.* p. 216.

Affray

An affray is an unlawful fight by one or more to the terror of other persons. There must be other persons present who do not take part in or encourage the fight, and are thereby put in fear. A common purpose need not be shown; nor is it necessary to produce a witness to testify that he was put in terror (*R.* v. *Taylor*,[42]). Unlike assault, where the mischief falls on the victim, in affray it falls on the bystander. An affray need not be in a public place. In *R.* v. *Button and Swain* [43] the House of Lords upheld convictions for an affray committed at a dance held by a darts league in a private scout hall, admission to which was by tickets distributed to members and their friends. There are no reported convictions for affray between 1845 and 1957,[44] but since 1957 the charge has been revived to deal with gangs who fight and disturb the peace, including football hooligans.

Unlawful Assembly

An unlawful assembly is an indictable common law offence. It arises where three or more persons *either* assemble to commit, or when assembled do commit, a breach of the peace; *or* assemble with intent to commit a crime by open force; *or* assemble for any common purpose, whether lawful or unlawful, in such manner as to give firm and courageous persons in the neighbourhood reasonable cause to fear that a breach of the peace will occur.[45] The gist of the offence is an assembly of three or more persons in such a manner or in such circumstances as to arouse a reasonable fear that a breach of the peace will occur. Curiously enough, there is no legal definition of " breach of the peace," but it is commonly associated with physical assault or fear of assault (strictly, assault and battery), or damage or threat of damage to property. In *R.* v. *Cunninghame Graham and Burns* (1888) [46] a meeting of the Metropolitan Radical Federation was held in Trafalgar Square on " Bloody Sunday " in November 1887, to demand the release of certain Irish patriots. There had been serious riots in the previous February, and the Police Commissioner had used his statutory power to forbid a meeting in Trafalgar Square. Graham and Burns at the head of about 150 persons attempted to

---

42 [1972] 3 W.L.R. 961 (C.A.). *Cf. R.* v. *Sharp* [1957] 1 Q.B. 552 (C.C.A.); *R.* v. *Woodrow* (1959) 43 Cr.App.R. 105 (C.C.A.); *R.* v. *Scarrow* (1968) 52 Cr.App.R. 591 (C.A.). A misreading of Bl.Com. IV, p. 145, led to the view held for over a century that affray must be committed in a public place. *Cf. R.* v. *Allan* [1965] Q.B. 130: mere presence, without encouragement of the participants.
43 [1966] A.C. 591.
44 Except one Irish case.
45 *R.* v. *Vincent* (1839) 3 St.Tr.(N.S.) 1037; *R.* v. *Billingham* (1825) 2 C. & P. 234.
46 16 Cox C.C. 420.

break through the police cordon, and were arrested. On indictment they were found not guilty of riot (*infra*) but guilty of unlawful assembly. Charles J. said it was for the judge to define an unlawful assembly, and for the jury to say whether in the circumstances of the case such assembly was unlawful. An assembly which begins innocently may become unlawful in view of the persons who take part and the conduct of the assembly at any particular time: " although you may have gathered together with a most innocent intention," said Charles J., " still, if while you are so gathered together you determine to do an act of violence, then you become guilty of unlawful assembly."

On the other hand, where people assemble for a lawful object without intending to cause a breach of the peace, even though they have reason to believe that there will be such a breach in consequence of their meeting being opposed by other persons, the former do not, according to the decision in *Beatty* v. *Gillbanks* (1882),[47] constitute an unlawful assembly. *Beatty* v. *Gillbanks* was an appeal to a Divisional Court against a binding-over order made by magistrates, who had found Beatty and two other officers of the Salvation Army guilty of unlawful assembly (which magistrates have no jurisdiction to try) as a preliminary to binding them over. The Divisional Court held that Beatty and the other Salvation Army officers had been wrongly held guilty of unlawful assembly merely because they had persisted, in spite of a justices' notice and a police direction, in holding their processions and meetings in Weston-super-Mare knowing that a rival organisation called the " Skeleton Army " systematically opposed them, with the result that considerable disturbance occurred. They were therefore wrongly bound over. The Salvation Army did not incite or intentionally provoke a breach of the peace, nor did they intend to meet force by force if opposed. " The finding of the justices comes to this," said Field J., " that a man may be indicted for doing a lawful act, if he knows that his doing it will cause another to do an unlawful act. There is no authority for such a proposition." It should be mentioned that the magistrates' notice prohibiting the processions and meetings, issued on the advice of the Home Secretary, was of no legal effect: it was merely a warning of the fact that disorder was likely to follow. The police direction with regard to the procession has now been superseded by section 3 of the Public Order Act 1936. It has been questioned whether this case laid down a general principle, or merely found on the facts of the case that Beatty and others did not cause the disturbance.[48] The judgment of Field J. indicates that he was laying down a general principle.

[47] 15 Cox C.C. 138; (1882) 9 Q.B.D. 308.
[48] Street, *op. cit.* p. 51.

A charge of unlawful assembly is not now often brought,[49] and later cases show that there are means of preventing or dispersing a meeting that is likely to lead to a breach of the peace. The police cannot guarantee a quiet hearing for everyone whose views arouse antagonism: otherwise, they might be expected to protect the meeting that is first on the scene. One might well ask why the Skeleton Army was not prosecuted. Perhaps it was for the reason that the Skeleton Army would not have come on the scene unless the Salvation Army had first started their procession.[50]

Prevention and dispersal of meetings

The executive have no power to prohibit a meeting beforehand, unless it is to be on government property. The police, however, have a primary duty to preserve the peace, and therefore may prevent a meeting from starting, or may order it to disperse at any time after it has started, if they reasonably believe that it is necessary to do so for the purpose of preserving or restoring public order. The reasonableness of this belief and of the consequent action may be questioned in subsequent legal proceedings, either in defence to a charge or as a cause of action in tort. In the Irish case of *O'Kelly* v. *Harvey* (1883),[51] it was held that a police officer may disperse a public meeting if he believes that there will be a breach of the peace and that there is no other way of preventing it. And in another Irish case, *Humphries* v. *Connor* (1864),[52] where a disturbance was caused by the fact that a Protestant woman, without intending to disturb the peace, wore an orange lily while walking through a crowd of Roman Catholics, a constable was held justified in removing the lily on the ground that it was necessary for the preservation of the peace. Similarly, the procession in *Beatty* v. *Gillbanks* (*supra*) could properly have been dispersed if the rival factions had come to blows.

Provocation is a different matter. In *Wise* v. *Dunning*,[53] Wise, a Protestant pastor who led a Protestant "Crusade" in Liverpool and held street meetings in Catholic districts, was held to have been properly bound over for deliberately using insulting words and gestures, intended or likely to result in a breach of the peace. Darling J. emphasised the provocation, although there was a local Act under which Wise might have been charged. Channell J. pointed out that although "the law does not as a rule regard an illegal act as being

---

49 But see *R.* v. *Caird*, *post*, p. 442; *R.* v. *Kamara* [1973] 2 W.L.R. 126.
50 There is reason to believe that there was local prejudice against the Salvation Army on the part of the authorities as well as the public, and it has been said that the Skeleton Army was financed by the publicans.
51 14 L.R.Ir. 105, 109.
52 17 Ir.C.L.R. 1.
53 [1902] 1 K.B. 167.

the natural consequence of a temptation which may be held out to commit it . . . the law does regard the infirmity of human temper to the extent of considering that a breach of the peace, although an illegal act, may be the natural consequence of insulting or abusive language or conduct." Wise's conduct would now be covered by the Public Order Act 1936.

A more recent case of considerable importance is *Duncan* v. *Jones*.[54] Mrs. Duncan, a Communist, was about to make a speech in a street opposite a training centre for the unemployed. On a former occasion she had done so, and a disturbance took place among sympathisers in the training centre. Jones, a police inspector, told her she must not hold a meeting there, but might do so a couple of hundred yards round the corner. Mrs. Duncan persisted in her attempt to hold a meeting, and Jones arrested her for wilfully obstructing a police officer in the execution of his duty. Her conviction was upheld by Quarter Sessions on the grounds that: (i) she must have known that a disturbance was probable; (ii) Jones reasonably apprehended a breach of the peace; (iii) Jones therefore had a duty to prevent the meeting; and (iv) Mrs. Duncan obstructed Jones in the execution of his duty. It may be noticed that obstructing a constable, which had been indictable only, was made a summary offence in 1885,[55] a few years after the case of *Beatty* v. *Gillbanks*. What is the effect of the decision in *Duncan* v. *Jones* on the principle laid down in *Beatty* v. *Gillbanks*? The audience in *Duncan* v. *Jones* was not hostile, but there was an atmosphere of excitement. Mrs. Duncan was not charged with obstructing the highway. The Divisional Court in *Duncan* v. *Jones* denied that the case raised any constitutional issue, and did not give the police any guidance as to how they should exercise their discretion in such cases. It has been pointed out that a charge which was intended to be a defensive weapon (obstructing a police officer) has come to be used by the police as a weapon of offence; and it has been suggested that the police should arrest for obstruction of the highway or prospective breach of the peace, or that they should have contrived that Mrs. Duncan technically assaulted Jones, and then left it to her to bring an action for assault or false imprisonment against Jones.[56] It appears that persons in Mrs. Duncan's position should obey the police, and then pursue any remedy in the courts afterwards.

---

[54] [1936] 1 K.B. 218. See E. C. S. Wade, " Police Powers and Public Meetings " (1937) 6 C.L.J. 175; T. C. Dainteth, " Disobeying a Policeman—A Fresh Look at *Duncan* v. *Jones* " [1966] P.L. 248.

[55] Prevention of Crimes Amendment Act 1885. Assaulting a constable, which would be an indictable common law offence, had been regulated by the Prevention of Crimes Act 1871. Both offences are now covered by the Police Act 1964.

[56] Dainteth, *op. cit.*

Prohibition or routing of processions

The Public Order Act 1936, s. 3, provides that: (i) a chief officer of police, if he has reasonable grounds for apprehending that a public procession may cause serious public disorder, may prescribe the route of the procession, or prohibit it from entering a given area; (ii) a chief constable in a town outside London, if he thinks that the powers under (i) are insufficient to prevent serious public disorder, shall apply to the local council for an order prohibiting the holding of all public processions or any class of public procession in the town for a period not exceeding three months. The council then may, with the consent of the Home Secretary, make such order; (iii) the Commissioner of the City of London Police, or the Commissioner of Metropolitan Police, may in similar circumstances and with the consent of the Home Secretary make a similar order relating to his police area or any part of it. The three months' period under (ii) and (iii) may, with the consent of the Home Secretary, be extended for a further three months; (iv) it is an offence not to comply with such directions or conditions, or to organise any public procession in contravention of such order. A spontaneous procession is " organised " by the person who indicates the route.[57]

Binding over

The power of magistrates to make a binding-over order is a kind of preventive justice. The order is that a person should enter into a recognisance (a bond whereby he binds himself under a penalty) with or without sureties (other persons who will vouch for him under penalty) to keep the peace and/or to be of good behaviour for a certain period. If that person commits a breach of the order, he and his sureties are liable to forfeit the whole or part of the sums in which they are bound. There is no legal limit to the amount of the recognisances or of the sureties, or to the period of the order (which is commonly twelve months). If the person concerned refuses to enter into a recognisance, or if he is unwilling or unable to find satisfactory sureties, the magistrates may commit him to prison for not more than six months or until he sooner complies with the order. In *Lansbury* v. *Riley*[58] George Lansbury M.P., who incited suffragettes to militant action, was bound over to be of good behaviour in the sum of £1,000 with two sureties of £500 each; as he was unable or unwilling to find the sureties he was committed to prison for three months. The power to bind over to keep the peace is probably of common law origin, and may have been exercised by the

---

[57] *Flockart* v. *Robertson* [1950] 1 All E.R. 1091 (D.C.) *per* Lord Goddard C.J.
[58] [1914] 3 K.B. 229 (D.C.); *Everett* v. *Ribbands* [1952] 2 Q.B. 198.

Conservators of the Peace. The power to bind over to be of good behaviour towards the Queen and her people is ascribed to the Justices of the Peace Act 1361.[59]

Under the Magistrates' Courts Act 1952, s. 91, the power on the complaint of any person to bind over another person to keep the peace or to be of good behaviour towards the complainant, must be exercised on complaint. It was said in R. v. Aubrey-Fletcher, ex p. Thompson,[60] that for making a binding-over order under the Magistrates' Courts Act there has to be a complaint adjudged to be true; whereas an order under the Justices of the Peace Act 1361 can be made at any time during proceedings if it emerges that there might be a breach of the peace. In that case, however, where the charge was one of insulting words whereby a breach of the peace might be occasioned under the Metropolitan Police Act 1839, that stage had not yet been reached.

The question when the magistrates can make a binding-over order is not free from doubt. It appears that they may make such an order: (i) where a breach of the peace has been committed, or is threatened, or is reasonably apprehended [61]; or (ii) where an offence against public order has been committed and is likely to be repeated.[62] Such an order is not a conviction and therefore at common law there was no appeal, but a right of appeal to Quarter Sessions (now the Crown Court) was given in 1956.[63]

Rout

A rout is a disturbance of the peace by three or more persons who assemble with the intention of doing something which if executed would amount to a riot (infra), and who actually make a motion towards the execution thereof but do not complete it. This is a common law offence supposed to fill the gap between unlawful assembly

---

[59] Lansbury v. Riley, supra; R. v. County of London Quarter Sessions, ex p. Commissioner of Metropolitan Police [1948] 1 All E.R. 72, per Lord Goddard C.J. The Act was amended by the Criminal Law Act 1967, Sched. 3, Pt. II. And see C. K. Allen, The Queen's Peace, pp. 61–66; Glanville Williams, "Preventive Justice and the Rule of Law" (1953) 16 M.L.R. 417. The Act of 1361 may in fact have been intended to empower justices to require sureties from persons who are of good fame, as distinct from the power to punish rioters and other offenders against the peace. Superior courts may bind over convicted persons to come up for sentence if called upon, e.g. Morris v. Crown Office [1970] 2 Q.B. 114 (C.A.), and are not limited to six months' imprisonment.

[60] [1969] 1 W.L.R. 872 (D.C.).

[61] Wilson v. Skeock (1949) 65 T.L.R. 418 (D.C.) per Lord Goddard C.J., is authority for saying a breach of the peace need not actually have been committed.

[62] See David Williams, op. cit. p. 94.

[63] Magistrates' Courts (Appeals from Binding-Over Orders) Act 1956. A case may be stated on a point of law for the Queen's Bench Division, e.g. Beatty v. Gillbanks, supra; and certiorari lies on a question of jurisdiction, e.g. R. v. Aubrey-Fletcher, supra.

and riot (in which the common purpose must be at least partly executed). The charge of rout was probably never much used, and there have been no prosecutions in modern times.

Riot

A riot or riotous assembly is a disturbance of the peace by three or more persons who assemble together with the intention mutually to assist one another, by force if necessary, in the execution of some enterprise of a private nature, whether lawful or unlawful, and afterwards actually execute the same in a violent and turbulent manner to the terror of the people.[64] It is a common law offence. In order to constitute a riot five elements have been said to be essential: (i) three or more persons; (ii) a common purpose, whether lawful or unlawful, of a private nature[65]; (iii) execution or inception of the common purpose; (iv) intent to help one another, by force if necessary, against anyone who may oppose them; (v) force or violence displayed in such a manner as to alarm at least one person of reasonable firmness (*Field* v. *Metropolitan Police Receiver*[66]). With regard to (v), the Court of Criminal Appeal expressed doubt whether it is necessary to produce at least one witness to prove that he was in fact alarmed.[67] In *R.* v. *Cunninghame Graham and Burns* (1888)[68] Charles J. told the jury that it did not matter whether the enterprise was lawful or unlawful, it must not be executed in a violent and turbulent manner to the alarm of the people.

In *R.* v. *Caird and Others*[69] several hundred students and others took part in a demonstration both outside and inside the Garden House Hotel at Cambridge, where a dinner with a Greek flavour was being held. It was a social function to encourage tourism in Greece, and there were no speeches. The demonstrators apparently disapproved of the Greek political regime, and thought it was insensitive of older and non-politically-minded citizens to attend the dinner. For a period lasting two and a half hours 300–400 persons assembled in front and at the back of the hotel with the common purpose of wrecking the dinner. They shouted, tried to stop people entering the hotel, attempted to break through the police cordon in a violent and frightening manner, stamped on the flat roof over the dining-room, broke windows of the dining-room and hurled missiles—including

---

64 Hawkins, *Pleas of the Crown*, I, p. 513.
65 If the common purpose was of a public or political nature, the offence would amount to treason: *R.* v. *Damaree* (1709) 15 St.Tr. 521.
66 [1907] 2 K.B. 853.
67 *R.* v. *Sharp* [1957] 1 Q.B. 552.
68 16 Cox C.C. 420; *ante*, p. 436.
69 (1970) 54 Cr.App.R. 499 (C.A.). O. Hood Phillips, " Limits of the Freedom to Demonstrate " (1970) 86 L.Q.R. 453.

lighted mole fuses—through. Tables were overturned, glass and crockery smashed, curtains torn down, chairs thrown, car tyres deflated, more than £2,000 damage done to the hotel, a police constable and a university proctor received serious injuries, many people received minor injuries, terrified women screamed and became hysterical. Sachs L.J. said in the Court of Appeal that it could not be disputed that there was a riotous assembly of most serious proportions; there was a concerted attempt by aggressive force of numbers to overpower the police, to embark on wrecking, and to terrify citizens engaged on peaceable and lawful pursuits. The borderline between unlawful assembly and riotous assembly was not easy to draw with precision. The assembly became riotous at least when alarming force or violence began to be used. Sentences varying from twelve to fifteen months' imprisonment, with Borstal for those under twenty-one were held to be proper in the circumstances.

A bystander, or a person who happens to find himself present at an unlawful assembly or riot, is not liable. The guilt of anyone accused depends on the fact of participation.[70]

The Riot Act 1714, which turned riot (a common law misdemeanour) into a felony in certain circumstances, was repealed by the Criminal Law Act 1967 on the occasion of the abolition of the distinction between felony and misdemeanour. Under section 3 of the 1967 Act it is lawful to use such force as is reasonable in the circumstances to suppress a riot.

Most of the cases on riot arise out of the Riot (Damage) Act 1886, which replaced the old law whereby the inhabitants of the hundred had to compensate persons who lost property owing to the conduct of rioters.[71] This Act provides that where premises are injured or the property therein is destroyed or stolen by any persons riotously and tumultuously assembled, compensation to the persons aggrieved is to be paid out of the local police fund. Thus in *Ford* v. *Metropolitan Police District Receiver*[72] it was held that when a good-humoured crowd entered an empty house on peace night in 1919, and took away the woodwork and flooring to make a bonfire, to the alarm of the next-door neighbour, their conduct embraced all the ingredients of a riot. In *Munday* v. *Metropolitan Police District Receiver*[73] the plaintiff recovered compensation for damage done by a large crowd which invaded his premises (assaulting his daughter and gardener in the process) in order to see a football match on the adjoining ground after the gates were closed. In *Dwyer (J. W.)* v.

70 *R.* v. *Atkinson* (1869) 11 Cox 330; *R.* v. *Caird, supra.*
71 See A. Samuels, " Compensation for Riot Damage " [1970] Crim.L.R. 336.
72 [1921] 2 K.B. 344. And see *Pitchers* v. *Surrey County Council* [1923] 2 K.B. 415; *Jarvis* v. *Surrey County Council* [1925] 1 K.B. 554.
73 [1949] 1 All E.R. 337.

Metropolitan Police District Receiver [74] it was held that the words
" riotously " and " tumultuously " involve two concepts, both of
which must be fulfilled for the purposes of the Act; and thus where
the plaintiff's shop was raided and robbed by four hooded men armed
with iron bars, and four persons in the shop were threatened but the
incident attracted no attention from outside, the claim failed as the
assembly was riotous but not tumultuous.

Demonstrations [75]

Demonstrations may be in favour of someone or something, for
example, when the local team win a football cup; but usually demonstrations are protests, and are therefore liable to lead to breach
of the peace, obstruction, damage to property, assault on the police,
abusive words and so on.[76] Planned demonstrations may amount to
conspiracy or incitement to commit an unlawful act.[77] A plea that the
accused were motivated by conscience will not affect the sentence, at
least if the offence has been repeated.[78] Sachs L.J. pointed out in
R. v. *Caird* that a demonstration may be unlawful even though
not accompanied by acts of violence; and that political or similar
motive is not the concern of the court. The place where a demonstration takes place is of the essence. What may be lawful in one's
own premises or in premises hired for the purpose may be unlawful
on someone else's premises, whether public or private. The rights
and liberties of the rest of the community must be protected.

II. TRADE UNIONS

Before 1971 [79]

Combinations of workers for the purpose of improving their working conditions were made illegal conspiracies by a series of statutes

[74] [1967] 2 Q.B. 970.
[75] See W. B. Fisse and J. B. Jones, " Demonstrations: Some Proposals for Law
Reform " (1971) 45 A.L.J. 593; K. J. Keith, " The Right to Protest " in *Essays
on Human Rights* (ed. Keith, N.Z., 1968) p. 49; O. Hood Phillips, " A Right to
Demonstrate? " (1970) 86 L.Q.R. 1; " Limits of the Freedom to Demonstrate,"
ibid. p. 453.
[76] *e.g. R.* v. *Caird* (riot and unlawful assembly); *Morris* v. *Crown Office* (contempt
of court); *Chandler* v. *D.P.P.* and *Adler* v. *George* (official secrets); *Arrowsmith* v.
Jenkins (obstruction of highway); *Papworth* v. *Coventry* (Metropolitan Police Act
1839); *Cozens* v. *Brutus* (Public Order Act 1936). And see *R.* v. *Farr and Brown*
[1970] Crim.L.R. 658 (lighted petrol bombs).
[77] *e.g. R.* v. *Clark* (incitement); *Bennion* v. *Hain, The Times,* August 22, 1972
(conspiracy).
[78] *R.* v. *Foley*; *R.* v. *Chandler*; *R.* v. *Randle* (1967) 52 Cr.App.R. 123 (C.A.).
[79] S. and B. Webb, *The History of Trade Unionism* (2nd ed. 1920); R. Y. Hedges
and A. Winterbottom, *Legal History of Trade Unionism* (1930). K. W. Wedderburn, *The Worker and the Law,* contains a useful though partisan account.

from the fourteenth century onwards, and this was the position until the Industrial Revolution was well under way. These statutes were consolidated by the Combination Act 1801, under which it was illegal for workmen to combine for obtaining increased wages, altering hours of work or preventing employers from engaging what workmen they wished, or to attend meetings for these purposes. By several Acts between 1824 and 1871, however, combinations for bona fide trade purposes, e.g. the regulation of wages and conditions, were made no longer criminal; but they might still be illegal associations at common law as being " in restraint of trade." More statutes were passed dealing ad hoc with political situations as they arose. Their general purpose was to redress the balance of bargaining power between capital and labour, with little regard for the general public, the consumers.

The Trade Union Act 1871 formed the basis of trade union law for the next century. The purposes of a trade union were no longer unlawful, either criminally or civilly, merely because they were in restraint of trade. Certain agreements between members of a trade union, although not illegal, were rendered unenforceable in the courts (s. 4). Registration of a trade union with the Chief Registrar of Friendly Societies had some advantages, but was not compulsory. A trade union remained an unincorporated association, although a registered union was regarded as having sufficient personality to sue in tort [80] and to be sued in contract.[81]

" Peaceful picketing," as therein defined, was declared lawful by the Trade Disputes Act 1906, s. 2. Section 4 of that Act, reversing the decision of the House of Lords in the *Taff Vale* case,[82] gave immunity to trade unions from actions for any tort committed by them or on their behalf. This immunity was not confined to torts committed in contemplation or furtherance of a trade dispute.[83] The Trade Union Act 1913, reversing the decision of the House of Lords in the *Osborne* case,[84] legalised the application of trade union funds for political purposes. The Trade Disputes Act 1965 nullified the decision of the House of Lords in *Rooks* v. *Barnard* [85] whereby a threat to strike, involving a breach of contract, might constitute the tort of intimidation. Meanwhile the Trade Disputes and Trade Unions Act 1927 had attempted to define the conditions in which a " general strike " was illegal. This followed the much criticised decision of Astbury J. in

[80] *National Union of General and Municipal Workers* v. *Gillian* [1946] K.B. 81 (C.A.).
[81] *Bonsor* v. *Musicians' Union* [1956] A.C. 104 (H.L.).
[82] *Taff Vale Ry.* v. *Amalgamated Society of Railway Servants* [1901] A.C. 426.
[83] *Vacher & Sons Ltd.* v. *London Society of Compositors* [1913] A.C. 107 (H.L.).
[84] *Amalgamated Society of Railway Servants* v. *Osborne* [1910] A.C. 87.
[85] [1964] A.C. 1129; *Morgan* v. *Fry* [1968] 2 Q.B. 710 (C.A.).

National Sailors' and Firemen's Union v. *Reed*,[86] which arose out of the General Strike of 1926.[87] The Act of 1927, however, was repealed by the Trade Disputes and Trade Unions Act 1946, and the law on the legality or otherwise of a general strike returned to its previous uncertain state.

The Industrial Relations Act 1971 [88]

This Act, repealing the whole of the Acts of 1871 and 1906, attempts to put the law of industrial relations on a new and coherent basis. Although industrial relations cannot—any more than personal relations generally—be regulated entirely by laws and courts, the object of the Act is to provide a legal framework within which industrial relations can operate, and a last resort when they show signs of breaking down. In other words, the Industrial Relations Act 1971 attempts to bring trade unions and employers within the "rule of law" that applies to everyone else. It is not possible here to do more than refer to some of the provisions that have most significance for the constitutional lawyer; nor is it probable that the citation of previous cases would be of much value.

Certain general principles are laid down for the guidance of those concerned, *viz.* collective bargaining; orderly procedures for settling disputes by negotiation, conciliation or arbitration; free association of workers and employers; and the freedom and security of workers (s. 1). The Secretary of State is to issue a code of practice, to be laid in draft for approval by each House (s. 2). Every worker, as between himself and his employer, has a right to join, or not to join, a trade union (s. 5), and a pre-entry closed shop agreement is void (s. 7). New minimum periods of notice to terminate contracts of employment are laid down (s. 19). Every employee has a right not to be unfairly dismissed (s. 22). Collective agreements in writing are conclusively presumed to be intended to be legally enforceable (s. 34),[89] and breach of a collective agreement is an unfair industrial practice cognisable by the Industrial Court (s. 36). No court other than the Industrial Court may construe or enforce such agreements (s. 129).

A " trade union " is defined as an organisation of workers which

---

[86] [1926] Ch. 536; Sir John Simon, *The General Strike* (1926); Henry Strauss, *Trade Unions and the Law* (1946); *cf.* Sir F. Pollock in (1926) 42 L.Q.R. 289; A. L. Goodhart, *Essays in Jurisprudence and the Common Law*, Chap. 11.

[87] See Keith Middlemas and John Barnes, *Baldwin* (1969) Chap. 15; Julian Symons, *The General Strike* (1957).

[88] Based on *Fair Deal at Work* (1970). *Cf.* the Labour Government's *In Place of Strife* (1969) Cmnd. 3888, following the *Report of the Donovan Commission* (1968) Cmnd. 3623. See R. W. Rideout, " The Industrial Relations Act 1971 " (1971) 34 M.L.R. 655; O. Kahn Freund Q.C., *Labour and the Law* (1972) Chap. 7.

[89] *Cf. Ford Motor Co. Ltd.* v. *A.U.E.F.W.* [1969] 2 Q.B. 303.

is for the time being registered as a trade union under the Act (s. 61). The Act confers certain privileges and immunities on trade unions as so defined, which are withheld from mere organisations of workers. A Chief Registrar of Trade Unions and Employers' Associations is established, who not only takes over the responsibilities of the Chief Registrar of Friendly Societies before the Act, but also has new functions such as the surveillance of the rules of trade unions, and the hearing of complaints by members of registered bodies (s. 63). A (registered) trade union is a corporation, in which property is vested and which can sue and be sued in its own name (s. 74). Unregistered associations of workers, although they remain unincorporated, may sue and be sued in their own name, and judgment may be enforced against the property belonging, or held in trust for, such association (s. 154).

In the case of both trade unions and unregistered organisations, however, judgment cannot be enforced against property which by its rules cannot be used for financing strikes or other industrial action (ss. 153 and 154). The Act introduces the concept of an " unfair industrial practice." It is an unfair industrial practice for any person, in contemplation or furtherance of an industrial dispute, knowingly to induce or threaten to induce another person to break a contract, unless the former is a (registered) trade union or is authorised to act on behalf of a (registered) trade union.[90] This provision (s. 96) is aimed at unofficial action.[91] Industrial action in support of an unfair industrial practice is itself an unfair industrial practice (s. 97). No court may by order of specific performance or injunction compel an employee to work or to take part in industrial action (s. 128).

The Act establishes a National Industrial Relations Court ("the Industrial Court ") with a status equivalent to that of the High Court.[92] The President is a lawyer, but the Court includes lay members with special knowledge or experience of industrial relations. Appeal lies on a question of law to the Court of Appeal or the Court of Session (s. 99). In emergencies the Secretary of State may apply to the Industrial Court for a " cooling-off " order to discontinue or defer industrial action (s. 138).[93] He may also apply to the Industrial Court for an order for a ballot to be taken, where it appears to him that there are reasons for doubting whether industrial action has the support

[90] *Heaton's Transport (St. Helen's) Ltd.* v. *Transport and General Workers' Union* [1972] 3 W.L.R. 431 (H.L.): liability of union for shop stewards.
[91] *Cf. Vacher & Sons Ltd.* v. *London Society of Compositors* [1913] A.C. 107; *Torquay Hotel Co. Ltd.* v. *Cousins* [1969] 2 Ch. 106.
[92] Including power to punish for contempt: *Churchman* v. *Joint Shop Stewards' Committee* [1972] 1 W.L.R. 1094 (C.A.).
[93] *Secretary of State for Employment* v. *ASLEF* [1972] 2 Q.B. 443 (NIRC).

of the workers concerned (s. 141).[94] Hitherto a government has had to rely on the powers given by the Emergency Powers Act 1920.

An act done in contemplation or furtherance of an industrial dispute is not actionable in tort on the ground only that: (a) it induces another person to break a contract, or (b) it threatens that a contract will be broken or will be prevented from being performed; and an agreement by two or more persons to do any act in contemplation or furtherance of an industrial dispute is not actionable in tort if the act is one which, if done without such agreement, would not be actionable in tort (s. 132).[95] Section 133 repeals the provisions of the Conspiracy and Protection of Property Act 1875 and the Electricity (Supply) Act 1919 which imposed penalties in certain circumstances on persons employed in the supply of gas, water or electricity who went on strike in breach of their contracts of employment; but section 5 of the 1875 Act still remains, which makes it a criminal offence wilfully and maliciously to break a contract of service, knowing or having reasonable cause to believe that it is likely to endanger human life or to cause serious bodily injury or to expose valuable property to destruction or serious injury.

The definition of " peaceful picketing " is amended. Where one or more persons, in contemplation or furtherance of an industrial dispute, attend at or near a place where a person works or carries on business, or any other place where a person happens to be (not being a place where he resides [96]), and do so only for the purpose of peacefully obtaining or communicating information or peacefully persuading him to work or not to work, that does not of itself constitute an offence under section 7 of the Conspiracy and Protection of Property Act 1875 (intimidation or annoyance by violence or otherwise), and it does not of itself constitute a tort (s. 134).[97]

Due notice given by or on behalf of an employee of his intention to strike does not terminate his contract of employment or amount to a repudiation of that contract (s. 147).[98] A " strike " is defined as a concerted stoppage of work by a group of workers, in contemplation or furtherance of an industrial dispute, whether they are parties to the dispute or not, and whether the stoppage is or is not in breach of their terms of employment (s. 167).

[94] *Secretary of State for Employment* v. *ASLEF (No.* 2) [1972] 2 Q.B. 455 (C.A.).
[95] *Cf. Rookes* v. *Barnard* [1964] A.C. 1129 (H.L.).
[96] This exception is new.
[97] *Cf. Piddington* v. *Bates* [1961] 1 W.L.R. 162 (D.C.), breach of peace apprehended; *Tynan* v. *Balmer* [1967] 1 Q.B. 91 (D.C.), unreasonable user of highway. Strike pickets have been charged with obstructing the police, obstructing the highway, threatening behaviour and possessing offensive weapons.
[98] *Cf. Rookes* v. *Barnard, supra*; *Stratford (J. T.) & Son Ltd.* v. *Lindley* [1965] A.C. 269 (H.L.); *Morgan* v. *Fry* [1968] 2 Q.B. 710, 725, *per* Lord Denning M.R.

Wrongful expulsion from trade union

It is a serious matter for a member of a trade union to be expelled from his union. Expulsion may be wrongful because it was done by unauthorised persons, or the union rules of procedure were not complied with, or the principles of natural justice have been infringed. In the last case the jurisdiction of the courts over domestic tribunals comes into play.[99] That jurisdiction cannot be ousted by contract.[1] Where the court finds that expulsion was wrongful, it will issue a declaration if there is no other appropriate remedy,[2] and if necessary an injunction against continuing to exclude the plaintiff from membership.[3] The same applies to the wrongful infliction of fines by a trade union.

A member who has been wrongfully expelled from his union will often suffer damage in the form of loss of wages, and it has been held by the House of Lords that he may recover damages against the union for breach of contract, if the express or implied terms of the contract can be shown.[4]

---

[99] *Post,* Chap. 29.

[1] *Lawlor* v. *Union of Post Office Workers* [1965] Ch. 712.

[2] *Barnard* v. *National Dock Labour Board* [1953] 2 Q.B. 18 (C.A.).

[3] *Lee* v. *Showmen's Guild of Great Britain* [1952] 2 Q.B. 329 (C.A.).

[4] *Bonsor* v. *Musicians' Union* [1956] A.C. 104 (H.L.); *Edwards* v. *Society of Graphical and Allied Trades* [1971] Ch. 354 (C.A.); *Leary* v. *National Union of Vehicle Builders* [1971] Ch. 34. See D. Lloyd, " Damages for Wrongful Expulsion from a Trade Union " (1956) 19 M.L.R. 121; " The Right to Work " [1957] C.L.P. 36; Trevor C. Thomas, " Trade Unions and their Members " [1956] C.L.J. 67; K. W. Wedderburn, " The Bonsor Affair: A Postscript " (1957) 20 M.L.R. 105.

It is a serious matter for a member of a trade union to be expelled from his union. Expulsion may be wrongful because it was borne by the constitution, or personnel, or the union rules, of procedure were not complied with, or the principles of natural justice have been changed. In any case the jurisdiction of the courts over domestic tribunals comes into play. That jurisdiction cannot be ousted by contract. Where the court finds that expulsion was wrongful it will issue a declaration if there is no other appropriate remedy, and if necessary an injunction against continuing to exclude the plaintiff from membership. The entire applies to the wrongful infliction of fines by a trade union.

A member who has been wrongfully expelled from his union will often suffer damage in the form of loss of wages and it has been held by the House of Lords that he may recover damages against the union for breach of contract, if the express or implied terms of the contract can be shown.

Part VI

ADMINISTRATIVE LAW

CHAPTER 26

LOCAL GOVERNMENT

I. GENERAL SURVEY

THIS account of local government authorities is confined to England and Wales. Local government in Scotland at the present day bears some resemblance to the English system, but it has quite a different history and is under the supervision of the Secretary of State for Scotland.[1] The organisation of local government in Northern Ireland is based on different legislation, its main peculiarities being that the county councils are rating authorities, there are no civil parishes, and the central supervision is exercised by the Northern Ireland Minister for Home Affairs.

It is only possible in the space available to give an outline of the structure of the various local authorities, their relations with one another and with the central government, and to say something about local government elections and finance and the source of their powers. It is not practicable to describe the detailed powers which the various local authorities possess in relation to specific services.

Development of local government [2]

The present structure of local government authorities in England and Wales is based on recent legislation, and most of their powers are based on nineteenth- and twentieth-century statutes, although counties, boroughs and parishes as units for various purposes are ancient. In the shire, hundred and vill is found the key to the present organisation of rural areas for local government purposes— the county, the district and the civil parish. An antithesis between centralisation and decentralisation runs through the history of the organisation of English government. In the early Middle Ages, both before and after the Norman Conquest, the chief royal officer for the control of local government was the sheriff of the county or shire, subject to the supervision of the King's Council. The general ad-

---

[1] See *Reform of Local Government in Scotland* (1971) Cmnd. 4583.
[2] Redlich and Hirst, *History of Local Government in England* (ed. B. Keith-Lucas, 2nd ed. 1970); W. A. Robson, *The Development of Local Government* (3rd ed. 1954); S. Webb, *The Evolution of Local Government* (ed. 1951); Holdsworth, *History of English Law*, Vol. X, pp. 126–339; *A Century of Municipal Progress 1835–1935* (ed. Laski, Jennings and Robson, 1935); K. B. S. Smellie, *A Hundred Years of Local Government* (2nd ed. 1950).

ministration was carried on in the county court, the assembly of the freeholders of the county over which the sheriff presided.

Over a period of centuries the sheriff gradually lost nearly all his functions, so that Maitland could say in 1885 that the whole history of English justice and police might be described as " the decline and fall of the sheriff." [3] After various experiments, the local administration of justice was given in the middle of the fourteenth century to justices of the peace. For nearly five hundred years, that is, until the year 1834, the control of local government outside the boroughs was mainly in the hands of these justices of the peace, for besides the judicial functions in which they displaced the sheriffs and the county and hundred courts, a long series of statutes cast on them numerous administrative duties concerning such matters as highways, poor relief, wages and licensing.[4] The justices themselves were controlled by the King's Council until the Star Chamber was abolished in 1640. For the next two hundred years local government was, subject to the legislative power of Parliament, almost autonomous: practically the only control was exercised by the courts in applying the doctrine of *ultra vires* and issuing prerogative writs.

The period from the Middle Ages down to the early nineteenth century also saw a great growth in the size and number of towns, and to the justices of the peace as local government authorities we must add the boroughs. Further, the statutory institution of *ad hoc* bodies for specific purposes, which began with the Statute of Sewers 1531, was increasingly adopted in the eighteenth century for such purposes as the poor law, turnpike roads and urban sanitation.

Modern local government, characterised by *locally elected councils*, was inaugurated by the Poor Law Amendment Act 1834 and the Municipal Corporations Act 1835. The former Act reorganised the administration of the poor law which, apart from police, had hitherto been the most important function of local government. The Municipal Corporations Act provided for an elected borough council in place of an oligarchy of co-opted burgesses. The process of creating elected councils was continued by the introduction, first, of county councils and county borough councils in 1888,[5] and then of urban district councils, rural district councils and parish councils in 1894.[6] *Ad hoc* authorities continued to be created during the nineteenth century for highways, schools and sanitation, but they gradually disappeared. The general principle in modern times was to have one local authority for

[3] *Justice and Police* (1885) p. 69. For the modern sheriff, see *The High Sheriff* (*The Times*, 1961).
[4] Sir Carleton Allen, *The Queen's Peace*, Chap. 5.
[5] Local Government Act 1888.
[6] Local Government Act 1894.

all services in its area, and this was largely brought about by 1930.[7] The Local Government Act 1933 consolidated the legislation relating to the structure of local government outside London, and remained the basis of the law for the next forty years.

The government of London has always stood apart from the general system, owing to the maintenance of the ancient privileges of the City of London and the great size and population of Greater London. The organisation outside the City was greatly simplified by the creation of the London County Council and the metropolitan borough councils in 1899,[8] and this was replaced by the reforms contained in the London Government Act 1963, which created the Greater London Council.

Since the last war there has also been consolidation, as well as reform, of the statute law relating to particular services such as town and country planning, housing, education, highways, and the national health service.

Acquisition of powers by local authorities

Local authorities acquire their powers, which are all statutory, in various ways. The exercise of their powers is subject to judicial control by virtue of the doctrine of *ultra vires*.[9]

Public general Acts may confer general powers such as the making of contracts, the bringing or defending of legal proceedings and the making of by-laws, on all local authorities or all authorities of a certain kind, *e.g.* Local Government Acts and London Government Acts. Powers relating to specific services are also granted by such statutes as Public Health Acts, Housing Acts, Town and Country Planning Acts, Education Acts and Social Services Acts; some are obligatory and others permissive.

Adoptive Acts are public general Acts that come into force for a particular authority only if and when the latter adopts it, either by formal resolution or by order of the Minister. Examples are certain provisions of the Public Health Acts.

Local Acts

A particular local authority may acquire powers by procuring the passing of a private Act, known in this case as a local Act.[10] The Local Government Act 1972 provides that county councils and district councils may promote or oppose local or personal Bills. The resolution must be passed by a majority of the total number of

---

[7] Local Government Act 1929; Poor Law Act 1930.
[8] London Government Act 1899.   [9] *Post*, Chap. 30.
[10] For the procedure in Parliament, see *ante*, Chap. 9.

members of the council after a meeting held after ten days' notice in the local Press; and, in the case of the promotion of a Bill, must be confirmed by a like majority at a further meeting held as soon as may be after fourteen days after the Bill has been deposited in Parliament.

The promotion of local Bills is in any event an expensive procedure, and its place has largely been taken in recent years (except in the larger county boroughs) by the method of Provisional Order or Special Procedure Orders where they are applicable (*infra*).

A local Bill may set out *standard clauses* contained in " model Bills " which have been found acceptable to the House of Commons, and have been printed with the sanction of the Speaker to act as a guide to parliamentary agents.

A local Bill may incorporate by reference certain clauses contained in *Clauses Acts, i.e.* public general Acts which set out clauses for this purpose. A number of Clauses Acts were passed in 1845–1847 and later relating to such matters as water, gas, electricity, markets and fairs, harbours and docks, and cemeteries. Some of these have now been incorporated by general legislation, in some cases by reference.

Provisional Order confirmation Acts [11]

Many of the particular powers of local authorities are—or were until recently—conferred by these Acts, which confirm *Provisional Orders* made under statutory powers by the Minister concerned.

Orders subject to special parliamentary procedure [12]

Since 1945, statutory powers which are expressed to be subject to " special parliamentary procedure " are acquired in accordance with the requirements of the Statutory Orders (Special Procedure) Act 1945.

Ministerial (or Special) Orders

Local authorities may put forward schemes (*e.g.* clearance schemes under the Housing Acts) for confirmation after public inquiry, by the appropriate Minister. A ministerial order, unless rejected by parliamentary resolution (which has no power to amend it), gives the local authority statutory powers.

Central government control [13]

Central Authority

The experiment made in 1834 of appointing poor law commissioners who were neither in Parliament nor responsible to Parliament

---

[11] *Ante*, Chap. 9. Procedure modified by the Local Government Act 1972.
[12] *Ante*, Chap. 9. Procedure modified by the Local Government Act 1972.
[13] See J. A. G. Griffith, *Central Departments and Local Authorities* (1966).

was not successful, and was superseded by other methods of central control. A Local Government Board with a President in Parliament displaced the existing Poor Law Board. The Local Government Board was the central department responsible for the general supervision of local government from 1871 until the Ministry of Health was created in 1919. Since 1951 the general supervision of the work of local government (other than personal health services) has been entrusted to various Ministries, and now comes under the Department of the Environment.

The central government exercises a considerable degree of administrative control over local authorities in the interests of the community as a whole; for what is administered locally is often a national policy. This supervision is closer in respect of some services than of others. The most effective single agency is the control over finance exercised by the Secretary of State, and by the Home Secretary in the case of the police. The various methods are only mentioned here very briefly and by way of illustration.

The main significance of these supervisory powers lies in their cumulative effect. Their mere existence is generally enough to ensure that local authorities exercise their functions, not only as laid down by law but in consultation with, and in accordance with the policy of, the appropriate central government department.

Orders and regulations

Extensive powers to issue orders and regulations are given to Ministers in relation to food and drugs, public health, housing, social security and water supply. The Education Act 1944, s. 99, provided that if a Minister was satisfied that a local education authority had failed to discharge any duty imposed on it by the Act, he might make an order and give directions for its execution, and might enforce such directions by mandamus.

Sanctioning of schemes

Often it is the duty of a local authority to prepare schemes for the administration of a particular service within its area, e.g. planning and schools, and to submit such schemes to the appropriate Minister for approval.

Control over officials is exemplified by the power given to the Minister to regulate the appointment, salaries and duties of public health inspectors. The Home Secretary issues regulations concerning the salaries, duties and uniforms of local police forces, and may veto the appointment of a chief constable or children's officer. The

Secretary of State for Education and Science may veto the appointment of a chief education officer.

Inspection

The Minister may provide for inspection of local welfare services in the regulations which he is empowered to issue by the Social Security Acts. Inspection by Home Office and Department of Education inspectors is also the chief means for securing that local police and education authorities are performing their duties and complying with regulations.

Inquiry

A Minister who is authorised to act by the Local Government Act 1972, and the Secretary of State concerned with local government, may cause a local inquiry to be held.

Confirmation of by-laws is required by the Home Secretary, the Secretary of State for the Environment or other appointed Minister. This check on the lawmaking powers of local authorities is in addition to the limits imposed by Parliament and enforced under the doctrine of *ultra vires* by the courts.

Acting in default

The Minister may take over certain functions relating to education or civil defence, if it appears after a local inquiry that the authority has failed to discharge such functions. In practice, this power is very seldom exercised, as the knowledge of its existence—let alone the mere threat of using the power—is generally sufficient to induce the local authority to discharge its functions.

Control over loans

The consent of the Secretary of State to the raising of loans by local authorities is required in most cases.

Control over grants

This is the most important kind of financial control exercised by the central government over local authorities. The Secretary of State has power to reduce the rate support grant in case of default. This power gives the Minister a general control over the whole field of local administration, and the only check upon its exercise is that the Minister is obliged to lay a report of the proposed reduction before Parliament for approval by resolution of the House of Commons.

Similarly, the Home Secretary or the Minister may withhold any portion of the grant for police or housing from any authority whose administration of such service falls below the minimum standard required, or is not in accordance with statutory duties or ministerial regulations.[14]

Admission to meetings

The Public Bodies (Admission to Meetings) Act 1960 [15] provided that any meeting of a local authority or education committee should be open to the public. A body may exclude the public whenever publicity would be prejudicial to the public interest by reason of the confidential nature of the business. Public notice must be given of meetings to which the public are entitled to be admitted, and copies of the agenda must be supplied on request to any newspaper. These provisions extend where any body to which the Act applies resolves itself into a committee. The power remains to exclude persons in order to suppress or prevent disorderly conduct at a meeting. The Local Government Act 1972 provides that every local authority shall unless otherwise decided by majority vote admit the public and the Press to all its meetings, including meetings of its committees.

II. LOCAL AUTHORITIES IN ENGLAND AND WALES
(EXCLUDING LONDON)

Areas and authorities

The Local Government Act 1972 [16] reorganised the structure of local government in England and Wales on a two-tier basis throughout the country. The Act retains important responsibilities at local level, and greatly reduces the number of authorities. Local authorities are given more discretion in certain fields, and greater freedom to arrange their committee structure, to delegate the exercise of their functions and to appoint officers. The Act consolidates most of the existing Local Government Acts, the Act of 1933 being largely repealed.

The country (outside London) is divided into counties, and the counties into districts. There are six new *metropolitan counties* of Tyne and Wear, Merseyside, Greater Manchester, West Yorkshire,

---

[14] It is the policy not to approve the promotion to chief constable of an officer who has served his whole career in the same force.

[15] Repealing the Local Authorities (Admission of the Press to Meetings) Act 1908.

[16] Based on *Local Government in England: Proposals for Reorganisation* (1971) Cmnd. 4584, and *The Reform of Local Government in Wales: Consultative Document* (H.M.S.O. 1971). *Cf. Report of Royal Commission on Local Government in England* (Maud), (1969) Cmnd. 4040, and the Labour Government's *Reform of Local Government in England* (1970) Cmnd. 4276.

South Yorkshire and the West Midlands. The *non-metropolitan counties* correspond roughly with the existing counties; but there are many boundary changes, some counties (*e.g.* Worcestershire and Herefordshire, Cumberland and Westmorland, and some Welsh counties) are merged, Avon (Bristol and Bath) is created, Glamorgan is divided into three, and Rutland disappears. Both metropolitan and non-metropolitan counties are divided into *districts*, the number of districts in the latter being reduced. Rural *parishes* continue in England, which does not include Monmouthshire.

"Local authorities" in England and Wales are county councils, the Greater London Council, district councils, London borough councils, parish councils and community councils.

The principal councils in England are the *county councils* and *district councils*, consisting of a chairman and councillors elected by the local government electors. Each council is a body corporate. Existing boroughs lost that status, but a district council may petition for a charter conferring the status of a borough. The chairman is elected annually by the council from among the councillors or persons qualified to be councillors.

In rural areas in England there is a *parish meeting* of the local government electors for the purpose of discussing parish affairs and exercising the functions conferred on parish meetings. A larger parish or group of parishes may have a *parish council*, consisting of a chairman and elected councillors. Parish councils have powers rather than duties.

In Wales (which includes Monmouthshire) every district is to consist of one or more *communities*. Communities in the first instance will cover the existing boroughs, urban districts and parishes. In place of parish meetings and councils, therefore, there will be *community meetings or councils* with similar executive powers, but greater ability to express local wishes and needs.

Changes in local government areas

Separate permanent *local government boundary commissions* for England and Wales are set up to review local government boundaries and local electoral arrangements. Both commissions are advisory and report to the Secretary of State, who may give effect by order to their recommendations. The Boundary Commission for England was given the task of recommending the pattern of new districts within the non-metropolitan counties. The Boundary Commission for Wales after 1974 will draw up a revised pattern of communities. No local authority may promote a Bill for forming, altering or abolishing any local government area, or for changing its status or electoral arrangements.

Proceedings and discharge of functions

County and district councillors and elected members of London authorities are entitled to a flat-rate attendance allowance to cover the time spent on council business. Such allowance is taxable, and payable as of right without proof of loss of earnings. Reimbursement of travelling and subsistence expenses continues.

A councillor who has any pecuniary interest, direct or indirect, in any contract or other matter which is being considered at a meeting, must disclose the fact and may not take part in the discussion or vote on it. Breach of this rule renders him liable on summary conviction to a fine not exceeding £200, unless he proves that he did not know that the matter was to be discussed, but prosecution is only by or on behalf of the Director of Public Prosecutions.

Meetings and proceedings of local authorities and their committees, parish meetings and their committees, and community meetings, are regulated by the provisions of Schedule 12.

Local authorities may generally, subject to exceptions, arrange for the discharge of their functions by committees, sub-committees, officers, or other local authorities; but they may not delegate the levying or issuing of a precept for a rate or the borrowing of money. They must appoint separate committees for education and for personal social services.

Miscellaneous powers of local authorities

Local authorities are given a general power to do anything (whether or not it involves expenditure) that is calculated to facilitate, or is conducive or incidental to, the discharge of their functions. A local authority is to appoint such officers as they think necessary; but there are certain officers—including chief constable, education officer and director of social services [17]—whom they must appoint.

County councils and district councils may acquire land compulsorily for the purpose of their functions,[18] and a district council may do so on behalf of a parish or community council. Local authorities may make contracts in accordance with their standing orders. A person entering into a contract with a local authority is not bound to inquire whether standing orders have been complied with, and non-compliance with such orders does not invalidate the contract.

Local authorities may incur expenditure not otherwise authorised, which in their opinion is in the interests of their area or its

[17] Police Act 1964; Education Act 1944; Local Authority (Social Services) Act 1970.
[18] Subject to the provisions of the Acquisition of Land (Authorisation Procedure) Act 1946.

inhabitants, not exceeding the product of a rate of two pence in the pound. A principal council may incur such expenditure as they consider necessary (including the making of grants or loans to other persons or bodies) to deal with an actual or imminent emergency or disaster involving destruction of or danger to life or property affecting the area or its inhabitants.

By-laws

Councils of non-metropolitan counties and metropolitan districts may make by-laws for the good rule and government of their area, and for the prevention and suppression of nuisances. By-laws made under this general power are subject to confirmation by the Secretary of State. Notice of intention to apply for confirmation must be given in the local Press, and a copy deposited for public inspection at the council offices. Printed copies of by-laws must be open to inspection at the council offices, and must be available for sale to the public. Offences against by-laws are punishable on summary conviction by a fine up to £20, and £5 a day for a continuing offence.

Functions

Non-metropolitan county councils and metropolitan district councils are the authorities for education, personal social services and libraries.[19]

The functions of county councils include: co-ordination of transport policies; highways generally; traffic; transport generally; police (subject to amalgamation); reserve powers of housing (e.g. overspill); refuse disposal (in England); environmental health; and fire (subject to amalgamation).

The functions of district councils include: local planning; municipal transport; urban roads and footpaths; housing (house-building, house management, slum clearance, house and area improvement, building regulations); refuse collection (in England); refuse disposal and collection (in Wales).

County councils and district councils have concurrent functions in relation to museums and art galleries; parks and open spaces; playing fields and swimming baths; and coast protection.

Commissioners for local administration

The Ombudsman system is to be extended to local government in April 1974, when the new councils come into operation under the 1972 Act. There will be an independent statutory Commissioner

---

[19] In Wales some district councils may be designated for this purpose.

for Local Administration, with a number of local commissioners for parts of England and Wales. The commissioner will be appointed by the Crown, but financed by local government.

Complaints of maladministration will usually be referred to the commissioner by local councillors, but in some circumstances a commissioner may take up a grievance direct. Excluded from the scheme are complaints concerning the merits of a council's action, matters in which the complainant has been at no disadvantage compared with other ratepayers, and complaints that can be remedied by appeal to a Ministry or the courts.

III. LONDON GOVERNMENT AUTHORITIES

In the earlier part of the nineteenth century the government of London outside the City was somewhat chaotic owing to the way in which the town had grown outwards from what we should now regard as a small nucleus. Its government was mainly in the hands of the justices and parish vestries.[20] There were also the Metropolitan Police under the Home Secretary, and the poor law guardians. The London County Council was created in 1888.[21] In 1899[22] the metropolitan borough councils, incorporated into the administrative county of London outside the City, displaced the vestries and district boards. There were also *ad hoc* authorities such as the Metropolitan Water Board (1902), the Thames Conservancy Board (1854), the Port of London Authority (1908) and the London Passenger Transport Board (1933).

The London Government Act 1963[23] reorganised the local government of London. Greater London was constituted as a local government area, the counties of London and Middlesex ceasing to exist.

The Local Government Act 1972 did not alter the structure of local government in London, but it applies its provisions relating to the working machinery of local authorities to those in Greater London, and it incorporates in a schedule the provisions of the London Government Act affecting the constitution of the Greater London authorities.

[20] A vestry was originally a meeting of the parishioners, and later of the ratepayers of the parish.

[21] Local Government Act 1888.

[22] London Government Act 1899.

[23] Based on *Report of Royal Commission on Local Government in Greater London* (1960) Cmnd. 1164; *London Government: Government Proposals for Reorganisation* (1961) Cmnd. 1562. See J. F. Garner, " London Government and its Reform " [1961] P.L. 256.

1. Greater London and the Greater London Council

Greater London is the administrative area comprising the London boroughs, the City and the Temples. The councillors are elected together trienially. The Council is required to appoint a clerk and a treasurer, and such other officers as it thinks necessary.

The Greater London Council is the traffic, planning, main drainage, fire, and theatre-licensing authority for the area, and the highway authority for metropolitan roads; but it may, subject to certain restrictions, delegate to a London borough council or the Common Council of the City any functions, except the borrowing or precepting power.

2. London boroughs

Thirty-two London boroughs were created. The twelve Inner London boroughs cover the areas of the former metropolitan boroughs, and the remaining twenty Outer London boroughs cover the areas formerly contained in neighbouring counties or county boroughs. The London boroughs are incorporated. Each London borough forms an electoral area returning two, three or four councillors to the Greater London Council, except that Westminster together with the City and the Temples forms one electoral area. Each London borough also forms a rating area.

The London borough councils and the Common Council of the City are general housing authorities. The borough councils are planning authorities for certain purposes. They are also the authorities for children, welfare of the old, most civil defence functions, food and drugs, and shops. The local education authorities are the Inner London Education Authority and the councils of the Outer London boroughs. The London boroughs also have all powers under public Acts that are not specifically allocated or excluded by the London Government Act 1963.

3. The Temple

The Temple has always claimed to be outside the jurisdiction of the City of London, mainly on the ground that it was so excluded when it was ecclesiastical property belonging to the Knights Templar, and was not among the formerly monastic properties over which the City was given jurisdiction by charter.[24] The Inner Temple and Middle Temple are within the City of London for judicial purposes. The London Government Act 1963 provided that any functions

---

[24] Other curious arguments put forward in 1668 by Sir Heneage Finch, Treasurer of the Inner Temple, are summarised in Williamson, *The History of the Temple, London*, p. 480.

exercisable by a London borough council (other than sewerage and public health) may by Order in Council be made exercisable by the Sub-Treasurer of Inner Temple or the Under-Treasurer of Middle Temple, or (as respects both the Temples) by the Common Council of the City of London. Expenses incurred by the Sub-Treasurer and the Under-Treasurer under the Act may be defrayed out of a general rate levied in their respective Inns.

4. City of London Corporation

The City of London Corporation is a body corporate by prescription, its full style according to a statute of 1690 being " The Mayor and Commonalty and Citizens of the City of London." The Corporation was not affected by the Municipal Corporations Acts 1835–1882, but it is governed—mostly in accordance with royal charters granted from time to time—by three courts. The City of London is a common law corporation with some financial resources that are not subject to statutory control.

(i) *The Court of Common Council* consists of the Lord Mayor, aldermen and common council men.[25] The Court of Common Council is in some respects the sole authority within its area. It controls the property of the Corporation; elects the City Solicitor and the Town Clerk; is responsible for housing and for certain Thames bridges; and is the market authority within a seven-mile radius. It also controls the City of London police force. Otherwise, in planning and many other important matters of local government it is subordinate to the Greater London Council.[26]

(ii) *The Court of Common Hall* consists of the Lord Mayor, Sheriff. not less than four aldermen, and those liverymen of the City companies who are freemen of the City. This is the body that annually nominates two aldermen for the office of Lord Mayor. It also elects the Chamberlain (treasurer) and the City auditors.

(iii) *The Court of Aldermen* consists of the Lord Mayor and aldermen. Some time before November 9 it elects the Lord Mayor for the coming year from among the two aldermen nominated by the Court of Common Hall. It also elects the Clerk to the Lord Mayor, the Clerk to the Guildhall Magistrates and the district surveyors.

---

[25] The franchise is restricted and in fact there is seldom a contest; Robson, *Government and Misgovernment of London*, p. 30.

[26] The Royal Commission recommended that the City of London should become a Greater London borough, while retaining its existing constitution.

IV. LOCAL GOVERNMENT ELECTIONS

1. Local government franchise

The franchise has been uniform for all local government elections since 1918. Until 1948 the local franchise was based on occupation as owner or tenant of premises in the area for a qualifying period of three months. The assimilation of the parliamentary and local franchise was effected by the Representation of the People Act 1948.[27] Remaining differences were that in local elections there was an alternative occupation qualification, removed in 1969,[28] and that peers have the right to vote.

The local government franchise under the Representation of the People Act 1949, as amended,[29] is enjoyed by:

(i) British subjects or citizens of the Republic of Ireland, who are

(ii) not subject to any legal incapacity, and who are

(iii) eighteen years of age or over on the date of the poll; and

(iv) resident [30] in the area on the qualifying date, or qualified as members of the services or as merchant seamen.

Legal incapacity includes conviction of corrupt or illegal practices at elections,[31] and being detained as a convicted person in a penal institution.[32]

The law governing the conduct of local elections was adapted by the Local Government Act 1972. Electoral areas are coterminous as far as practicable with parliamentary electoral areas. The areas in counties are electoral divisions, and in districts they are wards. Local elections are held under rules made by the Secretary of State. The qualifying date is October 10, and the registers come into force on the February 16 following.[33] Registration officers are appointed by the council of the district or London borough or the Common Council. Returning officers for county elections are appointed by the county council; for district, parish or community elections they are appointed by the district council; and for Greater London or London borough elections they are the " proper officer " of the borough. Electors on the register who are qualified to vote in that area at local but not parliamentary elections (i.e. peers) are distinguished by the letter L.

27 Replaced by the Representation of the People Act 1949.
28 Representation of the People Act 1969.
29 *Ibid.*
30 *Fox* v. *Stirk; Ricketts* v. *Cambridge City Electoral Registration Office* [1970] 2 Q.B. 463 (C.A.).
31 Representation of the People Act 1949.
32 Representation of the People Act 1969.
33 Electoral Registers Act 1953.

2. Qualifications and disqualifications for election

The qualifications for election as councillor are narrower than those sufficient for a Member of Parliament. A councillor must have some connection with the area for which he seeks election, while a Member of Parliament need not.

A person is *qualified* for election as a councillor under the Local Government Act 1972 [34] if on the day of nomination and the day of election he has attained the age of twenty-one years and is a British subject and: (a) he is a local government elector for the area; or (b) he has during the whole of the preceding twelve months occupied as owner or tenant any land or premises in that area; or (c) his principal place of work during that twelve months has been in that area; or (d) he has during the whole of those twelve months resided in that area; or (e) in the case of a parish or community council, he has during the whole of those twelve months resided within three miles of the parish or community.

A person is *disqualified* for election as a councillor under the Local Government Act 1972 if he: (a) holds any paid office under the local authority concerned, including local government officers and teachers in schools established or maintained by it; or (b) he is an undischarged bankrupt or has made a composition with his creditors; or (c) he has during the preceding five years been surcharged by a district auditor to an amount exceeding £500; or (d) he has within the preceding five years been sentenced to imprisonment for not less than three months; or (e) he has been convicted in certain cases for corrupt or illegal practices under the Representation of the People Act 1949.

V. LOCAL GOVERNMENT FINANCE

Every local authority is required to make an annual return of its income and expenditure to the Secretary of State. The returns are made up to March 31, and a summary must be laid by the Minister before Parliament.

1. Income of local authorities

Local authorities derive their income mainly from rates and grants-in-aid from the central government. A part of the income of the principal local authorities is derived from rents, profits on trading

[34] Replacing the Representation of the People Act 1949 as amended by the Local Authorities (Qualification of Members) Act 1971.

undertakings, and charges for licences and fees; but profits derived from these sources are generally applied towards the expenses and improvement of these services and to reduction of rates.

(a) *Rates*

Rates are taxes which Parliament empowers local authorities to levy.[35] There is no legal maximum, and the responsibility is owed only to the local government electors. Under the Local Government Act 1972 the "rating authorities" are the London borough councils and the district councils. The Greater London Council, county councils, parish and community councils have power to issue "precepts" (*i.e.* demands to meet their needs) on the rating authorities. Each rating authority, after considering the annual estimates of its various departments, "makes" a rate sufficient to meet its own needs and also the precepts it receives.

Rates are levied on the *occupiers* of "hereditaments" (land and buildings) in the area, according to their "rateable value." The rateable value of property is assessed with reference to the "gross annual value" of the property which is, in theory, the rent which a hypothetical yearly tenant might reasonably be expected to pay. Deductions for the estimated cost of insurance and repairs give the "net annual value," and this is equivalent to the rateable value. The valuation of dwelling-houses is carried out by district valuers of the Inland Revenue Department, on the principles laid down by the consolidating General Rate Act 1967. Appeals against assessment lie to local valuation courts, and thence to the Lands Tribunal, and on a point of law to the Court of Appeal. Crown property is immune,[36] and places of public worship and agricultural hereditaments are exempted from rates. Relief may be granted to charities, and to domestic ratepayers with low incomes.

Ever since the Poor Relief Act 1601 the sanction for non-payment of rates has been distress and sale of chattels. A defaulter was formerly regarded as an "offender," but the obligation may now be said to be quasi-contractual, although there is no right of action to recover rates.[37] The modern process, which was consolidated in the General Rates Act 1967, is for the rating authority to bring a summons before the magistrates' court, and (if there is no good defence) to apply for a warrant for distraint on goods. If the distrainable goods are insufficient, and the failure to pay is due to wilful refusal or culpable neglect, the debtor may be committed to prison for three months.

---

[35] *Re a Reference under the Government of Ireland Act 1920* [1936] **A.C.** 352.
[36] *Ante*, Chap. 13.
[37] *Liverpool Corporation* v. *Hope* [1938] 1 K.B. 751.

(b) *Government grants*

The government makes annual grants to local authorities under the authority of Parliament. The reasons for making government grants are to relieve the rates, especially where a service is imposed on local authorities by government policy; to encourage the provision of new services; to compensate for loss due to government activity, *e.g.* de-rating; and to equalise the resources of local authorities. Since the war, government grants to local authorities have exceeded the rates in value.

The old system of percentage grants based on expenditure was found to encourage extravagance, and it took no account of the need of the poorest authorities. The Local Government Act 1929 therefore provided for a block grant in aid of general income for most services. After the creation of the national health service, the Local Government Act 1948 provided for the payment of an exchequer equalisation grant to any authority falling below a minimum standard of financial resources. The Local Government Act 1958 introduced a new system of general grants for the purpose of economy and also to allow greater discretion to local authorities. In particular, the general grant now covered education as well as health services. This Act also provided for a rate deficiency grant to be payable to local authorities in respect of their " normal " expenditure if their penny rate product was less than the standard penny rate for their area. Specific grants continued to be paid for police (50 per cent.), highways (percentage) and housing (unit subsidy).

A new kind of grant was introduced by the Local Government Act 1966,[38] aimed at reducing the burden of rates and producing a fairer distribution of Exchequer assistance among local authorities. A rate support grant replaced the previous general and rate deficiency grants and certain specific grants, as an interim measure designed to prop up the existing system of local government finance until there was time to re-examine the whole position in the light of any conclusions reached by Royal Commissions. The problem was to relieve the domestic ratepayer of ever-rising rate demands, without either curtailing the services or handing over the financing of particular services to the central government. The Minister was given power, subject to approval by resolution of the House of Commons, to reduce the rate support grant in case of default.

The future of local government finance was the subject of a

[38] Cmnd. 2923 : *Local Government Finance in England and Wales.*

Green Paper in 1971.[39] The main problem in the system of central government grants is the relative weight of block grants to specific grants. Additional sources of local revenue are needed but without adding to the total burden of the ratepayer. A local income tax is rejected as impracticable. The suggestion is made that dwellings might be assessed on capital value instead of a hypothetical rent.

(c) Loans

The capital expenditure of local authorities is largely met out of loans. Apart from special statutes authorising loans to be raised for specific purposes, the Local Government Act 1933, s. 195, gave a general borrowing power to all local authorities for the purpose of acquiring land, erecting buildings or undertaking other permanent works in pursuance of an object which is itself within the authority's powers. The Local Government Act 1972 authorises local authorities to borrow money for purposes approved by the Secretary of State, and subject to any regulations made by him with the consent of the Treasury.

2. Expenditure of local authorities

The current expenditure of local authorities goes mostly towards the administration of such services as education, housing, highways, personal social services and police. The income and expenditure on trading undertakings more or less balance. Capital expenditure is accounted for largely by housing, trading undertakings and the construction of schools and other public works.

Audit

Under the Local Government Act 1972 all local authority accounts must be audited, either by a district auditor appointed by the Secretary of State with the consent of the Minister for the Civil Service, or by a private auditor. Private auditors may be appointed only by district councils to audit accounts that are not specifically made subject under the legislation to district audit. The Secretary of State may order an extraordinary audit by a district auditor of accounts subject to either district or private audit.

District auditors disallow any expenditure which is unlawful or unreasonably excessive, and they surcharge any expenditure disallowed on the persons responsible for incurring or authorising such

[39] Cmnd. 4741: *The Future Shape of Local Government Finance.*

expenditure, *e.g.* the members of the council who passed the resolution (*Roberts* v. *Hopwood* [40]). They also surcharge any sum not duly accounted for on the person by whom it should have been brought into account, and the amount of any loss or deficiency on the person by whose negligence or misconduct it has been incurred, *e.g.* a rate collector. Such a person must, however, be a member, officer or servant of the local authority.

CHAPTER 27

PUBLIC CORPORATIONS

I. NATURE AND PURPOSE OF PUBLIC CORPORATIONS [1]

In addition to the central government departments under the direct control of Ministers of the Crown, and the local government authorities elected by the local electors, public affairs in Great Britain are administered by or with the aid of various independent public corporations.[2] These bodies are created by statute, and they possess a considerable, though varying, degree of independence from ministerial and therefore parliamentary control. They exercise public functions—either over the whole country or within limited areas—primarily for the benefit of the public and not for profit. Their chief characteristics are best expressed negatively, namely, that they are neither government departments under the direct control of Ministers responsible to Parliament nor are they elected by the local electors.

It is difficult to generalise about these public corporations, and no neat classification of them is possible. The classification which we may tentatively adopt, with examples, is as follows:

(i) *Managerial—industrial or commercial*

Executive bodies set up to manage nationalised industries or branches of commerce, *e.g.* National Coal Board; British Railways Board; British Freight Corporation; British Steel Corporation; British Docks Board; British Waterways Board; Central Electricity Generating Board, Electricity Council and area electricity boards; South of

---

[1] See J. F. Garner, *Administrative Law* (3rd ed. 1970) Chap. 10; *Government Enterprise* (ed. W. Friedmann and J. F. Garner, 1970); J. A. G. Griffith and H. Street, *Principles of Administrative Law* (4th ed. 1967) Chap. 7; W. A. Robson, *Nationalised Industry and Public Ownership* (2nd ed. 1962); Herbert Morrison *Government and Parliament* (1954) Chap. 12; Sir Arthur Street, " Quasi-Government Bodies since 1918," in *British Government since 1918* (by Sir G. Campion and Others); *Public Enterprise* (ed. Robson); D. N. Chester, *The Nationalised Industries: A Statutory Analysis* (Institute of Public Administration, 2nd ed 1951); J. F. Garner, " New Public Corporations " [1966] P.L. 324; D. N. Chester " Public Corporations and the Classification of Administrative Bodies " (1953) 1 *Political Studies* 34; *Advisory Bodies* (ed. R. V. Vernon and N. Mansergh); *Law and Contemporary Problems* (School of Law, Duke University, U.S.A. 1951, Vol. 16.

[2] The term was first used in the Report of the Crawford Committee on Broadcasting in 1926 (Cmd. 2599).

Scotland Electricity Board, North of Scotland Hydro-electricity Board; Gas Council and area gas boards; British Overseas Airways Corporation, British European Airways Corporation and British Airports Authority; Post Office; Bank of England; United Kingdom Atomic Energy Authority.

The nationalisation of existing undertakings has generally involved the compulsory acquisition of all their assets, which are then vested in the corporation. Sometimes the government merely acquires the shares, and thus controls the corporation, as with the Bank of England and the former British Iron and Steel Corporation.

(ii) *Managerial—social services*

Executive bodies set up to manage certain social services, *e.g.* development corporations for the various New Towns; regional hospital boards; Housing Corporation; British Broadcasting Corporation.

(iii) *Regulatory and advisory*

(a) Bodies set up to regulate private enterprise in certain fields, *e.g.* agricultural marketing boards; Livestock Commission; Wheat Commission; Independent Television Authority.

(b) Bodies set up to advise Ministers with regard to the exercise of certain of their statutory powers, *e.g.* National Transport Advisory Council and the transport consultative committees; central advisory councils for education; Police Council; Central Health Services Council; National Insurance Advisory Committee.

The practice of setting up independent statutory authorities is not new, although it has become much more important as a result of the nationalisation measures introduced by the Labour Government in 1946–49. Earlier examples were the London Passenger Transport Board (1933), the British Broadcasting Corporation (1927), the Port of London Authority (1908); and previously the electricity commissioners, Forestry Commission, insurance commissions, Road Board and Unemployment Assistance Board, and in the nineteenth century the poor law commissioners (1834) followed by school boards, health boards and so on.

The purpose of setting up "independent" authorities was to ensure the nationalisation of some industry or service, or some form of state regulation, while keeping the actual administration outside the Civil Service, above party politics and free from detailed scrutiny in Parliament. Nationalised industrial and commercial corporations were expected to pay their own way like any private business, keep proper accounts and subject them to audit; but their day-to-day management is independent of the government and therefore, generally speaking, not subject to questions and debate in Parliament. Further, this device obviates a great increase in government departments and civil servants who would share the privileges of the Crown in litigation, and in ministerial offices with seats in the House of Commons. On the other hand, nationalisation has not necessarily led to a better service to the community; losses on some undertakings that formerly fell on shareholders are now borne by the consumer and taxpayer; and the hope of many that there would be no occasion for strikes in industrial undertakings has not been fulfilled.

II. LEGAL POSITION OF PUBLIC CORPORATIONS [3]

The main constitutional problems relate to the legal status of those public corporations that manage some nationalised industry or branch of commerce or public service, especially their liability in contract and tort, and the question of parliamentary supervision. The latter is discussed in section III below.

Appointment and powers

To ascertain the legal position of any public corporation it is necessary first of all to look at the particular Act of Parliament that created it, for no two of them are alike. It is generally provided that they are bodies corporate, with perpetual succession and a common seal and power to hold land. The chairmen and other members of the boards are appointed and may be removed by the competent Minister or by the Crown. Their members do not have to be representative of any particular interests. Their salaries are generally fixed by the Minister with the approval of the Treasury. As there are no shareholders to exercise any control over the board, the Acts provide that the Minister may set up advisory committees or councils to advise him.

The powers of a public corporation are set out in the constituent Act. They are subject to judicial determination by the doctrine of *ultra vires* (*Smith* v. *London Transport Executive* [4]), but their powers in some cases are very wide. There is generally no legal means by

---

[3] Glanville Williams, *Crown Proceedings* (1948) pp. 4–8, 21–28, 30–37, 85; J. A. G. Griffith, " Public Corporations as Crown Servants " 9 U.T.L.J. 169; H. Street, *Government Liability* (1953) pp. 28–36; E. A. Scammell, " Nationalisation in Legal Perspective " [1952] C.L.P. 30; W. Friedmann, " The New Public Corporations and the Law " (1947) 10 M.L.R. 233–254, 377–395; W. A. Robson, " The Public Corporations in Britain Today " (1959) 63 Harv. Law Rev. 1321–1348; Garner, *Administrative Law* (3rd ed.).

[4] [1951] A.C. 555 (H.L.); and see *post*, Chap. 30.

which these bodies may be compelled by private citizens to exercise their functions. The Minister might be able to bring mandamus in some cases, unless this is expressly excluded by statute. The Transport Act 1962, s. 3 (1), provided that it should be the "duty" of the Railways Board to provide railway services, and in connection therewith such other services and facilities as might appear to the Board to be expedient; but section 3 (4) went on to say that no such duty or liability should be enforceable by judicial proceedings. Similar provisions are contained in the Iron and Steel Act 1967, s. 3 (4), the Transport Act 1968, s. 1 (3), and the Post Office Act 1969, s. 9 (4). Exceptionally, the Transport Act 1968, s. 106 (1), allows any person to apply to the court for an order requiring the Waterways Board to maintain commercial and cruising waterways for public use. The Minister might be able to apply for mandamus or a declaration, unless that is expressly excluded by statute. He may give directions " of a general character " in the public interest. In some cases he has power to give specific directions, e.g. to the air corporations as to transport services between particular points.[5] The Minister has power to control capital expenditure and borrowing, and also to direct the use of surplus revenues. The ultimate sanction is his power to remove members from office.

The industrial and commercial corporations are independent in the day-to-day conduct of their business, and subject only to indirect ministerial control. The Minister's powers—notably that of giving general directions—are kept in the background; but their existence enables him to exert a fair amount of unofficial pressure, which may take the form of " requests."

Public corporations must keep proper accounts, as far as possible on commercial lines, and submit them to audit. The financial control of nationalised industries depends on the extent and method of subsidisation from public funds. Some corporations, such as the transport boards and the electricity and gas corporations, are financially independent, unless the Treasury is called upon to guarantee the raising of stock or temporary loans. At the other extreme some corporations, such as the British Broadcasting Corporation which operates under a licence from the Minister, derive all their capital and working income from money voted by Parliament. In between are corporations owning various degrees of financial independence.

Their annual accounts are audited by professional auditors appointed by, or with the approval of, the Minister. The Public Accounts Committee may examine accounts presented to Parliament. New principles were announced by the Chancellor of the Exchequer

---

5 Civil Aviation (Declaratory Provisions) Act 1971.

in 1961 as regards the finances of certain nationalised industries, whereby over a five-year period their surpluses on revenue account should be at least sufficient to cover deficits on that account.[6] Social service corporations are generally under closer ministerial direction. They may be financed wholly or partly as part of a departmental budget, and therefore subject to the closer public auditory control of the Comptroller and Auditor-General.

A public corporation must make an annual report to the Minister, who must lay it before Parliament together with a report of any action taken, or declined to be taken, by him. Any directions given by the Minister must be published in the board's report, unless he directs that publication would be contrary to the national interest. The Minister is responsible to Parliament for the exercise of his powers, such as they are, and also for failing to exercise them.

Liability to judicial proceedings

The question whether a public corporation is a servant or agent of the Crown is of considerable legal importance. If it is a servant or agent of the Crown, civil proceedings would be governed by the Crown Proceedings Act 1947 (unless it was set up by a later statute expressly or impliedly inconsistent with the Act), and the action (if available) would have to be brought by or against the authorised department or the Attorney-General. The corporation would also have the advantage of the Crown privileges relating to injunction, execution, discovery and interrogatories,[7] and would not be bound by Acts of Parliament (including rates and taxes) unless expressly or by necessary implication.[8] And this might well affect the position of individual members of the board and its employees.

If the corporation is not a servant or agent of the Crown, the Crown Proceedings Act does not apply: it would be liable in the ordinary way in contract and tort; its staff would be employees of the corporation and not Crown servants; and proceedings by or against it (in so far as not expressly excluded or limited by the statute) would be in the name of the corporation (*Mersey Docks and Harbour Board* v. *Gibbs*, 1866[9]).

Where the statute is explicit

The National Health Service Act 1946, s. 13, expressly stated that a regional hospital board, notwithstanding that it exercised func-

---

6 *The Financial and Economic Obligations of the Nationalised Industries* (1961) Cmnd. 1337.
7 *Post*, Chap. 32.   8 *Ante*, Chap. 13.
9 L.R. 1 H.L. 93; *Gallagher* v. *Post Office* [1970] 1 All E.R. 712; *Westwood* v. *Post Office, The Times*, November 24, 1972 (C.A.).

tions on behalf of the Minister, should be entitled to enforce rights and be liable for liabilities (including liability in tort) as if it were acting as a principal: proceedings were to be brought by or against the board in its own name, and it was not entitled to the privileges of the Crown in respect of discovery or production of documents.[10] Similar principles applied to a hospital management committee, although it exercised its functions on behalf of the regional hospital board.[11] On the other hand, the Crown might claim privilege in respect of its documents; and it was held in *Nottingham Area No. 1 Hospital Management Committee* v. *Owen*[12] that a hospital vested in the Minister of Health under the Act of 1946 was "premises occupied for the public service of the Crown" under the Public Health Act 1936, and that the justices had therefore no jurisdiction to make an order under the 1936 Act to abate a nuisance constituted by a smoking chimney.

Later Acts constituting public corporations have been explicit on the point, at least in cases where there might be doubt, as in the case of corporations that own or occupy land or have taken over functions formerly exercised by a Minister. Thus the Atomic Energy Authority Act 1954 provided that land occupied by the Authority was deemed for rating purposes to be occupied by the Crown for public purposes; otherwise the Authority was not to enjoy Crown privileges. The Electricity Act 1957, s. 38, stated: "It is hereby declared for the avoidance of doubt that neither the Electricity Council nor the Generating Board nor any of the Area Boards are to be treated as the servant or agent of the Crown or as enjoying any status, immunity or privilege of the Crown, and no property of the Council or any of those Boards is to be regarded as property of, or held on behalf of, the Crown." Similar provisions were made by the Transport Act 1968, s. 52 (5) with regard to the transport boards, and the New Towns Act 1965, s. 35 (3), with regard to the Commission for the New Towns. There are usually express provisions with regard to stamp duty, and in some cases income tax and rates.

Post Office

The purpose of the Post Office Act 1969 was that the Post Office should cease to be a government department and should become an independent corporation, and the Act is, of course, quite explicit on this point. The functions and powers formerly exercised by the Postmaster-General as a Minister of the Crown are transferred to

---

10 See O. R. Marshall, "Hospitals and the National Health Service Act" [1952] C.L.P. 81.
11 *Bullard* v. *Croydon Hospital Group Management Committee* [1953] 1 Q.B. 511.
12 [1958] 1 Q.B. 50 (D.C.).

the new corporation. The postal service is a public service derived from a prerogative monopoly of the Crown, and it has been held that there is no contractual relationship between the sender of a postal packet and the Post Office.[13] Section 30 of the Post Office Act applies to the new corporation a limitation of liability in tort similar to that contained in section 9 of the Crown Proceedings Act 1947.[14] Thus the liability of the Post Office is limited to loss of, or damage to, a *registered inland* [15] *postal packet* due to the wrongful act, neglect or default of an officer, servant or agent of the Post Office while dealing with the packet; and proceedings must be brought within *twelve months* instead of the usual six years. The amount recoverable is not to exceed (a) the market value of the postal packet, or (b) the compensation appropriate to the registration fee paid.[16] Section 29 provides that, otherwise, no proceedings in tort lie against the Post Office for any loss or damage arising out of the postal or telecommunication service. The Post Office is exempt, for example, from liability for loss of or damage to unregistered postal packets, and for defamation published by telegram, telephone or postmark.[17] It is further provided that (contrary to common law) no individual—whether officer, servant, agent or independent contractor of the Post Office—is subject, except at the suit of the Post Office, to any civil liability for any loss or damage from which the Post Office is exempt.

Where the statute is not explicit

Most of the earlier Acts creating public corporations were not explicit on the question whether the corporation was a servant or agent of the Crown. In so far as such Acts have not been replaced by later legislation, if the matter should come before the court it would be a question of interpretation.

In *Tamlin* v. *Hannaford* [18] the Court of Appeal held that the British Transport Commission [19] was not a servant or agent of the Crown. The question in issue was whether a house which had been leased from the Great Western Railway was withdrawn from the

---

13 *Triefus & Co.* v. *Post Office* [1957] 2 Q.B. 352 (C.A.); *Wadsworth* v. *Postmaster-General* (1939) 56 T.L.R. 1; Paul Jackson [1972] P.L. 97.
14 No action lay against the Crown at common law; the Crown Proceedings Act created the liability which it limited.
15 *i.e.* posted in the United Kingdom, the Isle of Man or the Channel Islands for delivery therein.
16 See *Building and Civil Engineering Holidays Scheme Management* v. *Post Office* [1966] 1 Q.B. 247.
17 *Boakes* v. *Postmaster-General, The Times,* October 27, 1962 (C.A.): postmark, " Remember that Road Accidents are Caused by People Like You."
18 [1951] 1 K.B. 18. And see *British Broadcasting Corporation* v. *Johns* [1965] Ch. 32.
19 Predecessor of the British Railways Board.

protection of the Rent Restriction Acts by reason of its being vested in the British Transport Commission under the Transport Act 1947.[20] In considering whether any subordinate body is entitled to the Crown privilege of not being bound by a statute unless Parliament shows an intention that it should be bound, said Denning L.J. in delivering the judgment of the Court, the question is not so much whether it is an " emanation of the Crown " [21] but whether it is properly to be regarded as a servant or agent of the Crown.[22] This depended on the true construction of the Transport Act 1947, especially the powers of the Minister in relation to the Commission [23] When Parliament intends that a new corporation should act on behalf of the Crown, it usually says so expressly.[24] In the absence of express provision the proper inference, in the case (at any rate) of a commercial corporation, is that it acts on its own behalf.

It is probable that none of the recently-created industrial or commercial corporations is a servant or agent of the Crown. None of them is in the list of " authorised departments " issued by the Treasury under the Crown Proceedings Act 1947, s. 17, although this is not conclusive as proceedings may be taken under that Act against the Attorney-General. Many proceedings have been brought by and against industrial corporations in their own names without the question being raised in court.[25]

III. Parliamentary Supervision of Public Corporations [26]

An important constitutional problem that has not yet been completely solved is how to secure adequate parliamentary supervision of public corporations in the interests of the consumer and taxpayer, while pursuing the policy of decentralisation and freedom from detailed control. As far as the industrial corporations are concerned, experience shows that it is extremely difficult to draw the line between

[20] Cf. Crown Lessees (Protection of Sub-Tenants) Act 1952, which extended to sub-tenants of Crown lands the benefit of the Rent Restriction Acts.
[21] Cf. Gilbert v. Trinity House Corporation (1886) 17 Q.B.D. 795.
[22] International Ry. v. Niagara Parks Commission [1941] A.C. 328 (P.C.).
[23] See Central Control Board (Liquor Traffic) v. Cannon Brewery Co. [1918] 2 Ch. 123; [1919] A.C. 757.
[24] e.g. Central Land Board (now dissolved); Town and Country Planning Act 1947; Glasgow Corporation v. Central Land Board, 1956 S.L.T. 41. Also the former National Assistance Board and Land Commission.
[25] e.g. National Coal Board v. Galley [1958] 1 W.L.R. 16.
[26] See Sir Ivor Jennings, Parliament (2nd ed. 1957) Chap. 10; Herbert Morrison, Government and Parliament (1954) Chap. 12; W. A. Robson, Nationalised Industry and Public Ownership, Chaps. 7, 8, 10; Report from the Select Committee on Nationalised Industries (1952) H.C. No. 332, I, pp. 130–133; A. H. Hanson, Parliament and Public Ownership (Hansard Society, 1961).

general policy and day-to-day administration. The powers of the board and of the Minister need to be more clearly defined, and the Minister's intervention should more often take the form of a definite, published direction. Parliament needs more information, and better opportunities to make constructive use of its supervisory powers. There has been some demand for the departmentalisation of some of these public services, *e.g.* transport, gas and electricity.[27] A possible solution is to abolish the theoretical distinction between general policy and day-to-day administration, and to make the board entirely responsible to the Minister. Conventions would then be developed whereby it was left to the Minister to decide in what matters he should intervene, and he would have to be prepared to defend his non-intervention.[28]

1. Debate

Members may criticise the working of nationalised industries in any debate on which the matter is relevant:

(a) *Debate on motions,* including motions specifically concerning one or more of the industries, "ballot motions" in private members' time, debates on the Address in reply to the Queen's Speech, the daily half-hour adjournment, and adjournment motions moved by a Minister. In the last two, ministerial responsibility is required, and matters involving legislation are not permitted. In a debate on the Queen's Speech any topic is relevant, and on a Consolidated Fund Bill or adjournment motion any topic is relevant except a proposal for legislation.

(b) *Debate in Supply*

A relevant vote can be arranged. The rule of relevance in debate requires ministerial responsibility, and legislative action is banned.

(c) *Debate on Bills* dealing with one or more of the industries.

(d) *Debate on motions to approve or annul orders* or other statutory instruments made by Ministers under the various nationalisation Acts.

(c) *Debate on annual report and accounts*

The annual reports and accounts of the various public corporations are required by statute to be laid before Parliament by the Minister concerned, together with the Minister's report on the exercise of his own functions. They are then the subject of debate, but these facilities also are strictly limited. The debate on each corporation

---

[27] But conversely, the Post Office has become a public corporation.
[28] Hanson, *op. cit* Chap. 8.

comes only once a year, usually a considerable time after the events reported; and the range open for debate is then so wide that there is little opportunity of discussing details.

2. Questions to Ministers

The other chief opportunity for members to acquire information about the nationalised industries is by putting questions to Ministers in the House. As has been seen, the rules of the House and parliamentary practice place on the putting of questions to Ministers limits which in relation to public corporations are stringent. Questions addressed to the Minister must relate to the public affairs with which he is *officially connected*, to proceedings pending in Parliament, or to matters of administration for which he is *responsible*.

Matters for which a Minister is responsible include matters which the nationalised industries are required by statute to lay before Parliament; and appointments, finance, and matters on which he himself has statutory powers or duties. A question may be asked concerning the exercise by a Minister of his power to give a general direction in the national interest to the board of a public corporation. Questions are also admissible concerning specific responsibilities set out in statutes relating to certain nationalised industries, for example, research and training schemes. Ministers have power to require information from the boards, and therefore questions whose purpose is purely to seek information are prima facie admissible; but Ministers are not bound to answer, and they often refuse on the ground that the matter falls within the day-to-day administration of the boards. Further questions dealing with the class of matters concerning which an answer has been refused may be ruled out of order, unless the Speaker rules that they raise a matter of " urgent public importance." But it was announced by the Leader of the House in 1960 that Ministers would consider sympathetically the extent to which they could properly reply to " questions of general policy relating to Ministers' responsibilities." In any case, if a member really seeks information he can ask the board direct, and they will often supply it.

3. Select Committee on Nationalised Industries

A Select Committee on Nationalised Industries was set up in 1956 [29]: " to examine the Reports and Accounts of the nationalised industries established by Statute whose controlling Boards are appointed by Ministers of the Crown and whose annual receipts are not wholly or mainly derived from moneys provided by Parliament

[29] (1952) H.C. No. 332, I; (1953) H.C. No. 235.

or advanced from the Exchequer." The power to examine the reports and accounts of the nationalised industries leaves it to the Committee to decide how far they should go behind the Minister and make inquiries in matters that are within the competence of the boards.

This Committee has issued a number of reports. The first report [30] dealt with the Scottish electricity boards. The second report,[31] on the National Coal Board, provided much fresh information on the working of one of the major nationalised industries.

CHAPTER 28

DELEGATED LEGISLATION [1]

I. NATURE AND PURPOSE OF DELEGATED LEGISLATION

THE delegation of lawmaking power by Parliament to other persons or bodies is no new practice, although it has greatly increased in frequency and importance in the nineteenth and twentieth centuries. The great increase in delegated legislation in modern times is due partly to collectivism and the development of the Welfare State, and partly to the need to cope with emergencies of various kinds, such as strikes and economic crises.

The judicial control of delegated legislation, exercised mainly under the doctrine of *ultra vires*, is discussed later in Chapter 30.

The executive has no inherent power, as it has in France, to issue ordinances or decrees filling out the details of statutes. The authority of an Act of Parliament is necessary (*Case of Proclamations*, 1610 [2]). As the government *ex hypothesi* commands a majority in Parliament, however, it can procure from Parliament any powers it thinks it needs. Such cases as come before the courts nowadays usually concern the interpretation of enabling Acts, rather than questioning the *vires* of delegated legislation.

We consider in this section the nature and purpose of delegated legislation, and in the next section the parliamentary safeguards that have been provided.

---

[1] *Report of Joint Committee on Delegated Legislation* (1971–72) H.L. 184 and H.C. 475; *Select Committee on Procedure: The Process of Legislation* (1970–71) H.C. 538, Part VI; *Report of the Committee on Ministers' Powers* (" Donoughmore Committee ") (1932) Cmd. 4060, s. II; Sir Carleton Allen, *Law and Orders* (3rd ed. 1965); " Statutory Instruments Today " (1955) 71 L.Q.R. 490; Sir Ivor Jennings, *Parliament* (2nd ed. 1957) Chap. 14; H. W. R. Wade, *Administrative Law* (3rd ed. 1971) Chap. 9; J. E. Kersell, *Parliamentary Supervision of Delegated Legislation* (1960); Sir Cecil Carr, *Concerning English Administrative Law* (1941) Chaps. 2, 3 and 5; " Parliamentary Control of Delegated Legislation " [1956] P.L. 200; *Delegated Legislation* (1921); Sieghart, *Government by Decree*, pp. 98–148; J. A. G. Griffith, " The Constitutional Significance of Delegated Legislation in England " (1950) 48 *Michigan Law Review* 1079; " The Place of Parliament in the Legislative Process " (1951) 14 M.L.R. 279, 425; B. Schwartz, *Law and the Executive in Britain*, Chaps. 2, 4, 6 and 9; J. Willis, *The Parliamentary Powers of English Government Departments* (1933).

[2] 12 Co.Rep. 74; (1610) 2 St.Tr. 723. The exception is the prerogative of the Crown to legislate for newly conquered or ceded territories; *post*, Chap. 34.

Forms of delegated legislation

Delegated legislation takes various forms and assumes a variety of names. The primary classification is according to the person or body which has the legislative power, of which for present purposes the chief are:

(i) *The Queen in Council*—power to issue Statutory Orders in Council, *e.g.* under the Emergency Powers Act 1920. This kind of delegated legislation has the most dignified and " national " character.

(ii) *Ministers and other heads of government departments*—power to issue departmental or ministerial regulations, rules, orders, etc. These are extremely numerous, and now much greater in bulk than Acts of Parliament.

(iii) *Local authorities*—power to make by-laws for their areas under the Local Government Act 1972, Public Health Acts, etc.

(iv) *Public corporations*—power conferred by their constituent Acts to make by-laws and other regulations for the purposes for which they were created.

(v) *Rule committees*—power to make rules for procedure in court, *e.g.* Rule Committee of the Supreme Court (Supreme Court of Judicature (Consolidation) Act 1925, s. 99 [3]); County Court Rule Committee (County Courts Acts [4]); and judges or committees with power to make rules of procedure relating to matrimonial causes, bankruptcy, legal aid, etc.

As has been seen, the Schedules to the House of Commons Disqualification Act 1957 may be revised by resolution of the House,[5] and certain taxes may be collected for a limited period by resolution of the Commons under the Provisional Collection of Taxes Act.[6] Legislation by the Queen and Commons under the Parliament Acts 1911 and 1949 may be regarded as a special kind of delegated legislation,[7] and " self-executing " Community regulations under the European Communities Act 1972 as a kind of subordinate legislation.[8]

Departmental pronouncements, rulings to officials, concessions to

---

[3] The Committee consists of the Lord Chancellor and four or more of the following persons: Lord Chief Justice, Master of the Rolls, President of the Family Division, four other judges of the Supreme Court, two practising barristers and two practising solicitors. These Rules must be laid before Parliament. See *Hume* v. *Somerton* (1890) 25 Q.B.D. 239.

[4] The Committee consists of five judges appointed by the Lord Chancellor. These Rules are put into force by the Lord Chancellor with the concurrence of the Rule Committee of the Supreme Court.

[5] *Ante*, Chap. 8.

[6] *Ante*, Chap. 10.

[7] *Ante*, Chap. 6.

[8] *Ante*, Chap. 4; *post*, p. 488.

taxpayers, etc. have become common in recent years. They have no legal force, but they cannot be lightly ignored unless one is prepared to test their interpretation of the law in the courts.[9]

Sub-delegation

The power of delegated legislation vested in one authority is itself sometimes delegated to another authority, and this sub-delegation may go through several stages in a hierarchy of lawmaking authorities. Thus section 1 (3) of the Emergency Powers (Defence) Act 1939, which gave power to issue Defence Regulations by Order in Council, stated that Defence Regulations might empower any authorities or persons to make orders, rules and by-laws for any of the purposes for which Defence Regulations might themselves be made. Ministerial orders were issued under the Regulations, directions under these orders, and licences under these directions.

Sub-delegation is only lawful if expressly or impliedly authorised by the enabling Act, for the prima facie principle is *delegatus non potest delegare*.[10] The requirement of authorisation applies throughout the hierarchy of rules, as does the doctrine of *ultra vires* below the enabling Act itself. Sub-delegation should not usually be required except in emergencies.

" Statutory Instruments "

The Statutory Instruments Act 1946, which is mainly concerned with the publication [11] of the more important kinds of delegated legislation, provides in section 1 that where by that Act or any subsequent Act power to make, confirm or approve orders, rules, regulations or other subordinate legislation is conferred on the Crown in Council or any Minister or government department, then *if the power is expressed to be exercisable by Order in Council or by Statutory Instrument*, as the case may be, any document by which that power is exercised shall be known as a " Statutory Instrument." The expression is also important in connection with laying before Parliament [12] and the work of the Select Committee on Statutory Instruments.[13] The term " Statutory Instrument " also extends to any

---

[9] See Allen, *op. cit.* pp. 182–193; R. E. Megarry, " Administrative Quasi-Legislation " (1944) 60 L.Q.R. 125, 215; B. Schwartz, *American Administrative Law*, pp. 34–35. Allen called it " Administrative Quasi-Law."

[10] *Allingham* v. *Minister of Agriculture* [1948] 1 All E.R. 780; S. A. de Smith, " Sub-delegation and Circulars " (1949) 12 M.L.R. 37; *post*, p. 524.

[11] *Post*, p. 494.

[12] *Post*, p. 489.

[13] *Post*, p. 492.

legislative instrument made after January 1, 1948, in exercise of a power conferred before that date to make " Statutory Rules " within the meaning of the (repealed) Rules Publication Act 1893.

The reasons for delegated legislation

In spite of much criticism it has been generally accepted since the report of the Committee on Ministers' Powers in 1932 that delegated legislation has come to stay in our legal system, and that there are the following legitimate reasons for its use:

(i) *Pressure on parliamentary time*

Parliament in its legislative work—especially in the House of Commons—barely has time to discuss essential principles. Much time can be saved, and amendments to Acts of Parliament obviated, by delegating the consideration of procedure and subordinate matters to Ministers and their departments.

(ii) *Technicality of subject-matter*

The subject-matter of modern legislation is often highly technical. Technical matters, as distinct from broad policy, are not susceptible to discussion in Parliament and therefore cannot readily be included in a Bill. Delegation to Ministers enables them to consult expert advisers and interested parties while the regulations are still in the draft stage.

(iii) *Flexibility*

In large and complex measures like the National Health Service Act it is not possible to foresee all the contingencies and local conditions for which provision will have to be made, and it would be difficult to settle all the administrative machinery in time for insertion in the Bill. Delegated legislation provides a degree of flexibility, as changes can be made from time to time in the light of experience without the necessity for a series of amending Acts, *e.g.* under Road Traffic Acts and National Insurance Acts. Further, it allows for experimentation, as in Town and Country Planning Acts.

(iv) *Emergency powers*

In emergencies, such as war, serious strikes and economic crises, there would often not be time to pass Acts of Parliament, even if (as may not be the case) Parliament is sitting. Within limits unlawful acts can be done bona fide on the authority of the government in the expectation of later being legalised by an Act of Indemnity, but this is clearly not a desirable proceeding. Hence the emergency powers delegated by the Defence of the Realm Acts 1914–15 and the Emergency Powers (Defence) Acts 1939–40 in two world wars, and the permanent peacetime provisions of the Emergency Powers Act 1920.

Exceptional types of delegated legislation

(i) *Power to impose taxation* [14]

Section 2 of the Emergency Powers (Defence) Act 1939 provided that the Treasury might by order impose, in connection with any scheme of control authorised by Defence Regulations (themselves delegated legislation), such charges as might be specified in the order. A " new economic regulator " introduced by the Finance Act 1961 empowered the Chancellor of the Exchequer at any time of the year to vary by order the main customs and excise revenue duties and purchase tax. The maximum change was to be 10 per cent. in either direction, and the power was given on a yearly basis only. The Chancellor of the Exchequer forthwith increased these duties by 10 per cent.

(ii) *Power to modify or adapt the enabling Act or other Acts of Parliament*

Parliament sometimes delegates to a Minister the power of modifying the enabling Act so far as may appear to him to be necessary for the purpose of bringing the Act into operation. Such provisions are usually transitional. [15]

Power to modify or adapt other Acts of Parliament was given, for example, by the Representation of the People Act 1945, s. 12. The alternative would often involve the drafting and passing of large numbers of amending Acts. The power is innocuous so long as Parliament is aware of what it is doing, and imposes a short time limit.

(iii) *Powers excluded from the jurisdiction of the courts*

The right of the citizen to ask the court to declare delegated legislation *ultra vires* may be expressly excluded by Parliament,[16] although it is not clear precisely what words in an Act will be held to have this effect.[17] The Committee on Ministers' Powers regarded such a clause as generally objectionable, and only justifiable in very exceptional cases, *viz.* in emergency legislation and in cases where

[14] See *Att.-Gen.* v. *Wilts United Dairies* (1922) 91 L.J.K.B. 897.
[15] By a far-fetched analogy to the Statute of Proclamations 1539 (repealed in 1547), which gave the King a limited power to legislate by proclamation, this kind of provision became known as " the Henry VIII clause."
[16] *Cf. Chester* v. *Bateson* [1920] 1 K.B. 829.
[17] See *post,* Chap. 30.

finality is desirable, e.g. Stock Regulations under which titles to property may be created or money raised, and Regulations under the Foreign Marriage Act 1892, on which the validity of marriages may depend. In these non-emergency cases, where property or status may be affected, the Committee suggested that the regulations should be open to challenge for a short initial period.

(iv) Community laws [18]

The European Communities Act 1972, s. 2 (1), provides for the application in this country of laws made by the Treaties and by existing or future self-executing Community Regulations, questions of interpretation and (in the case of Regulations) validity being decided by, or in accordance with principles laid down by, the European Court.[19] There is also a limited power under section 2 (2) to issue Statutory Instruments giving effect to Community Directives, and either laid in draft for approval by resolution of each House or subject to annulment by resolution of each House.

II. PARLIAMENTARY SAFEGUARDS FOR DELEGATED LEGISLATION [20]

Apart from the common law jurisdiction of the courts to prevent a power of delegated legislation from being exceeded by declaring its exercise void as *ultra vires* in cases that may be brought before them,[21] Parliament provides a number of safeguards—of varying degrees of efficacy—to secure the proper use of the power. No attempt has been made in this country to establish a uniform code of procedure for the making and testing of delegated legislation, such as has been provided in somewhat different circumstances [22] by the American

---

[18] *Ante*, Chap. 4, and *post*, p. 489.

[19] *Cf.* L. Blom-Cooper and G. Drewry, *Final Appeal* (1972) Chap. 20.

[20] Report from the Select Committee on Delegated Legislation (1953) H.C. No. 310, pp. xi–xxxiii; Report of Committee on Ministers' Powers (1932) Cmd. 4060, pp. 41–48, 64–70; J. E. Kersell, *Parliamentary Supervision of Delegated Legislation*; " Upper Chamber Scrutiny of Delegated Legislation " [1960] P.L. 46; K. C. Wheare, *Government by Committee* (1955) Chap. 8; Sir Cecil Carr, " Parliamentary Control of Delegated Legislation " [1956] P.L. 200; R. C. Fitzgerald, " Safeguards in Delegated Legislation " (1949) 27 Can.Bar Rev. 550; S. A. de Smith, " Delegated Legislation in England " (1949) 2 *Western Political Quarterly* 515.

[21] *Post*, Chap. 30.

[22] See B. Schwartz and H. W. R. Wade Q.C., *Legal Control of Government* (1972) App. 1; J. F. Garner, *Administrative Law* (3rd ed. 1970) App. 1; K. C. Davis, *Administrative Law* (1951) Chaps. 5 and 6; L. Jaffe, *Administrative Cases and Materials* (1953) pp. 110–111, 280–282; " The American Administrative Procedure Act " [1956] P.L. 218.

Administrative Procedure Act 1946. A Joint Select Committee of both Houses on Delegated Legislation reported in 1972.[23]

It has been suggested that there should be a Select Committee on European Affairs—either a Commons Committee or a Joint Committee of both Houses—to inquire into, and report on, the domestic consequences of proposals for Community Regulations. As Parliament will have no opportunity to approve or disapprove Community measures when once they are made, arrangements should be made for the Houses to be informed by the government in advance of such proposals, so that they could be scrutinised at every stage before final decisions are made by the Council of Ministers.[24]

1. Laying before Parliament

There is no general Act which requires delegated legislation to be laid before Parliament. Even the Statutory Instruments Act 1946 does not require all Statutory Instruments to be so laid. The enabling Act has to be examined in each case. Enabling Acts now usually require Statutory Instruments to be laid, although the British Nationality Act 1948 is an example of an Act that does not. Laying is usually before both Houses, except as regards financial matters when it is before the Commons only.

There is no uniformity in the requirements, which may take any of the following forms:

(a) " Negative parliamentary procedure "

(i) To be laid before Parliament with immediate effect, but *subject to annulment* (by Order in Council) following a resolution of either House (" *negative resolution* "), usually without prejudice to the validity of anything done thereunder before annulment. This is the commonest form. Before 1948 there was no uniform period for the passing of negative resolutions, but section 5 of the Statutory Instruments Act 1946 prescribes a period of forty days after laying, excluding any time during which Parliament is dissolved or prorogued or both Houses are adjourned (s. 7). Where an instrument is subject to negative resolution, a member of the Commons may move a " prayer " for its annulment at the end of the ordinary public business and a division can be taken.

---

[23] See *Report from Joint Committee on Delegated Legislation* (1971–72) H.L. 184 and H.C. 475; see Preface.

[24] The Joint Committee on Delegated Legislation, *ibid.*, covered delegated legislation to be made under the European Communities Act; and the *First Report from the Select Committee on European Secondary Legislation* (February 1973) made recommendations with regard to proposed EEC legislation. See Preface.

In practice instruments are never annulled,[25] because the Minister can count on the government's majority. Even if the government were " caught napping," the Minister could introduce another instrument in identical terms. The procedure by negative resolution was seldom used before 1943. There has not been enough time in recent years for members to debate prayers for annulment. No amendment of the instrument is possible, although as a result of criticism the Minister may withdraw it and submit another in a modified form. A better procedure might be to allow motions that a Statutory Instrument be referred to the government for consideration. The Select Committee on Procedure (1970–71) [26] recommended that " negative " instruments adversely reported on by the Scrutiny Committee (*infra*) should automatically become subject to affirmative procedure.

(ii) To be laid *in draft* before Parliament, but subject to a resolution that no further proceedings be taken. An adverse resolution may be passed by either House within forty days (Statutory Instruments Act 1946, s. 6), which stops further progress on that draft but does not prevent fresh drafts being laid. Prison Rules are made in this way.

(b) " *Affirmative parliamentary procedure* "

(i) To be laid before Parliament, either in draft or when made, but not to take effect until approved by *affirmative resolution* in each House. This is the second most common method. A Minister must present the instrument for approval, and for this the government has to find time in each House. No amendment is usually possible.

The Minister who introduces the enabling Act decides what method of laying (if any) shall be prescribed. There are no rules, but the practice is for the positive (affirmative) procedure to apply to the more important kinds of delegated legislation, *e.g.*: where the exercise of the power of delegated legislation would substantially affect Acts of Parliament, except merely consequential adaptations; the imposition of financial charges; skeleton powers, *i.e.* powers to make schemes where only the purpose is fixed by the enabling Act and the substance is left to delegated legislation; and other powers of an exceptional or politically important nature.

(ii) Sometimes an instrument is to be laid before Parliament with immediate effect, but will cease to have effect unless approved by resolution within the prescribed period. This method combines prompt operation with parliamentary control, *e.g.* regulations made under the Emergency Powers Act 1920; and also a method of imposing taxation, *e.g.* import duties, where prior notice is undesirable.

[25] Or, hardly ever: *cf. ante*, pp. 158–159.
[26] *The Process of Legislation* (1970–71) H.C. 538.

(c) *To be laid without further provision for control*

This method is now very uncommon. It is used where Parliament contemplates that a Minister should take some action, and merely demands to be kept informed of the action taken, *e.g.* the postponing order under the New Valuation Lists (Postponement) Act 1952.[27] No resolution is necessary for the instrument to take effect. Where an instrument is merely laid before the House, it is usually impracticable to find time during the ordinary business of the Commons to move an address for its annulment, and if it is raised on the motion for adjournment no division is allowed. Questions may be asked about regulations lying on the table of the House.

The procedure of the two Houses and the time available—especially in the Commons—are not adequate to take full advantage of the opportunity for control offered by the laying of regulations before Parliament. The procedure in the House of Lords is similar, but rather more serviceable. A peer can call attention to a regulation lying on the table by moving for papers, or can move a resolution to annul any regulation which is subject to annulment, and in either case a division can be taken. Neither House can propose an amendment to a regulation laid before it.

Local instruments, dealing with such matters as local authorities' powers, are far more numerous than general instruments. They are registered, but Parliament is usually not concerned with control or even information, and they are seldom required to be laid before Parliament.

Legal effect of the requirement of laying

The legal effect of the requirement that instruments are to be laid before Parliament is uncertain. Is it " mandatory " (imperative), so that the instrument is invalid if the requirement is not fulfilled; or merely " directory," imposing on a public officer a duty of imperfect obligation, but not affecting validity? It seems that so far as concerns instruments subject to negative resolution, and probably also those subject to affirmative resolution, the requirement is directory.[28] There is no penalty specified if the requirement is not observed. In 1944 it was discovered that the Home Secretary had for three years overlooked the requirement that National Fire Service Regulations should be laid before Parliament " as soon as may be " after they were

---

[27] Rules presented to Parliament in Command Paper are " laid before Parliament ": *R.* v. *Immigration Tribunal, ex p. Joyles* [1972] 1 W.L.R. 1390 (D.C.).

[28] It was so held by the West Indian Court of Appeal in *Springer* v. *Doorly* (1950) L.R.B.G. 10; (1950) 66 L.Q.R. 299. The regulations in that case were to be laid " as soon as possible." And see *Bailey* v. *Williamson* (1873) L.R. 8 Q.B. 118.

made.[29] An indemnity Act [30] was therefore passed indemnifying the Home Secretary against " all consequences whatsoever, if any " incurred by this failure. The Turks and Caicos Islands Order 1962 [31] was inadvertently not laid before Parliament, and was replaced retrospectively by another Order issued in 1965.[32]

Section 4 (1) of the Statutory Instruments Act 1946 provides that where any Statutory Instrument is required to be laid before Parliament after being made, a copy of the instrument shall be laid before each House before the instrument comes into operation, except in cases of urgency notified to the Lord Chancellor and the Speaker of the Commons.[33]

What constitutes " laying before the House " is for each House to decide. The Laying of Documents before Parliament (Interpretation) Act 1948 defined statutory references to " laying " as taking such action as is directed by virtue of any Standing Order or Sessional Order or other direction or practice of either House to constitute laying, even though it involves action taken when the House is not sitting.

2. Scrutinising committees [34]

Select Committee on Statutory Instruments

Following a debate in the Commons after the incident of the National Fire Service Regulations in 1944, a Select Committee on Statutory Rules and Orders was set up by the Commons, with terms of reference based on the recommendations of the Committee on Ministers' Powers. As a consequence of the Statutory Instruments Act 1946, the Committee was renamed the Select Committee on Statutory Instruments (commonly known as " the Scrutiny Committee "), and its terms of reference have been extended from time to time.

Its terms of reference are to consider all general instruments, whether or not laid before the House, with a view to determining whether the special attention of the House should be drawn to it on any of the following grounds, that:

[29] Fire Services (Emergency Provisions) Act 1941.
[30] National Fire Service Regulations (Indemnity) Act 1944. And see Price Control and other Orders (Indemnity) Act 1951. *Cf.* Documentary Evidence Act 1868. Sir Carleton Allen, *op. cit.* p. 146, remarked that the Home Secretary in 1944 " lost a unique opportunity of studying the prison system from the inside."
[31] No. 1649.
[32] No. 1861.
[33] Sections 4 and 5 do not apply to orders which are subject to special parliamentary procedure or to any other instrument which is required to be laid before Parliament before it comes into operation (s. 7 (3)). And see s. 4 (2), *post*, p. 495.
[34] And see Preface.

(i) it imposes a charge on the public revenues, or requires the payment of a fee to a public authority for services or a licence;

(ii) it is made in pursuance of an Act specifically excluding it from challenge in the courts;

(iii) it appears to make some unusual or unexpected use of the powers conferred by the statute under which it is made [35];

(iv) it purports to have retrospective effect, where the parent Act confers no such authority;

(v) there appears to have been unjustifiable delay in its publication, or in laying it before Parliament;

(vi) there appears to have been unjustifiable delay in notifying the Speaker where, on the ground of urgency, the instrument came into operation before being laid before Parliament;

(vii) for any special reason its form or purport calls for elucidation;

(viii) the drafting appears to be defective;

or on any other ground which does not infringe on its merits or on the policy behind it.[36]

The Scrutiny Committee has the assistance of Counsel to the Speaker. It may require the government department concerned to explain, either by memorandum or witness, any instrument under consideration; and the Committee is instructed, before drawing the special attention of the House to any instrument, to afford the department concerned an opportunity of furnishing an explanation. The Committee is concerned with matters of *form*, as set out in its terms of reference. It is not concerned with policy, which is a matter for Parliament. Nor is it concerned directly with *ultra vires*, which is a matter for the courts,[37] although an " unusual " use of the power delegated may cast doubt on its *vires*. The practice has developed of electing a member of the Opposition as chairman of the Scrutiny Committee, who would not be embarrassed by conflicting loyalties if the Committee criticises departmental action.

The Committee has not considered it necessary to draw the attention of the House to more than a very small proportion of the masses of instruments that it has scrutinised [38]; but the very existence of the Committee has had an indirect effect in bringing about some improve-

[35] *e.g.* Dutch Elm Disease (Local Authorities) Order 1971, No. 1708, made by the Forestry Commission under the Plant Health Act 1967, authorising local authorities to cut down diseased elms if the owner failed to do so, and to recover the cost from the owner. [36] (1970–71) H.C. 538: *The Process of Legislation.*

[37] Injunction does not lie to restrain a Minister from laying before Parliament a regulation alleged to be *ultra vires*: *Harper* v. *Home Secretary* [1955] Ch. 238; *Merricks* v. *Heathcoat-Amory* [1955] Ch. 567. See *post,* Chap. 31.

[38] *e.g.* fn. 35, *supra.*

ment in the form and nomenclature of ministerial regulations, and in encouraging the practice of providing explanatory notes. The Committee made proposals which led to the passing of the Statutory Instruments Act 1946. Reports of the Scrutiny Committee are sometimes debated.

House of Lords Special Orders Committee

The House of Lords since 1925 has had a Committee to consider any instruments laid before the House requiring an affirmative resolution ("Special Orders"), with certain exceptions such as regulations issued under the Emergency Powers Act 1920 and measures passed in accordance with the Church of England Assembly (Powers) Act 1919.[39] In the case of Special Orders of a public character, the Committee is to consider and report whether they have any doubt that the order is *intra vires*, or whether there is any other matter in the order or in the parent Act to which they think it expedient to call the attention of the House. No motion for an affirmative resolution may be moved before the report of the Committee has been laid before the House.

It has been suggested that these terms of reference should be enlarged so as to bring them into line with the House of Commons Scrutiny Committee, in particular, by including orders which are subject to negative resolution.

3. Other controls in Parliament

    (a) Motions of censure on the Minister responsible for the instrument.
    (b) Debate and possibly motion and division on supply.
    (c) Questions to Ministers. In either House questions may be asked about instruments lying on the table, but no debate is allowed on a question.

4. Publication

The Rules Publication Act 1893, s. 1, required *antecedent* publicity for limited classes of statutory rules. *Subsequent* publication was provided for by section 3, which required all statutory rules made after 1893 to be sent forthwith after they were made to the Queen's printer.

The Statutory Instruments Act 1946 repealed the Rules Publication Act 1893 and generalised the procedure for *subsequent* publication; but it made no provision for antecedent publicity, the reason given being that the practice of informal consultation with outside interests

[39] As modified by the Synodical Government Measure 1969

had become general. Immediately after the making of any " Statutory Instrument " as defined in section 1,[40] it is to be sent to the Queen's printer and numbered, and copies shall " as soon as possible " be printed and sold (s. 2). The Stationery Office is to publish lists showing the date on which every Statutory Instrument printed and sold by the Queen's printer was first *issued* by that office; and in any legal proceedings a copy of any list so published purporting to bear the imprint of the Queen's printer shall be received in evidence as a true copy, and an entry therein shall be conclusive evidence of the date on which any Statutory Instrument was first issued by the Stationery Office (s. 3 (1)).

Delegated legislation generally comes into operation when it is made, unless some other date is specified therein.[41] The Statutory Instruments Act 1946, s. 3 (2), however, provides that where any person is charged with an offence under a Statutory Instrument, it shall be a defence to prove that the instrument had not been " issued " by the Stationery Office at the date of the alleged contravention, unless it is proved that at that date reasonable steps had been taken for the purpose of bringing the purport of the instrument to the notice of the public, or of persons likely to be affected by it, or of the person charged.

Where any Statutory Instrument is required to be laid before Parliament after being made, copies sold by the Queen's printer must show the date on which it came or will come into operation; and either the date on which copies were laid before Parliament or a statement that such copies are to be laid before Parliament (s. 4 (2)).

The Treasury, with the concurrence of the Lord Chancellor and the Speaker of the Commons, is empowered to make regulations for the purposes of the Act, including the numbering, printing and publication of Statutory Instruments, and the exemption of any classes of Statutory Instrument from the requirement of being printed and sold (s. 8). The Statutory Instruments Regulations 1947 made thereunder are contained in S.I. 1948 No. 1, which begins the printed series of *Statutory Instruments* that replaces the previous *Statutory Rules and Orders.*

The Regulations exempt from the printing requirement Statutory Instruments which: are local, or are otherwise regularly printed as a series (Reg. 5), or temporary (Reg. 6); contain bulky Schedules (Reg. 7); or where it would be contrary to the public interest that they should

---

[40] *Ante*, p. 485.
[41] *Jones* v. *Robson* [1901] 1 Q.B. 680; but *cf. Johnson* v. *Sargant* [1918] 1 K.B. 101. An Act of Parliament comes into operation on the date on which it receives the Royal Assent (printed beneath the title), unless some other date is specified: Acts of Parliament (Commencement) Act 1793; *R.* v. *Smith* [1910] 1 K.B. 17.

be printed before coming into operation (Reg. 8). Such exemption requires the certificate of the " responsible authority," *i.e.* the authority that makes the instrument. In *Simmonds* v. *Newall* [42] a conviction for the offence of selling in contravention of an Iron and Steel Prices Order was quashed by the Divisional Court, because the Schedules had not been printed and no certificate had been issued under Regulation 7 exempting from printing, and presumably reasonable steps had not been taken under section 3 (2). Parker J. said it was not necessary to decide whether a Statutory Instrument is wholly invalid if it is required by section 2 to be printed and it is not printed, or whether section 3 (2) provides a defence whether the Statutory Instrument is required to be printed or not. In *R.* v. *Sheer Metalcraft*, [43] a prosecution for buying in contravention of an Iron and Steel Price Order, the Schedules had not been printed and no certificate of exemption had been issued; but the jury found the accused guilty, because sufficient steps had been taken to bring the Schedules to their notice. Streatfeild J. told the jury that a Statutory Instrument is " made " (*i.e.* effective) when it is made by the Minister and (presumably, where laying is required) laid before Parliament: whether a Statutory Instrument has been " issued " (*i.e.* printed) is a different question, which can be raised as a defence under section 3 (2). The neglect to print or to certify exemption from printing did not make the order invalid, and it was admissible in evidence.

5. Prior consultation [44]

Acts of Parliament delegating legislative power sometimes provide that the Minister may, or shall, consult interested bodies or an advisory committee before issuing regulations. The interested bodies may be specified in the Act or left to the Minister's discretion. The Minister is not usually bound to accept such advice. Thus the Minister must consult the Council on Tribunals before making procedural rules for tribunals that come under its supervision; and the Lord Chancellor must consult the Council before making procedural rules for statutory inquiries. [45] In some cases a draft scheme is to be prepared by the interested body (*e.g.* a local authority), and confirmed or approved by the Minister. Exceptionally, the Minister is required to submit draft regulations to an advisory committee, without being bound to accept their suggested amendments. Apart from such statutory provisions, the practice of consultation has now become generally established.

[42] [1953] 1 W.L.R. 846; *sub nom. Defiant Cycle Co.* v. *Newell* [1953] 2 All E.R. 38.
[43] [1954] 1 Q.B. 586.
[44] See J. F. Garner, " Consultation in Subordinate Legislation " [1964] P.L. 105.
[45] Tribunals and Inquiries Act 1971, ss. 10 and 11.

CHAPTER 29

ADMINISTRATIVE JURISDICTION [1]

Introduction

" Administrative jurisdiction " or " administrative justice " is a
name given to various ways of deciding disputes outside the ordinary
courts. It is not possible to define precisely what bodies constitute
the "ordinary courts," although this expression was used in the
Tribunals and Inquiries Acts 1958 and 1971. There are some bodies
that might be placed under the heading either of ordinary courts or
of special tribunals. Certain matters involving calculations of figures
or scientific problems, such as the assessment of rates and taxes, local
audit, patents, inventions and performing rights, have been considered
by Parliament unsuitable for the ordinary courts. Then there has been
a great increase of governmental activity, both central and local, under
statutory powers in the late nineteenth and twentieth centuries, and
a number of social services are provided in the Welfare State. Under
both these heads there are complex systems of regulation and control,
such as national insurance, pensions, the health service, education,
public transport, the regulation of agriculture, rent control, housing
and redevelopment, town and country planning and the consequent
compulsory acquisition of land. It is inevitable that disputes should
arise, or conflicts of rights and interests between the individual
citizen and the central or local government authority. The ordinary
courts are appropriate for the decision of purely legal rights; but in
many of the kinds of cases of which we are speaking, the question in
issue is not one of purely legal rights but a conflict between private
and public interests, bound up in a greater or lesser degree with
ministerial policy as outlined by statute.

Where Parliament does not consider the ordinary courts suitable for

---

[1] *Report of Committee on Administrative Tribunals and Enquiries* (" Franks Committee ") (1957) Cmnd. 218; *Memoranda submitted by Government Departments*
(6 vols., H.M.S.O. 1956); *Minutes of Evidence* (H.M.S.O. 1956–1957); *Report of
the Committee on Ministers' Powers* (1932) Cmd. 4060, s. III.

    J. F. Garner, *Administrative Law* (3rd ed. 1970); D. C. M. Yardley, *A Source
Book of English Administrative Law* (2nd ed. 1970); Sir Carleton Allen, *Adminis-
trative Jurisdiction* (reprinted from [1956] P.L. 13–109); Griffith and Street,
Principles of Administrative Law (4th ed. 1967); R. M. Jackson, *The Machinery
of Justice in England* (6th ed. 1972); W. A. Robson, *Justice and Administrative
Law* (3rd ed. 1951); H. W. R. Wade, *Administrative Law* (3rd ed. 1971); *Towards
Administrative Justice* (Michigan, 1963); Harry Street, *Justice in the Welfare
State* (1968); *The Citizen and the Administration* (the Whyatt Report by *Justice*,
1961).

the decision of such disputes, especially at first instance, it prescribes
one of three other methods of deciding them:
  (i) special (or administrative) tribunal;
  (ii) ministerial decision after statutory inquiry [2];
  (iii) ministerial decision, in which the Minister uses his discretion
        without any prescribed procedure.[3]

The Franks Committee [4] regarded both tribunals and other
administrative procedures as essential to our society. Preference
should be given, however, to entrusting adjudication to the ordinary
courts rather than to tribunals, unless there are clearly special reasons
which make a tribunal more appropriate. Similarly, a tribunal is
to be preferred to a Minister, but it is not always possible to express
policy in the form of regulations capable of being administered by an
independent tribunal. The Franks Committee examined the working
of administrative law in other countries, notably the United States
and France; but concluded that, although there are advantages in
comparative study, each country must work out for itself, within the
framework of its own institutions and way of life, the proper balance
between public and private interest.

I. Special Tribunals

These are independent statutory tribunals whose function is judicial.
They are often called "administrative tribunals," especially those
more closely related by appointment or policy to the Minister concerned, because the reasons for creating them are administrative.
The tribunals are so varied in composition, method of appointment,
functions and procedure, and in their relation to Ministers on the one
hand and the ordinary courts on the other, that a satisfactory formal
classification is impossible. There are about 2,000 of them, and
more than fifty different types. There is no complete list.[5] If one's
interest is primarily in administration, one can arrange them according
to the branch of government with which they are concerned, e.g.
agriculture, landlord and tenant, transport, national insurance and
health service. A professional lawyer would be more interested to
know that legal representation is allowed in some but not in others;
that some have a fairly definite code of procedure and others not;

---

2 *Post*, p. 504.
3 *Post*, p. 505.
4 (1957) Cmnd. 218, paras. 406–408; see *post*, p. 505. *Cf. Report of the Committee on Ministers' Powers* (1932) Cmd. 4060, pp. 115–118.
5 Exhaustive information down to 1957 is contained in the *Memoranda submitted
  by Government Departments* to the Franks Committee. See also N. D. Vandyk,
  Tribunals and Inquiries (1965); Garner, *op. cit.* Chap. 7.

that some have legal chairmen appointed by the Lord Chancellor and others are composed entirely of laymen appointed by the Minister, with many variations on this theme; that from some there is no appeal, while from others appeal lies to the Minister or to another ministerial tribunal or to the High Court or the Privy Council, and if there is an appeal it is probably on law [6] only but may be on both law and fact. The members of these tribunals are usually persons with knowledge and experience of the trade, industry or profession concerned.[7] Decisions of some of the more important tribunals are reported, but many are not.

Reasons for creating special tribunals

The reasons why Parliament increasingly confers powers of adjudication on special tribunals rather than on the ordinary courts may be stated positively as showing the greater suitability of such tribunals, or negatively as showing the inadequacy of the ordinary courts for the particular kind of work that has to be done. In the following summary we choose mainly the former method.

(i) *Expert knowledge*

Many of the questions that have to be decided under modern social legislation call for an expert knowledge of matters falling outside the training of the lawyer; also an understanding of the policy of the legislature and experience of administration. They are not primarily legal questions, although at some stage a judicial habit of mind may be required.

(ii) *Cheapness*

The vast number of questions that arise from day to day, affecting the interests of thousands of people, must be disposed of much more cheaply than can be done in the stately and costly courts of law. The speed and informality mentioned below contribute to the relative cheapness of administrative justice.

(iii) *Speed*

Again, if these multitudinous questions are to be disposed of without the delay that would clog the administrative machine and work great hardship on interested parties, institutions must be devised

---

[6] Including legal interpretations of such terms as " house," " rent," " services."
[7] W. E. Cavanagh and D. Newton, " The Membership of Two Administrative Tribunals " (1970) 48 *Public Administration* 449; " Administrative Tribunals How People Become Members " (1971) 49 *Public Administration* 197; S. Mc-Corquodale, " The Composition of the Administrative Tribunals " [1962] P.L. 298.

and procedure adopted that will dispatch the business much more speedily than the ordinary courts can do. Indeed, the courts would not have time to take over this work, in addition to what they already have, without being entirely reconstituted and so losing their present identity.

(iv) *Flexibility*

Although every body of men that has to make decisions evolves in course of time general working principles, and government departments tend to follow their own precedents, the new tribunals are not hampered by the rigid doctrine of binding precedent adhered to by the courts. They thus have greater freedom to develop new branches of law on the basis of modern social legislation and suitable to the needs of the Welfare State, as in times past the Court of Chancery developed Equity.[8] This does not mean that the decisions of tribunals are entirely capricious and unpredictable: there is a growing practice for some of them to publish selected decisions.

(v) *Informality*

Tribunals are not bound by such complex rules of procedure or such stringent rules of evidence as prevail in the ordinary courts. They may admit hearsay evidence; they must observe the rules of natural justice, but cross-examination is not essential.[9] Procedural rules of varying degrees of completeness are prescribed for some of these bodies, but the sources from which they derive their information are not usually restricted. This means that the layman is not at such a disadvantage in presenting his own case and following the proceedings as he is in the courts.

Examples of special tribunals

Tribunals concerned with property, taxes and rates include the Lands Tribunal, agricultural land tribunals, Special and General Commissioners of Income Tax, local valuation courts (rating), district auditors, rent tribunals (furnished houses), rent assessment committees,[10] the Patents Appeal Tribunal, the Performing Right Tribunal and the Royal Commission on Awards to Inventors.

Tribunals concerned with industry and industrial relations include the Industrial Court, courts of inquiry, the Transport Tribunal, the

---

8 *Cf. James* v. *Minister of Pensions* [1947] K.B. 867 (Denning J.).

9 *Miller* (T. A.) v. *Ministry of Housing and Local Government* [1968] 1 W.L.R. 992 (C.A.).

10 D. C. M. Yardley, " Rent Tribunals and Rent Assessment Committees " [1968] P.L. 135.

Chief Registrar of Trade Unions and Employers' Associations, industrial tribunals and national insurance (industrial injuries) tribunals.

Tribunals concerned with social welfare include social security appeal tribunals, national insurance tribunals, the Pensions Appeal Tribunal, the National Health Service Appeal Tribunal, medical boards, medical appeal tribunals, mental health review tribunals and the Chief Registrar of Friendly Societies.

To these one may add those concerned with immigration, namely, adjudicators and the Immigration Appeal Tribunal.

Domestic tribunals

Some disciplinary bodies set up for professional or other associations are established by statute, often with appeal to the courts, and therefore find a place here although they are not public authorities.

Another reason for including domestic tribunals here is that the supervisory or corrective jurisdiction of the High Court [11] is exercised over statutory domestic tribunals in a similar way to that over special or administrative tribunals, in that they must observe the principles of natural justice; and this supervisory jurisdiction over them provides useful precedents for administrative law.[12] However, whereas excess of jurisdiction renders a statutory tribunal liable to damages, excess of jurisdiction by a non-statutory tribunal does not, unless there is a breach of contract or malice.[13] Declaration and injunction lie against non-statutory tribunals, but not certiorari and prohibition.[14]

The Solicitors' Disciplinary Committee consists of past and present members of the Council of the Law Society appointed by the Master of the Rolls under the Solicitors Acts. The Committee may strike a solicitor off the rolls, suspend him from practice or fine him for professional misconduct. It is not a committee of the Law Society. Appeal lies from the Disciplinary Committee in certain cases to the

---

[11] Post, Chap. 31.

[12] Lord Justice Morris, " The Courts and Domestic Tribunals " (1953) 69 L.Q.R. 318; D. Lloyd, " The Disciplinary Powers of Professional Bodies " (1950) 13 M.L.R. 281 and (1952) 15 M.L.R. 413; J. D. B. Mitchell, " Domestic Tribunals and the Courts " (1956) 2 British Journal of Administrative Law 80; J. Gareth Miller, " The Disciplinary Jurisdiction of Professional Tribunals " (1962) 25 M.L.R. 531; Report of Departmental Committee on Powers of Subpoena of Disciplinary Tribunals (1960) Cmnd. 1033.

Natural justice does not necessarily involve the right to legal representation. Pett v. Greyhound Racing Association (No. 2) [1970] 1 Q.B. 46; Enderby Town Football Club v. Football Association [1971] 1 Ch. 591 (C.A.); [1971] 1 W.L.R. 81 (H.L.).

[13] Byrne v. Kinematograph Renters Association [1958] 1 W.L.R. 762.

[14] R. v. National Joint Council for the Craft of Dental Technicians, ex p. Neate [1953] 1 Q.B. 704 (D.C.).

Master of the Rolls, whose decision is final: in other cases to a Divisional Court of the Queen's Bench Division of the High Court and thence to the Court of Appeal.[15] The Committee's procedure is statutory. It sits in private, but exercises its functions judicially and gives its findings and order publicly. The publication of its findings and order is absolutely privileged from actions for defamation.[16]

Disciplinary committees have been created by statute for a number of other professions to hear complaints of misconduct and with power to strike members off the register. In the medical,[17] dental, optical and allied professions, appeal against removal from the register lies to the Judicial Committee of the Privy Council. In the professions of pharmacy and architecture [18] such appeal lies to the High Court.

The Masters of the Bench of each of the four Inns of Court have a customary jurisdiction, said to have been delegated by the judges, to disbar members of their Inn for professional misconduct. Such a tribunal is not a court of law: witnesses are not asked to take an oath and they may not be compelled to give evidence.[19] The Senate of the Inns of Court set up in 1966 now exercises by its Disciplinary Committee this customary jurisdiction, other than the carrying into effect of any sentence. Appeal by a barrister from disbarring or suspension lies to the Lord Chancellor and the judges of the High Court, but it is not the practice for those judges to sit who have already heard the matter as Benchers.[20]

15 *Re the Solicitors Act 1932* [1938] 1 K.B. 616; *Re A Solicitor (No. 2)* [1956] 1 W.L.R. 1312; *Re A Solicitor* [1969] 1 W.L.R. 1068 (D.C.). See T. G. Lund, " The Professional Discipline of Solicitors," *Administrative Tribunals at Work* (ed. R. S. W. Pollard) p. 118; (1955) 55 *Law Society's Gazette* 547.

16 *Addis* v. *Crocker* [1961] 1 Q.B. 11 (C.A.).

17 *H. J. Sloan* v. *General Medical Council* [1970] 1 W.L.R. 1130 (P.C.); *Libman* v. *General Medical Council* [1972] A.C. 217 (P.C.).

18 *Hughes* v. *Architects' Registration Council* [1957] 2 Q.B. 550 (D.C.).

19 *Re Marrinan, The Times,* June 28 and 29, July 1 and 4, 1957; *Seymour* v. *Butterworth* (1862) 3 F. & F. 381. And see *Report of Committee of Privy Councillors on Interception of Communications* (1957) Cmnd. 283. In 1963 an M.P. charged the Attorney-General before the Benchers of the Inner Temple with unprofessional conduct in having deceived the House of Commons by failing to reveal that there was reason to believe that Chief Enaharo (*ante,* p. 381) would not be allowed to choose his own counsel if he were tried in Nigeria. The Benchers heard the case in private, and held that the charges were unfounded: *The Times,* October 22 and 23, 1963.

20 *Re S. (A Barrister)* [1970] 1 Q.B. 160. *Re Marrinan, The Times,* July 5, September 29, October 1 and 3, 1957; *Lincoln* v. *Daniels* [1962] 1 Q.B. 237; *R. v Gray's Inn* (1780) 1 Doug.K.B. See also *Re Yankson, The Times,* January 14, 1971 (unsuccessful appeal to Visitors of Lincoln's Inn by 48-year-old Ghanaian to be allowed fifth attempt to take examinations).

An important group of domestic tribunals are those set up by trade unions.[21]

Universities in this country are mostly created by royal charter, although some are governed by private Acts of Parliament. The former (chartered corporations) ought to be classed as non-statutory bodies, their " statutes " being prerogative Orders in Council. Disciplinary powers of university authorities have been judicially described as " judicial "[22] or " quasi-judicial "[23]; and university disciplinary bodies or committees must observe the principles of natural justice as a matter of implied contract. Natural justice does not require the provision of an appeal against expulsion.[24] Even though the principles of natural justice have not been complied with, the court may refuse discretionary remedies.[25] It has been stated or presumed in several cases that—apart from the ordinary remedies of damages, declaration and injunction—certiorari would lie against university disciplinary authorities,[26] but in so far as they are not statutory bodies this is contrary to the principles of administrative law. A college prospectus containing the outline syllabus of a course of study forms part of a contract between the college and its students[27]; but domestic disputes between members of a university concerning the conduct of examinations, the classification of candidates and the conferment of degrees are within the exclusive jurisdiction of the Visitor, commonly the Queen in Council; *Thorne* v. *University of London*.[28] The High Court, said Diplock L.J. in that case, fortunately does not act as a court of appeal from university examiners.[29]

21 *Ante*, p. 449.
22 *Ceylon University* v. *Fernando* [1960] 1 W.L.R. 223 (P.C.), declaration refused because natural justice observed. See also *De Verteuil* v. *Knaggs* [1918] A.C. 551, 560; *cf. Ex p. Death* (1852) 18 Q.B. 647.
23 *Glynn* v. *University of Keele* [1971] 1 W.L.R. 487 (Pennycuick V.-C.), principles of natural justice not complied with, but court exercises discretion to refuse injunction; see H. W. R. Wade, " Nudism and Natural Justice " (1971) 87 L.Q.R. 320.   24 *Ward* v. *Bradford Corporation, The Times*, July 9, 1971 (C.A.)
25 *Glynn* v. *University of Keele, supra.*
26 *R.* v. *Aston University Senate, ex p. Roffey* [1969] 2 Q.B. 538 (D.C.); principles of natural justice not complied with, but court in its discretion refuses certiorari and mandamus because of delay in making application; *R.* v. *Oxford University, ex p. Bolchover, The Times*, October 7, 1970 (D.C.), expulsion not unfair, leave to apply for certiorari refused; *cf. Vidyadaya University Council* v. *Silva* [1965] 1 W.L.R. 77 (P.C.), certiorari not available for dismissal of Professor; see H. W. R. Wade, " Judicial Control of Universities " (1969) 85 L.Q.R. 468.
27 *D'Mello* v. *Loughborough College of Technology, The Times*, June 17, 1970, claim for damages dismissed as no breach of contract proved.
28 [1966] 2 Q.B. 237 (C.A.), following *R.* v. *Dunsheath, ex p. Meredith* [1951] 1 K.B. 127 (D.C.).
29 So in *Sammy* v. *Birkbeck College, The Times*, May 20, 1965 (C.A.), a student who failed to obtain the first-class degree he thought he deserved, lost his action against his former college for breach of contract, fraud and negligence.
    See further, J. W. Bridge, " Keeping Peace in the Universities: the Role of the Visitor " (1970) 86 L.Q.R. 531; S. A. de Smith, " University Discipline and

II. MINISTERIAL DECISIONS

The Whyatt Report [30] suggested that the individual should be entitled to an impartial adjudication of his dispute with authority, unless there are overriding considerations which make it necessary in the public interest that the Minister should retain responsibility for making the final decision.

1. After statutory inquiry

Parliament often provides that, before a decision is made by a Minister or other public authority which affects the rights of citizens, an inquiry must be held at which those whose interests are concerned may state their objections to the action proposed before a final decision is made. Inquiries are usually prescribed by statute before land is compulsorily acquired for such purposes as town development, slum clearance, the building of housing estates, schools and hospitals, and road improvement; and also before town and country planning schemes are confirmed. Inquiries may also be prescribed in relation to the provision of social services, and for other schemes of control. Most inquiries are arranged by the Ministry for the purposes of its own housing and planning cases and those of local authorities. The procedure provides a framework for a fair hearing in the weighing of the proposals of a public authority against the interests of persons affected by them. The Minister's eventual decision, which has a wide measure of discretion, is final.

Statutory rules of procedure have been made by the Lord Chancellor under the Tribunals and Inquiries Act for inquiries arising from the compulsory purchase of land by local authorities and by Ministers, and arising from planning appeals. The rules deal with a written statement of its case by the authority initiating or opposing the proposals, the persons entitled to appear, legal representation, evidence and cross-examination of witnesses, inspection of site, reasoned notification of decision, and the right to obtain a copy of the inspector's report.

Natural Justice " (1960) 23 M.L.R. 428; B. A. Hepple, " Natural Justice for Rusticated Students " [1969] C.L.J. 169; D. C. Holland, " The Student and the Law " (1969) 22 C.L.P. 61; W. A. Seavey, " Dismissal of Students: ' Due Process ' " (1957) 70 Harv.L.R. 1406; L. A. Sheridan, " Sacking Professors and Sending Down Students: Legal Control," in *Law, Justice and Equity* (ed. R. H. C. Holland and G. Schwarzenburger, 1967) p. 35; H. W. R. Wade, *Administrative Law* (3rd ed.) App.C.; " Private Government on the Campus— Judicial Review of University Expulsions " (1963) 72 Yale L.J. 1362.
[30] *The Citizen and the Administration,* Chap. 6.

2. Without statutory inquiry

Some Ministers have the power—often without appeal—to make decisions directly affecting the rights of individuals or other public authorities. This power of decision may be either original or appellate. In either case it may involve a dispute between a public authority and an individual or between two public (often local) authorities. The power is in a greater or less degree discretionary, usually there is no kind of appeal from it, and in the cases we are now considering no public inquiry or other form of procedure is prescribed by statute. Normally, therefore, citizens can only complain about these decisions through such political means as letters to Members of Parliament, questions in the House and motions in debates on the adjournment.

Examples are the Home Secretary's power to hear appeals from police officers against dismissal or reduction in pay, and his powers relating to prison administration; and the judicial functions of various Ministers in relation to such matters as bankruptcy, weights and measures, registration of business names and trademarks, licensing of road transport, and appeals from district auditors.

The Minister *may* hold an inquiry in many of these cases. The relevant parts of the Tribunals and Inquiries Act may be applied to such "discretionary inquiries" by Statutory Instrument, so as to bring them (if held) under rules of procedure.

III. TRIBUNALS AND INQUIRIES ACT

A Committee on Administrative Tribunals and Inquiries under the chairmanship of Sir Oliver Franks (now Lord Franks) was appointed by the Lord Chancellor: "To consider and make recommendations on: (a) The constitution and working of tribunals other than the ordinary courts of law, constituted under any Act of Parliament by a Minister of the Crown or for the purposes of a Minister's functions. (b) The working of such administrative procedures as include the holding of an inquiry or hearing by or on behalf of a Minister on an appeal or as the result of objections or representations, and in particular the procedure for the compulsory purchase of land." The Committee reported in 1957.[31]

The purpose of Parliament in providing that certain decisions

---

[31] (1957) Cmnd. 218. See E. C. S. Wade, "Administration under the Law" (1957) 73 L.Q.R. 470; W. A. Robson, "Administrative Justice and Injustice" [1958] P.L. 12; G. W. Keeton, "Administrative Tribunals and the Franks Report" (1958) 11 C.L.P. 88; G. Marshall, "The Franks Report on Administrative Tribunals and Enquiries" (1958) 35 *Public Administration* 347; J. Willis, "Administrative Decision and the Law" (1958) 13 U.T.L.J. 45.

should not be left to the ordinary courts but should be subject to special procedures, said the Committee, must have been to promote good administration; and the general characteristics that should mark these special procedures are " openness, fairness and impartiality." It was not possible to define the principles on which it had been decided that some adjudications should be made by tribunals and others by Ministers: the distinction was a fact that had to be accepted. Tribunals should be regarded as machinery provided by Parliament for adjudication, rather than (as the Committee on Ministers' Powers had suggested in 1932) as part of the machinery of administration.

The Government accepted most of the recommendations of the Franks Committee in the Tribunals and Inquiries Act 1958.[32] Certain reforms could be introduced by administrative directions to government departments or local authorities. The most important innovation made by the Act was the creation of a Council on Tribunals.[33] The Act also made further provision as to the appointment, qualifications and removal of the chairman and members, and as to the procedure, of certain tribunals; it provided for appeals to the courts from certain tribunals; it required the giving of reasons for certain decisions of tribunals and Ministers; and it extended the supervisory powers of the High Court. The Act was amended in 1959[34] and 1966,[35] and the law was consolidated by the Tribunals and Inquiries Act 1971.

Councils on Tribunals

Section 1 of the Tribunals and Inquiries Act 1971 provides for the continuance of the Council on Tribunals:

(a) to keep under review the constitution and working of the tribunals specified in Schedule 1,[36] and from time to time to report on their constitution and working;

(b) to consider and report on such particular matters as may be referred to the Council with respect to " tribunals other than the ordinary court of law," whether or not specified in Schedule 1; and

[32] H. W. R. Wade, Note in [1958] C.L.J. 129; J. A. G. Griffith, " Tribunals and Inquiries " (1959) 22 M.L.R. 125.

[33] The idea appeared to have originated with Professor W. A. Robson, who proposed a " Standing Council on Administrative Tribunals " (see Franks Report, *Minutes of Evidence*, p. 496), in addition to an Administrative Appeal Tribunal. It was reinforced by Dr. H. W. R. Wade's proposal for an " Administrative Court " (*ibid*. pp. 551–555).

[34] Town and Country Planning Act 1959, s. 33 (provision of rules of procedure for statutory inquiries).

[35] Tribunals and Inquiries Act 1966 (provision of rules of procedure for discretionary inquiries).

[36] Other tribunals may be added to Schedule 1 by Statutory Instrument.

(c) to consider and report on such matters as may be referred, or as the Council may determine to be of special importance, with respect to administrative procedures involving the holding by a Minister of a statutory inquiry.

The Council consists of ten to fifteen members appointed by the Lord Chancellor and the Secretary of State for Scotland. There is a Scottish Committee of the Council, consisting of two or three members of the Council and three or four other persons appointed by the Secretary of State. The chairmen of the Council and of the Scottish Committee are paid a salary, and the other members may be paid fees.

The Council reports to, and receives references from, the Lord Chancellor and the Secretary of State. The Council is required to make an annual report on its proceedings,[37] and the Lord Chancellor and the Secretary of State are to lay the annual report before Parliament, with such comments (if any) as they think fit.

Appointment of members of tribunals

The chairmen of some tribunals are appointed by the Lord Chancellor,[38] and the chairmen of certain other tribunals are selected by the appropriate Minister from a panel of persons appointed by the Lord Chancellor.[38]

The Council on Tribunals may make to the appropriate Minister general recommendations as to the appointment of members of the tribunals specified in Schedule 1 (i.e. those under the supervision of the Council), and also of the relevant panels, and the Minister " shall have regard " to such recommendations.

A Minister may not, with certain exceptions, terminate the appointment of a member of a tribunal specified in Schedule 1, or of a relevant panel, without the consent of the Lord Chancellor.[38]

Procedural Rules for tribunals and inquiries

Tribunals

The Minister must consult the Council on Tribunals before making or approving procedural rules for the tribunals that come under its supervision. There is now a right to legal representation before most statutory tribunals [39]; but legal aid is not yet available except before the Lands Tribunal.

---

[37] The annual reports of the Council on Tribunals are published by H.M.S.O.
[38] Or the Lord President of the Court of Session or the Lord Chief Justice of Northern Ireland.
[39] J. E. Alder, " Representation before Tribunals " [1972] P.L. 278.

Inquiries

The Lord Chancellor [40] may, after consulting the Council, make rules for regulating the procedure to be followed in connection with statutory inquiries held by or on behalf of Ministers. Such rules may regulate matters preparatory to, and subsequent to, statutory inquiries, as well as the conduct of such inquiries themselves. This power is exercisable by Statutory Instrument.

Appeals from tribunals to the High Court

A party to proceedings before most statutory tribunals, who is dissatisfied with the tribunal's decision on a point of law, may either appeal to the High Court or require the tribunal to state a case for the opinion of the High Court. The appeal or case stated is heard by a Divisional Court of the Queen's Bench Division. Appeal lies by leave of the High Court or of the Court of Appeal to the Court of Appeal,[41] and thence to the House of Lords.

There is no regularity as regards appeals on questions of fact or discretion. In some cases there is an appeal to a superior tribunal or to a Minister, in others there is no appeal.

Extension of supervisory powers of superior courts

Any provision in an Act passed *before* August 1, 1958, that any order or determination shall not be called into question in any court, or any similar provision which excludes any of the powers of the High Court, shall not prevent the removal of the proceedings into the High Court by order of certiorari or prejudice the powers of the High Court to make orders of mandamus.[42] This preserves, rather than " extends," the supervisory jurisdiction of the High Court over tribunals.[43] It does not, however, affect statutory provisions prescribing a special time limit within which applications to the High Court must be made; nor does it affect the discretion of the Home Secretary to grant or refuse applications under the British Nationality Act 1948. The section does not mention applications for a declaratory judgment.

Reasons to be given for decisions

Where a tribunal which comes under the supervision of the Council gives a decision, or a Minister notifies a decision made by him after holding a statutory inquiry, it is the duty of the tribunal or Minister

---

[40] Or the Lord President of the Court of Session. The Tribunals and Inquiries Act 1966 substituted the Secretary of State for Scotland.

[41] The Court of Session takes the place of the High Court and the Court of Appeal in relation to proceedings in Scotland.

[42] There is a corresponding provision in relation to Scotland.

[43] See *post*, Chap. 31.

to furnish a written or oral statement of the reasons for the decision *if requested to do so* by persons concerned. The statement may be refused, or the specification of the reasons restricted, on grounds of national security. Such a statement forms part of the decision and must be incorporated in the record, so that the order will be a " speaking order " for the purposes of certiorari.[44] This provision does not apply to a Minister's decision in connection with the making or approval of regulations, by-laws or orders of a legislative and not an executive character.

Work of the Council on Tribunals [45]

There are more than 2,000 tribunals under the supervision of the Council. The Council not only acts as a " watchdog " but also as a focus of information. It keeps under review the constitution and working of tribunals. With regard to statutory inquiries its function is to consider and report on such matters as may be referred to it by the Lord Chancellor or the Secretary of State, or as the Council may determine to be of special importance. It does not recommend the kinds of person who should be appointed to conduct inquiries. Complaints are digested by a complaints committee. The Council's powers are not executive but advisory, and it does not act as a court of appeal from tribunals. Nor does it seek to impose uniformity on all tribunals.

A special report on the *Chalk Pit* case [46] was made to the Lord Chancellor. Major Buxton, a landowner, complained to the Council [47] about the decision of a Minister to allow a firm to use a gravel pit adjoining his piggeries for the production of chalk. The inspector who conducted the inquiry reported that the production of chalk would result in dust being blown onto adjoining land, with serious detriment to animals and crops. Major Buxton alleged that the Minister consulted the Minister of Agriculture privately between the end of the inquiry and the announcement of his decision, thus stultifying the inquiry. The Council made a report to the Lord Chancellor on the problem of handling new factual evidence noted by Ministers after statutory inquiries; with the result that a Statutory Instrument was later issued directing a Minister to re-open an inquiry on request

---

44 Proper, adequate reasons must be given: *Re Poyser and Mills' Arbitration* [1964] 2 Q.B. 467.
45 *First Report of the Council on Tribunals*, H.M.S.O. 1960; The Marquess of Reading, " Tribunals and Inquiries " (1960) *Law Society's Gazette* 551; H. W. R. Wade, " The Council on Tribunals " [1960] P.L. 351; J. F. Garner, " The Council on Tribunals " [1965] P.L. 321.
46 See Griffith and Street, *A Casebook of Administrative Law* (1964) pp. 142–174.
47 He had been unsuccessful in the courts as he was not a " person aggrieved ": *Buxton* v. *Minister of Housing and Local Government* [1961] 1 Q.B. 278.

if he disagrees with the inspector on receiving new evidence (including expert opinion) or has considered a new issue of fact not raised at the inquiry.

Annual reports show that the Council has been consulted on rules of procedure for a number of tribunals and for Inquiries. It has made representations about accommodation, public hearings and legal aid. The Council is also consulted on Bills.

IV. PARLIAMENTARY COMMISSIONER FOR ADMINISTRATION [48]

Maladministration

Statutory and administrative reforms still did not touch the problem of "maladministration." This is the problem of complaints made by private citizens that a public authority, although it has acted within the law, has failed to observe the proper standards of administrative conduct. Such cases do not come within the jurisdiction either of the courts or of tribunals. Maladministration was described by Mr. Crossman in the debate on the Parliamentary Commissioner Bill as "bias, neglect, inattention, delay, incompetence, ineptitude, perversity, turpitude, arbitrariness and so on." [49] An example is the *Crichel Down* case,[50] where a landowner complained that the Ministry of Agriculture had refused to hand back to him after the war part of his land which had been requisitioned during the war and was no longer required by the Ministry for the purposes for which it had been requisitioned. In this particular case the Minister was induced by the outcry to hold a departmental inquiry, which criticised the conduct of certain officials in the Ministry, with the result that the officials were moved to different work and the Minister (although not personally involved) resigned his office. The citizen's

---

[48] *The Parliamentary Commissioner for Administration* (1965) Cmnd. 2767; *The Citizen and the Administration*, Part III, A report by *Justice* (Whyatt Report, 1961); *The Ombudsman: Citizen's Defender,* ed. D. C. Rowat (2nd ed. 1968); Sir Edmund Compton, "Parliamentary Commissioner for Administration" (1969) 10 J.S.P.T.L. 106; Paul Jackson, "The Work of the Parliamentary Commissioner for Administration" [1971] P.L. 39; Lord Lloyd of Hampstead, "The Parliamentary Commissioner" [1968] C.L.P. 53; Sir Alan Marre, "Some Thoughts on the Role of the Parliamentary Commissioner for Administration" (1972) 3 *Cambrian Law Rev.* 54.

See also Sir Guy Powles, "The Citizen's Rights against the Modern State" (1964) 13 I.C.L.Q. 761; C. C. Aikman, "The New Zealand Ombudsman" (1964) 42 *Can.Bar Rev.* 399; A. G. Davis, "The Ombudsman in New Zealand" (1962) *Jo. International Commission of Jurists,* 51; N. S. Marsh, "The Ombudsman in New Zealand" (1963) 1 N.Z.Univs. Law Rev. 71.

[49] 734 H.C. Deb., col. 51.

[50] (1954) Cmd. 9176; C. J. Hamson, "The Real Lesson of Crichel Down" (1954) 32 *Public Administration* 383. *Cf.* R. M. Jackson, "Judicial Review of Legislative Policy" (1955) 18 M.L.R. 571.

only remedies were for his Member of Parliament to ask a question in the House, to raise the matter in the debate on the adjournment or in debates on supply, to correspond with the Minister or to persuade the Minister to hold an *ad hoc* inquiry.

Parliamentary Commissioner for Administration

For some years there had been discussion on the suggestion [51] that a Parliamentary Commissioner, with an independent status like that of the Comptroller and Auditor-General, should be appointed for this country, whose functions would be similar to those of the Ombudsman [52] known to Scandinavian countries and then recently introduced into New Zealand. Hesitation in the past was due largely to the fear that the appointment of such an independent official would interfere with ministerial responsibility, which is stronger here than in Scandinavia; and to a less extent to the fact that it was difficult to foresee how much work would fall to a Commissioner in a country with a population much greater than that of any of the Scandinavian countries or New Zealand. In 1967 the Parliamentary Commissioner Act was passed.

Appointment

The Parliamentary Commissioner Act 1967 provides for a Parliamentary Commissioner of Administration to be appointed by letters patent. His salary is charged on the Consolidated Fund. He may be removed on an address from both Houses, and he is excluded from membership of the Commons. He is an *ex officio* member of the Council on Tribunals, whose functions (as in cases like the *Chalk Pit* case) overlap his own, and in some cases the citizen may choose whether to complain to the Commission or the Council.

Investigation of complaints

A person who thinks he has suffered injustice as a result of maladministration by a department or authority of the central government may complain to a member of the House of Commons in writing within twelve months from first having notice of the matter. The Commissioner has a discretion whether or not to conduct an investigation.[53] An investigation is conducted in private. The principal

---

[51] The suggestion for an Inspector-General of Administration was originally made by Professor F. H. Lawson in [1957] P.L. 92–95. The Government turned down the suggestion for a Parliamentary Commissioner in 1961: 640 H.C.Deb., cols. 1693–1756.

[52] One objection to the title " Ombudsman " in English-speaking countries is to form the plural, which in Danish is Ombudsmand.

[53] *Re Fletcher's Application* [1970] 2 All E.R. 527n. (C.A.); mandamus does not lie.

officer of the department or authority concerned must be given an opportunity to comment on the allegation. The complainant has no right to appear, but the Commissioner may see him if he thinks fit. The Commissioner has the same powers as the High Court to require a Minister, civil servants or other persons to furnish information or produce documents, excluding proceedings or papers of the Cabinet or a Cabinet committee. There is no Crown privilege [54] at the investigation stage; but a Minister may claim Crown privilege in respect of the *publication* or passing on of documents or information if their disclosure would in his opinion be prejudicial to the safety of the state or otherwise contrary to the public interest. The Official Secrets Acts would prevent the Commissioner from including such information in his reports.

Departments and authorities covered

The departments and authorities in respect of whom the Commissioner may investigate complaints are set out in Schedule 2. They include most of the central government departments, but do not cover local authorities, public corporations, the police or the National Health Service.[55] The list may be added to or reduced by Order in Council, the instrument being subject to annulment by resolution of either House. The Act applies to U.K. departments and authorities in Northern Ireland.[56]

Matters excluded from investigation are set out in Schedule 3. The excluded matters are within the functions of the departments listed in Schedule 2, *viz.*: foreign relations; action taken outside the United Kingdom; the government of H.M. overseas dominions; extradition, fugitive offenders, investigation of crime,[57] and security of the state (including passports); civil or criminal proceedings in any court, court-martial or international tribunal; the prerogative of mercy; medical matters; commercial contracts; personnel matters of the armed forces, civil service, teachers or police; the grant of honours, and royal charters. This list may be reduced by Order in Council.

---

[54] *Post*, Chap. 32.
[55] The Government in introducing the Local Government Bill in 1971 indicated their intention to establish a system of commissioners to investigate complaints by members of the public against local authorities; and the Secretary of State for Social Services announced in the Commons in February 1972 that commissioners would be appointed to deal with complaints (excluding clinical medical matters) by patients against the National Health Service. See Preface.
[56] The Northern Ireland Parliament in 1969 established a Commissioner for Complaints to deal with complaints against local authorities and other public bodies.
[57] *i.e.* by or on behalf of the Home Office.

Reports by Commissioner

Where the Commissioner conducts or decides not to conduct an investigation he must send a report to the member concerned; and when he conducts an investigation he must send a report to the principal officer of the department concerned. If he thinks injustice has been caused, and that it has not been or will not be remedied, he may lay a special report before each House.

The Commissioner must lay a general report annually before each House on the performance of his functions, and he may lay special reports from time to time.[58]

The Commissioner's reports in the first five years of his office show that more than half of the complaints received have been rejected as being outside his jurisdiction (*e.g.* personnel matters or police). Some injustice by maladministration has been found in 12 per cent. of the cases fully investigated, but none of them serious. The most frequent cause has been delay in the over-worked Inland Revenue department. The reports confirm the integrity of the Civil Service, and its freedom from bias or perversity. The Commissioner issued a special report on the *Sachsenhausen* case in 1967,[59] and the Foreign Secretary was prevailed upon to pay compensation.

Select Committee on the Parliamentary Commissioner for Administration

A Select Committee of the Commons was set up to deal with complaints by M.P.s who think the Commissioner has failed to deal properly with complaints forwarded by them, to consider what remedial action has been taken by the departments, and to recommend changes in the law. The Select Committee does not act as a court of appeal from the Commissioner's findings. In its first two annual reports the Committee criticised the narrow way in which the Commissioner was interpreting his jurisdiction.[60] It recommended an extension of the Commissioner's powers to cases where the departmental procedure for reviewing a rule, or the grounds for maintaining it, could be shown to be defective. The Committee has more than once recommended that the Commissioner should have power to investigate personnel matters and staffing within the Civil Service.

---

[58] With regard to absolute privilege from defamation, see *ante*, p. 416.
[59] (1967–68) H.C. 54. See G. F. Fry, " The Sachsenhausen Concentration Camp Case and the Convention of Ministerial Responsibility " [1970] P.L. 336.
[60] (1967–68) H.C. 258; (1967–68) H.C. 350. See Geoffrey Marshall in *The Commons in Transition* (ed. A. H. Hanson and B. Crick, 1970) Chap. 6.

CHAPTER 30

JUDICIAL CONTROL OF PUBLIC AUTHORITIES: I. LIABILITY [1]

I. EXCESS OR ABUSE OF POWERS

Judicial control of powers

We consider in this chapter the general principles in accordance with which the courts control the exercise of powers by public authorities other than Parliament and the ordinary courts themselves, and other than the Crown. The remedies available for this purpose are dealt with in the next chapter, and civil proceedings by and against the Crown in Chapter 32.

There is usually a discretion as to the manner in which a power shall be exercised, the sanction being parliamentary or administrative and not judicial: if not, there is a duty to exercise the power (if it is exercised at all) in the prescribed way. If there is no discretion whether to exercise the power or not, the so-called " power " is strictly a duty to act, although the duty is often not owed to or enforceable by a private individual. An administrative power is usually discretionary both as to whether it shall be exercised at all and as to the manner in which it shall be exercised. The exercise of their functions by local education authorities, for example, can often be enforced or restrained by the Minister.[2]

The courts have jurisdiction at common law to determine, in an action properly brought before them, whether the purported exercise of a power is authorised by law. If it is not so authorised, either because the alleged power does not exist or its scope is exceeded, the act is *ultra vires* and void. If a power is abused or exercised unreasonably, or if the principles of national justice (where applicable) are not observed, the act is illegal: the courts can declare it void and in some cases set it aside.[3] All these grounds for nullifying the

[1] See S. A. de Smith, *Judicial Review of Administrative Action* (2nd ed. 1968); H. W. R. Wade, *Administrative Law* (3rd ed. 1971); J. F. Garner, *Administrative Law* (3rd ed. 1970); D. C. M. Yardley, *A Source Book of English Administrative Law* (2nd ed. 1970); J. A. G. Griffith and H. Street, *Principles of Administrative Law* (4th ed. 1967); B. Schwartz and H. W. R. Wade Q.C., *Legal Control of Government* (1972); H. Street, *Governmental Liability* (1953). For the earlier period see G. E. Robinson, *Public Authorities and Legal Liability* (1925).
[2] *Cumings* v. *Birkenhead Corporation* [1972] Ch. 12; *Wood* v. *Ealing London Borough Council* [1967] Ch. 364.
[3] For the effect of declaring an exercise of power in public law *void* or *voidable*, see A. Rubinstein, *Jurisdiction and Illegality* (1965).

act of a public authority are regarded by some writers as falling under the heading of *ultra vires*, but it is convenient to deal with them separately.

Ultra Vires rule

The common law powers of public authorities are mostly part of the royal prerogative, and the jurisdiction of the courts over them was asserted in such cases as the *Case of Monopolies* (1602),[4] the *Case of Proclamations* (1610)[5] and *The Zamora*.[6] As regards the innumerable statutory powers, the question is one of interpretation of the statute concerned. The acts of a competent authority must fall within the four corners of the powers given by the legislature.[7] The court must examine the nature, objects and scheme of the legislation, and in the light of that examination must consider what is the exact area over which powers are given by the section under which the competent authority purports to act.[8]

A straightforward case on the validity of a statutory administrative power is *Att.-Gen.* v. *Fulham Corporation*,[9] where it was held that a local authority which had power under the Baths and Wash-houses Acts 1846 to 1878 to establish baths, wash-houses and open bathing places was not entitled to carry on the business of a laundry, and was acting *ultra vires* in washing or partly washing customers' clothes as distinct from providing facilities for persons to wash their own clothes. An example of the *ultra vires* exercise of a judicial power was *The King* v. *Minister of Transport, ex p. Upminster Services*,[10] where the Minister, who had power to hear appeals from traffic commissioners with regard to the grant of certain licences, exceeded his jurisdiction by laying down conditions as to the future holding of a licence.

An example of the principle in relation to delegated legislation is *Chester* v. *Bateson*,[11] in which it was held that a regulation made by

---

[4] 11 Co.Rep. 84b.

[5] 12 Co.Rep. 74.

[6] [1916] 2 A.C. 77.

[7] *Per* Lord Greene M.R. in *Carltona Ltd.* v. *Commissioners of Works* [1943] 2 All E.R. 560, 564.

[8] *Per* Sachs J., in *Commissioners of Customs and Excise* v. *Cure and Deeley Ltd.* [1962] 1 Q.B. 340.

[9] [1921] 1 Ch. 440.

[10] [1934] 1 K.B. 277. See also *The King* v. *Minister of Health, ex p. Davis* [1929] 1 K.B. 619; *Marriott* v. *Minister of Health* [1937] 1 K.B. 128.

[11] [1920] 1 K.B. 829 (D.C.). And see *Att.-Gen.* v. *Wilts United Dairies* (1921) 91 L.J.K.B. 897; (1921) 37 T.L.R. 884 (H.L.), no authority to impose charges; *McEldowney* v. *Forde* [1971] A.C. 632 (H.L.), regulations too vague and so arbitrary as to be unreasonable; *Hotel and Catering Industry Training Board* v. *Automobile Proprietary* [1969] 1 W.L.R. 697; [1969] 2 All E.R. 582 (H.L.).

the Minister under the Defence of the Realm Act 1914 was *ultra vires*
in that it made it an offence to take, without the consent of the
Minister, any proceedings in the courts for the recovery of possession
of houses occupied by workmen employed on war production in
special areas so long as they continued to pay their rent and to observe
the other conditions of the tenancy.   The imposition of reasonable
conditions for taking such proceedings might have been valid, but
the enabling Act gave the Minister no power to prohibit under penalty
judicial proceedings without his consent.   A landlord might wish
to question, or might be mistaken either in law or fact as to whether
the occupant was a workman so employed, or whether he had paid
his rent or violated some other condition of his tenancy.   Again, in
Commissioners of Customs and Excise v. *Cure and Deeley* [12] a
purchase tax regulation which provided that if any person furnished an
incomplete return the Commissioners might determine the amount
of tax appearing to them to be due and demand payment thereof,
which amount should be deemed to be the proper tax due unless within
seven days it was shown *to the satisfaction of the Commissioners*
that some other amount was due, was held *ultra vires* the Finance (No.
2) Act 1940.   The fact that a rule has been laid before the Houses
and not been annulled does not bar review by the courts,[13] and it is
immaterial that a Statutory Instrument has been affirmed by a resolution of both Houses.

Where the enabling Act requires a power to be exercised in a
certain *form*, the neglect of that form renders the exercise of the
power *ultra vires*.   Thus in *Jackson Stansfield & Sons* v. *Butterworth* [14] the Court of Appeal held that oral permission from a
borough surveyor to build in excess of the amount specified in the
licence was invalid since a written licence was contemplated by the
Act.

Again, where the enabling Act prescribes a particular *procedure*
for the exercise of a power, the exercise of the power is void if that
procedure is not followed.   In *R.* v. *Minister of Health, ex p. Yaffe* [15]
the Liverpool Corporation purported to make an improvement scheme

---

[12] [1962] 1 Q.B. 340.   The Purchase Tax Act 1963, s. 27 (2), later provided that
where a person did not keep proper accounts and the Commissioners estimated the
amount of tax due, the amount should be recoverable unless *in any action relating
thereto* the person liable proved the amount properly due and that amount was
less than the amount estimated.

[13] *Mackay* v. *Marks* [1916] 2 I.R. 241; *Institute of Patents Agents* v. *Lockwood*
[1894] A.C. 347, 366; cf. *Bowles* v. *Bank of England* [1913] 1 Ch. 57.

[14] [1948] 2 All E.R. 558.   *Cf. Howell* v. *Falmouth Boat Construction* [1951] A.C.
837.

[15] [1930] 2 K.B. 98.   *Cf. Minister of Health* v. *The King* (*on the prosecution of
Yaffe*) [1931] A.C. 494, where the House of Lords approved the principle laid
down by the Court of Appeal but upheld the scheme.

under a Housing Act which was approved by the Minister. The Minister had no power to confirm the scheme unless he had: (i) received a copy of something that was a scheme within the meaning of the Act, (ii) considered the petition, (iii) caused a local inquiry to be held, and (iv) been satisfied on the report as to certain matters specified in the Act. The Court of Appeal held that the Minister's order confirming the scheme was invalid, because at the local inquiry the necessary provisions with regard to the furnishing of plans had not been complied with. Similarly, the exercise of a power is *ultra vires* if any *preceding conditions* have not been fulfilled, such as the giving of requisite notices (*R.* v. *Surrey Justices* (1870) [16]), or an appeal made to the Minister in lieu of applying to the court.[17]

The exercise of a power may be invalid if the facts on which the exercise of the power must be based are not present ("jurisdictional facts"). Thus in *White and Collins* v. *Minister of Health*,[18] where there was power to acquire compulsorily any land that did not form part of a "park, garden or pleasure ground," the court set aside an order which had been confirmed by the Minister, because the land did form part of a park.[19]

By-laws are *ultra vires* if they are repugnant to the general law; but it is not easy to decide in what circumstances a by-law will be held invalid on that ground. It obviously must not be contrary to statute, although it can, of course, forbid what would otherwise be lawful at common law. In *Powell* v. *May* [20] a by-law made by a county council forbidding generally any person to frequent or use any street or other public place for the purpose of bookmaking or betting or wagering, was held invalid as being repugnant to the Street Betting Act 1906 and the Betting and Lotteries Act 1934, which would have allowed the appellant bookmaker certain defences.

Abuse of power

A power that is discretionary, *i.e.* not coupled with a duty, is abused or misused if it is exercised for an unauthorised purpose, if relevant considerations are disregarded or irrelevant considerations taken into account. Such abuse of power may be either in good faith or in bad faith. An authority acts in bad faith if it acts dishonestly, in order

[16] L.R. 5 Q.B. 466.
[17] *R.* v. *Minister of Health, ex p. Dore* [1927] 1 K.B. 765, arising out of *Roberts* v. *Hopwood* [1925] A.C. 578.
[18] [1939] 2 K.B. 838.
[19] *Cf.* D. M. Gordon, " Conditional or Contingent Jurisdiction of Tribunals " (1960) 1 *Univ.British Columbia Law Rev.* 185.
[20] [1946] K.B. 330. And see *Thomas* v. *Sutters* [1900] 1 Ch. 10; *White* v. *Morley* [1899] 2 Q.B. 30; *Gentel* v. *Rapps* [1902] 1 K.B. 160, 166; *R. and W. Paul Ltd.* v. *Wheat Commission* [1917] A.C. 139.

to achieve an object other than that for which it believes the power
has been given; or maliciously, if it acts out of personal animosity.
Thus a local authority which has the power of compulsory acquisition
of land for civic extensions or improvements would not be entitled to
acquire compulsorily if its purpose were merely to reap the benefit
of enhanced values (*Municipal Council of Sydney* v. *Campbell*[21]);
nor may an education authority which has power to dismiss teachers
on educational grounds dismiss them in order to effect economy (*Hanson* v. *Radcliffe Urban District Council*[22]). The court may infer the
purpose for which the enabling Act granted the power, and hold that
the power has been abused, *e.g.* where a local authority referred
tenancies in bulk to a rent tribunal so as in effect to turn the tribunal
into a general rent-fixing agency (*R.* v. *Paddington Rent Tribunal,
ex p. Bell Properties Ltd.*[23]). The High Court can control the exercise
of statutory powers if they are being exercised otherwise than in
accordance with the purpose for which they were conferred. Thus a
compulsory purchase order made in 1951 in order to provide a car
park was set aside as it was based on a notice to treat served in 1939
for the purpose of widening the street and creating a market hall
(*Grice* v. *Dudley Corporation*[24]).

The question is complicated where a power is exercised both for
an authorised and an unauthorised purpose.[25] The courts on the
whole have tried to find the true purpose for which the power was
exercised. Thus in *Westminster Corporation* v. *L. & N.W. Ry.*,[26]
where the local authority had power to construct underground public
conveniences, the court considered whether this was the true purpose
which the Corporation sought to effect in acquiring land compulsorily,
or whether it was merely a colourable device to enable it to make
a subway for pedestrians. The courts tend to avoid the question
of motive, which seems to be immaterial if the purpose is within the
statute (*Robins & Son Ltd.* v. *Minister of Health*[27]), for they must
not usurp the discretion given to administrative authorities.

The requirement of bona fides is not generally important in
practice, as good faith is presumed. Bad faith in public authorities

---

[21] [1925] A.C. 338.
[22] [1922] 2 Ch. 490.
[23] [1949] 1 K.B. 606.
[24] [1958] Ch. 339. And see *Webb* v. *Minister of Housing and Local Government*
[1965] 1 W.L.R. 755; [1965] 2 All E.R. 195 (C.A.), acquisition of land by coast
protection authority; J. Bennett Miller, " Administrative Necessity and the Abuse
of Power " [1960] P.L. 330.
[25] See *e.g. Earl Fitzwilliam's Wentworth Estate Co.* v. *Minister of Town and
Country Planning* [1951] 2 K.B. 284 (C.A.); [1952] A.C. 362 (H.L.).
[26] [1905] A.C. 426; and see *R.* v. *Brighton Corporation, ex p. Shoosmith* (1907)
96 L.T. 762.
[27] [1939] 1 K.B. 537.

is uncommon and difficult to prove. The question sometimes arises in connection with powers of a judicial nature, where it is related to the principles of natural justice.

Unreasonable use of power

"It is well settled," said Lord Macnaghten,[28] "that a public body invested with statutory powers . . . must take care not to exceed or abuse its powers. It must keep within the limits of the authority committed to it. It must act in good faith. And it must act reasonably. The last proposition is involved in the second, if not in the first." The decision of a public authority can be upset, said Lord Greene M.R. in *Associated Provincial Picture Houses Ltd.* v. *Wednesbury Corporation*,[29] if it is unreasonable in the sense that the court considers it to be a decision that no reasonable body could have made. It is not what the court itself considers unreasonable. One aspect of acting reasonably is calling one's own attention to matters which one is bound to consider, and excluding from consideration matters which are irrelevant. In that case the Court of Appeal held that the licensing authority's condition for the opening of cinemas on Sundays, *viz.* that no children under the age of fifteen should be admitted, was not unreasonable. Unreasonableness may be of such a degree as to amount to abuse of power. Thus in *Roberts* v. *Hopwood*[30] the House of Lords held that the minimum wage fixed by the Poplar Borough Council for its employees was so excessive in relation to the labour market that it contained an element of gratuity.

In *Kruse* v. *Johnson*[31] Kruse had been convicted under a county council by-law for conducting an open-air religious service within fifty yards of a dwelling-house in a village, and continuing to sing a hymn after being requested by a police constable to desist. A full Divisional Court considered the validity of the by-law: "No person shall sound or play upon any musical or noisy instrument or sing in any public place or highway within fifty yards of any dwelling-house after being required by any constable, or by an inmate of such house personally or by his or her servant, to desist." Lord Russell of Killowen C.J. said that local by-laws are not unreasonable merely because particular judges may think that they go farther than is necessary or convenient; but a court might hold them unreasonable

---

[28] *Westminster Corporation* v. *London and North Western Ry.* [1905] A.C. 426.
[29] [1948] 1 K.B. 223.
[30] [1925] A.C. 578. And see *Prescott* v. *Birmingham Corporation* [1955] Ch. 210; *cf.* Public Service Vehicles (Travel Concessions) Act 1955.
[31] [1898] 2 Q.B. 91. And see *Parker* v. *Bournemouth Corporation* (1902) 86 L.T. 449; *Arlidge* v. *Islington Corporation* [1909] 2 K.B. 127; *Taylor* v. *Brighton Borough Council* [1947] K.B. 736; as to Ministerial regulations, see *Sparks* v. *Ash Ltd.* [1943] K.B. 223.

if they were found to be partial or unequal in their operation between classes, or if they were manifestly unjust, disclosed bad faith, or involved such oppressive or gratuitous interference with the rights of those subject to them as could find no justification in the minds of reasonable men. Applying this test, the court held that the by-law was not unreasonable.

Principles of natural justice [32]

Certain principles of "natural justice" are incorporated into the common law. They were originally applied to the process by which courts themselves made their decisions. A breach of natural justice was one of the grounds on which the decision of a lower court could be upset by a higher court. In the course of time these principles came to be applied to the exercise by administrative authorities of powers of a judicial nature, at one period commonly called "quasi-judicial" powers. In other words, administrative authorities—Ministers, public officials, local government authorities and so on—are expected to observe the principles of natural justice whenever they act judicially. This requirement is enforced primarily by special remedies of the superior courts, notably the prerogative order (formerly writ) of certiorari. [33]

There is authority for regarding the requirements of "natural justice" as a special part of the *ultra vires* rule, on the ground that a decision made contrary to the principles of natural justice, when the rights of particular individuals are adversely affected, is no decision within the terms of the enabling Act. [34]

1. A man may not be a judge in his own cause

This, said the Committee on Ministers' Powers, is "the first and most fundamental principle of natural justice." [35] Thus in *Dimes* v. *Grand Junction Canal* (1852) [36] a decree of Lord Chancellor Cottenham, granting an injunction to a company and confirming its title, was held voidable and set aside by the House of Lords on the ground that he was a shareholder in the company, although it was not sug-

---

[32] Report of the Committee on Ministers' Powers (1932) Cmd. 4060, pp. 75–80; H. H. Marshall, *Natural Justice* (1959); G. J. Webber, "Natural Justice in Recent English Case Law" [1964] C.L.P. 17.

[33] *Post*, Chap. 31.

[34] *Spackman* v. *Plumstead District Board of Works* (1885) 10 App.Cas. 229, *per* Lord Selborne L.C.; *Errington* v. *Minister of Health* [1935] 1 K.B. 268, *per* Greer L.J., and p. 279, *per* Maugham L.J. *Cf. General Medical Council* v. *Spackman* [1943] A.C. 627, 640, *per* Lord Wright; *White* v. *Kuzych* [1951] A.C. 585 (P.C.) *per* Viscount Simon at p. 600.

[35] (1932) Cmd. 4060, p. 76.

[36] 3 H.L.C. 759.

gested that Lord Cottenham was influenced by the interest he had in the company. The principle is not confined to cases in which the person adjudicating is a party, but applies to a cause in which he has a personal interest. Lord Evershed M.R. once directed that an appeal should be heard by another division of the Court of Appeal on the ground that as Master of the Rolls he was an *ex officio* member of the Church Commissioners for England, who were parties to the action.[37] The interest need not be pecuniary or proprietary. In *R.* v. *Sunderland Justices* [38] the Court of Appeal set aside an order made by the borough justices on the ground that they had previously, as councillors, spoken in the council on the matter out of which the case arose.

Not only must the adjudicator be free from bias, but there must not even be the appearance of bias. The usual test is whether a real likelihood of bias has been created. In *The King* v. *Sussex Justices, ex p. McCarthy* [39] the conviction of McCarthy for a motoring offence was quashed because the clerk to the justices, a member of a firm of solicitors who were to represent M in civil proceedings arising out of the collision in connection with which McCarthy was charged, retired with the justices, although in fact he did not give them any advice on the conviction. Lord Hewart L.C.J. said in that case: " A long line of cases shows that it is not merely of some importance, but is of fundamental importance that justice should not only be done but should manifestly and undoubtedly be seen to be done." So where a chief constable was present at a meeting of a borough watch committee when it was deliberating whether to confirm the provisional dismissal by him of a police constable, the Court of Appeal held that the quasi-judicial proceedings of the watch committee were invalid, as it had failed to conform to the essential requirements of justice (*Cooper* v. *Wilson* [40]).

2. " *Audi alteram partem* "

Each party must have reasonable notice of the case he has to meet; and he must be given an opportunity of stating his case, and answering (if he can) any arguments put forward against it. So in *Cooper* v.

---

[37] *The Times*, October 30, 1956.
[38] [1901] 2 K.B. 357.
[39] [1924] 1 K.B. 256, 259. *Cf. R.* v. *Rand* (1866) L.R. 1 Q.B. 230; *R.* v. *Lower Munslow Justices, ex p. Pudge* [1950] 2 All E.R. 756. See also *R.* v. *East Kerrier Justices, ex p. Mundy* [1952] 2 Q.B. 719; *Practice Note (Justices' Clerks)* [1953] 1 W.L.R. 1416; [1953] 2 All E.R. 1306.
[40] [1937] 2 K.B. 309. See also *per* Lord Goddard C.J. in *R.* v. *Caernarvon Licensing Justices, ex p. Benson* (1949) 113 J.P. 23, 24. For a judge sitting on appeal from himself, see *Director of Public Prosecutions* v. *Beard* [1920] A.C. 479; *R.* v. *Lovegrove* [1951] 1 All E.R. 804.

Wandsworth Board of Works [41] a demolition order was quashed because the owner had no notice or opportunity to be heard. In criminal cases this elementary principle of justice is expressed in the saying that "no one ought to be condemned unheard." As was quaintly stated in *Dr. Bentley's Case* (1723) [42]: "Even God himself did not pass sentence upon Adam before he was called upon to make his defence." Most of the earlier cases in which the principle was applied concerned summary proceedings before justices and deprivation of office: in the latter part of the nineteenth century came housing and public health cases, and more recently planning cases. [43]

In *Ridge* v. *Baldwin* [44] the Chief Constable of Brighton brought an action against the members of the Watch Committee for a declaration that his dismissal was void. He had been acquitted at the Old Bailey on charges of corruption, but the judge in the trial of two of his subordinates cast aspersions on his leadership of the force, and remarked that a new chief constable was needed. The Watch Committee then dismissed him under the Municipal Corporations Act 1882, s. 191 (4), for neglect of duty, but without formulating any specific charge or giving him an opportunity to be heard except that his solicitor addressed the Committee at one of two meetings. The section cited empowered the Watch Committee to dismiss any constable for neglect of duty or unfitness. [45] The Chief Constable did not ask for reinstatement but he wanted to secure his pension rights, to which he would have been entitled if he had been asked to resign. The House of Lords, reversing a unanimous Court of Appeal, gave judgment for the Chief Constable. Their Lordships held that the rules of natural justice applied, so that the Watch Committee ought to have informed him of the charges and given him an opportunity to be heard. The Committee's decision was null and void; and therefore the Home Secretary's dismissal of his appeal, although " final and

---

[41] 14 C.B.(N.S.) 180. See also *Stafford* v. *Minister of Health* [1946] K.B. 621; *Re Pergamon Press* [1971] Ch. 388.

[42] *R.* v. *Chancellor of Cambridge University* (1716) 1 Str. 557.

[43] S. A. de Smith, " The Right to a Hearing in English Administrative Law " (1955) 68 Harv.Law Rev. 509.

[44] [1964] A.C. 40; applied in *Pillai* v. *City Council of Singapore* [1968] 1 W.L.R. 1278 (P.C.). *Malloch* v. *Aberdeen Corporation* [1971] 1 W.L.R. 1578; [1971] 2 All E.R. 1278 (H.L.). See also *Lapointe* v. *L'Association de Bienfaissance et de Retraite de la Police de Montréal* [1906] A.C. 535 (P.C.).

A. L. Goodhart, " *Ridge* v. *Baldwin*: Administration and Natural Justice " (1964) 80 L.Q.R. 105, doubts whether the decision was a correct interpretation of the statutes. *Cf.* A. W. Bradley, " A Failure of Justice and Defect of Police " [1964] C.L. 83; D. G. Benjafield and H. Whitmore, " The House of Lords and 'Natural Justice ' " (1963) 37 A.L.J. 140.

[45] These provisions are now replaced by the Police Act 1964, so that the authority of this case is now one of general principle only.

binding " according to the Police (Appeals) Act 1927, was of no effect.[46] Merely to describe a statutory function as " administrative," " judicial," " quasi-judicial," etc., said Lord Reid, is not in itself enough to settle the requirements of natural justice. Where officials and others have power to make decisions affecting the rights of individuals, the duty to act judicially can readily be inferred from the nature of the decision, and it is not necessary to look for any express judicial element, such as a duty to give a formal hearing.

It was established in *Ridge* v. *Baldwin* that failure to give a fair hearing renders the decision not merely voidable, but void. In the Privy Council, however, Lord Upjohn said in *Durayappah* v. *Fernando* [47] that he would prefer to describe such an order as a nullity.

Lord Denning M.R. said in *Schmidt* v. *Secretary of State for Home Affairs*,[48] that the hard and fast distinction between " judicial " and " administrative " functions for this purpose has been abandoned; a person is entitled to be heard if he has some " right, interest or legitimate expectation." In *Schmidt's* case it was held that the Home Secretary's decision in refusing an extension of residence to an alien scientologist did not fall into this category. Cases to which the maxim *audi alteram partem* do not apply include dismissal from service where the post is held at pleasure, and the Home Secretary's refusal to grant naturalisation.

The maxim *audi alteram partem*, where it applies, does not necessarily mean that a person is entitled to be heard orally.[49] The principles of natural justice are substantive principles, and do not prescribe even the most general rules of procedure. Thus in *Local Government Board* v. *Arlidge* [50] the House of Lords refused a house owner's application to quash a decision of the Local Government Board confirming a closing order made by a borough council, because the grounds of his application—namely, that he was not told which members of the Board gave the decision, and that he was not given an oral hearing or allowed to see the report of their inspector— were procedural, and the substantive principles of natural justice had

---

[46] As the dismissal was on the ground of misconduct rather than inefficiency, the Watch Committee ought also to have observed the procedure prescribed by the Police Discipline Regulations under the Police Act 1919.

[47] [1967] 2 A.C. 337 (P.C.), Minister's order dissolving a municipal council held voidable at the election of the council. Applied in *R.* v. *Aston University Senate, ex p. Roffey* [1969] 2 Q.B. 538 (D.C.). See H. W. R. Wade, " Unlawful Administrative Action: Void or Voidable? " (1967) 83 L.Q.R. 499; (1968) 84 L.Q.R. 95; M. B. Akehurst, " Void or Voidable?—Natural Justice and Unnatural Meanings " (1968) 31 M.L.R. 2, 138.

[48] [1969] 2 Ch. 149, 168.

[49] *Board of Education* v. *Rice* [1911] A.C. 179 (H.L.), *per* Lord Loreburn L.C. And see *Spackman* v. *Commissioner Public Works* (1885) 10 App.Cas. 229.

[50] [1915] A.C. 120.

been observed. Legal representation is not essential to a fair hearing,[51] and natural justice does not require that reasons for decisions should be given.[52]

Sub-delegation of powers [53]

The prima facie rule is that a person or body to whom powers are entrusted may not delegate them to another, *delegatus non potest delegare* [54]—unless expressly or impliedly authorised to do so. Thus in *Allingham* v. *Minister of Agriculture* [55] a Divisional Court held that the Bedfordshire War Agricultural Committee, to which the Minister of Agriculture had validly delegated his power under Defence Regulations to give directions with respect to the cultivation of land, and which had decided that sugar beet should be grown on eight acres of the appellant's land, had no power to delegate to their executive officer the power to specify the particular field to be cultivated. On the other hand, in *Smith* v. *London Transport Executive* [56] the Executive was validly acting as delegate of the British Transport Commission in operating a bus service. Certain powers, such as that conferred by Defence Regulations on the Home Secretary to intern persons of hostile origin or association,[57] must be exercised by the Minister personally; but generally it is contemplated that a Minister may authorise civil servants in his department to perform routine administrative functions on his behalf.[58] This is not delegation in the strict sense, for the act of the official is really the act of the Minister, who retains control and responsibility. In *Woollett* v. *Minister of Agriculture and Fisheries*,[59] where members of an agricultural land tribunal were to be appointed by the Minister, it was held that they could be appointed by X on behalf of the Minister, but not by X in his capacity as the secretary of the tribunal. In *Vine* v. *National Dock Labour Board*,[60] where the Board had purported to delegate its disciplinary

---

51 *Pett* v. *Greyhound Racing Association (No. 2)* [1970] 1 Q.B. 46.
52 *R.* v. *Gaming Board for Great Britain, ex p. Benaim* [1970] 2 Q.B. 417 (C.A.) (" *Crockford's Case* ").
53 See Carr, *Concerning English Administrative Law*, pp. 88–91; S. A. de Smith, " Sub-Delegation and Circulars " (1949) 12 M.L.R. 37; J. F. Garner, " The Delegation of Administrative Discretion " (1949) 27 *Public Administration* 115; Willis, " *Delegatus non potest delegare* " (1943) 21 Can.Bar Rev. 257.
54 *Delegata potestas non potest delegari:* 2 Co.Inst. 597.
55 [1948] 1 All E.R. 780 (D.C.). And see *Ellis* v. *Dubowski* [1921] 3 K.B. 621.
56 [1951] A.C. 555 (H.L.).
57 See *Liversidge* v. *Anderson* [1942] A.C. 206 (H.L.).
58 *Carltona Ltd.* v. *Commissioners of Works* [1943] 2 All E.R. 560 (requisitioning of land); *R.* v. *Skinner* [1968] 2 Q.B. 700 (C.A.) (approval of breathalyser).
59 [1955] 1 Q.B. 103.
60 [1957] A.C. 488; approving *Barnard* v. *National Dock Labour Board* [1953] 2 Q.B. 18 (C.A.).

powers to a committee, the House of Lords said that both the nature of the duty and the character of the person to whom it is entrusted have to be considered. Judicial authority cannot normally be sub-delegated; administrative powers sometimes may but often may not be sub-delegated; as regards the disciplinary powers in this case, whether called judicial or quasi-judicial, their Lordships held that they could not be sub-delegated.

When a power has been validly delegated by one authority to another, the exercise of the power by the latter must be within the power delegated by the former,[61] and any conditions attached to the delegation must be complied with.[62]

II. ORDINARY JUDICIAL CONTROL

Where a tort or breach of contract has been committed by a public authority, its liability may be said to be prima facie the same as that of a private individual. The authority is moreover responsible for the torts and contracts of its employees and agents in the same way as an ordinary individual or corporation.[63] This presumption, however, is subject to certain important qualifications. The great difference between public authorities and private individuals is that the former have so many and various *powers* conferred on them which ordinary individuals or corporations do not have, and which may cause harm to private citizens but the proper exercise of which does not entitle an injured person to a right of action. Local authorities, for example, have power to order houses to be demolished, to acquire land compulsorily, and to do works—such as the making of sewage farms—which would ordinarily constitute nuisances. These powers are given because the authority is acting on behalf of the public, and where public and private interests conflict, policy generally requires that the former must prevail.

On the other hand, public authorities are mostly the creations of statute, and have only such powers as are expressly conferred by

---

61 *Smith* v. *London Transport Executive, supra.*

62 *Blackpool Corporation* v. *Locker* [1948] 1 K.B. 349 (C.A.): Minister delegated to local authorities power to requisition houses, subject to making provision for disposal of furniture; requisition *ultra vires* because conditions not complied with.

63 For the purpose of this discussion it is assumed that the reader is acquainted with the general principles of vicarious liability in tort and contract which are part of the general law of tort and contract (including agency). For those who have not studied the law of tort and contract, a brief outline including vicarious liability and agency, is given in O. Hood Phillips, *A First Book of English Law* (6th ed.) Chaps. 17 and 18. Criminal liability, not discussed here, is generally personal only.

statute. The citizen may therefore find that a contract which he thought he had entered into is void as being beyond the power of the authority to make.

Further, when the citizen has a remedy he may find that it does not lie against the public authority, but only against the person who appeared to be (but who in law was not) the servant of that authority.

Lastly, the fact that a public authority has failed to perform some duty does not necessarily mean that a citizen can take proceedings against it either to compel it to perform the duty or for damages for failing to do so.

Liability in contract

Statutory public authorities, such as local authorities and public corporations, have a general power to make contracts in the discharge of their functions. They may have specific contractual powers as well. If a public authority enters into a contract in relation to some matter that is beyond its powers—a question of statutory interpretation—the contract is *ultra vires* and void.[64] For *intra vires* contracts, public authorities are generally liable in the ordinary way, e.g. a contract by a local authority to sell coke (*Bradford Corporation* v. *Myers* [65]).

Some countries, such as France, have a theory of " administrative contracts," whereby many of the contracts made by public authorities are governed by different rules from private-law contracts.[66] English law has no theory of " administrative " or " public " contracts, but a public authority cannot by contract bind itself not to exercise powers conferred on it by statute (*Ayr Harbour Trustees* v. *Oswald* (1883) [67]). The exact scope of this principle is not clear. It has been suggested that the underlying principle is that of governmental effectiveness, so that " no contract would be enforced in any case where some essential governmental activity would be thereby rendered impossible or seriously impeded." [68] Such a contract, it is suggested, is not void if it is the kind of contract that the authority has power to make, but

---

64 *Rhyl U.D.C.* v. *Rhyl Amusements* [1959] 1 W.L.R. 465; [1959] 1 All E.R. 257.
65 [1916] 1 A.C. 242.
66 M. Waline, *Droit Administratif* (9th ed.) Pt. III, tit. 2; H. Street, *Governmental Liability*, pp. 81–84; L. N. Brown and J. F. Garner, *French Administrative Law* (1967) Chap. 8. French public authorities may also enter into private-law contracts, *e.g.* a commercial lease.
67 8 App.Cas. 623 (H.L.), *per* Lord Blackburn at p. 634. And see *York Corporation* v. *Henry Leetham & Son* [1924] 1 Ch. 557; *Birkdale District Electricity Supply Co.* v. *Southport Corporation* [1926] A.C. 355, *per* Lord Birkenhead at p. 364; *William Cory & Son Ltd.* v. *City of London Corporation* [1951] 1 K.B. 8.
68 J. D. B. Mitchell, *The Contracts of Public Authorities* (1954), p. 7. And see Mitchell, " Limitations on the Contractual Liability of Public Authorities " (1950) 13 M.L.R. 318, 455; " Theory of Public Contract Law " (1951) 63 Jur.Rev. 60.

it is not specifically enforceable. This leaves open the question of compensation to the other contracting party, which is due in justice but for which the common law does not seem to make provision. If this suggestion is sound, it applies to public authorities generally the principle of Crown contracts stated in the *Amphitrite* case,[69] if that decision is kept within reasonable limits.

The old theory of freedom of contract is giving way in public law to standard forms of contract with large monopolies like the public corporations that provide electricity, gas and railway transport. Here the terms and conditions and the charges are regulated, and the consumer's only choice is to accept the terms *in toto* or reject the service altogether.

Liability for nuisance

There is a presumption that statutory powers are not intended to be exercised in such a way as to cause a nuisance, *e.g.* that the power of a local authority to build hospitals does not authorise the erection of a small-pox hospital in a residential area. If the power is *imperative*, *i.e.* imposes a duty to perform some act in a certain manner, so that it appears expressly or by necessary implication that it cannot be performed without causing a nuisance, then a nuisance may be committed [70]; but if the power is expressly or impliedly *permissive*, *i.e.* the performance of the act is merely rendered not illegal in itself, then ways and means must be found to prevent its causing a nuisance. The burden of proving that the power is imperative rests on the party purporting to act thereunder (*Metropolitan Asylum District* v. *Hill* (1881)[71]). Similar considerations arise where fumes from a power station injure neighbouring property (*Corporation of Manchester* v. *Farnworth*[72]).

A nuisance may be caused either by an act or an omission, so that where this tort is committed the distinction between misfeasance and non-feasance is irrelevant (*Pride of Derby Angling Association Ltd.* v. *British Celanese Ltd.*[73]).

Liability for negligence

Even where a statutory power is bound to interfere with private rights to some extent, the power must be exercised with due care

---

69 *Rederiaktiebolaget Amphitrite* v. *The King* [1921] 2 K.B. 500; *post*, Chap. 32.
70 See *Dormer* v. *Newcastle-upon-Tyne Corporation* [1940] 2 K.B. 204.
71 6 App.Cas. 193 (H.L.). *Cf. The Hammersmith Ry.* v. *Brand* (1869) L.R. 4 H.L. 171; *Edgington* v. *Swindon Corporation* [1939] 1 K.B. 86; *Marriage* v. *East Norfolk Rivers Catchment Board* [1950] 1 K.B. 284.
72 [1930] A.C. 171 (H.L.). See also *R.* v. *Epping (Waltham Abbey), ex p. Burlinson* [1947] 2 All E.R. 537 (D.C.).
73 [1953] Ch. 149 (C.A.).

towards those likely to be affected. Parliament never authorises the commission of negligence. The leading case is the decision of the House of Lords concerning one of the first large public corporations, *Mersey Docks and Harbour Board* v. *Gibbs* (1866),[74] where the Board was held liable to the owners of a ship and her cargo for damage caused by its negligence in leaving a mud bank at the entrance to the docks.

So local authorities have been held liable for damage caused by negligence due to leaving a heap of stones unlighted on the highway (*Foreman* v. *Corporation of Canterbury* (1871)[75]), due to failing to detect a leak in the water supply system (*Corporation of Manchester* v. *Markland*[76]), and to carelessly inserting or failing to maintain a traffic stud (*Skilton* v. *Epsom and Ewell Urban District Council*[77]). In *Fisher* v. *Ruislip and Northwood Urban District Council*,[78] where the local authority was held liable for failing to give reasonable notice of the existence of a surface air-raid shelter with which the plaintiff collided in the blackout, the Court of Appeal reviewed a number of "blackout" and similar cases arising out of the two world wars, and distinguished negligent misfeasance, where the authority has itself created the danger by the exercise of its power, from merely failing, by not exercising its powers, to prevent damage arising independently.

In *Gold* v. *Essex County Council*[79] the Council was held liable to damages for the negligence of its radiographer in covering a patient's face with lint instead of lead-lined rubber cloth, and in *Cassidy* v. *Ministry of Health*[80] the hospital authority was held liable for the neglect of a whole-time medical officer in post-operation treatment. A person who owes another a duty cannot escape responsibility by delegating it to someone else. Denning L.J. pointed out that the distinction between a servant (under a contract of service) and an independent contractor (under a contract for services) is only relevant to distinguish cases where an employer is or is not liable for "collateral" negligence or other tort. On the other hand, where the defendant admittedly owes a duty of care to the plaintiff, as where a person is accepted as a patient by a hospital authority and is injured by negligent treatment, the proper question is: who employed the person who caused the damage? If the patient himself employed him,

---

[74] L.R. 1 H.L. 93.   And see *Gore* v. *Van der Lann* [1967] 2 Q.B. 31 (C.A.), liability for negligence of municipal bus conductor to pensioner travelling with free pass.

[75] L.R. 6 Q.B. 214.

[76] [1934] 2 K.B. 101.

[77] [1937] 1 K.B. 112.

[78] [1945] K.B. 584.   *Cf. Baxter* v. *Stockton-on-Tees Corporation* [1959] 1 Q.B. 441 (C.A.).

[79] [1942] 2 K.B. 293 (C.A.).

[80] [1951] 2 K.B. 343 (C.A.).

the hospital authority is not liable; but if the hospital authority employed him it is liable, whether he is a physician, surgeon, radiographer, nurse or anyone else. It makes no difference that the treatment is " gratuitous." [81]

Failure to perform statutory duties [82]

Whether a public authority is liable in damages to a private individual for injury caused by the failure to perform a statutory duty, as opposed to the exercise of a discretionary power,[83] depends on the facts of the case and the interpretation of the statute imposing the duty. The plaintiff has to show that the duty was owed to himself and not merely to the public generally, that the damage he suffered was directly caused by the breach of duty, and that the damage was of the kind contemplated by the statute (*Groves* v. *Lord Wimborne* [84]). Usually the duty is owed to the public only and not to individuals, as in the case of a local authority whose failure to remove snow from the street caused a woman to fall and hurt herself (*Saunders* v. *Holborn District Board of Works* [85]). The provision of some other remedy, such as complaint to the Minister, will often be held to exclude an action for damages.

It is a general principle of common law that failure to perform a statutory duty is an indictable misdemeanour. Indictment is therefore the residuary remedy for non-performance of a duty by a public authority, although the cases where it is now appropriate are probably few. In *Clegg, Parkinson & Co.* v. *Earby Gas Co.*[86] a Divisional Court held that no action for damages lay by consumers for failure to perform the statutory duty of providing gas to the public, the remedy being that (if any) provided by the statute, and otherwise indictment.

A residuary remedy of limited application is mandamus.[87]

Highway authorities

The Highways Act 1959 provided that highways formerly repairable by the inhabitants at large—*i.e.* highways that existed before the Highway Act 1835 or which have been adopted—should be maintain-

---

[81] See Grunfeld, " Recent Developments in the Hospital Cases " (1954) 17 M.L.R. 547.

[82] See G. Sawer, " Non-Feasance Revisited " (1955) 19 M.L.R. 541, where early drainage cases are also discussed.

[83] *Cf. Shennard* v. *Glossop Corporation* [1921] 3 K.B. 132; *East Suffolk Rivers Catchment Board* v. *Kent* [1941] A.C. 74 (H.L.).

[84] [1898] 2 Q.B. 402, 415, *per* Vaughan Williams L.J.

[85] [1895] 1 Q.B. 64.

[86] [1896] 1 Q.B. 592.

[87] *Post,* Chap. 31.

able at the public expense by the highway authorities. The Act also abolished indictment for non-repair of highways. Any person who alleges that a highway is out of repair may serve notice on the highway authority. If the extent of repairs required is in dispute, the matter may be settled by the magistrates' court, but if liability is disputed the case goes to the Crown Court (s. 54).

The Highways (Miscellaneous Provisions) Act 1961, s. 1, abrogated the common law exemption of highway authorities from civil liability for damages arising from non-repair of the highway.[88] In an action against a highway authority for damage caused by failure to maintain a highway maintainable at the public expense, the authority will be liable unless they prove that they took such care as in all the circumstances was reasonably required of them as the highway authority to secure that that part of the highway was not dangerous to traffic.[89] The doctrine of contributory negligence applies.[90] Section 1 binds the Crown, i.e. the Minister as the highway authority for trunk roads.[91]

---

[88] Cf. Russell v. Men of Devon (1780) 2 T.R. 667; Cowley v. Newmarket Local Board [1892] A.C. 345.

[89] See Griffiths v. Liverpool Corporation [1967] 1 Q.B. 374 (C.A.), plaintiff injured by tripping over flagstone on pavement. Diplock L.J. said that the statutory duty is not based on negligence, but supersedes the common law of nuisance. See also Meggs v. Liverpool Corporation [1968] 1 W.L.R. 689 (C.A.); Bramwell v. Shaw [1971] R.T.R. 167.

[90] Burnside v. Emerson [1968] 1 W.L.R. 1490 (C.A.).

[91] Bright v. Att.-Gen. (1971) 115 S.J. 226 (C.A.).

CHAPTER 31

JUDICIAL CONTROL OF PUBLIC AUTHORITIES: II. REMEDIES [1]

I. ORDINARY REMEDIES AGAINST PUBLIC AUTHORITIES

1. Action for damages

When an injury is done to a citizen's person or property by a public authority acting *ultra vires* or in abuse of power, an action for damages may be brought in circumstances where an action would lie against a private individual. The actions most commonly brought are for trespass, false imprisonment,[2] negligence [3] and nuisance.[4]

Where a public authority is under a duty to do or to refrain from doing some act, and an individual suffers a particular injury peculiar to himself owing to the breach of that duty, he may bring an action unless this is expressly or impliedly excluded by statute.[5] In some cases he must join the Attorney-General as plaintiff. The duties of public authorities, however, are generally owed to the public only, and Parliament often specifies a particular remedy excluding private actions.[6]

If a public authority commits a breach of contract which it was within the powers of the authority to make, an action for damages will lie.[7]

2. Injunction and specific performance

Where a public authority threatens to do or to continue to do some unlawful act, such as a nuisance, an action may be brought for an injunction to restrain the authority from doing or continuing to do so. The breach of an injunction amounts to contempt of court. An injunction was originally an equitable remedy. It may be sought in

---

[1] See works cited *ante*, at p. 514n.; and J. F. Garner and A. R. Galbraith, *Judicial Control of the Administrative Process* (Ditchley Foundation, 1969); S. Galeotti, *The Judicial Control of Public Authorities in England and Wales* (1954).
[2] *Percy* v. *Glasgow Corporation* [1922] A.C. 299.
[3] *Mersey Docks and Harbour Board* v. *Gibbs* (1866) L.R. 1 H.L. 93.
[4] *Metropolitan Asylum District* v. *Hill* (1881) 6 App.Cas. 193.
[5] *Groves* v. *Lord Wimborne* [1898] 2 Q.B. 402, 415; *Ching* v. *Surrey County Council* [1910] 1 K.B. 736; *Oldham* v. *Sheffield Corporation* (1927) 136 L.T. 681.
[6] *Phillips* v. *Britannia Hygienic Laundry Co. Ltd.* [1923] 2 K.B. 832, 840; *Atkinson* v. *Newcastle Waterworks Co.* (1877) 2 Ex.D. 441; *Clegg, Parkinson & Co.* v. *Earby Gas Co.* [1896] 1 Q.B. 592, 594.
[7] *Armour* v. *Liverpool Corporation* [1939] Ch. 422.

addition to or instead of damages, but will only be granted at the discretion of the court exercised judicially and in the type of cases in which it would lie against a private individual. In *Pride of Derby Angling Association* v. *British Celanese Ltd.*[8] an injunction was granted against the Derby Corporation and the British Electricity Authority to restrain them from continuing a nuisance by polluting a river. Although injunction is discretionary and will not be granted if, for example, damages would be a sufficient remedy, yet there is a prima facie right to an injunction if the defendant threatens to continue the nuisance.

Injunction is the appropriate method, unless it is excluded by statute, for questioning the right of a person to hold a particular office.

An injunction sought by parents to restrain a local education authority from introducing a scheme for comprehensive schools was refused, partly on the ground that if an education authority did fail in its duty under the Education Act 1944 to provide sufficient schools, the only remedy under the Act was a complaint to the Minister.[9] But an injunction or interim injunction may be granted to restrain a local education authority from carrying out a reorganisation scheme without the necessary notices or contrary to the articles of government of a school.[10] Conversely, a local education authority may obtain an injunction to restrain an expelled student from entering college premises.[11]

An act done by a public authority generally affects the public, and the person to sue for an injunction on behalf of the public is the Attorney-General. In some cases he may allow his name to be used at the request (" on the relation ") of some individual (" the relator ") who is substantially the party affected. This is called a " relator action." [12] A citizen may claim an injunction against a public authority in his own name only where, in addition to the threatened breach of a public right, either some private right of his is affected or he will suffer some damage peculiar to himself (*Boyce* v. *Paddington Borough Council* [13]).

An action for specific performance of a contract may be brought against a public authority in similar circumstances to those in which

8 [1953] Ch. 149 (C.A.).
9 *Wood* v. *Ealing London Borough Council* [1967] Ch. 364.
10 *Bradbury* v. *Enfield L.B.C.* [1967] 1 W.L.R. 1311 (C.A.); *Lee* v. *Enfield L.B.C.* (1967) 111 S.J. 772. And see *Lee* v. *Department of Education and Science* (1967) 66 L.G.R. 211: declaration.
11 *Brighton Corporation* v. *Parry*, *The Times*, June 10, 1972.
12 *Att.-Gen.* v. *Wimbledon House Estate Co.* [1904] 2 Ch. 34; *Att.-Gen.* v. *Bastow* [1957] 1 Q.B. 514; *Att.-Gen.* v. *Smith* [1958] 2 Q.B. 173.
13 [1903] 1 Ch. 109.

specific performance would be granted against an ordinary corporation or private individual.[14] The contract must, of course, be one of the kind that is on principle enforceable against government authorities.[15]

3. Action for a declaration [16]

An action for a declaration asks for a " declaration of right." It may be brought in the High Court even though no damages or other relief is claimed. The claim is often brought together with a claim for an injunction, and similar rules apply with regard to suing in the plaintiff's own name or at his relation by the Attorney-General.[17] There must be a justiciable issue,[18] and this remedy cannot be brought in order to ask hypothetical questions.[19] A declaratory judgment cannot be directly enforced, but it may be assumed that a public authority will observe the law when the High Court declares what it is.

The action for a declaration is a convenient and flexible remedy of increasing importance against public authorities.[20] It is available to test the validity of delegated legislation, and the *vires* of decisions of tribunals whether statutory or voluntary.[21] But a declaratory judgment cannot quash a decision, and the remedy is not appropriate where the decision was within jurisdiction but there is error on the face of the record.[22]

In *Vine* v. *National Dock Labour Board* [23] the House of Lords granted a declaration that the plaintiff's dismissal was a nullity, as well as damages for wrongful dismissal. It was held that the disciplinary duty of the local board was too important to be delegated without express power and, although the jurisdiction to give a declara-

---

[14] *Crook* v. *Corporation of Seaford* (1871) L.R. 6 Ch. 551; *cf. Crampton* v. *Varna Ry.* (1872) 7 Ch.App. 562.

[15] See *ante*, p. 526.

[16] I. Zamir, *The Declaratory Judgment* (1962); E. Borchard, *Declaratory Judgments* (2nd ed. 1941), especially pp. 875–926; J. F. Garner, " *Locus standi* in Actions for a Declaration " (1968) 31 M.L.R. 512; G. J. Borrie, " The Advantages of the Declaratory Judgment in Administrative Law " (1955) 18 M.L.R. 138; K. C. Davis, *Administrative Law*, p. 729; S. A. de Smith, " The Province of Declaratory Judgment Redetermined " (1958) 21 M.L.R. 404.

[17] *Ante*, p. 532.

[18] *Cox* v. *Green* [1966] Ch. 216: a question of professional etiquette is not justiciable.

[19] *Re Barnato, Joel* v. *Sanger* [1949] Ch. 258.

[20] *Barber* v. *Manchester Regional Hospital Board* [1958] 1 W.L.R. 181; [1958] 1 All E.R. 322; *Price* v. *Sunderland Corporation* [1956] 1 W.L.R. 1253; [1956] 3 All E.R. 153: collection of money for school meals not a duty of teachers.

[21] *Davis* v. *Carew-Pole* [1956] 1 W.L.R. 833; [1956] 2 All E.R. 524; *Ceylon University* v. *Fernando* [1960] 1 W.L.R. 223; [1960] 1 All E.R. 631 (P.C.).

[22] *Punton* v. *Ministry of Pensions and National Insurance* [1964] 1 W.L.R. 226: decision of National Insurance Commissioner.

[23] [1957] A.C. 488; following *Barnard* v. *National Dock Labour Board* [1953] 2 Q.B. 18 (C.A.).

tory judgment was to be exercised cautiously, damages in this case would not be an adequate remedy. In *Francis* v. *Yiewsley and West Drayton Urban District Council*[24] the Court of Appeal granted a declaration that an enforcement notice relating to a caravan site was invalid, although the plaintiff had a statutory right of appeal to a magistrates' court and could have set up the invalidity of the notice as a defence to a prosecution. The House of Lords in *Pyx Granite Co.* v. *Ministry of Health*,[25] where an agreement concerning quarrying in Malvern Hills had been confirmed by private Act, granted a declaration that development was authorised. Their Lordships held that jurisdiction to grant a declaration was not ousted by the Town and Country Planning Act 1947, which provided for an application to the Minister to determine whether planning permission was needed: only a clear expression of intention in a statute would exclude the jurisdiction of the court. Declaration is useful in disputes between public authorities, or in cases where a public authority merely wants to know the extent of its powers. It is not necessarily excluded because other remedies, such as certiorari or mandamus, are available. The time limit for bringing the action is the usual period of six years: discovery and oral evidence are allowed.

II. SUPERVISORY JURISDICTION OF THE HIGH COURT[26]

" Prerogative writs " were writs brought by the King against his officers to compel them to exercise their functions properly or to prevent them from abusing their powers. They could be issued at various periods of their history either out of the Court of King's Bench or the Court of Chancery, or both. The term " prerogative writ " was applied to habeas corpus in the reign of James I; but it is not until Lord Mansfield[27] and Blackstone that we find it grouped with certiorari, prohibition and mandamus as " prerogative writs " because they were not directed immediately to the tribunal or person concerned but were supposed to issue from the King to a royal officer, such as the sheriff.[28] The chief prerogative writs were habeas corpus, prohibition, certiorari,

---

24 [1958] 1 Q.B. 478.
25 [1960] A.C. 260; *cf. Barraclough* v. *Brown* [1897] A.C. 615 (H.L.). And see S. A. de Smith, note in (1959) 22 M.L.R. 664.
26 See Lord Parker C.J., " Recent Developments in the Supervisory Powers of the Courts over Inferior Tribunals " (Lionel Cohen Lectures, 1959).
27 *R.* v. *Cowle* (1759) 2 Burr. 834, 855.
28 For an account of their origin and development, see S. A. de Smith, " The Prerogative Writs " (1951) 11 C.L.J. 40; D. C. M. Yardley, " The Scope of the Prerogative Orders in Administrative Law " (1957–1958) 12 N.I.L.Q. 78; de Smith, *Judicial Review of Administrative Action*, Chap. 8.

mandamus and *quo warranto*; but of these only the first remains as a writ,[29] the last has been abolished, and the others are now displaced by a modified procedure of orders.

At the present day a private citizen as well as a public authority may apply to the High Court for one of these orders, but this kind of remedy has certain special characteristics: (i) It has a special form of procedure which cannot be used together with, or as an alternative to, any other kind of remedy such as damages or injunction; (ii) It is obtainable only at the discretion of the court if cause is shown why it should be issued [30]; and the discretion will be exercised against the applicant if there has been undue delay in making the application, or his conduct has been unmeritorious or the case is trivial; (iii) It is subject to a special time-limit of six months; there is no discovery of documents and evidence is given on affidavit. The proceedings are brought in the name of the Crown, on behalf of (*ex parte*) the applicant.

This supervisory or corrective jurisdiction is exercised by a Divisional Court (Queen's Bench Division) of the High Court.[31]

1. Certiorari [32]

This is an order issued to an " inferior court " or a person or body exercising what the High Court regards as a " judicial " or " quasi-judicial " function, to have the record of the proceedings removed into the High Court for review, and (if bad) to be quashed. The Administration of Justice (Miscellaneous Provisions) Acts 1933 and 1938 simplified the procedure by abolishing the former writ, and requiring the applicant to show cause why the corresponding order should be issued. The applicant must be a " person aggrieved," that is, he must have suffered a peculiar grievance of his own beyond some inconvenience suffered by him in common with the rest of the public, but this requirement is construed broadly.[33] Certiorari differs

---

29 For habeas corpus, see *ante,* Chap. 23.

30 Declaration, injunction and specific performance are also discretionary.

31 For the procedure, see Griffits, *Guide to Crown Office Practice.* The Court of Appeal can assume jurisdiction on appeal from a Divisional Court which has refused the order.

32 The former writ of certiorari appears first to have been used against the Commissioners of Sewers charged by a statute of 1531 to see to the repair of sea walls, but most of the earlier cases were against justices. For the history, see Holdsworth, *History of English Law,* Vol. X, pp. 199–206; D. C. M. Yardley, " The Grounds for Certiorari and Prohibition " (1959) 37 Can.Bar Rev. 294; and *R.* v. *Northumberland Compensation Appeal Tribunal, ex p. Shaw* [1951] 1 K.B. 711, *per* Lord Goddard L.C.J.; [1952] 1 K.B. 338 *per* Denning L.J.

33 *R.* v. *Surrey Justices* (1870) L.R. 5 Q.B. 466; *R.* v. *Richmond Confirming Authority, ex p. Howitt* [1921] 1 K.B. 248; *R.* v. *Manchester Legal Aid Committee* [1952] 2 Q.B. 413. See D. C. M. Yardley, " Certiorari and the Problem of Locus Standi " (1955) 71 L.Q.R. 388.

from an appeal where the case is reheard on its merits, and it does not lie for the purpose of providing an appeal where none is granted by statute.[34]

What is an " inferior court " for this purpose, or whether a person or body exercises powers of a " judicial " or " quasi-judicial " nature, is a question for the High Court to decide. The former *locus classicus* was the dictum of Atkin L.J. in *R.* v. *Electricity Commissioners*[35]: " Whenever any body of persons having legal authority to determine questions affecting the rights of subjects, and having the duty to act judicially, act in excess of their legal authority, they are subject to the controlling jurisdiction of the King's Bench Division, exercised in these writs " (*i.e.* certiorari and prohibition). It was made clear in *Ridge* v. *Baldwin*[36] (a declaratory action) that authority to determine questions affecting the rights of subjects and the duty to act judicially are not two separate requirements: the latter is not additional to the former. Certiorari has been held to lie against a county court judge, a court-martial, the Patents Appeal Tribunal, the Medical Appeal Tribunal, a local valuation court, rent tribunals and a Minister holding a public inquiry.[37] In *R.* v. *Surrey Justices* (1870)[38] certiorari was granted because the justices had ordered a road to be closed without affixing the notices prescribed by statute; and in *Board of Education* v. *Rice*[39] certiorari and mandamus were granted against the Board of Education because, in a dispute between the managers of a school and the local education authority, they had not decided the question which the statute directed them to decide. In *R.* v. *Manchester Legal Aid Committee, ex p. Brand*[40] Parker J. concluded that a legal aid committee, being unconcerned with questions of policy and having to decide wholly on the facts of a particular case solely on the evidence before them, " must act judicially, not judiciously."

---

[34] *Cf.* Administration of Justice Act 1960, s. 16. For the distinction between certiorari and appeal, see *R.* v. *Jones, The Times,* December 3, 1968 (C.A.).

[35] [1924] 1 K.B. 171.

[36] [1964] A.C. 40, *per* Lord Reid; *cf. per* Lord Hewart C.J. in *R.* v. *Legislative Committee of the Church Assembly, ex p. Haynes-Smith* [1928] 1 K.B. 411. Atkin L.J.'s dictum is too wide as regards certiorari and ecclesiastical law; *post,* pp. 538–539.

[37] *R.* v. *Worthington-Evans, ex p. Madan* [1959] 2 Q.B. 145 (D.C.); *R.* v. *Hurst (Judge), ex p. Smith* [1960] 2 Q.B. 133 (D.C.); *Baldwin and Francis Ltd.* v. *Patents Appeal Tribunal* [1959] A.C. 663 (H.L.); *R.* v. *Medical Appeal Tribunal, ex p. Gilmore* [1957] 1 Q.B. 574 (C.A.); *R.* v. *East Norfolk Local Valuation Court* [1951] 1 All E.R. 743; *R.* v. *Fulham Rent Tribunal* [1951] 2 K.B. 1; *R.* v. *Paddington Rent Tribunal, ex p. Bell Properties* [1949] 1 K.B. 666; *Errington* v. *Minister of Health* [1935] 1 K.B. 249. Certiorari was not granted in *Re Mansergh* (1861) 1 B. & S. 400 (court-martial).

[38] L.R. 5 Q.B. 466.

[39] [1911] A.C. 179 (H.L.).

[40] [1952] 2 Q.B. 413 (D.C.).

The expression " quasi-judicial " function or power was frequently applied by the courts in the 1930s and 1940s to those functions of administrative authorities which the courts would control by means of certiorari.[41] The Committee on Ministers' Powers [42] described a quasi-judicial decision generally as " an administrative decision, some stage or some element of which possesses judicial characteristics." There was one practical test whether an act was administrative or judicial, said Sir Cecil Carr,[43] namely, the writ of certiorari. Thus in *Errington* v. *Minister of Health* [44] the Court of Appeal set aside a clearance order on the ground that, after objections had been taken, the Minister was acting quasi-judicially in considering whether to confirm the order, and therefore he acted improperly in hearing one side in the absence of the other. In *Franklin* v. *Minister of Town and Country Planning* [45] an application was made to quash the Minister's order under the New Towns Act 1946 designating Stevenage as the site of a " new town," on the ground that before considering objections the Minister had stated at a public meeting that he would make the order, and was therefore biased in considering any objections. The House of Lords, however, gave judgment for the Minister on the ground that his function in making the order was purely administrative, and the question of bias is only relevant in the exercise of a judicial or quasi-judicial function.

Scope of certiorari

The grounds on which certiorari lies are:

(i) *Want or excess of jurisdiction.* For this reason certiorari was granted against a licensing authority which had given permission to open a cinema on Sunday, whereas this was prohibited by statute [46]; and against a legal aid committee which had granted a legal aid certificate to a trustee in bankruptcy on the basis of the means of the

---

[41] *e.g.* Scott L.J. in *Cooper* v. *Wilson* [1937] 2 K.B. 309, 340; *Blackpool Corporation* v. *Locker* [1948] 1 K.B. 349, 367; Lord Thankerton in *Franklin* v. *Minister of Town and Country Planning* [1948] A.C. 87.

[42] (1932) Cmd. 4060. And see H. W. R. Wade, " ' Quasi-judicial ' and its Background " (1949) 10 C.L.J. 216, 237–240.

[43] *Concerning English Administrative Law*, p. 106. The argument was circular: if the function was judicial, certiorari lay; if certiorari lay, the function was judicial.

[44] [1935] 1 K.B. 249. *Cf. Frost* v. *Minister of Health* [1935] 1 K.B. 286 (before objections lodged, Minister was acting in purely administrative capacity); *Horn* v. *Minister of Health* [1937] 1 K.B. 164.

[45] [1948] A.C. 87. And see *Robinson* v. *Minister of Town and Country Planning* (the " *Plymouth* " case) [1947] K.B. 702 (C.A.); *B. Johnson & Co. (Builders) Ltd.* v. *Minister of Health* [1947] 2 All E.R. 395 (C.A.).

[46] *The King* v. *London County Council, ex p. Entertainments Protection Association* [1931] 2 K.B. 215.

bankrupt instead of the means of the trustee (*R*. v. *Manchester Legal Aid Committee, supra* [47]).

(ii) *Denial of natural justice.*[48] Certiorari has been issued at the instance of a ratepayer to quash the decision of a rural district council permitting a certain development of land, since one of the councillors who voted on the resolution was interested in the use of the land [49]; and to quash a decision of the General Medical Council removing a doctor's name from the medical register, because the Council had refused to hear certain evidence which it ought to have heard (*General Medical Council* v. *Spackman* [50]).

(iii) *Error on the face of the record.*[51] It was commonly thought at one time that certiorari was limited to cases of jurisdiction and natural justice, but the Court of Appeal held in *R*. v. *Northumberland Compensation Appeal Tribunal, ex p. Shaw* [52] that this remedy is also available where an inferior tribunal has issued a " speaking order " (*i.e.* an order showing the reasons on which it is based), and an error of law appears on its face.   In that case the applicant complained that the tribunal had made an error in computing the compensation to which he was entitled by statute for loss of employment on the nationalisation of the health service.   The award set out the manner in which the sum was computed, and this enabled the court to hold that the computation was not in accordance with the statutory regulations and that the decision must be quashed.   Error on the face of the record renders a decision voidable. There was usually no obligation on a tribunal to make a " speaking " or reasoned order before the Tribunals and Inquiries Act 1958, replaced by section 12 of the 1971 Act.[53]   Now that statutory tribunals and Ministers making decisions after statutory inquiry must make speaking orders, judicial control by error on the record may become more important than *ultra vires* control.

Certiorari does not lie to review subordinate legislation.[54]   It does

---

47 [1952] 2 Q.B. 413. See also *R*. v. *Fulham Rent Tribunal* [1951] 2 K.B. 1, on review of jurisdictional facts.
48 For the principles of natural justice, see *ante,* pp. 520 *et seq.*
49 *The King* v. *Hendon Rural District Council, ex p. Chorley* [1933] 2 K.B. 696.
50 [1943] A.C. 627 (H.L.).
51 See J. M. Fitzgerald and I. D. Elliott, " Certiorari: Errors of Law on the Face of the Record " (1964) 4 *Melbourne Univ.Law Rev.* 552.
52 [1952] 1 K.B. 338; confirming Divisional Court at [1951] 1 K.B. 711; following *Walsall Overseers* v. *London and North Western Ry.* (1879) 4 App.Cas. 30 (H.L.) and *R*. v. *Nat Bell Liquors Ltd.* [1922] 2 A.C. 128 (P.C.).
    And see *R*. v. *Patents Appeal Tribunal, ex p. Swift & Co.* [1962] 2 Q.B. 647 (D.C.); *R*. v. *Medical Appeal Tribunal, ex p. Gilmore* [1957] 1 Q.B. 574 (D.C.) *per* Denning L.J.
53 *Ante,* pp. 508–509.
54 *R*. v. *Legislative Committee of the Church Assembly, ex p. Haynes-Smith* [1928] 1 K.B. 411.

not lie against ecclesiastical courts, because ecclesiastical law is a different system of law from that administered in the High Court [55]; or against voluntary (*i.e.* non-statutory) domestic tribunals [56]; nor does it lie for dismissal of a person under an ordinary contract of employment.[57]

Licensing and disciplinary powers

Some licensing and disciplinary cases are not easy to reconcile with general principles. The liquor licensing functions of the justices have always been regarded as judicial for the purposes of reviews.[58] In *Nakkuda Ali* v. *Jayaratne* [59] the Privy Council classified as " administrative," and therefore not subject to certiorari, the cancellation of a trading licence by the Controller of Textiles under the Ceylon Defence Regulations. The grant of a licence in the first place was a privilege given after the general right to trade had been taken away by statute, and the Controller had to be satisfied about " unfitness." Lord Reid in *Ridge* v. *Baldwin* [60] seemed to regard Defence Regulation cases as being in a special category. In *R.* v. *Metropolitan Police Commissioner, ex p. Parker* [61] a Divisional Court similarly held that the power of the Commissioner of Police to revoke a taxi-driver's licence on the ground of unfitness could not be interfered with by certiorari or otherwise, although the driver complained that there had been a denial of natural justice as he had not been given an opportunity to rebut police allegations about the misuse of the taxi. Lord Goddard C.J. laid stress on the disciplinary nature of the power to revoke the licence, saying it was most undesirable that the free and proper disciplinary exercise of powers should be fettered by threats of judicial proceedings. He also pointed out that there was no order to be brought up to be quashed. This last case was applied by a

---

[55] *The King* v. *Chancellor of St. Edmundsbury and Ipswich Diocese* [1948] 1 K.B. 195. *Cf.* prohibition.

[56] *R.* v. *National Joint Council for the Craft of Dental Technicians, ex p. Neate* [1953] 1 Q.B. 704 (D.C.); *cf. R.* v. *Criminal Injuries Compensation Board, ex p. Lain* [1967] 2 Q.B. 864 (C.A.): certiorari may be issued against a public body set up by prerogative as part of an administrative scheme approved by both Houses and financed by parliamentary funds.

[57] *Vidyodaya University of Ceylon* v. *Silva* [1965] 1 W.L.R. 77; [1964] 3 All E.R. 865 (P.C.): dismissal of university professor. The remedy is an action for damages if the dismissal was in breach of contract.

[58] *R.* v. *Brighton Borough Justices, ex p. Jarvis* [1954] 1 W.L.R. 203; [1954] 1 All E.R. 197, *per* Lord Goddard C.J.

[59] [1951] A.C. 66. *Cf.* H. W. R. Wade, " The Twilight of Natural Justice? " (1951) 67 L.Q.R. 103.

[60] [1964] A.C. 40; *infra.*

[61] [1953] 1 W.L.R. 1150; [1953] 2 All E.R. 717. *Cf.* D. M. Gordon, " The Cab Driver's Licence Case " (1954) 70 L.Q.R. 203. And on both cases see D. C. M. Yardley, " Revocation of Licences—An English Dilemma " (1956) *Juridical Rev.* 240.

Divisional Court in *Ex p. Fry*,[62] where a chief fire officer had administered a caution to a fireman under statutory regulations for a disciplinary offence, namely, refusing to clean the uniform of a superior officer. The fireman alleged a denial of natural justice, but the Court of appeal upheld the refusal to grant certiorari in view of his conduct.

Ridge v. *Baldwin* [63] is now authority for saying that natural justice generally applies to licensing powers, although a large element of policy is involved; but there are few decisions concerning government departments or local authorities. Disciplinary powers no longer appear to be regarded as being in a special category. The conclusion seems to be that certiorari is applicable generally to licensing and disciplinary powers, but that the discretion of the court will often lead to its refusal.

2. Prohibition

The former writ of prohibition issued out of the King's Bench or other superior court directing the judge and parties to a suit in any inferior court to cease from the prosecution thereof on the ground that the cause did not belong to that jurisdiction.[64] The penalty for disobedience is committal for contempt. It was mainly by this writ that the common law courts in earlier days contested the jurisdiction of the Admiralty and ecclesiastical courts. The Administration of Justice (Miscellaneous Provisions) Acts 1933 and 1938 made the same procedural changes in prohibition as in certiorari.

The order of prohibition is now issued by a Divisional Court of the High Court to *prevent* an inferior court or tribunal from exceeding or continuing to exceed its jurisdiction or infringing the rules of natural justice. Prohibition is governed by similar principles to certiorari, except that it does not lie when once a final decision has been given. Thus in *R.* v. *Liverpool Corporation, ex p. Liverpool Taxi Fleet Operators' Association* [65] it was granted to prohibit a local authority from acting on a resolution with regard to the number of taxicab licences to be issued, without first hearing representations on behalf of interested persons. The court has a discretion as to the persons for whose benefit prohibition will issue.[66]

Prohibition has been granted, for example, against Electricity Commissioners to prevent them from holding an inquiry with a view

---

[62] [1954] 1 W.L.R. 730; [1954] 2 All E.R. 118.
[63] [1964] A.C. 40 (H.L.).
[64] Bl.Comm. iii, 105. See D. C. M. Yardley, "The Grounds for Certiorari and Prohibition" (1959) 37 Can.Bar Rev. 294.
[65] [1972] 2 Q.B. 299 (C.A.).
[66] D. C. M. Yardley, "Prohibition and Mandamus and the Problem of Locus Standi" (1957) 73 L.Q.R. 534.

to bringing into force an *ultra vires* scheme for the supply of electricity (*R.* v. *Electricity Commissioners* [67]); and against Income Tax Commissioners, an assessment committee and rent tribunals.[68] But it was decided in *The King* v. *Legislative Committee of the Church Assembly, ex p. Haynes-Smith,*[69] where application was made for an order to prohibit the Church Assembly from proceeding further with the Prayer Book Measure 1927, that it would not issue against a legislative or deliberative body. Nor will prohibition be issued to a military tribunal administering martial law (*Re Clifford and O'Sullivan* [70]).

Where a final decision has been made by the inferior court prohibition is obviously useless, but certiorari is available to enable the High Court to review and, if necessary, to quash the decision. Thus prohibition was the appropriate remedy to prevent the Minister of Health from proceeding to confirm an *ultra vires* housing scheme (*R.* v. *Minister of Health, ex p. Davis* [71]), but certiorari was appropriate when an *ultra vires* scheme had already been approved by the Minister (*Minister of Health* v. *R., ex p. Yaffe* [72]). Applications for certiorari and prohibition are often brought together, for example, to quash a decision already made by a rent tribunal and to prevent it continuing to exceed or abuse its jurisdiction (*R.* v. *Paddington Rent Tribunal, ex p. Bell Properties Ltd.*[73]).

Prohibition and mandamus were issued together in *R.* v. *Kent Police Authority, ex p. Godden* [74] where, on the compulsory retirement of a police inspector on the ground that he was permanently disabled, it was held that the inspector's medical advisers were entitled to see all the material placed before the medical practitioner appointed to make the decision about disablement.

3. Mandamus

"By Magna Carta," said Bowen L.J.,[75] "the Crown is bound neither to deny justice to anybody, nor to delay anybody in obtaining justice. If, therefore, there is no other means of obtaining justice, the writ of mandamus is granted to enable justice to be done." The

---

[67] [1929] 1 K.B. 171, *per* Atkin L.J. Certiorari was refused in that case.
[68] *Kensington Income Tax Commissioners* v. *Aramayo* [1916] 1 A.C. 215; *R.* v. *North Worcestershire Assessment Committee, ex p. Hadley* [1929] 2 K.B. 397; *R.* v. *Tottenham and District Rent Tribunal, ex p. Northfield* [1957] 1 Q.B. 103.
[69] [1928] 1 K.B. 411. The House of Commons rejected the Prayer Book Measure.
[70] [1921] 2 A.C. 570 (H.L.).
[71] [1929] 1 K.B. 619.
[72] [1931] A.C. 494.
[73] [1939] 1 K.B. 666.
[74] [1971] 2 Q.B. 662 (C.A.).
[75] *R.* v. *Commissioners of Inland Revenue, re Nathan* (1884) 12 Q.B.D. 461, 478; Bl.Comm. iii, 110. See D. C. M. Yardley, " The Purpose of Mandamus in English Law " (1959) *Juridical Rev.* 1.

penalty for disobedience is committal for contempt. The Administration of Justice (Miscellaneous Provisions) Acts 1933 and 1938 made the same procedural changes in mandamus as in certiorari and prohibition. The order of mandamus may be issued to any person or body (not necessarily an inferior court) commanding him or them to carry out some public duty. It is a residuary remedy of use where no other remedy is available.[76] An order will not be issued if an action in tort would lie, or if a more convenient procedure is available,[77] or if some other remedy is provided by statute (*Pasmore* v. *Oswaldtwistle Urban District Council*[78]). It may be issued on the application of the Crown, or of a private individual who has a specific right or an interest over and above that of the public generally.[79] It is doubtful whether a private citizen has a *locus standi* to obtain an order of mandamus for the enforcement by the police of the law against gaming clubs.[80]

Mandamus has been issued to compel the hearing of an appeal by a statutory tribunal,[81] the determination of a dispute between a local education authority and school managers (*Board of Education* v. *Rice*[82]), to procure the production of a local authority's accounts for inspection,[83] against a returning officer to declare a councillor elected,[84] against a county court judge to make a legal aid order,[85] and against the Board of Trade requiring them to investigate the affairs of the applicant company under the Companies Act.[86] Mandamus was not granted to compel the College of Physicians to admit an applicant (*R.* v. *Askew* (1768)[87]), to order a magistrate to hear a case covered by parliamentary privilege,[88] or to compel the Chairman of Convocation of London University to call a meeting, as the matter could have been put to the Visitor (*R.* v. *Dunsheath, ex p. Meredith*[89]).

[76] *R.* v. *Secretary of State for War* [1891] 2 Q.B. 326.
[77] *R.* v. *Charity Commissioners* [1897] 1 Q.B. 407; *Ex p. Jarett* (1946) 62 T.L.R. 230.
[78] [1898] A.C. 387.
[79] *R.* v. *Hereford Corporation, ex p. Harrowen* [1970] 1 W.L.R. 1424 (D.C.): ratepayer; *cf. R.* v. *Customs and Excise Commissioners, ex p. Cook* [1970] 1 W.L.R. 450 (D.C.). See D. C. M. Yardley, "Prohibition and Mandamus and the Problem of Locus Standi" (1957) 73 L.Q.R 534; S. M. Thio, "Locus Standi in Relation to Mandamus" [1966] P.L. 133.
[80] *R.* v. *Commissioner of Police of the Metropolis, ex p. Blackburn* [1968] 2 Q.B. 118 (C.A.): mandamus not granted on account of Commissioner's undertaking.
[81] *The King* v. *Housing Tribunal* [1920] 3 K.B. 334.
[82] [1911] A.C. 179.
[83] *R.* v. *Bedwellty U.D.C., ex p. Price* [1934] 1 K.B. 333.
[84] *R.* v. *Soothill, ex p. Ashdown, The Times,* April 2, 1955.
[85] *R.* v. *Judge Fraser Harris, ex p. The Law Society* [1955] 1 Q.B. 287.
[86] *R.* v. *Board of Trade, ex p. St. Martin's Preserving Co.* [1965] 1 Q.B. 603 (D.C.).
[87] 4 Burr. 2186.
[88] *R.* v. *Graham-Campbell, ex p. Herbert* [1935] 1 K.B. 594; *cf. R.* v. *Ogden, ex p. Long Ashton R.D.C.* [1963] 1 W.L.R. 274; [1963] 1 All E.R. 574 (D.C.).
[89] [1951] 1 K.B. 127. And see *Sammy* v. *Birkbeck College, The Times,* November 3, 1964, and May 20, 1965 (mandamus refused).

Mandamus is not available against the Crown itself, nor against a servant of the Crown to enforce a duty owed exclusively to the Crown (*R.* v. *Secretary of State for War*[90]; *The Queen* v. *Lords of the Treasury* (1872)[91]), because a third party cannot require an agent to perform a duty which he owes solely to his principal. But mandamus may be issued against Ministers or other Crown servants to enforce a statutory duty owed to the applicant as well as to the Crown (*The Queen* v. *Special Commissioners for Income Tax* (1888)[92]). In *Padfield* v. *Minister of Agriculture, Fisheries and Food*[93] the House of Lords held that where a Minister had by statute an unfettered discretion whether or not to refer a complaint to a committee, he must consider only relevant matters and exclude irrelevant ones, and that even where he gave no reasons he could be required by mandamus to consider the complaint lawfully.

Exclusion or restriction of the jurisdiction of the courts

Statutes have purported or appeared to exclude the jurisdiction of the courts by the use of various drafting formulae, though with scant success. The Tribunals and Inquiries Act 1971, s. 14 (replacing the Act of 1958, s. 11) now provides that any provision in an Act *passed before August 1, 1958,* that any order or determination shall not be called in question in any event, or any provision in such an Act which by similar words excludes any of the powers of the High Court, shall not prevent the use of the remedies of certiorari or mandamus. Exceptions are the British Nationality Act 1948, s. 26 (Home Secretary's discretion to grant or refuse an application under the Act), and Acts making special provision for applications to the High Court within a limited time.

It was held by the Court of Appeal in *R.* v. *Medical Appeal Tribunal, ex p. Gilmore*[94] that a formula like " any such order or decision shall be final " does not bar certiorari: it makes the decision final on the facts, but not final on the law. The formula that an order or rules made " shall have effect as if enacted in this Act "

---

[90] [1891] 2 Q.B. 326.

[91] L.R. 7 Q.B. 387. See E. C. S. Wade, " The Courts and the Administrative Process " (1947) 63 L.Q.R. 164.

[92] 21 Q.B.D. 313. And see *R.* v. *Board of Trade, St. Martin's Preserving Co.*, *supra.*

[93] [1968] A.C. 997.

[94] [1957] 1 Q.B. 575 (C.A.). And see *R.* v. *Minister of Transport, ex p. Upminster Services Ltd.* [1934] 1 K.B. 277. *Cf. Ex p. Ringer* (1909) 25 T.L.R. 718 (D.C.), " conclusive evidence that the requirements of this Act have been complied with."

has dicta of the House of Lords both for and against the exclusion of judicial control.[95]

A different kind of provision is that found in some Acts concerning planning and the compulsory acquisition of land, which set a *time limit* (commonly six weeks) in which the validity of the order may be challenged in the High Court, and specifying the permitted grounds of complaint as (a) *ultra vires* or (b) non-compliance with the statutory procedure, and stating that subject to these provisions the order may not be questioned in any legal proceedings. The main purpose of such provision is to limit the time within which an order or decision may be questioned in the courts, so as to ensure that the *title* to land acquired by a public authority for building, etc. should not remain uncertain after a short time. In *Smith* v. *East Elloe Rural District Council*[96] the House of Lords held, by a majority of three to two, that after the six weeks' period a compulsory purchase order could not be challenged even on the ground that it had been procured by bad faith. It was not necessary to decide whether the order could be challenged for bad faith within six weeks. Of the minority who thought the order could be challenged for bad faith after six weeks, Lord Reid thought this was not excluded by the statute and Lord Somervell thought such remedy lay under general principle. The majority decision was much criticised as offending against the principles of natural justice; but although justice may require compensation for loss brought about by fraud, that does not necessarily mean that an order on which title to land is based should be upset.

The whole question was considered by the House of Lords in *Anisminic* v. *Foreign Compensation Commission*.[97] The Foreign

---

95 *Institute of Patent Agents* v. *Lockwood* [1894] A.C. 347, *obiter dicta* that judicial review was excluded; *Minister of Health* v. *R., ex p. Yaffe* [1931] A.C. 494, *obiter dicta* that judicial review was not excluded; see *R.* v. *Minister of Health, ex p. Yaffe* [1930] 2 K.B. 98 (C.A.).

96 [1956] A.C. 736. The plaintiff had previously obtained damages against the council and contractors for trespass, as the continuance of wartime requisition was done in bad faith; *Smith* v. *East Elloe R.D.C.* [1952] *Current Property Law*. In subsequent proceedings by the plaintiff against the clerk and a representative of the Ministry for damages for conspiracy to injure, Diplock J. held that there was no conspiracy, that damages had already been recovered for trespass, and his Lordship was not satisfied that the clerk had in fact acted in bad faith: *Smith* v. *Pyewell, The Times,* April 29, 1959.

97 [1969] 2 A.C. 147. Browne J.'s judgment at first instance, which was upheld by the House of Lords, is reported at [1969] 2 A.C. 223. See H. W. R. Wade, " Constitutional and Administrative Aspect of the *Anisminic* Case " (1969) 85 L.Q.R. 198; B. C. Gould, " Anisminic and Jurisdictional Review " [1970] P.L. 258; D. M. Gordon, " What did the Anisminic Case decide? " (1971) 34 M.L.R. 1; note by S. A. de Smith in [1969] C.L.J. 161.

Cf. Foreign Compensation Act 1969, s. 3: No determination by the Commission may be called in question in any court of law, except (a) case stated on

Compensation Act 1950, s. 4, provided that "the determination by the Commission of any application made to them under this Act shall not be called in question in any court of law "; but the House of Lords (reversing the Court of Appeal) held by four to one that this provision did not prevent the court from making a declaration that the Commission's determination was a nullity. Lord Reid said: " It is one thing to question a determination which does exist: it is quite another thing to say that there is nothing to be questioned. . . . It is a well established principle that a provision ousting the ordinary jurisdiction of the court must be construed strictly. . . . No case has been cited in which any other form of words limiting the jurisdiction of the court has been held to protect a nullity. . . . Undoubtedly such a provision protects every determination which is not a nullity." Cases where the decision of a tribunal may be a nullity are: where it had no jurisdiction to enter into the inquiry; where it gave its decision in bad faith; where it made a decision which it had no power to make; where it failed to comply with the requirements of natural justice; where in good faith it decided the wrong question; and where it failed to take account of something of which it was required to take account, or based its decision on a matter which it ought not to have taken into account. Something much more specific than this Act would be required if it is to be held that Parliament intended to exclude the court's jurisdiction on any of these grounds.

The *East Elloe* case (*supra*) was distinguished in the *Anisminic* case. Lord Reid did not regard the former case (in which he had dissented) as very satisfactory. It is not certain, he said, whether the plaintiff was claiming that the authority which made the order had itself acted in bad faith, in which case the order would be a nullity; or whether she was alleging that the clerk had fraudulently misled the council and the Ministry, in which case the result would be quite different. The *Anisminic* case has been said to upset the *East Elloe* case, but this would put public authorities into a very difficult position. One suggestion is that *Anisminic* should apply only where there is a complete ouster of the court's jurisdiction, and perhaps where an order is *ultra vires* on its face; but that where the ouster is after a time limit, a longer period than six weeks ought to be prescribed.[98] Perhaps a distinction should be drawn in such cases between the quashing of an order and the award of compensation.

question of law to Court of Appeal concerning jurisdiction or interpretation of Order in Council, and (b) proceedings on ground that determination is contrary to natural justice.

[98] H. W. R. Wade, *Administrative Law* (3rd ed.) pp. 151–153.

Suggested reforms in administrative law [99]

It has been suggested both judicially and extra-judicially that the defects of certiorari—notably the attempt to distinguish between "judicial" and "administrative" acts—are such that it is ripe for replacement by the action for a declaration.[1]   Other inconveniences of certiorari are that it must be brought within six months, that no discovery is allowed, and that it cannot be combined with other remedies such as injunction or damages.   On the other hand, certiorari is governed by more precedents than declaration, and the result of an application is therefore more predictable.   Further, the procedural defects of certiorari could easily be removed by statute.[2]

Justice in a recent report recommended the enactment of a Statement of the Principles of Good Administration.[3]   This would include: (a) notice should be given to persons likely to be affected and an opportunity given to be heard; (b) an authority should ascertain all material facts before making decisions; (c) reasoned decisions should be made promptly and notified to persons likely to be affected; (d) prompt and accurate information should be given when reasonably requested.   Their second recommendation is the creation of an Administrative Division of the High Court,[4] to improve the remedies available to the citizen where there is failure to comply with the Principles.   Its jurisdiction would be both original and appellate.   In addition to the power to grant all existing High Court remedies, the Administrative Division would be able to remit a case for reconsideration, to vary or reverse a decision, and to award damages.   Assessors experienced in administrative matters would act where necessary.   A simple originating summons would obviate the need for the plaintiff to specify the remedy sought.

The Law Commission, asked by the Lord Chancellor to review existing remedies with a view to evolving a simpler and more effective procedure, has suggested that an "application for review" by the

---

[99] For a review of the various suggestions, see J. E. Trice, " Administrative Law Reform: A Survey " [1972] J.P.L. 418.

[1] See *e.g.* Sir Alfred Denning, *Freedom under the Law* (1949); *Pyx Granite Co. Ltd.* v. *Ministry of Housing and Local Government* [1958] 1 Q.B. 554 (C.A.) at p. 570; Lord MacDermott, *Protection from Power under English Law* (1957).

[2] H. W. R. Wade, " The Future of Certiorari " [1958] C.L.J. 218; D. M. Gordon, " Certiorari and Declaration as Alternative Remedies " (1959) 75 L.Q.R. 455; Louis L. Jaffe, " Research and Reform in English Administrative Law " [1968] P.L. 119, and comments by J. D. B. Mitchell at p. 201 and J. F. Garner at p. 212.

[3] " Administration under Law," Report by *Justice* (1971); *cf.* H. W. R. Wade, " Crossroads in Administrative Law " [1968] C.L.P. 75, suggesting an Administrative Bill of Rights.

[4] An Administrative Division of the High Court was established in New Zealand in 1968.

High Court should replace the present complex restrictive remedies.[5]
The court would be able to make orders quashing decisions, or en-
joining an administrative authority from acting illegally, or commanding it to act where it was under a duty to do so, or declaring an
administrative act invalid. Such orders would be available against
decisions made by local authorities, government departments, Ministers
and administrative tribunals. The primary object is not to assert
private rights, but to have illegal public acts and orders controlled
by the courts. Such judicial powers might possibly be exercisable
against universities, professional organisations and domestic tribunals,
i.e. organisations exercising a virtual monopoly in an important field
of human activity.

There is no wide support for the view that we should try to graft
on to our legal system an administrative law jurisdiction of the Con
tinental kind, administered by a court corresponding to the *Conseil
d'Etat*.[6]

---

[5] *Remedies in Administrative Law: Law Commission; Published Working Paper
No. 40* (1971). See J. E. Trice, " Administrative Law Reform and Planning Law "
(1972) 36 Conv.(N.S.) 375.

[6] J. D. B. Mitchell argues in favour of the French *droit administratif* as a model:
" The Causes and Consequences of the Absence of a System of Public Law in
the United Kingdom " [1965] P.L. 95; " The Present State of Public Law in the
U.K. " (1966) 15 I.C.L.Q. 133; " The Constitutional Implications of Judicial
Control of the Administration in the U.K." [1967] C.L.J. 46.

CHAPTER 32

CROWN PROCEEDINGS

I. LIABILITY OF THE CROWN

Introduction [1]

Two ancient and fundamental rules of English constitutional law
were abolished by the Crown Proceedings Act 1947. The first, that
proceedings against the Crown for breach of contract or restitution
of property could only be taken after obtaining a *fiat* by the inconvenient procedure of petition of right, was due to the principle that
the King could not be impleaded in his own courts. The second, that
the Crown could not be proceeded against at all in tort, was due to the
same principle coupled with the doctrine that " the King could do no
wrong." No action lay at common law against the Sovereign personally, whether for public or private acts. Also—contrary to the
law of agency and of master and servant—no action lay against the
Sovereign for breach of contract or torts committed by Ministers,
other officers or departments acting as servants or agents of the
Crown. In certain cases, however, a petition of right would lie. The
maxim " the King can do no wrong " meant not only that the King
could not be made liable by action, but also that wrong could not
be imputed to the King, and therefore he could not be said to have
authorised another to commit a wrong. This ruled out the maxim
qui facit per alium facit per se where the Crown was the employer.
As there is no concept of the state in English law, and as government
departments are merely groups of Crown servants, this meant that
the citizen could not claim satisfaction out of public funds for torts
committed by the Crown.

The immunity of the Crown at common law, subject to the limited
and inconvenient procedure by petition of right, became increasingly
serious in modern times owing to the growth of state activity, for
the Crown had become the largest employer, contractor and occupier
of property in the country. The grievance that it was necessary to
apply to the Home Secretary for a *fiat* before bringing a petition of
right was more a matter of form than of substance, for in practice
the Attorney-General always recommended that the *fiat* should be

---

[1] Gleeson E. Robinson, *Public Authorities and Legal Liability* (1925); G. S. Robert-
son, *Civil Proceedings by and against the Crown* (1908). For the history, see
Holdsworth, *History of English Law*, Vol. IX, pp. 7–45; " The History of
Remedies against the Crown " (1922) 38 L.Q.R. 141, 280.

granted where there was any sort of prima facie case against the Crown. On the other hand, the personal liability incurred by Crown servants for torts committed in their official capacity often failed to satisfy injured parties, who might not even know which individual was responsible; while the practice whereby the Treasury, in what it considered appropriate cases, paid ex gratia compensation where Crown servants were unsuccessful defendants was illogical, arbitrary and probably unlawful.

Matters came to a head at the end of the last war in two cases of persons injured by the condition of premises occupied by the Crown. In *Adams* v. *Naylor* [2] two boys were injured by a minefield which was negligently marked and fenced. An action was brought against an officer of the Royal Engineers, whose name had been supplied by the War Department as the responsible officer. It was not known who was personally responsible for the state of affairs at the time of the accident, and the House of Lords criticised *obiter* [3] the practice of government departments putting up " nominated " or " nominal " defendants as whipping-boys. Soon afterwards the Court of Appeal in *Royster* v. *Cavey* [4] felt constrained to follow the considered dicta of the House of Lords, where an employee in a Ministry of Supply ordnance factory, who had received personal injuries while so employed, wished to bring an action for negligence at common law and for breach of statutory duty under the Factories Act 1937. The plaintiff was supplied by the Treasury Solicitor with the name of the superintendent of the factory, but the latter had no connection with the factory at the time of the accident. The court held that it had no jurisdiction to try an action against him, as he was neither the occupier of the factory nor the plaintiff's employer. [5]

A comprehensive Crown Proceedings Bill [6] was then introduced by the Lord Chancellor, Viscount Jowitt. The Bill was privately examined by an informal committee of Law Lords and others, presided over by Viscount Simon, while the Lord Chancellor consulted all the other available judges. Lord Jowitt could therefore fairly claim that the Bill received " the unanimous approval of the entire Bench of Judges."

[2] [1946] A.C. 543.
[3] The case was decided on the Personal Injuries (Emergency Provisions) Act 1939.
[4] [1947] 1 K.B. 204.
[5] *Lane* v. *Cotton* (1701) 1 Ld.Raym. 646.
[6] Based partly on a draft Bill of 1927 (Cmd. 2842) prepared by a committee under two earlier Lord Chancellors, Birkenhead and Haldane. The delay was due largely to the misgivings of the Service Departments and the Post Office (then a government department).

Crown Proceedings Act 1947 [7]

The main objects of the Act were, as far as practicable, to make the Crown liable in tort in the same way as a private person, and to reform the rules of procedure governing civil litigation by and against the Crown, especially by allowing an action without a *fiat* where petition of right previously lay. The Act adopts the Anglo-American principle of treating the state (or " the Crown ") for the purpose of litigation as nearly as possible in the same way as a private citizen, instead of borrowing the Continental idea of a separate system of administrative law. The effect is to bring English constitutional law nearer in one way to the conception of " the rule of law " than it was when Dicey wrote.

Part V applies the Act with appropriate modifications to Scotland,[8] and section 53 provided for the extension of the Act by Order in Council to Northern Ireland with any necessary modifications. The Act is only concerned with the liability of the Crown in respect of the government in the United Kingdom (s. 40 (2)).

Right to sue the Crown in contract, etc.

" Section 1. *Where any person has a claim against the Crown after the commencement of this Act, and, if this Act had not been passed, the claim might have been enforced, subject to the grant of His Majesty's fiat, by petition of right, or might have been enforced by a proceeding provided by any statutory provision repealed by this Act, then, subject to the provisions of this Act, the claim may be enforced as of right, and without the fiat of His Majesty, by proceedings taken against the Crown for that purpose in accordance with the provisions of this Act.*"

This section gives the individual a right to sue the Crown without any *fiat* in cases where, if the Act had not been passed, he could (i) bring a petition of right or (ii) take any proceedings under special statutory provisions repealed by the Act, *e.g.* War Department Stores

---

[7] R. McM. Bell, *Crown Proceedings* (1948); J. R. Bickford Smith, *The Crown Proceedings Act, 1947* (1948); Glanville L. Williams, *Crown Proceedings* (1948); Sir Carleton Allen, *Law and Orders* (3rd ed. 1965) Chap. 10; H. Street, " Crown Proceedings Act, 1947 " (1948) 11 M.L.R. 129–142; Sir Thomas Barnes, " The Crown Proceedings Act, 1947 " (1948) 26 Can.Bar Rev. 387; G. H. Treitel, " Crown Proceedings: Some Recent Developments " [1957] P.L. 321.
   For comparative surveys, see H. Street, *Governmental Liability* (1953); B. Schwartz and H. W. R. Wade, *Legal Control of Government* (1972); L. Neville Brown and J. F. Garner, *French Administrative Law* (2nd ed. 1973); P. W. Hogg, *Liability of the Crown in Australia, New Zealand and the United Kingdom* (1971).
[8] J. R. Bickford Smith, *The Crown Proceedings Act, 1947* (1948) pp. 49–58 (by K. W. B. Middleton); Fraser, *Outline of Constitutional Law* (2nd ed.) Chap. 11; J. D. B. Mitchell, Constitutional Law (2nd ed. 1968) Chap. 17.

Act 1867. Proceedings by way of petition of right were abolished by section 13.

Most of the actions in contract brought against the Crown since the Act came into force have been settled out of court. Disputes over building contracts with the government usually go to arbitration.

Section 1 did not create a new cause of action, and so the limitations on the scope of the former petition of right continue to apply to this right of action.

Scope of petition of right [9]

The theory of the petition of right was that as the King was the fountain of justice, he would cause justice to be done as soon as the matter was brought to his notice. Petition of right lay first for the recovery of land of which the Crown had wrongly taken or retained possession, and for the recovery of chattels real and probably chattels personal. It also apparently lay for certain cases of damage caused by undue user of Crown property, such as the wrongful assertion of an easement causing damage.[10] When the law of contract developed, a petition of right came to be granted for breach of contract, at first for debt or liquidated damages (*e.g.* on a contract for goods supplied), and later for unliquidated damages.[11] In *Thomas* v. *The Queen* (1875) [12] it was held that Thomas, an engineer, was entitled to bring a petition of right claiming a reward and his expenses in respect of an artillery invention in accordance with an agreement with the Secretary of State for War. The remedy was also available to recover liquidated or unliquidated sums due under a statute where no other remedy was provided (*Att.-Gen.* v. *De Keyser's Royal Hotel Ltd.*[13]) and was probably available in quasi-contract.[14]

There were four limitations or exceptions to the availability of a petition of right:

(i) Owing to the prerogative immunity in tort, a petition of right did not lie for a pure tort, that is, a tort unconnected with the wrongful taking of property, such as negligence or trespass. Thus in *Viscount Canterbury* v. *Att.-Gen.* (1843) [15] an ex-Speaker failed in

---

[9] Clode, *Petition of Right* (1887); Holdsworth, *History of English Law*, Vol. IX, 7–45.

[10] *Tobin* v. *The Queen* (1864) 16 C.B.(N.S.) 310, *per* Erle C.J. at pp. 363–365.

[11] *The Bankers' Case* (1700) 14 St.Tr. 1.

[12] L.R. 10 Q.B. 31.

[13] [1920] A.C. 508 (H.L.). And see *Commercial and Estates Co. of Egypt* v. *Board of Trade* [1925] 1 K.B. 271 (angary; compensation payable by international law).

[14] *Cf. Brocklebank Ltd.* v. *R.* [1925] 1 K.B. 52. Since the Crown Proceedings Act, if not before, the question of waiver of tort is irrelevant. See further, Street, *Governmental Liability*, pp. 125–127; A. W. Mewett, "The Quasi-Contractual Liability of Governments" (1959–60) 13 U.T.L.J. 56.

[15] 1 Phillips 306; (1843) 12 L.J.Ch. 281.

his claim for compensation from the Crown for damage done to his furniture by the negligence of certain Crown servants who, by burning an excessive quantity of old Exchequer tallies, caused a fire which destroyed the Houses of Parliament in 1834. Similarly, in *Tobin* v. *The Queen* (1864) [16] the owners of a ship trading in palm oil off the coast of Africa failed in their claim for compensation from the Crown for the destruction of the ship and cargo by the captain of H.M.S. *Espoir*, who had falsely assumed that she was engaged in the slave trade which he had statutory authority to suppress. The same rule would apply to false imprisonment, conversion and libel.

(ii) Contracts of service with members of the armed forces are controlled by the prerogative.[17] The position of civilian officers and civil servants is in some respects not free from doubt.[18]

(iii) Contracts that fetter future executive action. During the First World War the Swedish (neutral) owners of *S. S. Amphitrite* were induced to send the ship to a British port by a letter from the British Legation at Stockholm stating that she would be released if she proceeded to the United Kingdom with a cargo of approved goods. The ship did so but was nevertheless refused a clearance, and the owners brought a petition of right for damages for breach of contract: *Rederiaktiebolaget Amphitrite* v. *The King*.[19] Rowlatt J. gave judgment for the Crown, on the ground that there was no enforceable contract. " It is not competent for the Government," said his Lordship, " by enforceable contract to fetter its future executive action, which must necessarily be determined by the needs of the community when the question arises. It cannot by contract hamper its freedom of action in matters which concern the welfare of the State." The judgment was an unconsidered one and no authorities were cited, but it is generally taken as an authority for the principle stated above. On the facts of the case it would have been sufficient to hold that the letter from the British Legation was merely an expression of present intention of what the government would do, and that the Crown did not intend to enter into contractual relations.[20] Rowlatt J. distinguished " commercial " contracts, on which the Crown can be

---

[16] C.B.(N.S.) 310; *supra*. The judgment of Erle C.J. suggests that an action would have lain against the captain.

[17] *Ante*, Chap. 17. And see Z. Cowen, " The Armed Forces of the Crown " (1950) 66 L.Q.R. 478.

[18] *Ante*, Chap. 16.

[19] [1921] 3 K.B. 500.

[20] This reasoning was approved by Denning J. in *Robertson* v. *Minister of Pensions* [1949] 1 K.B. 227, 231. And see *Australian Woollen Mills Ltd.* v. *Commonwealth of Australia* [1956] 1 W.L.R. 11; [1955] 3 All E.R. 711 (P.C.).

made liable. Otherwise the limits of the supposed rule are uncertain,[21] and in fact no subsequent English decision has been based on it.[22] The common law makes no provision for compensation in such cases.

(iv) *Contracts dependent on grant from Parliament.* In *Churchward* v. *R.* (1865) [23] Churchward contracted with the Admiralty Commissioners to maintain a mail service between Dover and the Continent for eleven years, expressly in consideration of an annual sum to be provided by Parliament. The Admiralty terminated the contract in the fourth year, and the Appropriation Act of that year provided that no part of the sum appropriated towards the post office packet service should be paid to Churchward after a certain date. Churchward naturally failed in his petition of right for breach of contract, but dicta in that case have led to the view that the provision of funds by Parliament is an implied precedent condition for the liability of the Crown on its contracts, and even for the validity of Crown contracts.[24] There is no good reason, however, why funds should be antecedently or specifically appropriated by Parliament in order that the Crown may make contracts through responsible Crown servants in the course of their official duties. Enforceability, on the other hand, is a different matter from validity, and the other party cannot obtain satisfaction from the Crown if parliamentary funds are not available when the time arrives for payment.[25]

The Petitions of Right Act 1860 provided a simpler procedure than that which existed at common law, following complaints by Army contractors during the Crimean War about the difficulty of recovering debts from the War Department.

A Crown servant is not personally liable at common law for the breach of a contract entered into by him in his official capacity. Thus

---

21 See Holdsworth in (1929) 45 L.Q.R. 166 for a strong criticism of the rule. According to one view, the *Amphitrite* case, if kept within due limits, supports the general principle of "governmental effectiveness": J. D. B. Mitchell, *The Contracts of Public Authorities*, pp. 27, 52. *Cf.* Street, *op. cit.* p. 98.

22 The *Amphitrite* case was followed by the High Court of Southern Rhodesia in *Waterfalls Town Management Board* v. *Minister of Housing* [1956] Rhod. and Ny. L.R. 691. It was not referred to in *Crown Land Commissioners* v. *Page* [1960] 2 Q.B. 274, where it was held that the Crown as lessor was not prevented by implied covenant for quiet enjoyment from exercising a statutory power to requisition from one of its tenants.

23 L.R. 1 Q.B. 173; 6 B. & S. 807.

24 (1865) L.R. 1 Q.B. 173, 209, *per* Shee J.; *Cf. per* Cockburn C.J. at pp. 200–201.

25 *Commercial Cable Co.* v. *Government of Newfoundland* [1916] 2 A.C. 610, 617 (P.C.) *per* Viscount Haldane; *Mackay* v. *Att.-Gen. for British Columbia* [1922] 1 A.C. 457, 461, *per* Viscount Haldane; *Commonwealth of Australia* v. *Kidman* (1926) 32 A.L.R. 1, 2–3 (P.C.) *per* Viscount Haldane; *New South Wales* v. *Bardolph* (1934) 52 C.L.R. 455, 474, *per* Evatt J. *Cf. Att.-Gen.* v. *Great Southern and Western Ry. of Ireland* [1925] A.C. 754, 773 779 (H.L.). See further, Colin Turpin, *Government Contracts* (1972).

in *Macbeath* v. *Haldimand* (1786) [26] the King's Bench held General Haldimand, Governor of Quebec, not liable for stores ordered by him from Macbeath for the Fort of Michilimakinac. The plaintiff knew that the goods were for government use, and that the defendant was not contracting personally. Thus stated, it is merely an application of the general law of agency. It is now clear that a petition of right would have lain before 1948 in the circumstances of this case.[27]

There were some statutory exceptions. Parliament occasionally used language referring to the bringing of actions by or against a government department or Minister in his official capacity, with or without incorporating that department or Minister. The effect of such language and the extent (if any) of liability to be sued depended on the interpretation of the words used in the particular statute. The matter was reviewed by the Court of Appeal in *Minister of Supply* v. *British Thomson-Houston Co.*,[28] where it was held that the War Department Stores Act 1867 rendered the Minister of Supply liable to be sued on official contracts concerning military stores. The Ministry of Transport Act 1919 expressly made the Minister officially liable in tort as well as contract.

Liability of the Crown in tort

" Section 2 (1). *Subject to the provisions of this Act, the Crown shall be subject to all those liabilities in tort to which, if it were a private person of full age and capacity, it would be subject*:

    (a) *in respect of torts committed by its servants or agents;*

    (b) *in respect of any breach of those duties which a person owes to his servants or agents at common law by reason of being their employer; and*

    (c) *in respect of any breach of the duties attaching at common law to the ownership, occupation, possession or control of property . . .*"

This is the most important section, which provided the *raison d'être* of the Act. The marginal note reads: " Liability of the Crown in tort," but the Act does not make the Crown liable generally in tort: subsection (1) makes the Crown liable in three classes of case:

    (a) *Vicarious liability to third parties for torts*, such as negligence or trespass committed by servants in the course of their employment, and for the authorised or ratified torts of independent contractors.

---

[26] 1 T.R. 172.
[27] *Thomas* v. *R.* (1875) L.R. 10 Q.B. 31. Few petitions of right on contracts were brought from the time of the Restoration, when the Sovereign came to rely almost entirely on parliamentary grants to finance the government of the country, until the Crimean War.
[28] [1943] K.B. 478.

At common law actions in tort could not be brought against government departments, for they are not legal entities but consist of a number of individual Crown servants. Nor could the injured party sue the head of the department or other superior officer of the Crown servant who committed the tort, because they are fellow servants of the Crown and do not stand to each other in the relation of master and servant [29]; unless the superior officer actually ordered or directed the commission of the tort, in which case it would also be his act.[30] The general rule was therefore that the action had to be brought against the actual wrongdoer or wrongdoers, and it had to be brought against them personally and not as servants or agents of the Crown or of the department, nor as a department. Thus in *Raleigh* v. *Goschen* [31] an action for trespass to land brought against Goschen (First Lord of the Admiralty), the Lords Commissioners of the Admiralty and the Director-General of Naval Works was dismissed on the ground that it should have been brought against the engineer employed by the Admiralty and/or the two marines who actually committed the trespass with him, and/or against such (if any) of the defendants personally as had actually ordered or directed the trespass.

A proviso to section 2 (1) adds that the Crown shall not be liable unless, apart from the Act, an action in tort would have lain against the servant or agent. This may be intended to preserve such defences as act of state or acting under prerogative or statutory powers (which in any case is provided for by section 11); but it has the effect of exempting the Crown in those exceptional cases where an ordinary employer is liable even though the servant who actually committed the tort cannot for some reason be sued.[32]

In *Dorset Yacht Co. Ltd.* v. *Home Office*,[33] where the plaintiff's yacht was damaged by Borstal trainees who had escaped from a nearby camp where they were under the control of Borstal officers, the House of Lords held as a preliminary issue that the Home Office owed a duty of care to the plaintiffs capable of giving rise to liability in damages if negligence could be proved. Lord Denning M.R. in the Court of Appeal said that the Crown would be similarly liable if it

---

[29] *Bainbridge* v. *Postmaster-General* [1906] 1 K.B. 178.
[30] *Lane* v. *Cotton* (1701) Ld.Raym. 646.
[31] [1898] 1 Ch. 73; the Admiralty wanted the land at Dartmouth in order to build a naval college. See also *Madrazo* v. *Willes* (1820) 3 B. & Ald. 353, and *Walker* v. *Baird* [1892] A.C. 491 (naval captains liable for wrongful damage to property inflicted in the supposed course of duty).
[32] *e.g. Smith* v. *Moss* [1940] 1 K.B. 424. And see *Twine* v. *Bean's Express Ltd.* [1946] 1 All E.R. 202, 204.
[33] [1970] A.C. 1004. In *Greenwell* v. *Prison Commissioners* (1951) 101 L.J. 486 the plaintiffs obtained damages in a county court for damage to their vehicle caused by boys who had escaped from an " open " Borstal. See C. J. Hamson, " Escaping Borstal Boys and the Immunity of Office " (1969) 27 C.L.J. 273.

negligently permitted prisoners to escape and they commit fore-seeable damage.[34]

(b) *Breach of common law duties owed by an employer to his employees, viz.* to supply proper plant, to provide a safe system of working and to select fit and competent fellow-servants.

(c) *Common law liability attaching to the ownership, occupation, possession or control of property.* This would include liability for nuisance; the rule in *Rylands* v. *Fletcher* (1866) [35]; liability for dangerous chattels, etc. The right to sue under section 2 is implied, for *ubi jus ibi remedium.*[36]

Section 2 (2) provides that, in those cases where the Crown is bound by *statutory duties* which are also binding on persons other than the Crown and its officers, the Crown shall be liable in tort for breach of such statutory duties if private persons are so liable.[37] In order to make the Crown liable under this subsection it must be shown, first, that the Crown is *bound* by the statute (*e.g.* Factories Act 1961; Occupiers' Liability Act 1957),[38] the presumption against this [39] being preserved by section 40 (2); secondly, that other persons (including local authorities or public corporations) are also bound by the statute; and thirdly, that other persons can be made liable in tort for such breach. Thus the Ministry of Transport owes a duty to take reasonable care when siting large road signs.[40] The liability of the Crown as a highway authority (*viz.* the Minister in relation to certain roads) is limited to that of a local authority (s. 40 (2)), but this has been greatly extended by the Highways (Miscellaneous Provisions) Act 1961.[41]

Where functions are conferred by law directly on an officer of the Crown, he is regarded for the purpose of this section as if he were acting as an agent under instructions from the Crown (subs. (3)). The Crown has the benefit of any statute regulating or limiting the liability of a government department or Crown officer (subs. (4)).

Subsection 5 excludes proceedings against the Crown for acts done by any person " while discharging or purporting to discharge any responsibilities of a judicial nature vested in him, or any responsibilities which he has in connection with the execution of judicial

---

[34] See *Greenwell* v. *Prison Commissioners, supra; cf. Ellis* v. *Home Office* [1953] 2 Q.B. 135 (C.A.).

[35] L.R. 1 Ex. 265; (1868) L.R. 3 H.L. 330.

[36] *Ashby* v. *White* (1703) 1 Smith L.C. (13th ed.) 251; 2 Ld.Raym. 320, 938.

[37] *Cf. Royster* v. *Cavey* [1947] K.B. 204; *Cooper* v. *Hawkins* [1904] 2 K.B. 164.

[38] *Pisicani* v. *Post Office, The Times,* May 11, 1967 (C.A.).

[39] *Ante,* p. 240.

[40] *Levine* v. *Morris* [1970] 1 W.L.R. 71 (C.A.).

[41] *Ante,* p. 530.

process." [42] Thus if judges, magistrates or constables exceed the limits of their immunity, they do not—even if they are regarded as Crown servants or agents [43]—render the Crown liable for torts committed while discharging or purporting to discharge their judicial functions.

Officers (i.e. Ministers and other servants: s. 38 (2)) who may render the Crown liable under section 2 are limited to those appointed directly or indirectly by the Crown and paid wholly out of the Consolidated Fund or moneys provided by Parliament, or holding an office which would normally be so paid (subs. (6)). This provision, which is narrower than the vague common law definition of a Crown servant, [44] covers unpaid temporary civil servants, but not police or other public officers forming part of the government of the country who are appointed or paid by local or other public authorities. [45]

Many actions against the Crown have been commenced in the High Court and county court, but most have been settled. A number of writs have been in running-down cases, involving the negligence of drivers of government-owned vehicles. [46]

Where the Crown is liable under Part I of the Act, section 4 applies to the Crown the law relating to indemnity and contribution between tortfeasors and contributory negligence. [47] It is presumed that the Crown is bound by certain statutes reforming the law of tort, whether passed before or after the Crown Proceedings Act, even though the intention to bind the Crown does not appear either in the Crown Proceedings Act or expressly or by necessary implication in such statutes themselves. Section 10 of the Crown Proceedings Act (infra) seems to imply that the Fatal Accidents Act 1846 (compensation for dependants of deceased) and the Law Reform (Miscellaneous Provisions) Act 1934, s. 1 (survival of causes of action on death) apply to the Crown. [48] But nothing is said about the Crown, for in-

---

[42] See A. Rubinstein, " Liability in Tort of Judicial Officers " (1963) 15 U.T.L.J. 317.

[43] Cf. Holdsworth, " The Constitutional Position of the Judges " (1932) 48 L.Q.R. 25–26; Lewis v. Cattle [1938] 2 K.B. 454 (police constable).

[44] Bank voor Handel en Scheepvaart N.V. v. Administrator of Hungarian Property [1954] A.C. 584 (H.L.).

[45] See, e.g. Police Act 1964 (police constable); Stanbury v. Exeter Corporation [1905] 2 K.B. 838 (agricultural inspector); Tamlin v. Hannaford [1950] 1 K.B. 18 (British Transport Commission).

[46] In Browning v. War Office [1963] 1 Q.B. 750 (C.A.), where a member of the United States Air Force was injured through the negligence of a driver of a British army lorry, the question in issue was the measure of damages.

[47] In particular, the Law Reform (Married Women and Tortfeasors) Act 1935 and the Law Reform (Contributory Negligence) Act 1945.

[48] In Levine v. Morris [1970] 1 W.L.R. 71 (C.A.) the personal representatives of a man killed in a motor accident successfully sued the Ministry of Transport as well as a private driver for negligence.

stance, in the Defamation Act 1952, which Act put the defendant in a better position than he was at common law.[49]

Section 3 makes the Crown liable if it authorises a servant or agent to infringe a patent, trademark or design or copyright.[50] The statutory right of the Crown is preserved to use patents on paying compensation assessed by the Treasury,[51] as are the rights of the Crown under the Atomic Energy Act 1946.

There are certain matters where the analogy between the Crown and the subject breaks down, for in these spheres the functions of the Crown involve responsibility of a kind which no subject undertakes. Examples are the defence of the realm and the maintenance of the armed forces.[52]

Provisions relating to the armed forces

Section 10 provides that where a member of the armed forces,[53] while he is on duty as such [54] or is on any land, premises, ship, aircraft or vehicle used for the purposes of the armed forces, is killed or suffers personal injury at the hands of another member of the armed forces acting as such, or as a consequence of the nature or condition of premises, vehicle, equipment, etc. used for the purposes of those forces, in circumstances that entitle to a pension, no action in tort shall lie against either the Crown or that other member of the armed forces or an officer of the Crown. This section refers only to death or personal injury which the Minister certifies to be pensionable. In such cases any common law action against the fellow member of the armed forces [55] is taken away, provided that the act was connected with the execution of his service duties, and was not done, for instance, out of private revenge. In *Adams* v. *War Office*,[56] A, a class Z reservist, was killed while on duty by the bursting of a shell fired by other members of the armed forces on duty. The Minister certified that A's death was attributable to service for the

---

[49] See G. H. Treitel, " Crown Proceedings: Some Recent Developments " [1957] P.L. 321, 322–326.

[50] The infringement of a patent or copyright is not properly classified as a tort, but it was held in *Feather* v. *Reg.* (1865) 6 B. & S. 257 that a petition of right was not appropriate.

[51] Since the Patent Act 1907 patents are effective against the Crown, but the Crown has a right to use patents on paying compensation. See *Pfizer Corporation* v. *Ministry of Health* [1965] A.C. 512 (H.L.), use of patented drugs by hospital under National Health Service.

[52] Also formerly the Post Office, *ante,* Chap. 27.

[53] Including pensionable members of any organisation established under the control of the Admiralty, the Army Council or the Air Council; s. 38 (5).

[54] Including civil defence duty: Civil Defence (Armed Forces) Act 1954.

[55] One soldier could sue another at common law for wrongful injury done to him when both were on duty: *Weaver* v. *Ward* (1616) Hob. 134.

[56] [1955] 1 W.L.R. 1116; [1955] 3 All E.R. 245.

purposes of entitlement to an award, but later decided that no award should be made as A's father did not satisfy the conditions of the royal warrant under which parents may claim a pension. A's father then claimed damages against the War Office for negligence, arguing that the Minister's certificate was void and therefore the exemption of the Crown under section 10 did not apply; but it was held that as the Minister's certificate had been issued, the Crown was exempt under section 10 even if no award was made.

As regards the Crown, the doctrine of common employment—which has been abolished for civilians [57]—is applied in an extended form to members of the armed forces. The section answers the question (raised by Lord Jowitt, not Tennyson) whether a trooper whose leg was shattered by a cannonball in the charge of the Light Brigade could recover damages on the ground that Raglan had blundered.

The Admiralty or a Secretary of State, " if satisfied " as to the facts, may issue a conclusive certificate as to whether a soldier, etc. was on duty, and whether the premises, etc. were being used for the purposes of the armed forces.

Acts done under prerogative or statutory powers

Section 11 states that nothing in the above provisions shall extinguish or abridge the prerogative or statutory powers of the Crown: in particular, the powers exercisable by the Crown, whether in peace or war, for the defence of the realm or the training or maintenance of the armed forces. Among prerogative powers not mentioned are those relating to the treatment of aliens, the employment of Crown servants and the principle of the *Amphitrite* case.[58] Statutory powers would include the billeting of soldiers.

The Admiralty or a Secretary of State, " if satisfied " as to the facts, may issue a conclusive certificate that the act was necessarily done in the exercise of the prerogative, for example that it was necessary for the sake of practice to fire guns that have broken windows or kept people awake at night. It remains the function of the court to decide whether, and to what extent, the alleged prerogative exists.[59] This section is of fundamental importance for the word " prerogative " has a very wide range.

No such certificate may be made in the case of statutory powers, and indeed their express preservation was not necessary.

[57] Law Reform (Personal Injuries) Act 1948.
[58] *Rederiaktiebolaget Amphitrite* v. *The King* [1921] 3 K.B. 500; *ante*, p. 552.
[59] *Case of Monopolies* (1602) 11 Co.Rep. 84b; *Case of Proclamations* (1610) 12 Co.Rep. 74; *Att.-Gen.* v. *De Keyser's Royal Hotel Ltd.* [1920] A.C. 506 (H.L.); *Burmah Oil Co.* v. *Lord Advocate* [1965] A.C. 75 (H.L.).

The Queen in her private capacity

The Act does not apply to proceedings by or against, nor does it authorise proceedings in tort to be brought against, the Queen in her private capacity (s. 40 (1)), or in right of the Duchy of Lancaster or Cornwall (s. 38 (3)). This preserves the Queen's personal immunity in tort; but it is uncertain whether for breach of contract (*e.g.* sale of groceries to Buckingham Palace) or wrongful detention of property by the Queen personally the subject can still proceed under the Petitions of Right Act 1860, or whether he is thrown back on the ancient common law petition of right.[60] There are in fact no reported instances of petitions of right against a Sovereign in his private capacity, but the doubt as to procedure is inconvenient as Her Majesty might legitimately wish to deny liability or dispute the amount.

II. CIVIL PROCEEDINGS BY AND AGAINST THE CROWN [61]

Jurisdiction and procedure

The Crown Proceedings Act 1947 provides that the civil proceedings [62] by and against the Crown which are allowed by Part I of the Act shall be heard in the High Court (s. 13) or the county court (s. 15) as in actions between subjects and in accordance with rules of court, and similar principles apply to appeals (s. 22).

The Treasury is required to publish a list of authorised government departments, and proceedings are to be instituted by or against the appropriate department, or—if there is, or appears to be, no appropriate department—the Attorney-General (s. 17). It will be noticed that proceedings under the Act are not taken by or against either the Queen or the ministerial head of the department.

No injunction, order for specific performance or for the recovery of land or delivery of property is to be issued against the Crown; but the court may make an order declaratory of the rights of the parties or declaring that the plaintiff is entitled to property or possession

---

[60] See *post*, p. 562.

[61] R. M. Bell, *Crown Proceedings* (1948); J. R. Bickford Smith, *The Crown Proceedings Act 1947* (1948); Glanville L. Williams, *Crown Proceedings* (1948); Carleton Allen, *Law and Orders* (3rd ed.) Chap. 10; S. A. de Smith, *Judicial Review of Administrative Action* (2nd ed. 1968); H. Street, *Governmental Liability* (1953); B. Schwartz and H. W. R. Wade Q.C., *Legal Control of Government* (1972). The procedure in Scotland is governed by Part V of the Crown Proceedings Act; see J. D. B. Mitchell, *Constitutional Law* (2nd ed. 1968) Chap. 17; Bickford Smith, *op. cit.* pp. 53–58, 100–106 (by J. W. B. Middleton); Fraser, *Outline of Constitutional Law* (2nd ed.) pp. 157–169.

[62] The Act does not apply to criminal or Prize proceedings; nor does it affect proceedings on the Crown side of the Queen's Bench Division, *e.g.* habeas corpus, certiorari, prohibition and mandamus (s. 38 (2)).

(s. 21). Thus in *Lee* v. *Department of Education and Science* (1967) [63] a declaration was granted that the period allowed by the Minister for the making of representations against his proposal to alter the articles of government of a grammar school was unreasonably short. The remedies provided by the Act may be additional to an order of mandamus (s. 40 (5)).

An action may be brought against the Attorney-General or (since the Crown Proceedings Act) against the appropriate authorised department, asking the court to declare what the law is on a given point where the Crown or servants of the Crown threaten to do something which is thought to be illegal. This remedy against the Crown originated in the Court of Exchequer.[64] In *Dyson* v. *Att.-Gen.*[65] the Court of Appeal held that this was a proper procedure where the plaintiff contended that a threat by the Inland Revenue Commissioners to impose a pecuniary penalty for neglecting to make certain returns within a specified time was illegal and *ultra vires* the Finance Act 1910. The action cannot be brought where a petition of right was formerly appropriate, *e.g.* for a money claim against the Treasury.[66]

Certain existing procedures which were already working satisfactorily were retained, *e.g.* relator actions, and proceedings by or against the Public Trustee, Charity Commissioners and Registrar of the Land Registry (s. 23). Proceedings against the Crown by petition of right and *monstrans de droit* were abolished, and the Petitions of Right Act 1860 was wholly repealed.[67]

Statutes relating to the limitation of actions now generally bind the Crown.[68]

---

[63] 66 L.G.R. 211. *Cf. International General Electric Co. of New York* v. *Customs and Excise Commissioners* [1962] Ch. 784; no jurisdiction to grant an interlocutory declaration against the Crown in cases where an interlocutory injunction might be granted against a private individual.

[64] *Pawlett* v. *Att.-Gen.* (1668) Hardr. 465.

[65] [1911] 1 K.B. 410. See also *Hodge* v. *Att.-Gen.* (1839) 3 Y. & Co.Ex. 342; *Esquimalt and Nanaimo Ry.* v *Wilson* [1920] A.C. 358 (P.C.).

[66] *Bombay and Persia Steam Navigation Co.* v. *Maclay* [1920] 3 K.B. 402, 408. Nor can the court make an interim (interlocutory) declaration against the Crown in such cases: *Underhill* v. *Ministry of Food* [1950] 1 All E.R. 591.

[67] *Cf. Franklin* v. *Att.-Gen.* [1973] 2 W.L.R. 225: Rhodesian government stock.

The following proceedings by the Crown were also abolished: Latin and English informations; writs of *capias ad respondendum, subpoena ad respondendum*, and appraisement; writs of *scire facias*; writs of extent and of *diem clausit extremum*; and writs of summons under Part V of the Crown Suits Act 1865.

[68] Law Reform (Limitations of Actions, etc.) Act 1954, s. 5; Limitation Act 1963, s. 5. But special periods apply to H.M. ships: Maritime Conventions Act 1911.

Proceedings against the Sovereign in her private capacity

The Petitions of Right Act 1860 contemplated that petitions of right could be brought against the Sovereign in her private capacity, for section 14 distinguished these from petitions relating to any public matter. In the case of public matters the Treasury were authorised to pay out of moneys legally applicable thereto or voted by Parliament for that purpose, while in the case of private matters the amount to which the suppliant was entitled was to be found out of such moneys as Her Majesty should be graciously pleased to direct. At first sight section 39 (1) and the Second Schedule to the Crown Proceedings Act appear to repeal the Petitions of Right Act completely; and as section 40 (1) of the Crown Proceedings Act provides that " nothing in this Act shall apply to proceedings by or against, or authorise proceedings in tort to be brought against, His Majesty in His private capacity," it would seem that a citizen in proceeding against the Queen in her private capacity (*e.g.* for groceries supplied to her at Buckingham Palace), is thrown back on the old common law procedure by petition of right—for it cannot be contemplated that the Act intended to render the subject altogether remediless in such cases. On the other hand, the saving clause in section 40 (1) above and the expression " subject to the provisions of this Act " in sections 1 and 13 could be held to mean that neither the abolition of petitions of right nor the repeal of the Petitions of Right Act applies to proceedings against Her Majesty in her private capacity. The latter is probably the better interpretation, although the draftsman has gone a clumsy way about it.

Judgments and execution

The Crown is put in the same position as subjects with regard to interest on debts, damages and costs (s. 24). The Act requires the appropriate department to pay any damages and costs certified in the order of the court; but no execution can be levied against the Crown,[69] and no person is individually liable under any order for payment by the Crown (s. 25).[70] On the other hand, the Crown relinquished its former prerogative modes of execution; and it lost its special rights to imprison for debt, except in two cases where the person would already have had the money, *viz.* failure to pay death duties or purchase tax (s. 26). The procedure for enforcing payment of fines, *e.g.* for smuggling, is retained.

[69] *Wick and Dennis' Case* (1589) 1 Leo. 190.
[70] It is still possible, however, to sue a Crown servant personally for damages in a case like *Raleigh* v. *Goschen* [1898] 1 Ch. 73 (*ante,* p. 555) although there does not seem to be much point in doing so.

Discovery and interrogatories

The Crown Proceedings Act allowed the court for the first time to require the Crown, *in civil proceedings to which the Crown is a party,* to make discovery of documents and to answer interrogatories (s. 28 (1)).[71] Discovery is routine practice in most civil actions. It consists of the disclosure of facts or documents in the form of sworn answers by one party to questions put by the other party, after approval by the court, as to facts or as to documents relating to the action which are or have been in his possession or power. Interrogatories require a court order, which is rather sparingly granted. They consist of written questions put by one party to the other, after approval by the court, on matters material to the action.

"Crown Privilege" [72]

The proviso to section 28 (1) preserves the rule—*applying also to actions to which the Crown is not a party,* and covering the trial as well as interlocutory proceedings—which authorises or requires the withholding of any document or the refusal to answer any question on the ground that the disclosure of the document or the answering of the question would be *injurious to the public interest.* The objection to such disclosure or answer is usually made by the head of the department concerned.

Subsection (2) goes further by providing that any rules of court made for the purpose of section 28 shall secure that the *existence* of a document will not be disclosed if, in the opinion of a Minister of the Crown, it would be injurious to the public interest [73] to disclose the existence thereof. This exception was necessary because the general rules of court require that the documents which the party

---

[71] And see Administration of Justice Act 1970, s. 35, applying Part III of the Act (Discovery and Related Procedures) to the Crown, including inspection of property before certain proceedings.

[72] See H. G. Hanbury, " Equality and Privilege in English Law " (1952) 68 L.Q.R. 173; P. Ingress Bell, " Crown Privilege " [1957] P.L. 28; J. E. S. Simon, " Evidence Excluded by Considerations of State Interest " [1955] C.L.J. 62; H. Street, " State Secrets—A Comparative Study " (1951) 14 M.L.R. 121; C. S. Emden, " Documents Privileged in Public Interest " (1923) 46 L.Q.R. 476; notes by F. K. H. Maher in (1963) 79 L.Q.R. 37; A. L. Goodhart, *op. cit.* p. 153; J. D. B. Mitchell, *op. cit.* p. 487; P. V. Baker in (1964) 80 L.Q.R. 24; Sir Carleton Allen, *op. cit.* p. 158. *Cf.* A. Wharam and J. A. T. Whitmore, " Crown Privilege in Criminal Cases " [1971] Crim.L.R. 675, 682.

[73] The Memorandum accompanying the Crown Proceedings Bill specified " defence, foreign affairs, and related matters." On the second reading, suggestions that " public security," " public safety " or " defence of the realm " should be substituted for " public interest " were not accepted by the government.

For the appalling case of *Odlum* v. *Stratton* (1946), see Allen, *Law and Orders* (3rd ed.) App. 2.

objects to producing should be set out in the affidavit of documents, and the Crown may wish to claim privilege for the fact that a document exists.

In *Duncan* v. *Cammell, Laird & Co.* (the *Thetis* case [74]) the dependants of sailors who were drowned in a new British submarine, *Thetis*, which sank on her trials just before the beginning of the last war, brought an action for compensation against the builders of *Thetis*. War had now begun, and the First Lord of the Admiralty's objection to the production of plans of the submarine in the possession of the contractors was upheld by the House of Lords. The two main criticisms of the judgment delivered by Viscount Simon L.C. were: first, the statement that Crown privilege extended to any class of documents which the public interest required to be withheld for " the proper functioning of the public service," which would include departmental files and minutes, as if the proper administration of justice was not also a public interest; and secondly, the ruling that an English [75] court would not inspect the documents concerned. These two statements came under increasing attack in 1965 in three cases in the Court of Appeal. In *Merricks* v. *Nott-Bower*,[76] an action for libel by two police officers against their superiors, the Court of Appeal stated that as the issue in *Duncan* v. *Cammell, Laird* was the national security, the dictum of the House of Lords concerning the " proper functioning of the public service " might be *obiter*. With regard to overriding the Minister's objection and ordering the production of documents, the Court of Appeal said that the English law relating to Crown privilege was—or ought to be—the same as the law in Scotland and Commonwealth countries. In *Re Grosvenor Hotel, London (No. 2)*,[77] where the issue was the renewal of the tenancy of Grosvenor Hotel, Victoria, the documents concerned consisted of correspondence between the British Transport Commission and the Minister of Transport and the Treasury Solicitor relating to the framing of government policy in respect of the exercise of the Minister's powers under the Transport Act 1962; and in *Wednesbury Borough Council* v. *Ministry of Housing and Local Government*,[78] an action by five local authorities relating to a local inquiry held to consider their objections to the Local Government Commission report on the Black Country, the documents

---

[74] [1942] A.C. 624; see *per* Viscount Simon L.C. at p. 638. *Cf. Robinson* v. *State of South Australia (No. 2)* [1931] A.C. 704 (P.C.); *Glasgow Corporation* v. *Central Land Board*, 1956 S.C. 1; 1956 S.L.T. 41, 46–47 (H.L.); *Corbett* v. *Social Security Commission* [1962] N.Z.L.R. 878.

[75] *Duncan* v. *Cammell, Laird* did not apply to Scotland; *cf. Glasgow Corporation* v. *Central Land Board, supra.*

[76] [1965] 1 Q.B. 57.

[77] [1965] Ch. 1210.

[78] [1965] 1 W.L.R. 261; [1965] 1 All E.R. 186.

concerned were departmental briefs for the guidance of Ministry inspectors appointed under the Local Government Act 1958, and correspondence between Ministry officials and the inspectors relating to the Black Country inquiry. In these two cases the Court of Appeal held that: (i) the court could override the Minister's objection and order production if it thought that the objection to discovery was not taken in good faith or was unreasonable; (ii) if the Minister wanted protection for a whole class of documents, he should describe the nature of the class and specify the reason why the documents should not be disclosed: the court would accept the Minister's statement that the documents contained, for example, military secrets, diplomatic exchanges or confidential reports on army officers; and (iii) the court itself could, if it thought fit, inspect the documents, ensuring that they were not disclosed to anyone else, although this was the ultimate power and would rarely be exercised. The interests of justice were not held to require this power to be exercised in either of these cases, and in fact it had not so far been exercised by an English court.

After the Practice Statement of 1966 [79] declaring that the House of Lords could overrule its own previous decisions, that court had the opportunity of reviewing the law relating to Crown privilege in *Conway* v. *Rimmer*.[80] In that case C, a former probationary police constable, brought an action for malicious prosecution against R, his former superintendent. The Home Secretary, on behalf of the police, objected to the production of reports made concerning the plaintiff during his probation—one of which was made for transmission to the Director of Public Prosecutions concerning the prosecution which was the subject-matter of these proceedings—on the ground that they belonged to classes of documents the production of any of which would be contrary to the public interest. The House of Lords held unanimously that: (i) the classes were not such that their production would obviously be contrary to the public interest; (ii) the Home Secretary's claim was therefore not conclusive; and (iii) the court might call for the documents, and decide after inspecting them whether an order for their production to the other party ought to be made. *Duncan* v. *Cammell, Laird* was not followed, and may be said to have been overruled so far as concerns the inspection by the court of documents in a civil case for which the Crown claims privilege. Otherwise the main effect of *Conway* v. *Rimmer* was to narrow the ratio of *Duncan* v. *Cammell, Laird* by holding that Viscount Simon's dicta were too wide, although the actual decision on the facts of the earlier case was undoubtedly right.

[79] [1966] 1 W.L.R. 1234; [1966] 3 All E.R. 77.
[80] [1968] A.C. 910, citing Scottish, Australian and American cases.

Lord Reid later in *Conway* v. *Rimmer* announced that he had examined the documents, and could find nothing in any of them the disclosure of which would be prejudicial to the proper administration of the local constabulary or to the general public interest. He was therefore of the opinion that they must be made available in the litigation. Their Lordships accordingly voted " that the defendant do produce for inspection at his solicitor's office to the plaintiff and his advisers on reasonable notice the five documents." [81]

The claim of Crown privilege is the personal responsibility of the ministerial head of the department, although if it does not appear that he has himself considered the documents he may be given an opportunity to swear a further affidavit.[82] Crown privilege cannot be claimed for whole classes of documents merely because some of them may be entitled to it: protection should be claimed on the basis of contents, bearing in mind the connection between the documents.[83] Oral evidence of the contents of a privileged document cannot be admitted, nor may a document which the court has ruled shall be withheld from production in the public interest be used by a witness to refresh his memory.[84]

In *Auten* v. *Rayner*,[85] an action for false imprisonment and malicious prosecution brought against a detective sergeant, the Home Secretary successfully claimed privilege for police reports made in the course of criminal proceedings. Communications between the Lord Chancellor's department, his local advisory committee and magistrates concerning the conduct of a magistrate have been held to be privileged.[86] In a petition for divorce brought by a soldier's wife, the War Office successfully claimed privilege for documents in its possession concerning reconciliation work carried out by welfare officers on behalf of the service authorities.[87] Crown privilege can be claimed for a document whoever possesses it and from wherever it has emanated.[88]

---

[81] *Conway* v. *Rimmer* (Note) [1968] A.C. 996; [1968] 2 All E.R. 304n. Nevertheless, the plaintiff eventually lost his action for malicious prosecution because he failed to prove want of reasonable or probable cause: *The Times*, December 17, 1969.

[82] *The Grosvenor Hotel, London (No. 1)* [1964] Ch. 464 (C.A.).

[83] *Crompton (Alfred) Amusement Machines* v. *Customs and Excise Commissioners* [1972] 2 Q.B. 102.

[84] *Gain* v. *Gain* [1961] 1 W.L.R. 1467; *sub nom. Gane* v. *Gane* [1962] 1 All E.R. 63. [85] [1958] 1 W.L.R. 1300; [1958] 3 All E.R. 566 (C.A.).

[86] *Iwi* v. *Montesole* [1958] Crim.L.R. 313.

[87] *Broome* v. *Broome* [1955] P. 190.

[88] *Cf. Whitehall* v. *Whitehall*, 1957 S.C. 30; 1957 S.L.T. 96, where the documents neither emanated from, nor came into the possession of, the Crown; *R.* v. *Lewes Justices, ex p. Secretary of State for Home Department* [1972] 3 W.L.R. 279 (H.L.), letter about R written by police officer to Gaming Board at Board's request immune from disclosure in the public interest, not as a question of Crown privilege.

Part VII

THE COMMONWEALTH

CHAPTER 33

THE UNITED KINGDOM AND THE COMMONWEALTH

I. THE UNITED KINGDOM

The United Kingdom consists of England, Wales [1] and Scotland, which constitute Great Britain, [2] together with Northern Ireland. [3] The United Kingdom is the state for the purpose of international relations.

It is proposed to say something in this section about those parts of the United Kingdom other than England.

Wales [4]

The *Statutum Walliae*, passed in 1284 after Edward I had defeated Llewelyn ap Griffith, declared that Wales was to be considered as incorporated into the Kingdom of England. The Principality was divided into the six counties of Caernarvon, Anglesey, Merioneth, Flint, Cardigan and Carmarthen, while the rest of Wales remained under the control of the Lords Marcher. Henry VIII completed the introduction of the English legal and administrative system into Wales. The union was effected by annexation rather than treaty. The Laws in Wales Act 1536 united Wales with England, and gave to Welshmen all the laws, rights and privileges of Englishmen. Welsh constituencies received representation in the English Parliament, and the Principality was divided into twelve counties on the English model for the purposes of local government. An Act of 1542 covered land tenure, courts and administration of justice. The Council of the Marches of Wales was not abolished until 1689. References to "England" in Acts of Parliament passed between 1746 and 1967 include Wales. [5]

The judicial systems of England and Wales were amalgamated in 1830. The Welsh Courts Act 1942 provides that the Welsh language may be used in any court in Wales by any party or witness who considers that he would otherwise be at a disadvantage by reason of his natural tongue being Welsh. Interpreters are provided at public expense. The proceedings are to be recorded in English.

---

[1] Laws in Wales Act 1536.
[2] Union with Scotland Act 1706.
[3] Union with Ireland Act 1800; Government of Ireland Act 1920.
[4] See William Rees, *The Union of England and Wales* (University of Wales Press, 1938); J. F. Rees, *Studies in Welsh History* (Cardiff, 1947); *Welsh Studies in Public Law* (1970); (1972) 50 *Public Administration* 333, 353.
[5] Wales and Berwick Act 1746; Welsh Language Act 1967, s. 4.

The Church of England in Wales and Monmouthshire was disestablished in 1914.[6]

After 1951 there was a Minister for Welsh Affairs, usually holding some other Cabinet rank, and since 1964 there has been a Secretary of State for Wales. The House of Commons has set up a Welsh Grand Committee to consider matters relating exclusively to Wales.

The capital of Wales has been declared to be Cardiff, and there is a tendency for Welsh affairs to be administered from government offices in that city.

Scotland [7]

The Kingdom of Scotland had a separate history from England until 1603, when James VI of Scotland succeeded Elizabeth I as James I of England. It was held in *Calvin's Case* (1607)[8] that persons born in Scotland after the union of the Crowns in 1603 were not aliens in England. This was merely a personal union, and was followed in 1707 by a union of the two Kingdoms into the United Kingdom of Great Britain. The treaty was ratified by both the English and Scottish Parliaments, which ceased to exist on the transference of their powers to the Parliament of Great Britain.

The Union with Scotland Act 1706 provided for the succession of the Crown of Great Britain in accordance with the English Act of Settlement. There was to be a Parliament of Great Britain, and provision was made for the representation of peers of Scotland in the House of Lords. Any law in force in either Kingdom inconsistent with the terms of the Union was to be void. There was no constitutional tradition in Scotland; constitutional government was beginning in England, and the development of conventions after the Union continued on the English lines.[9] Scots law was to remain in force unless and until altered by the Parliament of Great Britain. Public law might be assimilated, but by article 18 Scots private law was not to be changed "except for evident utility of the subjects within Scotland."

---

[6] Welsh Church Act 1914.
[7] For the constitutional and administrative law of Scotland, see T. B. Smith, *Scotland: The Development of its Laws and Constitution* (1962); J. D. B. Mitchell, *Constitutional Law* (2nd ed. 1968); *The British Commonwealth: Development of its Laws and Constitutions: I The United Kingdom*, pp. 603 *et seq.* (by T. B. Smith); D. Milne, *The Scottish Office*; T. B. Smith, "The Union of 1707 as Fundamental Law" [1957] P.L. 99; G. M. Trevelyan, *Ramillies and the Union with Scotland*, Chaps. 12–14; J. D. B. Mitchell, "The Royal Prerogative in Modern Scots Law" [1957] P.L. 304; W. I. R. Fraser, *Outline of Constitutional Law* (2nd ed.); C. de B. Murray, *How Scotland is Governed*; Bickford Smith, *Crown Proceedings Act 1947* (Scottish sections by K. W. B. Middleton); Dykes and Philip, *Chapters in Constitutional Law*.   [8] 7 Co.Rep. 1.
[9] *Cf. MacCormick* v. *Lord Advocate*, 1953 S.C. 396; 1953 S.L.T. 255.

The Church of Scotland

The Union Act makes the preservation of the Presbyterian Church in Scotland an essential term of the Union, and the Sovereign must take an oath for its preservation on his accession. The (Presbyterian) Church of Scotland was established in Scotland by Scottish legislation before the Union.[10] This establishment, which differs in various ways from that of the Church of England,[11] was confirmed by the Union Act, and by the Church of Scotland Act 1921, which declares the lawfulness of the scheduled " Articles Declaratory of the Constitution of the Church of Scotland in Matters Spiritual." A Regent appointed under the Regency Act 1937 may not assent to a Bill altering the constitution of the Church of Scotland. Parliament cannot, however, bind its successors, even probably as regards the provisions declared to be essential terms of the Union.[12]

Courts and appeals

Scotland has its own system of courts. The Court of Session consists of the Inner House and the Outer House. The five judges of the Outer House sitting separately have a superior civil jurisdiction. The Inner House hears civil appeals sitting in two divisions, one presided over by the Lord President and the other by the Lord Justice-Clerk. The High Court of Justiciary is a superior court of criminal jurisdiction, and is composed of the Lord Justice-General (the Lord President), the Lord Justice-Clerk and all the judges of the Court of Session. There is a Court of Criminal Appeal.

Article 19 of the Union Act provided that no causes in Scotland were to be heard by the Court of Chancery, Queen's Bench, Common Pleas " or any other Court in Westminster Hall," and " the said courts or any other of the like nature " should have no power to review the decisions of the Scottish courts. However, the House of Lords heard and allowed a civil appeal from the Court of Session in the *Case of Greenshields* (1709),[13] where an Episcopalian meeting-house was set up opposite St. Giles's Cathedral. The House of Lords have continued to hear civil appeals since, although this may not have been intended by those who negotiated the Union on behalf of Scotland.

---

[10] Acts of 1560, 1592, 1689 and 1690.

[11] See R. King Murray, " The Constitutional Position of the Church of Scotland " [1958] P.L. 155. The learned author of this article exaggerates, however, when he talks of the " sovereignty " of the Scottish Church: if the Church is established by statute, its rulemaking authority must be a delegated power.

[12] See *ante*, Chap. 4.

[13] *Greenshields* v. *Mags. of Edinburgh*, Robertson, App. 12. See Dicey and Rait, *Thoughts on the Union between England and Scotland*, pp. 194–195; Turberville, *The House of Lords in the Eighteenth Century*, pp. 94–95, 139–141. *Cf.* Scottish Episcopalians Act 1711.

As regards criminal cases, there was no appeal from the High Court of Justiciary to the Scottish Parliament before the Union, and it has been held that no appeal lies to the House of Lords from that court since the Union (*Mackintosh* v. *Lord Advocate* (1876)[14]).

Northern Ireland [15]

Ireland before 1800 had for centuries been a subordinate Kingdom of the English Crown. It had a Parliament (Houses of Lords and Commons) and a system of courts on the English model. Doubts were expressed at various times whether the English Parliament was competent to legislate for Ireland, and whether final appeal from Irish courts lay to the English or the Irish House of Lords. The executive in Ireland was definitely under the control of the English Government through the Lord-Lieutenant.

The Union with Ireland Act 1800 united the two Kingdoms of Great Britain and Ireland into the United Kingdom of Great Britain and Ireland, in a manner similar to the Union of 1707. The Act turned a personal union into a legislative union. The Union with Ireland, unlike that with Scotland, was not based on a treaty negotiated by commissioners representing each country, but was brought about by Acts of the British and Irish Parliaments following parallel resolutions passed by each Parliament in response to messages from the Crown. The Scottish Union was to a great extent treated as a precedent with regard to terms.

"Partition" of Ireland

The Government of Ireland Act 1920[16] provided for the setting up of two subordinate Parliaments, one for Northern Ireland and the other for Southern Ireland, with a government in each area responsible to its Parliament. The Lord-Lieutenant and a Council of Ireland would form a bond of union between North and South with a view

---

[14] 3 R.(H.L.) 34.
[15] H. Calvert, *Constitutional Law in Northern Ireland* (1968); *The British Commonwealth: Development of its Laws and Constitutions: I The United Kingdom* (1955) pp. 411 *et seq.* (by L. A. Sheridan); A. S. Quekett, *The Constitution of Northern Ireland* (1928–46); N. Mansergh, *The Government of Northern Ireland* (1936); V. T. H. Delany, *The Administration of Justice in Ireland* (2nd ed. 1965); A. G. Donaldson, "The Constitution of Northern Ireland: Its Origin and Development" (1955) 11 U.T.L.J. 1; "The Senate of Northern Ireland" [1958] P.L. 135; "Fundamental Rights in the Constitution of Northern Ireland" (1959) 37 Can.Bar Rev. 189; *Some Comparative Aspects of Irish Law* (1957); "Some Recent Developments in Irish Public Law" (1963) 15 U.T.L.J. 283; F. H. Newark, "The Constitution of Northern Ireland: the First Twenty-Five Years" (1948) 8 N.I.L.Q. 52; R. J. Lawrence, *The Government of Northern Ireland* (1965).
[16] Replacing the Government of Ireland Act 1914, which never came into force.

to eventual termination of partition. This Act was not effectively implemented in Southern Ireland; and following the Anglo-Irish Treaty of 1921, Ireland was accorded Dominion status similar to that of Canada by the Irish Free State (Agreement) Act 1922.

Northern Ireland, however, comprising the six counties of Antrim, Armagh, Down, Fermanagh, Londonderry and Tyrone, exercised its option to remain in the United Kingdom under the terms of the Government of Ireland Act 1920. That Act as amended [17] remains the basis of the Constitution of Northern Ireland. The status of Northern Ireland as part of the United Kingdom is "guaranteed" by the Ireland Act 1949, s. 1 (2).[18]

The Northern Ireland (Temporary Provisions) Act 1972 transferred all legislative and executive powers to the United Kingdom Parliament and the (new) Secretary of State for Northern Ireland. This provision was to expire after one year unless the United Kingdom Parliament resolved otherwise. Meanwhile the Northern Ireland Parliament stood prorogued.

Parliament

The Parliament of Northern Ireland, which meets at Stormont, near Belfast, consists of the Queen, the Senate and the House of Commons. The Senate is composed of the Lord Mayor of Belfast and the Mayor of Londonderry (ex officio) and twenty-four senators elected by the House of Commons for eight years, half the elected members retiring every four years. The House of Commons consists of fifty-two members, the franchise being the same as for the United Kingdom Parliament except that there is a residence qualification of three years. Peers have the franchise, as the Senate is not a house of peers. The offices, procedure and privileges of the House are similar to those of the House of Commons at Westminster.

The Parliament must be summoned at least once in every year, and the maximum duration of a Parliament is five years. The Parliament has no constituent power. Its legislative authority extends to the making of laws for the peace, order and good government of Northern Ireland, with certain exceptions and reservations. " Excepted matters " are matters of national concern which are outside its powers altogether, e.g. matters relating to the Crown, peace and war, defence and defence forces, foreign and inter-Commonwealth relations, naturalisation and control of aliens, external trade, coinage, wireless telegraphy, patents and copyright. " Reserved matters " are

---

[17] e.g. by Irish Free State (Consequential Provisions) Act 1922; various Northern Ireland (Miscellaneous Provisions) Acts, and the Northern Ireland Acts 1947 and 1962. The Northern Ireland Act 1972 legalised (retrospectively to 1920) the use of troops for certain civilian purposes. [18] Ante, Chap. 4.

certain matters reserved to the United Kingdom Parliament, in particular, postal services, and such taxation (including income tax and customs and excise duties) as the United Kingdom Parliament continues to levy.[19] The Parliament is forbidden to pass any law establishing or prohibiting the exercise of any particular religion, or imposing a general levy on capital.

The Senate may not amend money Bills. If the Senate rejects or fails to pass a money Bill, a joint sitting may be summoned in the same session. If a public Bill, other than a money Bill, is rejected by the Senate in two successive sessions, the two Houses may be summoned to a joint sitting and the Bill passed by a majority of the two Houses present. An Act of the United Kingdom Parliament is not, of course, invalid if it deals with a matter within the competence of the Northern Ireland Parliament. On the other hand, an Act of the Northern Ireland Parliament within its powers, if inconsistent with an Act of the United Kingdom Parliament, is void to the extent of such repugnancy.

The parliamentary electors of Northern Ireland are represented by twelve members in the United Kingdom House of Commons. A person is not entitled to vote at such an election unless he has been resident in Northern Ireland for three months before the qualifying date.[20]

The Governor or the Home Secretary may require the Judicial Committee of the Privy Council to give an opinion on the validity of legislation of the Northern Ireland Parliament.[21]

The Executive

Executive authority is in the hands of the Governor, who summons, prorogues and dissolves the Parliament on the advice of the Prime Minister of Northern Ireland. The Cabinet, which is the Executive Committee of the Privy Council of Northern Ireland, consists of the Prime Minister and the heads of the government departments.

The Secretary of State is the channel of communication between the Governments of the United Kingdom and Northern Ireland.

Courts and appeals

The Supreme Court of Judicature of Northern Ireland consists of the High Court and the Court of Appeal, which sit in Belfast.[22]

---

[19] United Kingdom taxation of Northern Ireland is appropriated to Northern Ireland, and Northern Ireland is supposed to make a contribution to United Kingdom expenditure.

[20] Representation of the People Act 1949, s. 1 (2).

[21] See *Re a Reference under the Government of Ireland Act 1920* [1936] A.C. 352.

[22] For the purpose of serving a writ out of the English jurisdiction, the word " Ireland " in the Rules of the Supreme Court is construed as meaning Northern

The Supreme Court has jurisdiction to review the constitutionality of Northern Ireland legislation.[23]

Appeal lies in civil cases from the Court of Appeal to the House of Lords, including appeals in questions relating to the validity of legislation of the Northern Ireland Parliament.[24] The right of appeal to the House of Lords in questions of constitutional validity may not be excluded by the Northern Ireland Parliament. Appeal to the House of Lords from the Court of Criminal Appeal lies under similar conditions as from the English Court of Appeal, criminal division.

II. THE BRITISH ISLANDS

The British Islands consist of the United Kingdom, the Isle of Man and the Channel Islands (Interpretation Act 1889, s. 18). Having dealt with the United Kingdom, it remains for us to discuss the Isle of Man and the Channel Islands. These are neither part of the United Kingdom nor are they colonies; but they are part of Her Majesty's dominions, and persons born in them are British subjects by birth. For the purposes of the British Nationality Act 1948 they are treated in a similar way to colonies, so as to fall within the citizenship of the United Kingdom and Colonies; but as a mark of their unique association with the Crown their citizens may, if they desire, be known as " citizens of the United Kingdom, Islands and Colonies."

The inclusion of the Channel Islands and the Isle of Man in the EEC has presented constitutional, administrative and economic difficulties. Accordingly, after consultation with them, the United Kingdom sought for the islands arrangements short of full membership, and proposed a form of association under Article 238 of the Treaty of Rome.[25]

Isle of Man [26]

The Isle of Man was formerly under the suzerainty of the Kings of Norway and Scotland, but Kings of England exercised some degree

Ireland: *Hume Pipe and Concrete Construction Co* v. *Moncrete Ltd.* [1942] 1 K.B. 189.

[23] Lord MacDermott, " The Supreme Court of Northern Ireland—Two Unusual Jurisdictions " (1954) J.S.P.T.L. 201.

[24] Act of Union 1800; Government of Ireland Act 1920; Government of Northern Ireland Act 1962. See *Gallagher* v. *Lynn* [1937] A.C. 863; *cf.* H. Calvert, " *Gallagher* v. *Lynn* Re-examined—A Legislative Fraud? " [1972] P.L. 11.

[25] *The United Kingdom and European Communities* (1971) Cmnd. 4715; K. R. Simmonds, " The British Islands and the Community ": I Jersey (1969) 6 C.M.L.Rev. 156; II Isle of Man (1970) 7 C.M.L.Rev. 454; III Guernsey (1971) 8 C.M.L.Rev. 475.

[26] See *The British Commonwealth: Development of its Laws and Constitutions: I The United Kingdom*, pp. 485 *et seq.* (by D. C. Holland); *Report of the Com-*

of control over the island after 1290 (Edward I), and the island finally came into the allegiance of the English Crown in 1399 (Henry IV). It was held more or less independently [27] by the Stanley family (Earls of Derby) as Lords of Man under letters patent until 1736, when it passed to the Duke of Atholl. The Crown bought out the Duke's regalities and customs rights in 1765.[28] To these were added the ecclesiastical patronage and other general manorial rights in 1825.[29] The island has retained its ancient internal constitution as modified by statute,[30] and has legislative autonomy in most respects. The island is, however, in strict theory subject to the authority of the United Kingdom Parliament, although Westminster legislation extending to the Isle of Man is, in practice, restricted to such matters as defence, postal services, wireless telegraphy, copyright, merchant shipping and civil aviation. The island is not part of the United Kingdom,[31] and therefore it is not bound by Acts of Parliament except where it is included either expressly or by necessary implication.[32]

The Legislature

The legislature, known as the Court of Tynwald,[33] consists of the Sovereign (usually represented by the Lieutenant-Governor), the Legislative Council and the House of Keys.[34] The Legislative Council, over which the Lieutenant-Governor presides, is composed of the Bishop of Sodor and Man,[35] the First Deemster, the Attorney-General,[36] and seven members elected by the House of Keys. The House of Keys consists of twenty-four members elected for five years. Legislation may be initiated in either branch of the legislature

mission on the Isle of Man Constitution (1959) (Chairman, Lord MacDermott); Report of the Joint Working Party on the Constitutional Relationship between the Isle of Man and the United Kingdom (1969); Commission on the Constitution: Joint Evidence of the Home Office and Tynwald (1970). For a general account, see R. H. Kinvig, History of the Isle of Man (2nd ed.).

[27] Although appeal lay to the Privy Council: Christian v. Corrin (1716) 1 P.Wms. 329.
[28] Isle of Man Purchase Act 1765.
[29] Duke of Atholl's Rights, Isle of Man, Act 1825.
[30] e.g. Isle of Man Constitution Acts 1961 to 1971, passed by the Manx legislature largely to implement recommendations of the MacDermott Commission (1959).
[31] Davison v. Farmer (1851) 6 Ex. 242.
[32] Sodor and Man (Bishop) v. Derby (Earl) (1751) 2 Ves.Sen. 337.
[33] Probably derived from Norse Thing-vollr or Thing-Wald = Parliament field or meeting-place of the assembly.
[34] The original of the term " Keys " is obscure: it is perhaps a corruption of a Manx Gaelic expression meaning " the twenty-four." The earliest use of the word " Keys " seems to have been in 1585.
[35] The Bishop cannot sit in the House of Lords.
[36] The Attorney-General has a seat but no vote: Isle of Man Constitution Act 1971, s. 1.

and is debated in each branch separately, although there are provisions for conferences.

Bills are signed in Tynwald at joint sittings of the branches: they require the confirmation of the Sovereign in Council and a declaration of the Royal Assent in Tynwald.[37]

The Executive

The Queen's representative is the Lieutenant-Governor, who summons Tynwald Court (being obliged to do so if a majority of either branch so request), and who is ultimately responsible, subject to the Home Secretary, for public order and the administration of justice. The public services are now almost entirely administered by a complex of Boards of Tynwald; monthly sittings of Tynwald Court, presided over by the Lieutenant-Governor, supervise the operation and financing of the public services. A confidential Executive Council was set up in 1961 [38] to advise the Lieutenant-Governor on all matters of principle, policy and legislation. It may be that what was intended to be an advisory body will ultimately assume the functions of a Cabinet.

Finance

The Isle of Man is in customs union with the United Kingdom under a " common purse " arrangement: differences in customs rates have been eliminated, and the customs union has been protected by inter-governmental agreements of 1957.[39] The Isle of Man Act 1958 enabled Tynwald to regulate customs, finances and harbours, so that the island is no longer subject to the control of the British Treasury. The Manx legislature levies an income tax. In financial matters the Lieutenant-Governor has ultimate responsibility and retains a power of veto; in practice, however, he shares financial control with the Finance Board of Tynwald.

The Home Secretary is the main channel of communication between the United Kingdom and the Isle of Man, and advises the Lieutenant-Governor.

Courts and appeals

The island has its own system of courts. Manx land law is largely Norse in origin and is unique. In most branches of private law Manx

---

[37] Before the Acts of Tynwald (Emergency Promulgation) Act 1916, Acts had to be promulgated in English and Manx at Tynwald Hill, St. John's, before they became law. Since the Act (s. 3) they cease to have force if they are not promulgated in the customary manner within twelve months.
[38] Isle of Man Constitution Act 1961, ss. 14–22, as modified by Isle of Man Constitution Act 1968, ss. 1–3.
[39] Cmnd. 317.

law has in recent times followed English law.[40] Appeal lies to the Judicial Committee of the Privy Council from the Staff of Government Division.[41]

The Channel Islands [42]

The Channel Islands formed part of the Duchy of Normandy, and remained to the King of England when the rest of Normandy reverted to France in the thirteenth century. They are not part of the United Kingdom. The common law of the Channel Islands is still the ancient custom of the Duchy, the principal authority being *Le Grand Coustumier du Pays et Duché de Normandie* which was compiled in the thirteenth century.

The islanders, though loyal to the Crown, affect to recognise the Sovereign only in right of the Duchy of Normandy, and they deny the right of the United Kingdom Parliament or the Queen in Council to legislate for them without the consent of the States (the legislatures) confirmed by registration in the local Royal Court. There can be no real doubt of the legislative competence of Parliament, which legislates for the islands in such matters as customs and excise, the armed forces, extradition, fisheries, telegraphs, Post Office, copyright, merchant shipping and civil aviation; but the efficacy of legislation by prerogative Orders in Council is uncertain. In practice, the consent of the States is obtained and the Act or Order is registered, the islanders asserting—contrary to the British view—that it is the local registration which gives it legal effect. The Crown appoints a Lieutenant-Governor for each of the Bailiwicks of Jersey and Guernsey, who summon the States and have powers, subject to the Home Secretary and the Secretary of State for Defence, in relation to the preservation of peace and defence.

The Home Secretary is the channel of communication between the Channel Islands and the Crown.

Jersey [43]

Legislative authority in Jersey is vested in the States, consisting of the Bailiff (nominated by the Crown) as president: the Attorney-

---

[40] See R. B. Moore, *The Isle of Man and International Law* (1926).

[41] For the history of appeals, see J. H. Smith, *Appeals to the Privy Council from the American Plantations,* pp. 171–174.

[42] See *The British Commonwealth: Development of its Laws and Constitutions: I The United Kingdom,* pp. 1141 *et seq.* (by L. A. Sheridan); *Report of Committee of Privy Council on Proposed Reforms in the Channel Islands* (1947) Cmd. 7074; J. H. Le Patourel, *The Medieval Administration of the Channel Islands, 1199–1399: Minquiers and Ecrehos Case,* I.C.J. Reports (1953) p. 47.

[43] See C. W. Duret Aubin, " Recent Constitutional Changes in Jersey " (1952) 1 I.C.L.Q. 491.

General, the Solicitor-General and the Dean of Jersey without votes; twelve senators elected for nine years, twenty-eight deputies elected for three years, and the twelve constables (mayors of parishes) elected for three years. Permanent legislation, as opposed to provisional laws, requires the consent of the Queen in Council. The Lieutenant-Governor may veto measures that he considers to be contrary to the Queen's interests, but he must furnish his reasons to the Home Secretary.

Civil and criminal jurisdiction is exercised by the Royal Court, presided over by the Bailiff.[44] Appeal lies as of right in civil cases to the Judicial Committee of the Privy Council.[45] There is no appeal to the Judicial Committee as of right in criminal cases; but it was held in *Renouf* v. *Att.-Gen. for Jersey*[46] that the prerogative power to grant special leave to appeal had never been relinquished, although special leave would only be granted where there was a grave miscarriage of justice.

Guernsey

The legislative and judicial institutions of Guernsey are substantially similar to those of Jersey, except that a Court of Appeal for both civil and criminal cases was established in 1961.

Alderney is a dependency of Guernsey, which has administrative and financial responsibility for many important services in the island and can legislate in respect of them. Otherwise the legislature of Alderney, which was reformed in 1948, is the States, consisting of an elected President and nine elected members.

Sark is also a dependency of Guernsey. It is still a feudal seignory held by the Seigneur (or Dame) de Sark.[47] Its legislature for local purposes is the Chief Pleas.

III. THE COMMONWEALTH [48]

1. Territories of the Commonwealth

The British Empire is a name that has now fallen into disuse. For a long time it was employed to mean all territories over which

---

[44] See C. d'O. Farran, " Judicial Machinery in the Channel Islands " (1955) I.C.L.Q. 46.
[45] For the early history of appeals, see J. H. Smith, *op. cit.* pp. 4 *et seq.*, 63 *et seq.*
[46] [1936] A.C. 445. For later cases, see *Quin* v. *The King, The Times,* November 8, 1951; *Manley-Casimir* v. *Att.-Gen. for Jersey, The Times,* February 12, 1965 (Jersey law and practice apply). [47] A. R. de Carteret, *The Story of Sark* (1956).
[48] See further on general matters, Sir Kenneth Roberts-Wray, *Commonwealth and Colonial Law* (1966) Chaps. 1 and 2; S. A. de Smith, *The Vocabulary of Commonwealth Relations* (1954). There are statutory definitions for particular purposes of some of the expressions used in this section.

the Crown exercised or claimed some degree of control, *viz.* the British Islands (including the United Kingdom), British India, British colonies, protectorates, and those self-governing colonies which in the early part of this century came to be known as the Dominions. The expression probably included protected states but not mandated (later trust) territories.

Her Majesty's dominions are all territories under the sovereignty of the Crown. A synonym sometimes used is " British territory." The expression would not ordinarily include protectorates [49] or trust territories, although it may do so for the purposes of particular statutes, *e.g.* the Foreign Judgments (Reciprocal Enforcement) Act 1933.

British possessions are any parts of Her Majesty's dominions exclusive of the United Kingdom.[50]

British colonies are any parts of Her Majesty's dominions excluding the British Islands, and excluding independent members of the Commonwealth, their provinces and states,[51] and associated states.[52] Persons born in a British colony are citizens of the United Kingdom and Colonies by birth.

British protectorates were territories under the protection of the Crown. They were not British territory, and did not form part of Her Majesty's dominions. The Crown was responsible for their defence and external affairs. Internally some were administered in a similar way to colonies (" protectorates " in the strict sense).[53] These are now virtually all independent. Others were administered, with varying degrees of British supervision, by their native rulers (" protected states ").[54] They are scheduled to the British Protec-

---

49 *Cf.* Roberts-Wray, *op. cit.* p. 23, where sovereignty in the sense of ownership is distinguished from sovereignty in the sense of governmental power. In the latter sense, the Crown may be said to have sovereignty in protectorates.

50 Interpretation Act 1889, s. 18 (2).

51 *Ibid.*, s. 18 (3), amended by the Statute of Westminster 1931, and the various Independence Acts passed since then. The original definition also excluded British India.

52 *Post*, p. 607.

53 Where the Crown had acquired jurisdiction in a foreign country by treaty, grant or other lawful means, this jurisdiction was exercised under the Foreign Jurisdiction Act 1890 (replacing the Foreign Jurisdiction Act 1843): *The Ionian Ships* (1855) 2 Spinks Ecc. & Adm. 212; *Papayanni* v. *Russian Steam Navigation Co.* (1863) 2 Moo.P.C.(N.S.) 161; *R.* v. *Earl of Crewe, ex p. Sekgome* [1910] 2 K.B. 576; *Re Southern Rhodesia* [1919] A.C. 211 (P.C.); *Sobhuza II* v. *Miller* [1926] A.C. 518; *North Charterland Exploration Co.* v. *R.* [1931] Ch. 169; *R.* v. *Ketter* [1940] 1 K.B. 787; *Nyali Ltd.* v. *Att.-Gen.* [1956] 1 Q.B. 1 (C.A.); *Ex p. Mwenya* [1960] 1 Q.B. 241 (C.A.). See Hall, *Foreign Jurisdiction of the British Crown*; Jenkyns, *British Rule and Jurisdiction beyond the Seas*; Oppenheim, *International Law*, I (8th ed. Lauterpacht) paras. 92–94.

54 *Mighell* v. *Sultan of Johore* [1894] 1 Q.B. 149; *Duff Development Co.* v. *Kelantan Government* [1924] A.C. 797 (H.L.); *Sultan of Johore* v. *Abubakar Tunku Aris Bendahar* [1952] A.C. 318.

torates, Protected States and Protected Persons Order 1969.[55] Their inhabitants, if they have not acquired the citizenship of an independent country, have the status of British protected persons.

British trust territories were former mandated territories whose administration was entrusted to the Crown by the allied and associated powers in 1919 to be executed on behalf of the League of Nations. After the last war they were administered under the name of trust territories by the United Kingdom or other Commonwealth governments on behalf of the Crown in accordance with the Charter of the United Nations. Trust territories were not British territory, and did not form part of Her Majesty's dominions.[56] All have now acquired independence. Their inhabitants, unless they have acquired the citizenship of an independent country, have the status of British Protected Persons.

Dependent territories

This is a non-technical term which has recently come into use to refer to all territories in the Commonwealth which are not independent. It is a convenient way of referring to colonies, protectorates, protected states and trust territories. They are sometimes described in statutes as all countries and territories for whose international relations Her Majesty's Government in the United Kingdom is responsible.

Dependencies

This is not a technical term.[57] It is sometimes used in the same sense as " dependent territories " [58] (*supra*), but is not popular there. It is better applied to miscellaneous territories, such as dependent territories placed under the authority of another (*e.g.* Ascension Island and Tristan da Cunha are dependencies of St. Helena); British possessions which are so small as to be virtually unadministered (*e.g.* the Great and Little Basses and Minicoy); and similar outposts under the jurisdiction of independent members of the Commonwealth.

---

[55] Made under the British Nationality Act 1948 and the British Nationality (No. 2) Act 1964. The remaining territories in 1969 included British Solomon Islands, Brunei, Canton Island, New Hebrides and Tonga.

[56] H. Duncan Hall, *Mandates, Dependencies and Trusteeship*; Oppenheim, *International Law*, I, paras. 94 *c* to 94 *o*; Clive Parry, " The Legal Nature of Trusteeship Agreements " (1950) B.Y.I.L. 164.

[57] *Re Maryon-Wilson's Estate* [1912] 1 Ch. 55, 66, *per* Farwell L.J.; *Re Brassey's Settlement* [1955] 1 W.L.R. 192; [1955] 1 All E.R. 577.

[58] For " multiple dependencies," see M. Wight, *British Colonial Constitutions, 1947*, p. 68.

Independent members of the Commonwealth

This clumsy expression covers—in addition to the United Kingdom —those countries still in the Commonwealth whose " Dominion status " was recognised by the Statute of Westminster 1931 (now Canada,[59] the Commonwealth of Australia [59] and New Zealand); and those former dependent territories that have since been granted independence by special statutes, *e.g.* India, Ceylon, Ghana and Nigeria, and whose membership has been agreed by the other members of the Commonwealth. No satisfactory generic name for these has yet been devised. Sometimes they are called " members of the Commonwealth " or " Commonwealth countries." Citizens of these countries are by English law British subjects or Commonwealth citizens under the British Nationality Act 1948, as amended.

States in association with Britain

A new kind of non-colonial status, falling short of independence, has been devised for some of the smaller islands in the Caribbean following the break-up of the Federation of the West Indies.

The Commonwealth

In 1884 Lord Rosebery said in a speech in Australia that " the Empire is a Commonwealth of Nations." [60] The name " British Empire " began to fall into disfavour between the Wars in those countries that were acquiring independence, and " the British Commonwealth of Nations " or " British Commonwealth " came into use, either as synonymous with the whole British Empire, or as referring to the independent parts as in " the British Empire and Commonwealth." The " British Commonwealth " then ousted " the British Empire " almost completely in popular usage. The Asian and African members, however, do not regard themselves as British, and prefer " the Commonwealth " simply. This last name on account of its shortness has come into general favour, except perhaps in the Commonwealth of Australia where it is ambiguous. The term now usually includes dependent territories as well as independent members.

---

59 The provinces of Canada and the states of Australia are *sui generis*: see *Mellenger* v. *New Brunswick Development Corporation* [1971] 1 W.L.R. 604 (C.A.).

60 " I say that these are no longer colonies in the ordinary sense of the term, but I claim that this is a nation. . . . There is no need for any nation, however great, leaving the Empire, because the Empire is a Commonwealth of Nations ": Robert Rhodes James, *Rosebery* (1963) p. 196.

2. The Crown in the Commonwealth [61]

At common law it was said that the Crown was one and indivisible throughout the King's dominions, and the King was everywhere present in his dominions.[62] Thus in *Williams* v. *Howarth*[63] the Privy Council held that the debt due from the Government of New South Wales in respect of the pay of a soldier who had fought in the Boer War (when New South Wales was a colony) was discharged by the payment of a smaller amount from the Imperial Government.

The question of the divisibility of the Crown came into issue after the Balfour Declaration of 1926 and the Statute of Westminster 1931. The question does not arise in connection with dependent territories of the United Kingdom, whose governments all represent the Queen of the United Kingdom. Nor does the question apply to republics in the Commonwealth or Malaysia, who merely recognise the Queen[64] as Head of the Commonwealth. There is only one Head of the Commonwealth. With these qualifications, when it is asked whether " the Crown " at the present day is " indivisible " throughout the Commonwealth, one has to consider, first, what is meant by " the Crown "—the Queen or the government?—and, if the latter, which government? Secondly, one has to determine which legal system is referred to—English law, the law of some other part of the Commonwealth, or international law?

" The Crown," as has been seen in Chapter 13, is not a precise legal term. Acts of Parliament usually refer to Her Majesty or Her Majesty in Council. Where the Crown is specifically referred to in a statute, it will be defined: thus in the Crown Proceedings Act 1947 it is defined as the Crown in right of Her Majesty's Government in the United Kingdom. Other Commonwealth territories have, or may have, statutes defining the liability of the Crown to proceedings in their courts.

There is one Queen,[65] although by accession proclamations in 1953

---

[61] Sir Ivor Jennings, *Constitutional Laws of the Commonwealth* (3rd ed.) I, pp. 18–25; J. E. S. Fawcett, *The British Commonwealth in International Law*, pp. 79–85; D. P. O'Connell, " The Crown in the British Commonwealth " (1957) 6 I.C.L.Q. 103. See also *post*, p. 628.

[62] See *Amalgamated Society of Engineers* v. *Adelaide Steamship Co.* (1920) 28 C.L.R. 129; *Re Bateman's Trusts* (1873) L.R. 15 Eq. 355; *Re Oriental Bank Corporation, ex p. The Crown* (1884) 28 Ch.D. 643.

[63] [1905] A.C. 551.   [64] *Semble*, the Queen of the United Kingdom.

[65] The accession of George VI, however, took effect in South Africa one day earlier, and in Eire one day later, than in the United Kingdom; but this was due to technical devices intended to demonstrate the new nationhood of those dominions, both of which are now republics outside the Commonwealth.

Physically there are two crowns, those of England and Scotland, the latter to be worn in Scotland; but the Kingdoms of England and Scotland are united.

Has each of the Queen's realms a throne? *cf.* Roberts-Wray, *op. cit.* p. 86, where it is suggested that there is more than one Queen, but only one throne.

and later statutes in some Commonwealth countries she has been accorded varying titles which indicate her special connection with those countries. The Queen or her representative (Governor-General, etc.) is a part of each legislature in the realms and colonies, and the government of each is carried on in her name,[66] on the advice of the Ministers of that territory in the case of independent members. The " common allegiance " of the non-republican members of the Commonwealth was confirmed in the London Declarations of 1949 and 1955, when the intention of India and Pakistan to become republics within the Commonwealth was announced. In addition to citizenship of the United Kingdom and Colonies, each independent member of the Commonwealth may have its own citizenship laws. All such citizens (British subjects or Commonwealth citizens) are treated in the same way in the United Kingdom,[67] but not necessarily in other Commonwealth countries. Their criminal liability under English law for things done in their own countries is assimilated to that of aliens by the British Nationality Act 1948, s. 3, so that their liability for treason would depend on the law of their own countries.

In ordinary language " the Crown " usually means the central government. But as there are now as many independent governments as there are independent countries of the Commonwealth, " the Crown " in any of these will usually mean the government of that country. This is especially so where statute has expressly or impliedly designated a particular fund to meet a debt.[68]

Further, disputes between member nations of the Commonwealth are possible, such as the dispute between India and Pakistan on the status of Kashmir. The Crown may at the same time be at war in respect of some Commonwealth territories and at peace in respect of others. In the Second World War not only did some Commonwealth countries make separate declarations of war against Germany and Japan, but Eire remained neutral throughout. Since the war the members of the Commonwealth have not pursued a common foreign policy. They differed, for example, over the Suez Canal intervention in 1956 and on the question of recognising Communist China. Some have entered into regional treaties with non-members to the exclusion of other members.

The conclusion seems to be that the common law doctrine of the indivisibility of the Crown has been modified, from the English law point of view, by legislation and constitutional convention. The Queen holds several offices as Head of State. The legal systems of

66 Except in protected states.
67 Except for the Immigration Act 1971; *ante*, Chap. 21.
68 *Att.-Gen.* v. *Great Southern and Western Ry. of Ireland* [1925] A.C. 754.

other Commonwealth countries generally regard the Crown as divisible, but within the federations it is indivisible for certain purposes. In international law the Crown is clearly divisible. Some writers would describe the relation of the Crown to the various Commonwealth countries as a new kind of personal union; others would say the Commonwealth contains several distinct kingdoms or realms; but no formula yet devised is adequate to explain all the facts.

CHAPTER 34

BRITISH COLONIES [1]

A BRITISH colony may be defined as any part of Her Majesty's dominions, excluding the British Islands, the independent members of the Commonwealth, their provinces and states, and associated states.[2] The Crown is immediately related to a colony as Sovereign. Colonies are under the sovereignty of the Crown both in the sense of governmental power and in the sense of ownership or belonging; whereas protectorates and trust territories are either regarded as not being under the sovereignty of the Crown or as being under that sovereignty only in the sense of governmental power.[3] This distinction affects such important matters as citizenship and lawmaking power. All persons born within a British colony are, as we have seen, citizens by birth of the United Kingdom and Colonies, and as such British subjects.[4]

The constitution of a colony is contained in several documents. The basic instrument is usually an Order in Council or letters patent, but sometimes an Act of Parliament. This provides for the government of the colony, and generally includes provisions relating to the composition and powers of the legislative and executive councils and the superior courts. Letters patent constitute the office of Governor and define his duties and powers. Royal instructions, issued from time to time by the Secretary of State, prescribe the manner in which the Governor is to exercise his functions. A Royal Commission appoints the Governor for the time being.

---

[1] Sir Kenneth Roberts-Wray, *Commonwealth and Colonial Law* (1966); *Changing Law in Developing Countries* (ed. J. N. D. Anderson, 1963); Sir Ivor Jennings, *Constitutional Laws of the British Commonwealth* (3rd ed. 1957) Vol. I; H. V. Wiseman, " The Cabinet in the Commonwealth " [1958] P.L. 326; Sir Hilary Blood, *The Smaller Territories* (1958); *Problems of Parliamentary Government in the Colonies* (ed. S. D. Bailey, 1953); Sir Ivor Jennings, *The Approach to Self-Government* (1956); Sir Keith Hancock, *Colonial Self-Government* (1956); O. Hood Phillips, " The Making of a Colonial Constitution " (1955) 71 L.Q.R. 51.

For the history, see Holdsworth, *History of English Law*, Vol. XI, pp. 35–139, 229–267; A. B. Keith, *Constitutional History of the First British Empire; Responsible Government in the Dominions* (2nd ed. 1928); M. Wight, *Development of the Legislative Council, 1606–1945; British Colonial Constitutions, 1947;* C. E. Carrington, *The British Overseas* (1950); Sir Alan Burns, *In Defence of Colonies.*

[2] *Ante*, p. 580.

[3] *Cf.* Roberts-Wray, *op. cit.* pp. 23, 625.

[4] Although they are subject to the Immigration Act 1971; *ante*, Chap. 21.

586

I. DEVELOPMENT OF COLONIAL GOVERNMENT

The "four British Empires"

The sixteenth and seventeenth centuries saw some colonial expansion, mainly for the purpose of trade. English colonial expansion was the result of private enterprise and not government policy. If British subjects took possession of territory by settlement, the authority of the Crown extended to them; if they took by conquest, they acquired for the Crown.[5]

The earliest colonial constitutions were letters patent to a proprietor or company, authorising him or it to trade and exercise jurisdiction within the area. Some jurisdiction was necessary, as with medieval boroughs, to protect trade. "Royal" colonies, in which the direct governmental authority was the Crown, came later, the first being Virginia in 1624 on the forfeiture of the charter. There was no doubt that the King had the prerogative power to control colonies. The question in the time of James I was whether Parliament should interfere. It was clear that Parliament had jurisdiction in settled colonies, and that the common law extended to settlers all the constitutional rights of Englishmen. The prerogative was more extensive in conquered colonies, which in the first instance the King could govern as he pleased, but the King could not without Parliament take away constitutional rights that he had granted.[6] Central political control over the colonies was vested in the Privy Council, which formed committees for trade and plantations. The first Secretary of State for the Colonies was established in 1854. Parliament interfered chiefly in revenue matters and the passing of Acts of trade and navigation, controlling the commercial relations of the Empire. Apart from the Governor's powers of veto and reservation, the Crown could disallow colonial Acts that affected the prerogative or conflicted with British statutes. The Crown also disallowed colonial Acts that conflicted with fundamental constitutional principles or the established principles of English law.

With the American declaration of independence in 1776 Britain lost thirteen North American colonies. She learned by this experience, and retained and developed "the second British Empire," which expression covers the period from the loss of the American colonies to the development of colonial self-government in the middle of the nineteenth century. The main common law principles relating to colonial government were established by the middle of the eighteenth

---

[5] *Campbell* v. *Hall* (1774) 1 Cowp. 204; (1774) 20 St.Tr. 287, 322–323.

[6] *Calvin's Case* (1609) 7 Co.Rep. 1 at f. 17b. Later, this meant when representative institutions had been granted.

century in such cases as *Campbell* v. *Hall* (1774).[7]   Later changes
were effected mostly by the development of constitutional conventions,
although there were a few important statutes, *e.g.* the Colonial Laws
Validity Act 1865 (mainly declaratory) and the British Settlements
Act 1887.

The expression " the third British Empire " is sometimes used to
describe the period of the development of self-government in certain
colonies, *e.g.* in Canada, Australia and New Zealand, from the
middle of the nineteenth century to the formal recognition of Dominion
status by the Statute of Westminster 1931; and the name "fourth
British Empire" has been given to the looser association of the
Commonwealth since the end of the Second World War.

British colonial policy since the war

The central purpose of British colonial policy at the end of the
last war was stated to be to guide the colonial territories to responsible
self-government within the Commonwealth in conditions that ensure
to the people both a fair standard of living and freedom from
oppression from any quarter.   This statement of policy was reiterated
in subsequent years by successive Secretaries of State.

In 1971 the remaining dependent territories were eighteen, with a
total population of 5,000,000, of whom 4,000,000 were in Hong Kong.
Most of them are islands in the West Indies, and the Atlantic, Pacific
and Indian oceans.[8]   They have a diversity of economic, social and
political problems, which are all the more difficult because they are
so small.   There are international disputes concerning Gibraltar,
British Honduras and the Falkland Islands.   The policy now is to
foster their economic and social development so as to increase their
revenue and create new sources of revenue, rather than direct monetary
aid.   The administrative problems of running the remaining dependent territories are internal problems affecting the desires and
aspirations of the inhabitants.   The Secretary of State is ultimately
responsible for their government, but this is discharged by a Governor
or Administrator working through the Civil Service.   Most of the
civil servants are local, but they are reinforced by British experts.

In pursuance of the dual policy of political advancement and
economic development, the United Kingdom Parliament has provided
large sums of capital for economic development and social welfare
in the colonies and other dependent territories.   Political changes
in the direction of self-government or independence have indeed been

[7] 1 Cowp. 204.
[8] The British Indian Ocean Territories, a group of islands between Mauritius and
Ceylon, were established as a British colony a few years ago.

so rapid in recent years that they have outstripped economic and social development. The constitutions of particular territories are nowadays so transitory that it is impracticable to describe them here individually.

Classification of colonies

(a) Colonies may be classified according to the manner in which they were acquired, which may have been as follows: (i) by *settlement* in territory where there was no population or only primitive tribes, or (ii) by *conquest or cession* of territory having an organised society. This distinction, which came to be recognised in the seventeenth century,[9] affects the constitutional position of the colony, especially the legislative power. It also determines the system of private law that prevails in a given colony. But both the private and the public law are subject to legislative changes, so that this distinction is now largely of historical interest.

(b) A more modern classification is that into (i) colonies *possessing responsible government* (commonly called " self-governing colonies "), and (ii) colonies *not possessing responsible government* (" non-self-governing colonies," formerly known as " Crown colonies "). This distinction rests on whether or not the executive is responsible for most purposes to the colonial legislature (to the lower House if that legislature is bicameral). Any remaining non-self-governing territories would be those with very small populations.

Settled colonies [10]

Settlement might be by: (i) occupation by British settlers under the authorisation of the Crown, *e.g.* Canada (excluding Quebec and Ontario), the Australian colonies [11] and some of the West Indies; (ii) recognition by the Crown, as British territory, of unauthorised settlements by British subjects, *e.g.* British Honduras, the Pitcairn Islands and Tristan da Cunha; or (iii) formal annexation of uninhabited islands or uninhabitable Arctic or Antarctic areas, *e.g.* some of the Pacific Islands, the Isles of Northern Canada, the Ross Dependency of New Zealand, the Falkland Islands and the British Antarctic Territory.

---

[9] See, *e.g. Calvin's Case* (1709) 7 Co.Rep. 1; *Blankard* v. *Galdy* (1609) 4 Mod. Rep. 215; (1609) 2 Salk. 411.

[10] As this topic is now mainly of historical interest, no distinction is made in the examples given between existing colonies and territories that have acquired independence since the last war.

[11] Penal settlements may have constituted a separate kind of colony: see *per* Eggleston J. in *Newbery* v. *The Queen* [1965] 7 F.L.R. 34, 39; and see (1965) 11 A.L.J. 409 *et seq.*

The law in settled colonies [12]

British settlers took with them the common law of England [13] and the statute law as existing at the time of settlement. Subsequent Acts of Parliament did not apply to the colony unless they were expressed to apply to that colony or to colonies generally.[14] The law, whether enacted or unenacted, that the settlers carried with them was only such as was applicable to their new situation and suitable to the condition of a young colony, a test which was often found difficult to apply (*Whicker* v. *Hume* (1858) [15]).

Conquered and ceded colonies [16]

Cession was usually the result of conquest. The varieties of acquisition by these two means were: (i) conquest only; (ii) conquest on terms of surrender; (iii) cession by treaty with a civilised state; (iv) voluntary cession by the inhabitants, *e.g.* Malta, Fiji. The Privy Council in *Sammut* v. *Strickland* [17] said that colonies acquired by voluntary cession, or by cession after conquest, were in the same position in British constitutional law as colonies acquired by conquest merely.

Legal system in conquered and ceded colonies [18]

The general rule was that in conquered or ceded colonies the existing legal system was retained unless and until it was altered or abrogated by the Crown (*Campbell* v. *Hall* (1774) *per* Lord Mansfield C.J.[19]). The legal system might, for example, be Roman-Dutch law, customary French law, the Code Napoléon, Hindu law, Mohammedan (Islamic) law or native African custom. Existing laws were abrogated if they were: (i) contrary to Acts of Parliament, whether general

---

12 See Roberts-Wray, *op. cit.* Chap. 11.
13 *Pictou Municipality* v. *Geldert* [1893] A.C. 524.
14 *Memorandum* (1722) 2 P.Wms. 74 (provisions of Statute of Frauds relating to formalities of will did not apply to Barbados, which was settled before 1677); *Lauderdale Peerage Case* (1885) 10 App.Cas. 692. See also *In the Goods of Foy* (1839) 2 Curt. 328; *New Zealand Loan Co.* v. *Morrison* [1898] A.C. 349.
15 7 H.L.C. 124, 161, *per* Lord Cranworth.
  In settled colonies where there was a small indigenous population, the native law might still be applied to the natives, *e.g.* the Maoris of New Zealand: see *Hoani Te Heuheu Tukino* v. *Aotea District Maori Land Board* [1941] A.C. 308 (P.C.). New Zealand should perhaps be regarded as having been voluntarily ceded by the inhabitants.
16 As this topic is now mainly of historical interest, no distinction is made here between existing colonies and territories that have acquired independence since the last war.
17 [1938] A.C. 678.
18 See Roberts-Wray, *loc. cit.*
19 1 Cowp. 204 (Grenada); following *Calvin's Case* (1609) 7 Co.Rep. 1, and *Blankard* v. *Galdy* (1693) 2 Salk. 411. And see *Forbes* v. *Cockrane* (1829) 2 B. & C. 448, 463; *R.* v. *Jizwa* (1894) 11 S.C. 387.

or particular, extending to the colony[20]; (ii) contrary to British constitutional principles[21]; or (iii) repugnant to the fundamental religious or ethical principles of Europeans.[22] The question whether torture, allowed by the law of Spain, could be permitted in Trinidad was discussed at length in *R.* v. *Picton* (1804–10)[23]: the court were clearly of the opinion that torture could not be allowed, but no judgment was given in that case. A similar question had been decided against the Governor of Minorca, who was sued for damages for confining the plaintiff in a ship preparatory to banishment from the island (*Fabrigas* v. *Mostyn* (1773)[24]). On the other hand, many pagan social customs have been recognised as continuing, such as polygamy among the Chinese of Penang.[25]

English law has been introduced by Act of Parliament or local legislation into some colonies acquired by conquest or cession. This refers to the common law and statute law as they existed at the date of the application of English law to the colony or at some specified date, and in so far as such law is not of a kind applicable only to England.[26] Subsequent Acts of Parliament do not apply, except expressly.[27]

II. LEGISLATIVE POWER AND THE COLONIES

Legislation for the colonies may be effected by: (1) the United Kingdom Parliament; (2) the Crown, under statutory powers or in some cases by virtue of the prerogative; and (3) colonial legislatures.

1. Legislation by the United Kingdom Parliament

There has never been any real doubt about the competence of Parliament to legislate for the colonies, nor, in view of the doctrine of the supremacy of Parliament, are there any legal restrictions on this power. From the middle of the nineteenth century, however, there was a convention against Parliament legislating without their consent for the self-governing colonies that became Dominions in 1931. A

---

[20] *Campbell* v. *Hall* (1774), *supra.*
[21] *Union Government Minister of Lands* v. *Whittaker's Estate* [1916] App.D.(S.A.) 203.
[22] *Calvin's Case* (1609) 7 Co.Rep. 1a, 17; *Blankard* v. *Galdy* (1693) 4 Mod.Rep. 215, 225a; (1693) 2 Salk. 411; *Memorandum* (1722) 2 P.Wms. 75; *Campbell* v. *Hall, supra.*
[23] 30 St.Tr. 225, 529, 883–955.
[24] 20 St.Tr. 175, 181; (1773) 1 Cowp. 161 (*Mostyn* v. *Fabrigas*).
[25] *Khoo Hooi Leong* v. *Khoo Chong Yeoh* [1930] A.C. 346 (P.C.): legitimacy of children of second wife.
[26] *Att.-Gen.* v. *Stewart* (1815) 2 Mer. 143, 160.
[27] *R.* v. *Vaughan* (1769) 4 Burr. 2494.

similar convention came to apply in the present century to a newer group of self-governing colonies, including Southern Rhodesia, Malta and the Gold Coast (now Ghana). Any doubt there may have been as to how far Acts of Parliament passed after the foundation of a given colony applied to that colony were set at rest by section 1 of the Colonial Laws Validity Act 1865, which states that " an Act of Parliament, or any provision thereof, shall . . . be said to extend to any Colony when it is made applicable to such Colony by the *express words or necessary intendment* of any Act of Parliament."

Where parliamentary authority is necessary or desirable for legislation in respect of colonies, Parliament usually prefers to authorise the issue of Orders in Council by the Crown. British Acts are used for matters of general concern, such as Admiralty jurisdiction, aerial navigation, armed forces, copyright, currency, extradition, foreign enlistment, fugitive offenders, international treaties, merchant shipping, nationality and citizenship, official secrets, reciprocal enforcement of judgments, and territorial waters jurisdiction; and also for constitutional changes where more than one colony are concerned, *e.g.* federations or amalgamated courts of appeal.

2. Legislation by the Crown

This may take the form of Orders in Council, proclamations or letters patent. Here it is necessary to distinguish between settled colonies on the one hand and conquered or ceded colonies on the other.

(a) *For settled colonies*

The prerogatives of the Crown, and the rights and immunities of British subjects, in colonies established by occupancy and settlement are similar to those that obtain in this country (*Kielley* v. *Carson* (1842) [28]). The Crown may constitute the office of Governor, and an Executive Council; appoint a Governor and issue royal instructions to him; establish courts of justice; and provide for the summoning of a legislature [29] with power to legislate and tax. In this way constitutions were first granted to Bermuda (1620) and most of the early American colonies. Any other form of constitution was thought to require at common law an Act of Parliament, as with the Australian colonies

---

[28] 4 Moo.P.C. 63, 84–85 (Newfoundland).
[29] Roberts-Wray, *op. cit.* p. 152, points out that there is little judicial authority for the common opinion that would limit the prerogative to the setting up of a *representative* legislature.

in 1823. Apart from its constituent power, the Crown could not at common law legislate for settled colonies.[30]

The British Settlements Acts 1887 and 1945. As the Crown had no direct lawmaking power at common law, legislation by the Imperial Parliament was also necessary to empower the Crown to make laws for such sparsely populated settlements as the Falkland Islands and those on the West Coast of Africa. General statutory powers were given to the Crown for this purpose by the British Settlements Act 1887.[31] The Act applies in effect to settled colonies that have not already been granted representative institutions. The power was used for the Straits Settlements[32] and certain settlements in the Western Pacific Islands.

The British Settlements Act 1887, as amended, provides that it shall be lawful for Her Majesty in Council from time to time to establish all such laws and institutions, to constitute such courts and officers, and to make such provisions and regulations for the proceedings of such courts and for the administration of justice as may appear to Her Majesty in Council to be necessary for the peace, order and good government of Her Majesty's subjects and others within any British settlement (as therein defined). The Queen may confer on any court in any British possession jurisdiction original or appellate in relation to any British settlement. Power is given to issue, alter and revoke Orders in Council for the purposes of the Act.

(b) *For conquered or ceded colonies*

The Crown has a prerogative power to legislate for conquered or ceded colonies, exercisable by Order in Council, proclamation or letters patent. This includes the power to establish any kind of constitution. When a representative legislature[33] has been granted to a colony, the prerogative power to legislate cannot be exercised while such grant is in force, as that would be repugnant to the grant, unless (as is now almost invariably the case) such power is expressly reserved in the grant (*Campbell* v. *Hall, infra*). Where the power to amend a colonial constitution by prerogative is reserved, it may be exercised retrospectively.[34] If, however, the representative government is *revoked*, whether by Imperial Act or by a valid exercise of the

---

[30] *Re Lord Bishop of Natal* (1865) 3 Moo.P.C.(N.S.) 115, 148, *per* Lord Chelmsford L.C.
[31] Consolidating the Acts of 1843 and 1860, and amended in 1945.
[32] Singapore, Penang and Malacca.
[33] A representative legislature is defined for the purposes of the Colonial Laws Validity Act 1865 as a colonial legislature comprising a legislative body of which (at least) one-half are elected by the inhabitants of the colony.
[34] *Abeyesekara* v. *Jayatilake* [1932] A.C. 260 (P.C.).

prerogative (*i.e.* in the latter case, where power to revoke was reserved), the prerogative power to legislate revives, even though such power of resumption has not been expressly reserved (*Sammut* v. *Strickland, infra*).

In *Campbell* v. *Hall* (1774) [35] the owner of a plantation in Grenada brought an action against a collector of customs to recover the amount of duty paid on sugar exported from the colony, on the ground that the duty was imposed without lawful authority. Grenada had been ceded by France in February 1763. After the issue of letters patent constituting the government of the colony, a royal proclamation was issued in October 1763 directing the Governor to summon a representative assembly, and in April 1764 a Governor was appointed by letters patent with power to summon such an assembly. The Governor arrived in the island and the Assembly met. Meanwhile, in July 1764, letters patent were issued by the Crown imposing a duty of $4\frac{1}{2}$ per cent. on produce exported from the island. The Court of King's Bench held in favour of the plaintiff, their opinion being delivered in one of Lord Mansfield C.J.'s most famous judgments. Lord Mansfield said that the Crown had irrecoverably granted that legislation for the island should be exercised in the representative assembly, and no power to legislate by prerogative had been reserved.

In *Sammut* v. *Strickland* [36] the question in issue was the validity of an Ordinance issued by the Governor of Malta in 1936 imposing customs duties on certain imports. Malta was acquired by voluntary cession of the inhabitants in 1802. In 1936, because responsible government granted in 1921 was breaking down, Parliament passed an Act [37] conferring on the Crown power to revoke or amend the Constitution of Malta. The Governor then issued the Ordinance concerned. The Privy Council held that: (i) colonies acquired by voluntary cession are in the same position in British constitutional law as colonies acquired by cession after conquest or by conquest merely; (ii) the correct interpretation of the decision in *Campbell* v. *Hall* is that if representative institutions are granted without the reservation of the power of concurrent legislation, the exercise of the prerogative of legislation is *suspended* while the legislative institutions continue to exist. There was no question in *Campbell* v. *Hall* of representative

[35] 1 Cowp. 204; (1774) Lofft 655; (1774) 20 St.Tr. 239.
[36] [1938] A.C. 678. There is some useful learning in the late Professor Berriedale Keith's argument for the respondents at pp. 683–691. This case was applied by Eggleston J. in *Newbery* v. *The Queen* [1965] 7 F.L.R. 34, in relation to the power of the Crown to place Norfolk Island under the authority of the Commonwealth of Australia. Norfolk Island was originally a penal settlement; after being vacated by the convicts it was occupied by the inhabitants of Pitcairn Island, who were descended from the mutineers of the *Bounty*.
[37] Malta (Letters Patent) Act 1936.

institutions having been revoked; (iii) although the Crown has no prerogative power to amend or revoke the grant unless such power is expressly reserved in the grant, it is not necessary for the Crown expressly to reserve the right to resume legislative power after lawful revocation of the grant (in this case by statute). To hold otherwise would be to leave the colony without a legislature, unless and until the Imperial Parliament should intervene.

3. Powers of colonial legislatures

Colonial legislatures are subordinate lawmaking bodies, and their powers depend on the statute, Orders in Council or letters patent granting them. They are invariably given a general power to make laws " for the peace, order and good government " of the colony. A colonial legislature is restricted as to the area of its powers, but in that area it is unrestricted and does not act as an agent or delegate.[38] No decision on the validity of colonial legislation appears to have turned on this expression, and the courts have never analysed the words. The expression is tautologous because " peace " and " order " come under " government," and " good " is not justiciable.[39] Such restrictions as there are on the making of laws with extraterritorial operation [40] are a deduction from the power to make laws " for " the territory, or perhaps for the government " of " the territory.[41]

Colonial legislatures, although subordinate, can themselves delegate their powers, e.g. to impose customs duties,[42] or to license road services for a fee.[43] On the other hand, a colonial legislature cannot abdicate its functions altogether. A Canadian Act which provided that laws might be passed or might cease to have effect by the votes of the electorate confirmed by proclamation, and without the concurrence of the legislature, would be void.[44]

A colonial legislature can bind its successors, since section 5 of the Colonial Laws Validity Act 1865 provides that colonial Acts shall be passed " in such manner and form as may from time to time be required by any . . . Colonial Law for the time being in force " in the colony. Hence it was held by the Privy Council in Att.-Gen. for New South Wales v. Trethowan [45] that an Act passed by the New

---

38 *Hodge* v. *R.* (1883) 9 App.Cas. 117, 131 (Ontario); *Powell* v. *Apollo Candle Co.* (1885) 10 App.Cas. 282 (New South Wales).
39 *Cf. Riel* v. *R.* (1880) 10 App.Cas. 675 (Canada); *D'Emden* v. *Pedder* (1904) 1 C.L.R. 91, 109 (Tasmania); *Croft* v. *Dunphy* [1933] A.C. 156 (Canada); *R.* v. *Fineberg* [1968] N.Z.L.R. 443 (New Zealand).
40 *Post*, p. 600.
41 See Roberts-Wray, *op. cit.* 369–370.
42 *Powell* v. *Apollo Candle Co., supra.*
43 *Cobb & Co.* v. *Kropp* [1967] 1 A.C. 141 (P.C.).
44 *Re Initiative and Referendum Act* [1919] A.C. 935 (P.C.).
45 [1932] A.C. 526; *ante*, p. 70.

South Wales Legislature in 1929 providing that no Bill to abolish the Legislative Council (the upper house) should be presented to the Governor for his assent unless it had been approved by a referendum, and that this provision should apply to any Bill repealing or amending the Act, was effective after a change of government in 1930 to prevent the abolition of the Legislative Council without a referendum having been held.

The Colonial Laws Validity Act 1865

The early common law rule was the rather vague one that a colonial Act was invalid if repugnant to English law, and so some of the colonial constitutions which were enacted before 1865 provided that the legislative assembly should not pass legislation which was repugnant to (i.e. inconsistent with) the law of England. A controversy arose in the early 1860s when Boothby J. of South Australia passed adverse judgments on certain Acts passed by the South Australian legislature. Some he held contrary to English law, and others invalid because the Governor had not reserved them for the royal pleasure. The two Houses of the South Australian Parliament passed addresses asking for his removal. The matter went, in accordance with constitutional practice, to the Secretary of State for the Colonies, who asked the Law Officers (Sir Roundell Palmer and Sir Robert Collier) to advise. Their opinion was that the colonial Acts were invalid if contrary to United Kingdom Acts; that royal instructions to reserve assent to certain classes of Bills were instructions to the Governor only, not affecting the validity of such Acts if he gave his assent; but that, as regards repugnance to English law, a distinction was to be drawn between the " fundamental " principles and the non-fundamental rules of English law.[46] Such a distinction, if it ever existed, was complicated and no longer practicable.

The result was the passing of the Colonial Laws Validity Act 1865, which applied to all Her Majesty's dominions except the Channel Islands, the Isle of Man and India.[47] The Act was intended to be declaratory. Certainly it was not restrictive, but if it made any change it enlarged the powers of colonial legislatures. It will be seen that

---

[46] Keith, *Responsible Government in the Dominions*, I, pp. 339–341. Addresses to remove Boothby J. were presented in 1862 and 1866, but the Law Officers did not advise his removal, especially as some of the Acts held invalid by him were so. In 1867 he was removed by the Governor in Council under the Colonial Leave of Absence Act 1782 (repealed in 1964) which applied to public officers, holding office under letters patent during good behaviour, who were guilty of misconduct or absent from the colony without leave. There was a right of appeal to . the Privy Council. See Keith, *op. cit.* II, pp. 1072–1073.

[47] Similar principles applied to India. The Act still applies to the Australian states, although they are no longer colonies.

sections 2, 3 and 4 do not go so far as the Law Officers' opinion.
Section 5 was included as the constituent power was also doubtful.
Section 7 expressly validated the South Australian Bills or Acts in
question.

(a) Repugnancy to United Kingdom statutes

The Colonial Laws Validity Act 1865, s. 2, provides that: "Any
Colonial Law which is or shall be in any respect repugnant to the
provisions of any *Act of Parliament* extending to the Colony to which
such Law may relate, or repugnant to any Order or Regulation made
under authority of such Act of Parliament, or having in the Colony
the force and effect of such Act, shall be read subject to such Act,
Order or Regulation, and shall, *to the extent of such repugnancy, but
not otherwise,* be and remain absolutely void and inoperative."

Section 3 provides that: "No Colonial Law shall be or be deemed
to have been void or inoperative on the ground of repugnancy to
the Law of England unless the same shall be repugnant to the provisions of some such Act of Parliament, Order or Regulation as
aforesaid."

A "colonial law" is defined in section 1 as including laws made
for a colony by the Queen in Council (whether statutory or prerogative)
as well as by the colonial legislature. It will be seen from the words
we have put in italics in section 2, that a colonial law is only void for
repugnancy if it is repugnant to an Act of Parliament or statutory
order, etc. made thereunder, and that it is only void to the extent of
such repugnancy. Section 3 makes the matter quite clear by expressing it in a different way.[48]

The validity of colonial laws may be tested in actions brought
before the courts of the colony, and on appeal to the Privy Council.[49]

(b) Effect of disregarding Governor's instructions

Section 4 provides that: "No Colonial Law, passed with the concurrence of or assented to by the Governor of any Colony, or to be
hereafter so passed or assented to, shall be or be deemed to have been
void or inoperative by reason only of any Instructions with reference
to such Law or the subject thereof which may have been given to
such Governor by or on behalf of Her Majesty, by any Instrument

---

[48] See *Phillips* v. *Eyre* (1870) L.R. 6 Q.B. 1
[49] A colonial legislature may debate, pass and present a Bill to the Governor—
without being impeded by declaration or injunction—although it would, if enacted,
be void under the Colonial Laws Validity Act as being repugnant to United
Kingdom statute; *Rediffusion (H.K.) Ltd.* v. *Att.-Gen. of Hong Kong* [1970]
A.C. 1136 (P.C.). See O. Hood Phillips, "Judicial Intervention in the Legislative
Process" (1971) 87 L.Q.R. 321.

other than the Letters Patent or Instrument authorising such Governor to concur in passing or to assent to Laws for the peace, order and good government of such Colony, even though such Instructions may be referred to in such Letters Patent or last-mentioned Instrument." Thus failure to observe royal instructions does not invalidate the Governor's assent to a Bill, unless such instructions are actually embodied—not merely referred to—in the principal instrument defining his general legislative authority, so as in effect to form part of the constitution of the colony. Apart from this exception, the Governor's failure to regard royal instructions is a matter between him and the Crown, which—though it might result in his recall—does not affect the validity of colonial laws assented to by him.[50]

(c) Power to establish courts

Section 5 of the Colonial Laws Validity Act 1865 provides that: " *Every Colonial Legislature* shall have, and be deemed at all times to have had, full power within its jurisdiction to establish *Courts of Judicature*, and to abolish and reconstitute the same, and to alter the constitution thereof, and to make provision for the administration of justice therein." Such laws must be passed in the appropriate manner and form, as mentioned below in connection with constitutional amendments.

(d) Constituent powers

Section 5 of the Act further provides that " every *Representative* Legislature shall, in respect to the Colony under its jurisdiction, have, and be deemed at all times to have had, full power to make laws respecting the *constitution, powers and procedure of such Legislature*; provided that such Laws shall have been passed *in such manner and form*[51] as may from time to time be required by any Act of Parliament, Letters Patent, Order in Council, or *Colonial Law* for the time being in force in the said Colony."

It will be seen that this part of section 5 applies only to a *representative* legislature, which is defined in section 1 of the Act as being " any Colonial Legislature which shall comprise a Legislative Body of which [at least] one half are elected by the inhabitants of the Colony." The expression " constitution " here refers to the composition of the legislature, not the general constitution of the colony.

---

[50] See D. B. Swinfen, " The Legal Status of Royal Instructions to Colonial Governors " [1968] *Juridical Rev.* 21.

[51] See *Att.-Gen. (N.S.W.)* v. *Trethowan* (1931) 44 C.L.R. 394 (High Ct. Austr.) *per* Dixon J. at pp. 425–427; Mr. Justice Owen Dixon, " The Law and the Constitution " (1935) 51 L.Q.R. 590, 602–604.

It probably has to remain a representative legislature,[52] and of course it cannot enlarge its own powers so as, for example, to make a unilateral declaration of independence. In *Madzimbamuto* v. *Lardner-Burke*,[53] an appeal from Southern Rhodesia after UDI, the Privy Council stated that: (i) The nature of the sovereignty of the Queen in the United Kingdom Parliament over a British colony must be determined by the constitutional law of the United Kingdom; (ii) the Queen in the United Kingdom Parliament was still sovereign in Southern Rhodesia at the relevant time (1965), and therefore the Rhodesia Act 1965 and Orders in Council passed thereunder were of full legal effect in Southern Rhodesia; and the convention under which the United Kingdom Parliament did not legislate without the consent of the Government of Southern Rhodesia, although important as a convention, had no effect in limiting the powers of the United Kingdom Parliament.

A colonial statute by describing itself as a Constitution Act does not *ipso facto* require any special procedure for its amendment. Thus it was held by the Judicial Committee in *McCawley* v. *The King*[54] that the Constitution Act 1867, passed by the Queensland legislature under the authority of an Imperial Act, could be amended in the ordinary way and did not require a special Amendment Bill, since it did not prescribe any specific manner or form. The constitutions of the Australian states (formerly colonies) were in this sense " uncontrolled " and not " controlled." A non-representative colonial legislature may have such constituent power from some other source than section 5 of the Colonial Laws Validity Act.[55] Conversely, such constituent power has in the past been expressly withdrawn or withheld from certain representative legislatures, *e.g.* some of those set up under the British Settlements Acts 1887 and 1945.

Where the constituent powers of a representative colonial legislature existing before 1865 were subject to specific limitation by Imperial Act ("entrenched clauses"), as was the case in New Zealand, it was uncertain whether section 5 was intended to remove

---

[52] *Taylor* v. *Att.-Gen.* (*Queensland*) (1917) 23 C.L.R. 457, 477, *per* Gavan Duffy and Rich JJ.

[53] [1969] 1 A.C. 645. See Roberts-Wray, *op. cit.* pp. 991–993; L. H. Leigh, "Rhodesia after UDI" [1966] P.L. 148; "Rhodesian Crisis—Criminal Liabilities" by B. A. Hepple, P. O'Higgins and C. C. Turpin [1966] Crim.L.R. 5, and by O. Hood Phillips, *ibid.* p. 68.

Southern Rhodesia has been a self-governing colony since 1923 although it was the modern practice for Acts of Parliament to mention it by name and not to include it among "colonies." Rhodesia made a Unilateral Declaration of Independence in 1965, and declared itself a republic on March 2, 1970.

[54] [1920] A.C. 691, *per* Lord Birkenhead L.C. See Mr. Justice Owen Dixon, "The Law and the Constitution" (1935) 51 L.Q.R. 590, 602–604.

[55] *Chenard & Co.* v. *Arissol* [1949] A.C. 127.

those restrictions.[56] After the war New Zealand thought it expedient to ask the United Kingdom Parliament to pass an Act [57] removing any legislative limitations that might remain.

A non-representative legislature is usually given power to frame its own Standing Orders. Colonial legislatures in general tend to follow the procedure of the House of Commons with greater or less degrees of variation. The Colonial Office, in consultation with the clerk and officers of the House of Commons, issued a draft code of model Standing Orders. This has been used as a guide, although with the development of representative and responsible government there has been a good deal of local revision.[58]

Extra-territorial legislation [59]

The power of a colonial legislature extends to the making of laws for the peace, order and good government *of the colony,* including its territorial waters. Special powers to legislate beyond these limits are conferred by the United Kingdom Parliament in such matters as defence and merchant shipping. Whether, apart from any special powers expressly conferred by Imperial Act, a colonial law purporting to have extra-territorial effect is for that reason necessarily void is uncertain. The Colonial Laws Validity Act 1865 does not deal with this question. There are dicta in *Macleod* v. *Att.-Gen. for New South Wales* [60] and other cases to the effect that such legislation is void; but some of the later cases, notably *Croft* v. *Dunphy,*[61] throw doubt on the principle that was thought to be established in *Macleod's* case. The dearth of decisions actually based on that principle [62] may

---

[56] *New Zealand and the Statute of Westminster* (ed. Beaglehole) Chap. 3; Currie, *New Zealand and the Statute of Westminster, 1931;* cf. *Hoani Te Heuheu Tukino* v. *Aotea District Maori Land Board* [1941] A.C. 308, 326 (P.C.).

[57] New Zealand Constitution (Amendment) Act 1947.

[58] F. G. Allen, " Procedure in Colonial Legislative Councils " (1955) *Parliamentary Affairs,* 396.

[59] See D. P. O'Connell, " The Doctrine of Colonial Extra-Territorial Legislative Incompetence " (1959) 75 L.Q.R. 318; cf. Sir John Salmond, " The Limitations of Colonial Legislative Power " (1917) 33 L.Q.R. 117.

The question is still of importance also with regard to the Australian states: see D. P. O'Connell, " Problems of Australian Coastal Jurisdiction " (1958) 34 B.Y.I.L. 199, 248 *et seq.*

The Southern Rhodesia (Constitution) Act 1961 made provision for Southern Rhodesian legislation to have extra-territorial effect.

[60] [1891] A.C. 455 (P.C.).

[61] [1933] A.C. 156 (P.C.); *post* p. 602. Lord Sankey L.C. in *British Coal Corporation* v. *The King* [1935] A.C. 500 (P.C.) referred to the doctrine forbidding extra-territorial legislation as " a doctrine of somewhat obscure extent."

[62] In *R.* v. *Lander* [1919] N.Z.L.R. 305, the Court of Appeal of New Zealand (Stout C.J. dissenting) followed *Macleod* v. *Att.-Gen. for New South Wales* in the case of a British subject who, while a member of the New Zealand Expeditionary Force, committed bigamy in England.

be due to the fact that colonial attorneys-general advise against the passing of legislation purporting to have extra-territorial effect.

In *Macleod* v. *Att.-Gen. for New South Wales* (*supra*) the Judicial Committee set aside the conviction by the courts of New South Wales, under an Act of the legislature of New South Wales, of a person who was married in New South Wales and who went through a second marriage ceremony in the United States. The New South Wales Act penalised bigamy, " whosoever " went through a second form of marriage and " wheresoever " such second marriage took place. On a literal interpretation, said the Judicial Committee, the Act would be so wide as regards both person and place that the colony could have no such jurisdiction either in constitutional law or by international law, and it was therefore necessary to search for a reasonable limitation. They held that " whosoever being married " meant " whosoever being married, and who is amenable, at the time of the offence committed, to the jurisdiction of the colony of New South Wales "; and that " wheresoever " meant " wheresoever in this colony the offence is committed." The case is therefore only authority for the principle that in interpreting a colonial law the presumption is that it is not intended to have extra-territorial effect. However, Lord Halsbury L.C. went on to say *obiter*: " Their Lordships think it right to add that they are of opinion that if the wider construction had been applied to the statute, and it was supposed that it was intended to comprehend cases so wide as those insisted on at the bar, it would have been beyond the jurisdiction of the Colony to enact such a law. Their jurisdiction is confined within their own territories . . . ."

Where extra-territorial legislation has been passed by a colonial legislature, the Privy Council have in fact acted on the maxim *ut res magis valeat quam pereat.* Thus in *Ashbury* v. *Ellis* [63] the Judicial Committee upheld the validity of a New Zealand Act allowing judicial proceedings to be conducted in certain cases without service of the writ on a defendant who was outside the jurisdiction. The judgment of the Privy Council in *Peninsular and Oriental Steam Navigation Co.* v. *Kingston* [64] implied that an Australian Act penalising the breaking of customs house seals on the high seas would be void, but it was held in that case that such breaking combined with *entering port with broken seals* was punishable under the Australian Act. In *Att.-Gen. for Canada* v. *Cain* [65] the Privy Council held that a Canadian Act which impliedly authorised the personal restraint of an alien immigrant into Canada to be exercised outside the territorial limits, for the

[63] [1893] A.C. 339.
[64] [1903] A.C. 471, 476–477.
[65] [1906] A.C. 542.

purpose of returning him to the country from which he came, was
not *ultra vires*. In *Croft* v. *Dunphy* [66] the question in issue was the
validity of a Canadian Act (passed before the Statute of Westminster)
authorising customs officers to board and examine any vessel hovering
in Canadian territorial waters and to bring the vessel into port.
Canadian territorial waters were defined as extending, in the case of
vessels registered in Canada, to *twelve* marine miles from the land.
According to English law and its view of international law at that
time, territorial waters extended to *three* marine miles from the land.
The Canadian Act was passed for the enforcement of the liquor
laws. The Privy Council upheld the validity of the Act, notwithstanding that it extended beyond the three-mile limit.

It will be noticed that these Privy Council cases concerned Canada,
Australia and New Zealand, when they were self-governing colonies
progressing towards independence. A similar latitude was allowed
to the Indian legislature under the Government of India Act 1935 in
Wallace v. *Commissioners of Income Tax, Bombay* (1948), [67] where
an Act imposing income tax on income accruing to any company if
the greater part of its income arose in British India, was held validly
to extend to a company registered in the United Kingdom. Lord
Uthwatt pointed out that the " general conception as to the scope
of income tax is that, given a sufficient territorial connection between
the person sought to be charged and the country seeking to tax him,
income tax may properly extend to that person in respect of his
foreign income," and said that Parliament must have intended to
confer such power on the Indian legislature in relation to " taxes on
income." It has accordingly been suggested [68] that the true principle
is that a subordinate legislature may legislate with extra-territorial
effect if there is a sufficient " territorial connection " with the person
affected or with a thing in which he is concerned. As regards a person,
the territorial connection would extend at least to his presence,
residence, domicile or carrying on of business in the legislating territory, but not to the ownership of shares in a foreign company which
carried on only part of its business in that country.

The Report of the Inter-Imperial Relations Committee of the
Imperial Conference, 1926, [69] referred to " the difference between
the legislative competence of the Parliament of Westminster and of
the Dominion Parliaments, in that Acts passed by the latter operate,
as a general rule, only within the territorial area of the Dominion

[66] [1933] A.C. 156.
[67] 75 I.A. 86 (P.C.).
[68] Roberts-Wray, *op. cit.* pp. 390–392. And see *Broken Hill South Ltd.* v. *Commissioner of Taxation (N.S.W.)* (1936) 56 C.L.R. 337, *per* Dixon J. at p. 375.
[69] Cmd. 2768.

concerned." The Report of the Conference on the Operation of Dominion Legislation, 1929 [70] said : " It would not seem to be possible in the present state of the authorities to come to definite conclusions regarding the competence of Dominion Parliaments to give their legislation extra-territorial operation."

Rejection, reservation and disallowance

(a) A colonial governor, as representative of the Queen and a constituent part of the colonial legislature, has power to *refuse his assent to Bills* submitted to him by the legislature, or may in some cases return Bills to the legislature with proposed amendments. The power to refuse assent exists at common law, and is implied in constituent Acts which provide that Bills shall not become law unless they receive the Governor's assent. The classes of cases in which the Governor should refuse his assent are commonly set out in his instructions.

(b) A Colonial Governor has power to *reserve* Bills submitted to him by the colonial legislature, by withholding his assent until Her Majesty's pleasure be taken thereon. This is a prerogative power which in most cases is embodied in the constituent Acts of the colonies. The exercise of this power by the Governor may, according to royal instructions, be either obligatory in the case of certain topics, or discretionary in all cases. Her Majesty's pleasure would be made known on the advice of the Secretary of State.[71]

(c) The Crown, acting on the advice of the Secretary of State, has the power to *disallow* or annul a colonial Act. The power exists at common law, but is embodied in most constituent Acts— especially in non-self-governing colonies—usually with a time limit of one or two years. Modern means of speedy communication have deprived this power of its former usefulness. Its continued existence is inconvenient, as lawyers and others in the colony cannot be certain until the prescribed period has elapsed whether the ordinance will continue in force. The power would rarely, if ever, be exercised in relation to a colony possessing fully responsible government unless general Commonwealth interests were involved.

Composition of colonial legislatures

There have been colonies with no legislative body, the sole law-making power in the colony being vested in the Governor or High

---

[70] Cmd. 3479. Hence section 3 of the Statute of Westminster 1931, relating to the Dominions.

[71] For the Governor's converse " reserved power " of certifying laws against the will of the legislature, see *post*, p. 605.

Commissioner. Where there is a legislative body—as there will be nowadays if there is a substantial population—it may be composed in varying proportions of one or more of the following elements: *ex officio* members, *i.e.* senior executive officers who are members by virtue of their office; nominated members, official or unofficial, appointed usually by the Crown or the Governor; elected members, chosen by an electorate whose franchise varies from colony to colony.

The legislative body may be unicameral, in which case it is usually called the Legislative Council or, when it is representative, the Legislative Assembly; or bicameral, in which case usually the upper house is called the Legislative Council and in the early stages of the colony's development is composed wholly or mainly of *ex officio* and nominated (official or unofficial) members, while the lower house is called the House of Assembly and is elected or contains an elected element. Where there is a federation there is a federal legislature as well as separate legislatures for each of the members of the federation.

There are almost as many varieties of colonial legislatures as there are colonies, and their constitutions are subject to frequent change. It is therefore not practicable here to attempt to describe them in detail. Post-war constitution-making tendencies have been to confer Legislative Councils on colonies which had no legislative body; to turn official majorities into unofficial majorities, elected minorities into elected majorities, and Assemblies with elected majorities into Assemblies wholly elected; to substitute universal adult suffrage (with racial quotas in mixed populations) for property or educational franchise qualifications; and to confer some degree of responsible government, especially as regards internal affairs, on colonies with wholly or mainly elected Assemblies.

III. EXECUTIVE POWER IN THE COLONIES

The powers of the Governor

Executive government in the colonies is carried on in the name of the Crown by Governors.[72] Governors are appointed by the Crown on the advice of the Secretary of State; and they are responsible to the Crown, although in many colonies the executive depends on the local legislature for supply. The office of Governor is created by letters patent; its duties are defined in instructions issued under the Sign

---

[72] In some colonies the representative of the Crown is called Lieutenant-Governor or High Commissioner, but for the present purposes it is convenient to describe them all as Governors.

Manual and Signet; and its occupant is designated, and his authority further delimited, by a commission. He is the agent of the Crown, exercising on its behalf an authority limited by the above instruments, by any further instructions or directions he may receive from the Crown through the Secretary of State, and by statute. Thus the powers of Governors vary; but generally they are empowered by their commission, and apart from statute, to appoint members of the Legislative and Executive Councils; to issue writs for the election of members to representative bodies, and to summon or dissolve such bodies; to appoint and dismiss Ministers (if any); to appoint officials; to assent or refuse assent to Bills, or to reserve them for the Crown's assent [73]; to authorise the expenditure of public funds; to remit penalties and pardon offenders.[74] If there is no representative government, they initiate taxation and appropriation measures and usually other Bills.

Where the legislature is representative but the colony is not self-governing, the Governor usually has a *reserved power* (commonly known as his " reserve power " or power of " certification "[75]), if he considers it expedient in the interests of public order, public faith or good government that a Bill introduced into the legislature but not passed by it within a reasonable time shall have effect, to declare that such Bill shall have effect as if it had been passed by the legislature. " Public order," etc. is defined to include the responsibility of the colony as a territory within the Commonwealth, and all matters pertaining to public officers. The Governor is required to report to a Secretary of State any such declaration and the reasons therefor, together with any written objections by members of the legislature.

In addition to these powers, commonly granted by the instruments appointing them, Governors have extensive and detailed authority conferred on them by various statutes in respect of customs, defence works, naturalisation of aliens, and many other matters.

The prerogative powers in relation to foreign affairs, war and peace are not delegated to the Governor of a colony.[76] " The prerogative of the Queen, when it has not been expressly limited by local law or statute," it has been stated,[77] " is as extensive in Her Majesty's colonial possessions as in Great Britain."

---

[73] *Ante*, p. 603.
[74] On this last point, see O. R. Marshall, " The Prerogative of Mercy " [1948] C.L.P. 104, 116–126; Roberts-Wray, *op. cit.* pp. 341 *et seq.*
[75] No certificate is in fact issued.
[76] See J. E. S. Fawcett, " Treaty Relations of British Overseas Territories " [1949] B.Y.I.L. 86.
[77] *Per* Lord Watson in *Liquidators of Maritime Bank of Canada* v. *Receiver-General of New Brunswick* [1892] A.C. 441.

Executive council and ministers

Executive Councils consisted at first of officials serving in this capacity *ex officio* or nominated by the Governor. At an early stage of development, nominated unofficial members are introduced. The unofficial element grows, and nomination may be made on the recommendation of the Legislative Council. The functions of an Executive Council in non-self-governing colonies (formerly known as " crown colonies ") is advisory only. The Governor may be required to consult the Council on certain matters, but he is not bound by its advice. When the legislature becomes representative (*i.e.* has an elected majority) the unofficial members of the Executive Council will probably be members of the legislature and leaders of opinion there, so that the Governor will try to avoid acting against their unanimous advice. Some territories have, or have had, a " membership system," whereby responsibility for certain government departments is assigned to members of the Executive Council, in order to give experience of political office to leading individuals before the political development of the territory is sufficiently advanced to produce elected Ministers. A membership system was introduced into Fiji in 1964.

The introduction of the ministerial system is the next stage in the development of a colony towards self-government. Departments are assigned by the Governor to unofficial members of the Executive Council as Ministers, who are also elected members of the legislature. The Governor is now instructed to act normally on the advice of the Executive Council, and the elected Ministers will by convention depend on the confidence of the legislature. Certain departments are retained by officials, including defence and external affairs. Finance will tend to be among those departments entrusted to Ministers. The Attorney-General's department and internal security may be retained by officials for a time. The Governor's reserved power in matters involving public order, public faith and good government [78] will be available in an emergency. The leader of the majority in the elected House may now be styled Chief Minister.

Development of internal self-government [79]

The last transitional stage before independence within (or outside) the Commonwealth is usually internal self-government, the United Kingdom retaining control only over defence and external affairs,[80]

[78] *Ante*, p. 605.
[79] See further, S. A. de Smith, *The New Commonwealth and its Constitutions* (1964) Chap. 2.
[80] Responsibility for defence and external affairs may be entrusted to a United Kingdom Commissioner, as in the pre-independence constitutions of Singapore and Malta. Also, a limited treaty-making power may be delegated under the authority of statute to a self-governing colony.

and the power to suspend the constitution in an emergency, for which the Secretary of State remains responsible to Parliament. All the other departments are now administered by elected Ministers holding the confidence of the legislature. A Public Service Commission and a Judicial Service Commission will be set up, and provision made for the independence of the judiciary, the Auditor-General and the Director of Public Prosecutions.

The Executive Council now becomes the Council of Ministers or Cabinet, operating as far as possible the conventions of the British Cabinet system, and the Chief Minister is styled Prime Minister. At some stage the Governor no longer summons or presides over the Council.

The description given above must be taken merely as typical. It may not exactly fit any particular territory. These developments in executive government should be considered alongside the typical development of colonial legislatures [81] in order to obtain a general picture of the growth of internal self-government in dependent territories since the Second World War. The chief remaining limitations are the subordination of the colonial legislature to the United Kingdom Parliament, and the lack of international personality.

The pre-independence constitutions of Singapore [82] and Malta, although they retained the legal status of colonies, gave them the name of " states."

States associated with the United Kingdom [83]

A new kind of non-colonial dependent status has been devised for certain of the smaller islands in the Eastern Caribbean following the break-up of the Federation of the West Indies in 1962 and the independence of Jamaica and Trinidad and Tobago. The West Indies Act 1967 provided that Antigua, Dominica, Grenada, St. Christopher-Nevis-Anguilla,[84] St. Lucia and St. Vincent should be states in association with the United Kingdom. They are no longer " colonies," nor are they independent. The United Kingdom retains legislative power and executive responsibility for defence, external affairs,

---

[81] *Ante*, pp. 603–604.

[82] See O. Hood Phillips, " The Constitution of the State of Singapore " [1960] P.L. 50.

[83] *Constitutional Proposals for Antigua, St. Kitts/Nevis/Anguilla, Dominica, St. Lucia, St. Vincent, Grenada* (1965) Cmnd. 2865; *Report of Antigua Constitutional Conference 1966*, Cmnd. 2963. And see Margaret Broderick, " Associated State-hood—A New Form of Decolonisation " (1968) 17 I.C.L.Q. 368. The scheme was influenced by the arrangement between New Zealand and the Cook Islands.

[84] Anguilla Act 1971 gives power in certain circumstances by Order in Council to sever Anguilla from St. Kitts/Nevis and to provide a separate constitution for Anguilla.

nationality and citizenship, the succession to the Throne and the Royal Style and Titles. The Crown has power by Order in Council in relation to defence and external affairs to change the law of an associated state, and by reason of war or other emergency such changes may derogate from fundamental rights in state constitutions.

The associated states have legislative powers similar to those of the Dominions under the Statute of Westminster,[85] section 2 of the Colonial Laws Validity Act ceasing to apply to them; except that legislation of an associated state may not be repugnant to the West Indies Act 1967, or to United Kingdom statutes relating to nationality or citizenship, the Royal Style and Titles, the succession to the Throne, defence or external affairs. A state has power to amend its constitution in the prescribed manner. The Governor represents the Queen, the British Government being represented by commissioners. A citizen of the United Kingdom and colonies connected with an associated state may be known as a citizen of the United Kingdom, associated states and colonies.

An associated state may not be merged or severed except at the request and with the consent of its legislature. Certain functions relating to external affairs may be delegated to governments of the associated states. If an associated state wishes to terminate its association, three months must elapse between the introduction of the Bill and the second reading, and the Bill must be passed by a two-thirds majority in the third reading and approved by a two-thirds majority at a referendum. A referendum is not required for union with an independent Commonwealth country in the Caribbean. The United Kingdom may terminate association by Order in Council, but the British Government has given assurances that it will give reasonable notice before terminating association.

[85] Post, Chap. 35.

CHAPTER 35

INDEPENDENCE WITHIN THE COMMONWEALTH

Development of dominion status [1]

The development of responsible government in the colonies originated in the report sent from North America by Lord Durham in 1839 to the British Government. Upper and Lower Canada already had representative assemblies. The gist of Lord Durham's Report was that it was a necessary consequence of the grant of representative institutions that the Governor should entrust the administration to such men as could command a majority. In other words, responsible Cabinet government should be introduced, and this could be effected simply by a change in the Governor's instructions. Responsible government was accordingly introduced into the united colonies of Ontario and Quebec under Lord Elgin in 1848. Full autonomy in internal affairs was gradually supplemented by a degree of autonomy in external affairs. The British North America Act 1867 implied the existence of responsible government in the new federal Dominion of Canada. The same principles came to be extended to Newfoundland, the Australian colonies (now states), New Zealand and the South African colonies during the latter part of the nineteenth century, to the federal Commonwealth of Australia in 1900, the Union of South Africa in 1909 and the Irish Free State when granted dominion status in 1922. The autonomy of the Dominions received further impetus by the recognition of Canada, Australia, New Zealand and South Africa as separate members of the League of Nations after the 1914–1918 war.

The Balfour Declaration of 1926 [2] described the position and mutual relations of the United Kingdom and the Dominions at that time as: " *autonomous Communities within the British Empire, equal in status, in no way subordinate one to another in any aspect of their domestic or external affairs, though united by a common allegiance to the Crown, and freely associated as members of the British Common-*

---

[1] Sir Ivor Jennings, *Constitutional Laws of the Commonwealth* (3rd ed.) Vol. I; A. B. Keith, *Responsible Government in the Dominions* (2nd ed. 1928); *The Dominions as Sovereign States* (1938); *Speeches and Documents on the British Dominions, 1918–1931*; Dawson, *The Development of Dominion Status, 1900–1936*; Hancock, *Survey of British Commonwealth Affairs*, I (1937); R. T. E. Latham, *The Law and the Commonwealth* (1937); G. E. H. Palmer, *Consultation and Co-operation in the British Commonwealth* (1934); *The Round Table*, No. 240 (Diamond Jubilee Special number, 1970).

[2] *Report of Imperial Conference, 1926,* Cmd. 2768.

609

wealth of Nations." The principles of equality and similarity appropriate to status, however, did not universally extend to function, *e.g.* diplomacy and defence. The Crown was the symbol of the free association of the members of what was then called the British Commonwealth of Nations, and they were united by a common allegiance to the Crown, based on the common status of British subjects. It was resolved at the Imperial Conference of 1926 [3] that a treaty applying only to one part of the Empire should be made on the advice of the government of that part, and should be stated to be made by the Sovereign on behalf of that part. Dominions might have their own seals for authenticating treaties if they wished. The mutual relations between the members of the Commonwealth were regarded as being governed, not by international law, but largely by conventions whose character was something between international law and constitutional law.

The principle that a dominion might exchange diplomatic representatives with a foreign country was recognised in 1920 in the case of Canada and the United States. The Dominions had come to possess their own armed forces. Although a dominion could not be compelled without its consent to give active assistance in a war in which the Crown was engaged, it was not generally admitted before 1939 that a dominion could remain technically neutral in such a war.

The Imperial Conferences of 1926 [3] and 1930 [4] resolved that the Sovereign should act on the direct advice of the dominion Ministers in relation to the appointment of the Governor-General, who was the representative of the Sovereign and not of the British Government. The power of reserving Bills of a dominion legislature, which had been rarely exercised, ought not to be exercised against the wishes of that dominion. The power of disallowing dominion legislation was by convention not exercised.

Conventions were formulated that any alteration in the law touching the succession to the Throne or the Royal Style and Titles should require the assent of the Parliaments of all the Dominions as well as of the Parliament of the United Kingdom [5]; and that laws thereafter made by the United Kingdom Parliament should not extend to any of the Dominions as part of the law of that dominion otherwise than at the request and with the consent of that dominion.[6] Further, uniformity of legislation as between the United Kingdom and the

---

[3] *Supra.*
[4] Cmd. 3717.
[5] *Report of the Conference on the Operation of Dominion Legislation, 1929,* Cmd. 3479.
[6] (1930) Cmd. 3717.

Dominions in such matters as the law of prize, fugitive offenders and extradition, could best be secured by the enactment of reciprocal statutes based on consultation and agreement.[7]

I. THE STATUTE OF WESTMINSTER 1931 [8]

The Statute of Westminster dealt only with legislative powers, and not exhaustively with them. The chief matters with regard to which legislation of the United Kingdom Parliament was required in order to reconcile the law relating to legislative powers with the conventional status of the Dominions were: (i) the operation of the Colonial Laws Validity Act 1865, which nullified dominion legislation repugnant to United Kingdom statute law; (ii) the doubtful rule that the Dominions could not pass legislation having extraterritorial effect; and (iii) the legally unfettered power of the United Kingdom Parliament to legislate for the Dominions. Attention was drawn to these matters by the Imperial Conference, 1926.[9] They were fully considered by the Conference on the Operation of Dominion Legislation, 1929,[10] whose resolutions were adopted by the Imperial Conference, 1930.[11] They determine the contents of the most important sections of the Statute of Westminster, which was passed by the Imperial Parliament in 1931 on the recommendation of the Imperial Conference, 1930, after the communication of resolutions of the Parliaments of the six Dominions.

The preamble recites: (i) the fact that the Imperial Conferences of 1926 and 1930 concurred in making certain declarations and resolutions; (ii) the convention relating to the law touching the succession to the Throne and the Royal Style and Titles; (iii) the convention with regard to legislation by the United Kingdom Parliament for the Dominions; (iv) that " it is necessary for the ratifying, confirming and establishing of certain of the said declarations and resolutions of the said Conferences that a law be made and enacted in due form by authority of the Parliament of the United Kingdom "; and (v) the request and consent of each of the six Dominions to the passing of the statute.

---

[7] (1926) Cmd. 2768; (1949) Cmd. 3479.

[8] K. C. Wheare, *The Statute of Westminster and Dominion Status* (5th ed.); *Constitutional Structure of the Commonwealth* (1960) Chap. 2. See also Jennings, *op. cit.*; Beaglehole (ed.), *New Zealand and the Statute of Westminster*; W. P. M. Kennedy, " The Imperial Conferences, 1926–1930: The Statute of Westminster " (1932) 48 L.Q.R. 191.

[9] Cmd. 2768.

[10] Cmd. 3479.

[11] Cmd. 3717. These Reports have been referred to by the Judicial Committee; see Jennings, " The Statute of Westminster and Appeals to the Privy Council " (1936) 52 L.Q.R. 173, 175–177.

Definitions

The statute defined the expression " dominion " in section 1 as meaning any of the following: Canada, the Commonwealth of Australia, New Zealand, the Union of South Africa,[12] the Irish Free State,[13] and Newfoundland.[14] Section 2 provides that, notwithstanding the Interpretation Act 1889, the expression " colony " shall not, in any subsequent Act of the United Kingdom Parliament, include a dominion or any province or state forming part of a dominion.

Repugnance of dominion legislation to United Kingdom statutes

Section 2 provides as follows:

" (1) *The Colonial Laws Validity Act 1865 shall not apply to any law made after the commencement of this Act by the Parliament of a Dominion.*

(2) No law and no provision of any law made after the commencement of this Act by the Parliament of a dominion shall be void or inoperative on the ground that it is repugnant to the law of England, or to the provisions of any existing or future Act of Parliament of the United Kingdom, or to any order, rule or regulation made under any such Act, and the powers of the Parliament of a dominion shall include the power to amend or repeal any such Act, order, rule or regulation in so far as the same is part of the law of the Dominion."

Subsection (2) was inserted in case the mere repeal of the Colonial Laws Validity Act as affecting the Dominions should leave them in the position in which they would have been at common law before 1865. It applies only to dominion legislation passed after the commencement of the Statute, but any void Act previously passed could be given validity by re-enactment. It covers " any existing or future Act " of the United Kingdom Parliament, but it is doubtful whether it extends to the amendment or repeal of the statute itself.

Section 2 might be construed in a narrow sense as merely abolishing the doctrine of repugnancy to United Kingdom statute law and as conferring no additional legislative power; or it might be construed in a wide sense (subject, in the case of Canada and Australia, to sections 7–9) as conferring full sovereign powers on dominion legislatures. The Statute had the effect of enabling an existing dominion

---

[12] South Africa became a republic and seceded from the Commonwealth in 1961. The provisions of the Statute of Westminster as affecting South Africa had been enacted as part of the law of the Union by the Status of the Union Act 1934.

[13] The Irish Free State, called Eire after 1937, seceded from the Commonwealth in 1949, and now calls herself the Republic of Ireland.

[14] The Statute never came into operation as regards Newfoundland, which is now a province of Canada.

THE STATUTE OF WESTMINSTER 1931

law to delegate wider powers than could have been delegated under it previously.[15]

Extraterritorial operation of dominion legislation

Section 3 states: "It is hereby *declared and enacted* that the Parliament of a Dominion has *full* power to make laws having extraterritorial operation."[16] This set at rest, so far as dominion legislation was concerned, any doubts that might have existed as a result of the dicta in *Macleod* v. *Att.-Gen. for New South Wales*.[17] In practice, territorial limitations on the operation of legislation of all legislatures are quite common, and arise from the express terms of statutes or from rules of construction applied by the courts as to the presumed intention of the legislature, regard being had to the comity of nations and other considerations. What this section was designed to get rid of was any *constitutional* limitations there may have been which placed Acts of dominion Parliaments in a different position in this respect from Acts of the Imperial Parliament. It did not mean that a dominion could alter the law of the United Kingdom or of other dominions or of foreign countries, but that it could pass legislation, *e.g.* in criminal matters, "which attaches significance for courts within the jurisdiction of facts and events occurring outside the jurisdiction." [8]

This was one of the adoptive clauses so far as Australia and New Zealand were concerned, and it may be noted that section 5 of the Emergency Powers (Defence) Act 1939 provided that the provisions of any Defence Acts passed by the Australian and New Zealand Parliaments, which purported to have extraterritorial effect (*inter alia*) as regards ships and aircraft registered in those dominions, should be deemed to have such operation.[19] This provision was inserted in the Emergency Powers Act, in accordance with convention, at the request and with the consent of the dominions concerned; but such request and consent did not have to be expressly declared in accordance with section 4 of the Statute of Westminster as Australia and New Zealand had not at that time adopted sections 2–6 of the Statute.

Extension of United Kingdom legislation to the dominions

Section 4 provides as follows: "*No Act of Parliament of the United Kingdom passed after the commencement of this Act shall*

---

[15] *Co-operative Committee on Japanese Canadians* v. *Att.-Gen. for Canada* [1947] A.C. 87 (P.C.).
[16] Author's italics.
[17] [1891] A.C. 455. See *ante*, pp. 600–601.
[18] Wheare, *The Statute of Westminster and Dominion Status*, p. 167.
[19] The adoption of sections 2–6 of the statute by Australia in 1942, however, dated back to the commencement of the war with Germany.

*extend, or be deemed to extend, to a Dominion as part of the law of
that Dominion, unless it is expressly declared in that Act that that
Dominion has requested, and consented to, the enactment thereof."*

The request and consent required is that of the *government* of
the dominion concerned, except that in the case of Australia section 9
(3) requires also the request and consent of the Commonwealth
Parliament. This exception was made at the request of Australia,
owing to the contingency (which has in fact occurred) that the Senate
might not be in agreement with the government. Section 4 only
applies to subsequent Acts of the United Kingdom Parliament, but
previous Acts may be repealed or amended by a dominion legislature
under section 2. The words " as part of the law of that dominion "
were substituted as better draftsmanship for the words recommended
by the Imperial Conference, 1930, " as part of the law in force in that
dominion."

It has been suggested that section 4 is merely a rule of construction, and not a limitation of the sovereign legislative powers of the
United Kingdom Parliament, in that it directs the courts that, unless
an Act of Parliament expressly declares that a dominion has requested
and consented thereto, the Act shall not be deemed to extend to that
dominion as part of its law.[20] The section, however, goes further
than that in expressing the intention of the legislature, for it says,
" No Act . . . *shall extend* or be deemed to extend. . . ." The strict
legal position—so far, at least, as British courts are concerned—was
stated *obiter* by the Judicial Committee in *British Coal Corporation* v.
The King,[21] to the effect that Parliament could—in the unlikely event
of its wanting to do so—either repeal section 4, or pass legislation
inconsistent with it by a clear expression of intention. Whether the
courts of a dominion to which the section applied would enforce such
a repealing Act, let alone a measure which was clearly inconsistent
with section 4, is another matter. Dixon C.J. said in *Copyright
Owners Reproduction Society* v. *E.M.I. (Australia) Pty. Ltd.* (1958)[22]
that there was a strong presumption that the United Kingdom Parliament would not legislate for a dominion without its consent even
before 1931, and there is therefore a rule of construction in the
Australian High Court that, in the absence of evidence of such consent,
a United Kingdom Act is not intended to apply to that country.[23]

The first Imperial Act affecting a dominion passed after the Statute
of Westminster was the Newfoundland Act 1934, by which the
dominion status of Newfoundland was suspended and the powers of

---

[20] Wheare, *op. cit.* pp. 153 *et seq.*
[21] [1935] A.C. 500, 520, *per* Lord Sankey L.C.
[22] 100 C.L.R. 597; (1958) 32 A.L.J.R. 306.
[23] See further, *ante*, pp. 60–63.

administration were entrusted to a Governor acting on the advice of a Commission. Convention required the request and consent of the Newfoundland Government, but section 4 of the Statute of Westminster did not apply, as Newfoundland had not adopted it. The Newfoundland Act recited that " an address has been presented to His Majesty by the Legislative Council and House of Assembly of Newfoundland in the terms set forth in the schedule to this Act." The preamble to His Majesty's Declaration of Abdication Act 1936 [24] recited that " the Dominion of Canada, pursuant to the provisions of section 4 of the Statute of Westminster 1931, has requested and consented to the enactment of this Act, and the Commonwealth of Australia, the Dominion of New Zealand, and the Union of South Africa have assented thereto." The Act made an alteration in the law touching the succession to the Throne and could, with the necessary consents, be made to extend to the Dominions. Section 4 of the Statute of Westminster only applied at that time to Canada, South Africa and the Irish Free State. South Africa was in a special position owing to the Status of the Union Act 1934, by which Union legislation was required to extend a law to the Union as part of the law of the Union (s. 2). The parliamentary institutions of Newfoundland were in suspense.

Merchant shipping legislation and Admiralty courts

Although it had been the practice since 1911 for United Kingdom Acts relating to merchant shipping and navigation to be so framed as not to extend to the Dominions, the law on this subject in the Dominions was still subject to the Merchant Shipping Act 1894, whereby Bills passed by the legislature of a " British possession " relating to ships registered in that possession, or regulating the coasting trade of that possession, should be reserved for the royal pleasure. Section 5 of the Statute of Westminster provided that the Parliament of a dominion should be excluded from these provisions of the Merchant Shipping Act. Instead of the Dominions severally repealing these sections under the power conferred by section 2 of the Statute and enacting special laws under the authority of sections 2 and 3, the way was clear for contemporaneous and (subject to local conditions) uniform arrangements to be made to implement the draft British Commonwealth Merchant Shipping Agreement prepared by the Conference of 1930.

---

[24] N. Mansergh, *Documents and Speeches on British Commonwealth Affairs, 1931–52,* I, pp. 179 *et seq.*; *Survey of British Commonwealth Affairs, 1931–39,* pp. 41–46; R. T. E. Latham, Appendix to *The Law and the Commonwealth*; K. H. Bailey in *Politica,* March and June 1938; Wheare, *op. cit.* pp. 278–290.

The Colonial Courts of Admiralty Act 1890 [25] abolished the former Vice-Admiralty courts and constituted colonial courts in the various colonies,[26] with a jurisdiction equivalent to the Admiralty jurisdiction of the English High Court as it stood in 1890.[27] The 1890 Act provided that any Bill passed by a colonial legislature altering the jurisdiction, practice or procedure in such courts should be reserved for the royal pleasure. Section 6 of the Statute of Westminster provided that these provisions should cease to have effect in any dominion.

Application of sections 2–6

Australia was not particularly keen on the passing of the Statute of Westminster, while New Zealand would probably have preferred that it should not be passed. Section 10 of the Statute accordingly provided that none of the sections 2–6 should extend to Australia, New Zealand or Newfoundland as part of the law of that dominion unless that section was adopted by the Parliament of that dominion. Adoption might date back to the commencement of the Statute, and it might at any time be revoked.

Australia adopted sections 2–6 by statute after Japan entered the war in 1942, as from the commencement of the war with Germany, *i.e.* September 3, 1939.[28] New Zealand adopted these sections by statute in 1947 without retrospective effect. Newfoundland was never in a position to adopt the sections.

Saving for certain dominion constitutions

Canada

Section 7: Canada was the only dominion that had no power to amend its Constitution Act. This limitation is to be accounted for partly by the relatively early date of the British North America Act 1867 and partly by the federal nature of its Constitution. When the Conference on the Operation of Dominion Legislation reported in 1929 the provinces had not been consulted about the proposed Imperial Act, and the Report of the Imperial Conference, 1930, shows that certain of the provinces protested against the proposed legislation—in

---

[25] See R. C. FitzGerald, " Admiralty and Prize Jurisdiction in the British Commonwealth of Nations " [1948] *Juridical Rev.* 106.

[26] Ireland was not a colony, but was subject to the Courts of Admiralty (Ireland) Act 1867.

[27] *The Yuri Maru* [1927] A.C. 906.

[28] It was held by the Court of Appeal of New South Wales in *ex p. Bennett; Re Cunningham* (1967) 86 W.N. (Pt. 2) (N.S.W.) 323, that the Statute of Westminster came into effect in Australia on September 3, 1939.

particular, section 2—until they had had an opportunity to determine whether their rights would be adversely affected. The saving clause relating to legislation by the Canadian Parliament (s. 7) reads: " (1) Nothing in this Act shall be deemed to apply to the repeal, amendment or alteration of the British North America Acts 1867 and 1930,[29] or any order, rule or regulation made thereunder . . . . (3) The powers conferred by this Act upon the Parliament of Canada . . . shall be restricted to the enactment of laws in relation to matters within the competence of the Parliament of Canada . . . ." If Canada wished for constitutional amendments, or to have constituent power, it was free— (*semble*) subject to consultation with the provinces— to ask the United Kingdom Parliament to pass the necessary legislation, which that Parliament would by convention be bound to do. This has now occurred, the British North America (No. 2) Act 1949 conferring on the Canadian Parliament a limited power of constitutional amendment by means of ordinary legislation.[30]

Sections 8 and 9: Australia

The Commonwealth of Australia Constitution Act 1900 provides the legal basis of federation under the Crown, which the recital states was intended to be indissoluble. Sections 1–8, which involve the federal principle, make no provision for their amendment by the Australian Parliament. The *Constitution*, which is contained in section 9 of the Constitution *Act*, can be altered by the Commonwealth Parliament, but only after a referendum.[31] This position is reserved by

---

[29] What about British North America Acts passed since 1930, *e.g.* the British North America Act 1964, empowering the Canadian Parliament to legislate with respect to old age pensioners?

[30] The exceptions are: (a) matters assigned exclusively to the provincial legislatures; (b) the rights or privileges of provincial legislatures or governments; (c) rights relating to schools and the use of the English and French languages; and (d) the requirements that Parliament should meet at least once a year, and that no House of Commons should continue for more than five years except in time of war or insurrection. Several drafts have been discussed between the Federation and the provinces of a Bill providing machinery for constitutional amendment of the excepted matters. See, *e.g.* Bora Laskin, " Amendment of the Constitution " (1963) 15 U.T.L.J. 190; P. Gerin-Lajoie, *Constitutional Amendment in Canada* (1950); W. S. Livingstone, *Federation and Constitutional Change* (1956); E. R. Alexander, " A Constitutional Strait Jacket for Canada " (1965) 43 Can.Bar Rev. 262; (1966–67) *McGill Law Journal*, Vol. 12, No. 4 (Confederation Centennial Edition, 1867–1967).

[31] The proposed amendment must be approved not only by a majority of all the votes, but also by a majority of the votes in a majority of the states. No amendment diminishing the proportionate representation of representatives of a state in the House of Representatives, or altering the limits of the state, or in any manner affecting the provisions of the Constitution in relation thereto, may become law unless the majority of the electors voting in that state approve the proposed law: Constitution of the Commonwealth, s. 128. Of the twenty constitutional amendments proposed since 1906, only five have been approved, and of these only

sections 8 and 9 (1) of the Statute of Westminster, which provide as follows: " 8. Nothing in this Act shall be deemed to confer any power to repeal or alter the Constitution or the Constitution Act of the Commonwealth of Australia . . . otherwise than in accordance with the law existing before the commencement of this Act. 9. (1) Nothing in this Act shall be deemed to authorise the Parliament of the Commonwealth of Australia to make laws on any matter within the authority of the States of Australia, not being a matter within the authority of the Parliament or Government of the Commonwealth of Australia." [32]

Section 8: New Zealand

" The Constitution of New Zealand," said the Conference on the Operation of Dominion Legislation, 1929, " is to be a very considerable extent alterable by the Parliament of New Zealand; but the powers of alteration conferred by the Constitution are subject to certain qualifications, and it is apparently a matter of doubt whether these qualifications have been removed by section 5 of the Colonial Laws Validity Act." As in the case of Canada and Australia, it was for New Zealand to make representations to the Imperial Parliament if it wished for further constituent power. Section 8 of the Statute of Westminster therefore provided that: " Nothing in this Act shall be deemed to confer any power to repeal or alter . . . the Constitution Act of the Dominion of New Zealand otherwise than in accordance with the law existing before the commencement of this Act." This section, of course, was not required until New Zealand should adopt section 2 of the statute. In 1947, when New Zealand adopted sections 2–6, she asked for and obtained an Imperial Act that gave her complete constituent powers.[33]

two were of much importance. See W. A. Wynes, *Legislative, Executive and Judicial Powers in Australia* (4th ed. 1970); G. Sawer, *Australian Federalism in the Courts* (Melbourne U.P. 1967). And see J. G. Starke, " The Effect on Australian Law of the Admission of the United Kingdom to the European Common Market " (1963) 37 A.L.J. 49.

[32] The constitutions of the Australian states, though written (based largely on United Kingdom statutes), are largely flexible (subject to retaining such fundamentals as the monarchy). State legislation remains subject to the Colonial Laws Validity Act 1865, but there is a convention that the United Kingdom Parliament would not legislate for the states without their consent: R. D. Lumb, *The Constitutions of the Australian States* (2nd ed. Brisbane, 1965).

[33] See J. C. Beaglehole (ed.), *New Zealand and the Statute of Westminster* (1944); A. E. Currie, *New Zealand and the Statute of Westminster, 1931* (1944); J. L. Robson (ed.), *New Zealand, Development of its Laws and Constitution* (2nd ed. 1967); New Zealand Constitution (Amendment) Act 1947.

II. THE COMMONWEALTH AT THE PRESENT DAY [34]

1. Grant of independence

While the grant to British colonies of responsible self-government within the Commonwealth is a matter for the United Kingdom Government and the territory concerned, the question of the admission of a territory to full and independent membership of the Commonwealth is one on which all existing members are consulted. From the Indian Independence Act and the Ceylon Independence Act of 1947, the grant of independence has been effected by Act of Parliament. Independence involves, first, the acquisition of international personality which is recognised by other countries. It leads to application, sponsored by the United Kingdom, for membership of the United Nations, which is invariably accepted. Independence also gives rise to complex problems of state succession.[35] Secondly, independence involves the freedom of the country concerned from dependence on the Parliament and Government of the United Kingdom.

Independence Acts

The Independence Act will therefore remove, in the manner of sections 2, 3 and 4 of the Statute of Westminster, the three legislative limitations of repugnancy, extra-territoriality and the powers of the United Kingdom Parliament. The doctrine of repugnancy [36] is abolished by a provision on the lines of section 2 of the Statute of Westminster, whereby no future law made by the Parliament of the territory concerned shall be void on the ground that it is repugnant to any existing or future Act of Parliament. This would probably include the Independence Act itself, even if it is not specifically mentioned. Section 3 of the Statute of Westminster, authorising legislation with

[34] Sir Kenneth Roberts-Wray, *Commonwealth and Colonial Law* (1966); Sir Ivor Jennings, *Constitutional Laws of the Commonwealth* (3rd ed. 1957, Vol. I); *The Commonwealth in Asia* (1951); *The Approach to Self-Government* (1956), *Problems of the New Commonwealth* (1958); K. C. Wheare, *The Constitutional Structure of the Commonwealth* (1960); S. A. de Smith, *The New Commonwealth and its Constitutions* (1964); *The Vocabulary of Commonwealth Relations* (1954); N. Mansergh, *Documents and Speeches on British Commonwealth Affairs, 1931–52*; *Commonwealth Perspectives* (1958); G. Marshall, *Parliamentary Sovereignty and the Commonwealth* (1957); Heather J. Harvey, *Consultation and Co-operation in the Commonwealth* (1952); J. E. S. Fawcett, *The British Commonwealth in International Law* (1963); *Changing Law in Developing Countries* (ed. J. N. D. Anderson, 1963); *Parliament as an Export* (ed. Sir Alan Burns, 1966); T. O. Elias, " The Commonwealth in Africa " (1968) 31 M.L.R. 284; L. Wolf-Phillips, " Post-Independence Constitutional Change in the Commonwealth " (1970) XVIII *Political Studies*, p. 18.

[35] See Roberts-Wray, *op. cit.* pp. 267–269; Fawcett, *op. cit.* Chap. 18. And see *The Effect of Independence on Treaties* (International Law Association, 1966).

[36] Colonial Laws Validity Act 1865, s. 2.

extra-territorial operation, was needed in relation to the Dominions in 1931, as that Statute did not make a definite break between dependence and independence: it was a statutory declaration of existing facts that had been brought about by gradual evolution. In the post-war Independence Acts this provision may not be necessary, as the power of extra-territorial legislation may be implied by independence, but it is inserted *ex abundante cautela*.

The provision that future Acts of the United Kingdom shall not apply to the country concerned has been modelled on section 4 of the Statute of Westminster. That section was followed closely in the case of Ceylon and Ghana. The Indian Independence Act, however, omitted the " request and consent " and substituted " unless it is expressly extended thereto " by a law of the Indian legislature. The Nigerian, Sierra Leone and later Acts merely omit the contingency that they might request and consent to United Kingdom legislation.

The powers of disallowance and reservation and the reserved power of certification were abolished by the Indian Independence Act. Disallowance has never been formally abolished for Canada, Australia and New Zealand, but by convention it is never exercised. In other cases of independence these extraneous powers will have been abolished by amendment to the pre-independence constitution.

Independence in the case of former colonies, *e.g.* Ghana, Nigeria and Malta, which involves the transfer of sovereignty to territories that previously had no international personality, is usually described in the Act as " fully responsible status " within the Commonwealth. Protectorates (*e.g.* formerly Uganda) and trust territories (*e.g.* formerly Tanganyika) are not within Her Majesty's dominions, and therefore Independence Acts have technically annexed them to the Crown in order that on the withdrawal of protection they might be granted independence within the Commonwealth. In the case of trust territories this process requires the approval of the United Nations. Provision is made that British protected persons retain that status unless and until they become citizens of the newly independent country. The independent Federation of Malaya was formed by agreement between the United Kingdom and the rulers of the protected Malay states, prior approval having been given by Act of Parliament.

The Statute of Westminster did not deal with executive powers, because their exercise was adequately governed by constitutional conventions, and the Statute was not intended at the time it was passed actually to confer independence. The Indian Independence Act 1947 provided that the United Kingdom Government should cease to be responsible for the government of India, and this has been followed in Acts granting independence to former colonies. Acts conferring independence on protectorates either do the same or provide that Her Majesty shall cease to have jurisdiction over the territory.

There is usually an Agreement between the United Kingdom and the territory concerned that the latter shall succeed to the rights and obligations affecting it arising out of international agreements.[37] Other countries appear to accept this. Sometimes the grant of independence is accompanied by an Agreement with the United Kingdom on external affairs, defence and public officers. This was so, for example, with Ceylon, Malaya, Nigeria, Singapore and Malta.[38] They do not all still remain in force. The External Affairs Agreement with Ceylon (now the Republic of Sri Lanka) was especially interesting as it referred to the conventions formulated in resolutions of previous Imperial Conferences.[39]

It is also necessary for Parliament to pass an Act continuing the law of the United Kingdom in force here in relation to the territory so far as it is applicable to its new constitutional status,[40] and to modify certain existing Acts of Parliament, e.g. the British Nationality Act 1948, s. 1 (3) (countries whose nationals are British subjects and Commonwealth citizens), the Army and Air Force and Naval Discipline Acts (Commonwealth forces); and Acts relating to visiting forces and diplomatic immunities.

Independence constitutions

The constitution of the newly-independent country will have been drafted by agreement between the Secretary of State and the local party in power, sometimes in consultation with opposition or minority parties. It is usually contained in an Order in Council or some other instrument separate from the Independence Act, as this is a quicker and more flexible way of getting parliamentary approval. When the constitution has come into operation in what is now an independent country, it cannot be challenged in the courts.[41]

In addition to Canada and Australia, a number of post-war constitutions of Commonwealth members have some kind of federal

---

[37] e.g. Cmnd. 2633 (Malta).

[38] Cmnd. 2423; Cmnd. 2410.

[39] Sir Ivor Jennings, The Constitution of Ceylon (3rd ed. 1953); " The Making of a Dominion Constitution " (1949) 65 L.Q.R. 456.

[40] e.g. Ghana (Consequential Provision) Act 1960; see Gohoho v. Guinea Press Ltd. [1963] 1 Q.B. 948 (C.A.): service of writ.

[41] Buck v. Att.-Gen. [1965] Ch. 745 (C.A.), affirming Wilberforce J. [1964] 3 W.L.R. 850.

form.[42]   These include India,[43] Nigeria,[44] Malaysia, Uganda and Kenya.

Most of the post-war constitutions include a declaration of fundamental rights, with power of judicial review.[45] The first was the Indian Constitution,[46] which came into force in 1950. Based partly on the American Bill of Rights and partly on the experience of English constitutional history, the fundamental rights and their qualifications in the Indian Constitutions are elaborated with great fullness. The Nigerian declaration of fundamental rights (1960) [47] formed the model for several later formulations in other Commonwealth countries, being derived not only from those in the Constitutions of Pakistan (1956) and Malaya (1957), which themselves borrowed extensively from India, but also from the European Convention for the Protection of Human Rights and Fundamental Freedoms (1950). One of the more recent examples is Malta (1964).[48] A special case is the " Bill of Rights " passed in 1960 by the Canadian Parliament, which cannot bind itself not to alter the law by express repeal.[49]

The topic of republics within the Commonwealth is discussed below.[50] The change from monarchy to republic has usually been made following a short interval after independence. Cyprus on the

---

[42] See further, de Smith, *The New Commonwealth and its Constitutions,* Chap. 7; K. C. Wheare, *Federal Government* (4th ed. 1963).

[43] Strictly a Union. See D. D. Basu, *Commentary on the Constitution of India* (5th ed.); H. M. Servai, *Constitutional Law of India* (1967); A. Gledhill, *The Republic of India: Development of its Laws and Constitution* (2nd ed. 1968).

[44] The Nigerian Federation, which has gone through a number of changes since independence, was said to be unique in that it was not formed from units that were previously separate countries. The divisions are mainly tribal.

[45] See Sir K. Roberts-Wray, " Human Rights in the Commonwealth " (1968) 17 I.C.L.Q. 908.

[46] See *Golak Nath* v. *State of Punjab,* A.I.R. 1967 S.C. 1643; O. Hood Phillips, " Fundamental Rights and Prospective Overruling in India " (1968) 84 L.Q.R. 173. And see Basu, *op. cit.* Vols. I and II (5th ed.): Gledhill, *Fundamental Rights in India* (1955); Sir Ivor Jennings, *Some Characteristics of the Indian Constitution* (1953).

[47] See Kalu Ezera, *Constitutional Developments in Nigeria* (1960); T. O. Elias, " The New Constitution of Nigeria and the Protection of Human Rights and Fundamental Freedoms " (1960) Jo.*International Commission of Jurists* 30; D. C. Holland, " Human Rights in Nigeria " [1962] C.L.P. 145. See further, de Smith, *op. cit.* Chap. 5.

[48] *Olivier* v. *Buttigieg* [1967] 1 A.C. 115 (P.C.). And see *Collymore* v. *Att.-Gen. of Trinidad and Tobago* [1970] A.C. 538; *Akar* v. *Att.-Gen. of Sierra Leone* [1970] A.C. 853; *Jaundos* v. *Att.-Gen. of Guyana* [1971] A.C. 972.

[49] In *R.* v. *Drybones* (1969) 9 D.L.R. (3d.) 473, the Canadian Supreme Court held by a majority of six to three that a Canadian statute which infringes freedoms declared in the Bill of Rights is " inoperative " unless it *expressly* declares that it shall operate notwithstanding the Bill of Rights. *Cf.* F. M. Auburn in (1970) 86 L.Q.R. 306; D. A. Schmeiser, *Civil Liberties in Canada* (1964); (1959) Can. Bar Rev. (Canadian Bill of Rights); F. R. Scott, *Civil Liberties and Canadian Federalism*; Bora Laskin, " Canada's Bill of Rights: A Dilemma for the Courts? " (1962) 11 I.C.L.Q. 519.

[50] *Post,* p. 626.

other hand became a republic immediately on independence, at first outside the Commonwealth but later joining it, and Zambia (formerly Northern Rhodesia) on independence became a republic within the Commonwealth.

Constitutional amendment usually requires some special procedure at least for altering provisions relating to federal distribution of powers, fundamental rights, and communal or minority guarantees. In *Bribery Commissioner* v. *Ranasinghe*,[51] an appeal from Ceylon, the Privy Council said: " a legislature has no power to ignore the conditions of law-making that are imposed by the instrument which itself regulates the power to make law. This restriction exists independently of the question whether a legislature is sovereign." These special provisions, however, may later be repealed by means of their own special procedure, as was done in the case of Ghana. But the basic Articles of the Cyprus Constitution (dealing with communal participation in government) cannot in any legal way be amended, except presumably with the consent of Greece, Turkey and the United Kingdom.[52]

Some members of the Commonwealth, a little time after achieving independence, wish to base a revised constitution on a local *grundnorm;* they assert the principle of constitutional " autochthony," that is, that their constitution is sprung from their native soil and not derived from a United Kingdom statute. Strictly, autochthony requires a breach in legal continuity, an actual or technical revolution.[53] A complete breach in legal continuity is attended by some risk if the local courts are independent and impartial. The notion of autochthony is hardly applicable at any rate to Canada, Australia or New Zealand.[54]

Dependent peoples usually want at first to adopt British methods of parliamentary and Cabinet government, adapted to suit local conditions. The main constitutional conventions are commonly formulated or incorporated by reference. The balance of power between conflicting ethnic, religious, linguistic or regional interests

---

51 [1965] A.C. 172.

52 Cyprus Act 1960; S.I. 1960 No. 1368; (1960) Cmnd. 1093, Appendix D. *Cf.* Achilles Emilianides, *The Zurich and London Agreements and the Cyprus Republic* (Athens, 1961).

53 Wheare, *The Constitutional Structure of the Commonwealth,* Chap. 4; *cf.* Kenneth Robinson, " Constitutional Autochthony in Ghana " (1961) 1 *Journal of Commonwealth Political Studies,* 41; " Constitutional Autochthony and the Transfer of Power," in *Essays in Imperial Government* (ed. Robinson and Madden, 1963) p. 249; Sir Ivor Jennings, *Constitutional Problems in Pakistan* (1957); A. Gledhill, " The Constitutional Crisis in Pakistan (1954–1955) " *Indian Year Book of International Affairs* (1955) p. 1.

54 Roberts-Wray, *op. cit.* pp. 289–295.

needs to be settled before independence.[55]   An independent country should be economically viable. It must provide for its own defence and the handling of external affairs. The governmental structure should not be too complex in relation to the population. Literacy is not essential for the franchise. Capable leaders can usually be found to fill the ministerial posts; but beyond this there is the urgent need for an honest and efficient civil service. The dearth of administrators is largely a question of education, and the main obstacle in the way of providing education is the cost.

The desire for independence is itself stimulated by British political ideas, and nationalism marks the later stage in the development of a dependent territory. There is in effect only one party, whose aim is to end " colonialism "; but the British political system presupposes two main parties or groups, one being an effective opposition capable of providing an alternative government. The one-party principle may be introduced before long, especially after the country has become a republic with a strong Presidential system. Thus the " Westminster model " of parliamentary democracy was soon abandoned in Pakistan and Ghana.

2. Full membership of the Commonwealth

The Commonwealth itself is not an international person. It is a kind of international organisation that does not fit into any of the recognised categories, such as federation, confederacy, real union or personal union.   " If we were to name the characteristic institutions which have in the past tended to bind the countries of the Commonwealth together," says one authority,[56] " we might point to the common allegiance to the Crown; the appellate jurisdiction of the Privy Council; responsible Cabinet government; the common status of British subjects; Imperial preference; the pound sterling; and the Royal Navy."   All these institutions, however, have changed much from what once they were.

The basic rules of the Commonwealth today are concerned mainly with the acquisition, continuance and discontinuance of membership.[57] They say little about the incidents of membership. They are conventions which have grown out of practice, and may be modified or discarded when that is thought convenient.   " Members decide what

---

[55] See S. A. de Smith, " Mauritius: Constitutionalism in a Plural Society " (1968) 31 M.L.R. 601; Claire Palley, " Constitutional Devices in multi-racial and multi-religious societies " (1969) 19 N.I.L.Q. 377.
[56] Fawcett, *op. cit.* p. 75. The Commonwealth does not correspond to the sterling area. Before the secession of South Africa, it might have been said to correspond (except for Canada) to the cricket-playing countries of the world.
[57] de Smith, *op. cit.* pp. 17–37.

they want to do," says Wheare,[58] " and then bring the rules up to date." In order that a country may be admitted to full membership of the Commonwealth, it must be: (i) independent; (ii) willing to recognise the Queen as head of the Commonwealth; and (iii) willing to co-operate. The only independent country to have entered the Commonwealth from outside is Cyprus, and that took place six months after the termination of its colonial status.

The grant of independence, as has been said, is decided by the United Kingdom.[59] Then, if its government so wishes, the United Kingdom invites the governments of the other full members of the Commonwealth to agree to its full membership, because they have equality of status. If they, or a majority of them, did not agree, the country concerned would become independent within the Commonwealth, but it would not be a *full* member. On the other hand, there appears to be no rule that the members must be unanimous: a minority probably cannot prevent its becoming a full member, although they might ignore it or even secede.

While both sentiment and self-interest may be said to operate in keeping the older dominions in the Commonwealth, self-interest predominates in determining new countries to join the Commonwealth; although even in them sentiment is not absent, especially among administrators, lawyers and educated persons generally. The advantages of the association to new members include continued financial aid; the secondment of skilled personnel, such as administrators and teachers; mutual trade; and co-operation of many kinds, such as the provision of diplomatic information and help in time of trouble. There are also unofficial links such as are formed by associations of Members of Parliament, lawyers, doctors, scientists and technologists. No disadvantages or limitations are involved in membership, and in fact no new member seceded [60] before (West) Pakistan early in 1972.

Secession

It has been recognised since 1947 that an independent member may leave the Commonwealth either by voluntary secession, or by terminating its allegiance to the Crown without obtaining the consent of the other members to its remaining a member. The secession of an independent member of the Commonwealth, to be fully effective, requires not only local legislation—which in this respect is beyond the powers of the legislatures of Canada and Australia—but also an

58 Wheare, *op. cit.* p. 119.
59 Or Australia, etc., in relation to their dependencies.
60 Burma left the Commonwealth on obtaining independence in 1947.

Act of the United Kingdom Parliament for such purposes as amending the British Nationality Act 1948.

The secession of Eire in 1948 was recognised by the other members. Recognition of the secession was made by the United Kingdom in the Ireland Act 1949, which nevertheless declares that the Republic of Ireland is not to be regarded as a foreign country nor are its citizens to be regarded as aliens. The Prime Minister of South Africa informed the meeting of Commonwealth Prime Ministers in March 1961 that South Africa intended to introduce a republican constitution, and that its Government wished South Africa to remain within the Commonwealth. In the light of the views expressed by other member governments and the indications of their future intentions regarding the racial policy of the South African Government, however, Dr. Verwoerd withdrew his application for South Africa's continuing membership of the Commonwealth as a republic.[61] The South Africa Act 1962 made provision for the operation of the law relating to South Africa as a foreign country, and amended the British Nationality Acts so that South Africans, unless they were also United Kingdom citizens or citizens of some other Commonwealth country, became aliens.

The Somaliland Protectorate on acquiring independence in 1960 joined the Republic of Somalia, and so left the Commonwealth.

Republics in the Commonwealth

The India (Consequential Provision) Act 1949 recognises that India [62] is a republic while remaining a member of the Commonwealth. Since its new Constitution came into force in 1950, India no longer owes allegiance to the Crown. The Queen is not Queen of India, but India recognises the Crown as the Head of the Commonwealth with which it is associated and of which it is a full member. Yet the Act of 1949 continues the provisions of the British Nationality Act 1948 and the Representation of the People Act 1949, whereby citizens of India are British subjects or Commonwealth citizens and as such have the right to vote in this country. The desire of India to remain a member of the Commonwealth after the coming into force of her republican Constitution was discussed at a meeting of Commonwealth Prime Ministers in 1949, which issued the following declaration [63]:

[61] See J. D. B. Miller, "South Africa's Departure" (1961) 1 *Journal of Commonwealth Political Studies*, 56.

[62] *i.e.* the former British India excluding Pakistan, but including most of the former Indian states.

[63] For the negotiations leading to this declaration, including recognition by India of the King as "Head of the Commonwealth," see J. W. Wheeler-Bennett, *King George VI*, pp. 719–731.

"The Governments of the United Kingdom, Canada, Australia, New Zealand, South Africa, India, Pakistan and Ceylon, whose countries are united as members of the British Commonwealth of Nations and owe a common allegiance to the Crown, which is also the symbol of their free association, have considered the impending constitutional changes in India.

The Government of India have informed the other Governments of the Commonwealth of the intention of the Indian people that under the new constitution which is about to be adopted India shall become a sovereign independent Republic. The Government of India have however declared and affirmed India's desire to continue her full membership of the Commonwealth of Nations and her acceptance of the King as the symbol of the free association of its independent member nations and as such the Head of the Commonwealth.

The Governments of the other countries of the Commonwealth, the basis of whose membership of the Commonwealth is not hereby changed, accept and recognise India's continuing membership in accordance with the terms of this declaration.

Accordingly, the United Kingdom, Canada, Australia, New Zealand, South Africa, India, Pakistan and Ceylon hereby declare that they remain united as free and equal members of the Commonwealth of Nations, freely co-operating in the pursuit of peace, liberty and progress."

It will be seen that this declaration modified the Balfour Declaration of 1926,[64] which was recited in the preamble to the Statute of Westminster 1931,[65] and dropped the term "British" as applied to the Commonwealth—at least in its relation to India.

Pakistan[66] did not complete her constitutional deliberations until 1956. In 1955 she also announced her intention of becoming a republic while remaining a full member of the Commonwealth. The Pakistan (Consequential Provision) Act 1956 made provision as regards the operation of existing law relating to Pakistan in view of this new status, and the Commonwealth Prime Ministers in London issued a Declaration in 1955 similar to that of 1949. Other republics in the Commonwealth now include Ceylon (Sri Lanka), Ghana, Cyprus, Nigeria, Tanzania, Kenya, Malawi, Zambia and the Gambia. The Federation of Malaysia has one of its own rulers as Head of State.

The existence of republics within the Commonwealth marks the end of that "common allegiance" which featured so prominently

[64] *Ante*, p. 609.
[65] *Ante*, p. 611.
[66] For later constitutional developments before (West) Pakistan seceded from the Commonwealth, see G. W. Choudhury, *Constitutional Development in Pakistan* (2nd ed. 1969).

in the Balfour Declaration of 1926; but the concept of allegiance, now that it has been divorced from British nationality, seems to have no legal significance except in the law of treason. The rule was established in the case of India in 1949, and has been followed in the other cases since, that if a member of the Commonwealth becomes a republic (or a separate monarchy) [67]—that is, renounces allegiance to the Crown—its continuance as a member requires the consent of the other members. The rule was applied in relation to South Africa in 1961, although South Africa's secession was really for a different reason. It may be suggested that the rule has now lost its original purpose, and that the change to republican status ought not to be made the occasion for the other members to review a country's fitness to remain a member. It is still the rule that a member's internal affairs may not be discussed at a Commonwealth Prime Ministers' Meeting without that member's consent.

The Queen and the Commonwealth [68]

The symbol of Commonwealth association is the Queen and Head of the Commonwealth, rather than the Crown. The Queen has adopted a new personal flag—initial E and Crown within a chaplet of roses— for use where the royal standard (especially associated with the United Kingdom) is inappropriate.

The convention recited in the preamble to the Statute of Westminster [69] still requires that an alteration by the United Kingdom Parliament in the law touching *the succession to the Throne* should have the assent of the Parliaments of all the Dominions or realms owing allegiance to the Crown.[70] They would presumably also need to pass their own legislation in order to make such an alteration in the law effective in their own countries. It is suggested that the republics and separate monarchies (such as Malaysia) in the Commonwealth need only be informed of the change made in the law identifying the Head of the Commonwealth, although as a matter of courtesy they would probably be kept informed of any preliminary discussions.

On the other hand, as regards a change made by one member in *the Royal Style and Titles* used by that member—at least within the bounds set by recent precedent—it seems that convention since 1952 no longer requires the assent of any of the other members. On the accession of Queen Elizabeth II in February 1952 proclamations were

[67] *e.g.* Malaya (now Malaysia).
[68] And see *ante*, pp. 583–585.
[69] *Ante*, p. 611.
[70] Suppose they do not all agree?

issued in the independent countries of the Commonwealth which, except in the case of New Zealand, differed from that issued in the United Kingdom. In Canada she was proclaimed (*inter alia*) as " Supreme Liege Lady in and over Canada "; in Australia as " Queen of this realm . . . Supreme Liege Lady in and over the Commonwealth of Australia "; in South Africa as " Sovereign in and over the Union of South Africa "; in Pakistan merely as " Queen of her Realms and Territories and Head of the Commonwealth "; and in Ceylon she was proclaimed in English, Sinhalese and Tamil as " Our Sovereign Queen." [71] India was already a republic and Mr. Nehru, the Prime Minister, contented himself with a congratulatory message to the Queen, adding: " May I also welcome you as the new Head of the Commonwealth." Later that year discussions were held between the members, and it was agreed that each one should adopt a title to suit its own circumstances but including a common element. As a result Canada, Australia and New Zealand in 1953 adopted the same royal titles as the United Kingdom, but incorporated a specific reference to their own territory, thus: " Elizabeth II, by the Grace of God of the United Kingdom, Canada [Australia, New Zealand] and Her other Realms and Territories, Queen, Head of the Commonwealth, Defender of the Faith." In the republics, as has been said, the Queen is recognised only as Head of the Commonwealth.

Her Majesty during her tour of the Commonwealth after her coronation opened sessions of the Parliaments of the Commonwealth of Australia, the Australian states, New Zealand and Ceylon; presided over the Executive Councils of New Zealand and New South Wales, and held in New Zealand what was probably the first meeting of the Privy Council outside the United Kingdom. She opened the Canadian Parliament and presided over the Privy Council of Canada in 1957.

War and neutrality

The prerogatives in relation to external affairs may be transferred to a Governor-General by statute, or delegated generally or specifically by royal instrument. Canada acquired a seal in 1934, and letters patent of 1947 empower the Governor General on the advice of Canadian Ministers to exercise all powers of the Crown in relation to Canada.

On the declaration of war by the United Kingdom against Germany on September 3, 1939, Australia and New Zealand announced that they too were at war with Germany. The Governor-General of

---

[71] All these countries described her as " Elizabeth the Second," although she was the first Elizabeth to reign over them as distinct Kingdoms: Wheare, *op. cit.* p. 168n: *cf. McCormick* v. *Lord Advocate*, 1953 S.C. 396.

South Africa, on the advice of the new government, issued a proclamation of war on September 6. The King, on the advice of his Canadian Ministers, issued a declaration of war on behalf of Canada on September 10. The Indian Congress objected to the assumption that India was automatically involved in a war in which the United Kingdom was engaged. In 1941 the Governor-General of Australia, acting under authority specifically assigned to him by the King on the advice of the Australian Government, issued declarations of war against Japan, and also (through the United States Ministers accredited to those countries) against Finland, Hungary and Rumania.[72] The Governor-General of New Zealand issued similar declarations at the same time as the United Kingdom.[73]

The experience of Eire in the Second World War shows that a member of the Commonwealth may remain neutral in a war in which the Crown is engaged. Eire's neutrality was at once recognised by the enemy belligerents, Germany and Italy, and also by the United States who, before her entry into the war in 1941, was the most important neutral.

Citizenship [74]

As has been seen in Chapter 21, there is no longer a common code of British nationality. The first sign of divergence was the Canadian Nationals Act 1921, and the crisis came with the Canadian Citizenship Act 1946. This led to a conference of legal experts on Commonwealth nationality and citizenship in 1947. Their proposal was that the United Kingdom and the other Commonwealth countries should each define their own citizenship, and that the citizens of the various Commonwealth countries should be recognised in every part of the Commonwealth as " British subjects " or " Commonwealth citizens."

This " common clause " has been adopted by the United Kingdom, Canada, Australia and New Zealand. It does not necessarily mean, however, that citizens of the United Kingdom and Colonies have in those other three countries the same citizenship and political rights as their citizens have in the United Kingdom.[75] Other Commonwealth countries recognise " Commonwealth citizens " in various ways. Generally, although they are not " aliens," their status appears to differ little from that of aliens, except that citizenship may be obtain-

---

[72] See P. H. Lane, " Australia: External Affairs Power " (1967) 40 A.L.J. 257.
[73] Mansergh, *Documents and Speeches on British Commonwealth Affairs, 1931–1952*, I, pp. 461 *et seq.*
[74] See Clive Parry, *Nationality and Citizenship Laws of the Commonwealth.*
[75] The latter are now subject to the Immigration Act 1971.

able by registration rather than naturalisation. Ceylon accords no rights to Commonwealth citizens, apart from distinguishing them from aliens.

Meetings of Commonwealth Prime Ministers

After the Imperial Conference of 1937 the practice of holding more or less regular Imperial Conferences, with fixed agenda and full published reports, was discontinued. There have since been *ad hoc* meetings of Commonwealth Prime Ministers in London to review the state of the war and to discuss post-war settlements; to discuss international relations, economic affairs and defence; to answer the question of India's continued membership of the Commonwealth after adopting a republican constitution; to discuss South Africa; to discuss the Common Market; the world political situation; the progress of British territories towards independence, and membership of the Commonwealth; the means of promoting closer co-operation between the peoples of the Commonwealth; world economic affairs; disarmament; trade and immigration.

There have also been other conferences from time to time below the Prime Minister level, for example, the British Commonwealth Conference on Nationality and Citizenship, 1947; and the Conference of Commonwealth Foreign Ministers at Colombo in 1950, which recommended the establishment of a Commonwealth Consultative Committee to plan developments for South and South-East Asia (" the Colombo Plan ").

The " inter se doctrine " [76]

This doctrine underlay much of the theory and some of the practice of the pre-war Commonwealth. Although it has now been largely abandoned, the Commonwealth cannot be fully understood without some mention of it. " The *inter se* doctrine asserted," says a leading authority,[77] " that those relations between countries of the Commonwealth, which, if subsisting between any of them and foreign countries, or between foreign countries, would be regarded as international relations governed by international law, were neither international

[76] Fawcett, *op. cit.* Chap. 15; *The* Inter Se *Doctrine of Commonwealth Relations* (1958); R. Y. Jennings, " The Commonwealth and International Law " (1953) B.Y.I.L. 320; Clive Parry, " Plural Nationality and Citizenship with Special Reference to the Commonwealth " (1953) B.Y.I.L. 244; *cf.* R. T. E. Latham, " The Law and the Commonwealth " in Hancock's *Survey of British Commonwealth Affairs*, I, pp. 602 *et seq.*; P. J. Noel-Baker, *The Present Juridical Status of the British Dominions in International Law* (1929) pp. 289 *et seq.*; Oppenheim, *International Law*, I (8th ed. Lauterpacht) paras. 94a–94bb.
[77] Fawcett, *The British Commonwealth in International Law*, p. 144.

relations nor governed by international law." The doctrine only applied to relations among self-governing (now independent) members of the Commonwealth, and not between the United Kingdom and colonies that had not attained dominion status. It was a constitutional convention derived from the principles of unity and indivisibility of the Crown and common allegiance of British subjects. The doctrine affected chiefly the practice relating to treaties before the last war, nationality and currency.

Since the war, treaty relations among members of the Commonwealth no longer appear to differ from those existing between other states. In the absence of any provision to the contrary, they would be governed by international law. Thus there have been formal agreements between Commonwealth countries relating to the transfer of territory; agreements between the United Kingdom and Ceylon and other members on external affairs and defence; a trusteeship agreement between the United Kingdom, Australia and New Zealand concerning the administration of Nauru [78]; agreements between Commonwealth countries relating to air services and telecommunications; and a treaty of mutual co-operation between Australia and New Zealand filed with the United Nations in 1944. On the other hand, when members of the Commonwealth accept the compulsory jurisdiction of the International Court of Justice, they tend to reserve disputes with Commonwealth countries.

No formal machinery has been devised for settling disputes between members of the Commonwealth. An advisory opinion of the Privy Council has been sought twice in disputes between Commonwealth members.[79] Settlement through the machinery of the United Nations has also been resorted to twice: between India and South Africa in 1946 over the treatment of Indians in the latter country, and between India and Pakistan over the future status of Kashmir in 1954.

Diplomatic representatives

The style and precedence of Commonwealth High Commissioners were discussed at the 1948 meeting of Commonwealth Prime Ministers. Since then, Commonwealth High Commissioners in the United Kingdom have been allowed to take precedence with ambassadors of foreign states and they have been accorded the title of " Excellency." Republican members of the Commonwealth may send ambassadors rather

---

[78] Nauru, formerly a trust territory administered on behalf of the Crown by Australia, was granted independence in 1968. It has been admitted as a " special member " of the Commonwealth, being entitled to attend all general Commonwealth meetings except conferences of heads of governments.

[79] *Re Cape Breton* (1846) 5 Moo.P.C. 259 (annexation of Cape Breton to Nova Scotia); *Re Labrador Boundary Dispute* (1927) 137 L.T. 187.

than High Commissioners to other Commonwealth countries. These representatives of Commonwealth governments in the United Kingdom were granted immunities similar to those of foreign diplomatic representatives in 1952.

Consultation and co-operation [80]

No official encouragement has been given to the drawing of a distinction between those Commonwealth countries which are of British origin and those which are not. Nevertheless, the distinction is there—in history, tradition and sentiment. Apart from these ties which are real in Canada, Australia and New Zealand, and the otherwise nebulous recognition of the Queen as the Head of the Commonwealth, the main practical manifestation of Commonwealth membership is the system of consultation.

Consultation, exchange of information and co-operation are found mainly in the fields of external affairs, defence, finance and economics, and education. There is also a fair degree of mutual help. The obligation to consult, however, is not clearly defined, and consultation tends to be a one-way traffic. The United Kingdom would not change any law affecting citizens of Commonwealth countries, such as the Fugitive Offenders Acts, without consulting the other members, and in this case probably trying to effect reciprocal arrangements. The principle obtains of non-intervention in each other's domestic affairs. Apart from express agreements, no positive obligations are involved in Commonwealth membership. Generally, there is no definite Commonwealth policy. In particular, there is no common foreign policy.

The media for consultation include the Crown and the Governors-General, meetings of Prime Ministers, other Ministers and officials, the exchange of High Commissioners, and regular communication between the Foreign Office and the Departments of External Affairs of Commonwealth countries.

There are also a number of official organs for co-operation covering such matters as agriculture and forestry, air transport, economics, scientific liaison, shipping, statistics and telecommunications. Collective defence has been a major preoccupation both in war and peace, but the recent tendency is for regional international arrangements such as the North Atlantic Treaty Organisation. The Commonwealth Prime Ministers' Meeting in 1964 considered that it might be desirable to establish a Commonwealth Foundation to administer a fund for increasing interchanges between Commonwealth organisations in professional fields. At the Meeting in 1965 the Prime Ministers decided that the Foundation should be established as a legal charity. The

[80] Harvey, *Consultation and Co-operation in the Commonwealth.*

Foundation is an autonomous body, maintaining a close liaison with the Commonwealth Secretariat, and is financed by contributions from Commonwealth governments.

The Commonwealth Secretariat [81]

The Commonwealth Prime Ministers' Meeting in 1964 also considered that a Commonwealth Secretariat would be a visible symbol of the spirit of co-operation which animates the Commonwealth. At the 1965 Meeting the Commonwealth Prime Ministers decided to establish forthwith a Commonwealth Secretariat which would be at the service of all Commonwealth governments.[82] The first Secretary-General was Mr. Arnold Smith, formerly of the Canadian Foreign Service. The Secretariat derives its functions from the authority of Commonwealth heads of government, and the Secretary-General has access to heads of government. The Secretariat has no executive functions. Among its chief purposes are to disseminate factual information to all member countries on matters of common concern; to assist existing agencies in the promotion of Commonwealth links; and to help to co-ordinate preparations for future meetings of Commonwealth heads of government and of other Commonwealth Ministers.

The Commonwealth Secretariat Act 1966 provides that the Secretariat shall have the legal capacity of a body corporate, and it and its staff have the privileges and immunities conferred by the Schedule. The certificate of a Secretary of State is conclusive as to any relevant fact. Written contracts entered into by the Secretariat are subject to arbitration.

---

[81] See *The Commonwealth Relations Office Year Book, 1966,* Chap. 3. Both the Commonwealth Secretariat and the Commonwealth Foundation are located at Marlborough House, London.

[82] Cmnd. 2713, *Agreed Memorandum on the Commonwealth Secretariat.*

CHAPTER 36

APPEALS TO THE PRIVY COUNCIL [1]

I. APPEALS FROM DEPENDENT TERRITORIES

As we have seen, the jurisdiction of the Council was abolished in the seventeenth century, except from overseas territories, *e.g.* the Channel Islands, the Isle of Man, colonies ("plantations"), and later India. The remaining jurisdiction rested on the prerogative of the King as the fountain or reservoir of justice; but its exercise came to be regulated by the Judicial Committee Acts of 1833 and 1844, which created the Judicial Committee of the Privy Council to hear all Privy Council appeals.[2] The Crown has the prerogative to determine what is the jurisdiction of the Judicial Committee.[3] The Colonial Courts of Admiralty Act 1890 provided for the continued hearing of appeals by the Privy Council from courts in any British possession invested with Admiralty jurisdiction where there was no right of appeal to a local court or on appeal from a local court. There is power to make rules of court.

A Privy Council decision (technically opinion) is binding on the courts of the country from which the appeal came, and also on the courts of other countries from which appeal lies to the Privy Council in cases where the law to be applied is the same in both countries.[4]

Appeals lie not only from the Channel Islands, the Isle of Man and the colonies, but also by virtue of the Foreign Jurisdiction Act 1890, s. 1, from protected states, as they formerly lay from protectorates and trust territories.

Appeals to the Judicial Committee from overseas territories fall into two main classes:

(1) Appeals by "right of grant."
(2) Appeals by "special leave" of the Privy Council.

---

[1] N. Bentwich, *Privy Council Practice* (3rd ed. 1937); Sir Kenneth Roberts-Wray, *Commonwealth and Colonial Law*, pp. 433–463; E. McWhinney, *Judicial Review in the English-Speaking World*. For the early history, see J. H. Smith, *Appeals to the Privy Council from the American Plantations.*

[2] *Ante*, Chap. 14.

[3] *Australian Consolidated Press* v. *Uren* [1969] 1 A.C. 590 (P.C.).

[4] *Fatuma Bin Salim Bakhshuwen* v. *Mohamed Bin Salim Bakhshuwen* [1952] A.C. 1 (P.C.); *Australian Consolidated Press* v. *Uren, supra*. See H. H. Marshall, "The Binding Effect of Decisions of the Judicial Committee of the Privy Council" (1968) 17 I.C.L.Q. 743; G. W. Bartholomew in (1952) 1 I.C.L.Q. 392; Roberts-Wray, *op. cit.* pp. 572–75.

1. Appeals by "right of grant"

These are called appeals "by right of grant" because the limits are defined by Imperial Act, Order in Council or local statute, although fundamentally the appeal is founded on "the prerogative right and, on all proper occasions, the duty, of the Queen in Council to exercise an appellate jurisdiction" (*R*. v. *Bertrand*, 1867 [5]). They fall into two groups: (a) appeals "as of right" in the narrow sense, and (b) appeals at the discretion of the local court. In so far as these appeals rest on Act of Parliament or Order issued thereunder, they cannot be limited or abolished by the colonial legislature.[6] Leave to appeal to the Privy Council must be obtained from the local court, usually the Supreme Court of the territory. Neither group of appeals by right of grant now in fact includes criminal cases.[7]

(a) Appeals "as of right"

Although this kind of appeal is called "as of right," application for leave to appeal has to be made to the local court; but the latter must grant leave to appeal if certain conditions are fulfilled.[8] These conditions vary in different territories, although there is now a fair degree of uniformity. Generally speaking, an appeal lies "as of right" where the decision complained of is a final judgment, the subject-matter involved is worth a specified minimum sum (often £500) varying from £300 to £2,000,[9] and the appellant fulfils the prescribed conditions, *e.g.* as to the time within which application is to be made.

(b) Appeals at the discretion of the local court

If these conditions are not fulfilled, *e.g.* because the sum involved is below the prescribed minimum or the judgment is not a final one, the local court may have a discretion to grant leave to appeal if it considers that the question is one which by reason of its great general or public importance or otherwise ought to be submitted to Her Majesty in Council.[10] It commonly requires security for costs.

---

[5] L.R. 1 P.C. 520.
[6] Colonial Laws Validity Act 1865, s. 2. But *cf.* associated states under the West Indies Act 1967; *ante*, p. 608.
[7] *Falkland Islands Co.* v. *R.* (1863) 1 Moo.P.C.(N.S.) 299; and see *Chung Chuck* v. *The King* [1930] A.C. 244.
[8] *Cf. Lopes* (*R. S.*) v. *Chettiar* [1968] A.C. 887 (P.C.).
[9] *Meghji Lakhamshi & Bros.* v. *Furniture Workshop* [1954] A.C. 80. *Cf. Hui Shiu Wing* v. *Cheung Yuk Lin* [1968] 3 W.L.R. 941; no appeal as of right in divorce cases from Hong Kong.
[10] The Court of Appeal of Malta refused leave to appeal to the Privy Council in *Strickland* v. *Laycock*, January 27, 1956.

2. Appeals by "special leave" of the Privy Council

These are sometimes still called " prerogative " appeals, although they are now regulated by the Judicial Committee Act 1844. The Judicial Committee may grant special leave to appeal where:

(i) there is no grant of the right of appeal from the local court; or

(ii) the local court has no power to grant leave to appeal in the particular case, that is, generally in criminal cases; or

(iii) the local court has power to grant leave to appeal in the particular case, but has refused leave [11]; or

(iv) appeal lies directly to the Privy Council under the Judicial Committee Act 1844 from a court which is not a court of final appeal, e.g. from the Australian states.

The power to grant special leave to appeal cannot be limited or abolished by the legislature of a dependent territory except under the authority of an Act of Parliament, first, because that would be repugnant to the Judicial Committee Acts of 1833 and 1844 and therefore void under the Colonial Laws Validity Act 1865; and, secondly, because it could only be effective if construed as having an extraterritorial operation, and a colonial Act cannot in general have extraterritorial operation. The decision of the Privy Council in *Nadan* v. *The King* [10] was explained in this way in *British Coal Corporation* v. *The King*,[13] although it would have been sufficient to base it on repugnancy to Imperial statute.

Special leave to appeal may be granted in criminal cases as well as civil cases, but different principles are applied.

(a) Civil cases [14]

The Judicial Committee will grant special leave to appeal in civil cases only " where the case is of gravity involving a matter of public interest or some important question of law, or affecting property of considerable amount, or where the case is otherwise of some public importance or of a very substantial character." [15] Thus special leave was granted where the question was whether gold and silver minerals discovered in British Columbia were vested in the Crown as represented by the Government of Canada or that of British Columbia.[16]

[11] *Davis* v. *Shaughnessy* [1932] A.C. 106.
[12] [1926] A.C. 482.
[13] [1935] A.C. 500 (P.C.); and see *Att.-Gen. for Ontario* v. *Att.-Gen. for Canada* [1947] A.C. 127 (P.C.).
[14] Application for certiorari or prohibition is civil: *Maliban Biscuit Manufactories* v. *R. Subramaniam* [1971] A.C. 988 (P.C.).
[15] *Prince* v. *Gagnon* (1882) 8 App.Cas. 103, 105; *Caldwell* v. *McLaren* (1883) 9 App.Cas. 295.
[16] *Att.-Gen. of British Columbia* v. *Att.-Gen. of Canada* (1889) 14 App.Cas. 295.

Special leave has been granted on important questions of law even though the amount involved was below the prescribed minimum for an appeal by right of grant [17]; in constitutional cases such as the interpretation of a colonial Act [18]; where the revenue rights of the Crown are concerned [19]; and where the colonial court acted without jurisdiction.[20] Cases where special leave is likely to be granted although the matter is not of great public importance include questions affecting status, the validity of marriage, the legitimacy of children and injury to character or professional reputation.[21]

On the other hand, special leave will not be granted to determine merely abstract rights, or purely hypothetical questions; or in election petitions; nor generally on questions of fact.

(b) *Criminal cases*

In *Re Dillet* (1887) [22] Lord Blackburn said of appeals in criminal cases: " the rule has been repeatedly laid down, and has been invariably followed, that Her Majesty will not review or interfere with the course of criminal proceedings, unless it is shown that, by a disregard of the forms of legal process, or by some violation of the principles of natural justice, or otherwise, substantial and grave injustice has been done." In that case Dillet, who was both a barrister and a solicitor, was convicted of perjury before the Chief Justice of the Supreme Court of British Honduras, who in effect acted as prosecutor, witness and judge, and he was sentenced to six months' imprisonment. After he had served his sentence, and as a consequence of his conviction, Dillet was struck off the roll of solicitors of that court. Special leave to appeal was granted on the ground that the conviction was obtained in a manner so unsatisfactory that the conviction alone ought not to be conclusive as a ground for striking him off the roll. On the hearing of the appeal, the verdict and conviction were set aside. As the appellant had already undergone his sentence it was unnecessary to order a new trial, but the order removing him from the roll of practitioners of the Supreme Court of British Honduras was reversed.

These principles were restated by the Board in 1914 in *Arnold* v. *The King-Emperor*.[23] " This Committee," it was there said, " is not

---

17 *Sun Fire Office* v. *Hart* (1889) 14 App.Cas. 98.
18 *Ex p. Gregory* [1901] A.C. 128.
19 *Re Att.-Gen. of Victoria* (1866) 3 Moo.P.C.(N.S.) 527.
20 *The Queen* v. *Price* (1854) 8 Moo.P.C. 203.
21 e.g. *Le Mesurier* v. *Le Mesurier* [1895] A.C. 517; *Att.-Gen. of the Gambia* v. *N'Jie* [1961] A.C. 617. And see *Re Dillet, infra.*
22 12 App.Cas. 459, approving *Falklands Islands Co.* v. *R.* (1863) 1 Moo.P.C.(N.S.) 299, 312.
23 [1914] A.C. 644.

a Court of Criminal Appeal. It may in general be stated that its practice is to the following effect: It is not guided by its own doubts of the appellant's innocence or suspicion of his guilt. It will not interfere with the course of the criminal law unless there has been such an interference with the elementary rights of an accused as has placed him outside of the pale of regular law, or unless, within that pale, there has been a violation of the natural principles of justice so demonstratively manifest as to convince their Lordships, first, that the result arrived at was opposite to the result which their Lordships would themselves have reached, and, secondly, that the same opposite result would have been reached by the local tribunal also if the alleged defect or misdirection had been avoided." These principles were laid down at a time when there was no system of criminal appeals in this country. Otherwise the Privy Council might have developed somewhat broader principles in hearing appeals from countries having no Court of Criminal Appeal; and it has been suggested that they might even now exercise their discretion more liberally in such cases.[24]

Special leave to appeal against conviction was granted in *Chang Hang Kiu* v. *Piggott*,[25] where grossly improper procedure led to conviction for perjury; in *Knowles* v. *The King*,[26] where on a charge of murder the jury were not told that they might return a verdict of manslaughter; in *Ras Behari Lal* v. *The King-Emperor* (1933),[27] where one of the members of the jury in a murder trial did not understand sufficient English to follow the proceedings; and in *Joseph* v. *The King*,[28] where the judge, instead of recording the opinion of the assessors and then delivering judgment himself as required by the local Criminal Code, treated the assessors as if they were a jury and passed sentence according to their finding without delivering his own opinion.

Where the Privy Council has jurisdiction, whether civil or criminal, it may hear an appeal from *either party*. Thus in *Att.-Gen. of Ceylon* v *K D I Perera*[29] the Judicial Committee allowed an appeal by the Crown against the decision of the Court of Criminal Appeal of Ceylon ordering a new trial (not an acquittal) of a person who had been convicted of murder by the court of first instance.

The Judicial Committee follow the usual practice of appellate courts in not granting leave to appeal in criminal cases on questions of fact. A misdirection to the jury is not by itself a sufficient ground

---

24 Roberts-Wray, *op. cit.* p. 445.
25 [1909] A.C. 312.
26 [1930] A.C. 366 (West Africa).
27 (1933) 60 Ind.App. 354.
28 [1948] A.C. 215 (Fiji; manslaughter).
29 [1953] A.C. 200; following *R.* v. *Bertrand* (1867) L.R. 1 P.C. 520.

for interference if either the local Appeal Court or the Judicial Committee itself is satisfied that the facts nevertheless indicate the guilt of the accused.[30] Appeals will not be heard from a military tribunal administering martial law (*Tilonko* v. *Att.-Gen. of Natal*[31]), or from courts-martial administering military law.[32] The petitioner will generally be expected to have availed himself of any right of appeal to the local courts before approaching the Privy Council.[33]

II. APPEALS FROM INDEPENDENT COMMONWEALTH COUNTRIES

Appeals and the Statute of Westminster

Immediately before the passing of the Statute of Westminster 1931, appeal lay by right of grant from the Court of Appeal of New Zealand, and in some cases directly from the Supreme Court of New Zealand with the leave of that court. Appeal by right of grant also lay from the superior courts of the Canadian provinces, and (in relation to their state jurisdiction) from the Supreme Courts of the Australian states. As has been pointed out, such right of appeal could be altered or abolished by a dominion legislature, subject to the provisions of the Colonial Laws Validity Act 1865.

Appeals by special leave

In 1931 appeal lay to the Privy Council by special leave from all the dominions mentioned in that statute. Australia and South Africa, however, had power to limit the matters in respect of which special leave could be asked, subject to the reservation of such Bills. With that exception, the Dominions before the passing of the Statute of Westminster could not restrict or abolish the jurisdiction of the Privy Council to grant special leave to appeal: (i) by reason of the Colonial Laws Validity Act 1865, s. 2, because the jurisdiction of the Judicial Committee rested on—or was regulated by—the Judicial Committee Acts 1833 and 1844; and (ii) because they could not legislate with extraterritorial effect, except for the peace, order and good government of their territory (*Nadan* v. *The King*[34]).

The general principles on which special leave from the Dominions was at that time granted were explained by Viscount Haldane in

---

30 *Attygale* v. *The King* [1936] A.C. 338.
31 [1907] A.C. 93, 461.
32 *Mohammad Yakub Khan* v. *R.* (1947) 63 T.L.R. 94.
33 See *Kenyatta* v. *R.* [1954] 1 W.L.R. 1053.
34 [1926] A.C. 482 (P.C.). For the Irish Free State, see *Performing Right Society* v. *Bray Urban District Council* [1930] A.C. 377.

Hull v. *McKenna.*[35] Generally, he said, the jurisdiction of dominion courts should be regarded as final: only in exceptional cases would the Judicial Committee use its discretion to grant leave to appeal. Leave was very sparingly granted in criminal cases. Otherwise, leave was more freely granted in *inter se* disputes from federal dominions (except in so far as limited by statute in the case of Australia) and from India than in cases from unitary dominions. This practice followed the wishes of the various dominions themselves.

The question of appeals to the Judicial Committee was discussed by the Imperial Conference of 1926, but no proposal was made beyond recording the understanding that " it was no part of the policy of His Majesty's Government in Great Britain that questions affecting judicial appeals should be determined otherwise than in accordance with the wishes of the part of the Empire primarily affected. It was, however, generally recognised that, where changes in the existing system were proposed which, while primarily affecting one part, raised issues in which other parts were also concerned, such changes ought only to be carried out after consultation and discussion."

The Imperial Conference, 1930, did not agree on any solution to the question of appeals from the Dominions to the Privy Council, and it seems fairly clear that the Statute of Westminster 1931, proposed by that Conference, was not intended to affect them. The Judicial Committee, however, held in 1935 that sections 2 and 3 enabled the Dominions to which that Statute applied to abolish all appeals to the Privy Council, including appeals by special leave. The same consequence followed without any doubt from the Indian Independence Act 1947 and subsequent Independence Acts affecting other territories.

The power of the Parliament of Canada to abolish appeals to the Privy Council from both dominion and provincial courts, including appeals by special leave, was upheld by the Judicial Committee as regards criminal cases (a federal matter) in *British Coal Corporation v. The King,*[36] and as regards civil cases (a provincial matter) in *Att.-Gen. for Ontario* v. *Att.-Gen. for Canada.*[37] This was the result of a liberal interpretation of the British North America Act 1867, s. 101, empowering the Parliament of Canada to constitute a General Court of Appeal for Canada, and a regard for the " sovereign " status of Canada after the Statute of Westminster.

---

[35] Reported in [1926] Ir.R. 402.
[36] [1935] A.C. 500. See W. Ivor Jennings, " The Statute of Westminster and Appeals " (1936) 52 L.Q.R. 173. For the Irish Free State, see *Moore* v. *Att.-Gen. for the Irish Free State* [1935] A.C. 484.
[37] [1947] A.C. 127. See C. G. Pierson, *Canada and the Privy Council* (1960).

Waning jurisdiction of the Privy Council [38]

South Africa abolished appeals to the Privy Council in 1950.[39] Otherwise the tendency has been to abolish the Privy Council's jurisdiction on assuming republican status, beginning with India (1949), Pakistan (1950), Cyprus (1960)[40] and Ghana (1960). The latest abolitions at the time of writing are by Ceylon, Malta and Sierra Leone in 1972.

The position of Australia is complicated.[41] From Australian federal courts there is no appeal as of right. Section 74 of the Australian Constitution limits appeals by special leave to the extent that the certificate of the Australian High Court is required on any question as to the limits *inter se* of the constitutional powers of (a) the Commonwealth and any state or states,[42] or (b) any two or more states. This certificate has only once been granted.[43] Other appeals by special leave have been frequent.[44] Apart from *inter se* questions,[45] the Australian Parliament has power under section 74 of the Constitution to limit the matters in which special leave may be asked; and in 1968 it abolished appeals to the Privy Council in matters involving federal law and jurisdiction, whether from the High Court or from state courts.[46] Appeals to the Privy Council in purely

---

[38] See H. H. Marshall, " The Judicial Committee of the Privy Council: a Waning Jurisdiction " (1964) 13 I.C.L.Q. 697; Enid M. Campbell, " The Decline of the Jurisdiction of the Judicial Committee of the Privy Council " (1959) 33 A.L.J. 196; Lord Normand, " The Judicial Committee of the Privy Council " [1950] C.L.P. 1. *Cf.* Sir Douglas Menzies, " Australia and the Judicial Committee of the Privy Council " (1968) 42 A.L.J. 79; Claire Palley, " The Judicial Committee of the Privy Council as Appellate Court—the Southern Rhodesian Experience " [1967] P.L. 8; J. M. Ganado, " The Contribution of the Privy Council in Questions of Maltese Civil Law " in *Law, Justice and Equity* (ed. R. H. C. Holland and G. Schwarzenberger, 1967) p. 35.

[39] There had long been criticism of the Privy Council's handling of Roman-Dutch private law in *Pearl Assurance Co. Ltd.* v. *Government of the Union of South Africa* [1934] A.C. 570.

[40] But appeal lies from the Senior Judge's Court of the Sovereign Base Areas.

[41] See Cowan, *Federal Jurisdiction in Australia* (1959) pp. 172–181; Colin Howard, *Australian Federal Constitutional Law* (2nd ed. 1972); G. Nettheim, " The Power to Abolish Appeals to the Privy Council from Australian Courts " (1965) 39 A.L.J. 39.

[42] *e.g. Nelungaloo Pty. Ltd.* v. *Commonwealth of Australia* [1951] A.C. 34.

[43] *Att.-Gen. for Australia* v. *Colonial Sugar Refining Co.* [1914] A.C. 237. See W. Jethro Brown, " The Nature of a Federal Commonwealth " (1914) 30 L.Q.R. 301.

[44] *e.g. James* v. *Commonwealth of Australia* [1936] A.C. 578; *Commonwealth of Australia* v. *Bank of New South Wales* [1950] A.C. 235; *Australian Consolidated Press* v. *Uren* [1969] 1 A.C. 590.

[45] To abolish appeals on *inter se* questions would require a constitutional amendment; meanwhile the High Court is unlikely to grant the necessary certificate for such an appeal.

[46] Privy Council (Limitation of Appeals) Act 1968; Judiciary Act 1968.

state matters continue to lie from the High Court of Australia by special leave, and directly from state courts both as of right and by special leave.[47] A state cannot abolish appeals by special leave because of the Colonial Laws Validity Act, s. 2.

From the New Zealand Court of Appeal appeal lies in most cases, and in exceptional cases directly from the Supreme Court.[48]

As Malaysia (formerly Malaya) became a monarchy not owing allegiance to the Queen, an arrangement was made whereby the Head of State should refer appeals, or applications for special leave to appeal, to the Judicial Committee in certain cases; the opinion of the Judicial Committee being then reported direct to the Head of State.[49] The Judicial Committee thus became part of the judicial system of Malaysia.

Appeals may lie from a republic to the Judicial Committee itself, and not to the Queen in Council.[50]

Proposed Commonwealth Court of Appeal [51]

We have noticed the tendency for Commonwealth countries to abolish appeals to the Privy Council on assuming republican status, if not before. This is no criticism of the objective impartiality of the Judicial Committee, as may be seen from the use made of that body as part of the machinery for the removal of judges. By statute in some independent Commonwealth countries, as well as in some self-governing colonies approaching independence, an investigatory tribunal is set up composed of persons who hold or have held high judicial office in some part of the Commonwealth, to consider whether there is a case for the removal of a judge for inability or misbehaviour. The tribunal recommends whether the question should be referred to the Judicial Committee of the Privy Council. If it is so referred, the advice of the Judicial Committee would be accepted.[52] But the criticisms of the Judicial Committee as a court of appeal are that it

---

[47] e.g. The Wagon Mound [1961] A.C. 388 (N.S.W.); Bloeman (F. J.) Pty. v. Council of the City of Gold Coast [1972] 3 W.L.R. 43 (Queensland).

[48] e.g. Lee v. Lee's Air Farming Ltd. [1961] A.C. 12; Boots Chemists (New Zealand) v. Chemists' Service Guild of New Zealand [1968] A.C. 457.

[49] Hussien (Shaabin Bin) v. Kam (Chong Fook) [1970] A.C. 492; Ningkan (Stephen Kalong) v. Government of Malaysia [1970] A.C. 379.

[50] e.g. Malawi Independence Act 1964, s. 5; Kenya Independence Act 1963, s. 6.

[51] See Gerald Gardiner and Andrew Martin, Law Reform Now (1963) p. 16; Nwabueze, The Machinery of Justice in Nigeria (1963) Chap. 10; H. H. Marshall, " A Commonwealth Court " (1965) Round Table No. 221, p. 6.

[52] If the Queen ceases to be Head of State in the country concerned, the Judicial Committee may be eliminated and the investigating tribunal itself recommend whether or not the judge should be removed.

appears to be virtually a British Court sitting in London; it cannot fully understand the background of the legal system it is applying; and its jurisdiction, based as it is largely on the prerogative to grant special leave to appeal to colonies, is inconsistent with independence, and especially with republican status. It is a harmless anomaly that the form of procedure is advisory rather than judicial; and this could be obviated by the method devised by Kenya and Malawi.[53]

The Commonwealth Prime Ministers' Conference in 1962 expressed the hope that the regular appointment of judges from other Commonwealth countries would strengthen the Judicial Committee and emphasise its importance as a Commonwealth link. It might have done so a generation ago, but it is obviously too late now. A more recent proposal, which has had a good deal of support, is to set up a peripatetic Commonwealth Court composed of judges from various Commonwealth countries. Its jurisdiction would be twofold: (i) as a final court of appeal in certain cases from the courts of the Commonwealth countries, and (ii) to determine justiciable disputes between Commonwealth countries. Some would add the jurisdiction of a Supreme Court for the enforcement of a Commonwealth Bill of Rights.

Procedural problems would have to be solved. Should appeal to the Commonwealth Court always be as of right? If not, on what principles should leave to appeal be granted? And on what principles should decisions of the courts of Commonwealth countries be upset—for any error, or only for a gross miscarriage of justice? Questions such as these could no doubt be settled by legal experts without undue difficulty. But there are more formidable obstacles to be overcome. One is that the United Kingdom would be expected to abolish the appellate jurisdiction of the House of Lords [54] and to accept for herself the new Commonwealth Court as the final court of appeal, at least in some cases, from British courts. Another question is the composition of the court. How would the judges be selected? Would some countries be willing to spare senior judges for this purpose? Would the composition be scrutinised by the country visited? Would the country visited always supply one of its own judges? Lastly, the question of the expense of a court going on circuit round the world is usually raised in discussion of this proposal; and certainly the fares and subsistence allowances would

---

53 *Supra*, p. 643.
54 The merger of the judicial functions of the House of Lords with those of the Privy Council was often discussed in the nineteenth century: Robert Stevens, " The Final Appeal: Reform of the House of Lords and Privy Council 1867– 1876 " (1964) 80 L.Q.R. 343.

amount to a significant item.   On the other hand, we should also take into account the cost to litigants of the present system.

A Commonwealth Law Ministers' Meeting in 1966 under the chairmanship of Lord Gardiner, the Lord Chancellor, considered a proposal for a Commonwealth Court of Appeal. Some countries expressed their approval, but the majority have not shown themselves interested.   Support came from the smaller Commonwealth countries that still used the Judicial Committee.

INDEX